Dedication

This book is dedicated to my late and loving husband, Theodore (Ted) Sizer Cochran, who died in 2002. For many years he encouraged me to keep writing when I was down, hovered around when I needed support, and left me alone when I was up against a deadline. He always believed I could write this book, even when I didn't.

Ted was a helicopter pilot (Air Force Rescue in Vietnam), an adventurer, and an enthusiastic sailor. He combined his passions with his love of history in the making of documentary films. His best was *Island of the Bounty* (winner of the CINE Golden Eagle Award), which he made after sailing to Pitcairn Island in the South Pacific to meet the descendents of the *Bounty* mutineers still living there. He loved the islanders and returned three times to visit—twice with me when he was a guest lecturer on the *Crystal Symphony* cruise ship.

He was happiest when sailing, particularly on his boat *Hakatai* on San Francisco Bay. I recently found a picture taken of him steering a tall ship. It is inscribed with part of a favorite poem, "Song from the Ship" (1850), by Thomas Lovell Beddoes, that creates the excitement he felt when beginning even a local voyage:

> The anchor heaves,
> The ship swings free,
> The sails swell full,
> To sea, to sea!

The love of sailing and tall ships that we shared inspired me to use nautical analogies in this book to add colorful imagery to otherwise rather dry concepts. I hope it makes them easier to remember; it made it easier to keep writing.

Ted's belief in me and in "Roberta" compelled me to finish this book. Even though I've had many loving and supportive people cheering me on, Ted was my first mate and head cheerleader—and always will be.

© Dan Pirano. Reprinted with special permission of King Features Syndicate.

Roberta's Rules of Order

Alice Collier Cochran

Roberta's
Rules of Order

Sail Through Meetings
for Stellar Results
Without the Gavel:
A Guide for Nonprofits
and Other Teams

JOSSEY-BASS
A Wiley Imprint
www.josseybass.com

Published by Jossey-Bass
A Wiley Imprint
989 Market Street, San Francisco, CA 94103-1741   www.josseybass.com

Jossey-Bass books and products are available through most bookstores. To contact Jossey-Bass directly call our Customer Care Department within the U.S. at 800-956-7739, outside the U.S. at 317-572-3986, or fax 317-572-4002.

Jossey-Bass also publishes its books in a variety of electronic formats. Some content that appears in print may not be available in electronic books.

Readers should be aware that Internet Web sites listed in this work may have changed or disappeared between when this work was written and when it is read.

Art on p. ii entitled *Twin Brigantines at Angels' Gate* is by Scott Kennedy, artist. Used with permission of the Los Angeles Maritime Institute. www.lamitopsail.org

On p. iii, the poetry quoted is from the "Song from the Ship," lines 15 and 16, by Thomas Lovell Beddoes. Online text copyright © 2003, Ian Lancashire for Department of English, University of Toronto. Published by the Web Development Group, Information Technology Services, University of Toronto Libraries.

TALL SHIPS CHALLENGE® and Tall Ships® are registered trademarks of the American Sail Training Association.

Library of Congress Cataloging-in-Publication Data

Cochran, Alice Collier, date.
    Roberta's rules of order : sail through meetings for stellar results without the gavel : a guide for nonprofits and other teams / Alice Collier Cochran.—1st ed.
          p. cm.
Includes bibliographical references and index.
    ISBN 0-7879-6423-9 (alk. paper)
  1. Business meetings. 2. Nonprofit organizations—Management.
3. Teams in the workplace. I. Title.
    HF5734.5.C63 2004
    658.4'56—dc22
                                                            2003026847

FIRST EDITION
          10 9 8 7 6 5 4 3 2 1

Contents

Part III: Select Easy Meeting Methods to Get All Hands on Deck (Southeast Course)

Part IV: Stay Focused While Riding the Tide of Diversity (Southwest Course)

Part V: Tuning the Governance Rigging (Northwest Course)

Figures, Exhibits, and Tables

Tables

Preface

Launching Roberta's Rules of Order: A Seaside Story

In the early 1990s, a small chemical plant on Carquinez Strait, east of San Francisco Bay, experienced a serious accident. There were several injuries and one worker was killed. Under pressure from the city and local citizens, the company formed a *community advisory panel* (CAP), a group intended to bring nearby residents and plant managers together to talk over issues of public concern. After the group had mutinied against two facilitators, the plant manager asked Interaction Associates (IA) to provide a facilitator. IA is an international consulting firm that specializes in collaborative planning and facilitation. As an affiliate consultant with experience facilitating another local CAP, I was asked to take on the assignment. As I soon learned, this group was different from the other CAP.

When I walked into the crowded room adjacent to city hall chambers that first evening, I was told that it had been the scene of angry meetings following the accident. Tonight seemed to be no exception. People looked severe, serious, or scared—or was that my projection? My first challenge from the group came when I was explaining my role as a neutral person, not working at the plant or living in the community. "Who's paying for you to be here?" someone asked loudly, knowing that everyone knew it was the plant manager. It was clearly an attempt to discredit my neutrality. I explained that my role was to be an outside person, neutral about the content but helpful with the process of having a discussion.

I asked the participants to help me stay in the objective role. I also suggested that if anyone wanted to make a donation toward IA's fee, I was sure the company would be grateful. There were no takers, but a few people seemed to warm up a bit.

The next challenge came when I was attempting to establish some guidelines for working together productively and respectfully. A harsh-speaking college professor insisted that we use Robert's Rules of Order. (It was clear that he was probably the only one in the room who knew all the rules—and how to use them like a sledgehammer.) Some grimaced and rolled their eyes. I saw an opening, so I quickly asked if the group would try using *Roberta's* Rules of Order. No one, including myself, knew exactly what I meant. However, they all laughed and looked relieved that I had something else in mind that might work. I didn't try to gain consensus! Somehow I survived that night and have continued to be this group's monthly CAP facilitator for over eleven years.

Over the years Roberta's Rules of Order have evolved through trial and error and a lot of insight from many colleagues and clients. I began writing about what I had learned on a slow laptop computer as I flew across the country on business trips. I had two goals beyond passing the time during endless flights and airport delays. The first goal was to apply to nonprofit, voluntary, or nongovernmental organizations (NGOs) what I was learning about running better corporate business meetings. Many nonprofits feel constrained because their bylaws state they should use Robert's Rules of Order as their official meeting method. I wanted to provide another option, an alternative to parliamentary procedure. My own experience of serving on nonprofit boards had shown me that when Robert's Rules of Order are abandoned out of frustration and the group attempts to make decisions without any structure, there is often a free-for-all. It was clear that some structure was needed even though for many smaller meetings, parliamentary procedure was unwieldy.

My second goal was to help the average person who had been newly elected to lead or to serve on an advisory council or nonprofit board of directors be successful. Many books about facilitating meetings and decision making in groups have been written for business managers or professional facilitators. Few have been written for nonprofit leaders and members.

Unfortunately the terms *nonprofit* and NGO refer to a tax or structural status and define these organizations by what they are *not* instead of by what they *are*—civic or religious organizations for public or mutual benefit. For the purpose of keeping things simple in this book, the term *nonprofit* refers to all private organizations and NGOs in the civil, volunteer, independent, or third sector economy. In addition, the material in this book can be equally useful for citizen and activist groups, business teams, informal affinity groups, and clubs that have a purpose and meet together to make decisions.

Roberta's Rules of Order is a synthesis of what I have learned over many years from colleagues and from experimenting with meeting processes and decision making. It is intended to synthesize methods that will help you simplify your group's procedures. Let's deep six the laborious meetings and heavy formal structures. My hope is that this book will make it easier for your group to make a difference. Jump on board!

San Rafael, California   Alice Collier Cochran
November 2003

Acknowledgments

Many organizations and individuals have developed methods that have influenced Roberta's Rules of Order. I've also learned many important practices from colleagues in the field of group facilitation and nonprofit leadership. As I have synthesized and simplified what I have learned over the years, I hope I have properly credited the sources. I thank them all for influencing my thinking.

In particular I thank Michael Doyle, for first introducing me to the skill of facilitation in 1979, and David Straus, who, with Michael, wrote the little yellow book, *How to Make Meetings Work*, that introduced me and many in the world to facilitation. David and Michael are founding fathers of Interaction Associates (IA), an international consulting firm that has pioneered and popularized methods for better meetings within and collaboration among organizations. My long-standing affiliation with Interaction Associates has given me valuable learning and invaluable colleagues. I would particularly like to thank Barry Rosen, former president of IA, for the enthusiastic encouragement he gave me many years ago to write this book for nonprofit organizations.

I would like to thank Suzanna Pollak, past executive director of the Marin Council of Agencies (now the Center for Volunteer and Nonprofit Leadership), and Matt O'Grady, associate director of The Management Center in San Francisco for introducing me to the National Center for Nonprofit Boards, now called BoardSource. BoardSource's workshops and excellent trainers helped me recognize the niche for this book. After an excerpt was published in the BoardSource periodical *The Board Member*, I began getting e-mails requesting a copy of the then unfinished book. That validation of the need for a book like this kept me writing.

I would like to thank organization effectiveness consultant Peter Block, who took time to talk with me at a conference when I was feeling "stuck" and encouraged me to keep going. He told me to write this material not for professional colleagues, who would find it familiar, but for the average citizen who has agreed to lead an organization or serve on a small board committee or team and is looking for a simple approach.

I am grateful for the encouragement I've received over the past ten years from many people, including colleagues, clients, and workshop participants. Among them, I want to acknowledge especially the gentle guidance of Leslie Keenan and Suzanne West, two excellent writing coaches, and Robin Gayle, a gifted therapist—all of whom have helped me stay focused and slowly make progress.

I also want to thank Dorothy Hearst, senior editor at Jossey-Bass, for her thoughtful feedback and helpful redirection given to me over the last few years. Without her belief in this book and her patience with my grief following my husband's death, I would not have finished it. I consider that these special women, along with many dear friends and relatives, have been part of my "crew," and they have my heartfelt thanks for helping me "stay the course."

The Author

A lice Collier Cochran has been an independent consultant since 1985, working to increase the success of nonprofit boards, advisory groups, and corporate teams by improving their structure, governance, planning, meetings, and decision making. Prior to 1985, she had careers in college student personnel and in corporate training and organization development. She developed and managed an award-winning quality improvement effort for a bank called the Work Improvement Network (WIN Teams).

Cochran has served as consulting editor for the American Management Association's training publication *Facilitating a Workshop* and has been featured in several articles in BoardSource's periodical for nonprofit leaders, *Board Member*. She has conducted workshops on Roberta's Rules of Order for such nonprofit management support organizations as BoardSource, CompassPoint, and the Center for Volunteer and Nonprofit Leadership. She has also copiloted the course "Leading Together," for board presidents and executive directors to attend together, designed by Interaction Associates and offered through the Interaction Institute for Social Change and the Management Center in San Francisco.

Cochran has been a board member of the San Francisco chapters of the American Society for Training and Development, the Bay Area Organization Development Network, the San Francisco guild of the International Association of Facilitators, and the Junior

League of San Francisco. She is currently on the board of the American Sail Training Association and the Marin Advisory Council of the American Cancer Society, and she is past president of the Golden Gate Tall Ships Society.

She earned her B.A. degree, in English, from Longwood University and her M.Ed. degree from Virginia Commonwealth University. She has been prepared by BoardSource to apply its board assessment method and to consult on effective nonprofit governance. She has also been trained by the Drucker Foundation to use its self-assessment tool for nonprofit organizations and by CompassPoint in nonprofit organization effectiveness.

She lives in San Rafael, California, loves spending summer time with family in Maine, and enjoys sailing on the tall ships and on traditional sailboats, including her catboat, *Kitty Sark*. She may be contacted at Alice@RobertasRulesOfOrder.org.

Roberta's Rules of Order

Bizarro
by Dan Piraro

Introduction

I have heard and seen the problems of many groups as they struggle with parliamentary procedure. Here is an example of what a new organization board president might write to me as he or she prepares to run the board meetings.

Dear Alice:

I recently read the information you contributed to The Board Member, *and was excited to learn that you are writing a book called* Roberta's Rules of Order. *I thought that perhaps Roberta could help me.*

I've just been elected the president of a small nonprofit organization. Our bylaws say we should use Robert's Rules of Order at all meetings. (By the way, our bylaws are over ten years old and in desperate need of revision to make them more relevant to what we're doing today.) The past president gave me a copy of Robert's Rules of Order, Newly Revised. I found that it has 643 pages and now I'm in a panic about our next meeting! Who was Robert, and why do we still follow his rules, anyway?

Our board of twelve members is pretty diverse in age and culture. There are a lot of strong personalities, more women than men, and people who are very busy. Many are corporate managers or executives. They are impatient and feel that using the parliamentary procedure outlined in Robert's Rules of Order is too complicated. Besides, it uses language that's from another century! We could benefit from rethinking our structure as well, since the board isn't keen on hierarchy. Everyone wants to be in charge! Right now we are

Using parliamentary procedure in our small and informal group

Having arguments about using consensus instead

Having meetings that lose focus and lack accomplishment

Lacking clear expectations of board members' roles and behavior

Not having good attendance at meetings

Using outdated and strangely worded bylaws

Including a lot of policies in the bylaws—which makes them very long

Not having very much fun

I would like to know how you suggest running our meetings and structuring ourselves in a way that is more modern. We need something easy to implement because I and the other board members are also working full-time. I'd appreciate it if you could help us.

Sincerely,

A New Board President

Dear New Board President:

You are not alone in your situation. There are more than 1.8 million registered nonprofit organizations today in the United States alone—and this number grows each year. There are many other clubs and affinity groups. Many presidents, board members, and executive directors have the same concerns. Although it's not necessary to follow parliamentary procedure in smaller groups, it is important to have a written method and to adhere to democratic principles. You'll find that Robert's Rules of Order states that smaller boards or teams can write or modify "special rules" that can be used instead of, or in combination with, parliamentary rules.

My book, Roberta's Rules of Order, will help you create these special rules for your organization. You'll learn many other methods that I've learned over the last twenty years of conducting workshops and consulting with corporations and nonprofits. Although the book is intended for nonprofits, these methods can improve the functioning of any decision-making team.

I've called my book Roberta's Rules of Order because I want to indicate that compared to Robert's rules these methods are

- Less formal (Roberta is a first name; Robert was Henry Robert's last name)

- More feminine (but not just for women) with a softer tone and nonmilitary language

- More flexible (so that you can customize them to fit your organization's culture)

One purpose of Roberta's Rules of Order is to provide a structure you can customize for meetings, decision making, and governance that allows for freer discussion among members about the issues they must deal with. Although Roberta's rules do not impose strong control, they do not eliminate structure. There are guidelines and special rules for meetings but they are short and easy to learn. Whenever there are rules, everyone should be able to read them, remember them, and use them easily.

The rules outlined in Roberta's Rules of Order *are based on the following seven beliefs:*

1. People tend to support what they help to create or at least to influence.
2. Starting with the problem is more logical than starting with the solution (a *motion* is a solution).
3. Solutions that allow most of the people involved to win something are worth striving for.
4. Consensus isn't always worth the struggle.
5. Productive interaction can arise out of mild chaos as well as out of controlled situations.
6. Everyone has something to offer and should express it—once.
7. The wisdom of the group is discovered through reasonably structured, not random, conversations.

It's important to start with these beliefs. Decide whether they are compatible with the values of your organization. Roberta's Rules of Order may or may not be a good "fit" with your group. Roberta's Rules of Order are intended to help the smaller decision-making groups that meet regularly—teams, committees, and boards of about a dozen members—use a less formal and more engaging approach. These groups may be social or sports clubs, professional or trade associations, Scout groups, volunteer fire departments, PTAs, school or college councils, hobby clubs or affinity groups, community choruses and other performing groups, arts cooperatives, charities, advocacy organizations, childcare or elder-care centers, homeowners or neighborhood associations, museums, recreational clubs, food or clothing distribution centers, or religious or spiritual organizations.

To make it easier to navigate through the book, I've used the sea and sailing—particularly in traditional ships—as a metaphor. It is a natural choice because the terminology of the sea permeates our language, and the imagery is fluid and vivid. Many people love to sail or to see traditional ships under sail, as I do.

Using the methods in this book, you will learn ten key strategies, including how to

1. Avoid motions that present a solution without clarifying the problem
2. Move a group from many ideas to closure and action
3. Select a decision-making method appropriate for the situation
4. Decide the most productive and easy way to meet
5. Develop a values-based mission and vision statement
6. Use an agenda format that helps you focus on your mission and steer the meeting
7. Plan an interactive annual meeting
8. Respect differences among group members
9. Simplify the way your organization is governed
10. Establish a flexible structure with less hierarchy and more shared responsibility

In a traditional sailing ship, you never go in a straight line but are always correcting for drift. In approaching this book, you can, if you wish, ignore the tendency to read a book linearly, from cover to cover. However, before selecting the course you will take, please read Chapters One and Two to get your bearings and learn the ropes. Feel free to tack (turn) around the compass sections and set your own course to find the information you need. Bring on board what's most useful, and cast off the rest.

Best wishes for your success as president. Please keep in touch; I'd appreciate hearing from you again.
Sincerely,
Alice Cochran
P.S. The following story will answer your question, "Who was Robert, and why do we still follow his rules, anyway?"

Who Was Robert, and Why Do We Still Follow His Rules?

First, let's look back into history to give credit where it's due. Anyone who has developed a method for structuring organizations and conducting business meetings, as Henry Robert did, has done a service to man- and womankind. To establish an objective context for this book, let's begin with the story of Henry Robert and how an embarrassing moment sent him on a search for a better approach to meetings.

San Francisco, 1865

In 1867, Major Henry Martyn Robert was extremely pleased about his new assignment in San Francisco with the Military Division of the Pacific. As a West Point graduate and engineer in the Army, he had moved throughout the country, but this was his favorite location. The United States was recovering from the Civil War and focusing on becoming one nation again. California was a long way away from his home in New England and the places where he had served the Union Army along the East Coast. He was ready for a change.

Having been an active member and leader himself in civic and cultural organizations, a value encouraged by his religious beliefs, Henry Robert continued this involvement in San Francisco. The men who led organizational meetings in that city in this era (no women participated at this time) had all come to San Francisco from other states in the Union and had usually had experience serving in the legislature of their home states. English settlers in the United States were familiar with the general parliamentary process as it was then used in England and had applied that process in the legislative bodies developed for each state. However, each state legislature, in adapting parliamentary procedure, also developed its own specific meeting rules. Because the different participants were used to different sets of rules, the meetings Robert attended were often confrontational, particularly when it came to deciding how to proceed with business. Given these procedural arguments, many meetings were not productive.

While living in New England in 1863, because of his training and military rank, he was asked to lead a church meeting. It was attended by a group of very vocal men who were not willing to listen to each other's points of view. Things didn't go well. The men argued about the procedures as much as the issues. The debate was rancorous, and the conflict escalated. People were shouting and trying to keep others from speaking. All that he had learned in the Army could not help Robert keep order and control. He had been mortified. After this personally embarrassing episode, he vowed that he would never be put in the position of leading a contentious meeting again without a standard set of procedures that would provide control in meetings.

Back to Early English Kings and Unruly Men

Henry Robert began his search for existing rules to govern meetings by studying early parliamentary law, the rules and customs for carrying out business in the English Parliament. He traced the origins of parliamentary procedure back to the Anglo-Saxon tribes that migrated in the fifth century A.D. to the island later called Great Britain. After the Norman Conquest in 1066, English kings assembled Great Councils of noblemen and court officials to give them advice and counsel. These were select groups of males who were trusted by the king. (Agreeing with the king was considered good for your health!)

The Great Council evolved into what we now know as the English Parliament during the thirteenth century. The word *parliament* was used at that time to describe any important meeting held for the purpose of discussion. However, it wasn't until the sixteenth century that *procedures* for these meetings were established. We can only imagine that there were outbursts of anger, duels, and a few people run through with swords before someone thought of having a meeting method everyone agreed to use. Many of these early rules are still the backbone of good meeting principles today.

Across the Ocean to a Different World

When English settlers came to the New World, they began to establish assemblies to govern their colonies. Each colony derived its own method of managing meetings from English parliamentary procedures and later incorporated this method into a state constitution. Because each state applied the procedures differently, there were many versions of meeting rules. Of course the people in each state thought their method was the Right Way.

By the late 1700s, Thomas Jefferson, while serving as vice president of the United States and presiding officer of the U.S. Senate, saw a need for consistency in procedures. He compiled a manual of parliamentary practice for use in the U.S. Senate in 1801, basing it on the English Parliament's written procedures. Initially, both the House and the Senate adopted the procedures in this manual, but the House later adopted a different set of procedures (which added a new dimension of confusion).

Although a number state legislatures also came to use Jefferson's rules (which the people of that era never actually called "Jefferson's Rules"), many variations of parliamentary procedure were still used all across the country. However, they also had some important similarities. They all upheld democratic principles guaranteed to those who met as a "deliberative body," usually a large, voting legislative group, that allowed meeting participants to determine through discussion courses of actions to be taken by the whole group.

Henry Robert's further search for the Holy Grail of meetings undoubtedly included the manual of parliamentary practice written in 1845 by Luther Cushing of the Massachusetts House of Representatives. This manual was commonly called *Cushing's Manual* (notice the new surname trend). It was intended for large decision-making "assemblies" that were *not* legislative in nature. This approach was a breakthrough. Cushing recognized the growing need to have a body of rules appropriate for the many cultural, scientific, charitable, and religious organizations that needed a structure for governing their group and meetings. In addition, he made an important distinction between large assemblies and small groups (the "ordinary organization"), *giving permission to the small ones—of about a dozen people—to write and adopt informal rules to supersede his rules*. This caveat is the key to the kingdom for smaller, modern organizations and the rationale for Roberta's Rules of Order.

Forward to Post–Civil War United States

The United States was changing rapidly as Henry Robert continued to develop his rules. Immigrants from European and Asian countries were beginning to move into cities settled primarily by the English. Men with less wealth and education than earlier participants typically had were becoming involved in civic organizations. Women still were not. (In those days, women, who were still wearing corsets and bustles, did not attend public meetings.)

New inventions were changing the country from an agrarian to an industrial society. This was a time of enormous social change. His forward-thinking wife urged him to make rules that would be fair for *anyone* attending meetings, including women. He came upon a list of "rules for deliberative assemblies" intended for groups that discuss and determine common action, most likely *Cushing's Manual*. He personally tested and modified his rules while taking a leadership role in civic, religious, and educational organizations, including the YMCA in later years.

Vision and Values

Henry Robert felt strongly about preserving the values of democracy and encouraging citizen participation in civic matters. He wanted the rules he was developing to protect the rights of individuals. The primary rights were the right of the majority to rule, the right of those in the minority to express their opinions, and the right of each person to have an equal vote. Robert also valued hierarchy and structure, a value perhaps related to his military background. His intent was to promote fairness, equality, and good decision making. Helping groups reach unanimous agreement was his goal. Folklore has it that he was very good at doing this himself and wanted to teach others how. He experimented with his rules as he led meetings himself, particularly in San Francisco, a place where new methods that broke with old traditions were welcomed.

His vision was a set of rules that would support the rights and values he saw as essential yet would fit in an easily carried "pocket guide." He published them in a pamphlet in San Francisco in 1869.

The Pocket Manual Expands

By 1874, Robert was living in Milwaukee and finishing his handwritten manuscript for the *Pocket Manual of Rules of Order for Deliberative Assemblies,* rules that a society or organization in any state could adopt as its parliamentary authority. Finding a publisher for this work was difficult. Not to be thwarted, he published four thousand copies himself and gave away one thousand of them to educators and church leaders. Two years later a publisher accepted the manual, changed the name to credit the author, and distributed *Robert's Rules of Order* across the country.

After several revisions, Robert's pocket manual grew to more than five hundred pages. He decided to include information that went beyond running meetings, addressing such matters as structuring a board of directors, determining the roles of officers, and setting up committees. He lived to see his book widely used and his contribution admired by many. He retired from the Army in 1901, as a brigadier general, and died twenty-two years later, in 1923.

Henry Robert could never have imagined that his book would be used as the primary authority for running meetings of boards of directors and business meetings of organizations across America for more than a century. He also would never have expected the growing criticism of his rules as stifling, restrictive, and overcontrolling. Wasn't order a good thing?

Given his frame of reference and the growing civic sector in the United States, his rules were appropriate and even progressive for his time. There have been other highly respected versions of parliamentary rules and many attempts to explain and simplify parliamentary procedure. However, *Robert's Rules of Order* (now in its tenth edition, with 643 pages, plus tables) is the best-known and most relied upon version of parliamentary procedure in nonprofit organizations today. Because bylaws should include the organization's decision-making method, the writers of those bylaws, usually lawyers, specify Robert's Rules of Order.

Moving On from Robert to Roberta

One of the common misperceptions about *Robert's Rules of Order* is that this book is only about making decisions in meetings. In fact it offers much more information that is valuable, although a bit overwhelming. For instance there are chapters on structuring the organization that discuss what to include in bylaws and that describe the roles of board officers. It can be a very useful tool if you don't get all entangled in the many chapters on motions. It's worth having as a reference and as a backup plan for large voting meetings.

A misperception about parliamentary procedure in general is that because it's effective in governmental and legislative situations, it's equally useful in smaller civic organizations. Often it's like using a hammer on a mosquito when a flexible flyswatter will do. Many authorities who have written simplified parliamentary procedures agree that what works in Congress, adapted from the English Parliament, is not appropriate for smaller civic and charitable decision-making groups. Do you really want to run your meetings like Congress? If you've ever watched a parliamentary debate or a congressional hearing on television, you'll understand how unsuited the method is for small boards of civic, religious, or charitable organizations.

Now let's look at the growing winds of change and the reasons why nonprofits and business teams have been chafing at the lines of control and moving away from Robert's rules and in the direction of Roberta's rules for many years.

Part I

A Gradual Sea Change
Toward More Flexibility

1

Shifting Shores from Robert's Rules to Roberta's

An easy way to visualize the process of managing a nonprofit organization is to think in terms of steering a traditional sailing ship on the sea. Using this metaphor, this book will help your organization voyage across open water from the shore that represents Robert's Rules of Order to the shore that represents Roberta's Rules of Order. In organizations as in sailing ships, regardless of their size, it takes a strong structural design and equipment, a skilled crew, and a forward focus to deal with the forces in the outside environment.

Think of a body of water with two opposing shorelines. Imagine that Robert's shore is due west, on your left, at 270 degrees on the compass, and Roberta's shore is due east, on your right, at 90 degrees. The sea in between, the site of your journey, both going forward and turning around, contains the key elements you will want to address to successfully adopt Roberta's Rules of Order. The cultural changes involved in the shift from the Robert's Rules of Order shoreline to the Roberta's Rules of Order shoreline are summarized in the following two lists of waypoints:

From Robert's Shore	To Roberta's Shore
Formality	Informality
Strict rules	Guidelines and agreements
Parliamentary procedures	Democratic principles and processes

1900s language	2000s common usage
Military terminology	Civilian terminology
One size fits all	Flexible, by culture
For English and European males	For members of a pluralistic society
Requires win-lose voting	Encourages win-win decisions
Two decision choices (yes or no)	Straw polls and multiple choices
Controlled	Relaxed
Complicated	Simple
Debate	Dialogue and conversation
Motions	Proposals precede motions

Moving from Robert's Shore to Roberta's Shore

The characteristics of these two shorelines describe organizational attitudes and methods that are very different. If your organization likes it on the Robert shore, then there is no reason to cast off and leave. However, if this shore's complexity frustrates your group's members, you're in good company. It may be time for the crew to *tack* and head to another shore.

If you choose to move from the Robert shore to the Roberta shore, you will be making a journey through some open water. It may be rough or smooth, depending on the course you take. Think of this journey not as a race to get to the other side but as a rally— a challenging course that requires you to periodically tack, or change direction (moving forward or even backward), with care. The order in which you decide to sail the course doesn't matter. However, on this passage you're encouraged to explore all directions of the compass at least once to get to the other shore. If you've already sailed one of the points of the compass, set your course for another. Decide your logical order, and proceed on the course you choose. Think of each chapter as a buoy or channel marker that guides the way into safe water.

The Reason for Rounding the Compass 360 Degrees

This book is focused on making a cultural shift, not just on adopting new meeting rules. Some organizations may find that Roberta's Rules of Order resemble what they're doing now but have never written down. Others may find these rules a major sea change yet believe the time has come to make that change.

Think of each of the four compass directions as a close look at one facet of an organization, as if you were using a pair of binoculars. This close look will give you essential details but not the entire seascape. The broader picture represents a culture, a collection of habits or behaviors that influence each other. For example, to change the way a group meets (one compass course) is a good start but will have little impact on how decisions are made (a different compass course). To affect decision making, you will need new sets of decision-making rules. Similarly, having more focused meetings won't help much if people don't attend. Nonprofits have also been known to change the way they make decisions in practice but ignore the governance documents that were written many years ago and that specify a decision-making method. Conversely, changing the bylaws may do little to change actual behavior in meetings.

Like wind, tide, and current, which together affect how well a boat performs, the way you run your meetings, the way you make decisions, and the way you govern the organization *together* affect how the organization performs.

Taking the Whole Journey

Roberta's Rules of Order is written in a way that helps you take the whole journey, not just a little jaunt. The only way to see real change in an organization's culture is to approach the organization as a vessel with interconnected parts—meetings, decision making, and governance. While working on these parts, you'll want to have a seaworthy craft and keep an eye on the elements. The three opposing elements to watch are the wind of simplicity or complexity, the tide of flexibility or rigidity, and the current of involvement or disengagement. *Roberta's Rules of Order* encourages the gentle elements of simplicity, flexibility, and involvement. Foster these elements in your organization and the journey will be easier.

However, if you don't believe in fostering these elements stop reading now! If they do fit with your organization's culture—or with the culture you want to create—please continue to read and to use what you learn to improve your organization. After all, working in nonprofits and in business teams is all about making a difference. It's hard to make a difference when everyone is tangled up in the rigging of procedural formality and blanketed in fog.

Using a Compass Rose for Direction

Following the first two introductory chapters (Part I), this book is divided into four parts that correspond to the four sections of a compass (Figure 1.1). The four primary points on a compass (north, south, east, and west) have been combined to indicate quarters or sections (northeast, northwest, southeast, and southwest). These are called courses. Although your group may begin with any section that seems most appropriate, this book begins with decision making (northeast on our compass) because it seems to be the direction that is the most difficult for many groups to navigate. The remaining parts address planning and running meetings (southeast), keeping conversations focused and productive (southwest), and equally important, the design of the organization's structure (northwest).

In a ship, the design of the hull is necessarily related to its function. Ships can, for example, go no faster than *hull speed,* the speed made possible by the design of the hull. Sleeker, lighter designs allow increased speed. A sturdy keel will keep the hull moving for-

Figure 1.1. Four Courses Using the Compass Rose.

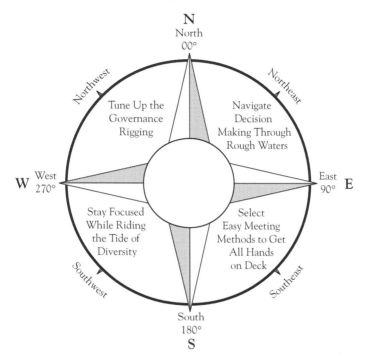

Note: See Parts II–V of the book in Table of Contents.

ward and prevent capsizing, except in extreme situations. Similarly, streamlining and simplifying its structure will help keep an organization flexible, nimble, and on the move.

Getting Under Way

As you sail your course you will become aware of some external forces—for example, the controversy and complexity surrounding decision making—that may cause you to change direction. Remember that the winds of change are always blowing. Just adjust your course, and don't get stalled or "in irons"—keep moving forward!

When you are ready, take the helm and chart your own course. Start wherever you find you need to begin, but continue to tack in each direction to cover all sections. The objective is to move through each of the major compass courses at least once and always keep making headway. The benefit is learning or being reminded of alternative methods of deciding, meeting, and interacting and of structuring the organization so that you can enjoy working together to fulfill your mission.

2

Rescuing Democratic Principles from Parliamentary Procedure

The Civil War has been over for a long time. When you compare how things are today to how they were over 125 years ago when Henry Robert first wrote his rules of order, it's obvious that our culture has changed. We are now living in a new millennium, with a more complex and pluralistic society. Yet as Peter Block, a renowned organizational effectiveness consultant and author, says, it is still the case that "many of our conventional ideas about gatherings find root in the beliefs of one Henry Martyn Robert and his rules. Now Robert's rules of order, or its grandchildren, invade every conference room and meeting hall. There is no escape" (Axelrod, 2000, p. ix). There have been efforts to simplify Robert's rules, but they are still clearly based on his original work, as are the many "new" and "modern" editions of *Robert's Rules of Order* and versions such as *Robert's Rules in Plain English* and *Robert's Rules with Illustrations*. *Cannon's Rules of Order*, an effort to return to the early practices of the English Parliament, is of course also based on parliamentary procedure.

Today's nonprofit organizations are less formal, faster paced, and have a more diverse membership than the organizations of Henry Robert's day. Think again of an older sailing ship. Although the design of the original vessel may still be seaworthy, many new materials for safety gear, rigging, and fabrics for sails have been developed to make this ship move more efficiently and to meet its crew's modern requirements. Similarly, in organizations, new flexible methods of participation are needed to meet the changing needs and expectations of organizational members.

In an effort to keep up with the times, organizations have rejected, altered, and ignored Robert's Rules of Order and other variations of parliamentary procedure. But when this system of rules is removed, it is like removing the sails from a sailboat—the vessel or organization has a hard time going forward. Something else needs to be put in place for propulsion. It doesn't need to be fancy, but it does need to be useful in many different situations. It also needs to apply democratic principles without using parliamentary procedure.

Protecting the Rights of Individuals

However cumbersome the procedures, the underlying principles of Robert's Rules of Order are the tenets of a democratic country. These principles protect the fundamental rights of individuals who are meeting as a group to make decisions together. No matter which method or procedure you use for running your organization and its meetings, it should not violate the following guaranteed democratic rights (Sturgis, 2000):

1. The right to assemble and organize
2. The right to propose ideas and speak without reprisal
3. The right of the majority to decide by voting on proposals and carrying out decisions
4. The right of the minority to protest and be protected

Other nations are fighting for these rights that we too often take for granted. These rights are the backbone of a democratic society and are not to be discarded lightly. The majority is given the right to decide, not the minority (as can happen when using consensus, discussed later). Protecting these rights even in small, informal organizations is important. It's the formal procedures, all the layers of protocol, rather than the democratic principles that are cumbersome.

Richard Axelrod (2000) names "embrace democracy" as one of four key principles for engaging people in large groups and carrying out organizational change. The democratic principles to be embraced are equity and fairness, maximum sharing of information, open decision-making processes, and freedom and autonomy. Axelrod makes the point that organizations are not governments and that everything in organizations doesn't boil down to a vote. However, he adds that the process of deciding should educate people and motivate them, not make them feel confused by procedure and limited in their participation.

Now let's contrast this democratic approach with characteristics of parliamentary procedure:

- Tight control is used to get results.

- Decisions must always be made by voting.

- Motions (solutions) are stated before problems are discussed.

- The chair has ultimate decision-making power.

- Voting is a win-lose proposition.

- The agenda is fixed: old business, new business, and so on.

- The language that describes roles is from the military.

- You need to be an expert in the procedural rules to run a good meeting.

Conflict over Procedures

When an organization's board has a healthy mix of older and younger members, it also has the potential for conflict. Although some of these members will have learned parliamentary procedure in the form of Robert's Rules of Order in their high school or college clubs and student councils, others have not. So to some this procedure represents an old-school way of thinking. To others it's the only orderly way to get things done. This schism is not always related to age; it may also stem from cultural teachings. People of Anglo-Saxon origin or from countries influenced by the British Empire may find more affinity with the structure of parliamentary procedure than do people whose traditions have roots in other parts of the world. For people from the latter cultures, parliamentary procedure lacks the spontaneity and focus on emotions and relationships with which they are more familiar.

According to Peter Block, "The contribution of Robert's Rules is the importance the book gives to the question of group process. The downside of the rules is the essentially legislative solution they offer to meetings and the way they promote the thinking that control and predictability are the keys to success" (Axelrod, 2000, p. ix).

Liz Guthridge (2002), a professional registered parliamentarian with the National Association of Parliamentarians, has a long love-hate relationship with Henry Robert. She sums up the conflict this way:

> You can't blame Robert that his rules don't fit today's time. After all he was an engineer in the army during the Civil War. He couldn't predict how the world would change. For example, he thought the San Francisco area was diverse in the late 1800s because the area had attracted people from all over the United States and the men had different ways of conducting meetings.

Can you imagine if he had to preside over meetings that included women, people of other nationalities, people of color, people of different sexual orientation and all the other diversity we encounter today? And he certainly didn't predict all the new technology, such as fax machines, conference calls, e-mail, video conferencing, etc. that have changed how people meet and interact with one another.

I propose that Robert's legacy should be the desire for social equality, not the preoccupation with order. We should honor his concepts, not follow his book of rules, as we do our organizational work. So rather than spend valuable time memorizing a guidebook, be true to what Robert intended. Replace his rules with common sense.

Taking the Opposite Tack

As often happens in social change, those who reject an approach often respond automatically with an opposite approach. Those who dislike using parliamentary procedure often promote reaching *consensus* as the alternative, but this may be an extreme choice for the group's culture. Think of a piece of rope, with one end of the line representing high control and structure and the other representing low control and structure (Figure 2.1). Organizations may jibe or switch from parliamentary procedure to consensus, going as far toward the opposite end of the rope as they can, failing to see that there are other options in between.

Figure 2.1. Control and Structure Continuum.

Decision-Making Opposites

High   **Low**

Parliamentary Procedure ——————————————————————— Consensus

Everyone knows what consensus means, right? Wrong! *Consensus* has multiple meanings, depending on the context. Often it's used to mean the opinion or will of the majority, as, for example, in the phrase "the consensus of the medical community." In some situations it means a unanimous decision (100 percent agreement), and in other cases it means that everyone understands the issues and agrees to go along with and implement the decision made by the group. A more specific term, *informed consent*, used by Hans and Anna Marie Bleicker in their workshops, means that even though people may not favor a decision, they often will support it based on the information they have learned about the issue. The difficulty for most organizations that seek consensus lies partly in this ambiguity of meaning. Moreover, when consensus means unanimity, a few individuals or even one individual can block a decision, making consensus a form of minority rule. (Notice that minority rule isn't included in the list of democratic principles!)

Organizations that use consensus successfully are generally those that are willing to spend the time and energy needed to reach each decision. They often share strong religious, humanistic, or spiritual beliefs that include a belief in the God-given insight of each individual and a commitment to hearing all viewpoints. They have a well-tested process and will go to great lengths to reach a consensus agreement. The decision-making process in communities of Friends (Quakers) exemplifies this approach.

Groups that don't use consensus successfully generally lack these shared beliefs and values. For various reasons, such as attempting to make decisions in a short time frame, they may put pressure on dissenting members to go along with the majority. This creates a false consensus and usually results in a backlash of hard feelings. Open resistance can result. Another problem is coming to a decision that has been watered down so much in order for everyone to agree to it that it misses the mark.

Training workshops and consulting services are now offered around the world to help the members of organizations be more collaborative. Corporate quality improvement efforts are shifting U.S. culture toward favoring collaborative decision making and consensus building. Often a nonprofit board member will have learned collaboration skills through his or her place of business but will meet with resistance when trying to apply collaborative concepts in the nonprofit board. Corporate teams don't have the same attachment to Robert's Rules of Order through expectation or bylaws as nonprofits do. The legal requirements and responsibilities of nonprofit boards make it important for them to have a codified method that is used fairly and consistently. One realistic concern is that without a vote there is nothing on record to show that a decision represented the will of the majority (see democratic right number 3, listed earlier). This may have negative consequences only if the decision is challenged legally, but unfortunately that is a possibility.

The Need for an Alternative

In 2001, in Santa Cruz, California, several local nonprofit management support organizations and BoardSource sponsored the conference "Exploring New Directions in Nonprofit Governance." The follow-up report written by BoardSource staff observed that some conference participants had "suggested simple adjustments to the way board business is conducted that could make a significant difference. I wish boards 'would use a method other than Robert's Rules to order business.' Many people complained that boards might be different if 'there were no limits' or if 'we didn't use Robert's Rules of Order.' Who sets the limits? Who imposes Robert's Rules? What's stopping you from eliminating the limits?" That's a good question. An article in *The Board Member* has reported that "many nonprofit organizations are examining alternative sources to traditional board meeting procedures. Some are looking for more informal ways to run meetings. Robert's Rules of Order is being set aside in favor of more unceremonious meetings" ("Old Rules of Order May Warrant Second Look," 2001, p. 5). The article concludes,

"Meetings should be conducted so that participants can make good decisions with reasonable outcomes, rather than focusing on monitoring procedure. While Robert's Rules has its place, having a choice is always a good alternative" (p. 5).

Permission to Break the Rules

Actually there is nothing to prevent boards from coming up with their own rules. According to the tenth edition of *Robert's Rules of Order*, they may create *standing*, or *special*, rules for conducting business meetings, rules that supplement or even supersede parliamentary procedure, particularly for smaller groups of "not more than about a dozen members" (Robert, 2000, p. 9). "About a dozen" is not a fixed number but an attempt to define small boards and committees. Special rules may be used in slightly larger boards when the group is particularly good at group process.

Anthony Mancuso, attorney and author of *How to Form a Nonprofit Corporation in All 50 States* (2000), explains the options open to those who are setting up nonprofit organizations. According to the bylaw section that specifies how the board will conduct business, he says:

> [You may] specify the rules of order, which will be used at directors' meetings. Some larger nonprofits will wish to specify "Robert's Rules of Order" here, but you may indicate any set of procedures for proposing, approving, and tabling motions that you wish. If you will have a small informal board . . . if you see no need to specify formal procedures for introducing and discussing items of business at board meetings or you may wish to specify "such procedures as may be approved from time to time by the board of directors" . . . to allow your board to *develop its own set of procedures for the conduct of meetings* [p. 7.15, emphasis added].

Finding the Right Balance

When a highly structured method is dropped and nothing structured is added in its place, a vacuum exists. This vacuum can create uncertainty. When members of a group know each other well and have developed trust among themselves, the vacuum can often be filled successfully with an informal approach. As one leader of such a group explained, "we just talk about something until we're sick of it and then we vote." This works well until the group changes membership or experiences high levels of conflict or controversy. As a participant in this second kind of group has put it, "sometimes our meetings can become a free-for-all."

What's missing is a middle ground that synthesizes and simplifies other approaches into something *chaordic.* This is a term coined by Dee Hock (1999), founder and former CEO of VISA, to describe his management approach, which blended chaos and order. *Roberta's Rules of Order* is an attempt to codify a chaordic meeting method, one that similarly balances chaos and order.

Think of having a set of special rules that are *rules of the road,* a term also used for navigation on the water. When you are sailing on a crowded bay, the only way to avoid collisions is to have rules that everyone uses. It's important to know who has the right of way when two boats approach each other and how to navigate the color-coded buoys down the channels.

Resource A contains Roberta's Special Rules for Meetings, a set of rules for small groups meeting for the purpose of decision making. These rules cover ten areas of process that will make a difference in your meetings (and they are cross-referenced to the appropriate chapters in this book). Group members need to talk about and modify these rules until they reflect the organization's meeting culture. Some are probably not very different from what your group is currently doing but may never have written down. As long as the group bases its rules on democratic principles and as long as the members agree as a group to use these written rules fairly and consistently, the group has a legitimate alternative to parliamentary procedure. You may want to preview these special rules now, but be aware that some of the terminology may not be clear until you have finished reading this book.

A Caveat

Roberta's Rules of Order are not meant to replace Robert's Rules of Order (or any other version of parliamentary procedure) in the occasional or annual large, voting civic or membership meetings for which the latter set of rules is intended. (For these meetings the services of a *parliamentarian* can be very helpful.) The purpose of Roberta's Rules of Order is to be an alternative method for smaller groups that meet regularly and are seeking less formality and more flexibility—as recommended in the tenth edition of *Robert's Rules of Order, Newly Revised* (2000).

However, before you use Roberta's Rules of Order as your future meeting rules, amend your bylaws to state that you will be using this method. Until then, use the voting method outlined in your existing bylaws, even if those bylaws are twenty years old, to make this and the other simplifications discussed in Chapter Fifteen and Resource A. Once you take this step you are likely to find that using a codified method other than parliamentary procedure allows your group to preserve democratic principles, improve its group process—and toss the gavel overboard.

Part II

Navigate Decision Making Through Rough Waters (Northeast Course)

3

Developing Proposals
Before Launching Motions

Roberta's Special Rules for Meetings (see template found in Resource A) encourage members of a group to develop written or verbal proposals that state the full situation and describe potential solutions. It recommends doing this *before* presenting a motion containing a single solution. The purpose of this chapter is to discuss the reasons for this approach and how to carry it out.

In this chapter you will learn

- The pitfalls inherent in a spontaneous motion from the floor

- Why it's advisable to discuss the problem before considering a solution

- How to state a simple proposal

- How to write a structured proposal

- How to identify the conditions for successful solutions

Problem: A Rogue Motion

The Village Improvement Society of a summer community was having its annual meeting on the third Saturday in August, as required in its bylaws. The location was a small church with wooden pews. Almost everyone was looking at someone else's back, a setting not conducive to discussion. Although the society made an effort to attract community members to attend, many chose other more interesting or relaxing activities that Saturday evening, particularly the younger people.

The meeting typically progressed through committee reports and on to elections. The nominating committee had just proposed the names of three new directors to serve on the board for the next three years. Nothing was handed out or said to describe the backgrounds of those nominated. It was assumed that everyone knew them. None of them was present.

The chairperson called for a motion to accept the slate. There was grumbling and muttering around the room. Someone spoke up: "Mr. Chairperson, I move that in order to be a director of this organization, you must be able to attend the annual meeting." Someone seconded this motion. This took the chair by surprise. After a brief discussion, this hasty motion was passed. In the future all proposed directors, regardless of circumstances, would have to be present at the annual meeting to be elected.

Hasty Motions Can Create Long-Term Problems

This well-intentioned civic organization, using Robert's Rules of Order, has just created a solution to a problem. But this solution does not necessarily improve the situation, and it has created another problem. The real though undiscussed issue is that the members of this community have for generations taken pride in knowing each other. Today, unfortunately, many of the regular summer residents do not know some of the newer year-round residents nominated for leadership roles. It makes them uneasy to elect "strangers." The new requirement to be present in order to be elected, if implemented, would prevent qualified people who vacation in this community in June or July from serving on the board.

Now the emphasis will have to be more on finding individuals who are available for one meeting than on finding those who are qualified and willing to serve.

In this case a hasty motion has compounded rather than solved a problem. Perhaps a request for a brief biography of each nominee or some other means of introducing those nominated would have been sufficient.

If a Motion Means Movement, Why Do We Get Stuck?

General synonyms for the word *motion* include *movement, action, impulse, gesture,* or *activity.* In the context of parliamentary procedure a motion is a statement, which can sound like a demand, that an action be taken or that an opinion be expressed by the group. It may be like a decision to tack when sailing—to change direction across the wind—quickly and abruptly. In organizations, as in sailing, there is usually a rationale, but often the situation and its alternatives aren't clearly analyzed in the pressure of the moment. Many times the problem is not described, understood, or even agreed to be a problem. Perhaps there is no problem but an opportunity whose benefits may not be clear. Once a motion is verbalized, however, the group focuses on whether or not to do it—not on whether the issue is clear and merits action at all. A motion sends a message that there are only two possible positions—you're either for it or against it.

Solutions Looking for Problems

A motion is sometimes a solution without an agreed-upon problem. Interaction Associates, a consulting firm focusing on collaborative planning and meeting facilitation, teaches that "if you can't get agreement on the problem or need, it will be hard to get agreement on the solution." Unless there is agreement on the problem and an understanding of the situation, the solution in the motion may not be appropriate. Groups need to reach agreement on the issues and needs in order to find the best solutions.

Interaction Associates defines a problem as "a situation that you or someone wants to change." This situation may not necessarily be negative—perhaps there is an opportunity to improve something. Because the language we use influences our thinking, it helps to state such situations broadly and positively.

Under Robert's Rules of Order an issue cannot be discussed until a motion has been made. Motions thus put the solution before the problem. By the time they get to discuss the problem, people have often taken up polarized positions. They have been put on the defensive by being forced to react quickly to a situation. We all know that once people take opposing positions, it's hard to make progress. By the time a motion is made it's often too late to have a constructive conversation.

The action that a motion advocates is often one person's "good idea" about or personal solution to something that is occurring. This is another reason why motions, whether verbal or written, usually state a request for a change in a way that encourages reactionary responses. When there is no agreed-upon problem, the reaction may be confusion, surprise, or an aggressive response to "kill" the motion. Immediately everyone begins to "debate" the merits of the pending change rather than to consider whether there is a need for change. During this effort to persuade others to think a particular way, having a meaningful dialogue, which requires keen listening and open-mindedness, is nearly impossible.

In short, starting with a motion (solution) makes it more difficult than it should be to reach a creative or multifaceted solution. Interaction Associates illustrates the process of solving problems with the diagram shown in Figure 3.1.

Figure 3.1. Problem-Solving Process.

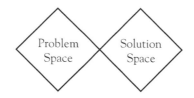

Source: Copyright Interaction Associates, Inc. Reproduced with permission.

Consider the Problem Before the Solution

As Figure 3.1 suggests, groups need to consider the problem before the solution. What goes on in the *problem space* is an effort to define, evaluate, and organize information that will determine the causes of the problem. Defining the problem and understanding its causes provides the best information to help find alternatives.

One maxim that has come out of quality improvement efforts in business is "problem solving is often cause reduction." This means that until we know the cause of a problem, we may be groping in the dark for a solution. Unless we define the problem and attack its causes, we may see the same problem over and over. It also implies that some situations may just have to be reduced until we can live with them, and may never be eliminated.

Offering Proposals

An alternative to a motion is a *proposal,* either *simple* or *structured.* A simple proposal is usually verbal. A structured proposal is written, prepared ahead of time by several individuals or group. A proposal differs from a motion in that it can be modified by the group and considered along with other proposals. A proposal emphasizes making full disclosure of information and reaching agreement on the problem before attempting to agree on a solution.

Simple Proposals

There are six steps to presenting a simple, stated proposal:

1. State the suggestion verbally to the group, and explain the need.
2. Clarify by answering questions for understanding.
3. Check for disagreement (objections); if none, then check for agreement. (*Stop* at this point if everyone agrees to the proposal.)
4. If there are objections, clarify issues as necessary and ask for statements of both pros and cons.
5. Ask for modifications or another proposal.
6. Check for disagreement; if none, then check for *substantial agreement*. If necessary vote (see Chapter Five for definition of substantial agreement and voting options).

For instance, the meeting leader might say:

1. John has proposed that we change our meeting night this year.
2. Is everyone aware that John isn't able to continue meeting on our usual night, the second Tuesday of the month, because he is taking a class at the community college? . . . Would anyone object to changing the date to make it possible for everyone to attend?
3. What day would someone suggest? . . . Jane proposes that we meet on the third Wednesday.
4. Is there anyone who couldn't regularly attend on the third Wednesday? [If someone cannot attend, continue by going through Step 5 on the previous list and asking for modifications or a new proposal.]

5. Does anyone disagree? . . . Do we have substantial agreement? If so, please mark your calendars for our regular meeting on the third Wednesday of each month.

It can be helpful to write even simple proposals on a flip chart for all to see. This makes it easier to discuss, perhaps modify, and reach agreement.

Structured Written Proposals

A structured proposal is written and prepared in advance of any discussion by the group. It is particularly important to do this when situations are complex or controversial. The proposal should be prepared by more than one person, although the actual writing may be done by one person on behalf of a team, task force, or committee. This usually results in a stronger, more acceptable proposal. Here are seven guidelines for writing a structured proposal:

1. Do it for any issue that is complex, controversial, or confusing.

2. Include information about the current situation (the problem or opportunity) and the proposed future situation (the recommended solutions).

3. Write and circulate the proposal in advance if possible.

4. Have more than one person present the proposal—the more the better.

5. Give everyone a chance to ask questions for clarification, speak for or against it (within a specified time limit), and suggest modifications.

6. Use the group's predetermined decision-making method to approve or not approve the proposed solution (see Chapter Five).

7. Include a suggested action plan for implementing the solution if it is approved.

Short Written Proposals

For a situation that is not very complex or controversial, a very brief written proposal may be sufficient. This proposal will still cover more than the typical motion, which usually has only a general rationale—only the good news—supporting it. This brief proposal should answer these four questions:

1. What is the situation that needs changing, and why does it need to be changed?

2. What are the probable causes of the situation? (Be cautious not to blame individuals.)

3. What is the recommendation (with costs and benefits), and why?

4. Who will carry out the change, and by when?

Extensive Written Proposals

When a situation is especially complex or controversial, a more extensive analysis of the problem may be advisable. Exhibit 3.1 outlines a suggested format for an in-depth structured proposal. This proposal should contain complete but brief statements and be limited to one or two pages. Your board can customize and adapt this outline to include other information you want to include in written proposals. Use the template in Resource B as a starting point. Exhibit 3.2 provides an example of a proposal constructed according to this outline.

Presenting the Written Proposal

When presenting a written proposal to a group, give group members time to read it. Request a few minutes of silence while they do this. Then go through the proposal section by section to clarify

Exhibit 3.1. A Structured Proposal: Outline with Key Questions.

The Current Situation

1. The Facts

What's the current situation? What are people seeing and perceiving?

When, where, and how often does the problem occur?

TIPS: Gather data and descriptive information that substantiate that a problem exists. How often is it happening, where or when? What's the talk on the street? What's verifiable?

2. The Cost or Other Impact

What is occurring or not occurring because of the situation?

What's the impact?

What is it currently costing?

What are the ramifications of solving and of not solving the problem?

TIPS: Give real numbers where possible. Describe any negative impact that this situation is having on the organization

3. The Main Causes

What are the reasons for the situation? Why does it exist?

TIPS: If you know why the problem exists, say so. If not, ask *why* questions (Why does X occur? Because of Y. Why does Y occur? And so on). Beware of reasons that seem simply to blame individuals. Think more systemically.

The Possible Solution(s)

4. Conditions for Success (including criteria or constraints)

What criteria would ensure success (for example, cost, resources, time)?

What are the optimum conditions?

What constraints exist?

TIPS: Conditions for success are the realistic boundaries that need to be considered. Writing this list may seem like a detour before looking at options, but it will help you objectively weigh the merits of multiple options. It may include some constraints or givens and some optimal conditions. The best way to write criteria is to make them as clear and simple as possible:

State each criterion as a closed-end question with a YES or NO (or UNKNOWN) answer.

State each criterion in the affirmative so that each YES means a positive or favorable response and NO is negative or unfavorable.

Exhibit 3.1. A Structured Proposal: Outline with Key Questions, Cont'd.

Consider criteria such as these for each option:

Mission: Does it fall within and support our mission?

Money: Will it cost less than _____ (amount)?

People: Will it require *no* additions to staff?

Ease: Can it be implemented easily?

Time: Can it be implemented within _____ (days/weeks/months)?

Impact: Is it likely to have a positive impact?

Resources: Is the necessary _____ (equipment, skill, and so forth) available?

Agree on the list before evaluating the alternatives or options.

5. Best Practices and Options

What are the possibilities? What are their advantages and disadvantages?

What has been successful elsewhere? How have others solved this?

What are the advantages and disadvantages (pros and cons) of several options? Use the criteria defined in the previous step, tallying the numbers of YES, NO, and UNKNOWN answers for each option and selecting the option or options with the most YES answers.

TIPS: Describe how other organizations have successfully solved this problem. List the solution or solutions that best meet your criteria. List any pros and cons or advantages and disadvantages that should be known. If there are a lot of UNKNOWN answers to your criteria, do more research before presenting a proposal.

6. Recommended Solution(s)

What is the recommended solution?

TIP: Using your research and best judgment, write a proposal recommending an action (or actions) and explaining why this action is preferred.

The Proposed Change

7. Suggested Action Steps

What will it take (time, money, people) to make this change successfully?

TIP: Prepare a timeline for the implementation that shows who needs to do what by when, and the resources or money needed. Request needed items.

Exhibit 3.2. A Brief Structured Proposal: Example.

The Current Situation

1. The Facts

The post office in our summer community is one of the smallest in the world. It has been a focal point of the community daily from June through August for decades. The U.S. Postal Service, as a cost-cutting measure, wishes to close it down and have all mail picked up from the post office in the nearest town, five miles away. It is staffed by the post office with someone "from away," and the residents miss having a postmaster who knows everyone, as was the case in the past. The post office hours have been shortened, and the end-of-summer closing date is now before Labor Day.

2. The Cost or Other Impact

The cost of the one summer employee for the post office has increased, and volume has decreased, causing a loss of revenue from stamps, special handling, and the like.

3. The Main Causes

The volume of mail for this summer post office has decreased due to several factors, including the increased use of e-mail and an increase in year-round residents who rely on the town post office in the winter and see no need to change their mailing address for three months in the summer.

The Possible Solution(s)

4. Conditions for Success

- It will keep the post office open.
- It will keep the mail being delivered daily to the community.
- It will require only one employee.

5. Best Practices and Options

- Close the post office.
- Keep it open with a different staffing arrangement.
- Hire a summer community member to serve as the postal worker, in the same way the library hires the summer librarian.
- Give the Postal Service final say on the person hired and trained as a postal worker.

Exhibit 3.2. A Brief Structured Proposal: Example, Cont'd.

There is an obvious disadvantage to the first option because postal services would be lost, as would a focal point of the community. There are more advantages to the other options because they allow the community to keep its valuable resource.

6. **Recommended Solution(s)**

   - That the community residents agree to raise the money through dues and donations to hire a summer resident at $3,500 per summer.

   - That the village post office have regular hours each day.

   - That the post office be open from June 1 through Labor Day.

The Proposed Change

7. **Suggested Action Steps**

   - Gather community support by circulating a petition to all served by the village post office by June.

   - Meet with the Postal Service regional manager to request that the summer post office be considered a privately subsidized "mailroom" of the main post office by next summer.

issues and answer any concerns. Try to reach tentative agreement as you proceed through the proposal. Then ask the presenting group to make a motion. For example, a representative of the group presenting the proposal shown in Exhibit 3.2 might say:

We move that the community association work with the regional Postal Service department to implement the proposal to keep the community post office open during the summers. We will allocate $3,500 to hire staff for the first year. This money will be solicited through the dues statement and a request for donations, but the association will cover any future shortfall.

Then they would use the group's predetermined decision-making method to finalize the decision (see Chapter Five).

Log Entry: Summary

In Western cultures groups have a tendency to jump directly into the *solution space* (Figure 3.1) in discussing a situation, particularly when people are impatient or conflict is present. You can help the members of your group by discussing the problem space first. (Is there a storm on the horizon?) Once the situation is understood, well defined, and analyzed, then encourage the group to proceed to the solution space. (Perhaps we should reef the sail and close the hatches.)

Proposals may be verbal or written. Written, structured proposals are recommended for any issue that is controversial, complex, or confusing (as discussed further in Chapter Four). When writing a proposal, follow or modify the outline shown here so that you give information about both problem and solution.

Proposals that include a clear statement of the problem, good analysis, and recommended solutions(s) are improvements on motions, which are only statements of an action, one solution.

Getting Under Way

- When presenting a simple verbal proposal, make sure the problem is understood before going any further.

- Agree on a format to use for written proposals.

- When solving a problem, be sure to agree on the conditions for success (the time, money, and effort that can reasonably be expended) so that you can make a good and acceptable decision.

Making Headway

Now that you know how to prepare a proposal that will consider the problem before the solution, we'll look next at the process of decision making. The following two chapters focus particularly on cautions about using consensus (Chapter Four) and on a range of alternative voting methods, including one for reaching substantial agreement, or concordance (Chapter Five).

Testing the Current
Before Heading for Consensus

The purpose of this chapter is to help you decide if and when consensus is the appropriate method for making decisions in your group.

In this chapter you will learn

- The definitions of two factors to consider: controversy and complexity

- How to use a decision-making square to assess levels of controversy and complexity

- What other factors to consider, and how important they are in your group

- How to find and use more information about a structured approach to consensus

Problem: Anticipating Complexity and Controversy

The governing board of a small church was split down the middle regarding its meeting method. Some members felt that the board, which had been using Robert's Rules of Order for as long as anyone could remember, should experiment with modern ways of running its meetings. Some members wanted to use consensus as is done in the Quaker community. The parish was known for being progressive and innovative in its worship services.

Many valued the process of building consensus and had seen it work well, particularly when the issues were clear and the solutions fairly obvious. However, some had seen how a few highly principled but very stubborn people could block moving forward because they wouldn't go along with a decision supported by the rest of the group.

In the coming year the board was facing two large projects. One was a very complex plan for repairing the church building's one-hundred-year-old foundation. The other was hiring a new minister to replace the beloved pastor who had recently retired. There had already been some controversy over appointing a pastor-nominating committee. There appeared to be rough waters ahead.

Most board members liked the intention behind a method of decision making in which everyone was heard and everyone agreed before proceeding. However, they didn't think that these complex and possibly controversial projects could get done, given the time frame, if the board switched to consensus decision making at this time.

Defining Consensus

Many groups, in an effort to avoid winner-take-all majority rule, have started to use consensus decision making for every situation. Not surprisingly, sometimes it doesn't succeed. Moreover, consensus can be variously defined. To some groups it means unanimity, or 100 percent agreement. To others it means general consent, or "I can live with it." In some circles it means "the sense of the group"—even if that group numbers in the thousands, as in issues of national policy.

In working groups, consensus is generally defined as everyone's agreeing to support moving ahead to implement the decision—or at least agreeing not to impede others as they move forward. All those participating (including those in the minority) should feel they've been listened to and that all issues have been aired. Everyone needs to have a clear understanding of the issues. The group has to provide a chance to think and talk together in some form of open dialogue (see Chapter Eleven). All this takes a lot of time, trust, and patience.

The important first step if your group wishes to use consensus decision making is to agree on the definition that the group will use. Then the group needs to take a look at and identify the various situations it might encounter in which consensus may not be possible or even appropriate. Next the group needs to set a limit on the time it will take to reach consensus in any situation. Answer this question, How long is too long for indecision to go on? Finally, after setting an appropriate time limit (a single meeting, a week, a month), the group needs to decide on the backup decision-making method it will use when group members cannot reach consensus, such as reaching a substantial agreement to move forward (see Chapter Five).

Navigating Through Controversy and Complexity

Why are some consensus decisions easy to make and some extremely difficult? In organizations that strive to make decisions by consensus, why does the process work well one time and not the next? Why does it often take so long and leave some people upset? When is consensus worth the struggle?

Organizations deciding when to use consensus as a decision-making process may need to consider a range of options and think *situationally*. In each situation, it will be helpful to consider two primary factors found in making a decision about any issue: the level of *controversy about* the issue and level of *complexity within* the issue. Think of these factors as strong tidal currents pushing against you as you try to move forward.

Issues are controversial when they

- Challenge personal values or beliefs.

- Put something at risk, including money or membership.

- Take something away or add something people feel strongly about.

- Involve a change that challenges "the way things have always been done."

Issues are complex when they

- Involve multiple groups or organizations.

- Are difficult to imagine having win-win solutions.

- Require legal advice.

- Affect the organization's bylaws or current mission.

The Decision-Making Square

For any issue, complexity may be high or low and controversy may be high or low. Figure 4.1 illustrates the four combinations of complexity and controversy that are possible. Each of the numbered corners represents a different combination:

Corner	Combination
1	Low Complexity combined with Low Controversy
2	High Complexity combined with Low Controversy
3	Low Complexity combined with High Controversy
4	High Complexity combined with High Controversy

In addition, in this model controversy is considered more difficult to deal with than complexity. When something is complex it may take more time, but it can often be broken down into smaller problems that can be dealt with separately. However, when something is controversial it often involves strong feelings and opinions related to beliefs and values. An issue may be highly complex and

Figure 4.1. Complexity-Controversy Matrix.

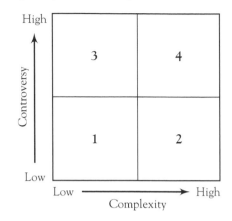

yet a group may reach agreement on it without too much difficulty, particularly if it's broken down into a series of small decisions. However, when an issue is highly controversial, people have more at stake, and it will be more difficult to reach agreement. Regardless of its level of complexity, such an issue may result in a large struggle. Therefore, issues that fall in Corner 1 generally are easy to find solutions for; in Corner 2 the decisions get harder. In Corner 3 decisions are generally very hard, and in Corner 4 they are almost impossible.

Corner	Agreement Difficulty	Consensus Success
1	Generally easy to agree	High
2	Harder to agree	↑
3	Very hard to agree	↓
4	Often impossible to agree	Low

The following example illustrates the four combinations of complexity and controversy and also shows how a situation may evolve in complexity and controversy over time.

Corner 1

The board of a mental health services agency in a midsize city was faced with hiring a new executive director (ED). Everyone understood the need for this position (Low Controversy) and knew that the board could use a nonprofit resource center's executive search service to assist it in the search. The board already had a few candidates in mind (Low Complexity).

Corner 2

Then the board learned that the Executive Search Service wouldn't be available to assist it for several months. Board members were clear that they wanted to move forward sooner (Low Controversy). They needed to form a team to begin the search. Although none of them was an expert in this area, five board members agreed to work together to begin to assess the organization's needs and write a new job description (High Complexity).

Corner 3

The members of the search team worked well together to get the preliminary work done. There was little disagreement about what role the new ED would be expected to play (Low Complexity). However, there was beginning to be disagreement about how to look for the right person. Some wanted to do a national search; others wanted to keep it local. Some wanted to find a woman; others argued that gender didn't matter. People were spending valuable meeting time arguing with each other. Several of the search team members stopped coming to meetings (High Controversy).

Corner 4

The outgoing ED, who had planned to stay three more months, was suddenly offered another job outside the state. He would be leaving in two weeks. The president of the board was impatient to have someone in the ED role before the organization's annual fund drive

(High Complexity). The search team leader had a friend she wanted to see in the position. This candidate was qualified on paper, but others on the team knew that she had a reputation for being coldly efficient and for alienating board members in her last position (High Controversy).

From this example of escalating levels of complexity and controversy, it is easy to see why consensus decision making gets harder as the levels get higher.

Other Factors to Consider

There are at least six other factors to consider in deciding whether to use consensus decision making. Think of them as environmental elements, such as wind and tide, that can work for or against you.

1. Size of the group making the decision
2. Time available to make the decision, and the urgency to make it
3. Support (buy-in) needed to implement the decision
4. Shared values about the inclusion of all stakeholders
5. Amount of trust among group members, and members' experience in working together
6. Track record of consensus successes and failures, often related to group culture

Think of a decision that needs to be made in your organization. Circle the conditions in Table 4.1 that will apply as your group makes that decision. Then determine whether your circles fall primarily in Column A, B, or C. If your circles are primarily in Column A, it will be easier to reach consensus (see Figure 4.2). If they are generally in Columns B and C, consensus may be possible but

Table 4.1. Evaluating Six Decision-Making Factors.

	A	B	C
Size of group	Small (1–15)	Medium (15–50)	Large (50–100+)
Time/urgency	Unlimited	Not rushed	Short
Support (buy-in) needed	High	Some	Not much
Shared values	Strong	Mixed	Weak
Trust	High	Moderate	Low
Consensus track record	Excellent	Good	Poor

Figure 4.2. Complexity-Controversy Matrix with Additional Factors.

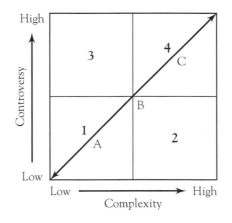

difficult. When the factors are primarily in Column C and the situation is high in both controversy and complexity (Corners 3 and 4), trying to reach consensus will be time consuming, difficult, and probably not worth the effort.

When you look at these factors in relation to the "square," it's easier to see that consensus decisions are not wise to attempt unless the factors are mostly in Columns A and B and the levels of complexity and controversy are low. Each board will need to decide when and whether it's wise to use consensus decision making.

Summary of Consensus Challenges

Critics say decision making by consensus equates with minority rule when individuals have veto power. It may not be upheld if legally challenged. This is often known as "the tyranny of the minority." Some point out that peer pressure and time constraints cause some groups to compromise too much and dumb down their decisions. Other groups are truly committed to getting everyone to agree on everything before moving forward and consequently spend too much time.

Groups that have the humanistic value or religious tradition of using consensus do it best. It's easier when the group believes that every person has a God-given wisdom that needs to be voiced as a part of the solution. Yet even Quaker communities, with a tradition of consensus decisions, can at times have difficulty achieving consensus. In most secular groups that belief and tradition are absent, and people have less patience with the process and each other.

When a group decides that consensus is its preferred decision-making method, that approach needs to be clearly written and agreed upon so it can be used consistently. Include this in your Special Rules for Meetings (see Resource A), in a way that shows *how* consensus will be reached. It's important that consensus not result in tyranny of the minority, or minority rule. Make the process available to everyone by including it in your *governance notebook* (see Chapter Fifteen).

The best approach is to consult the experts by purchasing a book or attending a workshop on consensus. Here is a synthesis of ideas from *Rules for Reaching Consensus*, by Saint and Lawson (1994); *On Conflict and Consensus*, by Butler and Rothstein (1991); and Interaction Associates (1994; 1997).

Launching into Consensus

Begin by making sure everyone is clear about the following three stages and foundation of reaching consensus. Clarify any questions about the process.

Start-Up: Foundation Agreements

- Agree on a definition of consensus.

- Agree on expectations for courteous behavior during dialogue.

- Agree on the process to be used (such as the stages discussed here).

- Agree on a backup decision-making method. (Who will decide if we cannot? Will we use a voting method after a certain time has passed?)

Stage 1

- Present the proposal or issue (as a handout or written on a flip chart).

- Encourage questions for understanding. Clarify factually without promoting or defending the issue.

- Give everyone an opportunity to voice his or her perspective and speak for or against the proposal.

- Call for consensus. If consensus exists, stop here and restate the agreement. If not, continue to Stage 2.

Stage 2: If Needed

- List what people like and what they have concerns about (in separate columns on a flip chart).

- Organize the related concerns into groups.

- Prioritize concerns (each person selects his or her two most important concerns; then list the concerns according to how many people selected each one).

- Discuss and modify the proposal in order to resolve concerns.

- Ask if any anyone wants to speak for or against the new proposal.

- Call for consensus. If consensus exists, stop here and restate the agreement. If not, continue to Stage 3.

Stage 3: If Needed

- Renegotiate time frame if necessary.

- Review mission and values of the organization.

- Restate remaining concerns.

- Encourage clarifying questions.

- Ask anyone to state reasons for or against the issue.

- Resolve one concern at a time.

- Take a nonbinding straw poll (ask for Yes or No or Gradients of Agreement; see Chapter Five).

- Ask for additional modifications ("What would it take for you to support this decision?").

- Call for consensus. If consensus exists, stop here and restate the agreement. If not, declare the proposal defeated.

The following are additional methods recommended by the experts to help groups reach consensus. These methods work best when the organization chooses to spend the time required to use them successfully.

Stand Aside

Stand aside is a term used by the Quaker community, those most experienced in building consensus decisions in a faith-based community. A person who chooses to stand aside is in effect saying, "Although I don't personally like this proposal, I will put the interest of the group first. Therefore I won't influence the decision and will support the will of the group." This option may be used when someone feels a conflict of interest, values, or some other personal reason for withdrawing from the decision making. This requires a *lot of trust* on the part of the member standing aside.

Postpone

If the group feels that a decision should not be made until more analysis or input is available, then the decision can be postponed. However, it's important to set a target date for reconsidering the decision. Be cautious with this tactic. It could be used to make an issue "disappear," such as when something is "postponed indefinitely" using Robert's Rules of Order.

Delegate to Modify

A proposal can be assigned to a subgroup (team, committee, or the like) that will add information, remove unacceptable portions, or otherwise modify it to fit the will of the group.

Eliminate Blocking or Veto

Blocking creates a situation in which one or two people (a minority) could hold back the group and cause a "tyranny of the minority." The concept of blocking or having a veto is what can make consensus bog down and keep groups from making truly democratic decisions.

Use the Backup Option

Decide on a backup method as your predetermined decision-making alternative. This could be delegating the decision with input to the executive committee, president, or executive director. It could also include one of several voting options (see Chapter Five for an explanation of voting options, including gaining substantial agreement or concordance).

Log Entry: Summary

Making group decisions can be difficult. When complexity and controversy are low and other supporting factors are in place, reaching consensus is easier. It gets more difficult as the supporting factors decrease and the levels of controversy and complexity increase.

If the situation is appropriate for consensus decisions, use a method clear to everyone and written into your special rules. Consensus is best suited to groups whose members have compatible values and a tradition of using this method successfully. Any group using consensus will need to spend the time required to do it well.

Getting Under Way

- Define consensus as it will be used in your organization. Agree on method or process you will use when reaching consensus, and write it down.

- Assess the situation surrounding major issues to determine the level of controversy and complexity.

- Assess the six other factors to consider, including the time limit. Decide if it's wise to spend the effort to reach consensus.

- Decide on a backup plan for making a decision if reaching consensus takes too long or becomes too difficult.

- If your organization's religious or humanistic values are so strong that members will accept only consensus decision making, then adopt a structured method that is written into your special rules for business meetings.

Making Headway

Knowing that consensus isn't always worth the struggle will keep your group from getting all tied up in knots when making decisions in situations with high levels of controversy and complexity. In the next chapter you'll learn ways to decide on your best options for making a decision when a vote is needed for the record.

5

Reaching for Concordance
When Consensus Is an Obstacle

The purpose of this chapter is to introduce options for reaching agreement, including a type of majority rule called *substantial agreement* or *concordance*.

In this chapter you will learn

- How to apply a range of decision-making options

- Why deciding by a simple majority can be divisive

- How to use concordance as a fallback to consensus

- How to use straw polling to identify levels of support and modify proposals

Problem: Disagreement About How to Decide

A condominium association that had functioned well for nearly twenty years was going through a transition. Many of the older and founding members were retiring and moving elsewhere. Younger members moving into the complex were joining the board. Now the members were more representative of the age range within the complex. However, with this shift came more conflict.

Everyone carried a different frame of reference, reflecting his or her age, values, and experience in organizational meetings. Some had learned about parliamentary procedure in their high school student government or a college sorority or fraternity. Others had never served on boards and had had a very different experience working in corporate quality improvement teams.

Some had found a good experience when using consensus decision making and others had not. The chairperson had seen one person block group agreement when that group was using consensus decision making, and she felt that this had resulted in minority rule.

Everyone on the association board supported majority rule, but board members were unsure how they should define majority. Was it always 50 percent plus one person? They feared being split down the middle on some difficult decisions, leaving half the group pleased and the others displeased. Someone told a story of a group that had been split down the middle on an issue, passed a motion by a very close vote, but then were always thwarted by the "losers" when they tried to implement the change. This association board was hoping to avoid these problems.

Deciding How You Will Decide

This board is typical of many that struggle with the best way to make decisions. One of the important things this and any group needs to agree on is its decision-making method—deciding *how* it will decide. (Until it makes this decision, the group is required to use the method stated in its bylaws.)

Many groups assume that the alternative to "majority rule" is consensus. As with other situations in our culture, we tend to think in terms of extremes (either-or choices). As discussed in Chapter Four, consensus can also mean that a few people can block a decision, allowing the minority to rule. There are other majority rule alternatives. It's possible to work hard to build consensus within a determined time limit but use a voting method to "finalize" the decision with a form of supermajority rule.

Why Avoid Simple Majority Rule?

Most bylaws state that meetings will be conducted using Robert's Rules of Order, which for most decisions provides a parliamentary method of *simple majority* rule (50 percent plus one). This is winner-take-all voting, producing clear winners and losers. A simple majority vote, particularly in a situation where there is lots of disagreement about a high-stakes issue, can result in some people feeling that they have gotten their way and others feeling they have lost something important. "Winners" feel happy; often "losers" feel mad. Sometimes the "winners" gloat, and the "losers" scheme how to get even or win the next time. A crew divided doesn't heal quickly. Some organizations have experienced a serious mutiny from which they have never recovered.

In cases involving a change of bylaws or rights of members, Robert's Rules of Order requires a two-thirds majority (also a *supermajority*). This produces a better indication of support but may still result in one-third of the group being disgruntled. Some states require a two-thirds vote in other situations as well. (For state-by-state information see *How to Form a Nonprofit Corporation in All 50 States*, Mancuso, 2000. For further clarification, contact the Office of the Secretary of State in your group's state of incorporation.)

One of the limitations of traditional voting is that it forces everyone into one of two positions—a *yes* position ("I agree") or a *no* position ("I disagree"). Yet those who vote yes may not all be in enthusiastic support of the idea. And saying no may result from anything like minor reservations to strong opposition. This terminology doesn't help us develop more ways to describe levels of agreement.

Full agreement is unanimity and a form of majority rule but is often confused with consensus. A unanimous vote means that everyone is willing to say yes to the decision as proposed and there is a vote to prove it. A consensus decision may mean that some have agreed to support the group whether they personally like the decision or not. There is usually a verbal agreement and no vote.

When a group wants to avoid the negative side of majority rule, it will often switch to using consensus. As we've seen in Chapter Four, when assessing the factors involved in decision making and the possibility of high controversy and complexity, this isn't always advisable. There's a tendency to neglect looking at the middle ground and alternative methods of decision making.

An Alternative to Both Simple Majority Rule and Consensus

Roberta's Special Rules for Meetings (see the template in Resource A) recommends seeking out the middle ground between consensus and simple majority rule. This option is to reach a *substantial agreement*. This means that at least 75 percent (or more) of those voting (given the presence of a quorum, which is discussed later in this chapter) approve a proposal.

Although a group may first strive for consensus, reaching substantial agreement may nevertheless be a more reasonable goal when the group is working within a stated time limit. The group predetermines its own comfort level with a target level of agreement, between 75 and 99 percent. This is then written in the group's special rules for meetings (Resource A).

Summarizing Ideas of Majority

Concepts of majority can be summarized by the percentages each one represents:

Simple majority	50% + 1
Supermajority	Usually 66% (2/3); higher than 50% + 1
Substantial majority	75% or more; a high supermajority
Unanimous	100%

Another way to visualize these concepts is to transfer them to the face of an analog clock (Figure 5.1).

Figure 5.1. Types of Majority Rule: By the Clock.

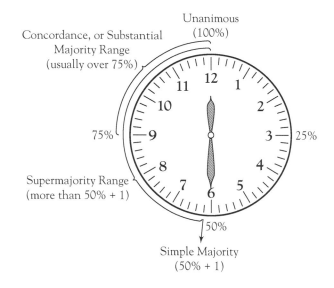

Simple Majority. A simple majority (50 percent plus 1) appears at the bottom of the clock, at 6:00 (plus one minute). Gaining a simple majority in some situations is hard, particularly in government elections or ballot initiatives. However, a simple majority vote of seven to five in a board with twelve members is highly divisive. Small groups that are polarized on an issue and split nearly in half may never recover from the conflict.

Supermajority. Moving on around the clock, we come to the supermajority. This includes the familiar two-thirds majority (66 percent), which falls at 8:00 on the clock. Sometimes it is defined as more or less, from 50 percent plus 1 to 99 percent. On the clock, it runs from 6:01 to 11:59.

The State of California is having trouble passing school bond measures that require a two-thirds majority vote, so the state is trying to reduce the required number of votes to a supermajority of 55 percent. Although the two-thirds majority vote is often hard to obtain on a controversial public issue, such as school bonds, a larger majority is preferable in a smaller group.

Substantial Majority. The substantial majority (more than 75 percent) is located between 9:00 and 11:59 on the clock. It is a form of supermajority that is on the last quarter of the clock. This is also called reaching a *substantial agreement* or the *sense of the group.* Another name for it is *concordance*—being in harmony or agreement.

It's necessary for your organization to decide how it will define substantial agreement, or concordance. Remember, this can be the backup voting plan when reaching consensus takes too long or seems impossible due to high controversy or the complexity of the issues.

Many groups that want more harmony than a simple majority offers when they act on a decision like the idea that at least 80 percent must agree in order to finalize a decision. For instance, concordance would be reached in a group of twelve with ten (83.33 percent) voting in favor of a proposal. (When working with these percentages, round down when the percentage ends in a fraction under 0.5 and up when the fractional amount is 0.5 or over.) In a group of twenty, sixteen voting yes would pass a proposal.

For example, using the clock face in Figure 5.1 and applying the twelve hours to a board of a dozen people, a simple majority is 7, a two-thirds supermajority is 8. A substantial majority is 9, if defined as 75 percent, or 10, if defined as 80 percent. Using the minutes of the clock to illustrate a group of sixty, such as a membership meeting, a simple majority is thirty-one, a two-thirds supermajority is forty, and a substantial majority is either forty-five (75 percent) or forty-eight (80 percent).

The Quorum Quandary

The concept of the *quorum* developed when voting could be done only in person and most people came to meetings on horseback. The mail wasn't reliable and e-mail wasn't conceivable. A quorum, a certain minimum number that must be in attendance before a vote can be taken, is required to make sure that nonprofits don't become personal clubs with a few making decisions for many people. The presence of a quorum means that enough people are at the meeting to make a fair decision for the rest of the group, all those who will be asked to support this decision. A quorum may also include those not present if they have had an opportunity to vote in advance of the meeting, such as by mail. Moreover, a quorum is necessary only for a group to make decisions (to close), not to generate ideas (open) or discuss and compare them (narrow).

A typical quorum is a simple majority (50 percent plus one) of the members unless otherwise stated in the bylaws or team's charter (Mancuso, 2000). Your group may specify a smaller or larger percentage. However because there are some restrictions on the minimum number, depending on the type of organization, it's best to consult the codes for your state by contacting the Office of the Secretary of State in your state. You may also wish to check the current publications available from Nolo Press in Berkeley, California. (See Resources.)

In larger membership organizations, the quorum often stated in the bylaws is one-third of the voting membership. Beware of going below one-third because special nonprofit rules may apply and a few people will end up making decisions for many others. For instance, in a membership organization of three hundred with a one-third quorum, one hundred people are needed to vote. If a decision is then made by a simple majority of those voting (50 percent plus one), as few as fifty-one people may make a decision for three hundred. (Bylaw and other structural changes usually need to be passed by two-thirds of a quorum, or seventy-five people in this example.)

We've all heard true stories of membership organizations with low quorum requirements and typically low meeting attendance that have made major changes that many members do not support. This leads only to ill-will and a destructive urge to "get even."

One approach to increasing participation is to modernize your voting method. People who may want to come to meetings may live too far away to battle traffic, be out of town on business frequently, or have other competing commitments. If you have organizational members, make it easy for them to vote as absentees by regular mail or fax. Develop a ballot that requires a signature, and make the deadline the day of the meeting. Use the same ballot at the meeting and count all ballots the same day. Use a list to check off each person who votes, ensuring only one ballot per member.

Groups with a secure Web site could permit electronic voting as long as each member can be identified and can vote only once. Because the codes governing nonprofits differ from state to state, it's a good idea to check with your state's Office of the Secretary of State before using electronic voting.

The voting method can be less complicated for a board or other smaller group. However, it's required by most states that everyone at an official board meeting be able to see or at least hear (via conference call) all the others in real time. (The use of the Web's chat features may alter the definition of "see and hear.") If a vote doesn't take place in the meeting, it should be done immediately as a continuation of the meeting where the issues were discussed. At the next board meeting the results can be reported and officially accepted.

Straw Polling to Test Agreement

A straw poll is an unofficial poll taken to gauge the amount of support for a proposal or idea. (The term *straw poll* originated from the ancient practice of throwing a straw up into the air to see which way the wind was blowing.) In Robert's Rules of Order taking a *straw poll* is not allowed. It's hard to understand why. One of our most democratic institutions, the jury system, allows straw polls to test the water, to see where people stand. Roberta's Rules of Order recommend using a nonbinding multiple-choice poll to test how people feel about an issue. Here are several examples of how multiple-choice options can be used as a polling device.

One method is to employ three colors—green, yellow, and red—to represent *go*, *slow*, and *no*. Green means, "I like the proposal as is"; yellow means, "I want more explanation and perhaps tweaking"; and red means, "I don't like it and would prefer to see it changed." An organization that was attempting to reach agreement on five guiding principles and thirteen goals to use in the measurement of its programs had a tight agenda. So each board member was given three colors in the form of five-inch by seven-inch sheets of paper. First, the board members clarified the information, and then they took a straw poll for each item, using the colored cards. Only those items for which people held up yellow or red cards were discussed further. This allowed more to be accomplished in a shorter time.

In an organization facing a great deal of change members were asked, "Based on your current understanding of this change, what is your readiness to support it?" They could choose one of five possible answers: (5) "I'm ready," (4) "I'm almost ready," (3) "I'm not yet ready," (2) "I'm not sure," and (1) "Count me out!" Everyone had a chance to respond by number. The total responses for each number were recorded for all to see. It was a quick way to take the temperature of the group.

Following this kind of poll, the discussion can focus on, for example, asking those who responded with numbers 1, 2, 3, and 4 what would it take for them to feel comfortable with moving up the scale. This can be a revealing and nonthreatening way for groups to discuss difficult issues.

The method just described of learning how much or little a person agrees with an idea or proposal is a modification of Sam Kaner and others' *Gradients of Agreement*, discussed in the *Facilitator's Guide to Participatory Decision-Making* (1996) and workshops taught by Kaner and his colleagues at Community at Work in San Francisco. There are often eight levels, but we'll simplify this to indicate various degrees of agreement or disagreement on a scale of 1 to 5.

Straw polls allow you to measure the "tide level" of a group. Higher is better than lower, when you can go aground and be stuck, going nowhere. Try using this method, as described here or modified to fit your organization, to test how much or little support there is for a proposal. Here is a summary of the Gradients of Agreement on a five-point scale:

Level	Response	Sample Statement
5	Enthusiastic response	"I endorse it enthusiastically."
4	Cautious support	"I support it with minor reservations."
3	Ambivalent support	"I have mixed feelings."
2	Little support	"I really don't like it."
1	No support	"I can't support it."

You might also want to include the following option when testing the levels of support for these gradients.

Level	Response	Sample Statement
0	Stand aside (see Chapter Four)	"I don't like this but I won't stand in the way of the group" (see Chapter Four). In this method, no blocking is allowed.

In a face-to-face meeting, the Gradients of Agreement can be easily applied by asking for a show of hands and recording responses on a flip chart. Do this after a proposal has been presented and clarified—but not yet modified. Sam Kaner and his coauthors (1996) suggest several variations, as discussed in the following sections, for finding out what everyone thinks and where each person stands on an issue. The best choice may depend on the size of the group and the time available.

Verbal Option: Pick One and Say Why

Go around the group and ask each person to state which level she or he supports and why. No discussion is allowed. Record each preference.

Silent and Speedy Options

Show of hands. Start with Level 5 and say, "Please raise your hand if you are at this level of support." Count the raised hands and record the number. Repeat for each level on down through 0.

Fist of five. Each person holds up the number of fingers that corresponds to their level choice.

Simultaneous declaration. Ask each person to write the number of his or her preference on a Post-it note. When finished, each person places the Post-it on a flip chart or holds it up for others to view.

Ballot. Ask each person to write his or her preference on a card and pass it to the leader to tally and report.

Modifying a Proposal Based on Initial Levels of Support

Once the levels of support are known, ask the members of the group these two questions:

"For those of you at Level 1 or 2, what would need to change for you to move to a higher level of support?"

"For those of you at Level 3 or 4, what would it take for you to be enthusiastic about this proposal, to move to Level 5?"

As these questions are answered, ask for recommendations for modifying the original proposal so that most people could move to Level 4 or 5 (enthusiastic or cautious support). Modify the proposal and test the levels of support again.

Making Support Quantifiable

Let's return to the example of the board that used colored cards to test support for program measurement goals. After the clarification, discussion, and modification resulting from its initial poll with the cards, the group was ready for a final poll, this time using the gradients of agreement scale. Group members had decided in advance that everyone needed to be between 4 and 5 on the scale for there to be agreement on the goals. After going through the goals one by one, they recommended to the team that was proposing the goals that certain goals needed more work on measurement. They decided to put these disputed numbers aside for the moment and take a straw poll to determine where everyone stood on support for the overall package. Each person called out his or her number (such as 4.3 or 4.6), and all were within the 4 to 5 range. The team was then charged with bringing the goals back to the next board meeting for a final look and vote. At that time a motion could be offered, "I move that we accept the team's revised proposal of goals and measurements for the coming year." And the board could take a binding vote, using the type of majority with which it is comfortable.

Consider a variation to use this method for preliminary decision making, perhaps via e-mail. You can add a number value to each level of the scale. (Remember, final decisions need to be approved at a regular meeting when a quorum is present, either in person or electronically.) For example, a level 5 vote would receive 5 points and so on, down to 1. Suppose your board has ten members ($N = 10$). Then the maximum number of points any proposal could get is 50 (10×5), assuming everyone selected level 5. The lowest possible number of points is 10 (10 × 1), assuming everyone selected level 1. This gives us a basis for determining a range.

Maximum Points If All Voted the Same

Level 5	10 × 5 = 50	Enthusiastic support
Level 4	10 × 4 = 40	Cautious support
Level 3	10 × 3 = 30	Ambivalent support
Level 2	10 × 2 = 20	Little support
Level 1	10 × 1 = 10	No support

Typically, of course, the total number of points a proposal receives will result from a mix of choices. For example, if five people on this ten-member board vote for Level 5 (25 points), four for Level 4 (16 points), and one for Level 2 (2 points), the total score will be 43. Each group needs to decide what different scores will mean and what its cut-off score will be between passing and not passing a proposal. Although the vote doesn't need to be unanimous, a proposal shouldn't pass if there is strong ambivalence. In this example where the maximum score is 50, a score between 40 and 50 would equal substantial agreement or concordance and be acceptable for passing a proposal. Here is a further possible breakdown of what this group's scores might mean in relation to a proposal using a ten-point range:

Score	*Meaning*
50	Is unanimously supported.
40–49	Is accepted as currently written.
30–39	Warrants further discussion to improve the proposal, then repoll.
20–29	Doesn't have enough support to proceed unless it is rewritten.
10–19	Is rejected as written.

At this point the group leader would say one of the following:

Score	Statement
50	"This proposal is accepted with unanimous support."
40–49	"This proposal is accepted with somewhat strong though not unanimous support."
30–39	"This proposal doesn't have enough support to be accepted or rejected. So we'll give everyone who has a reservation about it a chance to say what would improve the proposal enough to make it acceptable. Let's use our three-minute speaking limit for each person. Please pass if you have nothing to add."
20–29	"Given the negative feelings about this proposal, we'll defeat it now and consider it again only if it is rewritten to incorporate major changes."
10–19	"Due to lack of support, this proposal is defeated."

Handling an Impasse with a Backup Plan

It is also necessary to decide on one or more fallback options ahead of time, in the event that individuals with Level 3 and 4 support are at an impasse and cannot be moved to a higher level. The fallback option agreed to ahead of time could be to defer the decision to

- The leader (the president or the executive committee)

- The group, through a vote using a predetermined level of majority rule (simple, super, or substantial)

However you decide to use this straw-polling or preliminary voting method, be certain that everyone understands it and agrees on how to define the levels and that the group uses it consistently.

Log Entry: Summary

Each organization needs to decide the appropriate decision-making method for its culture. When certain conditions apply, consensus may be the best option. When consensus bogs the group down and time is running out, a voting method can be useful. This method may be either a predetermined type of supermajority (with a stated percentage that forms a substantial majority recommended) or an agreement to defer the decision to the leader(s) of the group.

Using a multiple-choice straw poll gives everyone an opportunity to express his or her concerns and influence the proposal. Discussing Gradients of Agreement allows all members of a group to express their opinions without taking a yes or no position.

Getting Under Way

- Talk together about the values of your organization or board regarding the most appropriate way to make decisions.

- Decide how you will make decisions, and write it into your special rules for business meetings (See Resource A).

- Use a straw poll that determines levels of support for a proposal to gain more understanding and agreement before making a final decision.

Making Headway

You have just completed the first course on the compass that we're using for this voyage—Navigate Decision Making Through Rough Waters. Now you know the options available for making decisions and can decide which ones make sense for your group. Before exploring further, take the time to apply this information.

Next we're going to shift to another course of the compass—
Select Easy Meeting Methods, to Get All Hands on Deck. Although you may already have a method for planning meetings, this
section could give you some different ideas and an easier format. If
you know you're already doing this well, select a different compass
course to cover next.

Part III

Select Easy Meeting Methods to Get All Hands on Deck (Southeast Course)

6

Balancing Traditional Meetings
with Modern Media

The purpose of this chapter is to encourage leaders to make the best use of face-to-face meetings and to become comfortable with electronic meetings when these are affordable and more convenient. In this chapter you will learn

- How to take advantage of the meeting space when group members meet in person

- Why balancing electronic meetings with face-to-face meetings makes sense

- What types of teleconferencing and other options to use

- What the advantages and disadvantages of telephone conference calls are

- How to apply courtesy guidelines for telephone conferencing

Problem: A Cranky Board

An active social club holds its monthly board meetings in the evenings. Members of the club live all over a metropolitan area with heavy commuter traffic. Everyone comes directly from work—most drive more than an hour to get there and cross at least one bridge during the rush hour. By the time they arrive they are tired, hungry, and often cranky.

Because this is a social club, with a nice clubhouse, members particularly value the time spent together. Several board members are lobbying to have the monthly meeting by conference call. Others really like interacting with other board members and would miss the face-to-face contact.

The Value of Meeting All Together

There is no substitute for a face-to-face meeting to build relationships and promote working together. Studies show that more than 75 percent of the communication between individuals comes from visual cues, such as body language, eye contact, and other physical reactions, in addition to tone of voice. Whenever possible, get people together to help build relationships and rapport, the bases of cooperation. Because of the value of these face-to-face meetings, let's look first at how to make the most of this type of meeting.

Choose the Location for Convenience, Comfort, and Focus

When looking for a location for a meeting, first consider the convenience to the members. It may be necessary to rotate the meeting location to make it fair—or equally inconvenient—for everyone.

For nonprofit organizations the cost of space can be an issue. You can request space from corporations, churches, banks, nonprofit technical assistance centers, or libraries and other public buildings. If the board is small or the house is large, it's nice to occasionally meet in someone's home. This informal setting helps people relax and get to know each other. These opportunities build relationships that develop trust.

Set Up the Room for Inclusion and Visibility

When you have access to a flexible space, move the tables around to create an open circle, like a horseshoe or a half-moon, in which everyone can have eye contact. The *America*, a famous sailing ship for which the international sailing race America's Cup was named, had a lovely semicircular cockpit for everyone to sit together (when not racing) and see forward. Keep that image in mind when setting up a room for a meeting.

When putting rectangular tables together, leave an open area. Focus everyone's attention by putting paper on the wall or placing a flip chart in front for visible note taking. If using an open "U" shape, avoid right angles. Bring the tables together at a 45-degree rather than a 90-degree angle, so everyone can see all the others. The tables will have small angular spaces between them that may make some people uncomfortable at first, but most like the elbowroom. Give everyone enough "personal space" so that people are not so close together they're uncomfortable. (Remember that different cultures have different preferences about closeness.)

If using a single table that is a large rectangle, select a focal point in the center of one of the long sides for the person leading the meeting. If the leader sits at the traditional head of the table, he or she is farther away from at least half of the participants. The best location is in the middle of the group. If someone is handicapped or in a wheelchair, make it easy for him or her to be seated among the others, not off to the side.

When the room is a narrow rectangle with a large, often immobile table, use three-quarters of the table and face the group toward the long side of the room. This allows more space to be used as a focal point for information. Use the wall for posting flip chart sheets or for projecting a presentation (only if other low-tech means of communicating aren't easy to see).

If possible, face the group away from outside doors, windows, and other distractions. Although the view may be great, a speaker turns into a faceless silhouette when standing in front of a bright window. Save the view for breaks.

Provide Food to Ease People into the Meeting

The best way to get a meeting to start on time and to provide time for informal connections is to offer a dinner or a social half hour before the meeting. In some urban areas people may have been driving for an hour in traffic and need a buffer zone before being able to settle down to productive work. Sharing a meal or refreshments is also a good way for group members to get to know each other informally. During this time people may also make announcements and distribute handouts for the meeting.

Sometimes having a meal to start the meeting can increase attendance. One community advisory panel (CAP) was having trouble with regular attendance, but when the hosting company offered a nice dinner half an hour before the start time "for those who wanted it," everybody came. This CAP has been meeting for eleven years with a consistent group every month. When people are volunteering their time, a meal is a nice reward. Similarly, the board of a church was having difficulty getting meetings started at 7:30 P.M. Now it offers a time to "commune" at 7:00, half an hour before the meeting. People can bring something to eat if they have missed dinner. This approach allows the meeting to start on time with everyone already present and "connected."

If your organization's budget can afford it, treat the board members to a modest meal. This is a fair exchange for their leadership and commitment to the organization. (It can be stated as a policy related to board compensation or reimbursement.) If the organization's budget is small or if this would be a political issue, have take-out foods delivered and ask everyone eating to chip in for the cost. This has been working well for years at the monthly meeting of one society's board.

If possible, avoid restaurants; the setting is just too distracting and generally unpredictable. If your group has to meet in a restaurant, make sure you have a quiet section or a separate room. When possible, have the meal first and then have the meeting. Avoid allowing a meal to continue into the meeting. When information and food compete, food wins. (Besides, who wants to perform a life-saving maneuver in the middle of a discussion?)

Have a Grace Period to Reduce Stress

It used to be easier to get from one place to another; now traffic can be so unpredictable that someone leaving with plenty of time can still arrive late. When people are driving or commuting to a meeting, anything can happen. Rather than increase their stress ("I'm late!"), give them a little leeway. If having a meal doesn't work for your group, then build in some social time to allow a fifteen-minute *grace period* at the beginning of the meeting for those who may be unavoidably late. Predictably, many meetings seem to lose at least fifteen minutes in the beginning anyway. People who come in late need time to get focused and to greet others. You might as well plan for it, as do movie theaters that run fifteen minutes of previews. Let everyone settle down before beginning.

Problem: A Commuting Meeting

A local unit of a national disease control organization used to have all its advisory board meetings in the county where the chapter office was located. Over the years the organization's structure has changed and several of the county offices have joined together to become a regional office. The national organization has just issued plans for consolidating further into larger regions.

Now, faced with the prospect of having to go farther to get to a meeting combining four counties, board members are balking at driving in commuter traffic because the trip often involves crossing the city. A task team is exploring electronic options.

The Need for an Electronic Meeting Alternative

Although most small nonprofits will continue to have face-to-face board meetings, several factors are pushing more organizations to provide alternative ways for those farthest from the primary meeting place to attend meetings.

- In large cities it's increasingly difficult to get through traffic, particularly during peak hours after work.

- Members of boards may miss meetings because of their work and travel schedules.

- Women or men with young children must arrange for baby-sitters.

- In some organizations board members live more than fifty miles from each other or from the primary meeting place.

In addition, if a board is national or international, meeting face-to-face is very expensive. Even if the meeting is held only quarterly, it can cost a board member or the organization a lot in travel expenses. The personal time lost is priceless. The need for another way to meet is obvious. This problem can also exist in a metropolitan area. One board in the Bay Area of San Francisco has a one-hundred-mile spread among its seven members. Telephone conferencing is often inexpensive in comparison to the personal toll and cost of traveling to meetings. Members may be willing to chip in to pay the conference call telephone bill rather than bear the costs and time lost to travel.

Because their members are communicating better between meetings now that they are using the Internet, some boards have reduced the frequency of their meetings from monthly to bimonthly. With the continuing invention of new media, boards can meet face-to-face only quarterly and conduct the rest of their business through electronic media.

Telephone Conference Calls

Several solutions are available; the easiest and most available at this time is to use the telephone. Let's start with the situation in which most of the members of the group meet face-to-face and a few others call into the meeting or meet in another location. The primary meeting location, the *host site*, can establish a *remote* telephone link through a telephone company. The telephone service provider gives your group a call-in phone number and code. This number will connect others with the host site. The simplest arrangement is to have one meeting site, with other members calling from work, home, or wherever is convenient for them. If there are two separate meeting sites with several people in each location, each site should have a person designated to lead the meeting. The best way to achieve clear sound from locations with multiple members is to purchase a piece of conference-calling equipment designed to pick up multiple voices. (It's very annoying to those listening by phone when one person's voice is muted by another's.)

Virtual Meeting Sites

Another option is to have no meeting place at all. Today you can set up an Internet chat room or other "virtual" arrangement, such as video conferencing, from your computer via the Web. At the appointed time, everyone joins the meeting. (It helps if the meeting leader is there first.) Each member can be welcomed and can enjoy chatting with others until everyone is present.

Start by having a *check-in* time when the meeting begins. Ask everyone to say the name of the location she or he is joining from and where she or he is physically—at a desk at work, in the living room at home, and so forth. This gives the members a visual cue, helping them see each other in their minds and making the situation feel a bit more real. All electronic (telephone, Internet, or video) meetings require a good agenda and some tight timekeeping, as they can be expensive. A less expensive telephone option may be to sublease a *bridge line* from another organization. Companies and individuals that conduct training or coaching *teleclasses* over the phone may own a line that you could arrange to use.

Advantages of Electronic Meetings

The obvious advantage of electronic meetings is having better attendance. This method supports today's more mobile and geographically dispersed lifestyles. It can also be cheaper for some members. With the cost of gasoline increasing and roads and airports becoming more congested, staying in one place is appealing.

Disadvantages of Electronic Meetings

The first and primary disadvantage of electronic meetings is frustration if the technology doesn't work. It's a good idea to practice before going live. Another disadvantage is the lack of visual cues—there is so much that's communicated by more than words. Taking away the visual element makes everyone have to work a little harder to be understood. For some organizations the price of long-distance telephone charges for a group meeting for several hours is also a deterrent.

Meetings that are poorly planned and badly run only get worse when there are multiple places or people on the line or on the computer. Nothing substitutes for a well-planned agenda and a leader who maintains the focus. A good set of courtesy guidelines specific to this type of meeting is also helpful (see Exhibit 6.1). Although some of these guidelines can be used in any meeting, the first three are particularly important for remote meetings.

Videoconferencing

Some large nonprofit corporations use television for meetings held with participants across the country. Although this usually isn't affordable for smaller nonprofits, check with other nonprofits or cor-

Exhibit 6.1. Remote Meeting Courtesy Guidelines.

Tips for Participants	Sounds Like
Say your name and location first.	"This is Jane in Los Angeles."
Say who you are each time you speak.	"This is Alice speaking. I believe that . . ."
Tell the group if you have to leave and when you return.	"This is Joe. I have to leave for five minutes." "This is Joe. I'm back."

Tips for the Leader	Sounds Like
Lead a check-in roll call.	"Would each of you please say your name and give your location?"
When asking for input, call everyone by name as you go around the group.	"Mary, what do you think? . . . Jim? . . . How about you, Steve?"
Give everyone a time limit.	"Under our courtesy guidelines, each person can take up to three minutes to respond."
Limit the number of "volleys" to two.	"It sounds like Joe and Mary have exchanged opinions with each other several times. What do others think? Jane?"
Announce time checks.	"It looks like we have only fifteen minutes left."
Check in periodically.	"Let's go around the group and respond. Let's go alphabetically by first name. Alice, please start."

porations to inquire about renting their facilities. Videoconferencing is also available at selected Kinko's locations for an hourly rate.

For more virtual video and Web-based meetings, it's possible to install a small camera on top of your home or office computer so you can be seen by others. Although this technology is available and constantly improving, it can be expensive when provided for every board member. For this to be a viable meeting option, everyone would need to be connected via the same technology. A word of caution: if you don't have a technically knowledgeable person available, be careful about attempting videoconferencing or Web meetings unaided.

Good Meeting Leadership Is Required

The need for all the methods previously mentioned for holding productive meetings is even more apparent in electronic meetings. Make sure each person has the same agenda and supporting material. It's a good idea to have a fax machine available in all locations for immediate transmittal. If the group is brainstorming ideas, narrowing options, or making decisions be sure there is someone acting as group recorder and keeping the list of things suggested or done, preferably in a way that makes the list visible to all in the group.

At the end of the meeting, wrap up with a summary of follow-through items, naming who is going to be doing what actions within a specific time limit. Write this summary down to share with all.

Problem: Communicating Between Meetings

The board of a private school had traditionally relied on the board secretary to take detailed minutes at each meeting, transcribe them, and mail them out. Because the secretary was a career woman with two children, she had many other responsibilities. By the time the board members received the minutes, the information could be several weeks old. There was so much detail that people generally only scanned the minutes. Although there was a section for follow-up action items, the time lag meant that many had already been done or forgotten.

The Power Is No Longer in the Pen

A primary goal for every group that meets should be to get every member connected to the Internet. All board members and others on committees or teams should acquire an e-mail account. In the new millennium, board members will be left behind without an e-mail address.

Although some boards rely on e-mail regularly, others are just getting started. But the power's in the keyboard these days. It's the best way to communicate quickly and efficiently with a group of people. However, although some people can't work without it, some hate it. Also nonprofits need to be aware of a possible *digital divide* between those who can afford the tools and those who cannot—and help to close it.

Each organization needs to address this issue, even if it requires using board development funds to purchase equipment or applying for a grant to do so. Some organizations have even purchased laptops or electronic palm-size notebooks to speed communication between members. Your group's board work can benefit when everyone has access to e-mail and begins to feel comfortable using it. Some may just need some technical support. At the very least, help those not on e-mail to get fax machines. Someone can be designated to fax the e-mail to these individuals. Regular mail is just too slow to use between meetings.

E-mail

E-mail is the most productive addition to communication for groups since the telephone. However, for some it takes some getting used to. E-mail is very helpful for planning meetings, communicating between meetings, and collaborating on projects—within an organization and among organizations. This and other future electronic tools will foster faster and easier communication. Use e-mail or a secure Internet tool for

- Sharing drafts of proposals and getting feedback

- Asking for and getting input into the content for agendas

- Posing and answering questions

- Sending requests and receiving information

- Reminding everyone of meetings and sending directions

Whatever we used to do by phone and regular mail can now happen faster on the Internet. E-mail also eliminates telephone tag. However, there are some drawbacks and things to avoid. For instance, e-mail messages can cause more misunderstandings. There is no tone of voice or facial expression to help interpret someone's meaning. People's choice of words can sometimes be confusing, particularly when people from different cultures and multiple languages are involved.

E-mail should not be used to send angry, accusatory messages of any kind. Beware of communication that can be hurtful and hard to retract. Adopt some basic guidelines, such as the following, for communicating electronically.

Ten E-Mail Guidelines

1. Avoid sending any message that accuses someone of wrongdoing, particularly when that e-mail could go to other people. If someone needs to be confronted, do it privately and in person if possible.

2. Read your e-mail over to yourself before sending it. Think about how it might be received. Is it clear, or could it be misinterpreted?

3. Keep a lot of white space in your messages. Use short statements and short paragraphs.

4. When writing about multiple topics, begin each discussion with a one- or two-word headline in capital letters. Better yet, send separate e-mails, one for each topic.

5. Other than for headlines or an isolated word for emphasis, don't use capital letters when writing messages. It comes across as if you're shouting.

6. When responding to a series of e-mails, restate the issue or give some context so the reader will know exactly what topic your reply concerns.

7. Set your font size at 12 points or larger so your message is easy to see.

8. Use a font that is not fancy and is easy to read.

9. Always check spelling and grammar before sending a message.

10. Be aware that not everyone checks e-mail frequently—you may need to call some individuals to ask them to log on.

Sticking to guidelines like these will help your group's e-mail communication add to group productivity. Also, periodically evaluate how your communication is working by asking for feedback: What's helpful? What's being harmed or hindered? What do we need to agree to do differently? Avoid the pitfalls as you use the tool of e-mail to enhance participation and productivity in your organization.

E-Groups

It's fairly easy these days to set up a group e-mail list, or an *e-group*. Once you have an e-group set up, you can use one address to communicate a message to everyone on the list at once. If you do not know how to do this, someone's teenager probably does. If not, call an e-mail service provider—some of them provide free services.

Although an e-group is easy to set up, it can produce too much mail for some. Set up some courtesy guidelines, such as a reminder that e-group mail should be sent only when everyone on the list needs to know something. Messages that matter to only a few members should be addressed only to them. (Newer boards tend to have a flurry of mail in the beginning, then it tapers off, but it's best to avoid overwhelming people in the first place.)

Web Pages

If your organization has a Web site, have your Web designer set up a separate page on the site for the board and for each working team or subgroup. Each page should represent the work of that group— meeting notes, action plans, goals, and so forth. These pages may be made secure and available to organizational members only. Authorized members can enter their secure area with a password and read information.

Another method, when the Web site isn't an option, is to use software called *groupware*, arranged through a Web service provider. This software allows all board members to read and make comments on a proposal between meetings. Each person has a password and can access the material and read the comments of all other members.

Internet Meetings

Web-based meeting management companies are also an option when you want to get everyone on the Internet at the same time. If you want to explore the best opportunities, get the most cyber-savvy person on your board to contact several Web meeting companies for a description of services and costs.

The options on the Internet are changing too rapidly to anticipate what will be available in the future. You can be assured this medium will continue to develop, offering new and amazing options. The best way to keep up with them is to use an Internet search engine, typing "Web meetings" into the search box. If you do contract with a company that specializes in Web meetings, be sure that it provides complete customer service, including training and a telephone help line.

Log Entry: Summary

Giving members a chance to ease into a meeting by providing a meal before the meeting or some refreshments and social time for fifteen to thirty minutes before starting will help them relax and be more focused. The location and room arrangement for a meeting can make a significant difference in the tone, the focus, and ultimately the results. Pay attention to comfort and to the visibility of members to each other and of any information displayed for the group.

Although face-to-face meetings are generally preferable for building relationships among members of boards, committees, or teams, electronic meetings are becoming more necessary. This is particularly true when people find they are spending more time and energy on getting to the meeting and back than on what they do in the meeting.

Although the transition will be easy for some and difficult for others, all boards need to be using electronic communication. The time for sending out board meeting summaries and agendas by "snail mail" is past. Take it slowly at first, helping those who don't feel comfortable get used to it—because it's here to stay.

Getting Under Way

- If distance isn't an issue, plan your meetings to be face-to-face; do team and committee work between meetings using electronic media.

- If distance is an issue, fax or e-mail the agenda and conduct the meeting by telephone or on the Web, or if the budget allows or you have some good friends in the right places, videoconference.

- Make sure each member has access to e-mail or a fax to speed up communications. Use e-mail between, but not in place of, meetings.

- Set up a secured portion of your Web site or other electronic option for board communication.

Making Headway

Once you've established the best way to meet, then it's time to plan for and conduct the meeting in a way that meets the expectations of your organization's mission and makes progress toward its vision.

Respecting Everyone's Time by Steering a Steady Course

The purpose of this chapter is to help you plan your group's meetings around people's needs and expectations while also keeping a focus on the mission and vision of the organization.

In this chapter you will learn

- How to focus the meeting on what's important to the participants

- Why it is important to answer twelve common questions in the first fifteen minutes

- How to use an easy agenda format that takes you around all the "spokes on the wheel" to a productive meeting

- Why it's helpful to put the mission statement or vision statement, or both, on the agenda

Problem: The Self-Defeating Public Meeting I

A county health coalition wanted to get more community involvement. Coalition leaders believed that making others aware of the high rates of cancer in the county was the first step. There had been articles in the newspaper, but now they wanted to have a community meeting.

The meeting was scheduled for 6:00 P.M. on a Wednesday night in the county supervisor's chambers. The ending time of the meeting wasn't specified. The chairs were fixed and the space was large. When people arrived they sat scattered throughout the room. Many people who lived in the county commuted to a nearby city to work. Because they had to drive a distance through rush hour traffic people arrived throughout the first half hour.

When participants arrived there was no agenda to tell them what to expect. A panel was asked to make brief presentations, but no one monitored the time. Some speakers were very long-winded. As a result, the time for input from the audience was cut short. Because there was no food available and it was around the dinner hour, people were hungry and grumpy. Some who had come on time started to leave at 7:30 P.M., not knowing how long the meeting would last. There were few people there at 8:00 P.M. when the coalition leaders had planned to ask for community response.

Are We Wasting Our Time Here?

Put yourself in the position of a participant in this meeting. Or think of the last time you went to a nonprofit organization's meeting (neighborhood association, PTA, community, or board meeting) and thought it was a good value for your time. A common complaint is that these meetings are often poorly planned and run. Is it any wonder that attendance is often low?

Many meetings aren't planned with the participants' interests in mind. What do *they* want to get out of it? Why are *they* choosing to attend? What do *they* need to know as soon as they arrive to feel they've made a good choice by attending? Have you ever attended community "involvement" meetings in which panel members gave speeches for three-quarters of the time? When you participate in a meeting, what do *you* want to know right away? Before you look at the list of typical questions that follows, think about all the concerns or questions you might have when you've just arrived at a meeting and you're waiting for it to begin. If any of your questions are not on this list, you may want to add them so you can also consider how best to answer them.

1. Why are we meeting anyway?
2. Will this be a good use of my time?
3. Is there an agenda?
4. How long will this take?
5. Who are these other people?
6. Are we going to accomplish something?
7. What happened as a result of the last meeting?
8. What's expected of me?
9. Will we get off on tangents (again)?
10. Will we be making decisions and, if so, how?
11. When will we take a break?
12. Where is the food?

Answering These Twelve Questions

How many times have you sat through meetings not knowing the answers to these questions? Most agendas structured under Robert's Rules of Order don't answer most of these questions, and the meetings leave people feeling uninvolved and sometimes annoyed. The answers should be made clear in the beginning of a meeting, either verbally or on the printed agenda. Once people know these answers, they can be more present mentally as well as physically and can participate more fully in the meeting. Here are tips on how to handle each of these questions when you are in the position of planning or leading a meeting. Thanks to IA and others for these ideas.

1. *Why are we meeting?* What is the purpose of this meeting? If there is a primary purpose for the meeting other than to conduct

the regular business of a board or ongoing group, a purpose statement such as "The purpose of this meeting is to plan our upcoming community forum" will help everyone to focus. For regular board meetings, it's helpful to put the organization's mission statement or vision statement, or both, at the top of the agenda to remind everyone of what's important.

2. *Will this be a good use of my time?* This is a key concern. No one wants to waste time in meetings. If you are the meeting leader, announce to all that you don't intend to waste their time. Go over the agenda to make sure it includes substance, and estimate how much time to allot to each section. Ask for everyone's help to stay on track.

3. *Is there an agenda?* You can answer this by sending an agenda out ahead of time via e-mail or passing one out in the beginning of the meeting. State the purpose of the meeting or the mission or vision of the organization on the top and organize the agenda around the meaningful results the meeting is intended to accomplish. Use discussion of goals or strategy to engage everyone's thinking toward the future. Avoid giving reports on what's already been decided or occurred. Put them in a handout or on the Web site. Try the format suggested later in this chapter for good results.

Include in your agenda an indication of the processes the meeting leader will use, such as brainstorming, categorizing, listing pros and cons, prioritizing, or other methods. Allow enough time for interaction and discussion.

4. *How long will this take?* Have you noticed that many meeting announcements tell when the meeting starts but not when it's going to end? Make the time the meeting is expected to end clear in the meeting notice and also at the beginning of the meeting.

Determine the time to be given to each topic. Calculate times in five-minute increments (five, ten, fifteen, twenty, and so on); almost everything takes at least five minutes. Appoint a timekeeper (remember the rabbit with the watch in *Alice in Wonderland?*) to remind speakers of the time. Make sure the group's meeting rules include a limit on the time each person may speak on a topic during discussions.

5. *Who are these other people?* Too many meetings of larger groups never help participants meet each other. If people haven't met or if some are new, allow time for brief introductions (see the discussion of helping people to connect later in this chapter). It's difficult for most people to feel comfortable enough to participate when they don't know the others in the room. Cooperation and decision making is based on trust, something that doesn't develop by accident. Take the time to build trust by helping people get to know each other and perhaps find something in common.

6. *Are we going to accomplish something?* Before spelling out the agenda, list the things that the group needs to accomplish or make a decision on at the meeting. Start with, "By the end of this meeting we need to accomplish the following." These items should be concrete, specific, tangible, or observable: for example, "We need to complete a draft of the budget for the next year." Go for the "meat," and tap into the thinking of those present about meaningful issues, goals, strategies, and plans. If a report intended to increase knowledge or understanding is presented, state why it will be useful: for example, "We will hear a report about the activities of the state legislature so that we can decide how to proceed with our advocacy effort."

7. *What happened as a result of the last meeting?* Hand out a summary (not detailed minutes) of the last meeting with the following information: who attended, what they decided, what actions were planned, and who is responsible for carrying out these actions (see Chapter Eight). An update on progress on these actions should be part of the agenda.

8. *What's expected of me?* If someone is expected to take a role in the meeting, put his or her name on the agenda. The more roles you can give away, the better. Make sure you let each person know ahead of time. (Have you ever arrived at a meeting and found you were supposed to present or say something, but you hadn't been told

in advance? Not nice!) Also, tell all the participants at the start of the meeting that you're glad they are there and that they are expected to contribute ideas, ask questions, give opinions, provide clarification, and help the meeting be productive (which includes staying on time).

9. *Will we get off on tangents?* If your group has a history drifting away from the topic, you may have difficulty changing this behavior. However, you can respect a roving speaker's concerns and get back on track by having a sheet of flip chart paper posted on the wall on which you can list items that come up but are not on the agenda. This list is sometimes called the *issues list,* the *parking lot,* or the *bin list.* (Facilitator lore says that the latter term refers to a *binnacle,* a French word referring to a cabinet located around the helm of a ship, where the compass was kept. It is not a trash bin.) Issues or questions on this list need to be discussed but probably at a later date. Make sure someone, either outside the meeting or during the next meeting, addresses each of these items.

10. *Will we be making decisions and, if so, how?* This is a very important question that should be clarified right away. Is this a decision-making meeting, or are the decisions being made elsewhere? Who will be making them, and by when? What will the decision-making method be? Clarifying the decision-making method in the beginning of the meeting will prevent many misunderstandings later. (See Chapter Five for decision-making options.) A common problem on larger boards is that too much of the decision making is done in the executive committee (see Chapter Thirteen), leaving the remaining board members bored from listening to reports. Make important decisions in meetings of the whole board.

11. *When will we take a break?* This is particularly important for smokers and those in the habit of checking messages regularly. Even though you may want to break them of these habits, just plan for a ten-minute break (which will take fifteen minutes) about every hour. Taking breaks will also increase everyone's attention span.

12. *Where is the food?* Have some food or at least nonalcoholic beverages or water available, particularly if the meeting is during a mealtime. Avoid serving alcohol as a part of any meeting. Save it for special events or receptions, but always provide an alternative. To ensure a more social and relaxed meeting (and to get people there on time) start with snacks or even dinner (see Chapter Six).

The Power of a Plan

These questions are on many people's minds when attending a meeting. Do what you can to answer them in the first fifteen minutes. The best way to accomplish this is to build the answers into a complete agenda, which addresses people's needs and engages them in the meeting.

Now, once again put yourself in the role of the person planning and leading a meeting. The first step is usually to develop a working plan, an expanded agenda. The agendas for most meetings, if they exist, usually consist of a list of topics, each described only by one word. Sometimes time frames are supplied, but sometimes time isn't mentioned, not even the meeting ending time. No wonder most meetings run over or don't accomplish what is planned. An agenda is often a good clue to an organization's general approach: Is it well thought out or seemingly thrown together at the last minute? Does looking at the agenda inspire confidence in the leadership and encourage people to participate?

Problem: The Self-Defeating Board Meeting II

The board of a prominent social club with a large facility in a metropolitan city has a monthly board meeting in the middle of the morning. The agenda format is taken from Robert's Rules of Order: call to order, committee reports, old business, new business, announcements. There is nothing to indicate what decisions need to be made. Committee reports and routine matters take a great deal of time.

There are no time limits listed on the agenda so every meeting goes over the time scheduled.

Because the meeting is held in the middle of the day, few younger working members are on the board. The average age of members is sixty. One of the primary issues is how to attract younger members to keep the club membership growing.

Problem: The Self-Defeating Board Meeting III

A respected organization that assists students who are underrepresented in the fields of math and science to enter college and the workforce has an advisory council. Included are representatives from secondary schools, colleges, and industry. The group now numbers twenty-five people, but only half usually attend the quarterly meetings.

The day of the meeting is structured into committee meetings in the morning and the full board meeting in the afternoon. Organization staff put a great deal of time into preparing reports for the committee meetings. An executive committee that also meets in the morning makes most of the important decisions. The afternoon agenda consists of a series of reports from the morning meetings. There is very little problem solving and decision making in the full group.

Most group members want to have a bigger impact, not just attend meetings to hear reports. Most feel that the format of the meetings is the problem and want it to change.

An Alternative Format

The type of agenda prescribed in Robert's Rules of Order is very dry, mechanical, and general. Old business is separated from new business as if that rather than urgency or potential impact were the most important distinction. On these agendas there is almost never a statement about the meeting purpose or a list of results to be accomplished.

Introductions are usually missing because it's assumed that people already know each other—as if they couldn't know more. There is little room for building relationships. According to Peter Block,

> We have the image that a good meeting is one where the presentation is clear and power pointed, things move quickly, there is little conflict and we don't waste time with feelings. . . .
>
> Human systems require patience, they grow out of conflict and succeed when feelings are connected to purpose. Meetings have deeper meaning than just to cover the content and decide something. Meetings are an important place where commitments and relationships are either chosen or denied [Axelrod, 2000].

Although you may already be using a better structure than Robert's rules recommend, take a look at an alternative model designed to answer participants' questions quickly and set a tone for participation. In this structure, the key word or phrase in the section title always starts with C, not to be cute but to help you remember. The key words are *complete, convene, connect, context, consent agenda, content, continue,* and *conclude*.

Another way to think of this model is as the wheel on a sailing ship (Figure 7.1). Consider that this wheel has eight spokes, each one taking the wheel a one-eighth turn. Each spoke has equal value, and all are necessary to make the ship turn safely. Notice the sections of the meeting inside the spaces between the spokes, beginning at the right of the spoke. The wheel needs to turn one complete revolution in a meeting—and another complete revolution in the next meeting, and so on. Once this format becomes familiar, it will be easy to recreate using a template you've made on your computer (see Resource C for sample agendas). Here are explanations of each section, moving clockwise on the wheel.

Figure 7.1. Eight Spokes to a Successful Meeting.

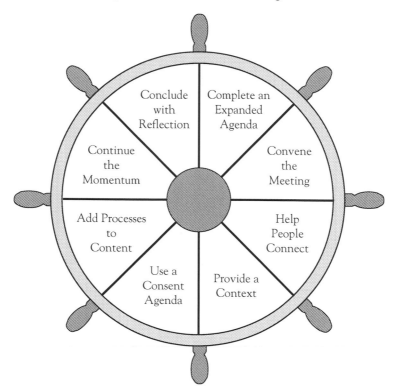

1. Complete an Expanded Agenda:
What Are We Going to Do at This Meeting?

An expanded agenda provides more information for members than the simple list of topics in categories as seen in Robert's Rules of Order. Start by stating the organization's mission and perhaps vision at the top. This keeps everyone focused on why the organization exists and what it is striving to become. If this is a special meeting (as opposed to a regular monthly meeting) state the meeting purpose.

Example

"The purpose of this meeting is to plan our next fundraising event."

The Grove Consultants International, known for the graphic techniques and predrawn templates used in facilitating meetings, has developed a helpful acronym for the information that participants need at the start of a meeting. It comes from the template "Meeting Startup" (Sibbet, 1996), which uses the acronym OARR. The last R stands for "roles" and refers to shared roles in meetings. The acronym has been modified, with permission, to spell OARS, as in rowing a boat together.

O for Outcomes, the intended results or accomplishments of the meeting

A for Agenda, what the group plans to do in the meeting

R for Rules, the ground rules or courtesy guidelines that will keep the meeting fair

S for Shared Roles, who will do what to share responsibility

Here is more detail about these items.

Outcomes

To inform people about what decisions are necessary, list the things the group intends to accomplish or needs to decide at this meeting. State them emphatically. Complete this sentence: "By the end of this meeting we will. . . ."

Example

"By the end of this board meeting we will assign board member roles and approve role descriptions."

Be sure these statements are specific and relate to intended results or desired outcomes.

Agenda

The agenda sets out the flow of the meeting. Put these items in a logical order, with impact and urgency being a consideration. If you

have a guest at the meeting who's there to talk on a particular subject, put that item first. Have you seen guests sit through a whole
meeting, waiting to make a short presentation? Try to avoid that
waste of their time.

For each item think of whether you are talking about it for the
first time (opening the discussion), focusing on options (narrowing
down the discussion), or making a decision (closing the discussion).
This helpful thought process comes from Interaction Associates (see
Chapter Twelve for more explanation). These *stages of discussion*
can be referred to more briefly as *open* (O), *narrow* (N), and *close*
(C). Put one of these words or its letter beside each agenda topic.
For example, placing "ONC" beside a topic would mean that you
plan to go through all three stages for it. This will also give you an
idea about the time to allot to the topic.

Put the most important or urgent items at the top of the list, and
for each one, determine whether you need to open, narrow, or close.
Now think of an appropriate process for each stage of each topic to
help the discussion stay on track. For example, brainstorming is a
familiar opening tool, and prioritizing using sticky dots is a popular
narrowing tool, as is discussing and weighing pros and cons. A closing tool might be taking a straw poll on a proposal using levels of
support before modifying it and voting (see Chapter Five). In some
cases you may get through the opening stage and then defer the subject to another meeting or delegate it to a team to narrow it down
and come back to the group with a recommendation.

As mentioned earlier, it helps to put the time limits on the
agenda in five-minute increments. Also, if you're thinking something will take ten minutes, give it fifteen or twenty. Remember,
more interaction takes more time but adds value. It's easier if clock
times are omitted except for the beginning and ending times.

Remember to allow a fifteen-minute *grace period* in the beginning for people to arrive and get settled (Chapter Six). It doesn't
make sense to start until people can get focused.

Spend at least five minutes at the beginning reviewing any previous agreements such as courtesy guidelines and a decision-making

method. Allow at least fifteen minutes at the end for reflection and action planning.

Rules

Develop a proposed list of meeting ground rules or courtesy guidelines—the ways to share responsibility for the success of the meeting.

Example

"We'll give each person our attention to speak for up to three minutes."

"We'll avoid making distractions and holding side conversations while someone is speaking."

"We'll turn off pagers and phones or set them to vibrate."

"We'll limit 'volleys' between two people to two before opening discussion up to others."

"Everyone gets to speak once before anyone gets to speak again."

If decisions are to be made, be ready to state the decision-making process.

Example

Decision-making agreement. "We will work to gain consensus (full support) through listening, questioning, and gaining understanding. If that does not occur within this meeting we will fall back to a vote. We need the substantial agreement of 80 percent to proceed" (see Chapter Five).

Shared Roles

The basic meeting roles are the *leader*, or president, executive director, or CEO (if applicable); the *timekeeper*; the *note taker*; and the *egalitarian*. The leader needs to ask for volunteers for roles and select those likely to do well in each role. The roles of *timekeeper* and *note taker* are familiar to most people. Sharing these roles will increase everyone's alertness and improve meetings right away. (See Figure 7.2.)

Figure 7.2. Shared Roles in Meetings.

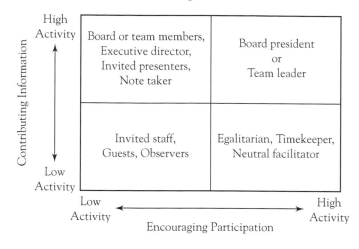

In boards the leader is generally the board president; in other groups he or she is the elected or appointed organizer of the group. In a meeting this role may become a balancing act between contributing information to the *content*—the subjects being discussed—and paying attention to the *process*—how people are interacting. While the president is leading, he or she is also helping others to participate fully by asking questions (see Chapter Twelve). It's best to remain as objective as possible regarding the content in order to keep others involved in the process. Both contributing and encouraging participation from others are difficult, so an egalitarian can take on the process focus.

Content and process always exist together, like two sides of a coin. According to Peter Block,

> We act as if "process" and "content" are somehow separate questions, and often at odds with each other.
>
> A good group process is needed wherever two or two hundred people meet, and the tension between process and content is a fool's dilemma. There is no need to

choose between the two—both are essential; they fail without each other [Axelrod, 2000].

Under Robert's Rules of Order a parliamentarian knows all the rules and instructs the group in how to follow them. Under Roberta's Rules of Order, everyone can easily know the rules and the parliamentarian is replaced by the egalitarian, a member of the group who is willing to keep an eye on the process and on how the participation is balanced. While filling this role, the member should generally not participate in the content of the conversations, unless he or she steps out of this role temporarily. To tap everyone's expertise, rotate this role frequently.

The timekeeper is one of the most important roles because he or she keeps the meeting moving and on time. Always have a timekeeper who is not the leader. (Consider giving the job to someone who gets irritated if the meeting runs overtime!)

The note taker makes an official record that a meeting took place. This person does not have to be the group's secretary. The note taker does not take standard blow-by-blow minutes (which can feel like a gale) but writes down the important things—who was there, what did they decide, what follow-through will be done by whom, and any context necessary to understand the decisions and follow-through needs. This becomes the *meeting summary*, to be sent to all in attendance.

It's important for the leader to give away all the roles he or she can to increase ownership of the success of the meeting and its results. These roles can be rotated to share the responsibility.

Three other helpful meeting roles are the *observer*, the *presenter*, and the *facilitator*. These roles are taken by individuals who are not regular members of the group.

Observers are generally invited guests or staff members who may need to become better informed about the group and its issues. Observers usually sit behind the group or to the side. They are primarily there to listen and they participate only when invited to do so by the leader.

Presenters are content experts who have been asked to present information to the group. They could be staff members, authorities on a subject, or any other individuals who are on the agenda to speak to the group. It's important that they know the time allowed for their presentation, including follow-up questions or discussion, and that the timekeeper keep them aware of the time.

When an important meeting is highly complex, includes controversy, or is a planning retreat (please call it a *planning advance!*), the group may decide to hire a process expert, or facilitator, to assist it. The facilitator contributes expertise to the agenda planning and guides the process of the meeting while remaining neutral about the meeting content.

2. Convene the Meeting: How Do We Get Started?

This is the official beginning of the meeting (the equivalent of the call to order in Robert's Rules of Order). Here's where you implement the working plan. As the leader, welcome everyone, state the meeting purpose, and go over the things that need to be accomplished at this meeting. Now is the time to use the OARS. Start by stating the outcomes, walking through the agenda, asking for support for the rules, or courtesy guidelines, and deciding the roles. Ask for volunteers to fill the roles (timekeeper, note taker, and so forth). Remind everyone of the agreed-upon decision-making process.

You may also want to make any necessary announcements at this point, rather than at the end of the meeting, and, depending on the culture of the group, an invocation or inspirational reading such as a passage or poem may be offered. The announcements get people to pay attention, and the invocation or reading helps them quiet down and get focused.

Example

"Let's begin our meeting with a brief poem about leadership. Jane, would you please read it?" (Be sure Jane knows that she will be called on to do this.)

3. Help People Connect to Each Other: Who's Here and What's on Their Minds?

Helping people connect to each other is a part of the beginning of a meeting that is often overlooked. (It may also be done before convening.) Somehow we forget that humans are hungry for feeling connected. And sometimes they're just hungry. As discussed previously, providing a meal or snacks can be a good way to start a meeting and help people connect.

This is also a chance to get everyone's voice in the room, to help them get settled and be present in mind as well as body. A *check-in*, in which people introduce themselves, should be very brief (with the help of time limits and a timekeeper) unless this is the kickoff for a multiday meeting and everyone is a stranger. In large groups (over twenty), ask people to introduce themselves in small groups of six or eight.

Here are a few suggestions. Ask people to state their names, something that identifies them (for example, if this is a neighborhood meeting, where they live), and perhaps something about them personally, such as a recent occurrence, a short good-news story, or one word that describes their state of mind. In some situations, ask what they expect to gain from the meeting or for a question they want answered before the meeting is over.

Most people like to tell their stories, and this helps to overcome barriers. Becoming better acquainted is the first step to building a good working relationship. Be creative, but watch the time.

4. Provide a Context: What Would Be Helpful to Know Before We Start?

Before beginning the working portion of the meeting, conduct a summary or recap of the last meeting, including what was agreed upon and set in motion. This is the time to give an update on action plans but defer items that are also on the agenda. Ask teams and committees to submit their progress reports in writing if it will take more than one minute to give a report verbally.

5. Use a Consent Agenda—
What Are the Quick Decisions That Can Be Made?

BoardSource (formerly The National Center for Nonprofit Boards) recommends having a *consent agenda* (or *consent calendar*) as a part of the working plan for a regular or decision-making meeting. A consent agenda presents routine decisions that don't need a lot of discussion. If *anyone* does want to discuss a particular item, he or she can request that it be removed from the consent agenda. It is then placed in the next section, where more discussion takes place. Items on the consent agenda might include appointments, the treasurer's report, a membership drive plan, and so forth. Usually such things have been discussed and recommended by a committee or subgroup. It's important, however, not to use this section to push through something controversial without discussion. This will feel like manipulation and will harm the level of trust and cooperation.

6. Approach the Content with Helpful Processes—
How Do We Complete Each Topic?

Now, use the content agenda you planned in logical order, and discuss each item, staying within the time allowed. If more time is needed for an item, get agreement from the group to take time away from something else. Keep the discussion moving through the stages of opening, narrowing, and closing as described earlier.

7. Continue the Momentum—
What Did We Accomplish and Now Need to Do?

Many times meetings seem to have no ending—people just start leaving. This next-to-last section of the working plan wraps things up in a way that makes it easy to continue to improve while moving forward. Make sure that the note taker has recorded all decisions or agreements, who is going to accomplish what task, and anything else that shouldn't get lost. (There's more about this in the next chapter.)

8. Conclude with Reflection—
How Well Did We Do and How Can We Improve?

Finally, take the time to ask for reflection ("What did you learn or gain?") and feedback ("What worked well and what needs work?"). We're often so busy rushing out the door that we miss a chance to talk about what we accomplished and valued—or what we wish to change. However, these exchanges keep meetings meaningful and continuously improving. Also, make sure the next meeting's logistics and preliminary agenda (or at least things to be accomplished) are clear before everyone leaves. (This topic is so important that it will be covered more thoroughly in the next chapter.)

Log Entry: Summary

The best way to prevent the typical problems in meetings is to anticipate the questions on people's minds and build the answers into the agenda and the activities at the beginning of the meeting. The prework to plan a meeting takes time, but doing it once will give you a template on your computer to use in the future. Breaking out of the old Robert's rules agenda will give everyone more information and mean less frustration. You'll find your group's meetings have a lighter, friendlier tone and are still productive.

Getting Under Way

- Develop an expanded agenda (see the examples in Resource C) to steer your next meeting, using the eight sections of the ship's wheel.

- Create an agenda-planning template on your computer to use each time you plan a meeting.

- Apply the OARS to remember the important things to do in planning and starting a meeting.

- Practice using this format to run your next meeting, and get feedback.

- Make modifications based on your feedback, and keep improving your working plan at each meeting.

Making Headway

Now that you've worked with a new agenda planning format and ways to lead the meeting, let's telescope in on the part of a meeting that people often breeze over—the ending. The next chapter will give you some ways to learn from each meeting to improve the next.

8

Ending with Reflection
and an Eye on the Horizon

The purpose of this chapter is to give leaders and participants methods for reflecting on their meeting experience in order to learn how to keep improving their meetings and other interactions. In this chapter you will learn

- How to solicit feedback about what to continue doing and what to change

- How to assess the success of the group on three dimensions—results, process, and relationships

- How to use a focused method to review information, discover meaning, explore feelings, and plan next steps

- How to write an action summary focused on decisions and follow through

Problem: The Ragged Ending

A suburban parks and recreation association meets bimonthly on a Saturday morning at the complex clubhouse. It used to have monthly evening meetings, but members agreed that meeting every other month for a little longer was preferable. Many members commute long distances to work and the evening traffic made it difficult to arrive on time.

Each member takes a turn bringing bagels and coffee to the meeting and setting up the room. After a little time for people to eat and greet, the meeting usually gets started by 9:15 A.M. By noon, if it isn't over, people start to leave, and there always seems to be someone who needs to leave earlier.

The end of the meeting is generally ragged and rushed. No one is clear on who's doing what to implement the decisions that were made that day. There is constant complaining about the lack of follow-through. Also, there never seems to be enough time to talk together about how people feel about their work together. Recently there have been tensions between some of the longer-term residents and the newcomers. Everyone tries to ignore it.

The Challenge of Endings

The ending of a meeting is always a challenge. The key is to make sure that all the participants can answer the following questions before leaving:

- What did we accomplish relative to what we intended?

- How well are we working together?

- How do I feel about how we're treating one another?

- Who's going to implement what we decided to do?

Interaction Associates has a simple and very helpful model for measuring the success of a meeting or the productivity of a team (see Figure 8.1). It's an equilateral triangle showing the needed balance in a meeting among achieving *results*, having a clear *process*, and maintaining positive *relationships* within the group. Interaction Associates calls this RPR (balancing results with process and relationships).

Figure 8.1. Dimensions of Success.

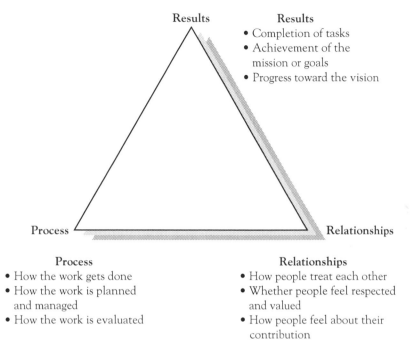

Results

Results
- Completion of tasks
- Achievement of the mission or goals
- Progress toward the vision

Process

Relationships

Process
- How the work gets done
- How the work is planned and managed
- How the work is evaluated

Relationships
- How people treat each other
- Whether people feel respected and valued
- How people feel about their contribution

Source: Copyright Interaction Associates, Inc. Reproduced with permission.

At the end of a meeting, it's helpful to schedule enough time to do the following:

Review the Intended Results: How Much Was Done?

As Stephen Covey (1989) has reminded us, the first step in planning is to "keep the end in mind." The same holds true for meetings. When your group reaches the end of the meeting, look at the list of what it expected to accomplish. How did it do? Can you literally check off each item? If not, will the unchecked items be taken care of by someone outside the meeting? If they aren't urgent, continue them to the next meeting and note them as priority agenda items. You're already building the next meeting's agenda. This is good!

Review the Process: How Did the Meeting Work?

For many years Interaction Associates has asked workshop partici-pants to list the problems with meetings. Every list proves the point that most problems relate to *process*—how the meeting was run—rather than *content*—what was discussed or accomplished. Improv-ing the process will greatly improve the meeting.

At the end of your group's meetings, ask the members for feed-back that will tell you what to continue or change for the next meeting. Ask two questions:

> "What worked well about this meeting?" Don't skip asking for kudos—we all need them. If you get comments only about the food, press for more substance.

> "What could we do better at our next meeting?" You're looking for suggestions for changes, such as finding an improved loca-tion or starting on time. Involve the group in planning how to implement at least one upgrade by the next meeting. Con-tinuing to ask for suggestions to make improvements will increase members' ownership and satisfaction.

Review Relationships:
How Do People Feel About Their Work Together?

This is more difficult to do than asking about results or process because people in groups are not always comfortable talking about their feelings. Ask for and offer acknowledgments and compliments for those who have contributed in a special way. They may have taken on a task on the group's behalf, managed an event, made the arrangements for the meeting, and so on. Encourage a culture of positive reinforcement rather than emphasizing what's not done well. Ken Blanchard and Spencer Johnson, in *The One Minute Man-ager* (1982), call this practice, "Catch 'em doing something right!" It will pay big dividends in creating a meeting culture of apprecia-tion and respect.

Some groups may be able to give honest feedback without offending others. This takes some practice and a few preventive ground rules or courtesy guidelines but is worth the effort. If there was anger or tension in the meeting, admit it, and ask if anyone wants to talk about how she or he feels about the interaction. If some people were hard on others, they may want to apologize. Encourage this. Blanchard and Johnson (1982) also discuss the One Minute Apology and how much positive impact an apology can have. Even one that lasts a few seconds can change the tone of a meeting before it ends.

The meeting leader can encourage participants to give each other feedback. They might use this phrasing: "When you said _____, I felt really _____." This may be enough, or it could be accompanied by a request: "Next time, I'd love for you to _____." Feedback may be positive: for example, "When you said you'd take on this project, I really felt grateful." However, it may also be negative: for example, "When I was speaking and you started talking too, I felt cut off. Next time I'd appreciate being able to finish my thoughts." (See Chapter Nine for more feedback techniques.)

When the positive feedback occurs, be thankful. When the negative feedback occurs, treat it not as a request to just one individual but as an example of something the whole group needs to address. If someone remarks on having been cut off while speaking, for example, reframe the comment as a need for the group to have and to reinforce courtesy guidelines such as "let each person speak for up to three minutes without interruption." If one individual is the primary offender, speak with him or her about it outside the meeting. Confrontation within the group is rarely productive as it puts people on the defensive and increases tension. Remember, this is a meeting of volunteers, not group therapy.

Reflect on the Meeting as a Whole

In the rush-rush world we live in, we've almost forgotten how to absorb what we've experienced and learn from it before moving on to the next event in our lives. This also applies to meetings. The

Institute of Cultural Affairs (ICA) teaches a method of gaining information from experience that seems to have universal appeal (Spencer, 1989). It is based on the premise that we experience things in four ways (see Figure 8.2):

- We perceive information as facts through our own personal filters (Objective level).

- We respond to them emotionally in positive and negative ways (Reflective level).

- We interpret their value and meaning, often using primarily assumptions (Interpretive level).

- We make choices based on that meaning (Decisional level).

Figure 8.2. Focused Conversation Method (ORID).

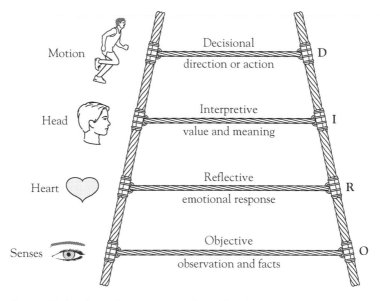

Source: Technology of Participations (ToP®), which is a registered trademark of the Institute of Cultural Affairs. Used with permission.

The ICA calls this method a Focused Conversation, or ORID, an acronym created from the names of the levels. It links to the Ladder of Inference, a model described by Chris Argyris (1990). When we "go up the ladder" we are often basing our opinions and actions on assumptions, not facts. Individuals and groups do this without realizing it. The best remedy is to make sure that observable behavior and factual information are clear and available to everyone.

Think of ORID as relating to parts of the body. The O (objective level) is what our eyes or ears can verify. The R (reflective level) is what we feel in our hearts. The I (interpretive level) is what we think as we analyze a situation. And the D (decisional level) is what we actually may do with our hands or feet. One of the keys is to be diligent about checking facts and comparing interpretations so that our information isn't based on assumptions. Using questions based on ORID to conduct a focused conversation at the end of a meeting can help a group learn more about each other. This understanding will be beneficial in future meetings. Here are some sample questions to ask:

- **O:** "What were some of the highlights or memorable moments of the meeting?" (Alternatively, use the agenda as a guide to reviewing what occurred during the meeting.)

- **R:** "How do you feel about the quality of our work together in the meeting?"

- **I:** "What new information or insight has been meaningful to you?"

- **D:** "Given what we did at this meeting, what is our most appropriate next step?"

For more detail and hundreds of possible questions, consult *The Art of Focused Conversation* (Stanfield, 1997). This pattern of reflecting and discussing can also be used at times other than closing a meeting as a way to help meeting participants talk about and listen to one another's observations, thoughts, and feelings.

Write Down Commitments to Take Action

When action planning is done at the end of a meeting, it's almost too late. The best way to capture what needs to be done is to have a piece of flip chart paper on the wall from the beginning of the meeting. Make three columns with these headings: "What," "By Whom," and "By When." During the course of the meeting, this becomes a list of the things individuals commit to do on behalf of the group. Here's the best way to make this procedure work well:

- Ask the note taker to capture the "what" on the list on the wall or on a separate sheet of paper as soon as he or she hears it. If someone volunteers to do it, capture the "who" also. Don't worry about stopping to fill it all in at the moment. Fill in the missing details in the last fifteen minutes of the meeting.

- Ask for volunteers to complete tasks, rather than assigning people. The more personal interest and choice are involved in completing a task, the better.

- Then ask for a backup partner for each original volunteer, in case that volunteer gets too busy or forgets. The partner has permission to remind the original volunteer and to help her or him out if necessary.

- You may also want to make a small copy of the list to include in each set of meeting notes. It makes it easy to keep track, using shading or color coding, of what's been completed and what still needs to be done. Don't take completed items off the list. Let it be a running record and reinforcement of accomplishments, however small the tasks (see Exhibit 8.2 later in the chapter and Resource D).

Prepare Follow-Up and a Summary

Everyone leaves a meeting with good intentions to do what they said they would do. However, in the moment we often forget the many other commitments we have. Everyone can benefit from a reminder, by regular mail or e-mail, between meetings. Request that the person planning the next agenda (or someone else willing to assist) follow up with the people named on the list before the next meeting. This lets the group leader know what has been completed and what needs to be included in the next agenda. This is also a good time to solicit items—and their intended results—for the next agenda.

After the meeting, prepare a meeting summary. Many meeting notes are too long. The term *minutes* originally referred to a minute-by-minute account of the meeting. Forget that! Each meeting needs a record to prove it occurred, but that record can be a simple summary. The basic information should answer these questions in a brief outline:

- What was accomplished, and what was decided?

- Who was at the meeting, and who was absent?

- What follow-up commitments were made for what actions?

- When and where is the next meeting?

- Who's handling the meeting management roles for the next meeting (leader, timekeeper, egalitarian, and so on)?

One of the best places to start the summary is with the meeting's intended results, as listed on the working plan. Which ones were accomplished? Which ones didn't get done and may be part of the next meeting? Customize your own format, using Exhibits 8.1, 8.2, and 8.3 as examples. Exhibits 8.1 and 8.2 show the summary and the follow-up action plan prepared as separate documents. Exhibit 8.3 shows a summary organized around a meeting's intended results. Try very hard to keep the summary to one page—your friends will bless you.

Exhibit 8.1. A Meeting Summary.

Meeting of the XYZ Organization	Telephone Conference Call
Board of Directors	

Date: January 7 at 7 P.M. Pacific Time (10:00 P.M. Eastern Time) for 60–90 Mins.

Purpose: To kick off the year with summary reports from each VP on his or her assessment of what's working and what needs work, and to make plans for the first quarter.

Present: All current members except Judy.

Decisions: The Board agreed on the following:

> Increase the postage on the newsletter to send it first class—Beth will implement.
>
> Hire a new program director—Mike will implement.
>
> Meet bimonthly (March and May) for the first half of the year, then switch to quarterly.
>
> Send out an association information insert in the next mailing—Jessika will implement.
>
> Elected Officers: President (Joe), Secretary (Beth), and Treasurer (Don).
>
> Create a secured Web site available to Ambassadors only—Joe will implement.

Decision Making: We will work toward consensus (full support) through listening, questioning, and gaining understanding. If consensus isn't reached by the end of the meeting (or another designated time limit), we will use concordance, or substantial agreement. We've agreed to define concordance as 80% approval of the board with everyone voting. On our board of 11 this means that 9 need to agree to implement a decision.

Follow-Up

> Joe will ask Judy to write an assessment report on her area and e-mail it to all next week. Beth will send out her report tomorrow.
>
> George and Mary will put together a proposal for increasing membership fees and send it out 10 days before the next meeting.
>
> Sally will draft a proposal within the next two weeks for developing a mentoring program for new board members.
>
> Barbara will put out a notice next week for a new volunteer Advertising Manager from the membership, to be on the job by the first of May.
>
> Jim will work on providing the Board with Web site access for display of information within a month.

Exhibit 8.1. A Meeting Summary, Cont'd.

Next Meeting Agenda Items

> A current membership e-mail list
>
> Obtaining grants for youth programs
>
> Expanding the Ambassadors program, particularly outside the U.S.

Next Meetings: March and May on the second Tuesday evening, beginning at 5:00 p.m. Pacific Time and 8:00 p.m. Eastern Time.

Exhibit 8.2. A Follow-Up Action Plan.

Meeting of: ABC Association—Board of Directors
Date: September 22–23, Chicago, Illinois

What	By Whom	By When
Make calls to collect outstanding 2001 dues from members	Jeff with help from others (he'll coordinate)	Mid-October
Provide incentives to get current members to pay dues early	Executive Committee will decide what to offer	Meeting on Sept. 28
Recruit members by region to the conference	Alice and Jim on West Coast; all board members	Two weeks— by Oct. 15
Get decision on scholarships for crew slots	Dave	Two weeks— by Oct. 15
Recruit members of other related organizations to the conference	Nancy	Two weeks— by Oct. 15
Send action plan and edited board meeting notes to office for distribution	Alice	Sept. 28
Contact new potential board members	Chris	Sept. 28
Craft letter to start Annual Appeal Generate mailing list Set goal to double income	Dave	Early October
Mail out letter with magazine as gift; send to those who donated last year as gift and incentive	Alex; coordinate with Dave and Peter	Send by Oct. 15
Send letter to XXX requesting funding of student grants to attend conference	Dave and Peter	Sept. 28

Exhibit 8.3. An Advisory Council Meeting Summary and Action Items.

Purpose: To begin the quarterly focus on the field programs along with regular Advisory Council business.

Summary: At this meeting we accomplished the following:

1. Gained knowledge of the precollege field programs in order to have a broader understanding of the statewide effort, including the schools program. Thanks to the staff members who came to share this information.

2. Were informed about the current situation from the University and the statewide perspective in order to understand the larger political and financial climate. Thanks to the Vice President of Outreach for the report and update.

3. Learned about the statewide overview, possible budget cuts, and potential scenarios. Thanks to the Executive Director for providing this information.

4. Received the current calendar for planning purposes. Members signed up to attend and assist with Competition Days in the spring.

5. Presented an award on behalf of the Council to the local Superintendent of Schools.

6. Reviewed the decisions made at the December meeting to form Task Teams, and heard a brief update of their ongoing work.

Follow-Up Action Items

The following progress updates will be made at the next meeting (May):

University Strategic Planning	Vice President
Statewide Budget	ED and Assoc. ED
Advisory Council Goals:	Jim and Team
Advisory Council Development:	Joan and Team
Advisory Council Governance	Susan and Joe
Advisory Council Strategic Planning	Mary and Team

Next Quarterly Meeting

Location rotates to Southern California. Program Focus on Community Colleges.

Log Entry: Summary

Organizations that have regularly scheduled meetings can fast-forward the action between meetings by spending the time to reflect on the meeting and plan the commitments to keep things moving ahead. Think of these ongoing meetings as a series of continuing loops of learning, with each meeting building on the previous meeting. By reflecting on and upgrading the results, processes, and relationships at the end of each meeting through a series of reflective questions or through using ORID for a focused conversation, your group will continue to improve the quality of its meetings as it implements what it learns.

Getting Under Way

- Build in time during or at the end of each meeting to talk about how things are going.

- Structure the discussion in one of three ways:

    Focus on what's working well that the group should continue, and what the group should do differently next time.

    Focus on how the group is doing in accomplishing *results*, using clear *processes*, and building *relationships* that make members respectful of each other.

    Use the ORID method to review, reflect, and plan.

- Develop a list of who is going to take care of what by the next meeting or designated date.

Making Headway

Traditionally one of the least enjoyable and dull meetings is the required annual meeting of a membership organization. The next chapter will provide ways to restructure these meetings to be more productive while engaging the input of members.

Polishing Up the Dull and Boring Annual Meetings

The purpose of this chapter is to provide ways to shift dry and boring annual membership meetings to a format that provides for interaction, enjoyment, and exchange of information.

In this chapter you will learn

- How to set a different tone when people walk into the room

- How to avoid verbal reports and use a "marketplace" to inform and gain volunteers

- Why have an open forum instead of a typical Q&A

- When to have a prevote issues discussion

Problem: Perfunctory Annual Meetings

The national association for a popular sport holds its annual membership meeting at its national conference—over lunch. While the meal is being served and eaten, the president of the organization tries to stop the conversations so that she or he can be heard. The agenda includes many committee reports as well as the election of new board members.

The committee reports are marginally interesting, but after the third one, they get boring. Some very exciting things have usually happened in the past year, but it's hard to hear and dessert is about to be served. The result of the election of directors is a forgone conclusion, based on a proposed slate of nominees for three-year terms. Although the information was mailed out ahead of the meeting, most people are not aware of the nominating process and cannot remember much about the proposed individuals.

At the end of the meeting, when the president dutifully asks if there is any other new business, it's rare for anyone to address the group. Yet throughout recent conferences, concerns about board decisions have been expressed informally. Members complain that nothing ever changes.

Going Through the Motions

Nonprofit organizations with members are required to have an annual membership meeting. Most do it with the enthusiasm of taking a long trip in a hot car through the desert. They just want to get to the other side quickly. In many organizations the real purpose and potential of these meetings has been lost.

Why are these meetings required? The purpose is to inform the membership of the "state of the organization" and to vote on bylaw changes or major issues affecting members. The opportunity that is often overlooked is the chance to build excitement and involvement in the organization for the *next* year. Think of it as an opportunity to present a snapshot of "where we are now" and to listen to the opinions of members.

If your group is currently using the most traditional—and the most boring—annual meeting format, it is probably following this agenda outline:

1. Call to order

2. Establishment of a quorum

3. Reading of the minutes of the last annual meeting (or accepting a motion not to read it)

4. Reading of reports of officers and all committees

5. Election of new directors

6. Motions (if there are some to come before the membership)

7. Adjourn (that is, run from the room)

This agenda accomplishes the most basic purpose of an annual meeting, to provide information and conduct voting. However, it's not structured in a way that will produce an engaging or particularly interesting meeting. In fact the meeting it produces will be boring. The part that can put everyone to sleep, particularly if it's held after lunch, is the reading of reports. This meeting agenda needs a major overhaul.

An Alternative Approach

Here are a number of techniques your group can use to hold large interactive meetings. Thanks to Kathie Dannemiller and associates for these methods.

Set an Informal and Lively Tone

When people enter a meeting room, they can sense the tone (formal or informal, dull or lively) by how the room is arranged and what they encounter. To set the tone for a more lively and informal meeting, give the following a try (see Figure 9.1):

Option A

- Set up the room with a series of round tables to encourage conversation. (If a round table is not available, two rectangular tables can be pushed together to make a square.) Sit six people in a semicircle at a table for eight. In a large meeting, using one semicircle or tables in a U-shape puts people too far away from one another.

- Set up rectangular or card tables and easels around the perimeter of the room with information about accomplishments from the past year. Allow time for everyone to visit these tables, like at a farmers' market.

- Place handouts with the agenda and any other pertinent information on the round tables. Using an in-basket in the center will keep things tidy.

- Use a music stand—or set the podium off to the side for notes only—so no one will stand behind it.

- Provide a hands-free microphone, or at least one with a long cord, to allow movement if the room is large.

- If an overhead or PowerPoint presentation is necessary, put the screen to one side at the front of the room.

- Eliminate the head table for board members; seat them among the group members at the round tables.

Option B

- If the group is too large to seat at tables in the room, set up chairs only in large concentric semicircles. Make sure that each person is able to see between the chairs of the row in front. Avoid straight military rows with each person having only a view of the back of someone else's head.

Revise the President's Role

Here's the role of the president or the individual delegated to run the meeting, such as a facilitator:

1. Convene the meeting, and welcome everyone with an overview of the meeting flow.

2. Give instructions to participants for introducing themselves to others at their table or in their small group and give them time to do this.

Figure 9.1. Annual Membership Meeting Room Arrangements.

OPTION A

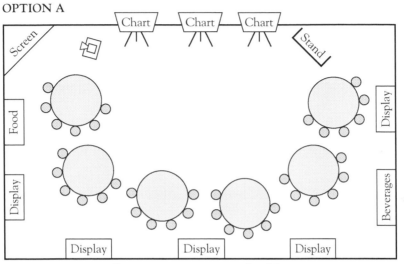

Seating arrangement with tables

OPTION B

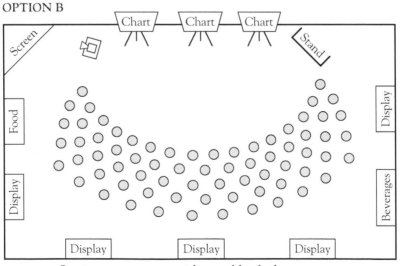

Seating arrangement without tables for larger groups

3. Preselect or have each table or small group select a table facilitator and timekeeper.

4. Announce that copies of the minutes of the last meeting are available in a handout or on the Web site.

5. Give a short summary (ten to fifteen minutes) of the accomplishments or major events of the year and also anything the organization had difficulty doing or regrets doing. Give a fair assessment of the current situation. Members will be asked to discuss this information at their tables and give feedback.

Conduct an Open Forum

Following these remarks, conduct an open forum for fifteen to thirty minutes. Ask each table to select a person to focus the discussion (facilitator), watch the time (timekeeper), and take notes, preferably on a laptop computer (note taker). Have each person at each table answer the following questions about the year's highlights and hindsights as well as hopes for the coming year (with the facilitator guiding each of the table's members to answer each question before moving to the next):

"What was a highlight for you about the past year?"

"In hindsight, what's your feeling about the current state of the organization? What is working well? What needs improvement?"

"What compliment would you like to give to this year's leadership? What do you hope will continue or change in the coming year?"

Ask each table to select a spokesperson who then summarizes that table's response (allow up to fifteen minutes for all the reports). Those in leadership positions should be coached to listen respectfully and to receive all comments without becoming defensive about past actions. "Thank you for sharing your opinion" is an appropriate response, for example.

Then thank members for their comments and collect the notes from each table or describe how they will be compiled. Promise that the board will read them and consider all ideas.

Present and Upgrade Goals

The following method of presenting and upgrading goals can also be used to get feedback on ideas for the coming year. This is generally a more positive exercise than identifying problems to solve. If the board has a proposal for goals for the year, always present these goals as tentative and subject to upgrades from the membership. Here's one way to do it:

1. Present the proposed goals. Explain how the board came up with them.

2. Answer questions about their meaning so everyone understands the intent.

3. Ask each table to discuss the goals, or assign specific goals to each table if there are more than four or five. (Having more goals might sound good initially, but it's better to have fewer goals and actually get them accomplished than to have more goals and never get them all done.)

4. Write the goals on separate large sheets of paper. Post them on the walls or windows around the room.

5. Ask the people at each table to choose a representative who will write the table's suggestions for changes or upgrades on each of the goals. If anyone would like to suggest an additional goal, write it on another large sheet and post it.

6. Take a break, and let everyone walk around the room and read the comments.

7. Take a straw poll by giving each person colored sticky dots to place on the goals she or he likes the most (limit each person's number of "dot votes" to one-third of the total number of goals posted).

8. Summarize the feedback from this activity, and tell the membership what the board will do with the information—the next steps.

Discuss the Financial Update

Distribute the financial summary for the full year in a simple and nearly self-explanatory format, such as a graph. Give everyone a chance to look it over (three to five minutes—the silence won't hurt) even if these members had access to the summary prior to the meeting. Ask the people at each table to help each other understand the summary. Again, the discussion will occur first at each table, and then a spokesperson will report for each table. Here are two questions for each person to answer:

> "How does the financial picture look to you? What has improved? What needs improvement?"

> "What questions for clarification do you have for either the president or the treasurer?"

Present Project Updates: Team and Committee "Bazaar"

Ask each project team and committee to write a one-page summary of its accomplishments, to be handed out to meeting participants. Set up a poster display showing each team's and committee's activities, on tables or on the walls. Ask each person to visit each table with four questions in mind:

1. "What did this group accomplish this year?"
2. "What difference did it make?"
3. "What ideas would I like to suggest for next year?"
4. "What would I be willing to get involved in myself?"

Have the one-page handout available at each station, along with a sign-up sheet for new volunteers.

One way to ensure a high number of visits to each project or committee is to hand out a trivia quiz with questions that can be answered only by going to each display table and learning about the activity. Or give people a card on which each project or committee places a star or a stamp. When quizzes or cards are completed, members put their names on them and drop them in a box for a prize drawing at the end of the meeting. Announce that "you must be present to win." This will keep more people to the end of the meeting. Similarly, giving out free raffle tickets at the beginning of the meeting and having a prize drawing at the end will add some fun and encourage people to stay until the meeting is over.

Convene a Business Meeting for Elections

Establish a quorum if voting is to occur (use written ballots and count them along with any mailed-in ballots).

Ask the *leadership selection team* (aka the nominating committee) to propose the slate of directors (and in some cases the officers) for the coming year. (Make sure the nominating process is open and clear to the members and that they have an opportunity to suggest candidates.) Provide time during the meeting for additional nominations.

If there is one person per office, ask for someone to move that the nominations be accepted as a slate. (Use a two-thirds majority vote or the agreed upon decision-making method.)

If more than one person is nominated for a particular position, first vote on the rest of the slate without that position. Then conduct the election for that position separately.

Solution: Discussion Before Decisions

Members of a worldwide organization come together once a year at an annual meeting to decide their position on major issues. Each chapter sends attendees who are voting delegates. Using Robert's Rules of Order in this situation makes sense. There are nearly six hundred attending each meeting.

Motions are prepared in advance and circulated. Even though a good attempt is made to educate everyone about the issues, the written material isn't always enough. Delegates began complaining about not being well enough informed to vote on some of the controversial issues. The leadership decided to do something new.

Now, the day before a voting meeting, the delegates arrive to attend an issue discussion. The room is set up with round tables when possible and random seating. The meeting starts with various experts presenting facts about the issues related to the pending motions. About 20 percent of the total meeting time is used for this type of information sharing.

The remaining 80 percent of the meeting time is designed for all present to talk. Each issue, assuming there are several, is given forty-five minutes to an hour. Each table appoints a leader and a note taker. The members at each table talk together to answer structured questions and to hear the pros and cons. One technique is to go around the table alternating pros and cons—with one person giving a pro on the issue and the next person a con and so on—regardless of personal belief. This gives everyone a chance to stretch his or her thinking.

Each individual is also asked to express his or her personal point of view. For some situations, there are "plants" in the groups to express an unpopular or unusual opinion. Near the end of the time limit for an issue, members are asked if they need more information to be ready to vote on that issue the next day. Most report that they are ready. Some talk late into the night about the issues. A summary of each table's discussion is verbally reported to the larger group for everyone to hear.

Liz Guthridge, veteran parliamentarian and business consultant, provided this excellent example. She also reports that the delegates at these meetings now feel far more informed and satisfied that they have heard lots of viewpoints before voting. The leadership feels that the quality of decision making has improved and that delegates are more energized.

Log Entry: Summary

Annual meetings, when conducted according to Robert's Rules of Order, are very dry. They are as dull as watching a sailboat race on a calm day. Although an annual membership meeting is required for nonprofits, the meeting format is flexible. There is no reason that they have to be boring. Use various ways to communicate suitable to the organization's culture—computers, videos, posters, skits, songs, or other creative means.

If you use Robert's Rules of Order for large voting meetings, think of ways to engage members to learn more beforehand. Try adding an issue discussion before the meeting, or devise some other way, perhaps using a Web site or on-line discussion, to help everyone think through and understand the issues before voting.

Getting Under Way

- Announce well in advance to your group's membership that the next annual meeting will experiment with a different, interactive format. Encourage attendance to both experience and evaluate the format.

- Plan an annual meeting this year that breaks the old mold, using some of the ideas in this chapter.

- Provide the members with more ways to learn about the issues and to offer feedback before decisions are made.

Making Headway

This chapter has provided means for breaking the tradition of passive annual meetings to make them more interactive and allow members to exchange more information. The next compass course includes some easy rules of the journey and things to be aware of when navigating around the natural obstacles found in diverse groups.

Part IV

Stay Focused While Riding the
Tide of Diversity (Southwest Course)

10

Expecting and Respecting Different Frames of Reference

The purpose of this chapter is to provide board members and meeting participants with an increased awareness of different ways we can work together in groups and benefit from our differences. In this chapter you will learn

- How culture influences reactions and participation in groups

- How to increase multicultural comfort in meetings

- Why it's valuable to encourage emotional expression and self-disclosure

- How courtesy guidelines and a member pledge can increase tolerance of different points of view

Problem: Opinions Based on Cultural Assumptions

The board of directors of an arts organization in a large city was having its monthly meeting. This time at least half the board was in attendance. Some people had stopped coming to the meetings after one of the more extroverted members had verbally attacked a small, quiet woman.

The woman was not completely fluent in English and had given another member the impression that she approved of a proposal he had presented, but then she voted against it. He said something about how people from her culture were always saying yes and agreeing with things but not really meaning it. She was upset but didn't show her feelings to the group. Other members didn't visibly react to the comment. Recently she and other members who are her friends haven't been coming to meetings.

We All Have Different Lenses

Have you ever attended a meeting where some people felt attacked and others felt that there had been a great discussion? As in the situation just described, have you said or done something that was interpreted by someone else to mean something other than what you intended? Why do we perceive situations so differently? It's as if each of us wears glasses that give us our own frame of reference. It can seem as though everyone is using a ship's telescope, which requires covering one eye and looking at a specific object. Often we zero in on different small things and then argue about who is seeing the whole reality and who is not. We also tend to make our assumptions, which drive our actions, on the basis of selected small bits of information. (Thanks to Susan Kirsch, management consultant, for this concept.)

We develop this selected focus from our life experiences, including where we were born, what age we are now, our native nationality, our family's size and dynamics, and many other influences. For example, we come from many different cultures and from families with varying degrees of comfort with confrontation and aggression. What one person thinks is being direct, another experiences as rudeness. Some of these influences are so subtle that perhaps we're unaware of them. What's important to remember, and hard to accept, is that no one's frame of reference is better than that of someone else. When our frame of reference affects our thinking, we form a point of view. If we could appreciate our different frames and welcome diverse thinking, we'd all be ahead. Not that easy!

Good sailors know to use the tidal current to their advantage, by allowing it to help them move forward whenever possible, rather than fighting against it. Diversity in organizations is a tide that can be used to everyone's advantage when we work with it.

Take a Multicultural Approach

In our multicultural country, particularly in urban areas, it's impossible to make generalities about how people behave simply from knowing their original culture. Many people's families have been living in America for generations—others have arrived more recently. Also, many behavioral and attitudinal differences can be attributed to personal style and comfort. So it's dangerous to judge people by means of stereotypes.

Exhibit 10.1 lists a few areas in which people's perceptions and behavior may differ—sometimes causing misunderstandings. Read the two statements following each number, and circle the one that best describes your own cultural preferences. Or try this revealing exercise. Ask the members of your team or board to circle the statements that are true for them, and then compare the results. How similar are the team or board members to one another in their choices? Are most of the circled choices on the right or left? Are most of the choices the same or different?

It's not just nationality that creates behavioral differences but also family influences, personality traits, and personal preferences. So how do we know how to behave around others? Talking about our similarities and differences helps us learn more about each other. Knowing more about each other is the first step to building trust through relationships. Trust is the foundation for successful group decision making.

Although generalizations in this area can result simply in stereotyping and shouldn't be used to make assumptions about a particular individual, the list on the left tends to profile the dominant culture in the United States—with some exceptions.

Exhibit 10.1. Cultural Differences.

In Some Cultures, People . . .	In Other Cultures, People . . .
1. Are uncomfortable with silence	Believe silence is a virtue
2. Express emotions freely	Hide emotions
3. Welcome confrontation	Avoid confrontation
4. Talk with their hands	Think pointing is rude
5. Expect direct eye contact	Consider direct eye contact disrespectful
6. Laugh or speak loudly to have fun	Believe laughing or speaking loudly is impolite
7. Discount the ideas of older people	Consider older people wise
8. Speak rapidly	Speak slowly and deliberately
9. Stand close to be friendly	Find standing close to be rude
10. Hug freely	Feel uncomfortable when touched
11. Talk about their feelings	Withhold feelings around strangers
12. Encourage autonomy and initiative	Encourage obedience and dependence
13. Are on a first-name basis with everyone	Prefer formal titles and surnames
14. Tend to be forceful and vocal	Tend to be listeners and observers
15. Want to get right down to business	Want social interaction first
16. Like to be punctual and start on time	Don't see punctuality as important
17. Want to move forward and act	Enjoy contemplating and reflecting
18. Separate the spiritual from business	Integrate spiritual beliefs into work

The Cultural Majority Is Changing

However, a change is occurring in our country. We have always been a country of immigrants and will continue to grow in diversity. The Caucasian majority will soon become the minority in some parts of the country. If we are to build successful relationships, we all need to be sensitive to the diverse frames of reference arising from our diverse backgrounds.

There are four major categories of differences that you should be aware of in meetings:

1. *Verbal expression.* Some people find loudness and talking (interrupting) while others are talking rude, whereas others think it is normal. Some people are uncomfortable speaking up in a meeting. They will appear nonparticipative but may be listening intently.

2. *Eye contact.* In some cultures people tend not to make direct eye contact because it is considered rude. Even when someone is seated directly across the table, they may not look at the other person. This can be misunderstood as avoidance or lack of assurance. Similarly, some people may interpret strong eye contact as being too aggressive, an attempt to put the other person on the spot.

3. *Body language.* The physical distance between individuals may be a source of comfort or discomfort. People from some cultures are more comfortable when they are seated close together in a meeting. Moving further apart may feel more comfortable to others but could be interpreted as unfriendly.

4. *Approach to time.* Some people highly value relating to others and being in a relaxed social atmosphere before and even during a meeting. They resent being rushed, whereas others value being on time and task oriented. This difference is a key source of discord in meetings.

Creating Multicultural Comfort

If your organization's goal is to serve the community, your board needs to become a reflection of the community. This will result in an increase in diversity. How do you run meetings to satisfy everyone? You obviously can't satisfy everyone completely. However, here are a few things to do that will help all participants feel included and able to contribute to the meeting, particularly if English is their second or third language.

Fifteen Techniques for Multicultural Meetings

1. Write things down for all to read, using a flip chart or handouts.

2. Emphasize the visual by using pictures and diagrams to convey ideas.

3. Let people write their own ideas on large Post-its and stick them on a flip chart (rather than having to verbalize them).

4. Go around the group to give everyone a chance to speak, but with no obligation to do so. (This is sometimes called a *whip-round, round-robin,* or *go-around.*)

5. Speak more slowly.

6. Pause often when speaking.

7. Check for understanding frequently.

8. Speak clearly, and emphasize or repeat important words.

9. Be concrete and specific when giving examples.

10. Strive to achieve harmony and balance in the meeting flow and surroundings.

11. Be aware that yes may mean any of the following:

    "Yes, I hear you" (but may not agree).

    "Yes, I understand you" (but may not agree).

    "Yes, I agree with you."

12. Schedule time *before* the meeting for a meal or refreshments and informal talking.

13. Spend time in the beginning of the meeting getting connected, or better acquainted, by asking everyone to say something about him- or herself (often called a *check-in*). Suggestions for how to do this follow.

14. Allow a minute or two of quiet time for thinking silently before brainstorming.

15. Encourage small-group conversations (in pairs or trios) to prime the pump before holding a large-group discussion.

Focusing on Relationships

When trust is present among the members of a group, it is easier for them to work together. Although trust is based on many things, one way to begin to develop it is to learn more about each other's frames of reference and personal preferences. Time allotted to getting to know each other—whether structured into the meeting or during dinners or outings—is time well spent for your organization. (See the discussion of results, process, and relationships in Chapter Eight.)

You can help build relationships within your group by encouraging people to make connections and find things that are mutually familiar. Without this common connection, people have more difficulty trusting each other. However, this requires some safe self-disclosure. To help group members find out more about each other's cultural influences, ask each person—on a retreat or in the beginning of a regular meeting—to participate in a check-in in which people learn something new about each other. Having these structured conversations is a good way to break down barriers and build trust. Even when group members think they know each other well, some answers will surprise people.

Select noninvasive questions that will get people sharing their feelings without feeling on the spot. Always give everyone the option to "pass," to say nothing and let the next person continue. Focusing on the positive is preferred to asking about the negative (it will come out anyway). Try using one of the following questions per meeting. To help people become more "present," be curious and ask:

"What's been a high point of your day [or week]?"

"What's new and exciting in your life since we last met?"

"Tell us some good news in your life."

"If you weren't here and had no other obligations, what would you be doing?"

"How did you (or are you planning to) spend your vacation?

"What's a word or phrase that sums up your state of mind right now?"

"What's your highest hope for this meeting?"

Cultural heritage is not always obvious, but it is influential. To help people share insightful information about their backgrounds, ask everyone to answer these questions at a retreat or a few at a time at a regular meeting:

"What's the origin of your first name, and of your last name?"

"Where were you born and where have you lived?"

"How many siblings do you have, and what was your birth order?"

"What was it like growing up in your family?"

"What is your favorite holiday, and how do you celebrate it?"

The Place for Emotions in Meetings

Anyone who has participated in meetings run with Robert's Rules of Order knows that they are highly structured and mechanical. People are expected to limit discussion to rational debate. The method was intentionally designed to control conflict. It includes having people address each other formally, without using first names, as "Mister," "Madam," or "Chair." Somehow, this reduces the leader to an inanimate object. Emotion is discouraged in order to minimize conflict—or the outward evidence of it. There is an assumption that using polite language will eliminate negative feelings—wrong! Negative feelings seem to leak through, given away by a harsh tone of voice, gesture, or facial expression. When you see and hear one person address another person as "my esteemed colleague," with teeth clenched and eyes like ice, it's obvious that there is emotion behind the words.

The result of this effort to control and suppress emotions in meetings is like turning off the cold water but also preventing the flow of the hot. The procedures, designed to control the words and behaviors of unruly men, also succeed in suppressing the more positive expressions. It's similar to not allowing yourself to feel hurt and pain in relationships, which can also limit your capacity to feel joy.

Suggestions for Group Members

Add Feelings to Your Language

Where is the joy in these meetings? Is anyone having fun? Are you? Have some members stopped coming or are they habitually absent? The "juice" of nonprofit boards is in the caring for the mission and the passion for its future. Are people on the board connecting on the level of shared concerns about which they feel deeply? If there are misunderstandings, it may be because the words people say can be interpreted to have meanings different from the ones they intended.

The language of feelings is more universally understood. If someone presents a rational argument, others tend to decide whether they agree or disagree on a rational level. If someone expresses feelings about an issue and uses words to communicate an emotion like love or fear, others tend to relate and potentially empathize. Feelings are more universal than ideas and more convincing than facts.

Although people may differ in opinions or not even understand each other's thinking, they can more readily relate to hurt, anger, frustration, joy, pride, and satisfaction. To eliminate emotions in discussions is to eliminate an element of life that is a rich resource for understanding and for finding common ground. Organizations that ignore the feelings of members miss an opportunity to build relationships. When a reservoir of shared emotions is part of the group's history, people can draw empathy from it when disagreements and conflict arise.

People from some cultures use expressions that are emotionally laden; compared to others they allow their feelings to be more on the surface. Whether excitement or disappointment, the emotion comes through naturally. People of other cultures are more reserved and reticent to disclose feelings. It's important to know the cultures of members of your group, not to stereotype but to be sensitive to their comfort level. The organization's culture is a composite of its members' cultures.

Practice Uncommon Courtesy

You and all other group members can take personal responsibility to do the following things to build positive working relationships:

- Practice questioning your assumptions, acknowledging differences, and looking for similarities. Be curious. Knowing more about other individuals' country of origin, number of siblings (and whether they were the firstborn, a middle child, and so on), where they were born and were raised, their preferred working style, and other personal perceptions can be very helpful.

- Be aware that some forms of joking can be hurtful. Never make fun of a nationality or physical trait. Always let the joke be at your own expense (silly me!), not someone else's.

- Be cautious that you never make one person the spokesperson for others of the same ethnic background (never say, for example, "Rosa, do you think the Latino community will agree with this?").

- If someone makes a remark that seems unfair, express your reaction privately. The person may not have been aware of how the remark could be interpreted and may benefit from being privately informed rather than publicly rebuked.

- Avoid interrupting someone to blurt out your ideas; if you disagree, count to ten silently. Make sure you've understood the other person's point before responding.

- It seems obvious, but please remember to say "excuse me" when you inadvertently interrupt and "please" when requesting something from others.

- Avoid making statements that imply someone is wrong and you are right. For example, "you" messages—such as, "you don't know what you're talking about," or even something a bit more subtle with the same tone—can have a damaging effect. We all like to believe we are "right," and can seldom see another point of view when we are on the defensive. Shift to "I" messages that do not blame anyone else—such as, "I see this differently because . . ."

- Pay attention to your tone of voice and body language. The words you're using may be benign, but the impact malignant. People often react more to the gestures and expressions they see and the way a voice sounds than to the words themselves. (Try saying out loud, "I wish you had told me this sooner," in three different tones— sad, matter-of-fact, and angry. Notice the differences in how you might react to these different tones.)

- If you even *suspect* you have offended someone, apologize. This brief effort can save hours or even years of hard feelings.

- If someone offers an apology, please *forgive* him or her. It will allow you both to be able to participate more fully in the meeting. If hard feelings continue, talk about it with the individual, not the group.

Maintain Focus in Meetings

As a participant in any meeting you can make a huge difference to the meeting's success. Consider the following list of suggestions, and act on as many as you can to keep the meeting focused and productive.

- If the group is too large for spontaneous discussion, signal the leader nonverbally when you wish to speak.

- When the meeting is going off track, ask the leader to make a *process check*, to redirect the discussion to the topic at hand.

- Limit comments and conversation with those sitting near you in order not to distract others.

- Concentrate to stay focused on the agenda, and avoid jumping ahead to other issues.

- Turn off cell phone ringers and set pagers to vibrate. If you must make or return a call, leave the room (out of earshot).

- If you know you have to leave early, tell the group at the beginning of the meeting. If others must leave too, it may be worthwhile to end early.

Ask Questions

One of the best roles you can play as a board or team member is the seeker of knowledge—ask a lot of questions with a sincere interest in learning. Ask questions that

- Are open when you want to allow many responses in order to get the most information. Such questions usually start with "What . . ." or "How . . .": for example, "What other options did you consider?"

- Are narrow or focused when you want to get specific information: for example, "How often does this happen?"

- Are closed when you want only a yes or no answer, when you want to limit the conversation or understand the process: for example, "Are there more items to discuss?"

- Inquire, rather than disguise the expression of an opinion: for example, "What do you think about . . . ?" rather than, "Don't you think that . . . ?"

- Ask about the meeting process when the method or topic is unclear: for example, "How much time do we want to spend on this issue?"

- Seek the opinion of someone who has been silent: for example, "Joe, we haven't heard from you. What do you think about this?"

Even if group members use all of these methods, if they don't also pay attention to their *tone*, communication can break down. Listen to how you and others are sounding. Are you sounding impatient, angry, annoyed, challenging, or sarcastic? Tone of voice will make or break how your communication is received. Be aware of the impact of *how* you sound on the meaning of *what* you say.

The Golden Rule

At meetings of religious, spiritual, and faith-based organizations, it may be helpful to remind everyone of the Golden Rule. What if our primary courtesy guideline was the Golden Rule? Chances are, we would both give and get more respect. Many people have observed the universality of the Golden Rule; versions of it appear in the writings of all the major religions. (The following wording is taken from a poster prepared by the Bahá'í Faith.)

> "Make thine own self the measure of others, and so abstain from causing hurt to them." Buddhism
>
> "Love thy neighbor as thyself." Judaism
>
> "And as ye would that men should do to you, do ye also to them likewise." Christianity
>
> "None of you truly believes until he wishes for his brother what he wishes for himself." Islam
>
> "Choose thou for thy neighbor that which thou choosest for thyself." Bahá'í Faith
>
> "Do not to others what ye do not wish done to yourself, and wish for others too what ye desire and long for for yourself." Hinduism

Member Courtesy Pledge

Another option is for all board, team, or committee members to agree to a courtesy pledge (see Exhibit 10.2). Acting on this pledge can prevent problems in relationships both during and outside of board meetings.

Log Entry: Summary

Every person develops a frame of reference from his or her early family background and personal experiences that influences his or her beliefs, thoughts, and behavior. The only way for you to understand

Exhibit 10.2. Member Courtesy Pledge.

As long as I am a Member of _____ I agree to

1. Speak to and about others as I would want them to speak to or about me.

2. Assume the best (rather than the worst) about others' intentions until I have all the facts.

3. Listen as an ally (rather than an adversary) to understand the point of view of others, whether or not I agree with them.

4. Speak my own opinion in a way that does not demean others, even if I disagree.

5. Speak for myself, using "I" messages and not blaming statements.

6. Speak kindly to others, and avoid aggressive nonverbal behavior and sarcasm when I do not agree with someone.

7. Keep confidential what is said in our meetings, particularly when it could be hurtful to any individual.

8. Speak with "one voice" as a board after decisions are made, regardless of personal opinion.

9. Never represent or speak on behalf of the Board outside of our meeting, unless requested to do so.

Signature: _____

Date: _____

---

others' differences is to get to know them better. Spending time talking about culture, family, and experiences helps to build trusting relationships. Expressing your feelings is appropriate when it helps others understand your passion and point of view.

Everyone shares the responsibility for successful communication in meetings. It's fair to insist on courteous behavior and to ask all group members to agree to treat each other gently and with respect.

Getting Under Way

- Plan times in which group members can learn more about each other's cultural backgrounds and personal interests.

- Encourage others and yourself to speak from the heart about feelings as well as opinions.

- Work together to develop a member pledge that everyone can agree to sign and follow.

Making Headway

In this chapter we focused on the importance of cultural awareness and sensitive communication. The next chapter builds on this information with methods to increase listening and substitute dialogue for debate.

Tacking Away from Debate Toward Dialogue

The purpose of this chapter is to eliminate traditional debate and introduce dialogue as a tool to increase listening and respectful conversations in meetings. This chapter focuses primarily on the responsibilities of board or other group members.

In this chapter you will learn

- Why motions produce debate

- What the difference is between a debate and a dialogue

- What beliefs and behaviors are needed to have respectful conversations

- Why it's sometimes useful to have an egalitarian instead of a parliamentarian

- How to be a constructive participant in a group discussion

Problem: A Controversial Issue

The public policy committee of a large local chapter of a national charitable organization has been working on a controversial issue. The committee wants the board to support a motion regarding the right of women to have reproductive choices. If the board approves it, then the motion will go to the general membership for a vote. After months of research, writing, and internal debate, the committee is ready to bring a motion to the board in support of pro-choice.

This is the first formal or official discussion of the issue with the board, although there have been plenty of heated informal discussions. By now there are definite camps for and against the motion. There are also some board members who believe the organization should not take a position on this issue at all. Everyone is expecting this discussion to be a free-for-all.

Supporting a Motion Means Taking a Position

When a person or group drafts a motion to present to a board or a broader membership, the motion generally represents a position taken by that group. It preferably includes the group's best thinking about how to solve a problem or move the organization in a particular direction. This position, or *stand*, is a potential source of conflict. Those who work with individuals and groups on reducing conflict know that the strong positions they take can create conflict. However, when there is disclosure of personal values, needs, interests, and desires, there is an increase in common understanding and effort to reach agreement.

Any controversial issue as complex as the one just described is difficult to resolve in a way that doesn't polarize a group. The Robert's Rules of Order method of proposing motions requires that a group take a stand on an issue. Those who have worked hard at researching it understand the situation clearly. However, everyone else may still be in the dark. How does the larger group, which now has to vote, learn enough about the situation to make an informed decision?

Robert's Rules of Order assume that following a motion there is debate. But what is the definition of *debate?* According to *Webster's Unabridged Dictionary*, to debate means "to contend, discuss opposing reasons, argue, take part in a formal argument, a controversy; to fight or quarrel." Debating is about winning, convincing, coming out on top. It's very sad that our high schools and colleges have debate clubs to teach young people how to be good at this skill, but not how to be good at listening. Have you ever heard of a listening club?

We generally structure a debate as opposing points of view, the *pros* for the motion and the *cons* against the motion. There is usually a chance to ask questions, expecting that all anyone needs is clarification. Often the answers become more justification for a stronger position.

A recent e-mail notice to members of a large charitable organization read:

> Please review the motions sent to you prior to the meeting and bring your comments to the meeting. Each motion will be read prior to opening it up for discussion from the membership.
>
> All members are invited to speak during the discussion. In an effort to ensure that the discussion is meaningful, please formulate your comments in either a PRO (in favor of the motion), CON (against the motion), or QUESTION format.

This is considered "opening it up for discussion." This may well just add to the polarization.

One way to prevent this polarization is, as discussed in Chapter Three, to use a written structured proposal, which provides more information than a typical motion. Taking time to look at the bigger picture and understand the problem and issues is a key to reaching an agreement. The proposal format includes an analysis of the problem as well as alternative solutions. Although there is a recommended solution, the thinking process that led to its selection is made clear. A proposal can be floated like a trial balloon before the time for decision making. And it presents enough information that it can be the basis not for *debate* but for *dialogue*.

Using Dialogue: A Powerful Conversation

Imagine what could happen if the argumentative approach of debating shifted to a more inquisitive approach with the goal of understanding the total situation. Would we be more likely to find a common ground or a creative solution that does not polarize us? Even in the case of something as complex and controversial as reproductive choice, groups with very different views have made progress in gaining understanding and finding areas of agreement through dialogue. Worldwide forums are being held via the Internet to increase dialogue on cultural, religious, and political issues.

Particularly when members of a group meet together, there is an opportunity for a structured conversation to increase that understanding. This structured conversation may be called a *focused conversation* or a *dialogue*. What is *dialogue?* In *Webster's Unabridged Dictionary* it is defined as "talking together, a conversation, an interchange, a discussion of ideas, especially when open and frank, as in seeking mutual understanding and harmony." Unfortunately the skills for carrying out these activities are not taught in many places. Often it is only as a result of destructive and even deadly conflict in our schools that students are now being taught the method of dialogue in conflict resolution workshops. Some businesses have begun to recognize the value of dialogue and to teach these skills to employees. Occasionally board members who have learned the techniques elsewhere introduce them into nonprofit organizations.

Dialogue Sounds Simple but Isn't Easy

In our modern culture we often see conversation as one of two things: a chance to impress others with our expertise or an opportunity to persuade others to another way of thinking. In contrast, one of the best-known contemporary advocates of dialogue, David Bohm (1996; see also Ellinor and Gerard, 1998), has observed that breakthroughs in science and in group discussions come from "being open to the flow of the larger intelligence" or "the wisdom of the whole." Although this approach, this openness, was practiced by the ancient Greeks, indigenous tribes, and American Indians, it has nearly disappeared in the modern world.

A dialogue is nearly impossible unless everyone involved believes the following five statements:

1. There is a collective wisdom in the group that exceeds that of any individual: all of us is smarter than any of us.

2. Every person needs to be given the opportunity to be heard.

3. Understanding how others think and why they believe something is valuable.

4. All points of view are valid.

5. There is no one right way to view something, or one right answer.

Unless everyone in your group believes these five statements, don't attempt a dialogue. It will not work, regardless of the techniques used. Additionally, it helps if everyone shares these traits—curiosity about and sincere interest in what others think, a respect for the other individuals in the group, and a desire to learn something that could change one's own thinking. These, not coincidentally, are the same beliefs and traits required to reach consensus (see Chapter Four). Groups that do not exemplify them will not reach deep understanding and true agreement. Like consensus, dialogue works best in smaller groups with shared values. It requires stopping other things and taking the time to really listen to understand. If your group is serious about reaching a consensus, include the practice of dialogue.

The Basic Dialogue Method

The actual technique of dialogue is straightforward. However, for a dialogue to be successful, everyone participating needs to understand and support

- The five beliefs behind the use of dialogue.

- The value of using dialogue to explore the particular situation at hand.

- The content that will be discussed. Use an open-ended focused question to guide the dialogue and explore all the issues (not a question that can be answered yes or no): for example, "What are the best uses of our time and talent in our community?"

- How the dialogue will be conducted, by whom, and for how long.

On sailing ships the command to stop doing something, like hauling on a line, is *belay*. In a dialogue we need to belay some of the reactions and responses that may feel automatic. In order for a dialogue to succeed, certain behaviors need to be belayed (as also discussed in Chapter Ten):

- To truly understand another person's point of view, put your assumptions and judgments on hold, at least temporarily. Think of putting them in pause mode or putting mental brackets around them.

- Don't make statements of opinion disguised as questions. Ask curiosity questions for understanding, not to make a point. For example, ask, "What's the history of this in our group?" rather than, "Can we really do this well considering our track record?"

- Avoid interrupting others who are speaking. Take notes if you want to remember something; respond during your turn to speak.

At the same time, these behaviors need to be constantly practiced:

- Talk about your feelings: for example, "I'm really afraid of the new direction to serve adults because I'm concerned about losing our focus on children." Learning about colleagues' beliefs, values, and heart's desires, not just their thoughts, will make a dialogue meaningful and sometimes magical.

- Listen for the underlying meaning in what's being said, but beware of making assumptions based on limited information.

- Practice nondefensive listening. If something is said you don't like, take a deep breath and remain silent until it's your turn to speak.

- Honor time limits agreed upon by the group.

- Keep the conversation confidential and within the group.

It's important to emphasize that the first step is to explore the issues, interests, needs, and concerns before reacting to a position or considering the solution. Dialogue is about listening with curiosity to understand other people's beliefs, values, and feelings before working on the solutions.

The Role of the Egalitarian

In a situation with the potential for tension, it's helpful to have one person who stays out of the fray and keeps an eye on how things are going. In most meetings everyone has opinions about the content. Some want to express them strongly. It's helpful to have someone focus primarily on how things are going, on the meeting process. This includes making sure everyone has an equal chance to speak and be heard. (This happens only when others are *listening*.) In Robert's Rules of Order this person is someone who has been trained in all the rules and can be a referee. In Roberta's Rules of Order this person's role is to keep the conversation balanced, fair, and equal. This is the role introduced in Chapter Seven as the *egalitarian*. Using the analogy of a sailing ship, you could compare the egalitarian's role to that of the ship's cook. The cook is in a neutral but nurturing position. He or she doesn't stand watch and so is not involved in the same responsibilities as others. The cook sees the bigger picture and the interaction among the ship's crew when they come together. Ships' cooks play a very important role because they provide a necessary service that keeps everyone content and productive.

The egalitarian needs to be someone who does not have an emotional attachment to the issue or someone who is able take a neutral position for the duration of the dialogue. The role of the egalitarian is to keep a focus on the process—how the dialogue is working—so others can focus on sharing content information and learning. This role can be rotated among the group members, giving everyone a new perspective on the importance of process in meetings. Rotating the role also helps the group avoid losing the content knowledge of the same person at each meeting. The leader of the group can also practice this role by remaining neutral, although as discussed in Chapter Seven this is difficult if he or she also needs to be a contributor to the content. Having an egalitarian to assist the leader is better.

Here are a few things the egalitarian may say or do to make it easier for others to participate:

- Set up the room for a dialogue, with the seats in a circle or semicircle, without a table to form a barrier, if possible. Make sure people can see each other's eyes.

- Write the focus question for the dialogue on a flip chart or whiteboard to keep it visible in front of the group.

- Go around the group, either in sequence or randomly, giving each person "a turn" to speak at least once. Individuals may always pass, choosing not to speak.

- Help the group agree on a dialogue time limit, determined by the depth of the question and the time available.

- Use a stick or wand as a *talking stick*, a technique derived from the practice in some Native American councils. Possession of the stick indicates whose turn it is to speak. When the speaker is done, he or she passes the stick to the next person who is to speak.

- Ask the group's permission to reinforce the process guidelines, and then do it fairly.

- Respectfully ask those who feel they must respond to something just said to wait their turn. Keep individuals' "airtime" equal.

- If the group agrees on a time limit for each speaker, use a timer. Three minutes is a good amount of time. (An old-fashioned three-minute egg timer works well. The egalitarian can pass it to the person speaking who then monitors his or her own time.)

One thing the egalitarian does not do is take notes on what people say. The egalitarian treats this dialogue like a thoughtful conversation among friends in his or her own home.

Suggestions for Dialogue Participants

The appropriate time for a dialogue is when the group is genuinely ready to explore the varying points of view and perspectives of its members. Dialogue doesn't happen by accident. Those participating must have the interest and willingness to learn from each other and respect their points of view. When it's their turn to speak, they should be encouraged to do so with conscious thought and to adhere to these guidelines:

- State ideas clearly, succinctly, and with the appropriate level of feeling.

- Clarify general words and phrases with specific descriptions: for example, "communication problems" may mean "not returning e-mail messages."

- Give specific examples to illustrate ideas: for example, "Yesterday at noon I saw five people waiting for someone to help them at the check-in counter."

- Express positive emotions and praise for others freely: for example, "I really appreciate that Judy opened the office early today."

- Never speak for more than the time agreed to by the group. Share the airtime.

- Avoid starting sentences with verbs, unless adding "please": for example, change "Get that done this week," to "Please get that done this week," or to "I'd really like it if you could get this done this week. Is that possible?"

- Avoid closed-end statements that expect agreement: for example, instead of saying, "Don't you think that . . ." or, "Aren't you glad we didn't do that?" say, "What do you think?"

Listening: A Key to Dialogue

If you're a good listener, you'll learn more and appear wiser. Here are a few suggestions to help you and others in your group to be better listeners:

- Listening is an inside effort. Practice being interested and curious about what people are thinking and saying rather than forming negative judgments.

- Listen to learn. Try to learn all you can rather than say all you want.

- Listen for key words and phrases to remember—jot them down.

- Listen for the meaning behind the words. Ask yourself, "Am I clear about what this person means?"

- To check your understanding of someone's point of view, restate the message in your own words and ask for confirmation. Example: "Am I correct in understanding that you're opposed to this because of the cost?"

- Restrain yourself—don't feel you have to spontaneously comment on everything.

- Be aware that feelings such as fear or worry make it harder to listen. Admitting these feelings may help you get beyond them to listen more openly.

As a group member your role is to be as constructive as possible. Practicing listening and participating in meaningful dialogue will increase trust and cooperation among group members.

Log Entry: Summary

The custom of putting motions on the table sets up a debate in which people take opposing positions for or against a particular direction. The effort to debate triggers people to take polarized positions. A more productive way to prepare to make decisions is to focus on understanding the problem and people's points of view before going further into looking for a solution.

Dialogue, although simple procedurally, requires a group to agree on the value of the dialogue method and then follow specific guidelines to ensure real listening and learning. The responsibility to do this well is on each person. The outcome is always interesting, usually enlightening, and often opens new ways to approach old problems.

Getting Under Way

- Talk within the group to find out whether or not all members are in agreement with the beliefs and values necessary to use dialogue well.

- Agree on courtesy guidelines to use when having a dialogue or conversation.

- Select someone to take the role of egalitarian initially, and then frequently rotate that role.

- Get agreement that the group will experiment with ways to reduce debate and increase dialogue—then do it!

Making Headway

The next chapter builds on the guidelines for dialogue and presents several ways to structure a group conversation through employing the specific stages of opening, narrowing, and closing. These will keep you off the shoals of discussion and from sailing around in circles.

Streamlining Discussions with a Clear Destination

The purpose of this chapter is to provide ways for board or team leaders to structure discussions, using three stages: open, narrow, and close.

In this chapter you will learn

- How to avoid discussions that turn into arguments

- How to lead a group through three phases of a discussion to open, narrow, and close

- How to identify and work through the *groan zone*

- How to use opening, narrowing, and closing questions to explore the problem and then the solution

Problem: A Free-for-All Takes Its Toll

The board of a country club was involved in long-range planning. Some members were strongly in favor of adding more tennis courts. Other members wanted to see additions to the exercise room. A third group wanted to construct a swimming pool.

Whenever there was a membership meeting to "discuss" the planning, people became argumentative and more and more polarized on the issues. The discussion became a free-for-all as people defended their positions, which sounded like solutions. As frustration grew, so did the volume. Some people ducked out early.

Little progress was being made, and the issues were always referred back to the strategic planning committee for more research. Tension was growing in the club, with people separating into opposing camps. Recently the popular annual dinner dance had had fewer attendees than in previous years.

A Recipe for an Argument

One of the most dangerous items to see on a meeting agenda is the word *discussion*. What is a discussion? As we've seen in the previous chapter, when people enter into a discussion with a fixed point of view, they tend to stick to their position and end up forming distinct camps. When a discussion has no structure, it can often go nowhere positive.

If you take the wheel of a ship and lash it down turned in one direction, the ship will go in circles. When a discussion is locked into familiar patterns of argument, debate, and dispute, it can continue to go in circles. What's needed is a method for steering the discussion through logical developmental stages.

The Stages of a Discussion: Open, Narrow, and Close

According to Interaction Associates, there are three stages to any discussion: *open, narrow,* and *close.* Interaction Associates teaches this concept and illustrates it as three sections of a diamond shape (see Figure 12.1). To be more specific, *opening* means gathering information and generating all the possibilities or options. *Narrowing* involves understanding and organizing the information. This may require research and evaluation. *Closing* means coming to a conclusion of the conversation or reaching an agreement on the best actions. Although decision making happens in closing, it's what

Figure 12.1. Stages of a Discussion.

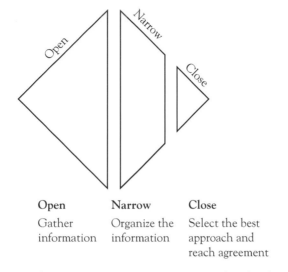

Open	**Narrow**	**Close**
Gather information	Organize the information	Select the best approach and reach agreement

Source: Copyright Interaction Associates, Inc. Reproduced with permission.

occurs in opening and narrowing that will make good win-win decisions possible.

Open

In the opening stage you need to ask your group to keep an open mind. Many groups use brainstorming at this stage, a process that encourages people to engage in free thinking, to build on each other's ideas, and to refrain from discussing and evaluating those ideas until the brainstorming is over. In some groups this is also called *divergent thinking,* or *branching out without limits.*

Narrow

In the next stage the group narrows down the options. Yes, there is life after brainstorming. However, many groups get stuck in this stage because it is harder for groups to let go of ideas than to generate them. In contrast to the divergent thinking of the opening stage, narrowing requires *convergent thinking*. Convergent thinking occurs as the group begins to evaluate alternatives, sort ideas into categories, and summarize and synthesize key information. At this point the group begins dropping some ideas or options in favor of others. The difficulty occurs when groups start to polarize, owing to either/or thinking. People start thinking that they are "right" and others are "wrong." At this stage they have a hard time listening and being open to others' points of view. Sam Kaner, founder of Community at Work and one of the best thinkers today about group process and decision making, has appropriately called this impasse point the *groan zone*.

As Kaner and his coauthors (1996) point out, it's hard for people to shift from expressing their own views to understanding other people's perspectives, particularly when there are a lot of perspectives or high emotions. People who do not feel understood will repeat themselves or become more insistent. Others will resist. The result is usually frustration and lack of movement toward closure. Because of the discomfort in this groan zone, some people will try to avoid disagreement and conflict by bringing discussions to a close quickly. It's this effort to avoid the discomfort that endangers good group decisions. Although easy issues or proposals suffer no harm from quick closure, others need far more exploration.

Close

The closing stage—the final coming together of convergence of ideas—is the most difficult because it requires reaching an agreement. Interaction Associates points out that in this stage we begin using either/or thinking (as if there are only two choices and they are mutually exclusive) to find a solution. Either we do A or we do B. The shift you can help group members make is toward *both/and* thinking. This means that it may be possible to implement both A and B—if not in their entirety, then perhaps by using parts of solution A and parts of solution B. This may result in some negotiating (adding or dropping solution features). The result should feel more like a creative, win-win solution than like a compromise in which everyone tends to lose something they want.

Solution: Moving from Either/Or to Both/And Thinking

A women's organization that provided career transition services in a major city was in agreement that it needed to expand its services to reach women in suburban locations. The board included members from two outlying counties, and they disagreed on the location of the new services. One faction wanted to expand further south and one further north. Each assumed that budget constraints made this an either/or choice. The conflict was escalating, and no decision was being made.

Finally two of the board members, one from each faction, met and explored other options. One woman knew of a great location south of the city that was owned by another nonprofit service organization that was looking for a compatible tenant. The other woman knew of a church in a poor neighborhood north of the city with a history of community service. This church was willing to offer free space as long as organization activities didn't interfere with church activities held on the weekends. The organization's services were conducted primarily in the evenings on weekdays.

These two proposed locations fit the criteria and the established budget. The board enthusiastically approved both solutions.

Using Open, Narrow, and Close in Problem Solving

Now let's return to the concept from Interaction Associates of separating group problem-solving activities into a *problem space* and a *solution space* (see Figure 3.1 on page 37). Leaders can use the stages of opening, narrowing, and closing in both the problem space and the solution space, so that the group can have a focused conversation.

The Problem Space

In the problem space the members of your group will be considering their perceptions, current knowledge, feelings, and willingness to work together. It may be necessary to define the problem tentatively, do research, and then redefine it in light of new knowledge. Using opening, narrowing, and closing questions can focus people's thinking and conversation.

Opening Stage

- How does everyone see the situation?

- For whom is it a problem?

- What do we know about this problem?

- Does this group have the authority and expertise to work on it? If not, who does?

- Is this a problem worth spending our time on? If not, what else can we do about it?

Narrowing Stage

- How should we define the problem preliminarily?

- What research needs to be done?

- Does the situation represent more than one problem?

- How can we break the problem into smaller problems?

Closing Stage

- What are the primary causes of (reasons for) the problem?

- What is this problem causing or affecting?

- How should we redefine it, now that we know the causes and impact?

The answers to these questions will help members decide whether the group should take the issue further.

The Solution Space

It's important to realize that lots of problems cannot be totally solved. All the group may be able to do is to learn a lot and then reduce the causes of the situation. This may result in a more tolerable situation by at least changing some of the impact. If group members agree to work on the issue and to solve it or at least mitigate it, then proceed to the solution space. Here are some questions that can guide group members' dialogue as they develop solutions:

Opening Stage

- Which key cause can we affect the most?

- What are all the options for solving or reducing this problem?

Narrowing Stage

- What are the key criteria we could use to select the best options?

- What options meet the most criteria?

- What are the facts and our intuition telling us?

Closing Stage

- Which option(s) would the group agree to implement?

- Who will take responsibility for the implementation?

One payoff for separating the problem space from the solution space is that the more work you do to answer the problem space questions, the easier it will be to answer the solution space questions.

Interaction Associates has another great saying, "Go slow to go fast," which is a shorthand way of saying that you should start slowly to end up finishing faster. You might say this to a group when you want to encourage participants to focus on the problem before seeking the solution.

Log Entry: Summary

As a meeting leader you can guide a discussion through three logical stages: opening, to gather or generate information; narrowing, to evaluate, select, and eliminate information; and closing, to select the best course of action from the information the group has. This process can be applied to problem solving. By using opening, narrowing, and closing questions to lead a structured discussion about the problem first, you can help your group reach agreement on the problem before proceeding to consider solutions. Using these tools gives a group a destination in a discussion and keeps it from going in circles.

Getting Under Way

- Place a diagram on the wall of your meeting space that shows the progression of opening, narrowing, and closing as the three stages of a productive discussion.

- Use the questions in each of these three stages to guide people's thinking during the meeting.

- Complete each stage before moving on to the next.

- When problem solving, apply the stages of opening, narrowing, and closing to explore issues related to the problem before applying these stages to developing the solution.

Making Headway

The previous courses in this book have focused on people in groups and how they can successfully meet and interact to get work done. The next course takes yet another tack to focus on the underlying decisions that structure an organization. This structure needs to be written down and used consistently to create lasting change.

Part V

Tuning the Governance Rigging (Northwest Course)

Building a Strong Yet Flexible Structure

The purpose of this chapter is to help you find the right balance of authority, responsibility, and roles to avoid both overstructuring and understructuring.

In this chapter you will learn

- Why some form of structure is necessary, but too much can sink you

- How to apply seven principles of democratic structuring

- How to clarify what's expected of board members

- Why the power of an executive committee should be limited

- Why it's better for boards to be smaller

Problem and Response: The Pull and Tug of Structure

The newly elected board of a regional professional association in a large metropolitan area had been functioning for nearly two months. Due to the near dissolution of the organization over the last two years and a complete turnover on the board, all the board members were new. Several former board members were assisting as a transition team. The seven-member board was functioning well as a leaderless team of seven.

Each new board member was elected to provide oversight for a particular function—Web and e-commerce, communications and publications, membership and marketing, member involvement, special programs, evening events, and finance and operations. Leadership was emerging but so was conflict.

Two of the values of the organization reflected in the board were collaboration and teamwork. When faced with their state's requirement for elected board officers, board members were resistant. Some were concerned about establishing a hierarchy on what was emerging as a self-directed team. They had each been elected to the board to head an area of responsibility, and most were reluctant to take on more work. Some thought the unstructured leadership that was emerging was sufficient. Others thought it was too informal and perhaps temporary. Overall, an understanding that the board needed both structure and flexibility was winning the day.

Casting Off Structure Isn't the Answer

In 1970, at the height of the women's movement, Jo Freeman wrote "The Tyranny of Structurelessness," an insightful article that discussed the consciousness-raising groups that were a popular part of the women's movement and were intended to be highly egalitarian and leaderless *rap groups* (when rap meant talking, not singing). They encouraged enlightening conversation about women and their changing roles in society. These groups were usually able to maintain their momentum until members decided that there was something that they wanted to accomplish beyond talk. Then the groups often began to come apart. But why?

In general, the women's movement had rejected the notion of organization and structure, as if both were inherently bad. This was a reaction against an overstructured society that had excluded most women from the hierarchy. When the focus of these groups changed, the members were unwilling to evolve an appropriate structure. Using our sailing analogy, it's as if the groups became dead in the water, or becalmed. This happens when the elements change, as when the wind dies, but it also happens when the crew lets the lines controlling the sails go slack. The boat then rounds up into the wind and stops. Because there is no wind filling the sail, the momentum stops. In other words, because there is no control, the boat will not go forward.

Structure Is Never Absent

Freeman's premise is that it is impossible for a purposeful grouping of human beings to persist over time without some form of structure. If the structure isn't formal, it will emerge informally. However, informal structures without formal leaders can be just as oppressive as highly formal structures. The leadership that emerges naturally is not always constructive. Those with strong personalities or large egos take charge. When there is no selection process for leadership roles, leaders are not empowered by the group. Without an explicit decision-making process, decisions are often made by a few. Freeman's conclusion is that structure isn't bad and it isn't absent. Therefore, it's better to make a conscious choice to develop a flexible structure appropriate to the group's mission than to let something evolve that could destroy the group. She encourages trial and error to find and customize the right approach. Her ideas are still appropriate today for organizations wanting to have structure without unnecessary hierarchy.

Structuring the Board and Setting Expectations for Its Members

Freeman presents *principles of democratic structuring*. Her ideas can be organized into the following seven categories:

1. *Distribute and delegate authority.* Use a democratic process to give authority to those who are willing and who have an interest in taking a leadership role or carrying out a task. Spread authority among as many people as possible. This

gives many individuals an opportunity to serve and to learn. Determine what jobs need to be done, and select a board member to oversee each job with the help of a team.

2. *Clarify responsibility.* Make it clear that anyone in authority is responsible to the board and to the larger group. A board leader or member cannot make decisions for the whole board unless that decision has been delegated. The board must convene to make decisions and then speak to the outside world with one voice (Carver and Carver, 1996).

3. *Rotate roles.* Balance power and increase commitment by rotating tasks and leadership roles. The secretary of state for each state sets guidelines for rotating officers and board members, to keep nonprofits from becoming personal clubs. Within those limits, boards may set their own policy and add additional roles.

4. *Allocate tasks using criteria.* Use ability, interest, and responsibility as primary criteria to select leaders for specific tasks. Everyone needs a clear area of responsibility. Provide learning and support for new members. A mentoring program is one way to do this.

5. *Diffuse information.* Information is power and everyone should have equal access to it as rapidly as possible. The Internet makes this principle easy to implement. Establish an informative and interactive Web site to post agendas and meeting summaries for all to see.

6. *Provide access to resources.* When possible give all members a chance to access resources and learn new skills. This may include sending members to networking conferences and leadership workshops. (See the Resources section at the end of the book for a list of Web sites.)

7. *Create opportunities to influence decisions.* When an organization has general members, create opportunities for them to provide input and influence decisions *before* those decisions

are made. For example, give members a chance to discuss and vote on goals and to modify mission and vision statements.

There are simple but powerful changes that any board can make to shift its culture to be more inclusive and democratic. This isn't just about voting—it is about being more egalitarian, inclusive, and fair.

Put Your Collaborative Policy in Writing

To begin with, when an organization wishes to operate more collaboratively and less as a hierarchy, it is useful to have a policy statement to this effect. Here's an example of collaborative leadership expectations expressed as an operations policy that you can complete:

> The officers of _____ organization hold their elected position for a maximum of _____ years. While carrying out the duties required by the State of _____, we agree to operate in a courteous and collaborative manner. As members we will confer with the full board before making statements or agreements that the board needs to support.
>
> Each board member will provide oversight and quality assurance for a particular area (attach a list) while working with the other board members as a team to govern the organization. As a board we will convene to make policy decisions and we will speak with one voice outside of the board meetings, regardless of personal opinion.

Changing the terminology a group uses can also send a message of change.

Find Terminology That Fits Your Group's Culture

Although changing terminology may seem unimportant, consider that the way we speak influences the way we think. This in turn changes how we relate to each other. For example, using military terminology to describe roles in organizations may have been appropriate following the Civil War, but today it seems heavy handed. (When was the last time you saw a sergeant at arms?) Words derived from inanimate objects, like *chair*, *floor*, and *table*, today seem impersonal and antiquated.

For legal and fiduciary reasons the organizational roles required by your state's secretary of state are called *officers*. When a group reports its officers annually to the Office of the Secretary of State, it must use the terms prescribed—*president*, *secretary*, and *treasurer*. This how the group represents itself and its leadership to the outside world. However, its internal labels can be more creative. If the word *officers* sounds too much like the military, use other titles internally. A woman's organization refers to its chairwoman as *head goddess*. Other options that have been used by various groups include *chief*, *wizard*, and *factotum* (Jack or Jill of all trades). Some groups like *scribe* or *recorder* better than *secretary*. Some organizations refer to the board as the *leadership team* or the *association coordinating team* (ACT). To refer to your group, consider using the term *crew*, *team*, or *council*. Have fun. Make the titles and terminology reflect your organization's culture.

Establish Board Member Expectations

One reason boards may not accomplish all their goals is that they have some members who are not clear about what they are there to do. Vague descriptions like raising funds, supporting the staff, or serving on a committee are often used. One of the best ways to clarify a board member's responsibility is to elect that member to fill a particular functional role. Think of a crew on a large ship. Yes, there are the traditional officers, but there are also many specialists. Crew members are generally hired for their particular skills. Each person on a ship has a role assignment, such as cook, bosun, or engineer. And everyone is assigned to a *watch*, which rotates responsibility for essential tasks. While on watch each person has a specific task, such as bow lookout. No one stands around idle. Each person's task is clear, and she or he is held accountable for doing it on behalf of the entire crew. They depend on each other for safety.

Each organization needs to identify its essential functions. Most, for example, will need individuals to oversee organizational use of the Web, to ensure the quality of publications, to keep an eye on operations, to plan regular programs, and to handle special events that require yearlong planning. Almost all boards need someone good at marketing and fundraising. Here are a few examples of board roles that can be customized for your organization. Use the title *vice president, director,* or *team leader* of

- Publications: printed and e-newsletter

- Marketing: outreach to maintain and grow membership

- Events and special programs or projects

- Income or fund development (finance)

- Education (or membership) development

- Ambassadors or liaisons to other organizations

- The Web site, electronic communication, and e-commerce

- Educational conferences and learning events

- Membership involvement and volunteering

- Organizational effectiveness and leadership development

- Future (or strategic) planning

- Public relations and media communication

Add to this list any other roles your group needs, or subtract those you don't need. Then write brief role descriptions with clear boundaries between roles. Once they have identified their necessary roles and areas, organizations know how many board members they need and are better able to recruit the right people to do the work. Being an enthusiastic supporter of the mission is important but isn't enough to keep an organization functioning well. BoardSource suggests taking a *zero-based planning* approach to committees or teams. Assume each year that you're starting over and forming only the committees or task teams you really need. A few, like leadership development (nominating) and fundraising, may carry over from year to year, but at least there should be a transfusion of new energy and direction (for more information, see Bobowick, Hughes, and Lakey, 2001).

Many grassroots organizations place representatives of their stakeholder groups on the board. However, it is better to avoid having *members at large* or members that represent only a constituency or point of view. All members should be able to carry out a specific board task. For example, if an educational organization feels it needs a teacher on the board, it should make sure that this teacher also brings a particular talent or skill that the organization needs. Perhaps she or he could be vice president or director of community outreach to schools.

In large organizations with paid staff, beware of electing board members to duplicate the roles of staff members. This can set up a conflict, with the staff member feeling as though he or she is reporting to the board member instead of to the executive director.

Expand Involvement in Organizational Leadership

When board members head up a particular functional area, they should be expected to develop a team of organizational members to work with them. Ideally, each vice president or director will recruit, with help from others, more talent from the community or the membership. In this way, these board members will become team leaders and not independent contributors. Their role becomes one of cultivating and mentoring potential leaders who can in turn move easily into the board roles.

Many boards call these subgroups *committees*, but you may want to eliminate the word *committee* (standing or ad hoc) altogether and use the term *workgroup* or *task team*. When the task is done and the work is over—whenever that is—the team disbands. Look at the word *committee*—it means a body to which work is committed. Even though the trust and confidence this implies is a good thing, it also implies the baggage of never-ending tasks, boring meetings, and more-work-to-do-when-I'm-already-busy-and-don't-have-any-more-time. This is unfortunate but true. Some organizations like to reserve the term *committee* for subgroups that are typically ongoing (standing), such as the committee for fund development. They use the term *team* for subgroups with a time-limited objective or focus, such as those that plan an event. Using the word *team* instead of *committee* may seem a semantics game, but *serving on a committee* connotes being involved in something open-ended and not always productive. *Serving on a team* suggests having a specific task and a time limit. This is more motivating. Even if these teams continue from year to year, as leadership development (nominating), board governance, and other such groups typically do, they should be renewed each year with revised goals, new timelines, and some new members.

Exhibit 13.1 presents a request for nominations used by the International Association of Facilitators (IAF). The IAF's executive leadership is called the E-Team and its board of directors is called the Association Coordinating Team (ACT). This highly participative nomination process was to fill ACT and E-Team roles. It was sent out to the entire membership, approximately one thousand people, by an e-mail listserve. It offers a good example of job descriptions, alternative terminology for roles, selection criteria, and a participative nominating process.

Select Board Members Beyond the Board's Immediate Circle

A word of caution—small nonprofit boards can effectively become clubs of personal friends. Be sure to appoint or elect (the latter is more democratic) a small team to take on the tasks of recruitment

Exhibit 13.1. A Request for Nominations.

Dear IAF Members:

As Past-Chair, this year I am responsible for the Nominations process for the "vacant" IAF E-Team leadership roles. We are trying to do something a little different this year in asking the whole IAF membership to recommend and nominate IAF members they feel would best suit the roles and serve IAF and its members.

THE PROCESS FOR NOMINATING CANDIDATES

Review the role definitions and the criteria for selection outlined below and put forward IAF members for the vacant role(s).

It is important that the nominated people are aware they are being nominated and that they meet the criteria. You as the person nominating another should outline in a brief synopsis why you think the person is suited for the role and how they meet the criteria. It is also important that the person you have nominated has some input to the nomination synopsis, as we would like to know why they think they would be suitable as well!

From these nominations the Nominations Committee will produce a slate of people, assessed against the criteria, for the vacant roles, and this will be sent back to the entire IAF membership for a vote. The "nominations" results will be announced at the upcoming IAF conference.

THE CRITERIA FOR SELECTION

Association Related

- Should have attended at least one IAF conference
- Has been an IAF member for at least one year
- Reflects and has demonstrated sharing the IAF core values
- Should ideally be attending the upcoming conference
- May have already contributed to the IAF in some way
- Should have been asked if they mind being nominated!

Leadership

- Has proven leadership skills and experience, preferably proven in an IAF role previously or in a similar role outside IAF
- Has strong communication skills and is willing and able to communicate
- Is able to look at the whole picture, visionary and strategic pieces

Exhibit 13.1. A Request for Nominations, Cont'd.

Commitment & Energy

- Will put in the required time and effort to attend meetings and contribute between meetings; this amount of time should not be underestimated as it is considerable
- Is willing to accept responsibility
- Is passionate about the profession of Facilitation

Personal Attributes

- Is thoughtful and thorough
- Is objective
- Is a proven problem solver and a person good at implementing
- Is able to work collaboratively and able to work with those already in existing roles
- And, finally, has something specific that they might like to accomplish while in office

We look forward to receiving your nominations for these important roles.
Thank you for participating.

Source: International Association of Facilitators.

and orientation. This *leadership selection team* is also known as the *nominating committee*. This group should solicit nominations, take all names of individuals suggested by existing board members (or by the larger membership in a membership organization), and contact these potential nominees. In this conversation potential board members should be informed of the expectations of serving on this board. They need to be told at least the following:

- Their potential role or area of oversight, such as public relations
- What the role requires (position description)
- The meeting frequency and the attendance policy
- Whether they are expected to make a financial contribution, and if so, how much

They should also be asked these questions and more developed by the board:

"What do you think you could contribute to the mission of the organization?"

"What direct or related experience do you have?"

"Whom may we contact for a character reference? Who has worked directly with you on a job or volunteer project?"

If there are criteria for the selection of board members, ask additional questions to see whether these potential nominees meet the criteria. Meet with them in person if possible and answer all their questions. Exhibit 13.2 is an example of the expectations a small nonprofit affinity group has of its board members. You can customize these expectations to fit your organization.

Help Board Members Assess Their Performance

John Carver and Miriam Mayhew Carver, in their booklet *Your Roles and Responsibilities as a Board Member* (1996), suggest ways for individuals to be better board members. Their approach works well if you have talented staff on board. If there is no staff, board members must do it all. However, the questions in Exhibit 13.3, borrowed from the Carvers and others, are good reminders to everyone to think strategically and be a constructive member of the team. These are ten questions that all board members can use to assess themselves individually. Check each question that can be answered yes. Then pick one or two questions that you did not check, repent, and resolve to change.

Electing Board Leaders

Paralleling the requirements for for-profit corporations, all nonprofits must elect officers (there's that military influence again). These officers are generally elected from the board by the board.

Exhibit 13.2. Board Member Service Agreement.

Fill in the blanks as a board and check off if you agree.

As a member of this Board of Directors, I agree to

- Be responsible for the legal compliance and the financial health of the organization.

- Make a minimum _____ year commitment to serve on the board.

- Pay membership dues and contribute $_____ to the organization annually or solicit from others.

- Oversee _____ [an area of responsibility] for the year, and recruit a team of 3 to 5 others to help.

- Work as a team member to plan _____.

- Work _____ (amount of time) at the fundraiser.

- Attend monthly meetings (missing no more than 3 a year).

- Attend membership meetings, and assist with preparation and hosting.

- Contribute articles or information to the quarterly newsletter.

- Always speak respectfully, and uphold the meeting courtesy guidelines (ground rules) we agree on.

- Help the board work as a team to support each other and accomplish the organization's mission.

- Support the decisions made by the board, and allow the board to speak with one voice, as a body.

- Follow through on commitments made at meetings and to others.

Name _____   Date _____

Identify Leadership Roles and Responsibilities

In most states only two or three officers are required—president (or chairperson), secretary, and treasurer. The president cannot also be the treasurer. If only two officers are required, you can combine the secretary's and treasurer's roles. However, it helps to spread the responsibilities and select at least four officers: president or chairperson, senior or first vice president (or vice chairperson), secretary, and treasurer. If your board has a vice president, that person is the backup for times when the president is traveling or otherwise

Exhibit 13.3. Checklist: How Am I Doing as a Board Member?

Check if your answer is YES.

☐ Do I think upward and outward, not downward and inward (focusing on strategy and not operations)?

☐ Do I look at the whole picture and not the parts?

☐ Am I focused on the outside world, not the management and staff, if we have them?

☐ Am I searching for substance, the ends, results, and benefits?

☐ Do I provide strategic resources for the organization and its leaders?

☐ Am I focusing on strategic issues, not activities?

☐ Am I a supportive team member with good, trusting relationships on the board?

☐ Do I approach interactions in and out of meetings as an ally who adds value?

☐ Do I promote exploration and outreach to new territory, not old turf?

☐ Do I support the decisions of this board publicly, regardless of my personal opinion?

Source: Adapted from Carver and Carver, 1996.

unavailable. Ideally, the vice president will also be the person in training for the president's role the following year. He or she can also oversee leadership development and succession planning.

The following lists contain the basic responsibilities of the officers and executive directors of smaller organizations. These are not all inclusive, so be sure to customize them to fit your group's situation, adding responsibilities as necessary. For more specific descriptions of board roles, see the sample job descriptions in *The Policy Sampler* (Fletcher, 2000).

Board President, Chairperson, or Team Leader

• Initiate and lead the board and membership meetings, or delegate that role to someone else.

• Plan the expanded board meeting agenda (with the executive director or executive committee).

- Help recruit and involve others in serving in work-groups or on task teams.

- Serve as the spokesperson for the organization, or delegate that role.

- Be responsible for the management of the organization (or work closely with the executive director).

First Vice President, President Elect, or Leader-in-Waiting

- Fulfill the responsibilities of the board chair in her or his absence or by request.

- Ensure that there is board training and development and identification of potential new members.

Treasurer, Finance Officer, or Moneybags

- Manage the board's financial responsibilities, with the help of a finance team.

- Ensure that regular financial reports and updates are given to the board at each meeting.

- Prepare (or assist the executive director or administrative manager in preparing) the annual operating budget.

- Arrange for a periodic independent audit.

- File or oversee the filing of financial forms for nonprofit organizations with the secretary of state or IRS.

Secretary, Scribe, Note Taker, or Record Keeper

- Send out information to board members in advance of the board meeting.

- Write board meeting summary notes with follow-up actions listed and send out notes to board members, or delegate and oversee these tasks.

- Keep a current governance notebook (see Chapter Fifteen) with official papers.

- Communicate with the secretary of state when necessary: for example, to file changes to the articles of incorporation or other documents.

Executive Director or Chief Executive Officer

- Hire and supervise any employees of the organization.

- Work as a partner with the board president to plan all board (and membership) meetings and agendas.

- Participate fully in the board meetings.

- Ensure that board decisions are being implemented, and report progress on goals to the board.

- Clarify his or her role with the board president to ensure good communication and avoid possible duplication and conflict (ongoing).

Use a Simple Election Process

It's helpful if the bylaws are written so that the membership elects the board of directors and then the board elects its own officers and decides how to divide responsibilities. Although there has to be an official election, in small organizations it is often done somewhat informally—more like a selection process. Here's a seven-step method for a small board:

1. Discuss the need for officer positions, and decide on the number of officers (unless specified in the bylaws).

2. Clarify the role expectations (customize the previous lists).

3. Seek nominations; each person says whether he or she is willing or not willing to serve in one of these officer roles for the specified time and whether he or she would like to nominate another board member.

4. Be sure that anyone nominated by someone else is willing to serve.

5. Ask candidates questions related to their potential roles; each person can do this.

6. Speak in favor of candidates; each person can speak about anyone she or he would like to support for a role.

7. If more than one person is nominated for any position, vote by written ballot; otherwise declare a slate of nominated officers and call for a voice vote.

Beware of the Too Powerful Executive Committee

One of the best reasons for having a small board (around a baker's dozen) is that it usually does not need an executive committee. Larger boards often form a board-within-a-board, a small group called the *executive committee* or *leadership team*, to expedite decision making. However, this committee can become *the* decision-making body for the board, leaving all the others wondering why they are serving at all. This is one of the reasons for board boredom and defection—board members' feeling that they are window dressing and not doing anything of consequence.

Some executive committees overstep their role by deciding things that should be the subject of a full board decision. An original rationale for this committee was that it could make itself available to act on behalf of the full board between meetings and in case of an emergency when it would be difficult to gather the full board. Unfortunately this reasoning is still used to justify the making of many decisions without full board involvement, even though today we have e-mail and ways to hold meetings electronically.

The powers of the executive committee should be written in the bylaws. According to Marla Bobowick, Sandra Hughes, and Berit Lakey (2001), the legitimate role of the executive committee is to

- Make emergency decisions when having a board meeting is impossible, not inconvenient.

- Make decisions on legal and financial matters after consultation with the board.

- Implement decisions made by the board.

- Inform the board of the time and agenda of its meetings and any decisions made.

When the organization has an executive director (ED) and staff, the role of the executive committee is to

- Support and give guidance to the ED.

- Work closely with the ED on personnel matters.

- Develop a process for evaluating the ED.

The executive committees should *not*

- Amend bylaws.

- Determine its own role in the organization.

- Elect or remove board members.

- Hire or fire the chief executive without board consent.

- Approve or change the budget.

- Make major structural changes—programs, mergers, collaborations, or dissolution—or any high-impact decisions without the consent of the board.

Consider Slimming Down Your Board

If your organization has a large board, consider reducing it to a smaller, *governing* board—the reason to have a board in the first place is so it can govern. Many boards become too large because of the tendency to fill them with financial supporters or representatives of all the organization's stakeholders. Neither is necessary. For aid in specific areas, create supporting *advisory councils*.

The best way to slim down the board is to separate the governing and legal responsibilities from the other functions. This will be a relief to some people. Your leadership selection team (nominating committee) should look for good managers for the governing board, fundraisers for a *financial advisory council*, and community or constituent representatives for a *community council of advisers*. Whenever possible avoid confusion by referring to these advisory groups as *councils* instead of *boards* and do not refer to their members as *directors*. Save those terms for one group, the board of directors.

An advisory council needs its own charter to be successful (see Chapter Fifteen). This will specify its purpose and expectations. Advisory councils cannot be left adrift. A board member should chair any advisory council, hold regular meetings, and make reports to the governing board.

Solution: Bringing a Phantom Board Back to Life

A musical organization, an affinity group, had been started twenty years ago in the college dorm room of its visionary founder. For many years it blossomed under his energetic leadership and was served by a small but enthusiastic board. Recently the founder had married, had a child, expanded his career, and started traveling frequently. Although his passion was still there, there wasn't enough time to do the work required. His desire was to hire an executive director. However, the board had shrunk to two active members; it had become a *phantom board*. The founder had been president beyond the limitation set by the secretary of state. In order to hire an ED, even a part-time one, there needed to be a functioning board of directors to do the hiring and to supervise the ED.

The current and most recent members of the board lived all over the country. The founder decided to bring in a consultant from a local nonprofit management support organization to conduct a search for a new ED. The consultant's first step was an assessment of the current state of affairs. Current and former board members were interviewed to learn what was currently working well and what had caused interest in serving on the board to decline. Each individual was polled regarding his or her interest in serving again and was asked for recommendations about others who might serve.

Five of these current and former board members, some living on the East Coast and some on the West Coast, agreed to participate in a two-hour telephone conference call meeting. The only time at which they were all available was 10:00 P.M. Eastern time (7:00 P.M. Pacific time). The primary purpose was to understand the responsibilities of the board and decide on the categories of tasks that needed oversight. The consultant facilitated the conference call. As a result of this meeting the following positions were created to serve the organization.

The new board was to have four officers (president, first vice president, secretary, and treasurer), and seven functional roles called *focus areas* of responsibility. The title of vice president was added to elevate the importance of the roles of overseeing the focus areas. (When you can't give money, titles help.) Given the needs, the ideal board size was determined to be seven to eleven members. For this transition year the board members' roles were vice president of

1. Publications, the Web, and e-commerce, including a printed newsletter, an e-newsletter, and on-line marketing

2. Membership and marketing, outreach to maintain and grow membership

3. Events and special programs or projects, including community awards

4. Income development and finance (also treasurer), including nonmember income, merchandising, and CDs

5. Inner-city programs, with an emphasis on expanding to include more young people

6. Education and scholastic, with a focus on schools and colleges

7. Local organizations (state and national) and liaisons

They decided that the first task would be to assess each focus area for what's working and what's not and to recommend to the board what to continue or change.

Each person was asked to let the consultant know privately the following:

- If she or he was willing and able to make a commitment for at least a year

- If she or he would serve for at least a year, in which oversight role (or a new combination of roles)

- If a different role breakdown worked better and, if so, to make a proposal

- Who else with talent she or he would recommend to serve in a particular role

As a result of the first conference call meeting each of the new vice presidents was asked to do an assessment of his or her area, describing the current situation—what was working well and what needed improvement—and making some proposals. These assessments were sent to each member via a group e-mail. One of the more experienced leaders, who had been previously involved, took a shot at drafting a set of bylaws.

Another two-hour conference call meeting was held several months later. One of the business items was to decide on the board's decision-making method. Members agreed to strive to gain consensus (full support) through listening, questioning, and gaining understanding. If consensus did not occur within the time allowed on the agenda, they would use a substantial majority or concordance of 80 percent agreeing to move forward. (For example, on a board of eight members, six would need to agree for something to be approved and implemented.)

Each person summarized what he or she had learned, informed the board of decisions made, and asked for input and agreement for decisions that would commit the board to spending money or establishing a new direction. Each member was expending effort on behalf of the organization and making progress. Several important decisions were made by the whole group by roll-call vote using concordance.

The newly constituted board was still lacking a board president. Three others had agreed to be first vice president, secretary, and treasurer. Those who had served before were burned out and fully committed in their careers. There was a definite need for new energy. One of the new VPs had impressed everyone with his analysis of the area he was overseeing. He was emerging as a natural leader. He was nominated by one of the others to serve as president for a year and was given some time to think about it. When he said he was willing, there was audible excitement and relief that things would be in good hands. There was unanimous agreement that he was the right choice for the newly transformed board.

Several issues needed work outside the meeting, including the next draft of the bylaws and a way of involving the organization's far-flung stakeholders. Although there was still a lot to be done, new life had been breathed into the organization, with talented people taking on defined roles and working collaboratively.

Log Entry: Summary

Nonprofits must comply with the officer requirements in their state of incorporation. Beyond that, your group may use different terminology internally and write specific expectations that board leaders will take a collaborative approach. However, beware of the tyranny of structurelessness and define an internal structure, with specific roles and titles, that complements the culture of the organization. When it involves more people in leadership and officer roles and forms task teams utilizing members or stakeholders, the board will be more focused and productive.

Getting Under Way

- Determine the current needs of the organization, and decide what talent is needed on the board. Give these roles titles, write brief role descriptions, and find candidates to fill these positions. (If there is a staff, make sure board roles don't duplicate staff roles.)

- Assess your organization's approach against the seven principles of democratic structuring for boards. Make an action plan to incorporate more of these principles.

- Modify or develop a board member service agreement that states the expectations for board members. Reinforce this agreement fairly once established.

- Use terminology that fits your organization's culture when referring to your leadership.

- Modify or develop your own list of criteria for your dream team of board members.

Making Headway

In this chapter you've considered alternatives to traditional board responsibilities, roles, committees, and anachronistic terminology. In the next chapter you'll clarify your organization's values, include them in the mission, and establish a vision for the future—three key markers along the channel to Roberta's shore.

Plotting Your Course with Mission, Vision, and Values

The purpose of this chapter is to help each organization become clear about its values and then incorporate their essence into its mission and vision. A mission statement tells why an organization exists, and a vision statement describes what it wants to be proud of in the future. The three markers of mission, vision, and values form a channel that establishes the direction and boundaries of the organization.

In this chapter you will learn

- How the purpose statement found in the articles of incorporation and the mission statement differ

- Why your organization should be explicit about its values

- How to write mission and vision statements

Problem: Things Change in One Hundred Years

The board of directors of a one-hundred-year-old chapel in a summer community were in an enviable position. They were informed that the will of a long-term summer resident had bequeathed to the chapel society an annual gift. In addition, a solid mutual fund had been building assets in the society's treasury. In the last several years a scholarship subcommittee had embarked on a model program to provide scholarships to members of the local year-round community. The purpose was to stimulate local high school students to further their education.

Although there was substantial agreement that the scholarship program was worth continuing, someone observed that the original statement of purpose didn't mention community outreach or distributing funds for nonreligious purposes. In addition, at a recent meeting several board members had brought up the idea of funding a worthy cause in another community. Their rationale was that there was enough money to benefit these other people with different needs. Although some agreed with that sentiment, they believed the chapel's funding efforts should concentrate on the local community and nearby town.

Because there was no agreed-upon mission or vision statement that could have further clarified the chapel's scope, discussion over the upcoming decisions was expected to be tense.

Developing a Values-Based Mission Statement

Nonprofit organizations are required by each state's secretary of state to write and register a purpose or objective statement in the organization's articles of incorporation. This usually amounts to a dry sentence that describes the organization in general terms. This general approach is taken intentionally, to give the organization some flexibility in the future without having to file a change to the articles. Unfortunately this general and often dated statement sometimes doubles for a mission statement. Let's look at writing a current values-based mission statement first, then at how to describe the future in a vision statement.

Although there are many approaches to writing or rewriting a mission statement, very few reflect the values of the organization or focus on what is attractive to those outside the group. Most mission statements are written for internal purposes, not to communicate to potential members why they might want to join or to funders why they might want to give money. Most mission statements are flat and dull as unpolished brass. Take a look at your current mission statement and put it to this test:

- Does it communicate some feeling?

- Does it make people care or possibly cry?

- If your organization has general members, would it compel anyone to join because doing so would serve their interests?

- Would it inspire anyone to help your organization personally or financially?

If the answer to most of these questions is no, then read further. If the answer to all of them is yes, pat yourself on the back and skip to the next chapter.

Raising a New Set of Sails

Think of writing an inspiring mission statement as putting a fresh set of sails on a sailing ship. It could still go forward with the old sails that are tattered and torn, but not as well. The new sails, the restated mission of the organization, will fill with wind better, withstand the weather longer, and help the organization reach hull speed, the fastest it can go.

For example, compare the impact of these two mission statements. A national conservation club once had this mission statement, which was adequate as a statement of purpose but which lacked juice, or inspiration:

> Our mission is to influence public, private and corporate policies and actions through Club programs at the local, national and international levels.

Then the club revised its statement to better reflect the values
of the organization and its members, who are the lifeblood of the
organization:

> Building on generations of success, we inspire people to
> join in protecting earth's natural treasures and vitality.
> Through our efforts, individuals magnify their power to
> restore the places where they live and preserve the places
> they love.

Now the mission states the reason why the organization exists
from the members' *point of view.* Doesn't it make you feel that you
could make a difference in the world if you joined?

As in the initial example of the chapel, it's often when times
change and people raise legitimate questions about the organization's boundaries and focus that it becomes important to have an
effective mission statement. A mission statement reaffirms the organization's promise to its community and its members. It makes a
public statement about what the organization values and intends to
do. A mission statement should

- Clarify shared expectations

- Inspire members or others to be involved

- Direct passion and energy

- Increase focus and direction, like a beacon of light

Every nonprofit organization needs to develop or periodically
revise its mission statement to give a focus to, differentiate, or limit
the scope of activities. Such a statement can inspire board, staff,
and members. It can also be used to recruit donors to support the
organization.

An effective mission statement tells why the organization exists and what *wouldn't* be occurring without this organization. It tells what the organization does and for whom. It is important for membership organizations to think from the point of view of the members. Why do existing members need this organization? What would make others want to be a part of it? The mission should also state or imply a key philosophy or primary values. The shorter the statement the better; one or two sentences is preferable. In summary, the mission statement tells

- Why the organization exists

- What makes the organization unique

- What *wouldn't* get done without it

- What the organization's primary values are

Connecting Values and Mission

Many organizations jump right into writing a mission statement and then wonder why it's difficult. One organization had such a difficult time that the board president said he hoped it would never come up again. Can you relate to that? It is difficult because the conversation about mission taps into the core of what people care about, based on their personal beliefs.

A *value* can be defined as a major philosophical belief. An organization's values are the beliefs from which it operates. These values form the foundation that supports and drives the mission. They are a mirror reflection of the collective values of the leadership and, ideally, the membership. The more widely the values held by all these individuals differ, the more complex the process of determining the mission becomes. And what's important to remember in this process is that no one is wrong. In his or her own mind, everyone is right. So just having a conversation about beliefs and values is a good beginning to finding common ground for agreement.

Evoking the Organization's Values

A nonprofit organization dedicated to conflict resolution in a multi-cultural city described its values this way:

> We believe in the following values, which we strive to apply both internally and externally and make congru-ent with our actions. We believe in
>
> • Taking a nonviolent, constructive response to conflict.
>
> • Sharing responsibility for communication and conflict outcomes.
>
> • Preventing the escalation of conflict.
>
> • Providing excellent and relevant services.
>
> • Building and supporting community.
>
> We strengthen the capacity of people in the local area to manage conflict through constructive interaction.
>
> Believing that conflict is an inevitable part of life, we involve community volunteers who offer accessible con-flict management training, mediation, and facilitation services.

Similarly, the members of your organization can start a mission statement process by agreeing on a list of shared values. Here are some steps to follow when determining the values with your board.

Before the Board Meeting

1. Ask the board members and any other appropriate stakehold-ers invited to participate to list the values they hold close to their hearts about the organization. First, provide them with several examples. Then ask them to consider what attracted them to be involved and what keeps them involved. Finally,

ask them to submit one or two key values that explain for them why the organization exists.

2. Have everyone involved fax or e-mail their value statements to a designated person, who compiles them. The compiler should also indicate the number of times each value is mentioned. These numbers will indicate areas of agreement.

3. Give everyone an opportunity to receive the compiled list and think about it before the next board meeting or retreat (preferably called an *advance*).

4. Explain the straw poll method, outlined in the following sections, that will ask everyone to select the one-third of the value statements he or she most strongly supports.

During the Board Meeting or the Advance

1. Write the value statements on a flip chart, giving each one a letter (A to Z and going on to AA to ZZ if necessary). Post the statements on the wall in the meeting room.

2. Ask for questions for clarification only—no debate or lobbying for or against any item at this stage.

3. Ask board members to take the time to select the one-third of the statements that they feel most strongly committed to support.

Using the Process

This multiple voting method is a type of straw poll, called N (or number of items) over 3, or N/3, by Interaction Associates. It's a handy method for creating a shorter list from a longer list, as a first step toward agreeing on the most important items. Everyone is allowed a number of votes equal to one-third of the list. For a list of twenty-seven items, for example, each person receives nine votes and can select nine items. If dividing by three produces a fraction, round up to the next highest number. For example, for a list of twenty-eight items, each person receives ten votes.

No one has to use all her or his allotted votes—but there is no vote sharing. There is also no *weighted* choices—that is, people may not use all their votes on one item or give more than one vote to any item. This is not a binding vote, only a straw poll. The process is intended to see where there is the most agreement within the group.

1. When everyone is ready, hand out sticky colored dots, sticky stars, or a marker and ask people to indicate their preferences by sticking a dot on the flip chart sheet for each preferred statement.

2. When all have indicated their preferences, tally the votes. Then, starting with the statements with the most votes, go through them one by one and check for agreement before an item is put on the *working short list*. Each item that goes on this list should be there because of a conscious choice made by the group as a result of discussing why it should or shouldn't be on the list, not simply as the result of the tallies.

3. If the working list has over a dozen items, or if the group feels that there are too many, ask people to speak for or against any statement ("What I suggest keeping . . ." and "What I suggest dropping . . ."), giving specific reasons.

4. If the group wishes to, conduct an *N/3* poll on the new list to produce an even shorter working list. Then use the group's agreed-upon decision-making method (see Chapter Five) to make a final decision on a list of values that will be formally considered the organization's values. This list might begin with the words, "We believe in . . . ."

Polling Outside the Meeting

Although taking a straw poll between meetings means that people don't have the benefit of hearing each other's points of view and learning about each other's personal values, it's possible to do the first round of an $N/3$ by having each person fax or e-mail a sheet that contains all the items, marked to show their choices, to one individual to tally.

1. When using an electronic method, allow an opportunity for board members to ask about the meaning of any words or concepts before they vote.

2. It's best to have the discussion leading up to a final decision in person or at least by conference call. Remember, it's the conversation that counts as much as the content on the list. It's through the talking and listening that shared meaning and common understanding are built.

3. Not everyone needs to agree with every item on the list. However, all items on the list should be directly related to the organization's purpose as stated in the articles of incorporation. If this is not true, those articles should be revised.

Drafting the Mission Statement

Now that your organization has created a list of shared values, those values will influence the quality of the mission statement. (Be careful, however, that they don't enlarge it. The values influence the mission statement but are not incorporated into it verbatim. Keep a separate list of the agreed-upon value statements.) With the values clarification exercise behind you, developing the mission statement should be easier.

Although an individual can write the mission statement for a group, most people won't feel committed to it. The process of getting agreement on a statement is key to its value. Some organizations want to avoid taking the time involved ("We're too busy going in circles!") and are concerned about raising conflict. However, these are the organizations that are likely to benefit the most from developing or revising their mission statements.

Here's an example of moving from values to mission. A progressive Christian church articulated its values in a *statement of faith*. Here are two excerpts:

> Jesus Christ is the foundation to our path to God, but we recognize that he represents one of many ways to know God.

> We find more grace in the search for meaning than in absolute certainty, more in the questions than in the answers.

After gaining general agreement on the statement of faith, board members approved this mission statement:

> We are a loving and spiritual family founded on the teachings of Jesus. We provide a nourishing environment for the spiritual growth of all beings to serve and support others. We encourage open-minded exploration to understand, embrace and celebrate the Grace of God.

This statement has been very helpful in the church's search for a new pastor because it expresses the organization's values and describes what it provides for members.

Once the board or team feels good about a draft of the mission statement, then it's time to take it to a wider audience for reactions and upgrades (remember, people tend to support the things they help create or influence). Sometimes it's helpful to provide two draft versions that members can choose between or combine. This work can be done at a membership meeting or through the mail or e-mail. For example, the following two versions of a mission statement were presented for feedback at the quarterly meeting of a yacht club:

Mission A

The mission of this yacht club is to provide its members with a warm and friendly club that actively promotes and supports high-quality yachting and yachting educational programs along with social activities taking place in an attractive environment with excellent views and facilities.

Mission B

This yacht club is dedicated to advancing, promoting, sharing, and improving member knowledge, proficiency, and enjoyment related to yachting, racing, cruising, and participation in boating and sailing activities. The club is also dedicated to the development of young sailors. Our clubhouse provides a congenial, warm environment and social venue in which members and guests enjoy high-quality year-round activities and social events, along with spectacular views of the bay.

The votes between these two versions were very close. Which one do you like better? How would you consolidate them to get the best from each one?

It's the Conversation That Counts

When discussing values when developing or revising a mission statement, it's the conversation that's important. The purpose is to talk about the options. Creative conflict has a purpose. It reveals what motivates people. People understand each other better when they express their beliefs and the personal feelings behind their thoughts. The statement of mission is merely what the organization makes public to the world. Everyone needs to stand behind what the statement represents.

In the process of discussing values and developing a mission, many topics can come up. Often highly specific ideas expressing expectations for behavior and for the way the organization operates are raised. The conflict resolution organization described earlier discovered that in addition to listing values, they wanted to list the ideals related to their interactions with clients and each other. They decided to be explicit about how they approach their work and developed the following statements about the ideals they strive to demonstrate in and through the organization:

We strive for . . .
- Quality of service and internal processes
- Inclusion and diversity in our services
- Understanding and empathy
- Collaboration and teamwork
- Open communication and information sharing
- Staying current and useful
- Self-awareness and reflection
- Volunteer involvement
- Continuous learning: personal and professional growth
- Having fun

The final ideal is vitally important. Who says you can't have fun doing important work? Without enjoying what we do, motivation is hard to sustain. Volunteers, even board members, will disappear. Without joy, the statements of values and mission alone won't keep us going.

Looking Forward with a Vision Statement

Although it's very important to have a mission statement, it's even more powerful to have a vision statement. This statement describes the *preferred and possible future* of your organization at a specific point of time. This is your mission accomplished. Think of it like a warm, tropical port for sailors making a cold passage.

A vision statement answers these questions:

"What do we hope the future will be like?"

"What will be taking place?"

"What will we or others observe?"

"What will people be saying?"

"What will we feel proud of?"

"What will we be able to brag about?"

"How will it feel?"

There are many ways to carry out visioning. To begin with, some people don't like that name, so it may be better to call this process *creating preferred future* (or *possible future*) *scenarios*. The important thing is to keep the vision future focused but also practical and possible. Here's one way to get group involvement in developing a vision statement, inspired by the Technology of Participation from the Institute of Cultural Affairs and other methods of "affinity diagramming":

Ten Steps to a Vision Statement

1. Bring the board members and other key stakeholders together at a meeting. Begin the process by suggesting that they sit in a relaxed position and take a deep breath. They may close their eyes if they wish. Tell them that for about five minutes you are going to ask them to relax and imagine that they are in the year _____ (you decide) and are observing the positive changes that have occurred over the years.

2. Suggest that they let their imaginations wander. Help them by offering questions such as these as they think. State the questions *slowly*, with a *pause* after each one:

"Who's being served? What are their ages, interests and needs?"

"How many people are around? What are they doing?"

"What's the atmosphere like? What's the tone or ambiance as you walk in?"

"How are people treating each other?"

"How many people are on the staff? What are their roles?"

"What services are provided? What activities are offered?"

"What has been written in a recent newspaper article that praises the organization?"

3. Tell them you want them to keep thinking for a minute and then, when ready, to spend a little time writing down their thoughts.

4. After everyone has finished writing, ask the participants to spend three to five minutes sharing their images, in groups of two or three. (This will be loud and will raise the energy in the room—enjoy it!)

5. After five minutes, hand out large Post-its, and ask for the pairs or trios to write down the images, words, and phrases they would like to see included in the organization's shared vision. Instruct them to write only one idea per sheet and to print large, using a dark marker.

6. Stick the Post-its on sheets of flip chart paper on the wall, and invite a few people to work on behalf of the group, organizing the Post-its into clusters of ideas that sound alike. This will put the duplicates together.

7. Clarify what is in each cluster with a headline that names the category with a few key words. (Write each headline on another Post-it and place it above the cluster.) Use action words, as in this example, "Adding New Programs." At this stage there is no need for agreement on each of the ideas, but work hard to reach agreement on the cluster headlines.

8. Here's a good opportunity to reflect on what's on the wall by using the ORID Focused Conversation method (see Chapter Eight).

9. This is a good time to take a break or to end the session. Ask for a few volunteers to write a draft of a proposed vision statement, using the agreed-upon headlines. This statement should be only a few sentences long and should capture the main ideas. The key is to write it in the *present* tense as if it were *already true*. If those drafting the statement are having trouble agreeing on a single version, ask them to come back with two proposed statements.

10. Once the vision statement is presented (open), take suggestions for upgrades (narrow), and check for agreement (close). If there are two statements, select one to modify, incorporating the best phrases from the other.

Here's an example of a vision statement, a possible future, developed from a list of possible images and activities for a countywide breast cancer resource center:

> The Center is empowering hundreds of women each month to make informed decisions based on current information from our library and electronic resources. Trained volunteers assist them in a comfortable setting. Women in our county think of The Center as the first place to start when seeking information and support about breast cancer.

Here's another example, this time from a sailing and boating club:

> This is one of the premier yacht clubs on the bay. It has an outstanding reputation for its advancement and support of all age groups in yachting, cruising, and racing activities. The club's world-class view of the city and the

bay coupled with its high-quality service and food offerings complements the wide-variety year-round social activities and events that create camaraderie among members and guests.

The value of a vision statement is that it sets up a positive tension between what the organization's impact is now and what the leaders and members of the organization want it to be in the future. The pull of the future is strong. It acts like a magnet to draw energy and resources. Many organizations have found that the vision they thought would take at least five years to accomplish happened much more quickly. Reaching agreement on the future description—or even knowing there isn't agreement—can help an organization plan. As with sailing, there is usually a gap between "where we are" and "where we want to be." Organizations make the crossing between the current mission and the future vision by charting a realistic course, often called a strategic plan.

Log Entry: Summary

Focusing on the values of the organization as expressed by the board members is a recommended step toward writing a meaningful mission statement. Most nonprofit organizations are value driven. Making those values explicit and communicating them publicly can help people relate to the heart of the organization.

Remember that the mission tells *why* the organization exists. It tells what would be lacking if the organization disappeared. It reveals what the organization feels strongly about philosophically and generally describes its niche market. The trick is to do this in a few sentences!

Once your board has crafted a mission statement, it can move on to create a brief vision statement that describes the future when the mission has been accomplished. The positive tension between mission and vision statements will help your organization make realistic plans and move forward quickly.

Getting Under Way

- Use the process suggested in this chapter to learn the beliefs and passions that drive people's commitment to your organization.

- If your organization has an existing mission statement, determine whether it is a dry statement of purpose in disguise or an inspiring and compelling statement of intention.

- If it's a dry statement of purpose put it aside and start from scratch. Use the process outlined for developing a mission statement.

- If it's an inspiring statement decide whether to revise it. Even a conversation about it can be enlightening.

- Develop a vision statement, using the suggested process or a similar one.

- If your organization has members, circulate a draft for input.

- Publicize the organization's values, mission, and vision to members, clients, potential supporters, and donors.

- Include one or both statements on each meeting's agenda. This is why you're all meeting—to fulfill this mission and reach this vision.

Making Headway

Now that you have a clear sense of your organization's mission and vision and the values that drive them, it's important to make decisions about whether to revise the governance documents, such as bylaws, to make more progress.

Overhauling Your Bylaws

The purpose of this chapter is to give you some tools to revitalize and simplify your supporting governing structure. In this chapter you will learn

- What governance is, and why that term is used in nonprofits

- How to use thirty questions to simplify your bylaws

- Why a governance notebook is of value

Problem: The Disappearing Board

The informal leader of a singles ski group founded a nonprofit mutual-benefit organization fifteen years ago for those interested in skiing. Initially the organization had a small board, and board members worked well together for several years. Most board members were the founder's friends. Over the next few years, a number of board members married, some moved away, and some just lost interest in skiing. Now, about ten years later, there is no official leadership other than the founder and a few other people. The original bylaws cannot be located. The organization still puts out a newsletter that announces the group's few skiing trips.

A younger group of single people has a similar club that is very active. They would like to join forces with the older group but aren't sure they want to become a nonprofit. They have been functioning well as an affinity group that doesn't have dues or a need for voting members. Their approach is more informal and they dread having to write new bylaws.

A Necessary Overhaul

The term *overhaul* comes from the command to a ship's crew to "overhaul" the buntlines and clewlines—the smaller lines that furl a square-rigged sail. This simply means to take the slack out and get the lines in order to work again. Sometimes organizations come to a point that requires them to overhaul their governance structure. Their options are to revitalize, to dissolve, or to merge with another group. If the group continues or merges, then a number of decisions made earlier about governance structure need to be made again. This is a good time to rethink the whole structure and take a fresh approach.

What Is Governance?

Legend says that the members of the Massachusetts Bay Colony sat around a flat board, probably placed on two tree stumps, to talk about the common good of the colonists. This meeting became known as "the board meeting." We can only imagine that after discussing issues of survival and mutual support, they began to see a need for reaching agreements about how they would govern as a group.

Let's start with the word *governing*, a term often used in the nonprofit field. *Governing*, derived from an ancient Greek word meaning "to steer," generally means controlling or influencing. It also still applies to piloting or steering a ship. The ship's helm, which moves the rudder that controls the ship's direction, is called the *governail* or *governal*. On an engine there is often a *governor* that keeps the motor running within certain limits—so it doesn't spin out of control. Those who steer or govern a nonprofit are, among other things, responsible for controlling it and maintaining or changing its design. Without a good design, a ship may not be seaworthy. As discussed in Chapter One, a ship can go only as fast as it is designed to go, or its hull speed. A boat designed to sail for pleasure will never win a race against one designed to race. The same is true for nonprofits. A cumbersome design—a large board and many committees—may slow the organization down. Have you seen organizations drifting along, not getting anywhere? Eventually they may even spring leaks and go down.

The design of a nonprofit is established by its *articles of incorporation* and *bylaws*. These documents are like the hull of a wooden boat—the planking that is carefully selected and fitted to hold the boat together. Whether the organization is in its initial informal stages or has chosen to incorporate, it still needs bylaws or at least a simple set of written and agreed-upon statements about how it will operate, such as a team charter. Let's start with the legal documents and use the sailing ship analogy.

Articles of Incorporation: The Bowsprit

Think of the articles of incorporation as your organization's bowsprit, the rounded pole forward from the pointed end of a sailboat. Larger ships usually have a bowsprit to hold more sails; smaller boats may not. Similarly, not all small clubs, affinity groups, and new organizations will file articles of incorporation as nonprofits for the tax advantages. Some will use a fiscal agent with official nonprofit status to manage their money. However, organizations that wish to be approved for tax-exempt status must file articles of incorporation with their state's secretary of state, along with a set of bylaws. These documents help the tax authorities determine eligibility for exempt status.

It's best to be clear and thorough but not overly wordy in these documents. Simple statements with a clear meaning will be welcomed not only by the government entities that review them but also by the boards of directors who need to uphold them if the organization is to retain its nonprofit status. The process of doing this will be enlightening and will help the governing group develop into a team. The articles of incorporation usually include the official name, a statement of specific purpose, a statement that the group is not organized for the private gain of any individual and that no part of the net income or assets will benefit any director, officer, or member. It is also necessary to state (either in the articles or the bylaws) that if the organization is dissolved, any remaining assets after payment of debts will be distributed to a nonprofit fund, foundation, or another tax-exempt organization.

Keeping Track of the Papers

It's important to keep copies of articles of incorporation and the bylaws, along with other legal and informative documents, in an official *governance notebook*, as members of the board of directors will rotate and new boards may otherwise lose track of the original documents. One practical approach is to buy a three-ring binder, a three-hole punch, and a set of eight dividers. Make labels that say: (1) "Articles of Incorporation," (2) "Bylaws," (3) "Operating Policies" or "Standing Rules," (3) "Special Meeting Rules," (4) "Mission and Vision Statements and Values," (5) "Board Roles," (6) "Meeting Records," (7) "Current Goals," and (8) "Future Plan" or "Strategic Plan." Think of this as your *log book*, like the log book on a ship, the place where official notations about activities and progress are kept.

If your organization is considered a charitable or other type of nonprofit, remember that it is first a legal corporation, and second a tax-exempt organization because it meets specific conditions. If your board doesn't follow the rules in your state (contact your secretary of state's office for the relevant codes), it may put the organization in jeopardy of losing that valued status. That would be a shame and one your board wouldn't want to explain to those it serves. If you want to ignore the rules, then pay the taxes! Disregarding them is a reckless option. Just as ships must have safety features and pass inspections to be licensed to operate, it's important to follow the rules to keep your organization's nonprofit status active.

The Bylaws: Making Your Ship Seaworthy

Bylaws are what give an organization a structure and boundaries. How the board will govern or steer the organization depends on the decisions made when writing the bylaws. Like the strong planks in the hull of a wooden ship, all fastened together and sealed to be seaworthy, the bylaws give you a vessel in which to operate. The bylaws could also be likened to the governing rules for operating a sail training ship. These rules address who can be a member (qualifications for jobs), who's in charge of what (officers and other positions), when crew members will meet as a group (muster on deck) for watches, how other practical matters (such as safety drills) will be handled. In general it explains the way the organization (ship) operates.

Let's put bylaws in an historical context. The term *bylaw* dates back to the thirteenth century, when it meant a "rule of the village." "Bye-laws" (Old English) were the rules everyone had to live by that kept civil society acting civil. The earliest meetings were gatherings of elders, generally the men of a community. They came together to make decisions or at least offer opinions on matters of community importance. They also met to make bylaws as needed and to administer justice on behalf of the larger group. After all these centuries, some of the language still remains. Bylaws are still the working agreements that everyone needs to live by in the organization.

Developing Original Bylaws

Incorporated organizations must have a set of bylaws. Along with the articles of incorporation, they communicate how an organization will be governed and are a means of determining tax-exempt status.

Why did typical bylaws get so complicated? Perhaps because most are written by lawyers. Someone with writing skills should write them; lawyers should review them for compliance with state and even federal law. Although bylaws are required for legal corporations, it is not required that they be written in obtuse language and "legalese." When your board is developing bylaws, the rule of thumb is to be clear and complete without being overly descriptive. You'll want to be somewhat general, both to provide flexibility for future organizational activities and, in a membership organization, to ensure that the bylaws will be passed by the general membership (most states require bylaws to be approved by at least a two-thirds vote).

For the best model for writing new bylaws, contact Nolo Press for its book *How to Form a Nonprofit Corporation in All 50 States* (Mancuso, 2000). Another resource is *Bylaws: Writing, Amending, Revising* (Stephens, 2000). It is also helpful to review your organization's legal obligations according to your state's codes governing corporations. For example, in California the nonprofit codes are found in the general corporations code book. The nonprofit section is divided into parts that address public benefit or charitable, mutual benefit, religious, and special categories. You may also find these codes on your secretary of state's Web site. Reviewing these codes may not be the most exciting thing you have ever done, but it will nevertheless enlighten you about the requirements to which your organization and its board members are committing themselves.

Updating Bylaws

Do you know how old your organization's bylaws are? A good guess would be "as old as the organization." For some reason most board members evade eye contact when asked if they've even read the bylaws. Few will volunteer to update them. *Roberta's Rules of Order* aims to change that pattern and make updating easy. Bylaws can be modified as long as doing so doesn't change the organization's basic purpose (in the articles of incorporation) or violate any nonprofit corporate codes.

When updating bylaws you may want to read the old ones, then put them aside, and start from scratch. It's important to be clear and specific, but it's also important not to include information that can easily become obsolete or lock the organization into specific dates, times, and arrangements. Save these details for operating policies (see Chapter Sixteen). The process suggested here results in simplified, or "bare bones," bylaws.

First decide on the major headings. Each heading along with its content is an *article* (not to be confused with the articles of incorporation). The most common article headings in bylaws are "Name," "Purpose," "Members," "Board of Directors," "Officers," "Executive Committee" (if applicable), "Standing Committees" (or "Teams") if applicable, "Meetings," "Decision Making and Amendments," and "Changing the Bylaws." Each article is made up of one or more statements called *sections*. (In the following outline, the Roman numerals designate bylaw articles, and the Arabic numerals designate sections within each article.)

Next answer the following thirty questions in simple declarative sentences (you may decide that for your organization some are redundant or not applicable), and you will have the information needed for bare bones bylaws. (Also see the template in Resource E.) You do not need to repeat what was included in the articles of incorporation, policy, or roles, such as job descriptions. There may be additional information requested by your state of incorporation, so check for the latest requirements on the Web site. You may also add other information, but remember not to make it too detailed or restrictive—a common mistake.

Thirty Simple Questions for Creating Bare Bones Bylaws

I. Name (also in articles of incorporation)

1. What is our organization called?

II. Purpose (also in articles of incorporation)

2. What is our purpose?

III. Members

3. Are there voting members, and if so, who can be one?
4. Are there any membership categories or classes?
5. How does someone become a member?
6. How can a member resign or be removed?
7. Are there any honorary members?
8. Are there dues, and if so, how often are they collected?

IV. Board of Directors or Leadership Team

9. How many board members are there?
10. How many members need to be present to make decisions? (What is the quorum?)
11. How often are the regular board meetings?
12. How are our leaders (board members) selected (what's the nominating procedure)?
13. How is the board elected? (In a membership organization, the voting procedure should include members.)
14. What are the term limits or other restrictions?
15. How can a director be removed from the board?
16. If there is an executive board, who serves on it?
17. How will the organization protect directors from liability or lawsuit?
18. Will the board members be compensated? (Usually no.)

V. Officers

19. How many officers are there, and what are their roles?

20. How long are officers allowed to serve?

21. Who elects the officers—the members or the board?

VI. Meetings

22. How often are regular meetings held, and how will members be told?

23. Is there an annual business meeting or report to members?

24. Who can call a special meeting and how?

25. What constitutes enough members (a quorum) to make decisions? (See Chapter Five.)

26. When and how can electronic meetings be used?

VII. Decision Making

27. What procedures for group decision making will be used? (Use Resource A to customize your own special rules for business meetings.)

VIII. Changing the Bylaws

28. How can these bylaws be changed (by what majority)?

29. Who is entitled to vote on these changes?

IX. Dissolving the Organization

30. What will happen to the assets if the organization is dissolved? (Omit this section if the information is stated in the articles of incorporation.)

Here's how to make the updating process more or less painless. Ask if there are a few board members who really like to structure organizations (there are "governance geeks" around) and who would be willing to answer these thirty questions in writing and recommend answers to the whole board for discussion (open), modifications if needed (narrow), and agreement (close). Exhibit 15.1 is an example of an affinity group's revision to bare bones bylaws. The original bylaws were written by a lawyer and were twenty pages long!

Exhibit 15.1. Bare Bones Bylaws.

Bylaws of the Golden Gate Tall Ships Society
A California Public Benefit Corporation

I. NAME

The name of the organization is the Golden Gate Tall Ships Society
(GGTSS). It is located within the San Francisco Bay Area with a mailing
address in Sausalito, California.

II. PURPOSE/MISSION

Building on San Francisco Bay's rich nautical tall ship heritage, the Golden
Gate Tall Ships Society promotes the renaissance of traditional sailing ships.
We provide youth with scholarships for lifelong learning through sail training
and our members with traditional sailing experiences.

III. MEMBERS

1. Anyone who supports the mission and who pays annual membership dues,
   determined by the Board of Directors, may be a member.

2. There will be a roster of members that is kept current and available to all
   members.

3. All members whose memberships are current will be eligible to vote.

4. Any member may inspect any corporate records upon written request to the
   President.

5. Membership and all rights of members shall be automatically terminated due
   to voluntary resignation, the death of a member or the nonpayment of dues.

6. Members will be terminated within 60 days of nonpayment of dues after
   receiving written notice within 30 days. This notice will be sent by e-mail,
   if available, and by first-class mail to the last known address.

7. Members not attending a meeting to elect officers will be given the opportunity to vote by mail or electronically.

IV. OFFICERS/LEADERSHIP ROLES

1. There will be a President, Secretary, and Treasurer of the corporation.
   These positions will be elected by the Board of Directors annually and
   reported to the Secretary of State.

2. The President will prepare for and preside at meetings unless he/she
   designates another member.

Exhibit 15.1. Bare Bones Bylaws, Cont'd.

3. The Secretary will keep current or oversee others maintaining all corporate records, and oversee keeping a current membership roster and minutes of meetings. He/she will also file all required forms with the Secretary of State.

4. The Treasurer will prepare a monthly or quarterly financial report and maintain the corporation's financial records and accounts.

5. Officers will serve for a minimum of one year and a maximum of three years, in accordance with California Public Benefit Corporation codes.

V. MEETINGS

1. An annual meeting to elect officers will be held each year.

2. The Board of Directors or five percent of the membership may call other special meetings of members.

3. An annual report will be written by the President and published in the newsletter or mailed to members.

4. Members will be notified of a voting meeting by e-mail or regular mail fifteen (15) days before the date of the meeting.

5. The notice of any meeting at which Directors are to be elected will include the names of those nominated.

6. A quorum will be one-third of the members entitled to vote either in person or by absentee ballot.

VI. BOARD OF DIRECTORS/LEADERSHIP TEAM

1. There will be at least three and no more than twelve members of the Board of Directors.

2. The Directors will be residents of California and members of the Corporation.

3. The Directors will serve without compensation.

4. Each year the Board members will select primary areas of responsibility and solicit the participation of members to accomplish those tasks.

5. Board meetings will be held at least six times a year and may be called by any two Directors with forty-eight hours' notice delivered in person or electronically.

6. A simple majority of the Board members constitutes a quorum.

7. Meeting locations will be rotated to be convenient for most members.

Exhibit 15.1. Bare Bones Bylaws, Cont'd.

8. Meetings can also be conducted by conference telephone call.

9. When necessary, Board members may vote on an issue without a meeting by giving written consent using e-mail, provided the issue is clearly defined in writing and everyone has been given three days to respond.

10. The Board shall appoint a person(s) to form a nominating team for elections who will develop a slate of Directors and conduct the elections.

11. Board members may be removed if declared of unsound mind by a Court, if convicted of a felony, or if they fail to attend (3) three meetings of the Board within a single year.

12. Vacancies on the Board may be filled by a majority of the Directors.

VII. PROCEDURES FOR DISCUSSION AND DECISIONS

The Board of Directors will adopt or write Special Rules (from *Roberta's Rules of Order*) to provide a method to reach substantial agreement. In membership meetings when there is a need to vote on an issue, a proposal will be presented first for group discussion. This proposal can be modified. When the issue(s) is fully understood and/or modified, then a motion to accept or reject the proposal can be made and voted upon. Any situations not covered by Special Rules will default to *The Modern Rules of Order* (American Bar Association) and secondarily to *Robert's Rules of Order*.

VIII. AMENDMENTS/MODIFICATIONS

A majority of members attending a regular meeting, provided there is a quorum, may amend these bylaws. Mail or electronic (e-mail) ballots can also be used to vote.

A Shorter Option: The Team Charter

Groups that are not yet incorporated don't need bylaws but may write their own rules (called *un-bylaws* by one unincorporated group) or may create a *charter* like that used by business teams. (This is not the same as formal articles of incorporation, which are sometimes referred to as an organization's *charter*.) A charter will describe the informal group's operating principles to its members and stakeholders. It answers the question, What makes this group or team unique and its practices fair? A team charter may be written for sub-

groups—committees, workgroups, or task teams—within an organization that also has bylaws. When a group is a collaborative or
alliance, in which representatives of several organizations participate, writing a team charter is very useful. Taking time to complete
this charter before taking on the primary task of the collaborative
or alliance has proved invaluable in preventing confusion, mis-
direction, and conflict that are all too common.

Team charters are common in corporations. The following paragraphs borrow ideas from *Teams in Action* (Interaction Associates,
1994) and other corporate training programs.

To prepare their charter team members need to reach agreement
on answers to the following ten questions (taken in any order). (See
Exhibit 15.2 for an example of a charter for a board development
team, formerly a nominating committee, and also use the template
in Resource F.)

Ten Basic Questions for Creating a Team Charter

1. What is our mission or purpose?

2. What are the major goals or results we will strive to achieve?

3. What is our image of success (vision) at the end of our effort
   together?

4. What is the scope of our responsibilities, including the
   boundaries of our authority?

5. What decision-making method will we use?

6. What are the roles and responsibilities of team members,
   including the team leader?

7. What are our courtesy guidelines, or ground rules, for behavior at our meetings?

8. What are our expectations of one another regarding meeting
   frequency and attendance at meetings?

9. With what other groups do we need to cooperate or coordinate?

10. When will this team be expected to disband?

Exhibit 15.2. A Team Charter.

Team Charter for the Board Development Team
(Formerly Nominating Committee)

1. Our mission is to strengthen the Board of Directors and ensure its continuation.

2. Our goals are

   • Provide training and development opportunities for our current Board.

   • Conduct a biannual assessment of the Board's success.

   • Search for and develop a qualified pool of Board candidates each year.

3. We will have been successful if the Board has been fully staffed with qualified people who work together constructively to further the mission of this organization.

4. We recommend the criteria for Board selection, with the approval of the membership. We work with the Board to identify the roles that need to be filled. We recommend candidates to fill the vacant positions, subject to approval by the membership. We do not recommend officers; the Board members select them.

5. We make decisions by attempting to reach consensus (full support), but if that is not accomplished by the end of our meetings, we vote to reach concordance (substantial majority of 80 percent).

6. The Board member in the position of VP of Organization Effectiveness chairs the team. We rotate the roles of notetaker, timekeeper, and meeting logistics coordinator.

7. We use the courtesy guidelines recommended by *Roberta's Rules of Order.*

8. We meet quarterly and each member is expected to attend three out of four meetings.

9. We coordinate with the Board and the Board Governance Team, who are updating the bylaws.

10. Team members are appointed for two years, with at least one member rotating off and being replaced each year.

If the charter is for a task team, answer three more questions:

11. Who are the sponsoring board members (or others) with whom we need to communicate?

12. What is the time limit for our project?

13. If the project has phases, what are the milestones or desired results for each phase?

Log Entry: Summary

The governance of an organization is the place to start to determine the seaworthiness of the organization. Are the bylaws clearly written and up to date? Are things being done according to legal code and common sense? Taking a new approach to your group's governance by writing bare bones bylaws or a team charter will be like a fresh breeze that will keep you moving forward.

Getting Under Way Checklist

- Ask two to three board members with a high tolerance for detail to form a board governance team to draft answers to the bare bones bylaws questions.

- Consider the draft at a board meeting or during a longer planning meeting.

- Once board members reach agreement, submit a draft to the general membership for additional input (if yours is a membership organization).

- Ask teams and committees to complete team charters.

- If your group is a newly formed organization and doesn't intend to incorporate as a registered organization, complete the team charter.

Making Headway

Now that you have addressed major governance issues by revising your organization's bylaws, the final chapter in this book takes you through the everyday workings of your organization. Remember the details you took out of the bylaws? (This was like removing ballast from a ship in order to go faster.) These are your operating policies, which need to be written separately and put in your governance notebook.

Staying on an Even Keel
with Simple Operating Policies

The purpose of this chapter is to help your organization update its operating policies and keep this policy detail separate from its bylaws.

In this chapter you will learn

- How to use operating policies to keep your organization on course

- How to work with six major categories of policies

- How to use twenty key questions to determine policies

- How to write simple operation policy statements

Problem: Outdated Policies

A nonprofit professional association affiliated with a national organization had just elected a new board. One part of the board's initial work was to review bylaws and policies. A team of board members working on this issue found that the bylaws were laden with old policies and information that could be omitted or put into separate operations policies. There were also descriptions of roles, responsibilities, and committees that were outdated. The team, with the board's approval, set to work to simplify the organization's nearly twenty-year-old bylaws, reducing them from twenty-three pages to two or three pages.

Other board members were reviewing the existing policies. Those that they could find were written at least ten years ago. Some referred to policies for submitting articles from a professional journal that was no longer being published. Others established pricing structures that were now totally inadequate for the annual educational conference. These policies had once been useful but were now mostly irrelevant.

Policies: The Stabilizer Under the Surface

Have you taken a look at the policies of your organization lately? Do any exist? If so, are they up to date? Are they buried in the bylaws where they are hard to find and even harder to revise? Policies are guidelines, sometimes referred to as *standing rules*, for recurring situations that need to be managed consistently and fairly every time they occur. Policies communicate to everyone what is accepted and what isn't in the organization's operations.

Our sailing metaphor continues to apply. Sailboats have a centerboard, or keel, a heavy fin attached to the hull and not visible from the surface of the water. The keel is essential to staying upright and moving forward, instead of sideways, while under way. Like a keel, simple, written policies aren't visible to the public but are essential to give the organization stability.

Many sail training ships operating in the United States are nonprofit organizations managed by boards of directors. Each ship's board makes policies that are to be carried out by the officers operating the vessel and that address such issues as safety guidelines for port visits, guests aboard, and provisioning the ship (arranging for supplies and food). Similarly, other types of nonprofit governing boards write policies so that individuals can carry out everyday activities in ways that keep the organization *safe*, meaning financially solvent and out of legal jeopardy.

One of the best resources for boards is *The Policy Sampler: A Resource for Nonprofit Boards* (Fletcher, 2000). The policy, defined here by John Tropman from his book *Policy Management in the Human Services* (1984) is a practice that

- Is written down

- Is approved by the board

- Serves as a guide for action for board, staff, and members

He calls it the "meat on the bylaw bones." This becomes even more important when you have bare bones bylaws.

Specific operating policies should not be in the bylaws because they may need to be changed frequently. Policies that are separate from the bylaws are easier to change than bylaws. However, beware of getting too detailed in operating policies too by including procedures. Procedures for use of equipment and program application steps, for example, are necessary, but it's better to let staff or a team develop them and to keep them in a separate section in the governance notebook.

Carver and Carver (1996) advocate an approach to governance in which boards shift their attention and their meeting agendas to establishing Policies rather than focusing on the organization's day-to-day tasks of operation and implementation, which are to be handled by staff. Of course this works when there *is* a paid staff, which is not the case for many small nonprofits. This type of Policy (capital "P") involves making major decisions about organizational direction, such as changing the type of clients served. Organizations also have policies with a small "p"; these are the specific *operating policies*. Although all boards can benefit from focusing more on making Policy that wisely guides the organization, they also need to know more mundane policies, such as how to get reimbursed for travel expenses.

Boards may produce operating policies in many areas, as *The Policy Sampler* (Fletcher, 2000) attests; however, small nonprofits generally need to pay most attention to policies in the following six areas: finance; ethics; board and management; programs, workshops, and conferences; committees and task teams; and governance and organizational effectiveness. If your board discusses the following questions and agrees on the answers, it will develop its own policies in these areas. (See Resource G.)

Twenty Questions for Determining Operating Policies

I. Finance

   1. Who has check signing authority?

   2. What are the dollar limits of this authority?

II. Ethics

   3. How do we handle confidentiality?

   4. How do we handle a real or perceived conflict of interest?

III. Board and Management

   5. Who manages the association other than the board?

   6. What are the expectations and privileges of serving on the board?

   7. How are board members protected legally (indemnification)?

   8. How are board members rewarded without receiving compensation?

   9. What do board members and others get reimbursed for and how?

IV. Programs, Workshops, and Conferences

   10. What is our registration policy for programs?

   11. For whom do we allow fee waivers?

   12. If we give discounts, how do we define eligibility?

V. Committees and Task Teams

   13. Which committees and task teams exist?

14. Which are ongoing (standing) and which are temporary (ad hoc)?
15. How long does membership last?
16. How does a board member join a committee or team?

VI. Governance and Organizational Effectiveness

17. How do we go about assessing our effectiveness?
18. How do we do long-range planning?
19. How do we plan for the succession of leaders?
20. How do we orient new board members?

An Option When Changing Policies

When a policy change is proposed, it may be presented as a policy table or spreadsheet, such as the one shown in Table 16.1 for a proposed change in conference rates for a professional association. The change was to increase fees, offer a student rate, and add a volunteer discount. The board heard the rationale, considered these options, made modifications, and adopted the proposed policy as modified.

Examples

Here are some examples of board policies for a generic organization referred to as ABC. Exact numerical amounts mentioned in these policies are of course also examples, *not* suggested amounts. Actual

Table 16.1. Proposed Policy Change in Table Form.

	Member Rate	Nonmember Rate	Student Rate
Current policy			
Early bird	$130	$205	None
Later and on-site	160	235	
Proposed policy			
Early bird	$195	$270	$100 mem./$135
Later and on-site	250	325	125 mem./175
Volunteer discount	75	75	Fee waived/N/A

amounts are to be set by your board. (These examples are modified from those in *The Policy Sampler*, Fletcher, 2000.)

Common General Policies

Check Signing Authority

The board chair and treasurer and the executive director are authorized to sign checks. These three individuals shall be bonded.

Checks up to $500 require one signature. Checks over $500 and up to $10,000 require two signatures. All checks over $10,000 require two signatures, one of which must be the board chairperson's.

Financial Policy: Borrowing Money

Money may be borrowed when necessary to fund operations and expansion. Money may be borrowed only as required to meet those needs and must be consistent with sound fiscal and management processes. Borrowing money is not intended to replace inadequate planning or spending above budgeted levels.

Borrowing should be within appropriate limits and approved by the board prior to the time it is needed. Amounts should be borrowed at the lowest available interest rates.

Ethics: Conflict of Interest

Board members and employees of ABC have an obligation to avoid conflicts of interest. An actual, potential, or perceived conflict of interest occurs when a person is in a position to influence a decision that may result in a personal gain. This includes having influence on purchases, contracts, or leases.

It is a conflict of interest to receive a substantial gift or special consideration as a result of any transaction or business dealings involving ABC organization. Any real or potential conflict of interest should be reported to an officer of the corporation. The board member involved may be asked to resign or to refrain from voting in situations where the conflict may be present.

Board-Specific Policies

Indemnification

Each officer, each member of the board of directors, and employees or members elected or appointed to committees according to the bylaws shall be entitled to indemnification by ABC organization against all expenses (including attorney's fees), judgments, claims, and amounts paid in settlement arising from any claim. This includes proceedings related to his or her status as a representative of ABC to the fullest extent permitted by the Articles of Incorporation of ABC, the laws of the state, and the Bylaws.

Compensation

Board members shall serve without compensation. Board members shall be allowed reasonable reimbursement of expenses incurred in the performance of their duties, including attendance at board authorized meetings and conferences.

Expense Reimbursement

Travel expenses of board members who reside at least 150 miles from the site of the board meeting may be reimbursed, including overnight expenses, for attending the regularly scheduled board and required committee or team meetings.

A voucher should be filled out and returned to the Treasurer at the meeting. Receipts for expenses over $25 must accompany the voucher. A check will be sent to reimburse the board member within two weeks.

Log Entry: Summary

The best way to keep your group's bylaws from becoming complicated is to take out the policies that are not required to be in the bylaws. These policies apply to operations in such areas as finance, ethics, board and management, programs, committees and task teams, and governance and organizational effectiveness.

Getting Under Way

- Examine your organization's bylaws again to be certain you've eliminated operating policies.

- Evaluate and rewrite existing policies for clarity and simplicity.

- Answer the twenty key questions and write simple statements.

- Put these statements into your official governance notebook behind the tab labeled "Operating Policies."

Making Headway

You've completed the final chapter of this book, and your passage is almost over. You've visited the Roberta's Rules of Order shore, which has simpler, up-to-date, and user-friendly methods for meeting, conversing, organizing, and deciding. It's your choice whether to remain or return. Now your organization has more options and can make the choice to use whichever method is more appropriate for your organization. Please continue on . . .

Conclusion

The final step if you choose to use Roberta's Rules of Order is to customize your organization's own special rules for meetings. In Resource A you'll find a suggested set of these rules for nonprofit boards and other small groups that interact and make decisions. You and the other members of your group can begin by reading these suggested rules with your organization in mind. Then modify them as needed, and agree on how to fill in the blank portions. Each section supplies the number of the chapter that you may wish to review while working on these rules.

The important thing is to make these special rules your own. If they don't feel right, modify them until they make sense for your organization. The key is reaching agreement among the members of your board or other group and using the same rules in the same way each time. The result should be more productive and enjoyable meetings, more enthusiastic member participation, and an organization that more easily achieves its mission. Good luck on this important voyage!

The analogy to sailing ships has been used to describe visually the concepts discussed in the book to make it easier to "see" and remember. (To quote Nancy Richardson, a fellow board member of the American Sail Training Association and former pluralism and adult development consultant for Girl Scouts of the USA who has fun with words, "use Roberta's Rules of Order through smooth and rough waters, frustrating calms, exhilarating downwind runs and sudden squalls." Wishing you fair winds and following seas on your exciting voyage!

Resources

Resource A

Roberta's Special Rules for Meetings Template

The Template

Rule 1: Use of Special Rules [See Chapter Two]

(a) These special Rules for Meetings are to be used as the regular business meeting method of the _____ organization. The rules are subordinate to (1) the organization's bylaws, (2) the Articles of Incorporation, and (3) current State and Federal laws for nonprofit public or mutual benefit organizations.

(b) These Special Rules may be further modified by Concordance, or "substantial agreement," of the Board of Directors. For this organization substantial agreement is defined as a _____% majority. This does not prevent striving for consensus. Once these Special Rules are approved, all committees, teams, or task forces in the organization will use them for their business meetings.

Rule 2: Meeting Roles [See Chapter Seven]

(a) The President of the organization, or a member she or he appoints, will preside at the meeting and be called the Leader. She or he will appoint a Timekeeper and a Note Taker.

(b) The Leader is responsible for conducting a focused meeting with the help of a designated Egalitarian. The Leader will remain fair and impartial. The Leader will make the final decisions regarding the meeting content and Agenda after gathering input.

(c) The Egalitarian will remain neutral and focus on the meeting process to help reinforce the group's agreed-upon meeting Courtesy Guidelines. The Leader and the Egalitarian will confer on matters of meeting process. The Egalitarian will make the final decision on the fairness of the meeting process.

(d) All participants will help create and be asked to uphold the meeting Courtesy Guidelines. Participants will strive to reach a consensus agreement, but if it cannot be reached within _____ [time period], the final decision will be made by a _____% substantial majority vote, or concordance. [See options and definitions, Chapter Five.]

(e) The Note Taker will take brief notes during the meeting, on paper or a flip chart. As "tangential topics" come up, he or she will make a list for future discussion. He or she will write a summary of the meeting and distribute it to members within _____ days [or weeks]. He or she will send it by e-mail, fax, or if these options are not available, by regular mail. [See the suggested outline in Chapter Eight.]

(f) The Timekeeper will keep the Leader and the group aware of time. If the group has agreed upon a specified time limit for any individual to speak, the Timekeeper will give the speaker a one-minute warning. At the end of the time, the speaker will be asked to stop. This person cannot speak again until all the others have had an opportunity.

(g) Any Board member may present a verbal or written Proposal to the Board for consideration. Any group of members (more than one person) may bring a Proposal to the Board [this applies only to membership organizations].

Rule 3: Meeting Agenda [See Chapter Seven]

(a) The Leader, with suggestions from the members of the group, will draft an Agenda. It will include the organization's mission, the meeting purpose (if other than a regular meeting), and the meeting outcomes or intended results. The Agenda will focus on accomplishing the current major strategies or goals of the organization.

(b) The Agenda will state expected start and end times, topics in order of priority (policy, urgency, or impact), estimated time limits in minutes for each topic, and the name of the person leading presentation and dialogue on each topic.

(c) Whenever possible the Agenda and other pertinent material will be distributed in advance by e-mail, fax, or regular mail.

Rule 4: Quorum [Chapter Five]

(a) A quorum is not required to hold a meeting. However, no decision can be made that obligates the whole group without a quorum present in person or connected electronically. For this organization a quorum is defined as _____ members. [See definition in Chapter Five.]

(b) If the Leader determines that a quorum is present at the beginning of the meeting and the Agenda includes items to be decided, the decision making can continue even if members leave and a quorum is no longer present.

Rule 5: Electronic Meetings and Attendance [See Chapter Six]

(a) Members who cannot conveniently attend a meeting due to distance or logistical problems may attend any meeting electronically as long as everyone can be connected clearly. A designated person will make the arrangements and the costs will be covered by _____.

(b) Members who miss more than _____ meetings, in person or electronically, may be asked to resign.

(c) Participants will follow the guidelines for electronic meetings.

Rule 6: Starting the Meeting [See Chapter Six]

(a) The tone of the meeting will be informal and friendly. Members will be given a chance to relax, with social time and food preceding the meeting to allow a 15- to 30-minute transition period.

(b) There will be an opportunity in the beginning for everyone to "check in" briefly, update the group on any personal news, or make announcements of interest to the group.

(c) Anyone visiting a meeting will be introduced to everyone, and the group members to the visitor, with every attempt to include the visitor quickly.

(d) If desired there may be an invocation, spiritual practice, or moment of meditation or reflection to set a positive tone.

(e) Members will be given a chance to read and modify the Agenda at the beginning of the meeting. The group will reach concordance on the Agenda before proceeding.

(f) The first discussion will be about the meeting purpose, objectives, roles, expected behaviors (Courtesy Guidelines), and decision-making method for all appropriate items. The group will reach concordance before proceeding.

Rule 7: Routine Reports and Consent Agenda [See Chapter Seven]

(a) The Meeting Summary of the previous meeting and routine reports not requiring individual consideration will be placed on the Agenda at the beginning in a Consent Agenda section. This information will be provided to participants ahead of time or before the start of the meeting.

(b) The Consent Agenda items will not be discussed individually unless *any* member requests that an item be removed from this section and placed on the regular Agenda as a separate item for discussion. The Leader will check with the group for agreement to file routine reports as part of the organization's records.

Rule 8: Discussion of Issues [See Chapters Three and Eleven]

(a) Any item may be discussed that is on or added to the Agenda prior to or at the beginning of the meeting. A motion or a second is not required.

(b) The member(s) who presents an issue for consideration should present it in the form of a Simple (verbal) or Structured (written) Proposal. Written Proposals should address the problem and its causes before the solution. [See suggested structure in Chapter Three.]

(c) When possible, Structured Proposals will be available for members to read in advance of the meeting.

(d) All members will be given an opportunity to speak or ask questions. No one member may speak a second time until all wanting to speak have spoken once.

(e) When discussing a Proposal, the Leader or Egalitarian will structure the discussion to proceed from opening (idea generation) to narrowing (evaluating ideas) to closing (making decisions).

(f) The Leader or Egalitarian will ensure that the discussion is balanced between pros and cons and all points of view are encouraged.

(g) Any member can suggest changes to a Proposal. The Proposal can be modified by group concordance. If the changes are not agreed upon, another member may present a different Proposal.

(h) Up to three Proposals on the same issue may be presented for consideration. If more than one Proposal is being considered, each should be presented in writing, and they should be discussed one at a time.

Rule 9: Decision Making [See Chapter Five]

(a) All members will be given an opportunity to speak at least once and not more than twice on each Proposal.

(b) After a Proposal has been presented and thoroughly discussed, the Leader will ask if the group is in agreement with the Proposal. No one member or a minority may block a decision.

(c) If there is no concordance, the leader will call for a nonbinding simple straw poll (show of hands) and further discussion. As a result of the discussion, the Leader may suggest or request modifications and check again for concordance.

(d) Following the modifications, the Leader will check again to determine if there is concordance or lack of substantial agreement.

(e) If there is no concordance, the Leader will ask for a show of gradient levels, in a multiple-choice, nonbinding poll.

(f) After the polling the members will be asked to voice their concerns and suggest a change in the Proposal that would result in their support for the Proposal—or at least move their support up a level.

(g) If there isn't enough time or interest to continue discussing the Proposal, the group can "vote whether to vote." A _____% majority approval is necessary to require a dual (yes/no) vote. When a dual (yes/no) vote is taken, a _____% majority (concordance) is required to pass the Proposal.

(h) Votes may be by show of hands or written ballot. Any member may request a written ballot.

(i) If more than one Proposal is being considered, the group may decide to use a plurality vote and the Proposal with the highest number of votes would be approved.

Rule 10: Ending the Meeting [Chapter Eight]

(a) There will be time on the Agenda at the end of the meeting for the Leader to summarize the progress made at the meeting in relation to the organization's Mission or Goals.

(b) The Note Taker will summarize the agreements made and the follow-up action steps agreed to by the group, clarifying the tasks, the person(s) responsible, and task time limits.

(c) The members will remark on their personal experience (meaning, learning, or impressions) during the meeting and make suggestions on what to continue doing and what to change to improve future meetings. The Leader and Egalitarian will implement feasible ideas at the next meeting.

(d) When the Agenda is complete, or the time established for the end of the meeting is reached, the Leader will close the meeting. The meeting can continue after the established time limit only if there is substantial agreement to extend the meeting for a specified time period.

(e) The Note Taker will send out a Meeting Summary and Action Plan within _____ [time period].

Parliamentary Rules Backup

In addition to these special rules, you will find traditional parliamentary procedure very useful in highly complex and controversial situations when there is a need for a more formal structure for debate (should you choose to encourage it) and voting. It is hoped that this situation is the exception, rather than the norm.

For larger boards, contentious large groups in the public sector, or large, final decision-making membership meetings of any organization, the newly revised tenth edition of *Robert's Rules of Order* (Robert, 2000) could be your best friend. Although this version is still long (643 pages not counting tables and charts), the writing is clearer than it was in previous editions, and this edition provides additional information beyond motions and voting. There are many other versions of parliamentary procedure, but Robert's Rules of Order is the best known, particularly in nonprofits. (For a list of other versions, visit the Web site parliamentaryprocedure.org or parliamentarians.org.)

Another *much* shorter and very useful option is a streamlined and very simple version of parliamentary procedure called *The Modern Rules of Order* (Tortorice, 1999) published by the American Bar Association (ABA). This is most likely all you'll need.

Insert This Paragraph into Your Bylaws

The business meetings of _____
organization will be run by the attached agreed-upon Special Rules for Meetings adopted from *Roberta's Rules of Order*. For situations that warrant more formal parliamentary procedure, we will use [choose one]

The Modern Rules of Order (2nd ed.), American Bar Association, 1999.

Robert's Rules of Order (Newly revised, 10th ed.), Perseus, 2000.

Resource B

Structured Proposal Template

The Current Situation

1. The Facts ("The situation is . . .")

2. The Cost or Other Impact ("This costs us [or affects us] in the following ways . . .")

3. The Main Causes ("The reason[s] the problem exists is [are] . . .")

The Possible Solution(s)

4. Conditions for Success ("A solution needs to include . . .")

5. Best Practices and Options ("Several options are . . .")

6. Recommended Solution(s) (based on the information given here) ("Therefore we recommend that . . .")

The Proposed Change

7. Suggested Action Steps ("If the proposal is approved, the following will need to be implemented . . .")

Resource C

Planning an Expanded Agenda

The Template

[Name of Organization]
[Date] [Time] [Place]
[Mission Statement]

Outcomes [or Intended Results] for this meeting:

By the end of this meeting we will accomplish the following:

-
-
-

Sections and Topics	Leader	Time (minutes)
Connect:		
Refreshments		
Check-in, announcements		
Convene:		
Welcome, cover OARS		
Consent Agenda:		

Sections and Topics	Leader	Time (minutes)

Context:
  Review notes/actions
  from last meeting

Content [with "open,"
"narrow," "close"]:

  •

  •

  •

  •

  •

  •

Continue:
  Summarize, action plans,
  next meeting

Conclude:
  Reflection: what to
  continue or change

Example of Meeting Agenda: I

Golden Gate Tall Ships Society
(See the new bylaws of this organization in Exhibit 15.1.)
BOARD MEETING
6:30 to 8:30 P.M. (Dinner Dutch Treat at 6:00)
Hyde Street Pier, San Francisco

Mission: Building on San Francisco Bay's rich nautical tall ship heritage, the Golden Gate Tall Ships Society promotes the renaissance of traditional sailing ships. We provide youth with scholarships for lifelong learning through sail training and our members with traditional sailing experiences.

Tonight's Outcomes

By the end of this meeting we will accomplish the following:

- Make plans for coverage and logistics at Festival of the Sea

- Decide on raffle prize for fundraiser

- Hear report from Marin City kids on *Hawaiian Chieftain* and *Alma* sail

- Plan October sailing event

- Get invitations out for the reception on tall ship *Dewaruci* (following the meeting)

Sections and Topics	Leader	Time
Connect:	All	6:00 P.M.
Dinner and conversation		(30 min.)
Check-in and announcements		
Convene:	Alice	6:30 (15)
Welcome, tonight's outcomes, agenda, and roles		
Consent Calendar:	Gale	(10)
Finances and Membership		
Chieftain, *Alma*, and *Concordia* sails		
Context:		
Review notes and actions from last meeting		

Sections and Topics	Leader	Time
Update from ASTA Conference	Alice	(5)
Content:		
Festival of the Sea: close on logistics	Ethan	(45)
October sail for Blue Angels: close on charter	Bill	(15)
Dewaruci: raffle donations: open on options	Pam	(5)
Continue:		
Summarize, action plans, feedback, next meeting	All	(10)
Conclude:		
Reflection: what to continue or change		(15) 8:30 End

Example of Meeting Agenda: II

Bay Area Organization Development Network
BOARD MEETING—PROPOSED AGENDA
4:00–7:00 P.M.—CoVision Office

Today's Outcomes

By the end of this meeting we need to accomplish the following:

- Finalize October 20th Details

- Update on Neighborhood Salons

- Update on Best in the West

- Comment on Draft of Potential Member Brochure

- Consider the Proposal for a Learning Event in Monterey

- Finalize Nominating Procedure

- Finalize Fall Newsletter

Section	Who	Time
Connect	All	15 mins.
Check-In (2 mins. each)		
Convene:	Susan	5
Today's outcomes, agenda, roles (rotate Facilitator/Recorder)		
Consent agenda		10
Finances, Membership, Administration— What do we need to approve?		
Context		
Review notes/actions from last meeting	All	
Updates/accomplishments since last meeting		
Content topics (Inform, Open, Narrow, or Close)		2 hrs.
Marketing materials, cost (C)	All	15
Neighborhood Salons (NC)		
East Bay, SF Salons report and plans (C)	Joe	15
Best in the West—chair, format, speakers	Mary	15
Input for potential member brochure (O)	All	10
Proposal for a program in Monterey (ON)	Jim	10
Nominating process—proposal (ONC)	Lenny	
Fall newsletter theme (C)	Anne	20
Other items?		10

Section	Who	Time
Continue		
Summarize, action plans, next meeting's agenda	All	15
Conclude		
Acknowledgments and reflection	Susan/All	10

Example of Meeting Agenda: III

A Continuous Improvement Effort
Meetings of an Advisory Council

An organization in a state university system gives academic assistance to students who are underrepresented in specific fields. The programs are innovative and are seen as a model for other states. The organization has many success stories and a proven track record of helping students with potential through high school and college and into the job market. This group has an advisory council that represents the multiple business and educational sectors involved in this project. This council has representatives from secondary schools, colleges, and industry. It holds quarterly meetings.

Before Continuous Improvement

Traditionally the day of each meeting was structured to have committee meetings in the morning and the full council meeting in the afternoon. The committees paralleled the work of organization staff. The staff put a great deal of time into preparing reports for these committee meetings. They also attended the meetings and sometimes felt "grilled" by council members about program actions or decisions. The executive committee of the council also met in the morning and made most of the important decisions. Committee members reported those decisions to the council in the afternoon.

The council met as a whole in the afternoon for only three hours. Its agenda consisted of a series of reports from all the morning meetings. A typical agenda looked like this:

Advisory Council Meeting Agenda
1:30–4:30 P.M.

    I. Call to Order

   II. Report from the Associate Vice President

  III. Report from the Executive Director

  IV. Report from the Council Chair

   V. Reports of the Standing Committees

  VI. Old Business

 VII. New Business

VIII. Adjourn

Very little interaction, problem solving, and decision making took place in the full council. Most of the important issue discussions and decisions occurred at the executive committee meeting. Meetings were usually held close to an airport serving the city of the organization's statewide office.

As part of a continuous improvement effort, a council self-assessment was conducted, using tools available from BoardSource. It was helpful in clarifying the role of an advisory council as compared to the role of a governing board. This council had evolved into a hybrid, causing some confusion.

One of the concerns brought up was about meetings. There were generally as many staff members as board members at the meetings. Most council members wanted to have a bigger impact on the organization and talk about the important issues, not just attend meetings to hear reports. A clear message from the survey was that members desired more council involvement before decisions were made, and a chance to use the meetings for more interactive discussion.

After Continuous Improvement

The council president, executive director, and staff worked with a governance consultant and facilitator (the author) to improve the meetings and other aspects of the council. As a result the following meeting changes occurred:

- There is a new agenda format that states the intended results of the meeting.

- The council meetings are longer but also livelier.

- A portion of each meeting showcases field programs around the state.

- The meetings rotate around the state to be closer to the programs and to share the burden of traveling to meetings.

- Local program managers and other supporters are invited to lunch with the council.

- Issues, such as the budget process and goals, are brought to the full council for input.

- Standing committees that paralleled staff functions have been dropped and task teams related to needs identified in the assessment have been formed.

- The meeting room arrangement has been changed to allow more eye contact and interaction.

- A short summary of the meeting uses the intended result to assess progress.

- The executive committee has been expanded to include more council members and now meets by conference call between council meetings to plan the agenda.

- Staff members who manage the field programs now attend the meetings only when their program is being discussed. A few staff members (in the areas of communication, measurement, and public relations) who work with all programs attend all council meetings.

- Two field representatives regularly attend council meetings as observers, and others are invited when the focus is on their program area.

- Newly formed task teams are meeting by conference call between meetings and in person by arrangement an hour before the meeting.

- Proposals are developed by a task team or staff member, presented for clarification, discussed, and upgraded. Straw polls and a check of levels of support are used before voting.

The following is an example of the council's new meeting agenda:

Advisory Council Meeting Agenda
10:00 to 4:30 p.m.

Purpose: To begin the quarterly focus on the field programs along with regular council business.

Intended Results: By the end of this meeting everyone will

- Gain more knowledge of the precollege field programs so that the council can have a broader understanding of statewide programs.

- Receive information about the current situation from the university and statewide perspective in order to understand the larger political and financial climate.

- Have an opportunity to get clarification and discuss future financial scenarios.

Targeted Time	Agenda Item	Lead Person(s)
9:00 (60 mins.)	Task Team meetings	By arrangement through executive assistant
9:30 (15)	Coffee and conversation	
10:00 (15)	Welcome and introductions	
	Purpose and intended results	Council president
	Overview of today's agenda flow and roles	Facilitator
10:15	Field focus— precollege programs	Staff
	Open forum	Council members
12:15 (60)	Lunch with invited guests	
1:15 (15)	Council Business Meeting:	
	Opening the meeting	Council president
	Review of December decisions and continuing efforts: Strategic Planning, Governance, and Continuous Improvement	
1:30 (30)	Task Team updates	Group leaders
2:00 (45)	University overview	Assistant VP
	Strategic Review Panel report	
	Executive Leadership Team update	Executive Director
	Open forum	Council members
2:45 (15)	Break	

Targeted Time	Agenda Item	Lead Person(s)
3:00 (15)	Statewide overview— big picture	Executive director
3:15 (45)	Statewide budget: current situation, forecasting scenarios, potential impact	Associate director
	Focused conversation	Council members
4:00 (15)	Wrap-up—calendar handout	Council president
	Action items	
4:15	Reflection	Facilitator

Resource D

Follow-Up Action Plan Template

Meeting:
Date:
Attending:

Actions We Agreed On to Be Completed

What (Action/Activity)	By Whom	By When

Resource E

Writing Bare Bones Bylaws Template

The Template

Using the work done in Chapter Fifteen and the example at the end of this resource, work with the other board members to complete this template by filling in the blanks. This work will customize simplified bylaws for your organization.

I. NAME

The name of the organization is _____. It is located in _____, with a mailing address of
_____.

II. PURPOSE/MISSION

_____
_____

III. MEMBERS

1. _____ may be a member.
2. There will be a roster of members that is kept current and available to all members.

3. _____ will be eligible to vote.

4. _____ may inspect any corporate records upon _____.

5. Membership and all rights of members shall be automatically terminated due to _____.

6. Members will be terminated _____.
This notice will be sent by _____.

7. Members not attending a meeting to elect officers _____ [will or will not] be given the opportunity to vote by _____ _____.

IV. OFFICERS/LEADERSHIP ROLES

1. The officers of the Corporation will be _____.
These positions will be elected by _____ and reported to the Secretary of State. Their term will be for _____.

2. _____ will prepare for and preside at meetings unless he or she designates another member.

3. _____ will keep current or oversee others maintaining all corporate records, oversee keeping a current membership roster and minutes of meetings. He or she will also file all required forms with the Secretary of State.

4. _____ will prepare a monthly or quarterly financial report and maintain the Corporation's financial records and accounts.

5. Officers will serve for a minimum of _____ and a maximum of _____ in accordance with _____ [State] Public Benefit Corporation law.

V. MEETINGS

1. An annual meeting will be held _____.

2. _____ may call other special meetings of members.

3. An annual report will be written by _____ and distributed to _____.

4. Members will be notified of a voting meeting by _____ days before the date of the meeting.

5. The notice of any meeting at which Directors are to be elected will include _____.

6. A quorum to elect officers and vote on bylaws will be _____ _____ of the members entitled to vote either in person or electronically.

VI. BOARD OF DIRECTORS/LEADERSHIP TEAM

1. There will be at least _____ and no more than _____ members of the Board of Directors.

2. The Directors will be residents of _____ and members of the Corporation.

3. The Directors _____ [will/will not] receive compensation.

4. Each year the Board members will _____ _____.

5. Board meetings will be held _____ a year and may be called by _____.

6. A _____ of the Board members constitutes a quorum.

7. The meeting location will be _____ _____.

8. Meetings can also be conducted _____
   _____.

9. When necessary, Board members may vote on an issue by
   _____.

10. The Board shall appoint _____ for
    elections, who will develop a slate of nominees and conduct
    the elections.

11. Board members may be removed if _____
    _____.

12. Vacancies on the Board may be filled by _____
    _____.

VII. PROCEDURES FOR DECISION MAKING

The Board of Directors will use _____
as its written method for deliberation and decision making.

VIII. AMENDMENTS/MODIFICATIONS

_____ may change these
bylaws. Changes may be voted upon by _____
_____.

Resource F

Task or Project Team Charter Template

Complete this information for any working group to provide clarity and focus.

Team name _____

1. The mission of this team is to

   _____
   _____.

2. Our major goals [and objectives] are

   _____
   _____.

3. By the end of this project [or effort or year] we will have been successful if [vision statement of change]

   _____
   _____.

4. Our team leadership and roles are

   _____.

5. The boundaries of our authority as a group [or as individuals] are

   _____
   _____
   _____.

6. When in meetings, we will use the following courtesy guidelines:

   _____

   _____

   _____.

7. We will meet _____ and expect that members will miss no more than _____ meetings.

8. In completing our work, we will work closely with

   _____

   _____.

9. We will communicate by _____ [method and frequency].

10. The timeline for the project [or team] is from _____ to _____.

11. We expect to accomplish the following milestones or goals:
    -
    -
    -

12. Names of team members:

Resource G

Basic Operating Policies Template

Use the following template to decide on the key elements of your organization's policies. Ask someone to act as scribe, taking notes during the board's discussion of these questions and writing up a draft. The policy examples in Chapter Sixteen offer a guide to formatting this draft.

I. Finance

1. Who has check signing authority?

   _____

2. What are the dollar limits of this authority?

   _____

II. Ethics

3. How do we handle confidentiality?

   _____

4. How do we handle real or perceived conflict of interest?

   _____

III. Board and Management

5. Who manages the association other than the board?

   _____

6. What are the expectations and privileges of serving on the board?

_____

7. How are board members legally protected (indemnification)?

_____

8. How are board members rewarded without compensation?

_____

9. What do board members and others get reimbursed for and how?

_____

IV. Programs, Workshops, and Conferences

10. What is our registration policy for programs?

_____

11. For whom do we allow fee waivers?

_____

12. If we give discounts, how do we define eligibility?

_____

V. Committees or Task Teams

13. Which committees and task teams exist?

_____

14. Which are ongoing and which are temporary?

_____

15. How long does membership last?

_____

16. How does a board member join a committee or team?

_____

VI. Governance or Organizational Development

17. How do we go about assessing our effectiveness?

_____

18. How do we do long-range planning?

_____

19. How do we plan for the succession of leaders?

_____

20. How do we orient new board members?

_____

VII. Others

Resource H

Roberta's Web Resources

Following is a list of selected organizations with national or international services that coordinate and support the efforts of nonprofit and nongovernmental organizations. Visit each Web site for more information about conferences, services, training workshops, and links to other resources.

Alliance for Nonprofit   allianceonline.org
Management

This is a professional association working to improve the management and governance of nonprofits. Most nonprofit management support organizations (MSOs) are members of the Alliance.

BoardSource   boardsource.org

Formerly the National Center for Nonprofit Boards, BoardSource is dedicated to helping build strong and effective nonprofit boards. It publishes many useful pamphlets, an assessment tool for boards, and a magazine, *Board Member*.

CharityChannel   charitychannel.com

This is an online resource that helps connect nonprofits to information shared by others in the sector. It includes a newsletter, book reviews, job postings, and a consultant registry.

Idealist   idealist.org

Connected to Action Without Borders, Idealist connects people, organizations, and resources around the world. The Web site provides a list of organizations by country and by state within the United States that work on behalf of nonprofits.

Independent Sector   independentsector.org

Independent Sector is a coalition of generally larger nonprofits, foundations, and corporations that strive to strengthen the independent sector, including charitable, educational, religious, health, and social welfare organizations.

Internet Nonprofit Center   nonprofits.org

The Internet Nonprofit Center provides information for and about nonprofits via the Web, including publishing nonprofit FAQ's and providing access to information in their on-line library.

Leader to Leader Institute   leadertoleader.org

Formerly the Drucker Foundation, the Leader to Leader Institute offers workshops in self-assessment and business-nonprofit alliances in order to strengthen the leadership of the social sector.

National Council of   ncna.org
Nonprofit Associations

This organization represents the views and concerns of state and regional associations of nonprofits at the national level.

The Nonprofit Quarterly   nonprofitquarterly.org

Each issue of the Nonprofit Quarterly, a print magazine, focuses on a theme relevant to managing nonprofits.

Society for Nonprofit   snpo.org
Organizations

The Society for Nonprofit Organizations promotes excellence in nonprofit management, governance, and leadership. It also provides wide-ranging education, training, and support services through its Learning Institute and publishes *Nonprofit World*.

Following are other organizations serving nonprofits that are mentioned in *Roberta's Rules of Order*:

The Center for Volunteer and   centerforleadershipmarin.org
Nonprofit Leadership of Marin

Formerly the Marin Council of Agencies and the Volunteer Center, the Center for Volunteer and Nonprofit Leadership provides networking through affinity group meetings, training, and support for nonprofits in Marin County, California.

Community at Work   communityatwork.org

Community at Work specializes in training people in the skills and concepts of group decision making and collaborative process design to reach sustainable agreements.

CompassPoint   compasspoint.org

CompassPoint Nonprofit Services is a nonprofit training, consulting, and research organization. Among other services, it offers *Board Café*, a short electronic newsletter for board members.

The Grove Consultants   grove.com
International

The Grove has pioneered productive visual tools and templates for achieving and "seeing" results. Its catalog of Graphic Guides and products is available online.

Institute of Cultural Affairs   ica-usa.org

The primary objective of the Institute of Cultural Affairs is to promote positive change in communities, organizations, and individual lives in the United States and around the world. ICA offers training in the Technology of Participation, as well as other seminars, facilitation, and collaborative consulting services.

Interaction Associates   interactionassociates.com

Interaction Associates is a global provider of collaborative change consulting and workplace learning solutions. It is the first firm of its kind to fund and support a nonprofit institute—the Interaction Institute for Social Change.

Interaction Institute   interactioninstitute.org
for Social Change

The Interaction Institute for Social Change provides training, consulting, and facilitation services to community leaders, nongovernmental organizations, and other nonprofit groups that are committed to social justice and civic responsibility.

The Management Center   tmcenter.org

TMC is a leading resource for nonprofit management support in Northern California. It publishes *Opportunity Knocks* for nonprofit job seekers online.

Nolo Press   nolo.com

Nolo Press publishes reliable, plain-English books on legal matters, and provides software, forms, and an informative Web site.

Following are traditional sail training organizations mentioned in *Roberta's Rules of Order*—in case you're interested in renewing your spirit by sailing or just seeing the pictures.

American Sail Training   sailtraining.org
Association

American Sail Training Association is a thirty-year-old professional association of organizations operating traditional sail training ships around the world and their supporters. They organize an annual TALL SHIPS CHALLENGE® in the United States and publish the *Sail Tall Ships®* directory of member ships.

TALL SHIPS CHALLENGE® and Tall Ships® are registered trademarks of the American Sail Training Association.

Golden Gate Tall Ships® Society   ggtss.org

Formerly the Sausalito Tall Ships Society, the Golden Gate Tall Ships Society holds sailing fundraisers and provides scholarships to young people from the San Francisco area to sail on American Sail Training Association vessels.

Los Angeles Maritime Institute   lamitopsail.org

The Los Angeles Maritime Institute owns and operates two brigantines and a schooner for youth sail training. This training is called the Topsail Youth Program and is offered to students in the Los Angeles schools. Other programs serve adults.

References

Argyris, C. *Overcoming Organizational Defenses: Facilitating Organizational Learning*. Needham Heights, Mass.: Allyn & Bacon, 1990.

Axelrod, R. *Terms of Engagement: Changing the Way We Change Organizations*. San Francisco: Berrett-Koehler, 2000.

Beddoes, T. L. "Song from the Ship." In *Death's Jest-Book, or The Fool's Tragedy*. London: W. Pickering, 1850. (B-11 4357 Fisher Rare Book Library)

Blanchard, K., and Johnson, S. *The One Minute Manager*. New York: Morrow, 1982.

Block, P. Foreword. In R. Axelrod, *Terms of Engagement: Changing the Way We Change Organizations*. San Francisco: Berrett-Koehler, 2000.

"Board of the Future." *Board Member*, Special Edition, 1999, 8(5).

"Boards in Motion: How to Have Better Board Meetings." *Board Member*, 1999, 8(8).

Bobowick, M. J., Hughes, R., and Lakey, B. M. *Transforming Board Structure: Strategies for Committees and Task Forces*. Washington, D.C.: BoardSource, 2001.

Bohm, D. *On Dialogue*. New York: Routledge, 1996.

Butler, C.T.L., and Rothstein, A. *On Conflict and Consensus: A Handbook on Formal Consensus Decisionmaking*. Cambridge, Mass.: Food Not Bombs, 1991.

California Corporations Code. Eagan, Minn.: West Group, 2001.

Carver, J. *Planning Better Board Meetings*. Carver Guide 5. San Francisco: Jossey-Bass, 1997.

Carver, J., and Carver, M. M. *Your Roles and Responsibilities as a Board Member*. Carver Guide 2. San Francisco: Jossey-Bass, 1996.

Covey, S. *Seven Habits of Highly Effective People*. New York: Simon & Schuster, 1989.

Creighton, J., and Adams, J. *Cyber Meetings*. Philadelphia: Xlibris, 2002.

Cushing, L. *Cushing's Manual: Rules of Proceeding and Debate in Deliberative Assemblies*. Boston: William J. Reynolds, 1845.

Dannemiller Tyson Associates. *Whole-Scale Change: Unleashing the Magic in Organizations*. San Francisco: Berrett-Koehler, 2000.

Doyle, M., and Straus, D. *How to Make Meetings Work*. New York: Berkeley Publishing Group, 1982.

Ellinor, L., and Gerard, G. *Dialogue: Rediscover the Transforming Power of Conversation*. New York: Wiley, 1998.

Fletcher, K. *The Policy Sampler: A Resource for Nonprofit Boards*. Washington, D.C.: BoardSource, 2000.

Freeman, J. "The Tyranny of Structurelessness." *Berkeley Journal of Sociology*, 1970, 3, 151–164.

Guthridge, L. "Don't Blame Robert." Speech to Toastmasters, Jan. 8, 2002.

Hock, D. *Birth of the Chaordic Age*. San Francisco: Berrett-Koehler, 1999.

Interaction Associates. *Teams in Action Participants Workbook*. San Francisco: Interaction Associates, 1994.

Interaction Associates. *Essential Facilitation Participants Workbook* (3rd. ed.). San Francisco: Interaction Associates, 1997.

Jefferson, T. *A Manual of Parliamentary Practice for Use in the Senate of the United States* (Jefferson's Manual). Washington City: Dans and Force, 1801.

Kaner, S., and others. *Facilitator's Guide to Participatory Decision-Making*. Gabriola Island, B.C.: New Society Publishers, 1996.

Kirsch, S. "The Manager as Communicator." Materials from course at Golden Gate University, San Francisco, 1991.

Lakey, B. *Nonprofit Governance: Steering Your Organization with Authority and Accountability*. Washington, D.C.: BoardSource, 2000.

Mancuso, A. *How to Form a Nonprofit Corporation in All 50 States*. (4th ed.) Berkeley, Calif.: Nolo Press, 2000.

Masaoka, J. *All Hands on Board: The Board of Directors in an All-Volunteer Organization*. San Francisco: National Center for Nonprofit Boards and CompassPoint, 1999.

"Old Rules of Order May Warrant Second Look." *The Board Member*, 2001, 10(7), p. 5.

Robert, H. M. *Pocket Manual of Rules of Order for Deliberative Assemblies (Robert's Rules of Order)*. Chicago: S. C. Griggs, 1876.

Robert, H. M. *Robert's Rules of Order*. (Newly revised, 10th ed.) Cambridge, Mass.: Perseus, 2000.

Saint, S., and Lawson, J. R. *Rules for Reaching Consensus: A Modern Approach to Decision Making*. San Francisco: Jossey-Bass/Pfeiffer, 1994.

Sibbet, D. *Graphic Guide: Meeting Start Up*. San Francisco: Grove Consultants International, 1996.

Spencer, L. *Winning Through Participation: Meeting the Challenge of Corporate Chance With the Technology of Participation*. Dubuque, Iowa: Kendall/Hunt, 1989.

Stanfield, R. B. (ed.). *The Art of Focused Conversation*. Toronto: Canadian Institute of Cultural Affairs, 1997.

Stephens, J. *Bylaws: Writing, Amending, Revising* (2nd ed.). Clearwater, Fla.: Frederick, 2000.

Straus, D. *How to Make Collaboration Work*. San Francisco: Berrett-Koehler, 2002.

Sturgis, A. *Standard Code of Parliamentary Procedure* (4th ed.). Wilmington, Del.: American Institute of Parliamentarians, 2000.

To the Summit and Back: A Report on the California Summit—Exploring New Directions in Nonprofit Governance. Santa Cruz, Calif.: BoardSource, 2001.

Tortorice, D. A. *The Modern Rules of Order: A Guide for Conducting Business Meetings*. (2nd ed.) Chicago: American Bar Association, 1999.

Tropman, J. *Policy Management in the Human Services*. New York: Columbia University Press, 1984.

Index

A WAR OF NERVES

A WAR OF NERVES

Soldiers and Psychiatrists in the Twentieth Century

BEN SHEPHARD

Harvard University Press
Cambridge, Massachusetts
2001

Library of Congress Cataloging-in-Publication Data
Shephard, Ben, 1948–
A war of nerves : soldiers and psychiatrists in the twentieth
century / Ben Shephard.
p. cm.
Includes bibliographical references and index.
ISBN 0-674-00592-9
1. Military psychiatry—History—20th century. 2. Soldiers—Psychological
aspects—History—20th century. 3. War neuroses—History—20th century
I. Title
RC550 . S535 2001
616.89'0088'355—dc21   00-066367

For Sue

'There are nice and nasty neurotics.'
David Eder, 1916

'The jealousies of medical people – you wouldn't believe it.'
Graham Greene, *Ministry of Fear*, 1943

'We don't want any damned psychiatrists making our boys sick.'
US General, 1944

'Military psychiatry is to psychiatry as military music is to music.'
Dr Chaim Shatan, 1996

CONTENTS

ILLUSTRATIONS

A shell-shocked soldier *(British Pathé)*

Dr Gordon Holmes *(Wellcome Institute for the History of Medicine)*

Charles Myers *(Joan Rumens)*

The Duchess of Westminster's hospital, le Touquet *(Imperial War Museum)*

Private Meek *(British Pathé)*

Hypnotising a soldier *(National Library of Medicine)*

The 'Kauffman cure'

Thomas W. Salmon

William Brown, W. H. R. Rivers and Grafton Elliot Smith

Frederick R. Hanson

Moe Kaufman *(Paul Kaufman)*

Roy R. Grinker *(Roy R. Grinker, Jr)*

John Rickman interviewing an officer cadet *(Imperial War Museum)*

Officer Cadets taking a Thematic Aperception Test *(Imperial War Museum)*

A German soldier, Frankfurt, 1946 *(AKG)*

German troops at Cassino *(Robert Hunt Library)*

An American patrol in Vietnam *(Robert Hunt Library)*

ACKNOWLEDGEMENTS

The author and publisher wish to thank the following for the use of copyright material. Random House and the Estate of C. Day Lewis for lines from 'Where are the War Poets?' from *The Complete Poems* by C. Day Lewis (Sinclair-Stevenson, 1992) © in this edition. George Sassoon for extracts from *Sherston's Progress* by Siegfried Sassoon, copyright Siegfried Sassoon by kind permission of George Sassoon. Faber and Faber for lines from 'Bete Noire' by Keith Douglas. Spike Milligan Productions for extracts from Spike Milligan, *Mussolini, His Part in my Downfall* and Spike Milligan, *Where Have All the Bullets Gone?* International Universities Press for the English translation of Freud's testimony to the 1920 Vienna Court of Enquiry, published in the *Annual of Psychoanalysis*, Vol II (Gunther, 1974) and extracts from K. R. Eissler, *Freud as an Expert Witness* (1986). Every effort has been made to trace and contact the copyright holders of all material reproduced in this book. The author and publisher will be glad to rectify any omissions at the earliest opportunity.

For their co-operation, assistance and (where appropriate) permission to quote from their collections, I want to thank librarians and archivists at the American Psychiatric Association, BBC Archives, Bristol University Library, the British Library, the British Psycho-Analytical Society, the British Psychological Society, Cambridge University Library, German Historical Institute, Glasgow University Library, Guy's Hospital, Liddell Hart Centre for Military Archives (King's College London), Liddle Collection (University of Leeds), Imperial War Museum (Departments of Documents and of Film), Institute of Neurology, Institute of Psychiatry, Medical Research Council, Mt Sinai Hospital, National Institutes of Health, National Library of Scotland, Department of Psychology, Cambridge University, Public Record Office, Royal College of Physicians, Royal College of Psychiatrists, Royal College of Surgeons, Royal London Hospital, St John's College (Cambridge), Tavistock Clinic, and Wellcome Institute for the History of Medicine (apologies to Catherine Burgin for a neurasthenic outburst about copyright) – and the incomparable London Library. A travel grant from the Wellcome Trust enabled me to visit the United States in 1992. My thanks to the Trust and to Dr David Allen.

I could not have found my way through the labyrinth without the kindness of many strangers (some of whom have become my friends) and the love and support of my family and friends. Blundering into other people's territory, I have met with fellowship and encouragement from Peter Barham, W. F. Bynum, Michael J. Clark, Roger Cooter, Ann Dally, John Forrester, Gerald Grob, Mark Harrison, Rhodri Hayward, Lisa Herschbach, Paul Lerner, Hilary Marland, Roy Porter, Ulf Schmidt and Mathew Thomson among medical historians; Paul Addison, Antony Beevor, Brian Bond, Jeremy Crang, Noble Frankland, John Keegan, John Peaty, and Julian Putkowski among military historians; and Anton Obholzer, Ray Dolan, Caroline Garland, Craig Fees, Tom Harrison, Jennifer Johns, Malcolm Pines, and Michael Shepherd among clinicians. Sir Michael Howard corresponded with me on some points and has generously allowed me to quote from his letters.

For interviews or supplying material, I thank Lord Adrian, Alex Baker, Lucy Baruch, Arthur S. Blank (Jr.), Thomas C. Bond, John Bowlby, Norman Marshall Camp, Jack Chalker, Alan Costall, John Crammer, Adam Curle, Peter Dally, Jonathan R. T. Davidson, Pat de Maré, Arthur Egendorf, Bernard C. Glueck, Bonnie L. Green, Roy R. Grinker (Jr.), Bernard A. Heeney, Herbert Hendin, Stephen Hirsch, Harry C. Holloway, Kathleen Holmes, Mardi J. Horowitz, Philip James, Peggy Jay, Franklin D. Jones, Jennifer Johns, Paul Kaufman, Robert Kee, Lawrence C. Kolb, Denis Leigh, Theodore Lidz, Ian McDonald, John Mackenzie, James MacKeith, Stephen MacKeith, Ian MacGregor, Jim MacGregor, Heli Meltsner, R. S. Morton, Edmund Myers, Eric Newby, Roderick Ørner, Roger Pitman, Henry R. Rollin, John Rowlands, Joan Rumens, Arieh Shalev, Chaim Shatan, Peter Schurr, Herbert Spiegel, David Stafford-Clark, Ronald Symonds, Derek Summerfield, Michael Trimble, Peter Watson, Simon Wessely, Douglas Wickenden, John Wishart, and Michael Yealland.

My thanks to those who gave me the chance to road-test bits of the book at the Universities of Bristol, Cambridge, Edinburgh, Manchester and Warwick; the Military History Seminar, University of London; the Tavistock Clinic; the Royal Military Academy, Sandhurst; the Institute for Group Analysis; and the Wellcome Institute. Equally to Ferdinand Mount, Will Eaves, Orlando May and Maren Meinhardt of *The Times Literary Supplement* for letting me put some of my thoughts into print.

Among old comrades-in-arms, David Cohen, Anne Fleming, Nigel Miller, Brian Moser, David Parker, André Singer and Vicki Wegg-Prosser helped to point the way. Whatever I know of story-telling has been learnt from Ted Childs, Jeremy Isaacs, Bruce Norman, Phillip Whitehead and Zvi Dor-Ner. Peter Elstob, Barrie Pitt, and David Mason gave me a start in military history.

I owe a particular debt, for inspiring me to begin and then complete this project, to Martha and David Caute, the late Stephen MacKeith, Hugh Freeman, Ruth Leys, Allan Young and Catherine Merridale. All have given generously of themselves. Support along the road has also come from James Donald, Roger Smith, Ruth and Chris Keil, John Dollar and Stephen Lowenstein. Chapters or sections have been read by David Caute, Roger Smith, Jonathan Bird, Ann Dally, Paul Ferris, Christopher Francis, Noble Frankland, Hugh Freeman, Chris Keil and Catherine Merridale. I alone am responsible for the final product.

My agent, Peter Robinson, found me a publisher. The text has benefited greatly from Steve Cox's wisdom and humanity and Matthew Parker's skill and judgement. Dan Franklin, who originally commissioned the book, is now its publisher; his patience and loyalty have sustained me.

My children, Louisa and Joe, have kept me sane. Prosper and Esmond Devas have kept me laughing. Marylla and Julian Hunt, Caroline Moser and Peter Sollis, and Stewart and Catherine Boyd have provided hospitality and encouragement. My greatest debt is to Sue, who has kept the ship afloat, given love and counsel, and somehow managed to write a wonderful book of her own in a fraction of the time.

INTRODUCTION

In March 1918, Dr Harold Hills arrived at the Headquarters of the British Fourth Army on the Western Front and announced himself as its newly-appointed Neurologist.

A staff officer said, 'What's a neurologist?'
  'Someone who has made a special study of the nervous system.'
  'Anything to do with nerves?'
  'Yes.'
  He went to the door, opened it and called out, 'They have sent a man to look after our nerves.' There were shouts of laughter.[1]

Many doctors were sent to look after soldiers' nerves during the twentieth century, a time of tumultuous military conflict and of continuous development in psychological medicine. They carried many labels – psychiatrists, neurologists, psychologists – and earned many nicknames – 'shrinks', 'trick-cyclists', 'nut-pickers'.

Psychiatrists were brought in because they seemed to have ways of alleviating the suffering of war; because the military could no longer cope; or because, in an age of total war, they offered a way of reassuring civilian society that everything possible was being done for the soldier.

Psychiatrists saw the effects of battle on the human mind and recorded them with wonderful eloquence. War horrified, appalled, yet also excited them. It provided an extreme environment, a laboratory in which every theory could be tested literally to destruction; war shattered the mind, but in an intellectually absorbing way. These conflicting emotions pervade the medical literature; even as the doctors record the horrors, they marvel at the way the mind refracts and mediates them. A soldier admitted to Maida Vale hospital in London in January 1915 had completely lost his memory after being blown up by a shell at Ypres in October 1914. He had been sent first to a hospital in Manchester and now spoke with a Lancashire accent. But under hypnosis, he regained his memory, and, in the soft burr of his native Wiltshire, described 'with very manifest expressions of emotion' the 'horror of a bombardment by high explosive shells'. But when he came out of hypnosis, he could remember nothing and talked again in a Manchester accent. Try as they would, the doctors were unable to re-unite his two personalities. After 25 'sittings' he was discharged, a case of 'lost personality'.[2]

It was not just the effects on memory that were fascinating. Emotion, too, seemed to operate in strange ways. A generation later, a psychiatrist with the United States Eighth Air Force described how the pilot of a B-17 bomber was able to come seemingly untouched through a dreadful experience:

On his tenth mission the plane in front of him exploded, and what he took for a piece of debris flew back towards him. It turned out to be the body of one of the gunners, which hit directly in the Number Two propeller. The body was splattered over the windscreen and froze there. In order to see, it was necessary for the pilot to borrow a knife from the engineer and to scrape the windscreen. He had a momentary twinge of nausea, but the incident meant but little to him. As he did not know the man, the horrifying spectacle was at a psychological distance.

But two missions later, his own plane and crew were heavily damaged and he was himself involved in emotionally distressing events. Memories of the first incident came back to haunt and disturb him. He could no longer fly.[3]

The problem for the psychiatrists, though, was that they could not simply respond to their patients' suffering and tease out the intellectual puzzles they posed: they were also supposed to send them back into battle. They were military doctors, there to 'conserve the fighting strength', to help win the war. How could the needs of the military and the individual patient be reconciled? Some had no difficulty squaring this circle and even became skilful at offering the military what they wanted to hear. Others felt guilty about sending young men back into battle. Dr Tom Main spoke in 1945 of the 'emotional by-products' of the work – bitterness and impotence, anger, or a 'guilt-driven compassion for . . . others who have undertaken risks of death in battle' – that led to 'sentimentality and anger about neurotic soldiers' and clouded doctors' clinical judgement. The pressures drove some to suicide and ruined the lives of others.[4]

With experience, doctors' perspectives changed. They came to see that a man's capacity to endure in war was determined by many things – heredity, upbringing, 'character', the society he came from, how he felt about the war, his relationship to his fellow soldiers, the length of time he had been fighting, whether his wife had been unfaithful – quite apart from the military circumstances in which he found himself. They realised, too, that in the military context collective factors often mattered more than individual ones. A very high proportion of the men Dr William Brown treated in 1917 came from the same units; 'the better the discipline in any division, the less shell-shock there was in that division.'[5]

With experience many learnt, too, the value of self-denial. They recognised that doctors could do harm as well as good; that it was often wiser not to use medical terminology or to let a soldier think that he was ill. At times, the psychiatrist had to be 'cruel only to be kind'; it might even be in the man's own best interest – as well as the Army's – to send him back into combat.

Then there were issues about treatment. Should a soldier just be left to recover or should the psychiatrist help him to bring to the surface the memories and emotions of the battlefield? Many influential writers promoted the metaphor of catharsis, assuming it was better to 'get it off your chest' rather than to 'bottle it up'; but practical experience suggested that much depended on the personality of the psychiatrist and that 'methods of revival were often extremely painful for the patient'. An experienced and undogmatic British psychiatrist acknowledged in 1931 that 'physicians who encouraged their patient to repress still further their emotional experiences sometimes succeeded in making them fit to stand the strain of life.'[6]

There was also the question of compensation. Governments, of course, were reluctant to pay pensions to the mental casualties of war, but there was also some evidence that pensions did not actually help war veterans, that they 'only made them worse'.[7]

Finally, doctors learned that public opinion was an important factor in the treatment of soldiers with psychological problems. It helped to determine how they themselves felt about their work, and how their patients responded to treatment. But public opinion was not constant. In the Great War there was considerable public concern about shell-shock, which led, one eminent psychiatrist believed, to a 'wave of sentimentality' that made 'sane treatment of shell-shock' much more difficult. In contrast, in Britain during the Second World War (though not in the United States) civilians had too many problems of their own – bombing, evacuation, rationing – to spare much sympathy for the soldier who had broken down. During and after the Vietnam War, public attitudes changed several times and the stereotype of the Vietnam veteran in the media went from being a psychopathic baby-killer to an innocent victim.[8]

A War of Nerves explores the psychological problems soldiers developed in the World Wars and during and after Vietnam, and describes the steps doctors took to counter them. Medically speaking, it covers the diagnostic eras of shell-shock, battle fatigue and Post-Traumatic Stress Disorder.

To tell this story, the historian has to try to correct long-standing imbalances and to confront modern misconceptions. The imbalances go back to the Great War, when a great deal was written about shell-shock by doctors serving at Base, rather than at forward hospitals, and very little was written about what went on in the front line. This bias was partly redressed by the public inquiry into shell-shock the British held after the war and by the handsome volume called *Neuropsychiatry* the Americans published; yet only the Australians, among the combatants, produced an adequate historical study of the episode. The Second World War, too, generated an enormous, vivid, but lop-sided literature, much of it written by self-serving doctors. Medical writing on the war in Vietnam is massively outweighed by the torrent of publications on its aftermath.

The misconceptions derive from the developments since 1980. Until recently, medicine was a world apart and medical history mostly left to retired doctors.

Military psychiatry was a subject of deep obscurity, of interest in peacetime only to a handful of serving doctors. The American psychoanalyst Abram Kardiner complained in 1959 that 'the neuroses incidental to war alternate between being the urgent topic of the times and being completely and utterly neglected.' It was, he thought, 'hard to find a province of psychiatry where there is less discipline.'[9]

Then, in the 1980s, this all changed. Vietnam brought a sudden rediscovery of military psychiatry, not just by doctors working with veterans but, for the first time, by historians. Energised by the women's movement and by Michel Foucault's critique of traditional medical history, they dragged the subject back into the headlights of fashion and illuminated some aspects of it, most notably concepts of mental health before 1914. The downside to this, however, was that these writers were interested in issues of gender and power, not in the overall record, and mostly concentrated on aspects of the subject that resonated emotionally with modern readers: the First World War and issues such as race and sexuality.[10]

As a result, much attention was focused on the famous meeting in 1917, at Craiglockhart Hospital near Edinburgh, of the poet Siegfried Sassoon and the psychologist and anthropologist Dr William Rivers. Rivers was a humane and sympathetic figure, whose pioneering use of quasi-Freudian psychoanalysis offered a powerful contrast to the vicious methods of electrical torture used by other doctors to drive soldiers back to the war. Uniquely, both doctor and patient left eloquent accounts of their encounter.

This emphasis was popularised by the British novelist Pat Barker, in a trilogy of novels about Rivers and Sassoon published in the 1990s to great critical and commercial success. Barker drew skilfully on some of the literature, but she also projected backwards a great deal of modern baggage derived from the women's movement and the 1980s 'counselling culture'. She brought the subject back into the public mind, but in a lop-sided way.[11]

Neither Rivers nor Sassoon was in any way typical. Sassoon, a homosexual, was a gallant soldier but had publicly denounced the war; Rivers, though 'a great and good man', worked only with soldiers evacuated back to England and had more rapport with officers than with other ranks. He was, too, a man of his time, believing that educated people were evolutionarily more advanced than the uneducated.

If Rivers provides one modern point of reference, Post-Traumatic Stress Disorder constitutes the other. This term, created by the American Psychiatric Association (APA) in 1980, has gained public currency in a way unheard of since 'shell-shock' in 1914. Yet its significance is widely misunderstood. PTSD is a cumbersome phrase devised by a cumbersome committee. It embodies certain new assumptions about how trauma affects its victims, but it does not rest on any specific scientific breakthrough nor offer any great step forward in treatment. Yet press reporting frequently gives that impression.

This bipolar view, now standard in the media, completely ignores the important historical fact that the problem of war neurosis was comparatively well handled in the Second World War.[12]

The clinical literature of the war neuroses is so rich that it is easy for the historian to pull together a collage of horror and pathos. But to understand why, in the past, ordinary people were able to come through the horrors of war, we have to look at the overall record, not just at the gripping psychopathology. To get at the historical truth, the case histories must be reconciled with another, less enticing body of writing: official histories, war diaries, regimental histories, Pentagon memoranda – dull, managerial, impersonal in tone and full of military euphemism, the 'tough school'. We also have to explore the complex implications of Dr Paul Davis's 1945 assessment of the psychology of the soldier who has broken down:

Amidst a welter of different emotions he will be subject predominantly to feelings of acute anxiety and of exhaustion, of shame at having broken down, of relief at being out of the fighting, of depression and irritability, of hatred for and at the same time fear of the enemy, and so on. But the uppermost factor in his mind must be that he has – temporarily at any rate – failed in his duty as a soldier, whether he openly accuses himself of [it] as not infrequently occurs, or whether he seeks partially to excuse his conduct: he has fallen out of the group of which he was a part and is now separated from it and has to face alone an overwhelming flood of painful emotions.[13]

Finally, we must see the shell-shocked soldier not simply as a victim, silently suffering, powerless to help himself, but as an agent, using his medical symptoms as a weapon of resistance to military authority. The Tommy of Great War memoirs – brave, resourceful, loyal, but as quick to spot a soft option as a drink, a cosy billet or French mam'selle; a survivor not averse to 'swinging the lead' on the right occasion – is hardly recognisable in the pious modern literature.

Fortunately it is now becoming easier to take this more nuanced view. Over the past decade scholars have done much to clarify the social context of shell-shock, the tangled issues of pensions, French and German policy in the First World War and the complex medical politics which went into the 'invention' of Post-Traumatic Stress Disorder. My debts to Marc Ollivier Roudebush, Paul Lerner, Martin Stone, Wilbur J. Scott and many others will be apparent to those who know this field.

*   *   *

There is a compelling reason to take a much wider look at what happened in the past: we are making a mess of this problem today and need to relearn the lesson that, in treating the aftermath of war, good intentions are not enough.

The 1970s saw a long and impassioned campaign, in which many prominent American psychiatrists were involved, to win recognition for the psychological problems of Vietnam veterans. It seemed by 1980 that this movement had gained all its objectives: Congress had been persuaded to provide generous out-patient counselling to Vietnam vets and the American Psychiatric Association had agreed to include in its new, comprehensive system of psychiatric classification a category specially tailored to cover their needs and help them to get treatment, called Post-Traumatic Stress Disorder (or PTSD).[14]

The men and women who agitated on behalf of Vietnam veterans were honourable and admirable people. But by the 1990s it had become clear that the prescriptions so readily embraced two decades earlier had not greatly helped the patient population they were intend for; rather, by creating the term PTSD and making treatment available in the Veterans' Administration, the psychiatric profession had turned many veterans into chronic cases of PTSD. Similarly, the popularisation of the concept of 'trauma' in the 1980s was coming to be seen as a mixed blessing. Today, the clinical literature, once so full of hope and optimism, has a chastened and mystified note. Patients, a respected psychiatrist has conceded, are entitled to ask what results 'twenty years of passionate rhetoric about trauma and the treatment of trauma' has actually produced; it is time to put the 'naivete' of the recent past behind us. Another doctor has spoken of the 'potentially explosive impact' of stress-related diagnoses on 'societal approaches to responsibility and accountability.'[15]

It is becoming increasingly clear that doctors of the PTSD generation have gone through the same learning process as the World War One doctors. Indeed, there appears to be a recurring cycle with the war neuroses: the problem is first denied, then exaggerated, then understood, and finally, forgotten. In the ferment of war this cycle is speeded up; in the languid, well-funded peacetime of the 1980s it has taken two decades for the wheel to turn.

This book argues that throughout the twentieth century there was a dialogue in military psychology between the tough and the tender approaches; or, to put it another way, between the 'realists' and the 'dramatists'. 'Dramatists' were interested in teasing out the fascinating complexities of patients' symptoms and writing them up; 'realists', in getting them fighting again quickly. The 'dramatic' tradition survives as literature; the 'realist' as medico-military lore. Both have their merits, but things worked best when the two strands interacted in creative tension.

Every war is different. Every time there is a war, different social attitudes to fundamental questions like fear, madness and social obligation will redefine the role of military psychiatry in a different way. Medicine will be different; and symptoms; so, too, will military and institutional circumstances.

Societies and cultures differ, also. In particular, the record of the United States in handling war neurosis stands rather apart. Yet in spite of this it has somehow dominated the subject. In the 1970s the American 'realist' tradition was completely discredited by its role in Vietnam and the field was left clear to the 'dramatists' – full of complex emotions about Vietnam and the atrocities committed there, burdened with the aftertows of Auschwitz, Hiroshima and My Lai; most of them completely ignorant of the hard unglamorous lessons of the past. The result has been to standardise a model of post-traumatic illness derived from one of the most ill-conceived, morally confused and disastrous conflicts ever waged – Vietnam – and from one of the most dreadful events in modern human history – the Holocaust.

Psychiatry has a mixed record. Undoubted successes, such as the scheme for rehabilitating prisoners of war after the Second World War, have been offset by numerous disasters. Much of the work of psychiatrists is, in reality, marginal to the military effort and serves more as a receptacle, a sponge for absorbing public concern about war. Equally, it is vitally important for returning soldiers to receive love and sympathy from their families; a job and a relationship matter more than any psychiatric treatment. Yet overemphasis on public understanding can also have disastrous consequences.

This book focuses primarily on the British and Americans, who have passed this baton to and fro over the past eighty years; but it also makes occasional forays behind French and German lines for comparative purposes. Individuals loom large in this account, not in order to emphasise some 'great man' interpretation but because individuals matter in military psychiatry, just as they do in military history.

Like all medical history, *A War of Nerves* contains an inherent source-bias; we hear more from doctors than from patients. However hard he tries, the historian cannot even the account, cannot give the patients an equal voice, because most chose not to recount their experiences. In a fragment of verse drafted before going to his death in a tank in Normandy, the English poet Keith Douglas wrote about the 'beast on my back' he quietly carried after his experiences in the desert campaign:

> Yes, I too have a particular monster
> a toad or worm curled in the belly
> stirring, eating at times I cannot foretell, he
> is the thing I can admit only once to
> anyone, never to those who have not their own.[16]

PROLOGUE

THE SHOCK OF THE SHELL

In the winter of 1914/15 strange cases began to arrive at the hospitals and casualty clearing stations of the British Army in France. These soldiers were not wounded, yet they could neither see, smell nor taste properly. Some were unable to stand up, speak, urinate or defecate; some had lost their memories; others vomited uncontrollably. Many suffered from 'the shakes'.

One was a private soldier, aged 20, who had been moving from one front-line trench to another when he was caught in barbed wire. As he tried to disentangle himself he was 'found' by the German artillery.

Immediately after one of the shells burst in front of him, his sight, he said, became blurred. Another shell, which then burst behind him gave him a greater shock, 'like a punch on the head without any pain after it'. The shell in front cut his haversack clean away and bruised his side.[1]

Crying, shivering and frightened that he was going blind, the private was led to a dressing station. Five days later he arrived at the Base Hospital at le Touquet where the Cambridge psychologist C. S. Myers was working. After ten days' treatment he was evacuated to England.

That unknown private was the first recorded case of 'shell-shock' – one of three described by Dr Myers in an article of February 1915 in which he coined the term 'shell-shock', or rather introduced into the medical literature a phrase already current in the Army. Shell-shock seemed an appropriate term: nearly all Myers' early cases and many of those that swelled the medical press during 1915 had 'followed from the shock of an exploding shell', precipitating a sudden collapse.[2]

The experience of being shelled seemed to leave men blinded, deaf, dumb, semi-paralysed, in a state of stupor, and very often suffering from amnesia. Some could remember nothing between the moment of the explosion and coming to in hospital; others could remember nothing at all. A number of these patients also showed physical symptoms, such as extraordinary, unnatural ways of walking, that astonished the doctors who examined them in England:

you never dreamt of such gaits – the craziest, un-text book things. One fellow was just like [the trapeze artist] Blondin on a tight-rope . . . with the feet far apart, the arms out, the man balancing himself and making several attempts with his hind foot before taking a step.[3]

'I wish you could be here,' wrote the Professor of Medicine at Oxford to a colleague in July 1915, 'in this orgie of neuroses and psychoses and gaits and paralyses. I cannot imagine what has got into the central nervous system of the men . . . Hysterical dumbness, deafness, blindness, anaesthesia galore. I suppose it was the shock and the strain but I wonder if it was ever thus in previous wars?' Trench warfare was then some nine months old; already it was becoming obvious that the new 'industrial' form of warfare, in which vast armies in fixed positions systematically bombarded each other with high explosive artillery, was producing an epidemic of shell-shock.

But no one was quite sure how the symptoms were created. Were the men suffering physical damage to their nervous system or some strange kind of emotional shock? During 1915 a fierce debate erupted in the halls and journals of British medicine. Just about every specialist who had treated shell-shocked patients in England weighed in. It was hardly surprising that many leant towards a physical explanation of shell-shock. What could be more 'physical' than to have a high explosive shell land a few feet away from you? In those far-off, innocent days the very idea that frail human flesh should be exposed to sustained battery by high explosive was shocking. The doctors wrote, with a sense of Vorticist dislocation, of the horror of men destroyed by machines. The image of shells bombarding the nervous system pervades the medical literature. Even at second hand, the doctors felt the shattering, unravelling force of

The detonation, the flash, the heat of the explosion, the air concussion, the upheaval of the ground, and the acrid suffocating fumes [that] combine in producing a violent assault on practically all the senses simultaneously.[4]

Behind this sense of physical outrage lay a pyrotechnic revolution that, since the last major European war in 1870, had transformed warfare. Modern chemistry had brought nitro-glycerine and gun-cotton to the battlefield. Shells now contained *high* explosive – lyddite, cordite, melinite – 'materials which, unlike gunpowder, combusted totally and instantaneously, making no smoke to betray the position of the firer and leaving little deposit in the barrel to slow down the rate of fire and increasing the range of weapons to an hitherto inconceivable extent.' Artillery could now be deployed from miles behind the front line; mounted on recoilless carriages, the guns could keep firing, without tedious resighting, as fast as their crews could reload. Death could come suddenly and without warning from out of the sky.[5]

In 1915 the gruesome science of wound ballistics was still in its infancy; no one quite understood how the *physical* forces let loose by these shells worked on the body and the nervous system. What happened if you were near, but not directly in the path of an exploding shell? A French civil engineer called Arnoux ingeniously worked out with an aneroid barometer that 'the dynamic pressure exerted by the surrounding air on bodies within a few yards of the exploding shells' was over 10,000 kilos per square metre, which sounded quite lethal. Yet after observing the effect of exploding heavy charges of gun-cotton on pigs, the British physiologist L. E. Hill concluded that 'a few feet of air was enough to save the pigs from damage', and by 1915 countless soldiers in France could testify to similar escapes.[6]

Particular amazement was caused by 'fatal shell-shock without external signs of injury', cases where shellfire caused instantaneous death in groups of men without actually wounding them externally. At Gallipoli, the journalist Ashmead Bartlett found a group of seven Turks sitting together, with their rifles across their knees.

One man has his arm across the neck of his friend and a smile on his face as if they had been cracking a joke when death overwhelmed them. All now have the appearance of being merely asleep; for of the several I can only see one who shows any outward injury.

Several possible explanations were advanced for this quite common occurrence. A British military doctor thought that explosions caused some kind of concussion of the central nervous system. The noted neurologist, Dr F. W. Mott, wondered whether in these cases carbon monoxide poisoning was the fatal agent. Several years would pass before post-mortem work clarified this question, but the debate on 'fatal shell-shock' undoubtedly influenced the simultaneous attempt to understand those living cases of loss of memory, blindness, and paralysis to which the name shell-shock had also become attached.[7]

As the doctors argued the causes, in the public mind these soldiers were simply seen as having 'been exposed to, and had suffered from, the *physical* [my italics] effects of explosion of projectiles.' The vivid terse name, shell-shock, quickly took root in the popular imagination.[8]

1

DOCTORS' MINDS

One hot July afternoon in 1914, Vera Brittain attended Speech Day at Uppingham School. She always remembered that day as 'the one perfect summer idyll that I ever experienced, as well as my last carefree entertainment before the flood.' 'The lovely legacy of a vanished world,' she wrote in *Testament of Youth*, 'it is etched with minute precision on the tablets of my memory. Never again, for me and my generation, would there be any festival the joy of which no cloud could darken and no remembrance invalidate.'[1]

An Edwardian summer, a lost idyll shattered by the 'guns of August': it is an historical cliché now; yet one found in almost every memoir of that era, and centred usually round a particular occasion. Many doctors looked back in this way to an event that had marked the high-water point of the Victorian professional world of frock-coats and servants, the last time that the 'whole contemporary field of medicine' was assembled together before it fragmented into specialisms – the Seventeenth International Medical Congress of 1913.[2]

Eight thousand physicians, 'drawn from all parts of the civilised world', descended on London for a week of argument and entertainment, inaugurated in the Albert Hall by Prince Arthur of Connaught. When not making speeches or attending garden parties, they visited hospitals and asylums, examined sewage works, inspected the school children of London, explored the new 'Garden Suburb' in Hampstead, and went to Broadmoor and Stratford-on-Avon. At Bethlem Hospital an exhibition of drawings and paintings by inmates of asylums – appealing 'more to the student of mental diseases than the art student' – had been organised.[3]

Dr Paul Ehrlich, inventor of the 'magic bullet' for syphilis, gave a keynote address. Sir Ronald Ross, tamer of malaria, was there. The American brain surgeon, Harvey Cushing, spoke. The latest research on 'the beat of the heart', 'radium for skin diseases', the use of a barium meal with X-rays, transplantation of the kidneys, the 'role of the rat' in plague and 'the intellect of dwarfs' was unveiled. For the academically minded, there was medical history and 'New Evidence of the Antiquity of Man' provided by the Piltdown Skull. At Westminster Abbey, the Bishop of London, taking as his text Philippians, iii, 21 – 'the body of our humiliation' – urged doctors to use their ever greater powers to be 'messengers of God'; a suffragettes' demonstration muffled his message. Down the road, the Archbishop of Westminster, preferring Matthew, xxv, 36 – 'I was sick and ye visited me' – urged 'those called to the ministry of healing' to 'see Jesus Christ, even in the least of His brethren.'

After the opening ceremony, the doctors split off into twenty-six sections, scattered across London. Discussion of the disorders of the mind was, however, divided between the two sections of Psychiatry and Neurology. This split, which was to help shape the response to shell-shock, reflected a de facto division in the profession between psychiatrists – asylum medical officers, who looked after poor and severely disturbed patients and had low professional status – and neurologists – doctors in private practice treating richer patients and milder mental disorders, who had high status.[4]

As a medical student in the 1890s, the future psychoanalyst Ernest Jones once heard a satirical friend speculate about what asylum doctors – 'alienists'– discussed at their meetings. 'I suppose,' his friend said, 'they read papers on an improved variety of the Chubb lock' – his point being that they were just glorified medical gaolers. The trebling of the asylum population in fifty years had turned the great hospitals erected earlier in the century into overcrowded warehouses of the mad. There were about 165,000 registered lunatics in Britain's asylums in 1913, some 78,000 men to 87,000 women, and the psychiatrists who worked in them had little time to relate to patients or do research work. That year the medical press was full of complaints from alienists about the isolation and backwardness of their profession.[5]

Congress delegates were taken to one British asylum where original research was being performed, Claybury in Essex, to hear Dr Frederick Mott talk about the work done in its pathological laboratory on General Paralysis of the Insane. This terrible condition, which led eventually to seizures, paralysis, dementia and death, accounted for almost a fifth of male admissions to London County Asylums and had only recently been finally confirmed as a symptom of terminal syphilis. It took ten years to incubate, said Dr Mott, had not yielded to anti-syphilitic remedies and was still impossible to treat. Like Aids a century later, General Paralysis of the Insane was a 'lifestyle' illness; or, as the Victorians put it, a 'moral' disorder, the 'wages of sin'. But it was also biological, causing damage to the brain easily visible after death to a pathologist like Dr Mott, so it also fitted into the dominantly biological view of mental disorder, according to which most mental illness was believed to be organic. Mott spoke in another lecture of the 'neuropathic inheritance', the way madness passed from generation to generation. He himself had been able to obtain the brains of mental patients who were related and to compare their fissures and convolutional patterns, confirming the role of heredity in insanity and showing how in successive generations madness tended to intensify and come on at an earlier age. 'Nature,' said Dr Mott, 'is always trying to end or mend a degenerate stock.'[6]

To be confined to an asylum was a terrible step carrying stigma and shame: the 'disaster of committal'. There was, however, growing concern among younger psychiatrists that no facilities existed in Britain for treating 'borderline' cases, patients with milder mental problems. There was particular interest in a talk about a 'Psychiatric Clinic' recently opened in the United States, on a German model. The London County Council was about to create a similar clinic, with money given by the noted psychiatrist Henry Maudsley.

But, for the medical high-flyer, the real prestige and money lay not in asylum psychiatry, but in working as a 'Nerve-specialist'.

*   *   *

In 1894 the *Spectator* magazine noticed that the meaning of the words 'nerve' and 'nervous' was changing. Once, people had spoken of 'nerve' as a 'synonym for force or strength', 'nervousness' had 'denoted courage and vigour', and the 'nervous' man was 'one in whom all the elements of strength were well strung and under control'. Now they more often spoke of 'nerves', in the plural, and 'nervousness' had come to mean a 'timidity that borders on cowardice'. People more commonly thought about weak nerves than strong ones.[7]

Why had this happened? The *Spectator* acknowledged that 'the nerves of modern men were often put to a heavier strain than nature had intended them to bear.' 'Competitive examinations, luxurious indulgences, railway journeys and the daily Press' were all elements of modern life which 'conduce[d] to living fast rather than living long.' But a change in attitudes was also noted; the British were becoming softer: 'Men talk about their nerves today who certainly would never have spoken about them a hundred years ago.' It was becoming commonplace to hear someone announce that he had given up hunting or polo-playing because 'he has lost his nerve'. Instances of such 'weak surrender' were becoming more plentiful. In fact, 'between popular folly and the indulgent doubts of doctors, nervous disorders are making far greater strides among us than the stress of modern life would really justify.'

The suggestion that men's nerves were being undermined by their doctors was taken up a year later by one of the country's most eminent medical men, Sir Clifford Allbutt. There was no doubt, he wrote in the *Contemporary Review*, 'that men pay more heed to the approaches and events of disease than in former days; they are more set to learn of their physicians the causes and nature of the diseases under which they suffer; and above all they love to call their ailments by new names . . . what was "liver" fifty years ago has become "nerves".'[8]

The 'stir in neurotic circles', Allbutt believed, 'first began with the woman-kind.' He did not specify quite when. Doctors specialising in female patients had become very prosperous as 'the suburban sofa was exchanged for the back parlours of Harley Street'; fashionable spas in Europe, too, had done good business. With the arrival of the 'New Woman' of the 1890s, however, said Allbutt, 'both sexes began to chant nerves together, to compare symptoms, to speculate together on physiological problems and to worry out their cures hand in hand.'

Neurology, the diagnosis and treatment of nervous disorders, emerged in the 1860s as one of the earliest specialisms in medicine. Its prestige was then enhanced by a heroic period of medical research, much of it based on fearsome experiments on animals. By 1910, medicine had established that nerve cells (or neurons) in the brain communicate with each other across synapses; neurologists knew how messages pass between the brain and the peripheral nerves, understood how the spinal cord works and had a pretty good idea of how the autonomic nervous system organises the glands and involuntary muscles of the body. Although not in agreement on the subject, doctors had also learned a great deal about the way that control of the body's functions is distributed in the brain.[9]

However, from the start, neurologists had to be concerned not just with tangible physical defects of the brain and nervous system, observable under the pathologist's microscope, but also with more subjective and shadowy 'nervous' complaints. There were, too, different national traditions. The pre-eminent British centre, the National Hospital for the Paralysed and Epileptic, in Queen Square in the Bloomsbury district of London, excelled at the organic rather than the psychological end of this spectrum, using meticulous observation and new diagnostic equipment to explore the physical changes to the brain or nervous system in conditions like epilepsy, general paralysis and tumour.[10]

'Queen Square' produced medical giants: Sir William Gowers wrote the standard textbook of neurology; Sir David Ferrier charted the brain's geography by experimenting on animals; Sir Victor Horsley pioneered surgery in the brain. Above all, John Hughlings Jackson combined painstaking clinical examination with speculation about the place of the nervous system in human evolution. Many of these men were also highly eccentric. Hughlings Jackson was too impatient to sit through an evening in the theatre and would get off trains before reaching his destination, demanding alternative transport from bemused stationmasters. Gowers' enthusiasm for Pitman's shorthand led him to stop total strangers in the street and ask them if they used the system; one young man who admitted that he did not, was told, 'You are a fool and will fail in life.' But they were not very interested in their patients as people; Jackson could never remember their names. An American trained at the hospital recalled the 'impatience with psychological problems' shown there.[11]

Like all British consultants at this time, the Queen Square physicians lived a Jekyll-and-Hyde life. To obtain eminence in medicine, the newly qualified doctor had to get into one of the great London teaching hospitals and there work unpaid on patients. Because they were working-class, he treated them without much respect and used them for research and teaching purposes; they, in their turn, were considered fortunate to be treated for free. However, to earn a living, the doctor had also to work privately and as soon as he had any status in the hospital world, he would set up in Harley Street and see paying patients two or three days a week. These were of his own class and towards them he had to behave quite differently than towards his free patients. He gave them time and listened sympathetically to their problems because, if they didn't like him, they'd go to another doctor they did like. This was particularly true of the Queen Square neurologists: 'they got their intellectual stimulation from their morbid anatomy and their income from rich neurotics.' This tradition of approaching diagnosis and treatment differently depending on the class of the patient would be important to the handling of shell-shock.[12]

Their private patients mostly had *psychoneuroses*, nervous disorders that fell somewhere in the borderland between sanity and madness, for which no clear physical cause could be found. In the 1900s, these fell into two main categories, *hysteria* and *neurasthenia*, and the diagnostic rule of thumb, pungently expressed by one American neurologist, was: 'Finding the patient lachrymose and emotional [the doctor] calls the disorder hysteria; if depressed and inert, he calls it neurasthenia.'[13]

Hysterical patients would come to the doctor with complaints like paralysed arms and shaking legs, which seemed to be caused by malfunctions of the nervous system but for which medical examination could find no physical explanation. The term 'hysteria' derives from the Greek word for the womb and until the late nineteenth century it was thought of as a condition found only in female patients. Most British doctors believed it to be much commoner in women than men and to 'have a special proclivity to affect the Latin, Slavonic and Jewish races.'[14]

Certainly the French seemed to have a special affinity with the condition. The great Jean-Martin Charcot (1825–1893), Professor of Neurology at the Salpêtrière in Paris, was one of the first doctors to take hysteria seriously, 'as a genuine ailment rather than the malingerer's refuge'. By experimenting with hypnosis, he showed that hysterical symptoms like paralysis of the arm could be artificially produced and then removed; he used photography to 'add a new dimension of concrete reality to what had previously been fleeting if not dubious phenomena.' The result was to objectify hysteria. He also convinced his contemporaries that hysteria was not confined to women and was not 'simply related to the vagaries of the female reproductive system'. Hysteria in men, Charcot believed, was usually traumatic in origin.[15]

But in Anglo-Saxon countries, Charcot had a dubious reputation, particularly among the older doctors. The theatricality of his clinics, where the patients paraded their symptoms before vast audiences, was not to everyone's taste and it was widely suspected that some of his professional *hysteriques* 'rehearsed' their symptoms, which never seemed to turn up outside the Salpêtrière. This detachment continued after Charcot's death. The writings on hysteria of his pupils and successors, Joseph Babinski, Jules Dejerine, Pierre Janet and Sigmund Freud, were reported in the English medical press, but as one Queen Square doctor wrote, 'here in England, hysteria has never been cultivated . . . [it] has been left to itself.'[16]

Neurasthenia, the second major category of nervous disorder, was an American invention, a term coined by the New York neurologist Charles Beard in 1869. Neurasthenia was essentially nervous exhaustion, brought about by overwork or overindulgence, but its elastic boundaries also took in what would now be called depression, mood disorders and an 'identity crisis'. Flattering his patients, Beard characterised the neurasthenic in very sympathetic terms, as a casualty of the dynamism of American life. Neurasthenia for him was a 'disease of civilisation', brought about by 'the complex agencies of modern life': 'steam power, the periodic press, the telegraph, the sciences, and the mental activity of women.'[17]

Neurasthenia was quickly taken up in Europe, especially in Germany. In the process, it gradually lost its class specificity; the neurasthenic ceased to be an aspiring Yankee and became, in countries where doctors worked for the state and had working-class clientele, an artisan or booking clerk. The stock treatment for neurasthenia was the 'cure' devised by the great Philadelphia neurologist, Silas Weir Mitchell, which involved isolation, 'entire rest' and 'excessive feeding' with a milk diet. The 'Weir Mitchell cure', advertised by numerous institutions, was felt to be especially effective with female patients. Male neurasthenics were seldom subjected to the full rigours of the cure and usually escaped with rest, fresh air or foreign cruises.[18]

The rationale of such cures was that the body contained a finite amount of 'nerve force' that was in danger of being exhausted. The stock metaphors used by doctors were financial and electrical; patients were 'overdrawn at the bank' or their 'batteries were run down'. Analogies with nineteenth-century physics were also common and provided the rationale for one of the mainstays of treatment, the application of mild electric current to the body. Electrical treatments were thought to recharge drained nervous batteries without drawing on the patient's own reserves.[19]

But when increasingly sophisticated investigation of the nervous system failed to produce any confirmation of the 'nerve force' hypothesis, purists like Sir William Gowers at Queen Square lost faith in 'neurasthenia' and removed it from their textbooks. But the profession as a whole clung to it as a respectable label, 'a great comfort both to doctors and to the friend of patients.' The very vagueness of the term enhanced its usefulness; it 'managed,' a German psychiatrist said, 'to explain subjective bodily symptoms in terms of objective physical disease, thus removing any suggestion of the patient's own part in them'; and was particularly useful as a way for men to preserve 'an ethos of fortitude'.[20]

Whether 'real' or 'socially constructed' by doctors and wider society, these mental disorders were felt to be on the increase in the 1900s. 'Nervous breakdown is the disease of our age,' one doctor wrote in 1909, using the popular term which was by then replacing 'shattered nerves' or 'broken health'. 'If the psychoneuroses continue to increase at the present rate,' Dr Hugh Crichton-Miller told the British Medical Association in 1912, 'our sons will not starve.'[21]

Literary people were particularly prone to nervous breakdowns; there is scarcely an Edwardian writer who did not have one. Oscar Wilde found it comforting to have all the symptoms of neurasthenia: 'It makes one a perfect type.' Virginia Woolf famously saw five different doctors and underwent the Weir Mitchell cure, later avenging herself on the doctor concerned in her novel *Mrs Dalloway*. Rupert Brooke – sexually confused, revolted by the mechanics of sex – consulted Dr Maurice Craig in Harley Street, who made no attempt to probe his state of mind and simply urged him to eat and sleep his way back to health. Ford Madox Ford, never one to stint himself, saw *nineteen* specialists between 1903 and 1906 and underwent treatments which ranged from 'being fed one grape every quarter of an hour for sixteen hours out of the day' to having 'indecent photographs of a singular banality' flashed before his eyes. Theodore Roosevelt and the artist Frederic Remington were among numerous Americans sent out West to recover from neurasthenia.[22]

Some observers believed, however, that there was a more widespread break-down of nerves going far beyond the professional classes and 'brain workers'. In his analysis of British public opinion during the Boer War, *The Psychology of Jingoism*, the liberal journalist J. A. Hobson argued that 'the bad conditions of town life' in the great industrial centres 'lowered the vitality of the inhabitants, [and] operate with peculiar force upon their nervous organisation.' Hobson believed the 'nervous wear and tear' imposed by the 'constant struggle for a livelihood' was 'quite apparent in the features of the town population' and 'mark[ed] them out with tolerable distinctness from country folk.' 'In every nation,' he wrote, 'which has proceeded far in modern industrialism, the prevalence of neurotic diseases attests the general nervous strain to which the population is subjected.' The German nerve specialist Dr Wilhelm Erb blamed 'the Growing Nervousness of our Time' on the political upheavals of the nineteenth century and the 'rapid growth of large cities with all its unfortunate consequences: the creation of mighty industrial centres filled with proletarians.' The Austrian psychiatrist Krafft-Ebing wrote that 'nervousness is rising fatally'. The French sociologist Durkheim, in his study of suicide, reached similar conclusions.[23]

At the turn of the century, exhaustion became a common theme in scientific research and popular discourse; one response to the numbing pressures of modernity was a cult of athleticism. Cycling, professional football and rambling all began to flourish, leaving Sir Clifford Allbutt amazed 'at the physical splendour and dashing energy of our young friends today'; the world seemed 'to have filled with Apollos and Dianas'. Sport, though, was not simply a spontaneous response to urbanism. It was seen by many as a way of restoring enfeebled will and arresting moral decline. In France, Baron de Coubertin founded the Olympic movement in order to 'halt the universal neurosis of modern life.' He believed sport to be 'an incomparable psychic instrument, and a dynamic to which one can profitably appeal in the treatment of many psychoneuroses.'[24]

Another response to modern pressures was the emergence of a new kind of doctor, the *psychotherapist*. There has always been an important psychological element in all medicine; 'the distinctive British contribution to psychotherapy,' Edward Shorter remarks, 'had always been the suggestive effect of a brass plate on a Harley Street door.' But therapies explicitly addressed to the mind were a novelty, a reflection, in part, of the decline of religion. In the 1890s a group of doctors in the French provincial town of Nancy began to claim great success in using hypnosis to cure painful physical conditions and developed a rationale for hypnosis quite different from that of Charcot. They 'viewed it as a universal and powerful therapeutic tool, and for this reason wished to popularize rather than limit its usage.' The Nancy school also developed the idea of non-hypnotic suggestion.[25]

These techniques were then taken further by two Swiss-born physicians. Paul Dubois ran a luxurious sanatorium in Berne and published in 1904 what Edward Shorter has called 'the most influential work on psychotherapy written before Freud'. His method was to befriend his patients and then use rational persuasion to convince them that their ailments were imaginary. His friend, Jules-Joseph Dejerine, primarily a neurologist and Charcot's successor at the Salpêtrière in Paris, developed a brand of psychotherapy based even more on forming an emotional bond with his patients, believing that psychotherapy worked only 'when the person you are doing it to has confessed to you his entire life, that is to say when he puts absolute confidence in you.'[26]

In 1908 a British doctor visiting Paris was able to compare Dejerine's clinic with that of his great rival Joseph Babinski. Both were intensely dramatic, especially after the lack of interest shown in hysteria at Guy's Hospital in London. Much of the drama derived from the liberties French medical deities took with their patients' dignity. Babinski, in his clinic at La Pitié Hospital, followed the Charcot tradition and usually required his male patients to appear completely naked and his female ones to wear only knickers. This enabled him to examine their limbs quite freely and to devise innumerable tests for distinguishing organic from mental disorders, the most famous being 'Babinski's sign', an upward movement of the big toe when the sole of the foot is tickled.[27]

A huge man, of Polish origin and commanding presence, Babinski believed that 'every case of hysteria was curable by reversing the psychological process which had given rise to the symptoms from which the patient was suffering.' This meant, in practice, that as soon as hysteria was diagnosed in a patient, Babinski would start his cure. 'He used various forms of suggestion,' the visiting Englishman noted, 'especially the painful application of faradic electricity, together with vigorous persuasion [and] gave the patients no explanation of the nature or cause of his symptoms.' Yet it seemed, 'his somewhat crude methods [known as *traitement brusqué*] were extremely successful and were . . . rarely followed by relapse or development of other hysterical symptoms.' Crossing Paris to the Salpêtrière hospital, the Englishman found Dejerine employing a completely different approach. 'Dejerine always had a large audience at his Out-Patient clinic. He sat at a table on a platform facing the patient with whom he carried on a conversation which all could hear. So absorbed was the patient that he took not the slightest notice of the audience and willingly discussed every detail of his domestic and other troubles.'[28]

Dubois and Dejerine's methods had considerable influence on their English colleagues. A speaker at the 1913 Congress praised 'the masterly way in which patients are seductively led from their morbid mentality and made to view themselves and their surroundings in a proper perspective.' There was, he said, increasing recognition of 'the mental effect of suggestion as a curative agent', particularly if combined 'with the detachment of the patient from the sympathetic environment of injudicious friends.' An English translation of Dejerine's *Psychoneuroses* appeared in 1913. 'The subject of psychotherapy,' said one writer, 'is in the air and one sees references to it on all sides.'[29]

By 1913, however, the medical cutting-edge had moved on; newer fashions were arriving from abroad. The 'mish-mash of hypnotism' and 'positive per-suasion' had begun to be supplanted by the much more systematic form of psychotherapy that we now call psychoanalysis. Its two main pioneers were two former pupils of Charcot, both of whom were led by extensive work with compliant hysterical patients to devise new theories of the workings of the mind. Until recently, Pierre Janet (1859–1947) was forgotten outside France, but in the 1900s his reputation stood higher than Freud's. Whereas Babinski simply believed that hysteria was caused by suggestion – by the patient persuading himself that he had a disease and therefore developing its symptoms – Janet's long experience with hysterics led him to come up with a more complex psychological hypothesis. He found that nearly all hysterics had amnesia; they could not remember what had produced their symptoms but, under hypnosis, recalled memories, usually of a traumatic character, which had been forgotten.[30]

Janet concluded that hysteria was caused by the splitting of the personality into a conscious and subconscious part, the subconscious being responsible for the paralyses, fits and other symptoms. He called this process *dissociation* – the splitting of the mind. In the absence of medical evidence, however, Janet stopped short of offering much explanation of exactly why such divisions in the mind produced hysteria and other illnesses.

That was Sigmund Freud's great contribution. Though trained in a rigorously physical school of neurology, Freud's time with Charcot, observation of an hysterical patient under the care of his Viennese friend Breuer, and extraordinarily bold intellectual imagination led him gradually to cast aside the restraints of orthodox medicine and to develop a system of ideas which, starting from the narrow field of hysteria, would within a decade offer an entire alternative view of the mind. Hysteria, Freud argued in 1895, was produced by the sup-pression of emotions, memories and experiences. The memories were repressed – flung into the 'unconscious' – to avoid the mental conflict that their presence in the conscious mind would otherwise have produced. In some cases, though, the repressed emotions were hysterically 'converted' into physical symptoms. Only by bringing these memories to the surface through a process called 'abreaction', could 'catharsis' be achieved and mental health restored.[31]

To achieve this purpose, Freud originally used hypnosis, but was not particularly good at it and found it too difficult to control; by 1905 he was relying on the analysis of dreams – 'the royal road to the unconscious' – and on long analysis through 'free association' as his preferred therapeutic weapons. He had also concluded, mainly on the strength of his own self-analysis, that the origins of all mental disorders, not simply hysteria, lay in the sexual conflicts of childhood. Unlike Janet, Freud was careful to build up a 'Movement' around his work, which by 1914 comprised a small core of disciples in Vienna and an outer shell of adherents in Europe and the United States. Some younger doctors in

Britain had by then become aware of his writings and begun to popularise them.[32]

It is often suggested that the early British Freudians were a persecuted sect, like the early Christians. In fact, the medical press in 1913 is packed with coverage of psychoanalysis, much of it favourable, and Freud was acknowledged to be an important authority on neurasthenia. The great difficulty most British doctors had with Freud was his insistence that all neuroses derived from sexual conflicts and his emphasis on sexuality in children, which they considered revolting. 'The sex theories are not the whole of Freud's work,' wrote a physician at the Middlesex Hospital. 'They are not even its most important part. Freud's great contribution to science has been his demonstration of the [unconscious] mechanisms underlying so much of normal and abnormal life.'[33]

The 1913 Medical Congress in London devoted an entire session to psychoanalysis and may even have invited Freud to address it. In the end, however, the main speech was made by Pierre Janet, who read 'a brilliant and witty paper of considerable length' criticising Freud for 'borrowing his terms and attaching new meanings to them.' Janet agreed with Freud in thinking that traumatic events could leave 'memory' in the mind but sharply disagreed with Freud's view that trauma always existed, and that it was always a 'trauma of an undoubtedly sexual character'. Janet was followed to the rostrum by Freud's former disciple Carl Gustav Jung, who had himself recently broken with the master. He, too, attacked 'the sexual basis of all neurosis' as 'too narrow a standpoint.' It was left to Freud's London representative, Ernest Jones, to defend Freudian psychoanalysis. The discussion that followed 'seemed likely on one or two points to take an acrimonious tinge.'

* * *

The wranglings of psychoanalysts would have been of no interest to Britain's working-class population as it went about its Friday evening routines in August 1913. 'At week-ends,' Robert Roberts recalled of his boyhood in Salford, 'people purged themselves with great doses of black draught, senna pods, cascara and their young with Gregory powder, liquorice powder and California syrup of figs. For all these on Friday they came to the shop in constant procession. Through the advice of doctors and wide advertisement the working class had an awful fear of constipation, a condition brought on by the kind of food they ate.' Yet these people, he added, 'had to be seriously ill before a household would saddle itself with the expense of calling a doctor.'[34]

But they, too, had their culture of nerves. If the well-to-do took nerves to their doctors, nerves were vectored into the working-class by an alliance between patent medicine and the New Journalism. The advertising of quack cures had a long history in England, but the creation of a mass press, launched by Lord Northcliffe's *Daily Mail* in 1896, gave medical advertisers new power to reach a wide audience. The Edwardian era was 'the Golden age' of advertising when 'an advertiser, unhampered by codes of ethics, scarcely restricted by legislation, unconfused by market research theorists, could pit his wits against the world and score spectacular successes.'

> Are you in the full glory of manly strength?
> Are you a man in every sense of the word?

asked an advertisement in 1915. Readers who doubted their own potency were urged to write for a booklet on 'electricity, the road to Health.'

> The Ajax Dry Cell Battery pours a stream of new life into your weakened body and Courage, Ambition and Energy will fire your soul again.[35]

At this time a large proportion of press advertising was medical. 'In the pages of a single magazine,' a social investigator reported in 1912, 'one may find advertised guaranteed cures for almost every disease that human nature is heir to.' 'Millions of the new literates,' recalled Roberts, 'were reading newspaper advertisements without the knowledge to gauge their worth. Innumerable nostrums, some harmless, some vicious, found ready sale among the ignorant.' Many of the products offered cures for nerve complaints.[36]

In the United States, the more genteel sections of the press began to break their dependence on patent medicine advertising, but in Britain the impetus for reform had to come from outside. The British Medical Association campaigned against 'secret remedies', using as its weapon chemical analysis of the medicines. *More Secret Remedies* (1912) showed, for example, that the popular nerve tonic 'Phosferine', widely advertised as 'the greatest of all tonics, a proven remedy' for 'nervous debility', 'brain fag' and much else, contained nothing but alcohol, quinine, phosphoric acid and a little sulphuric acid.[37]

Phosferine was evidently a bit strong for some. The makers of 'Dr Hartmann's Antineurasthin', advertised as 'a brain and nerve food' specially intended for 'The Twentieth Century Disease', emphasised that it had 'none of the depressing reaction that follows the administration of artificial drug stimulants.' This, they claimed, was 'a special brain and nerve nutrient, and not a brain and nerve drug-irritant.'

> No longer need the brain worker struggle on under the cloud of fear of failing powers of brain and body. He or she may, by including Antineurasthin as an article vitally necessary in the daily dietary, build up and maintain that perfect balance of mental and physical power which alone can uphold health and happiness.

Chemical analysis showed that Antineurasthin contained 'about a teaspoonsful of beaten-up egg and a wineglassful of skim milk.' The BMA's campaign led to the setting up a House of Commons Select Committee on Patent Medicines which, with fine timing,published a damning report on the industry in August 1914. Its recommendations were not implemented until 1941.[38]

*   *   *

There was, though, another way for the poor to have 'nerves', by being involved in accidents. In 1913, the Manchester surgeon William Thorburn gave a paper on 'traumatic neurosis', based on his experience in treating some 5,000 cases, including a large number of people thrown into the sea when the pier at the seaside resort of Morecambe collapsed in 1885. Until the mid-nineteenth century, he said, accidents had been 'isolated or sporadic occurrences.' 'The victims were generally left to shift for themselves; public interest was hardly concerned with their affairs; the law practically ignored them; the press did not interview them.'[39]

The railway had changed all that. 'Railway collisions, their sudden occurrence, their dramatic setting, association of large numbers of injured, the social prominence of many victims, the wide publication of newspaper reports, and the growing importance of financial claim,' had all, Thorburn argued, 'created a lurid mental picture in the injured, and indirectly affected the general public in such a way as to prepare a fertile soil for nervous disturbance, while, owing to the nature of the railway collision, there appeared also many cases characterised by great pain in the back.' There had indeed been violent medical controversy in the late nineteenth century on the question of 'railway spine' – whether the back pains complained of by railway accident victims were caused by physical damage to their spines or were 'hysterical' or 'psychological' in nature. Those who argued the psychological case had eventually prevailed, thus saving the railway companies large sums in damages. 'Railway spine' first brought to medical attention the thorny problem of the role played in patients' symptoms by the prospect of receiving compensation. 'The worry and uncertainty of litigation after accidents of this sort are often an aggravating factor,' declared one standard medical text. A prominent London neurologist was more sympathetic. While 'patients with a low power of resistance' were, of course, 'especially liable to become neurasthenic from any accidental cause,' it should also be remembered that 'even healthy individuals, without neuropathic taint, may be rendered neurasthenic, as a result of overstrain, or trauma, plus emotion.'[40]

The issue of compensation was given greater importance by the 1911 National Insurance Act, which provided general compensation for sickness. The 1913 London Congress heard a long address from Britain's leading authority on malingering, the wheedling Aberdonian Dr John Collie, warning of the need to take special precautions to prevent abuse. Out and out malingering was rare, he believed, but there were many unintentionally dishonest people who remained long on the sick list 'as a result of an introspection which savours of cowardice, a bad heredity, or a pessimistic temperament.' Collie also drew on the newly-fashionable discipline of psychology to argue that sick and injured workmen 'unconsciously' valued 'their abnormal sensations in so far as they influence the continuance of sick pay' and seemed to be 'congenitally incapable of appreciating ordinary moral obligations when it rests with them to decide whether they shall or shall not return to work.' It was quite wrong, he said, to think that only the 'highly strung and delicately nurtured' used their symptoms for compensation. 'The stolid, respectable working man, when taken out of his normal somewhat humdrum existence and placed in a suitable environment,' was quite as likely to 'react to his surroundings and, as result, ultimately succumb to the temptations of the pettifogging lawyer.'

* * *

The Section of the 1913 Congress devoted to Military Medicine heard papers on 'sanitary organization in the tropics', 'caisson disease in divers', the 'physiology of exercise', the evacuation of the wounded and the treatment of syphilis.

Nothing, however, was said about the role of nerves in war. No attempt was made to follow up a report, given to a German medical congress in 1907, on *Kriegsneurosen*, nervous troubles observed in Russian officers during the war with Japan two years before. The symptoms, a German doctor had reported, were 'like those observed in traumatic neurosis or the "railway brain" of civilians – partly of a neurasthenic and hysterical and partly of a hypochondriacal character.'[41]

This lack of concern reflected the fact that there were still no specialist neurologists or psychiatrists in the Royal Army Medical Corps in 1913. The Army itself was, as H. G. Wells wrote, 'a thing aloof . . . it had developed all the characteristics of a caste . . . it was inadaptable and conservative.' Yet the shocks of the Anglo-Boer War of 1899–1902 had forced the Army to analyse its own reduced effectiveness. When it was noticed that recruits to the Army turned out to be smaller than they had been in the 1840s, widespread fears that the race was 'degenerating' seemed also to be confirmed.[42]

The torrent of rhetoric about 'degeneration' continued in the educated weeklies of the 1900s; only psychic phenomena receiving more space. Levels of lunacy, alcoholism and mental deficiency were all rising, confirming to biologically-minded doctors like Frederick Mott at Claybury Asylum that the country's racial stock was declining. What made it all the more alarming was that while the middle-class birth-rate was beginning to fall sharply, that of the very poor – the 'residuum' – remained high. 'The brain of this country,' declared Mrs Tweedie of the newly-founded Eugenics Education Society, 'is not keeping pace with the growth of weak-minded imbecility and vice.' 'Have We the Grit of our Forefathers?' asked the influential peer Lord Meath, who found signs of a 'decadent spirit' amongst portions of all classes.[43]

Such fears of genetic dilution were not confined to Britain. They led French psychologists to introduce intelligence testing in schools and their American colleagues to create the Intelligence Quotient ('IQ'), as a way of assessing the intelligence of immigrants. In Britain, though, particular attention focused on the question of mental retardation. 'The multiplication of the Feeble-minded' was 'a terrible danger to the race,' wrote Winston Churchill, then Liberal Home Secretary, in 1912.[44]

Many army officers had similar worries. Their particular fear, according to Tim Travers, was that 'the traditional military qualities of the army and the nation were being eroded and undermined' by 'too much individualism and too little discipline; the rise of unpatriotic working-class politics; the instability of the town-bred masses, especially in case of an invasion, and the declining military virility of the nation.' But military men were themselves divided about the solution. Some, like Lord Roberts and Colonel Baden-Powell, favoured conscription, believing that 'the solution to Britain's moral decay and decline in military qualities' was 'to discipline the nation by imposing compulsory military service upon its youth.' Others, like General Sir Ian Hamilton 'felt that the military instincts of the race were best expressed by the *esprit de corps* and primordial enthusiasm of the volunteer spirit.' A vigorous war of pamphlets ensued.[45]

Both schools of thought agreed, however, on the vital importance of *morale* in modern warfare. Only the will of the soldier to fight, it was believed, could prevail against the new technologies of war, and reverse the imbalance between the offensive and the defensive brought about by the arrival of the machine-gun and modern artillery. Throughout the 1900s, military minds had wrestled with the implications of the new weaponry before ultimately concluding that only by re-emphasising the offensive could the 'fire-swept zone' created by the new technologies of war be overcome.

So, the 'human factor' remained predominant. Military thinkers disagreed, however, as to whether the soldier's will to fight was best mobilised by sterner discipline or by the inculcation of such vague abstractions as 'racial cohesion' or 'national fighting instinct' and a sense of duty, honour and self-sacrifice. It became fashionable to talk about 'the psychological battlefield' and a few military intellectuals turned to ideas popularised by the French psychologist, le Bon, in his studies of crowd behaviour during the Commune of 1870, to argue that in battle, as in the crowd, the individual lost his rational powers of self-preservation and surrendered to the 'irrational collective mentality of the crowd'. The genuine military commander, it was suggested, had 'hypnotic powers of leadership' and conferred on the 'crowd/regiment the forward action of his will power, literally willing and compelling victory.' In fact this proved to be a more accurate prophecy of inter-war fascism than of the 1914–18 war.[46]

This apart, however, no systematic attempt was made to apply to military tactics the large body of academic research then being done on subjects like exhaustion. Nor, for all the agonising over 'degeneration' and deficiency in the population, did the Army think to change its recruitment methods.

*   *   *

Edwardians took for granted an equation between masculinity, virility, courage and emotional self-control. 'For the best part of a hundred years,' the military historian Sir Michael Howard has written, 'war did indeed "define masculinity" in British society. War was a test of manhood.'[47]

The military code of honour derived from the landed aristocracy, a class which had always regarded war as its ultimate justification, and which kept in training when there was not a war to be fought by duelling, hunting and dangerous activities of various kinds. With the 'socialisation' of the middle-classes by public schools in the nineteenth century the same mindset was transmitted to them. The English public school education, the Clarendon commission had declared in 1864, was 'an instrument for the training of character'. 'The English people,' the commission went on, 'were indebted to these schools for the qualities on which they pique themselves most – for their capacity to govern others and control themselves, their aptitude for combining freedom with order, their public spirit, their vigour and manliness of character, their strong but not slavish respect for public opinion, their love of healthy sports and exercise.'[48]

From about this time also, attempts were made to 'extend Christian manliness to working-class adolescents' through organisations like the Boys' Brigade, the Lads' Drill Association, and the Boy Scouts, which offered young men a chance to savour physical activity and adventure, while instilling in them (in varying degrees) patriotism, religion and a diluted version of the public school ethic. Much has recently been written about such 'character factories', one view being that while they attracted the upwardly aspiring upper-working-class or lower-middle-class young (or their parents), they had less appeal to the 'lumpen-proletariat', for whom the attainment of manliness continued to require 'an elongated "rite of passage" . . . through swaggering, brawling and the oblivion induced by either alcohol or violence.'[49]

Public schoolboys were taught that emotional self-control – repression, as the Freudians would call it – was one of the cornerstones of character. The 'stiff upper lip' left its mark on late-Victorian psychiatry in a distaste for therapies based on 'self-absorption', which were thought to encourage 'morbid introspection' or 'unnatural egotism'. The dominant view was that patients needed to learn 'not the indulgence but a forgetfulness of their feelings, not the observation but the renunciation of self, not introspection, but useful action.'[50]

But although we tend to think of the British as always having had stiff upper-lips the history of emotions is more complicated than that. 'Emotional display,' Michael Howard argues, had been 'quite normal among the British upper-classes until the early nineteenth century. Self-control came in with the Victorians, as did sombre decorum in dress, largely as a result of the spread of bourgeois Evangelism upward from the middle classes. It is significant that the "role model" for the English gentleman well into our own century was the cool, low-key Duke of Wellington, a man famous for his understatements; not the romantically heroic Lord Nelson with his bravura public displays of emotion.' Before the arrival of the public schools there was an early Victorian cult of male domesticity and sensitivity (evoked in *David Copperfield*); in the 1890s there was a 'decadent' counterattack, brought to an end by the scandalous arrest of Oscar Wilde. Then, in the late 1900s, virility and manliness again came under fire, and new currents of opposition began to flow, which equated self-control with hypocrisy and so-cial repression. This mood is powerfully expressed in a moment in E. M. Forster's *Longest Journey* where the hero Rickie urges a girl whose fiancé has just been killed, to express her feelings, to 'mind'.

'It's the worst thing that can ever happen to you in all your life, and you've got to mind it – you've got to mind it. They'll come saying, "Bear up – trust to time." No, no: they're wrong. Mind it.'[51]

A recent historian of Edwardian Britain has argued that it was a society with two faces. One was masculine and reaching out to the colonies. 'Imperial visions,' José Harris has written, 'injected a powerful strain of hierarchy, militarism, "frontier mentality", administrative rationality and masculine civic virtue into British political culture.' The other face, however, was feminine and inward-looking; 'domestic political forces were running in quite the opposite direction, towards egalitarianism, "progressivism", consumerism, popular democracy, feminism and women's rights.' The approach to shell-shock by the British Army, medical profession and public would in part be shaped by this division.[52]

On 16 August 1913, the Seventeenth International Congress of Medicine drew to a close. In his farewell address, the President implored the representatives of the great nations 'to make their undoubted influence felt in the direction of blessed peace.'

A year later, their countries were at war with each other.

SHELL-SHOCK IN FRANCE

In December 1914, alarming reports reached the War Office in London that large numbers of soldiers were being evacuated from the British Expeditionary Force in Europe with 'nervous and mental shock'. Some 7–10% of all officers and 3–4% of all ranks, it was said, were being sent home suffering from nervous or mental breakdown. Dr William Aldren Turner, an experienced Queen Square neurologist, was sent out to France to investigate.[1]

Aldren Turner reported that during the heavy fighting in October 1914, when the British Army held the Germans before the Flemish town of Ypres but lost a third of its own strength, there had indeed been a rash of cases where men had become paralysed under shellfire or had been reduced by exhaustion and strain to a state of collapse. Many of them were showing peculiar symptoms. Unfortunately, however, Dr Turner was unable to stay in France to deal with this problem; he had to return to medical commitments in London. Nor could his Queen Square colleague, Dr Gordon Holmes, working in a hospital in Boulogne, help; he was overwhelmed by the enormous number of head wounds requiring brain surgery. However, there happened to be on the staff of a wartime hospital established in the casino at le Touquet, a distinguished psychologist from Cambridge University, Dr Charles Myers, who *was* available. They had urged him to take on the 'psychological work'.

Dr Myers was summoned to London. Charming, intelligent, he had just been made a Fellow of the Royal Society (for his academic work). As we have seen, he had already treated three cases of shell-shock at le Touquet and written an article on the subject in the medical journal, the *Lancet*. He seemed ideal.[2]

Charles Myers came from a prosperous London Jewish family. A sunny, successful type, his mother's favourite, he had reached Cambridge at sixteen and there taken up the new discipline of psychology. He was, in every sense, a man of wide culture: a fine musician who had, as a young graduate, taken part in a pioneering anthropological expedition to New Guinea, which for the first time used the techniques of modern science to study 'primitive' people. Myers had spent a year studying the islanders' hearing, sense of smell, reaction times, rhythm and music, while his Cambridge colleagues W. H. R. Rivers and William McDougall had explored their marriage customs and tested their vision and sensibility to pain.[3]

Myers qualified as a doctor but had never practised. Instead, he helped Rivers to run the tiny Cambridge psychology department. When Rivers turned to anthropology, Myers took it over himself, paying out of his own pocket for a laboratory equipped in the latest German manner. His *Textbook of Experimental Psychology* and pioneering work on ethnographic music helped to make the 1900s 'perhaps the most exciting decade in psychology since the death of Aristotle'. His real talents, though, were social and administrative. Few could resist his winning smile, his encouragement and his hospitality.[4]

Already 41 years old in 1914, Myers had had a struggle to find a role in the war, but he was a skilful networker. Eventually, he went to Paris and persuaded the Duchess of Westminster to take him on to the staff of the hospital she was establishing at le Touquet. But that proved a frustrating experience for initially he was not allowed by the other doctors there to see patients. However, while in Paris, Myers had, with his usual energy and resourcefulness, visited the French neurologist Dejerine at the Salpêtrière hospital, where he had noticed many interesting cases of soldiers who had become dumb or partially paralysed. A Cambridge colleague had also shown him 'a queer case of aphasia [lack of speech]' in Boulogne. He had thus been alerted to the risk of 'hysterical and neurasthenic breakdown' in men who had been exposed to the 'shattering effects of the great German shells'.

Sure enough, when, after many false alarms, the first train load of patients arrived at the Hospital at le Touquet, Myers found his first British shell-shock case. Others soon followed. The other doctors showing no interest in these patients, Myers was allowed to make 'certain investigations' and quickly established that shelling sometimes affected the senses of vision, taste, and hearing.

There was no doubting Myers' interest in the problem. 'It was clear to me,' he wrote twenty years later, 'that my previous psychological training and my present interests fitted me for the treatment of these cases.' Thus it was that a university don with no previous experience of military medicine or asylum psychiatry, who had scarcely practised as a doctor, became chief 'Specialist in Nervous Shock' to the British Army in France. As so often in wartime, the readiness was all.[5]

On 16 March 1915, Myers packed his baggage into an ambulance and drove the five miles up the coast to Boulogne to take up his new duties. The next day, his diary records, he saw in the 'Base' hospitals nearby a dozen 'most interesting cases – including one of incessant terror bordering on acute mania; this a boy absolutely impervious to his surroundings, dodging shells from under the bed clothes.' A week later, Myers had sole charge of some 20 cases and, with a car and driver scrounged from the Red Cross, was energetically touring the hospitals. By the end of the month, he could record 'a remarkably successful first session with a mute patient, very considerably restoring his power of speech' and a 'pleasant drive' over to an Indian hospital to examine 'some neurasthenia cases characterised by a peculiar stoop in the walk.' Myers' role quickly expanded. Appointed to 'arrange the dispatch of mental and nervous cases from France to England', he was rapidly drawn into giving advice in courts martial, handling psychiatric and neurological cases for which he had little training and trying to overhaul the administrative procedures of army medicine. His elevation to the rank of Lt.-Colonel early in 1916 was an essential part of the process; by then Myers had learnt the importance of rank to the military machine.

His mood of purposeful energy was not, however, to last; in time it was replaced by frustration, anger, and eventually, bitterness. In retrospect Myers felt that he had been ceaselessly struggling against 'errors of omission, commission and especially of wasteful procrastination.' He believed that despite all his efforts, an unnecessary human tragedy took place, ruining many lives that could have been saved. The Army, for its part, would come to feel that the intervention of Myers and other psychologists simply made the task of winning the war more difficult.[6]

At the core of it all was a conflict between two models of human behaviour: the Army's – simple, robust, and clear, but increasingly inadequate to meet the strains and pressures of modern weapons unleashed on a conscript force – and that towards which Myers and his colleagues were groping – more shaded and complex, but much harder to define and much easier to abuse.

Myers' new colleagues, the Royal Army Medical Corps, were not a body of men greatly respected in the medical profession. Coaching army doctors for their examinations, Ernest Jones found them 'a jolly lot', 'recruited from that part of the profession who put adventure or an easy life before interest in their scientific activities.' To a prominent medical academic, they were the 'dregs' of the medical schools.[7]

In fact it was a little more complicated than that. Medicine then was an anxious business economically, calling for social skills and top hats, and many years of waiting for such crumbs as smart consultants chose to hand out. It was also very cliquey. Anyone without private means or connections found it hard to get established – Conan Doyle was a famous example of a doctor who got bored waiting for patients. Army medicine offered an escape from the rat race that many were happy to take, especially the products of the less fashionable Irish and Scottish medical schools. The RAMC did also have some pockets of excellence, most notably the Indian Medical Service, where tropical medicine was pioneered.

But the overall culture of the RAMC remained profoundly cautious and conservative, cut off from the wider world of science and preoccupied by its arcane administrative rituals. 'N. B. R.' – No Bloody Research – was a famous RAMC battle cry. During the Boer War of 1899–1902, the negligence of Army doctors and a failure to educate soldiers in elementary habits of hygiene ('Tommy doesn't understand it and his officer regards it as a fad') resulted in five times more soldiers dying from disease than from enemy bullets. When this disaster was exposed by numerous newspaper stories and a Royal Commission, the RAMC was forced to let some fresh air into its closed world and obliged to make contact with civilian medicine. Indeed, between 1905 and 1910 its energetic and forward-looking administrator, Sir Alfred Keogh, recruited most of the London hospital consultants into the Army reserve for the war he knew was coming, and brought about a transformation in attitude and performance without which trench warfare would have been impossible: the men would simply have died of typhoid and cholera.[8]

The emphasis, though, was on surgery and sanitation. Mental medicine, neurology even, remained a black hole as far as the RAMC was concerned, so that reports on the after-effects of shellfire written by Army surgeons after the Boer War and the Balkan War of 1912–13 (which read today as premonitions of shell-shock) were never followed up. During his entire period in France, Charles Myers 'never met with a regular officer who had any specialist's training and experience in mental or nervous diseases and disorders.'[9]

Wartime control of the RAMC was divided between the Medical Overlord in London, Sir Alfred Keogh, and his counterpart in France, Sir Arthur Sloggett. They were very different men. The son of an Irish magistrate, Keogh was an intellectual as Army doctors went, trusted by London consultants and friendly with Liberal politicians like R. B. Haldane, whose Army reforms he had helped implement. Called out of retirement in 1914, Keogh coped admirably with an administrative nightmare and showed great sensitivity to popular opinion.[10]

If Keogh represented some of the more 'feminine' sides of Edwardian public culture, Sir Arthur Sloggett embodied the masculine. He was the classic RAMC type: the rollicking man of action.

... Entered RAMC 1881 ... served Indian frontier 1884; Dongola Expeditionary Force 1896 as Senior MO; Soudan 1897 and 1898 including Khartoum (dangerously wounded, horse shot, despatches, promoted, 3rd class Medjedie, 2 clasps); South Africa 1899–1903 ...[11]

He looked the part, too – the neatly trimmed moustache, the jaunty walk, the bantering manner: 'We'll make a dashin' Captain of you,' he said mockingly when welcoming the portly Charles Myers into the RAMC. Sloggett had made sure that the 'best brands of champagne procurable in Cairo' were carted two thousand miles up the Nile in 1898, and then been shot through the chest at the Battle of Omdurman, surviving because 'my heart was in my boots'. He enlivened Sir Douglas Haig's 'New Year beano' in 1916 with 'yarns, some of which were libellous and few of which would have passed muster in a drawing room' and boasted to his 'old Egyptian' friend, Winston Churchill, 'that he [could] give the best dinner in St Omer, with fabulous tales of his port and brandy.' But Sloggett was more than just a crony. If he knew little about academic medicine, he was respected as a tough-minded administrator, 'efficient and wise.'[12]

If Keogh had the ear of politicians and do-gooders, Sloggett, in his château behind the lines, was much more immediately under the sway of the Army machine, notably that section most responsible for discipline, the Adjutant-General's office. As Myers quickly discovered, the issues of shell-shock and discipline were intricately interwoven.

Military medicine is always practised within a service culture, especially with the British, who did not have conscript soldiers as the Europeans did. The 'Old Army' – the pre-1914 British Regular Army – was based on a set of traditional values, like the officers' code recalled, half a century later, by a captain in a Scottish regiment.

Psychologists, sociologists and the like had not yet been invented so there was no pernicious jargon to cloud simple issues. Right was right and wrong was wrong and the Ten Commandments were an admirable guide . . . A coward was not someone with a 'complex' (we would not have known what it was) but just a despicable creature . . . Frugality, austerity, and self-control were then perfectly acceptable. We believed in honour, patriotism, self-sacrifice and duty and we clearly understood what was meant by a 'gentleman'.[13]

Towards the rank and file, the Army had an even more rough and ready model of human psychology, and its own clear-cut labels. Men were either sick, well, wounded or mad; anyone neither sick, wounded, nor mad but nonetheless unwilling to or incapable of fighting was necessarily a coward, to be shot if necessary. The model was crude, but had seemed to serve effectively enough the Army's purpose: to take poor human material, mainly 'economic drop outs', and forge it into a blunt but reliable instrument of war.

Discipline was tough and often arbitrary; the conditions, usually poor; the men, ignorant and uneducated. But harsh physical training and carefully inculcated regimental spirit provided great internal cohesion and strength. The attitude to mental disorder was closely interwoven with the complex masculine codes – of honour, superstition, self-control and comradeship – on which the Army was based. Mental illness was equated with weakness and lack of self-control, something to be treated by disciplinary methods until it reached the point where committal to an asylum became necessary.[14]

Although the Army had behind it centuries of experience of the psychological effects of war, it had never been its official practice to do much about them. 'No doubt there were men who from one cause or another broke down in every campaign,' the military historian Sir John Fortescue conceded in 1922; but, as such cases were dismissed as 'not differing greatly from cowardice', no adequate · records of them survived. On the other hand, he added, 'large numbers of men went out of their minds in the old campaigns, as they still do'; it was tacitly understood that 'even the bravest man cannot endure to be under fire for more than a certain number of consecutive days' and 'tired old soldiers in former wars' used to disappear mysteriously for periods of rest and recovery.[15]

The virtues of the Old Army emerged clearly in the early battles of the war: regular soldiers showed great resilience in the long retreat from Mons in the autumn of 1914 and the rapidity of their musketry (which the Germans took for machine-gun fire) quickly became part of British folklore. Even then, though, another facet was beginning to appear. A doctor noticed, among soldiers evacuated back to England, 'the number of patients who had apparently had an unfortunate childhood' and 'seemed to have enlisted in the army to escape from a world which had been hard on them from their early years.' In the opinion of another doctor, the Army of 1914 'contained a proportion of wasters and half-wits who broke down easily.'[16]

These virtues or shortcomings rapidly became academic, for by the end of 1914 the 'old' Army had ceased to exist, bled to death in the battles of that autumn. In its place came Territorials and the mass of young volunteers who answered Kitchener's call to the colours. Amid the chaos and confusion of recruiting, no proper attempt was made to assess even the physical health of these men, an important, but probably unavoidable, failure of policy. 'The whole country,' one medical examiner later recalled, 'was simply seething with recruits.'

They were medically examined, I say it without fear of contradiction, in the most haphazard manner. 20 to 30% of the men were never medically examined at all. I know of one doctor who medically examined 400 men per day for ten days and he didn't work 24 hours a day. Large numbers of people joined up who were quite unfit for service life, let alone trench warfare.[17]

Proper medical examination of recruits was not established until late in 1917. Even then, the primary emphasis remained on physical health rather than psychological or mental strength. In 1915 the idea of 'intelligence' as something measurable was still in its infancy and had certainly not penetrated the British Army. The only mental defects recognised by military recruiters were syphilis, lunacy (for which an asylum certificate was required) and epilepsy. Many officers believed that the less intelligent recruit actually made a better soldier, just as they preferred countrymen to 'stunted creatures' from the towns.[18]

Moreover, doctors were not important people in the Army's traditional culture; the Royal Army Medical Corps had had great difficulty in establishing itself. If military doctors knew their place and did not speak unless spoken to, they also knew that their job was to prevent 'wastage' or, in modern American terms, 'keep up the fighting strength'. They knew that 'all wounds and sickness in an Army are a military problem' because they offered the soldier a means of escape, an honourable exit from the battlefield, and that their job was to prevent malingering. Wounds were wounds, inflicted by the enemy, and therefore honourable (unless of course they were self-inflicted and the Adjutant-General's office always kept a close eye out for those), but the doctor who joined the Army during the war found himself having to invert normal civilian practice and go to great lengths to deny that a soldier was sick, 'unless an audible death rattle could prevent him from doing so.' Usually the soldier would be given a 'brisk' laxative and have his card marked with the hated words 'Medicine and Duty'.[19]

But Charles Myers came from a different background. He was an academic scientist, accustomed to speaking his mind; the role of the silent servant of the

military machine did not come easily to him. Intellectually intrigued
enigma of shell-shock, he continued to publish papers and, to get a clearer
of how the condition developed, spent several weeks working at Casua
Clearing Stations, the makeshift hospitals a few miles from the line where soldiers
arrived fresh from the front and the first diagnosis of their condition was made.
He also kept a close eye on what the French were doing. By the middle of 1916,
Myers had seen over two thousand cases of shell-shock.[20]

At the same time, he took practical initiatives. His first battle was to get the
Army to acknowledge shell-shock as something distinct from the traditional
categories of wounded, sick, well or mad and to provide separate facilities for its
treatment in France, so that 'innocent men who had mentally broken down
under the strain of warfare' were not flung together with the genuinely insane,
epileptics and criminals, or put into general wards with wounded soldiers (who
mocked and taunted them). It took almost a year to get much done, but by the
middle of 1916 specialist facilities for the treatment of shell-shock were at last
provided in Boulogne.

However, most cases of shell-shock continued to be evacuated back to
England, where they were often left to moulder unattended, and from where they
seldom returned. Myers soon saw that both for the men and for the Army, this
was unnecessary. By treating soldiers as if they were mad (or 'mental' as Sloggett
continued to call them), the Army was often pushing them into genuine insanity.
Yet many patients, far from suffering from some rare and incurable nervous
disease or deep-seated mental disorder, were just badly shook-up or temporarily
confused. Myers believed that they could often, if treated quickly and expertly,
get over their problems and go back to the war; or, at any rate, resume normal
civilian life and not be a burden to the state in years to come; the issue of war
pensions and their cost was already looming.

In line with this conviction, Myers began in May 1916 to press the case for
treating shell-shock even earlier, not at the Base but at specialist hospitals only a
few miles from the front. He was convinced, from his own experience and that of
the French, that such an innovation would dramatically reduce the levels of
'wastage'. He was in fact putting forward the principle of 'proximity' on which
all modern military psychiatry is based. But he met with strong opposition,
particularly from the Adjutant-General's department. The traditional view that
'we can't be lumbered with lunatics in Army areas' proved hard to shake.[21]

Myers also came to realise that there were other elements in the equation that
were out of his control.

* * *

The Western Front, as Paul Fussell has shown, was never isolated from the
political and social pressures of London and Paris. The officer/poets studied by
Fussell read the literary weeklies in the trenches; the men read the popular papers;
doctors kept up with the medical journals. As a result, events in France reflected
the mood at home, and the handling of shell-shock was considerably affected by

subject going on in Britain. Indeed, one important witness
ontested domain' of shell-shock was 'in a great part grabbed
he general community; which largely set ... the policy to
: least, the medical service and profession [had] to conform.'[22]
an early example of a common modern phenomenon: a
zed with scientific qualifications, taken up by public opinion
in an oversimplified way. 'This class of case,' a doctor noticed,
'aroused more general interest and attention and sympathy than any other.' The
early medical model of shell-shock, dominated by the image of the shell itself – a
violent, concussive *deus ex machina*, which arrived from out of the heavens and
left the soldier a shattered, gibbering wreck, his nerves destroyed and his special
senses, like eyesight and hearing, impaired – imbedded itself, in a crude and oversimplified way, in the public imagination.[23]

Historians have yet to explore in detail the coverage of shell-shock in the
popular press, though one doctor said later that 'two years of vivid journalese in
the home press prepared the minds of the drafts.' Certainly, a glance at two mass-
circulation papers in September 1915 shows that trench warfare was grafted easily
on to the pre-war culture of 'nerves'. An enormous advertising campaign for the
drug Phosferine (denounced by the BMA in 1912), carried photographs and
endorsements from serving soldiers who told readers how, 'in the nerve-racking
atmosphere of the trenches, just as much as in Civil Life after a hard day's work,'
the tonic generated the 'vital energy to overcome the dulling of the senses, the
numbing of the faculties, caused by the tremendous cannonade.' The drug
claimed to provide the 'extra nerve force to overcome the bodily discomforts, the
brain fatigue experienced under shellfire.'[24]

We do, however, know how shell-shock was presented to more literate readers.
'The effects of severe shelling,' *The Times* reported early in 1915, 'tend to show
themselves in a dazed state which may on the one hand be developed into
complete unconsciousness, on the other lightened till a condition comparable to
neurasthenia is observed.'

The soldier, having passed into this state of lessened control, becomes a prey to his
primitive instincts. He may be so affected that changes occur in his sense perceptions; he
may become blind or deaf or lose the sense of smell or taste. He is cut off from his normal
self and the associations that go to make up that self. Like a carriage which has lost its
driver he is liable to all manner of accidents. At night insomnia troubles him and such
sleep as he gets is full of visions; past experiences on the battlefield are recalled vividly; the
will that can brace a man against fear is lacking.[25]

The fact that phrases like 'wounds of consciousness' or 'the wounded mind' filled
the newspapers and that questions were asked in Parliament about the 'nerve-
shattered soldier' had a direct affect on military policy. Late in 1915, the Army
Council in London broke with past practice and for the first time officially
recognised the existence of a grey area between cowardice and madness. It tried,
however, to impose on shell-shock the traditional military distinction between

'battle casualties' and sickness: between wounds – which carried honour and dignity – and simple breakdown, which did not. This distinction was to be defined by 'enemy action' – whether or not the soldier had been under enemy shellfire. The Army in France was instructed that 'Shell-shock and shell concussion cases should have the letter W prefixed to the report of the casualty, if it was due to the enemy: in that case the patient would be entitled to rank as "wounded" and to wear on his arm a "wound stripe".' If, however, the man's breakdown did not follow a shell explosion, it was not thought to be 'due to the enemy'; and he was to labelled 'Shell-shock, S' (for sickness) and was not entitled to a wound stripe or a pension.[26]

The effect of this policy was further to exacerbate an already confused situation. Depending on circumstances, a shell-shocked soldier might earn a wound stripe and a pension (provided his condition was caused by enemy action), be shot for cowardice, or simply be told to pull himself together by his medical officer and sent back to duty. The Army Council's writ did not always have much impact on medical practice at the front, where doctors continued to label patients 'Mental' or 'Insane' or even 'GOK' (God Only Knows) before sending them to the Base. But it soon became clear that soldiers were quick to respond to the Army Council's invitation and were seizing on the advantages of shell-shock. 'We have seen too many dirty sneaks go down the line under the term shell-shock,' medical officers complained to Myers, 'to feel any great sympathy with the condition.' The word had become a 'parrot cry', on the tongue of all officers and men, the 'invariable answer' soldiers evacuated to Aid Posts gave to doctors' enquiries. 'Shell shock should be abolished,' Myers was told. 'The men have got to know the term and will tell you quite glibly that they are suffering from shell shock when really a very different description might be applied to their condition.'[27]

Myers was in 'hearty agreement' with these views, having 'also seen too many men at Base Hospitals and Casualty Clearing Stations boasting that they were "suffering from shellshock, Sir," when there was nothing appreciably amiss with them save funk.' 'It had,' he wrote later, 'proved impossible to legislate for the bad, without doing injustice to the good, soldier.' Some men were being given an easy option out of the trenches and were taking it, whereas others, who were genuinely suffering, were being denied proper treatment. He cited the case of an artillery officer who tried to keep going after a bombardment, collapsed, and ended up being labelled 'Nervousness' (by which was meant 'Shell-shock S') while two of his men, who gave way immediately, were sent down the line marked 'Shell-shock W', because their mental condition originated (according to regulations) 'immediately on their exposure to the effects of a specific explosion due to enemy action.' The two soldiers, 'by giving way immediately, became entitled to rank as wounded and wear a wound stripe'; the officer, by bravely refusing to do so, was sent down later stigmatised as 'nervous'.[28]

It was at about this point, in mid-1916, that a further complication occurred:

medical opinion, although by no means unanimous, began to shift. The dominant voice in Britain in the first two years of the war had been F. W. Mott, the pathologist to the London County Council and prolific writer and publicist for a strongly 'biological' view of mental health. Early in 1916, Mott gave a set of long, rambling lectures on 'the Effects of High Explosive on the Central Nervous System', based on his experience handling shell-shock cases at the Maudsley Hospital in South London. Where Charles Myers had brought to 'shell-shock' a psychologist's alertness to the special senses and the workings of the mind, Fred Mott had spent the previous twenty years dissecting the brains of London's lunatics. Many passages in the lectures reflect that approach. Mott argued that exposure to shellfire brought about structural or pathological changes in the central nervous system, which caused the blindness, deafness, paralysis, and other odd symptoms from which his patients were suffering. Perhaps tiny particles from shells damaged the brain; perhaps it was the effects of explosive gases.[29]

Elsewhere, though, Mott acknowledged that 'concussion' was not the whole story. He was well aware that by this time there was growing evidence that psychological factors were also involved. What role, he asked, did the soldier's state of mind prior to the explosion play in his behaviour after it? Were people of different temperament and emotional history affected in different ways? How did the symptoms of shell-shocked soldiers compare with those of the victims of civil disasters, such as railway accidents? How did the sustained experience of fear affect the soldier?

Mott struggled to reconcile his dogmatic pre-war views on the hereditary origins of mental disorder with the human suffering among 'normal' young men that now confronted him daily at the Maudsley. He argued that shell-shock was more likely to occur in 'individuals of a neuropathic or psychopathic pre-disposition' but accepted, too, that the privations of trench life, 'combined with fearful tension and misapprehension, may so lower the vital resistance of the strongest nervous system that a shell bursting near . . . is sufficient to lead to a sudden loss of consciousness.' He also acknowledged that in many cases 'psychic trauma' was exerting a continuous influence on the 'subconscious mind'.

Mott had worked only on soldiers evacuated to England. It was not till three months later, in June 1916, that the first authoritative study of shell-shock in British troops in France appeared. Harold Wiltshire, an experienced London physician, had spent a year at a base hospital in France, seen 150 cases of shell-shock, and compared notes with doctors at the front. He therefore spoke from roughly the same vantage point as Charles Myers.[30]

Wiltshire's article dealt a devastating blow to the idea that the symptoms of shell-shock were produced by the physical effects of exploding shells. For a start, he had never found such symptoms in genuinely wounded men, even though they had been even more exposed to the physical and chemical effects of shell explosions than the unwounded. Their cheerfulness was strikingly different from the morose gloom of the shell-shocked. Secondly, it was rare to find much evidence of physical concussion on shell-shock patients; indeed many of them, it turned out, had not been near an exploding shell. The real cause of their problem, said Wiltshire, was psychological (what he called 'psychic'); the prolonged strain of trench warfare wore down their resistance until 'these men were in a position of psychic tension in which they could have been knocked down by the proverbial feather and the effect of the blows was psychic rather than physical.'

Sometimes an explosion did knock them down, but, more commonly it was a 'sudden psychic shock', especially 'horrible sights', that administered the *coup de grâce*. One man was 'suffering from the mental shock caused by having to clear away the remains of a number of men killed by a shell.' Another was the only survivor of a shell explosion. Wiltshire speculated whether such sights were so damaging because, by revealing the real effects of shellfire, they destroyed the illusions on which a soldier's self-control was based. He also noted the extraordinary way in which the memory 'repressed' sights and emotions that it could not cope with.

So, by mid-1916, the doctors had finally come to the crucial understanding that, as Myers put it twenty years later, shell-shock does

Not depend for [its] causation on the physical force (or the chemical effects) of the bursting shell. [It] may also occur when the soldier is remote from the exploding missile, provided that he be subject to an emotional disturbance or mental strain sufficiently severe . . . Moreover in men already worn out or having previously suffered from the disorder, the final cause of the breakdown may be so slight, and its onset so gradual, that its origin hardly deserves the name of 'shock'. 'Shell-shock', therefore, is a singularly ill-chosen term; and in other respects . . . has proved a singularly harmful one . . . In the vast majority of cases the signs of 'shell-shock' appear traceable to psychic causes, especially, in the early cases, to the emotions of extreme and sudden horror and fright . . . Wartime 'shell-shock' was in fact very similar to peace-time 'hysteria' and 'neurasthenia'.[31]

Among British doctors, 'shell-shock' was now dead and discredited. Though Wiltshire had felt obliged to use the phrase, he thought it meaningless because it was applied indiscriminately to everything 'from concussion to sheer funk' whether due to shell explosions or not. By mid-1916, with the Battle of the Somme looming, informed medical opinion in London spoke of 'war neuroses' and 'functional nervous disorders' and did its best to play down its own part in creating the 'new and mysterious malady' of shell-shock. But if shell-shock had died in Harley Street, it remained very much alive in the British Army and among the general public; it was one of those words like harpoons which, 'once they have gone in, are very hard to get out again.' It was shell-shock's very vagueness which made it so useful, offering a neutral, physical label for a psychological condition. Shell-shock could thereby be accommodated within traditional ideas of courage and cowardice, even if the complex psychological reality revealed by Myers and Wiltshire's work in France now posed a head-on challenge to those values.[32]

The Army in France, having given official recognition to the idea of shell-shock could not abandon it as readily as the London doctors. When, therefore, Charles Myers (who had, of course, himself introduced the phrase shell-shock into the medical literature) proposed in June 1916 that it should be abandoned by the

Army and replaced by two conditions called 'concussion' and 'nervous shock', combined with proper facilities for forward treatment of cases near the front line, he had little immediate response. In spite of Wiltshire's evidence, the misleading categories 'Shell-shock W' and 'Shell-shock S' continued to be used.[33]

And while the medics and top brass argued, the men in the line struggled to live with their fears.

TRENCH WORK

In August 1915 Lieutenant Anthony Alfands had his first taste of trench warfare.

> I must say it is a devilish affair altogether. You sit like rabbits in a burrow and just wait for
> something to come and blow you to hell. You don't see the enemy and you kill very few
> of them. But you shell them very often. They do the same . . . as I write our heavies are
> pounding away like anything . . .
>
> It gets on one's nerves waiting always for the next bang. If one or two land unpleasantly
> near one's fore trench the usual effect is that you imagine every other shell is coming
> around and about the same place. If they do you lie flat on the trench and trust to luck.
> If they don't come near you well and good. Nerves seem to be the one vital thing for a
> soldier, nerves good and strong and better still no nerves.[1]

Alfands caught brilliantly the essence of trench warfare, the reason why it took
such terrible psychological toll – the powerless waiting for an impersonal death.
During 1915, Charles Wilson, the medical officer of the 1/Royal Fusiliers,
watched the effect that prolonged exposure to the trenches in the Ypres salient
was having on his men, how it was changing their perceptions of the war and of
each other. Each was discovering, once the 'Julian Grenfell mood of eager
enterprise' wore off, that the war was a matter of survival, of endurance. Of all the
things that preyed on the nerves and the senses – the noise, the filth, the smell,
the squalor, the horrors – shellfire was the worst. 'The acid test of a man in the
trenches was high explosive,' wrote Wilson, 'it taught us things about ourselves
we had not known till then.'[2]

The first thing you learnt – the easy bit – was how to tell the different types of
shell apart. There was the five-nine (called a Jack Johnson, after the black
American boxer, because of its black smoke), the whizz-bang and the four-two.
There was the 'minnie' or *Minenwerfer* which, according to General James Jack,
'you could see coming high in the air and dodge . . . if there is room and one
keeps cool.' Later on there were other, new-fangled weapons. Each had its special
noise and characteristics in the air, as distinctive as a teacher's tread down a
corridor, and its own special way of raining destruction on the ground. Guy
Chapman met an officer who could perfectly mimic them all, and Ford Madox

Ford wrote an entire letter to Joseph Conrad about shell noises. The war memoirs of the 1930s are a sustained threnody to the shell.[3]

The next lesson was in taking cover. Robert Graves claimed that you could usually hear a shell coming and take cover; he objected more to rifle fire. Most, though, found it an agonising experience, 'this loneliness in the face of shellfire.'

There is no one who can help you. You stand alone with soft frail flesh against the might of high explosive. Oh, how one loves mother earth. She is the one protector whose aid one can invoke. In her bosom is some chance of safety. How persistent she is, imperturbable. Better than strong timber or steel that splatter and warp.[4]

Then, after the wait – the explosion, which Guy Chapman remembered filled him with a 'terror in which my body seemed to dissolve and my spirit beat panic-stricken as a bird in the abyss of winter waves.'[5]

By 1915, soldiers had learned that shells could come unannounced. You might be talking to someone one minute and then, bang, a second later he would be gone. You might escape completely unmarked physically, but you might then collapse emotionally. Sometimes shellfire would provoke a sudden, dramatic nervous breakdown. Arthur Osburn, a doctor with the Irish Fusiliers, tells with unpleasant relish the story of a staff officer who ventured up to the front line for the first time – 'pink tabs on his collar and a decoration on his smart uniform' – and found himself under the kind of intense shellfire that troops in the line frequently had to endure. He promptly 'moaned and jibbered and shook his head grovelling on the ground.' When the shelling suddenly grew heavier, he appeared 'to be suddenly seized with a fresh access of terror. Wildly and incoherently he made efforts to conceal himself beneath the remains of a broken chair and the mud wall of the shelter.' Then, suddenly, spasmodically he began to dig furiously with his fingers. 'This was a case of complete loss of nerve and self-control. Driven mad with terror, slobbering and moaning, he clawed and scrabbled violently in the mud, his head under the chair. It was like a terrified and overrun fox going to ground, trying to dig his way back to safety through the very bowels of the earth.'[6]

The troops saw for themselves, as the doctors had, that often it was not the actual explosion that did the damage. In late 1915, Private Hiram Sturdy helped carry to a dressing station an Ayrshire farmer, 'muttering, slavering and shaking from head to foot, a big strong son of the soil.' He had been

Sheltering from one of those hell spasms and a shell buried itself almost at his feet and it was that few seconds' interval, waiting on the explosion, waiting to be hurled up in the air in pieces, that broke Jock. He collapsed, fell over at the knees, shivering and muttering and the shell never burst.[7]

Dramatic cases like these were exceptional. Most men hardened themselves and did their best to live with their fears. Much, of course, depended on their circumstances. There were quiet places in the line, and busy ones. To survive a month of spasmodic shellfire in a quiet sector was one sort of achievement; to live

through a day of sustained artillery barrage in a battle, whe
bursting every few feet, quite another.

Notions of courage began to change. 'We came to think le
performed on the spur of the moment, to value more the wort
was prepared to see the thing through,' wrote Charles Wilson.
like Wilson began to recognise the tell-tale signs of imminen
look for them. One day in late 1915, Wilson found himself shaking like a leaf
during a bombardment. He managed to contain his fear and told no one; a few
weeks later he noticed a sergeant alongside him also 'shivering like a reed in the
wind'.[8]

Everyone was afraid, except for a few lucky people who did not know fear.
Everyone struggled by his own methods to control that fear, to keep going. 'The
management of fear' is the subject of nearly all Great War literature; one of the
greatest of all war novels, Frederic Manning's *The Middle Part of Fortune*, is about
little else. Its protagonist, Bourne, is a man who has learnt to manage his fear,
just; to control himself over the stages of the cycle of trench warfare – in the front
line (for three or four days), in billets behind the line (another three or four days),
on leave (occasionally), back into the line, in battle. Bourne has devised a variety
and rhythm of activities, mainly involving scavenging for wine and food, with
which he occupies himself when out of the line and, like all soldiers of the Great
War, bitterly resents the High Command's efforts to keep him busy.[9]

Bourne manages to keep going (and is killed in battle). But many did not: by
the end of 1915 it was a commonplace to see men slowly crack up, gradually
become more and more affected by the conditions till eventually they would cease
to function altogether. Billy Tyrrell, a young doctor from Belfast, before the war
legendary in Ulster as an athlete and rugby-player, served with a battalion
deployed in the Ypres salient for three months on end. 'Three times . . . the other
Officers had been scuppered and the Battalion practically washed out.' After the
third time, he recollected in 1921, 'I knew I was approaching the end of my
tether.' They were then detailed for an especially difficult attack; Tyrrell was sent
on ten days' special leave to get fit for it, to 'fatten' as the troops called it.[10]

The attack went ahead on 4 July 1915. On the first day, the British managed,
at fairly small cost, to take all three German lines in the salient at Pilkem Ridge.
Tyrell's battalion, hitherto in reserve, was then put in to hold the new British
front line (the old German reserve trench). 'We all knew that after such a
successful attack, the real trouble and heavy casualties would occur when the
counterattack and shelling developed . . .'

Situations like this were a particular nightmare because the Germans knew
every detail of the position and could enfilade it with shellfire. On the evening of
5 July 1915, as Tyrrell was sitting in a German dug-out having a 'Council of
War', a 5.9-inch shell arrived, killing three officers on the spot and wounding
three more. Tyrrell escaped with singed hair. 'For the fourth time I was Senior
Officer and in charge of the situation, and the fact that I was responsible and in
charge saved my reason at the time.'

rid of the wounded, pushed the dead to one side, and tried to carry on with the
ly of bombs, ammunition, water and rations. All this time the casualties in our front
e were terrific, and our poor Battalion was being rapidly blotted out. It was a question
of holding out at all.

Eventually, 'sometime later', two senior officers came up to relieve Tyrrell.

As soon they had taken over responsibility I just shrank into one of the dug-outs. I knew
then that I could do no more . . . Then the dug-out was struck by an exceptionally big
shell which blew the whole thing down on top of me and that is all I can remember till I
came to again, I think about three or four hours later. What saved me was those huge trees
which formed the roof of the dug-out, they locked together when the dug-out was blown
in; about an hour after this happened two of my stout fellows came and dug me out.
When I came to I drank three quarters of a glass of neat whisky and carried on until we
were finally relieved by the West Riding Battalion . . .
    I mustered what remained of my Battalion behind the line, two Officer boys and less
than 300 men and proceeded to march them out. Just before dawn we met our
quartermaster, who had heard something of what had happened and came to meet us.
Now he had had previous experience of this kind of thing and ought to have known better
than to do what he did.
    He brought up all the Officers' horses and there were no Officers to ride them.
    When I saw the horses and realised what happened, it finished me. I broke down and I
do not mind telling you I cried for a week.

It took deep reserves of character and a strong sense of duty to keep going as long
as Tyrrell did. The final breakdown was the result of extraordinary pressures over
many months culminating in several days of shellfire, the loss of many men from
his unit and the strain of taking command for the fourth time. Nor was it
irreversible; Tyrrell was 'foolish for a week' and then rejoined his unit.
    But what of men of different timber? How did they cope? A sequence of letters
in the Liddle collection charts one such struggle. Robert Wingham was 22 in
1915. The second son of a solicitor, he volunteered to fight but it was with no
carefree spring in his step that he set off to France. 'Kid, it's a terrible adventure
before me,' he wrote to his fiancée Nell Cobden in September 1915, 'but I do
hope I shall play my part well.'[11]

Nell, if I die, please remember right up to the end of your days that I died loving you and
thinking of you always – and if I come back, why, we will make amends for the horrors I
am about to endure and we will live our lives and be very happy.

Then, in a series of wonderfully expressive letters, he describes taking part in the
famously-mismanaged Battle of Loos: 'It's marvellous how one can grow used to
terrible sights and assist terribly wounded men without a tremor. But these things
leave their mark on all of us.' He also shared the horror of artillery bombardment:
'My God, it's the most terrible thing in the world to live through.'
    Wingham was an imaginative, sensitive, vulnerable man. It was bad luck for

him that in October 1915 he had to undergo the classic Western Front horror. He 'escaped being blown to pieces by a miracle . . . One of my men received the full force of a burst just as I was handing him a note to take round. The poor fellow was blown to pieces – all over me – it was awful. The shock of it has rather taken my nerve away for this kind of work.'

Thereafter, the letters get increasingly self-pitying, about the cold, the water in the trenches, the shelling. It's no great surprise to read, on 29 December 1915: 'that bomb has done its work together with eight weeks' continuous bombardment. My health went all to pieces and they've sent me home.' By April 1916, 'the panic is dying away' and Wingham spent the rest of the war in Palestine, writing endless letters of complaint to his faithful Nell.

It is interesting to compare Wingham's letters to the behaviour under fire of a group of Northumberland Fusiliers, as witnessed by their doctor.

Two chaps go for water and one returns. Says a pal to him, 'Well, where's Bill?' 'A bloody whizzbang took his head off' may not appear sympathetic, but is the only way of looking at the thing and remaining sane. You may be certain, however, that the same man would carry Bill ten miles if there was any chance of fixing his head on again. They are great men, but rough outwardly.[12]

* * *

Robert Wingham had lasted a mere three months on the Western Front. Did that make him a coward or a hero? Probably his gloomy disposition made him unpopular, but being directly 'shelled' gave his condition a certain legitimacy. But what did his fellow officers think of him? It is striking – and moving – to come across real compassion for others' sufferings in surviving correspondence. Lieutenant W. H. Round (himself killed on the Somme in 1916) wrote home in late 1915:

Some people if they have a really bad time do lose their nerve completely (even the strongest nerved in the beginning) and it is actually as much of a sacrifice to lose one's nerve in a trench as to lose one's arm in fact I'm not sure that it is not more so, added to which when you get back people are in no way inclined to sympathize with you but rather tend to think 'Oh he can't be much good; he's lost his nerve'. Which only goes to show that they know absolutely nothing of the circumstances out here. They are circumstances under which any nerve would give. That's why I always feel particularly sorry for those people, far more so than for the wounded.[13]

Round wrote as an officer, of a fellow-officer. As the Irish doctor Arthur Osburn noticed, a 'natural and quite excusable freemasonry amongst ex-Public school boys' led officers to protect each other and come down on the charitable side of the 'thin yellow line' between cowardice and honourable breakdown. They could be less considerate towards their men. Hiram Sturdy, a private in the Royal Regiment of Artillery, saw an infantryman in 'a bad state of nervousness' and was told that it was shell-shock.

But the men who have the power won't have him sent back. Perhaps they call it cowardice, but whatever it is he is no use to himself and pitiful to see, but I suppose if he gets killed he will be a hero then. That is not cowardice and he should be sent back, is the verdict of his mates and when that is said in the line by his own chums one can take it to be true, as they are pretty good judges.[14]

An important voice in such a decision lay, of course, with the front-line medical officer, in whom the different strands of medical care and military discipline converged. On 31 July 1915, Dr Henry Wynyard Kaye of 43rd Field Ambulance reported 'great discussions on the right way of dealing with cases of nerves and nervous breakdown . . . I think we have arrived at a method which is a good compromise of our duty to the individual patient and to the Army as whole – not an easy matter . . . It is important to bear in mind that the nerves of say 98% of them up there are being put to as high a test as possible and therefore every moral stimulus must be applied to keep as many as possible up to the collar in fairness to all those who "stick it out" with such splendid endurance.'[15]

Kaye was under enormous pressure himself, living through 'an everlasting nightmare of blood-stained men', and had only contempt for two colleagues who broke down. The first 'seemed to have no self-control or moral stamina. He was reduced to the state of a frightened child, though I believe a CO worth the name could probably have made half a man of him.' The second was 'reduced to a state of drivelling fear which was humiliating to behold as he had not even the decency to be ashamed of it.'

Was a more general problem of morale developing? At times, Charles Wilson thought so. 'One gets to know the people who will hang on,' he wrote in September 1915, 'and on the other hand tales come along of others less staunch. A perceptible change of heart is abroad, there is a weakening of the resolve to stick by the regiment even among good fellows.' Wilson began to speculate as to which types were most vulnerable. In general, he felt, it was blank, unimaginative people who fared best, and sensitive, imaginative ones who were soonest in trouble. But it was clear at the same time that there was no longer a place for the stupid man. 'It is not what happens out here but what men think may happen that finds the flaw in them,' he wrote, 'yet it is the thinking soldier that lasts in modern war.'[16]

How widespread a problem was shell-shock at the beginning of 1916? Figures are scarce and unreliable, although according to one estimate some 24,000 cases of shell-shock were sent back to England in the year to April 1916. At this stage of the war much depended on circumstances and the unit the man was serving with; however, official files make clear that until 1916, shell-shock did not 'affect sufficient important people or sufficiently great numbers of people to register in the minds of the military authorities as a serious threat to military efficiency.' It was left to the medical men and they themselves were more preoccupied with other issues, most notably gas.[17]

But the Battle of the Somme would change all that.

4

THE SOMME

Shell Shock! Do they know what it means? Men become like weak children, crying and waving their arms madly, clinging to the nearest man and praying not to be left alone.

Garfield Powell, 23 July 1916[1]

Months before the British attacked in the rolling chalk downland of the Somme valley on 1 July 1916, the medical preparations began. Roads were dug, railways laid, cities of tents assembled, hospital wards cleared for the expected influx of wounded. Ten miles behind the front line, near the railhead at Corbie, No. 34 Casualty Clearing Station prepared a large hospital, mainly of tents, for the one thousand patients which, the staff were told, might be the extent of casualties per division on the first day of the battle. After treating several hundred 'friendly' casualties of the laborious British artillery barrage, they began to suspect that their resources might be a bit slender for the casualties of the coming 'push'.[2]

Indeed they were. In the worst day in its history, the British Army lost 57,000 men, of whom more than a third were killed. So heavily did the dead and wounded lie in no-man's land that it took days, in some cases weeks, for stretcher-bearers to reach and recover them. Even so, the medical services were overwhelmed. In the first 48 hours after 1 July nearly 4,000 wounded men were brought to No. 34 CCS alone. Howard Somervell, then newly qualified, was a surgeon there:

Never in the whole war did we see such a terrible sight. Streams of motor ambulances a mile long waited to be unloaded. Though many ambulance trains went out at one side of our camp, the wounded had to lie not merely in our tents and shelters and in the adjacent farm-buildings, but the whole area of the camp, a field of five or six acres, was completely covered with stretchers placed side by side, each with its suffering or dying man upon it. Orderlies went about giving drinks and food, and dressing wounds where possible.

We surgeons were hard at it in the operating-theatre, a good hut holding four tables. Occasionally we made a brief look around to select from the thousands of patients those few fortunate ones whose life or limbs we had time to save. It was a terrible business. Even now I am haunted by the touching look of the young, bright, anxious eyes, as we passed along the rows of sufferers.

Hardly ever did any of them say a word, except to ask for water or relief from pain. I don't remember a single man in all those thousands who even suggested we should save him and not the fellow next to him. Silently beseeching they lay, as we rapidly surveyed them to see who was most worthwhile saving. Abdominal cases and others requiring long operations simply had to be left to die. Saving a life by amputation, which can be done in a few minutes, or saving of limbs by the wide opening of wounds, had to be thought of first. There, all around us, lying maimed and battered and dying, was the flower of Britain's youth – a terrible sight if ever there was one, yet full of courage and unselfishness and beauty.[3]

This was only the beginning; the battle was to last another four months and claim another half a million casualties. Sir Douglas Haig was not deflected by the losses on the first day, and was only temporarily stayed by the doubts about his strategy that the War Cabinet voiced at the end of July 1916. Determined to wring a draw out of his opponent he persisted and persisted till finally the November mud forced him to stop (only on 29 October could the weary staff of No. 34 CCS report the 'first comparatively slack day since 1 July').[4]

The nature of the fighting on the Somme soon changed. Whereas on the first day machine-guns mowed down the men like ears of wheat, in the long series of grinding attritional fights that followed it was artillery – used with increasing sophistication – that took the heaviest toll. The headlong, doomed bravery of 1 July gave way to a more long-drawn-out battle to survive. Working at a field ambulance, William Johnson saw its effects.

Although much has been written tending to multiply the causes of the nervous disorders of war, there were only two factors of overwhelming importance, namely prolonged fighting and heavy bombardments . . . The type of warfare practised during the Somme battles of 1916 provided ideal conditions for the development of these disorders. The 'artillery preparation' of the attacking force called for an 'artillery reply' from the opposite side. This duel frequently lasted several hours or even days and during this period of waiting the nerves of all were on edge. Then after the attack, came the reckoning of the losses amongst comrades and it was not unlikely that, owing to the call for troops, the whole acute process might be repeated. Little by little men became worn down by such experience and despite their best efforts the time would come when it was impossible to keep their thoughts from preying on the ordeals and sights of the battlefield. In such instances a breakdown occurred slowly; a gradual change would be noticed in the demeanour and behaviour of the patient and he would eventually reach hospital with the report that he was 'quite useless in the line'.[5]

There was, also, another factor about the later Somme fighting to which he did not refer – the sense of utter *futility*. His Australian counterpart was more forthright about the 'degeneration of the offensive into a crude contest in attrition devoid of surprise or tactical refinement.'

It became difficult for the soldier to regard his tasks as part of an intelligent plan. Lacking thus the firm 'shield of faith' the troops in the latter stages of the offensive . . . were thrown into the inferno morally disarmed save for the traditions of their race and army and the strength of their own character.[6]

On the Somme, shell-shock and 'nervous disorders of war', hitherto a marginal medical problem, became a major drain on manpower. According to the British official history, 'In the first few weeks [of July 1916] several thousand soldiers were rapidly passed out of the battle zone on account of nervous disorders and many of them were evacuated to England.' The inadequate official figures show that the numbers of men returned as 'shellshock battle casualties' – suffering 'shell-shock' after actually being shelled (Shell-shock W) – tripled in the last six months of 1916 to some 16,000 cases. Between 26 July and 11 August a single unit, 2 Division, had 501 cases of 'shell-shock wounded' as compared to 2,400 wounded. These are the only surviving British figures and do not cover 'Shell-shock Sick'. They probably need to be multiplied by at least three to give a real sense of the scale of the problem.[7]

Were thousands of soldiers genuinely becoming paralysed and incapable of continuing? Or, as the Army believed, were 'large numbers of men desert[ing] from the line on the claim that they had shell shock'? Did the knowledge that a condition called 'shell-shock' existed, offering a real escape from the battlefield (and often months of recovery in England), encourage soldiers to develop its symptoms? Was this the first of those 'evacuation syndromes' which became familiar in later wars? The evidence does not permit a comprehensive answer, but a few well-recorded incidents give revealing glimpses of how shell-shock began to surface.[8]

There were some cases of nervous collapse on the very first day of the Somme – at a Casualty Clearing Station at Daours the war correspondent Philip Gibbs saw 'shell-shocked boys weeping or moaning, and shaking with an ague.' There were also some units which failed to leave their trenches or declined to carry through the attack – though Sir Douglas Haig's suspicions on this score were often unjust and unfounded. In general, however, it is astonishing and terrifying how bravely the men of the New Armies, feared and distrusted by their commanders though they were, fought on 1 July. One brigade

advanced in line after line, dressed as if on parade, and not a man shirked going through the extremely heavy barrage, or facing the machine-gun and rifle fire that finally wiped them out. [Its commander, General Rees] saw the lines which advanced in such admirable order melting away under the fire. Yet not a man wavered, broke the ranks, or attempted to come back.[9]

Buoyed up with hope and excitement, the men went calmly and uncomplainingly to their deaths. The same thing had happened at Gallipoli, where very few cases of mental breakdown were reported at the time of the first landing, something a psychologist attributed 'partly to the protective influence of the sthenic emotions [nervous excitement] which actuated almost all the men.' There was, however, bound to be a later reaction to the events of 1 July, as survivors digested the scale of the experience they had been through. Yet the High Command, only partly aware of the scale of British casualties and still pursuing fantasies of finishing off the German reserves, pressed on with the attack. William

Johnson's division was 'kept in until practically everybody was done up and there one saw the men streaming down.' 'There was nothing wrong with them,' he said in 1921, 'except that they were absolutely fagged out, and could not go over the top again. They had been over about 11 times in a fortnight and simply could not do it again. The only thing was for them to come down sick.'[10]

The gulf between higher command's priorities and the realities on the ground is evident in one of the few well-documented episodes of shell-shock at this time. In the first hour of the attack on 1 July 1916, the 11th Battalion of the Border Regiment, a unit made of shepherds, domestic servants, miners and clerks from the 'hills and dales of Cumberland and Westmorland', lost its colonel – a retired colonial cavalryman who had raised, recruited, trained and commanded the battalion – and all of its officers. By the end of the day, 490 men had gone, too, making a total of 516 out of a token strength of 850 officers and men (such losses were by no means unique that day; indeed 20 units fared even worse, the 10th West Yorkshire losing 710 men and the Newfoundlanders 684). The 11/Border was then withdrawn from the line for a week.[11]

On the evening of 9/10 July, the officers temporarily in charge of the battalion (which now numbered only 250) were ordered to select 100 men for a trench raid. Shortly before it was due to go ahead, they learnt that 'a number of men were reporting sick and saying they could not go over.' The men asked to see the Medical Officer 'as they said they were suffering from shell shock'. Exceptionally, they were allowed to do so. Lieutenant Kirkwood, the doctor, reported that the men were unfit and, unusually for an army doctor, spelt out why this was:

1) The attack on 1st July . . . had a most demoralising effect and the men had not recovered their mental equilibrium.
2) The few days' rest at Contay sorting out deceased comrades' kits did not improve their mental state.
3) Carrying up rations under heavy and incessant shellfire.
4) Digging out the dead in the trenches and carrying them down as well as living in the atmosphere of decomposed bodies.
5) Exposure in open trenches under continuous shelling and without sleep.
6) Twenty men that day (9th July) had been sent to the Advanced Dressing Station suffering from shell shock.

Ignoring this report, the Brigadier ordered the raid to go ahead. When it proved a disastrous failure, an inquiry was ordered. It quickly emerged that the Brigadier had been 'suffering from fever' and 'had no idea that the men were not fit mentally to act as ordered.' He in turn blamed the non-commissioned officers in the battalion for not setting a 'good example in the absence of officers.' But it was on Lt. Kirkwood, the doctor, that the full wrath of the Army descended. By objectively describing conditions on the front, by presuming implicitly to question the leadership, he had hit a very raw nerve indeed. For, horrible as the experiences he described were, they were common to practically the entire army. Indeed many units had had a far worse time.

The Reserve Army Commander, the tough cavalryman, Sir Hubert Gough, considered it 'inconceivable how men who pledged themselves to fight and uphold the honour of the country could degrade themselves in such a manner and show an utter want of the manly spirit and courage which at least is expected of every soldier and every Britisher.' But he directed his real fury at Kirkwood, the doctor:

The certificate which he signed and the reasons given by him in support of it conclusively prove that he has no conception of the duties and responsibilities of a regimental MO, and so long as he is allowed to remain in the service he will be a source of danger to it . . . sympathy for sick and wounded men under his treatment is a good attribute for a doctor, but it is not for a MO to inform a CO that his men are not in a fit state to carry out a military operation.

Brushing aside all objections, Gough demanded that Kirkwood be dismissed. Finally, Sir Arthur Sloggett, the senior medical man in France, became involved. He was commendably forthright:

The whole case is deplorable. A brigadier in total ignorance of the state of a battalion in his brigade – the OC of that Battn in 'a prostrate condition'. The MO appears to have been made a scapegoat.

But he knew better than to defend Kirkwood, and simply asked that 'with the alarming shortage of MOs now,' he be allowed to work at the Base. History does not record Kirkwood's fate; presumably, though, news of his dismissal travelled quickly round his fellow medical officers. Just as commanders who refused to attack were being 'degummed' (retired and sent home), so a doctor who showed 'undue sympathy' would soon be sent packing.

More alarming to the authorities, however, was the case of the Australians. On 16 August, the medical director of I Anzac Corps was ordered to explain the levels of shell-shock in his units. The Australians were latecomers to the Somme; it was not till 23 July, when things got seriously bogged down, that Anzac units hitherto deployed to the north were brought down to reinforce the Somme front. They were good, strong soldiers, many of them Gallipoli veterans, and they swept their way into the village of Pozières – which had eluded the British earlier in July – 'like a pack of hungry dogs [that] had tasted blood.'[12]

But there was no comparable advance elsewhere and for the next seven weeks the Australians were 'shelled to bits' in the inevitable counterattack. In the end 22,826 Australians fell 'to win a few yards of ground'. On 24 July an Anzac counted some 75 shells, 9.2s and larger, landing within five minutes in an area of some four acres:

All day long the ground rocked and swayed backwards and forwards from the concussion . . . men were driven stark staring mad and more than one of them rushed out of the trench over towards the Germans. [A]ny amount of them could be seen crying and sobbing like children their nerves completely gone . . . we were nearly all in a state of silliness and half dazed.[13]

The shelling at Pozières, wrote the Australian historian Bean, 'did not merely probe character and nerve; it laid them stark naked . . . The strain eventually became so great that what is rightly known as courage – the will to persist – would not suffice since, however keen his will, the machinery of the man's self-control might become deranged.' During the battle, an Australian lieutenant wrote

I have had much luck and kept my nerve so far. The awful difficulty is to keep it. The bravest of all often lose it – one becomes a gibbering maniac . . . Only the men you have trusted and believed in before proved equal to it. One or two of my friends stood splendidly, like granite rocks round which the seas raged in vain. They were all junior officers; but many other fine men broke to pieces. Everyone called it shell-shock but shell-shock [i.e. shell concussion] is very rare. What 90% get is justifiable funk due to the collapse of the helm of self-control.[14]

It was hardly surprising that a large percentage (at times over 50%) of the casualties evacuated from this inferno should have been suffering from one or other form of nervous disorder, not least from lack of sleep. Nor that, 'after the battle a narrower conception of duty prevailed.' But, in his report, I Anzac Corps' doctor also conceded that his men's will to continue might be being sapped by the knowledge that shell-shock offered 'an easy and honourable quittance by withdrawing as "wounded".' Later he added that the fact that 'shell-shock had been written up greatly in the lay and medical press' had further encouraged its symptoms to appear and that some inexperienced medical officers had been 'over soft hearted'.[15]

Both these episodes lead the modern reader to ask whether failures in leadership were responsible for the great escalation of 'shell-shock'. Or was the quality of troops declining? As the historian Tim Travers has shown, those questions were addressed, at the height of the battle, by elements in the leadership itself, when Divisional Commanders were asked by the Chief of Staff of Fourth Army for 'comments on recent operations', early in August 1916. While many chose caution, some were surprisingly outspoken. There was a division, too, between those who laid the recent lack of progress at the higher command's door and those who blamed the men.[16]

General Ivor Maxse of 18th Division, for example, painted a devastating picture of the staff's handling of the July battles:

When attacks are ordered to take place 'immediately' on woods, villages etc. in the open, unreconnoitred, without time for preliminary arrangements, by fresh troops hastily moved forward, companies are directed to 'take this place at all costs' and this order has been obeyed quite literally.

He then added, sarcastically,

I would venture most humbly to suggest that when such orders are given over the telephone it should be distinctly understood that some sort of 'look' must be taken at the ground by subordinate commanders before they march their men in close formation into an artillery barrage.[17]

General Kentish, whose 14th Brigade had been in the thick of very heavy fighting, also criticised the failure to 'give time to local commanders to organise their attack.' Then, in a section headed 'the limits of endurance of the infantry soldier', he spelt out something obvious on the ground but not to higher command – that any unit which suffered heavy losses needed time out of the line to recover before being thrown back into the fray – at least 28 days, said Kentish. He also went out of his way to defend the non-Regular soldiers: 'It is not true that the New Armies are slow'.[18]

That was precisely what the opposite school said. They believed that the problem was not so much the staff's handling of the battles as the failure of junior officers and New Army soldiers to exploit opportunities as they arose. 'The spirit of the men, is splendid, wrote General Bridges, 'but they labour under the disadvantage of being of unsporting habits and lacking those soldier instincts which generations of military service alone can supply.' These generals blamed the men for digging in too soon and their officers for not pressing on. Discipline in the ranks was also much too slack; 'We are much too easy-going an army.'[19]

Unsurprisingly, Haig and his Army commanders sided with the tougher view. They saw no realistic alternative to the strategy already being pursued: only by the 'use of energy and weight and mass' could the British Army hope to prevail; the ill-trained troops of the New Army were hardly capable of anything better. High casualties were accepted as inevitable – in May 1916 the Adjutant-General's department had estimated that an attack by 30 divisions would lead to 195,000 casualties. The sheer scale of the war, the rolling leviathan of logistics, was making such numbers (larger than the size of the British Army in peacetime) seem quite normal. Indeed, Haig was to complain on 4 September 1916 of a Division whose casualties were less than a thousand in a day and it became accepted that attacks that failed with considerable casualties were given a sympathetic hearing at Army and GHQ, whereas attacks that failed with light casualties were inevitably condemned. By now the High Command had begun to evolve the necessary distancing euphemisms, referring to men and casualties in banking language, such as 'no more money in the till'. 'Wastage' had become the standard term for discussing casualties.[20]

Commanders were also physically remote, many miles behind the lines, relying for their knowledge of battlefield conditions on communications that were often poor and on staff officers who seldom visited the front. This was especially true of Haig, whose daily routine (including his afternoon ride) went on with obsessive regularity throughout the autumn. Some generals can take criticism. Haig, though, was not temperamentally inclined to listen to advice from subordinates or to welcome dissent at his meetings. He liked 'thrusters' – generals like Gough, who brushed aside obstacles and was always willing to attack; and he was ruthless in getting rid of faint hearts. 'It was common talk that no Divisional Commander dared say his infantry were unfit to attack for fear of being sent home,' or 'degummed' in Army parlance. At the height of the battle, on 26 July 1916, a Divisional Commander complained that 'at the present time, most Brigadiers and Battalion Commanders believe that if they hold a wood lightly, as I suggest, and then lose it, they would be degummed, not so much for losing the wood as for not losing enough men in trying to hold it.'[21]

The outburst of *glasnost* inside Fourth Army was short-lived. General Kentish, the most outspoken critic, was sent home. Others hastened to fall back into line. 'I quite agree that it is dangerous to try to deduce too much from experiences of particular divisions,' one Corps Commander wrote, hastily dissociating himself from a very interesting questionnaire about tactical lessons of the battle. The heavy casualties were officially blamed on the 'lack of ingrained discipline' in the men.[22]

There were certainly few signs of any change of thought in the handling of the Battle of the Ancre in October 1916; the letters that junior officers who had fought in that battle wrote to the official historian in the 1930s are full of anger. 'The Army Commander and his staff simply had no conception of the condition of the forward area . . . the ground was one huge morass of slimy mud with very deep places where there were shell holes.' The Ancre was 'the only occasion when I saw men drop dead from exhaustion from their efforts to get out of the mud . . . the very worst occasion I came across of what appeared to be the cruel, useless sacrifice of life . . . the climatic conditions alone made it clear from the start to the very stupidest brain that no success could possibly result.'[23]

All of this had its effect on the men. The Ancre, said J. F. C. Fuller, was 'the only battle in which I had direct evidence that British troops deserted in considerable numbers to the enemy . . . this was due to the low nervous condition produced by the appalling surroundings of the battle. If a crowd of men are reduced to a low nervous condition, "shell shock" so called, becomes contagious.'[24]

*   *   *

In one way, however, the British Army was quick to absorb the lessons of the Somme battle. On 2 August 1916, by which time some 200,000 British soldiers had been killed or wounded, GHQ began to call for 'economy in men and reserves'. A week later the Adjutant-General's office intervened to clamp down on one of the main perceived areas of 'wastage' – the numbers of men being evacuated for shell-shock.[25]

Sloggett, the Director-General of Medical Services, was too wily an operator to let this threat to his powers go unchallenged. He insisted that the classification of wounds could not be a purely disciplinary matter, involving as it must 'technical medical questions', guidance on which could 'only emanate from this office'; but took steps himself to stem the flow of evacuees. Alarm bells sounded, memos flew, Assistant Directors-General of Medical Services scurried to and fro in their cars. On 21 August, Armies were told not to evacuate shell-shock cases to the base 'unless there are definite lesions and symptoms which require prolonged hospital treatment'. Two days later the chief doctor of Fourth Army gave instructions that 'the number of cases arriving at the Casualty Clearing Stations with a tally marked shellshock must somehow be reduced.' An Australian proposal for tightening up shell-shock procedures was quickly forwarded to the Adjutant-General as a sign that the medical authorities could handle the problem on their own.[26]

This was Charles Myers' opportunity. As we have seen, long before this panic over 'wastage' arose, he had been proposing that 'shell-shock' cases should not be evacuated directly to England but treated at special centres close to the line. In the past, the authorities' fears that the establishment of such centres 'would open up a flood-gate for wastage from the army which no one would be able to control' had made them reject his ideas; but now that the overriding imperative was to keep as many men as possible in France, they were more receptive.[27]

Myers was master of the hour – quick, energetic, adaptable. Suddenly he was an important man; in late August 1916 he was made Consulting Psychologist to the Army. He toured the front line, interviewed generals, inspected dressing stations. In a long memorandum he hammered home his conviction that to deal with the problem it was necessary to create special centres near the line using treatment based on:

1) Promptness of action
2) Suitable environment
3) Psychotherapeutic measures.[28]

A miracle happened: this time, Sir Arthur Sloggett took up Myers' scheme and pushed it through. In November 1916, sweeping aside the hesitations and doubts of the Adjutant-General, he set up the first special treatment centre, at a converted Casualty Clearing Station and appointed Dr William Brown, a highly qualified academic psychologist and former pupil of Myers, to run it. The British Army, it seemed, was getting into bed with psychology.

But it was not to be. Myers began to fall from grace as rapidly as he had attained it. On 4 December 1916, only days after having had the satisfaction of seeing the first special treatment centre at work, he was told by Sloggett that it was 'inadvisable from a General Staff point of view' to publish an article on shell-shock in the medical journals. Myers' efforts to circulate its contents to Army medical officers were also frustrated. A month later, just as Myers was about to suggest that he move his own base from Abbeville closer to the line (and to the treatment centres where his work now lay) he was dumbfounded to learn that under a new arrangement, he would cease to be Consulting Psychologist to the Army and instead 'have control of shellshock, mental and neurological cases in the southern end of the front.' Control of these matters in the northern – and, it soon turned out, militarily more important – sector was to be given to his one-time dining companion, Dr Gordon Holmes.[29]

Myers tried to resist but was slapped down. His protests that he was now expected to undertake specialist neurological work – such as diagnosing brain disorders – for which he was quite unqualified, were simply ignored. His new title, significantly, was to be Neurologist to the South Sector.[30]

This was a bitter blow. Myers retreated to England on sick leave. Twenty years later, the wound still festered. He felt particular anger towards Gordon Holmes who had eased his own passage into the military early in 1915. At that time, preoccupied with his own work on brain injuries, Holmes had urged Myers to take the 'psychological' work off his back. Since then shell-shock, from being a minor and obscure problem, had become one of the 'hot' fields in Army medicine and Holmes – or so Myers felt – had invaded it not because he was actually interested, but because his Harley Street territorial instincts had been aroused.

Colonel Holmes had previously told me that functional 'nervous' disorders always formed a very large part of the civilian neurologist's practice. Naturally, therefore, he was little disposed to relinquish in Army life what was so important a source of income in time of peace. Although he confessed that (like most 'pure' neurologists) he took little interest in such cases.[31]

Where Charles Myers was a tubby, sensitive, cultured Jewish intellectual, his mother's favourite, Gordon Holmes was an athletic, choleric Irishman who had lost his mother before he was ten. Forty-one years old, tall, broad-shouldered, myopic, he was the coming man of British neurology and a formidable antagonist.

The son of an Anglo-Irish landowner – 'a solitary, enclosed boy whose most deeply rooted characteristic of shyness was reinforced by his mother's early death and his father's early remarriage' – Holmes developed a passion for walking and wild life which led him to read medicine at Trinity College, Dublin. After studying in Frankfurt, he landed a job at Queen Square in London in 1901 and over the next decade established himself.[32]

As a student, Holmes spent months patiently dissecting the brain of a dog; as a consultant, he was notable – even among British neurologists – for his physical, anatomical approach to the brain and its functions. His gifts as a 'restless, indefatigable investigator' were married to a down-to-earth practical mind and he was never given to mystical speculations about the big questions of life. While working at Boulogne on an 'amazing number of head and spinal wounds', Holmes had seized the opportunity presented by this 'vast unwanted experiment in neurology', to establish, with meticulous accuracy, that wounds in the back of the cerebral hemispheres of the brain produced corresponding patches of blindness in vision. He quickly earned Sloggett's respect and trust and in 1916 was made Consulting Neurologist to the Army. By then his work on wounds was nearly completed and, with shell-shock attracting so much attention, it was natural that Holmes should become interested.[33]

Holmes had worked briefly in a Dublin mental hospital and written the odd article on general paralysis of the insane and neurasthenia, but was not much interested in the problems of mental disorder, sharing the 'impatience with psychological problems' of his mentors at Queen Square. By temperament, he was 'volcanic', 'tempestuous', and 'not endowed with wit, nor any broad sense of humour.' Though much loved by some of his students for his warm, impulsive nature, he could when angry be a terrifying physical force, known to lift up erring pupils by the scruff of the neck and shake them or to twist an arm 'to emphasise a fault in [a] clinical description.' His thoroughness in examining patients was sometimes matched by a rough insensitivity to their problems and, at Queen Square, he had 'fought with most of his colleagues and come to blows with some.'[34]

His break with Myers, though, was more than just a clash of temperament. Holmes shared the tough attitudes of the Army. His pre-war medical experience made him a pessimist about human behaviour, an instinctive disciplinarian. There are also some signs that he was alarmed by some of Charles Myers' methods. He said after the war that he had been 'impressed by the failures of the psychoanalysts and hypnotists'; and in 1916 a like-minded colleague warned that 'the sentimental introspective condition' such methods produced was 'decidedly opposed to any satisfactory military operations'. 'Hysteria,' Holmes and his school of thought believed, 'spreads by suggestion from one person to another and has got to be dealt with in no uncertain fashion. Otherwise, the best army in the world finds itself in hospital.'[35]

Towards the treatment of soldiers, too, Holmes and Myers represented two completely different philosophies, the former believing that the doctor should simply remove physical symptoms in the soldier; the latter that he should look for their underlying psychological causes. In an unpublished report he wrote in late 1916, Myers tried hard to meet the disciplinary needs of the Army; yet insisted that the therapeutic needs of the individual must also be addressed.

Between wilful cowardice, contributory negligence (i.e. want of effort against loss of self-control) and total irresponsibility for the shock, every stage and condition of shell-shock may be found. It follows, then, that each case must receive individual attention and treatment, based on its own merits ... The guiding principles of psycho-therapeutic treatment at the earliest stages should consist in the re-education of the patient so as to restore his memory, self-confidence, and self-control. For this restoration of his normal self, a judicious admixture of persuasion, suggestion, explanation and scolding is required.[36]

Myers was particularly interested in cases of lost memory, which he treated in the standard French manner, with hypnosis, an approach Gordon Holmes would never have considered. Inexperienced as a hypnotist, Myers had found that his first attempts demanded 'even more self-mastery' than his first operation. But he had been encouraged by some of the results and had begun patiently hypnotising patients over and over again. He would recover their lost memories of the past and by using post-hypnotic suggestion – that is, talking to them firmly the moment they emerged from hypnosis – would restore those memories to the conscious mind. Myers claimed that when patients were re-united with their memory they were able to reclaim their personalities; their physical symptoms – paralysis and so on – then disappeared automatically.

No one who has witnessed the unfeigned delight with which these patients, on waking from hypnosis, hail their recovery from such disorders, can have any hesitation as to the impetus thus given towards a final cure. Such restoration of past emotional scenes constitutes a first step towards obtaining that volitional control which the individual must finally acquire if he is to be healed.[37]

Myers, together with his protégé William Brown, was using a simple psychological model, derived from the French neurologists Janet and Dejerine, according to which the mind bundles away, out of consciousness, experiences and emotions it is unable to cope with.

The origin of the symptoms [Brown wrote] is to be found in the intense emotion of fear caused by the shell explosion, of which they are the objective physical manifestations . . .
    The attempted repression and control of the fearful emotion at its inception brings about a splitting of the mind [what Janet called 'dissociation'] which appears later as an amnesia of greater or lesser extent, often involving other losses of function also, such as dumbness, deafness, tremulousness and paralysis.[38]

Whatever the strengths of the theory, Myers himself never became an expert hypnotist; he lacked 'the common touch'. An article written in January 1916 revealed that of the 23 cases he himself had by then treated, only six patients were 'apparently complete cures' and another six were 'distinctly improved'. Yet eight patients had failed to be hypnotised and three had shown 'no improvement after hypnosis'. After the initial excitement he was forced to admit that there was 'slow progress in certain areas'. The case for Myers' approach was, therefore, far from proven.[39]

    By late 1916 Myers was becoming noticeably tougher, less focused on the small number of hypnotic patients he was able to spend time with and more concerned with detecting malingering amongst the huge new intake of shell-shock cases. But the mere fact that he had used hypnosis at all, with its 'savour of the uncanny, the mysterious and the unknown', had alarmed some in the Army medical hierarchy. Myers was told by the commandant of one military hospital 'that he would in no circumstances countenance its employment because the reputation of his unit would suffer thereby.' Even fifteen years after the war, the mere mention of hypnotism could raise a jolly, masculine laugh in RAMC circles.[40]

    In contrast, Holmes' methods were much less alarming to Army doctors and the Adjutant-General's office. Gordon Holmes came from a different tradition: back in 1887, confronted by the eternal problem of the relationship between the mind and the brain, the great neurological 'sage' John Hughlings Jackson had laid down the 'doctrine of concomitance'; that is, that 'in investigating nervous diseases, one could simply ignore the mind and its connections with the brain.' The Queen Square method was to do just that. Hysterical mutes would be tricked into speaking, 'paralysed' muscles activated by electric shock, and little attempt was made to probe the psychological causes of the problem.[41]

In June 1917, as the Army began to limber up for another great offensive, the boundaries between Holmes and Myers were again re-drawn. It was made clear that control of the forthcoming battle, to be fought in Flanders, would rest with Gordon Holmes; Myers, after two and a half years of struggle, was going to be a bystander. A couple of months later, writing to his old tutor William Rivers, he expressed some of his bitterness and frustration.

I have found some of the most successful MOs among those men who were neither neurologists nor psychiatrists. The pure neurologist is hopeless. Yet Holmes is given overall the now active part of our line for mental and nervous cases.[42]

By then it was early August of 1917. Passchendaele was in full swing.

PSYCHIATRY AT THE FRONT, 1917–18

Men going into action support themselves with a sort of enforced hysterical cheerfulness, but no one could be cheerful in the Third Battle of Ypres.

Charles Carrington[1]

Historians still argue about whether the thirteen battles the British Army fought in Flanders between 31 July and 12 November 1917 – usually known as 'Passchendaele' – achieved anything militarily. No one has ever disputed that the experience of fighting there surpassed in sheer unpleasantness any other in the war. To the historian Cruttwell, it was 'the culmination of horror'; to Edmund Blunden, 'murder, not only to the troops but to their singing faiths and hopes.' Partly, it was the sheer physical conditions; nature and modern weaponry conspired there to create a world which scarcely seemed to belong to this earth.

The rain [Cruttwell recalled] was pitiless, the ubiquitous mud speedily engulfed man and beast if a step was taken astray from the narrow duckboards, upon which descended a perpetual storm of shells and gas . . . Some of the pictures preserve an aspect of the macabre grotesqueness of this blasted and mangled land. Long-distance gun-fire and the art of night-bombing had developed so much during the last year that troops were kept in a fever of perpetual apprehension. Men's nerves were badly frayed before they took part in the fighting, and had little chance of healing when they were withdrawn from it.[2]

You might think, from many such accounts, that Passchendaele was a breeding ground for shell-shock, an environment so extreme as to challenge anyone's sanity. Haig himself described the Army in December 1917 as 'much exhausted' – dramatic language for him; that month the British Cabinet was told that 'cases of drunkenness, desertion and psychological disorders were increasing; that men from the front frequently spoke with great bitterness about "the waste of life during the continued hammerings against the Ypres Ridge".'[3]

Yet according to Gordon Holmes' official figures, there was less shell-shock at Passchendaele than at the Somme – 5,346 cases in an Army of half a million men, a rate of about 1%. Were soldiers less frightened? Or had the Army acquired a desperate professionalism in survival, a skill in keeping men going where

ould have broken? Or was it, perhaps, that the entire Army was
shell-shock and in no mood to let individual soldiers escape?[4]
lanation was bureaucratic: elaborate new arrangements were
ntrol the two varieties of officially-recognised shell-shock. The
office, while reluctantly agreeing after the Somme that new
specialist treatment centres could be set up, was determined to use them for its
own disciplinary purposes; in particular, to clamp down on 'Shell-shock W' by
making sure that men *really* had been blown up. 'Nerve failure,' it was pronounced, could no longer be 'classified as a wound on medical authority alone'
and all cases of 'shell-shock wounded' must be held near the front line until such
time as the genuineness of their case could be established, by reference back to
their unit. By June 1917 the inevitable form – known as AF 3436 – had been
devised and, as Passchendaele loomed, the medical authorities fussed over the
procedures needed to apply it.[5]

Trying to reconcile the needs of medicine and of discipline, the Army had
created something wonderfully baroque. On the one hand, it had listened to
Myers' arguments and created, just behind the front line, special treatment
centres for shell-shock; and all shell-shock cases were now to be given the initial
blanket label 'NYDN' – 'Not Yet Diagnosed Nervous' – and sent back to these
centres for specialist attention. But, because of the Adjutant-General's distrust of
doctors, no patient could receive that specialist attention until Form AF 3436
had been sent off to the man's unit and filled in by his commanding officer. This
meant that officers in the front line had to waste time filling in yet another
fatuous piece of bumf from HQ, while badly-affected patients had to wait for
treatment (the whole point of the centres, as originally conceived, being that
treatment would be *immediate*). It also created log-jams in the wards: when the
Director of Medical Services at Fifth Army rang No. 62 Casualty Clearing Station
on 2 August to ask why they still had 1,203 NYDN patients, he was told that 'AF
3436 had not been sent in for the latest arrivals . . . [and] few of the previous ones
had been returned.'[6]

But, from the Army's point of view, it was all worth the effort: Form AF 3436
revealed what some had long suspected, that many men who claimed to have
been blown up by a shell had not in fact been near an explosion. Some had simply
lied in order to earn themselves the extra perks of a wound, but there were also,
one front-line doctor believed, 'a lot of men who tell you they were buried by a
shell who are not telling the truth at all. They only *think* they are.' After months
of living with the fear of being blown up, 'the thing becomes real to them – it is
what they are thinking of day in and day out. They think they were buried by a
shell and they gradually come to believe that it was absolutely true.'[7]

It turned out that only a tiny proportion of 'Shell-shock W' cases – between 4
and 10% – were actually *commotional*; the vast majority were of *emotional* origin.
And so, by this elaborate means, the dimmest Medical Officer came to understand what Myers and Wiltshire had long since known – that the problem was
more psychological than physical, and 'shell-shock' an inappropriate label.[8]

The long-term effect of AF 3436 was to kill off at last the term 'shell-shock' in the Army. 'What was once a disease had in 1917 become a stigma' and by 1918 a 'forbidden term'. In the Army, as elsewhere, it proved difficult to come up with a satisfactory alternative – the various replacements lacked its punchiness – while the frequent changes of nomenclature dealt further blows to the reliability of Army statistics. The saga of 'shell-shock' came to its final end in September 1918 when 'Shell-shock W' was abolished.[9]

More immediately, though, the chaos produced by AF 3436 led to a further important change in method, which had a dramatic effect on the shell-shock rate. Halfway through the Passchendaele battles, it was decided that it was no longer necessary to send all cases to the special Casualty Clearing Station; if a doctor felt the man was just 'temporarily shaken', he could keep him even nearer the front.[10]

In this final stage in the tug of war between the needs of medicine and discipline, much of the power over shell-shock was thus being returned to the doctors – not to 'psychologists' or 'neurologists' but to ordinary Regimental Medical Officers. They, of course, varied as to temperament, experience, and inclination. There was Colonel Rogers of the 4/Black Watch, for example: a tower of paternalistic good sense, full of jovial wisdom born of experience. 'It is a great mistake to look on men as malingerers,' Rogers said after the war.

I must confess that when I went to France I was inclined to look on men far too much as malingerers, and I very quickly changed my opinion. I think there is far more in psychology.

Yet Rogers also believed it was a big mistake to 'send your cases down the line' – to evacuate them back.

You must send your *commotional* cases down the line. But when you get these *emotional* cases, unless they are very bad, if you have a hold of the men and they know you and you know them (and there is a good deal more in the man knowing you than in you knowing the man) . . . you are able to explain to him that there is really nothing wrong with him, give him a rest at the aid post if necessary and a day or two's sleep, go up with him to the front line, and, when there, see him often, sit down beside him and talk to him about the war and look through his periscope and let the man see you taking an interest in him.

He accepted, of course, that there were some cases he could not handle in the line. On one occasion, two officers and an orderly had been shelled near a communication trench.

The two officers stood it quite well, but the man simply collapsed and crumpled up. He was brought down to my aid post and I saw it was a case I must evacuate. He was there with terrified expression, cold face, sweat pouring off his body, unable to speak though he tried to do so . . .

Rogers' other great quality was to recognise that, in the end, 'humanity has only a certain limit of endurance'. He learned to read the signs of approaching breakdown and on one occasion – noticing that the troops no longer sang on going up into the trenches – was courageous enough to ask that his unit be moved to a less dangerous sector.[11]

RMOs who lacked Rogers' bluff humanity devised other techniques for keeping the troops 'up to the collar'. The commonest and most effective was what would now be called peer-group pressure, fanning the soldier's fear of losing face in front of his mates. In the Royal Fusiliers, according to Charles Wilson, 'shell-shock throughout the battalion was looked on as a disgrace. The man knew he would be looked upon with little sympathy. No doubt there were cases of hardship but it was the only way of keeping up morale, as shell-shock was very infectious.'[12]

The combined effect of the treatment centres, the new procedures, and the increased power of Regimental Medical Officers was that 'cases became much fewer as the Passchendaele operations continued, although the shellfire never slackened.' 'The rapid decrease in numbers,' I Anzac Corps doctor wrote, 'shows that except in the gravest form (which is very rare) the whole matter rests upon *a power of inhibition and control* being fully exercised.'[13]

One can only speculate as to what the long-term effects of being kept 'up to the collar' were for the hundreds of thousands of men who survived. 'It is curious to note how the spirit of the troops has changed even from two years ago,' a doctor working in a Field Ambulance at Passchendaele wrote to his wife late in 1917.

If anything it is more admirable: there is more patience and self-sacrifice: but it is infinitely pathetic to witness. No keen curiosity now, no careless enthusiasm, not even hate to carry them on: but instead a sense of duty, and a bowing down to the inevitable – the inevitable power which drives them on from behind.

The troops have settled down to war as slaves to their task: if they fall short of what is expected they risk discomfort, punishment, even death: whereas if they please their masters there are certain rewards to be won in the form of holiday and rest from the line. It is a sad spectacle to see free citizens of a civilised empire thus degraded.[14]

*   *   *

By this stage of the war, doctors on the Western Front had considerable experience of nervous disorders and a good deal of common ground had emerged. Everyone now knew that the incidence of shell-shock was likely to be higher in certain situations and groups of men. During periods of heavy fighting, even battle-hardened troops might break after prolonged service in the line. The signs of approaching breakdown were also becoming familiar to RMOs:

The wild fighting type becomes quiet and moody
The sullen type becomes excitable and talkative
The careful man becomes suddenly reckless
The previously well-behaved man perpetrates petty crimes[15]

The tank general J. F. C. Fuller later described how 'wear and tear an sapping of his nervous powers' often imposed a cycle on a soldier:

The normal healthy man arriving from England showed definite signs of physical fear when first coming under fire. This fear very shortly wore off and was replaced by a kind of callousness which sometimes increased when until a man took very little trouble to protect himself ... When this condition was well advanced a man became liable to breakdown mentally or to show a nervousness which may be defined rather as a mental terror than a physical fear ... First of all the man was healthily afraid of what was happening, then he became callous and after that he sometimes became obsessed with fear. [16]

Types thought most at risk were fresh troops, newly arrived in the line; 'old soldiers' over 40, especially if married; rapidly-trained volunteers; and specialists working in conditions of great danger – machine-gunners, engineers and tank crewmen. Doctors were also learning to distinguish between rough categories – pure 'commotional' shell-shock, a soldier blown up by a shell, on the one hand; the various varieties of 'emotional' shell-shock – exhaustion, 'neurasthenia' or nervous collapse, 'hysteria', and 'confusion' on the other. Each required slightly different treatment. [17]

Everyone agreed that soldiers suffering from simple exhaustion only needed a few days' proper rest before being able to resume their duties. But the other categories were more contentious. By 1917 the typical 'neurasthenic' was an officer or sergeant who – like Captain Stanhope in R. C. Sherriff's play *Journey's End* – had spent months, years even, trying to control his fears before finally breaking down. He would arrive looking pale and haggard, his palms sweating, his eyeballs protruding, 'with the look of a man who cannot drive himself one step further'. He might well be suffering from lack of sleep and nightmarish dreams and he would be very irritable and hard to deal with.

The 'hysteric', usually an ordinary soldier, often quite young, was the type of man Myers had originally seen in the winter of 1914/15. He would usually be suffering from tremors and twitches, dumbness and partial vision, paralysed limbs or deformed gait, that is, from external physical symptoms.

This division in symptoms between officers and men might seem suspiciously neat, but nobody questioned it at the time. The rationale seemed obvious:

The private soldier [Dr Henry Head explained] has only to obey, he has no responsibility for the war. The officer, on the other hand, is repressing all the time because first of all he must not show fear in any circumstances. In some circumstances all men are afraid and therefore he has to suppress all that. Then again ... in the British army he has to think of his men as a father thinks of his children. It is to a great extent anxiety of behalf of others. It is this sense of responsibility which makes so many young officers break down. [18]

Why, though, did the men develop physical symptoms – trembling, deafness, dumbness, twitching, stupor and all the rest? Head believed that:

being heavily shelled in the trenches he knew he could not run away.
ion of running away, but then he fell victim to a substituted condition
aralysed from the waist downwards or had some other disability which
e for him to remain in the trenches. That is where fear is transformed in
ysteria.

slow

57

Cases of this sort eventually came to be known by the Freudian label 'conversion hysterias' because the emotion of fear was hysterically 'converted' into physical symptoms. Neurasthenia and hysteria often overlapped with the final rough category – the 'confused': either emotionally weak individuals who had been near a shell explosion and had broken down, or quite normal people who had 'been through an experience of overwhelming severity or horror', perhaps after long exposure to the war had sapped their resistance.

* * *

Rifleman John Maxwell of the Rifle Brigade was buried by a shell at Passchendaele in August 1917 and dragged out from his trench 'absolutely shell-shocked'. Unable to speak and barely able to walk, he had to be 'half dragged' to the 'doctor's dug-out a bit in the rear', where the RMO put a NYDN – 'Not Yet Diagnosed Nervous' – ticket on him. Next, Maxwell was dragged to a first-aid station further to the rear. By now he could not walk at all, so he was put on a stretcher, taken to an ambulance, and driven to the specialist shell-shock ward, a group of tents alongside No. 62 Casualty Clearing Station at Haringhe (popularly known as 'Bandagehem'), about twelve miles back from the line; he was so covered in mud they had to cut his clothes off.[19]

There were numerous other cases there. 'Genuine shell shock in the acute stages,' a visitor noted, was 'very pitiful.' He saw one soldier with 'pronounced general tremor, an anguished expression, and semi-conscious'; another 'still more suporous and jerking about, every few minutes – as though falling in his sleep or having a strong electric current passed through him.'[20]

Although Gordon Holmes was in overall charge, the hands-on work at No. 62 CCS was in the hands of a young doctor called William Johnson who had treated hysterical patients at Guy's Hospital and studied briefly with the French neurologists. Equally importantly, Johnson had spent almost three years with a field ambulance and won the Military Cross for his bravery during the battle of the Somme. He had 'been there'.[21]

Like Holmes, Johnson was what the Army wanted, tough and down-to-earth. He was convinced that the public fuss had left soldiers believing shell-shock was 'a definite disease and that the term meant some mysterious change in the nervous system.' 'The usual thing,' Johnson later said, 'when one admitted a case and asked the man "Well, what do you complain of?" was to have the almost invariable answer "Shell-shock, sir" as if it was a concrete disease . . . I have had men coming up with photographs of themselves from the illustrated papers – Private A. B. suffering from shell-shock . . . Young soldiers prepare to become a case of shell-shock almost before the first shell drops near them. The very fact of the noise of the explosion causes a certain amount of emotional upset and that is sufficient to send them over the borderline.'[22]

Johnson found that simply to de-mystify the whole subject of shell-shock was often to effect a cure:

To the soldier's mind it was as much an entity as scarlet fever, with the further addition that, being incurable, shell-shock was more to be dreaded. In quite a number of cases the eradication of this false belief from the patient's mind was all that was needed to effect a rapid recovery from his symptoms. To explain to a man that his symptoms were the result of disordered emotional conditions due to his rough experiences in the line, and not, as he imagined, to some serious disturbance of his nervous system produced by bursting shells became the most frequent and successful form of psychotherapy . . . it not infrequently ended in the man coming forward voluntarily for duty, after having been given a much needed fortnight's rest in hospital.[23]

In line with this approach, Johnson paid little attention to amnesia which, he had noticed, was usually very short-term; hypnotism, far from being the key to the secrets of the mind, was for him just 'a simple and efficacious way of providing sleep'. Johnson even suggested that alarming medical terms like 'neurasthenia' should be replaced by simpler labels like 'exhaustion' (a suggestion followed a generation later).

Johnson's simple approach was also determined by the numbers he had to handle. For all the success of 'inhibition and control', Johnson still had to treat (and fill in forms for) 5,345 cases during the four months of the Passchendaele battles of autumn 1917 – an average of about 60 a day. Mostly, he relied on rest, an 'atmosphere of cure', and a few firm words of reassurance, but he also made deft use of some of the standard tricks for removing symptoms quickly. Soldiers who had become deaf and mute, for example, could easily be persuaded to speak again.

Twenty minutes would suffice to restore a man's speech and hearing, and, taking the first case that came to hand, he wrote a few simple directions upon a slate, made the patient imitate his own breathing with as little effort as possible, persuaded him to make a sighing sound, to phonate on a few words and then go through the alphabet; with a simple remark that of course he could now hear quite well, he dismissed the man well within the estimated time.[24]

According to Gordon Holmes, it was found in most Centres that the quickest way to restore a patient's speech was to tell him 'he would be given electricity to help him along': 'almost invariably he got his speech back within half an hour.' Having lost his symptoms, the soldier was then given a good rest for a few days and then given 'systematic exercise' by an instructor.[25]

As he grew more experienced, Johnson was able to treat in France one of the most difficult and intractable groups of cases – men who trembled all over. Instead of sending them back to England, you could, he discovered, by a judicious mixture of isolation, rest, persuasion, rubbing with oil and 'vigorous' massage by 'a professional rubber who was accustomed to train men for athletics', make their symptoms go away. The actual techniques used, though, were not important in themselves. 'The personality of the medical officer,' Johnson argued, 'is always of greater importance than the particular method.' Clearly his own calm, undemonstrative manner, patient firmness, ability to keep control of numerous patients and long experience at the front made him particularly good with hysterical cases. 'If the patient's confidence had been obtained,' he wrote after the war, 'it was possible to dissipate his hysterical manifestation without laying a finger on him.'[26]

Yet Johnson's up-beat tone is not borne out by the American neurosurgeon, Harvey Cushing, who visited No. 62 CCS in October 1917 and found the atmosphere there 'very dismal . . . a dumping ground for MOs who can't wriggle out – none of them appear at all interested in, or acquainted with, psychiatry.' Johnson also seems to have been much less assured with 'neurasthenic' officers, whom he clearly despised.

Did the tough, 'no frills' approach *work*? To take first the Army's yardstick, of the 5,000 odd cases treated during the Passchendaele period, 55% were returned direct to their units and a further 29% – mainly 'neurasthenics' – spent a month doing agricultural labour in France before returning to the front. That sounds impressive, but, as Johnson acknowledged, a great many of these patients were simply suffering from exhaustion. Over the remaining thirteen months of the war he treated another 3,000-odd cases, fewer of whom had simple exhaustion. This time the results were less impressive: 44% were evacuated to the base and 56% remained in the army area, most of them being given a month's farm work before going back to their units. Johnson's overall conclusion was that 'a majority' of cases, after perhaps two or three weeks in hospital, eventually went back to their units.[27]

We will never know how many of these men broke down again on returning to duty; a small sample carried out by Gordon Holmes suggested that about 10% relapsed – he did not say how quickly – and about 3% relapsed more than once. Anecdotal evidence suggests the true figure for relapses was much higher. 'Psychological cases sent back to front-line duty,' a doctor recalled twenty years later, 'if they did not relapse, were generally quite useless, as no one felt inclined to trust them in emergency.'[28]

*   *   *

Passchendaele was not the only battle the British fought that autumn; at Cambrai, in the Southern Sector, a bold but abortive attempt was made to use the new weapon, the tank. Cambrai was exceptional in another way. Soldiers who broke down there were handled not by Holmes and Johnson but by Charles Myers and his protégé, William Brown, using rather different methods.

Brown was a man of formidable academic qualifications. A mathematician and philosopher who took up academic psychology and graduated in medicine, he was by 1914 Reader in Psychology at London University and a well-known academic expert on hypnosis. He had then gained wide experience in shell-shock hospitals. Like Johnson, William Brown put great emphasis on the need for early treatment and the importance of the doctor being confident and up-beat – 'enthusiastic expectation of a rapid recovery' was an 'essential condition of success'; he used brisk 'persuasion' to get lighter cases back to the line. Nor did he mind using tricks to remove symptoms; he would, for example, make a sudden noise by banging books together to frighten a 'deaf' patient into hearing again.[29]

The crucial difference, though, was that where appropriate, Brown addressed the underlying psychological causes rather than just the symptoms. 'Long talks' brought about 're-education and mental analysis' in neurasthenic patients and hypnosis was used to treat major hysterical cases – about 15% of the total. His technique, described in books written after the war, is worth quoting at length.

The patient would be brought into hospital lying on a stretcher, perhaps dumb, trembling violently, perspiring profusely, his face showing an expression of great terror, his eyes either with a fixed stare or rolling from side to side. When one questioned him and got him to answer in writing he would tell one that he was unable to remember what had happened to him. In some way or other he had been knocked out and had come to find that he was paralysed and unable to speak.[30]

I interview him alone in my office and tell him in a tone of conviction that I shall restore his speech to him in a few seconds if he will do exactly what I say. I then urge him to lie down upon a couch, close his eyes and think of sleep. I urge him to give himself up to sleep, to let sleep come to him, as it assuredly will. I tell him that he is getting drowsy, his limbs are getting heavy with sleep, all his muscles are relaxed, he is breathing more and more slowly, more and more deeply. Above all, that his eyelids are getting heavy, as heavy as lead, that he feels disinclined to open them however hard he tries. At this stage, which generally supervenes within two or three minutes, he really cannot open his eyes. This is a stage of very light hypnosis quite sufficient for my purposes.

I now tell him that the moment I put my hand on his forehead he will seem to be back again in the trenches, in the firing line, in the fighting, as the case may be, and will live again through the experiences he had when the shock occurred. This I say in a tone of absolute conviction, as if there is not the slightest shadow of possibility of my words not coming true. I then place my hand on his forehead. He immediately begins to twist and turn on the couch and shouts out in a terror-stricken voice. He talks as he talked at the time when he received the shock. He really does live again through the experiences of that awful time. Sometimes he speaks as if in dialogue, punctuated with intervals of silence corresponding to the remarks of his interlocutor, like a person speaking at the telephone. At other times he indulges in imprecations [pleading] and soliloquy. In some cases he is able to reply to my questions and give an account of his experiences. In others he cannot do so, but continues to writhe and talk as if he were still in the throes of the actual experience. In every case he speaks and acts as if he were again under the influence of the terrifying emotion. It is as if this emotion had been originally repressed, and the power of speech with it, and is now being worked off and worked out . . .[31]

Charles Myers had used hypnosis only to revive the soldier's memory and had used such persuasions as 'Now when I put my hand on your forehead, you will be back in the trenches again, but you will not be unduly afraid, you will be able to live through it all calmly and to tell me all that happened to you.' But Brown had learnt by experience to go straight for the emotion, the terror. 'That emotion,' he claimed, 'has been pent up in these patients, under strain of attempted self-control, and . . . liberation of such emotion (known as "abreaction") produces a resolution of the functional symptoms.' Unlike Myers, Brown was a skilful hypnotist – 'a kind of wizard, who mesmerises when he likes,' according to one of his patients, the poet Wilfred Owen.[32]

Overall, Brown claimed to achieve dramatic results by his methods, returning 70% of soldiers 'to the line' after a fortnight's rest and treatment. In theory, then, his 'psychological' methods were just as effective in reducing 'wastage' as Johnson's more disciplinary ones. But by the time Brown's claims appeared in print, in August 1918, the balance on the Western Front had long since tilted against him and Myers. In fact, by the autumn of 1917 Charles Myers had lost all stomach for his work. Looking after a rump of his former empire while Holmes and Johnson handled the battle of Passchendaele was more than he could bear. In October 1917, on a visit to London he re-established contact with his original patron, the Army medical supremo at home, Sir Alfred Keogh, and was invited to help sort out shell-shock arrangements at home. Gratefully, Myers accepted. Two months later William Brown followed him back to England. For the last year of the war Holmes and Johnson had undisputed control of the arrangements in France and, as a result, they later claimed, were able dramatically to reduce the level of shell-shock. It may be, though, that shell-shock was expressing itself in other ways.[33]

*   *   *

The mustard gas attacks in July 1917 were not the first use of this weapon; as early as April 1915 the Germans had introduced chlorine gas. Their chemical industry was the largest in the world and, with the British naval blockade increasingly denying them the nitrate needed for making high explosive, it was perhaps inevitable that they should turn to this new weapon. The initial results were devastating. The British, after much desperate improvising and the conscripting of chemistry dons, had responded at Loos in September of that year with mixed results. Thereafter, Robert Harris has written, 'a chemical arms race developed, in the rush of which there was no time to worry about ethics.' Phosgene was the next chemical to be tried, by the Germans in December 1915, and by the British at the Somme the following July.[34]

Accounts of the effects of these gas attacks are so horrifying that one might wonder why they did not bring the war to an end then and there. Soldiers caught in the chemical storm watched helplessly as their vital organs slowly collapsed about them. Phosgene victims, after a couple of days of mild irritation of eyes and throat, developed 'an abundant flow of thin watery fluid, often streaked with blood, which simply flows from the mouth as the dying patient loses the power to expel it. After death the foam from this fluid may dry to a white efflorescence around the mouth.'[35]

But in the early years, the physical problems of manufacturing, handling and delivering the new weapon were so great that it could only be used locally, and, though in some instances entire stretches of the front collapsed before it, these breakthroughs were never followed up quickly enough. Then, in the last year of the war, gas began to move centre stage. New methods of delivering chemical weapons had been developed – the Livens projector, the Stokes Mortar, above all, the gas shell fired by the artillery – which made gas easier to handle. By 1918, 'between a third and a fifth of all shells were being filled with gas' and 'chemical warfare, once an unexpected and terrifying experience, was now an ever-present threat.' The next chemical to issue from Dr Haber's laboratories in Berlin – dichlorethyl sulphide, commonly know as mustard gas – was several degrees nastier than its predecessors. Soldiers exposed to mustard gas at first experienced only minor irritation of the eyes and throat, but within a few hours came 'intolerable pain in the eyes'. When some of the milder cases were evacuated each soldier had to be led like a blind man by an orderly to the ambulance car.[36]

Then the skin would develop burn blisters – great yellow, swollen disfigurations of the neck or groin. Finally, about two days after being attacked, men began to die, not from the burns but from the 'havoc the gas wrought in the throat and lungs'. A post-mortem conducted ten days after the first exposure to the gas recorded its horrible effects on the body. The victim's larynx and vocal chords were 'swollen and very red', his windpipe filled with 'thin, frothy fluid' and there were 'six ounces of blood stained fluid in the left lung.' Both heart and lungs had doubled in weight and the veins of the brain 'contained innumerable small bubbles of gas.'[37]

To see a flesh-and-blood human being, your comrade perhaps, mutate into a slimy creature – 'the white eyes writhing in his face', 'the blood . . . gargling from the froth-corrupted lungs' – was a terrible experience, bringing to the surface fundamental fears. Gas was – and has remained – as much a psychological as a physical weapon. Foul air entering the throat arouses in everyone a primitive fear of being choked or asphyxiated and triggers the instincts of self-preservation which go with it. Time and again during the Great War, gas attacks led to panic, and attempts by the military to devise countermeasures had only limited success.

Until early 1917 there was no proper gas mask. Troops had to face the chlorine attacks of 1915 with little more than bits of cloth soaked in urine over their faces. The 'P' helmet, which arrived later in the year, was very uncomfortable to wear and apt to leak in prolonged use. The 'box respirator' of 1917 looked more like a modern gas mask and was considered 'effective' by the medical authorities, but it did nothing to calm the fear of the troops. 'The mere mention of gas,' Colonel Rogers of the Black Watch recalled, 'could put the "Wind up" the Battalion at once, even if they had gas masks which, they were told, were perfectly safe.'[38]

Nor did training necessarily help. After 1915, every soldier on the Western Front had to attend a 'gas course' at one of the 'anti-gas schools' that had sprung up. He would spend 'an hour immersed in a cloud of gas', supposedly to give him 'confidence in his respirator'; he would be taught to put his gas mask on in less than six seconds and given basic instruction in recognising symptoms. It is a perennial question whether preventive training prepares the soldier to cope with psychological disorders or encourages him to develop their symptoms. Doctors in France were in no doubt that gas training, especially when combined with the whole terrifying ritual of the gas alarm – when screaming sirens could be heard up and down the line – could have disastrous effects. An eyewitness recalled that:

With men trained to believe that a light sniff of gas meant death, and with nerves highly strung by being shelled for long periods and with the presence of not a few who really had been gassed, it is no wonder that a gas alarm went beyond all bounds. It was remarked as a joke that if someone yelled 'gas', everyone in France would put on a mask. Two or three alarms a night was common. Gas shock was as frequent as shellshock.[39]

There was a dramatic illustration of this in 1918, when 'American troops, who had been constantly warned about gas and hastily drilled in meeting it but had no experience of it in action, were brought suddenly into the line.' Large numbers of them passed through Australian aid posts 'complaining, with obvious sincerity, of having been "gassed" but . . . present[ing] no symptoms or physical signs suggesting that they had actually inhaled any form of poison gas in amounts sufficient to be harmful.'[40]

The psychological effects of gas were not confined to the Americans nor to the inexperienced. 'After July 1917,' according to Charles Wilson, gas 'partly usurped the role of high explosive in bringing to a head a natural unfitness for war.' Gassed men, he thought, were 'an expression of trench fatigue, a menace when the manhood of the nation had been picked over.' This was plainly seen in March 1918, when, in a desperate bid to end the war before the Americans arrived, the German Army launched a sudden, unexpected offensive in France spearheaded by hundreds of thousands of rounds of mustard gas. Seven thousand British soldiers a week 'flooded into the field hospitals.'[41]

The gas crisis of March 1918 provoked within the British Army a reaction very similar to the shell-shock crisis of August 1916. Most of the cases were thought by the medical authorities to be 'hysterical'. 'Almost all were very light,' said T. R. Elliott, the Cambridge don acting as one of the Army's consultants. He thought it 'desirable to prevent the impression gaining ground that men who have inhaled a little mustard gas will get 3 or 4 months away in England.' Instead of languishing in hospitals at home, they should be kept in France and 'handled with the firmness that is needed to ensure a quick return to duty.'[42]

In the end the Army was obliged to set up specialist treatment centres for gas cases, based on those created for shell-shock; many of the problems of treatment, pensions, and psychological after-effects found in shell-shock would be duplicated.

But there was also another manifestation of the strain of war. In the later years of the conflict Army doctors were struggling to contain an epidemic of heart disorders. Soldiers have always had troubles of the heart: when in 1864 the British built a huge military hospital at Netley in Hampshire to serve the Empire, many cases of cardiac disorder soon appeared. This was, on the face of it, hardly surprising considering the 'tight-fitting tunics, the weight of accoutrements and sometimes of busbies, the diet and the drink, the temperature and the climate, and the extraordinary exertions demanded of the men.' Various Army committees sat and blamed the problem on 'tight accoutrements and over-exertion.' The weight of kit was reduced, soldiers were allowed to 'open their jackets', and 'setting up drill', said to 'over-expand the chest', was stopped. But still the condition persisted.[43]

Across the Atlantic, physicians working during the American Civil War had noticed similar problems among soldiers in the Union armies. Dr Henry Hartshorne attributed an 'affectation' which he called *muscular exhaustion of the heart* to 'great and prolonged exertion with the most unfavourable conditions possible – privation of rest, deficient food, bad water and malaria.' In 1871, Dr Jacob Da Costa wrote a famous article describing some 300 cases of *irritable heart*, men suffering from palpitations, cardiac pain, rapid pulse, respiratory problems and nervous and digestive disorders brought about by 'quick and long marches, heavy work . . . or even slight exertion in those whose constitution has been impaired.' Believing the special nerve centres at the base of the heart to be over-stimulated, Da Costa treated them with a veritable pharmacy of drugs – digitalis, aconite, veratrum viride, gelsemium, belladonna, opium, hyoscyamus, cannabis indica, strichnine and acetate of lead. However, rest alone may well have been primarily responsible for the fairly high rates of return he was able to achieve.[44]

Da Costa acknowledged that this ailment was not peculiar to soldiers but thought it unlikely ever to recur in such numbers again 'for so many men called, by the tap of the drum, from civil pursuits and sent without previous training into the field, is not a state of things likely often to happen.' But it did recur. In August 1914, the British Army's retreat from Mons, involving rapid marching for several sleepless days, produced many cases of chest pains, shortness of breath and heart palpitations which doctors had difficulty in diagnosing or treating. Nor did the switch to static trench warfare make much difference. Throughout 1915 and 1916, hospitals in Britain were 'receiving large numbers of recruits or of soldiers back from France who complained of pains in the chest . . . palpitations and giddiness on exertion.' Among them was the writer A. A. Milne, sent home suffering from 'shortness of breath and a racing heart.' In these cases, though, no organic diseases of the heart could be found. The condition acquired a new name, *Disordered Action of the Heart* (DAH).[45]

DAH posed a problem to the Army very similar to that of shell-shock. The numbers evacuated from France were so large that by the end of 1916 specialist treatment centres for DAH were being created in the Boulogne area, in which 'heart cases' could be assessed. By this means, the military managed eventually to hang on to some 50–60% of DAH cases, a saving of some 15,000 soldiers. Even so, by March 1918, some 36,569 men had been discharged from the Army and

Navy for cardio-vascular disorders and DAH would eventually become the third leading cause of discharge from the Army.[46]

In Harley Street and Whitehall, too, DAH provoked a debate similar to that over shell-shock. Heart specialists were divided along generational lines: the older school of cardiologists, concerned with precise anatomical lesions to the heart, pitted against the 'new cardiology', which took a more relaxed, 'global' view of the heart's functions. Most regimental medical officers in France had been trained by the old school to regard any irregularity of heart function, like murmurs or palpitations, as a sign of life-threatening heart disease; whereas the view among fashionable London consultants was that such symptoms were not significant in themselves – the important point was the body's overall capacity to handle exertion.[47]

The War Office's priority being to minimise 'wastage' and pensions, it found the latter approach better suited to its needs. In 1916, the Medical Research Council established two specialist hospitals in Britain, in which these cases were concentrated, and began dishing out money to an energetic young medical researcher, Thomas Lewis. By February 1917, Lewis had concluded that symptoms like breathlessness, pain, exhaustion, giddiness and fainting were not usually signs of heart trouble at all but merely 'exaggerated manifestations of healthy response to effort' – often brought about, he thought, by infection. A more appropriate term, he suggested, would be *Effort Syndrome*.[48]

Lewis and his colleagues then devised a programme of 'graduated exercises' intended to make it possible for 50% of soldiers to be returned to duty after only six weeks in hospital. It took some doing, for 'once a recruit . . . had been told he had "soldier's heart", it was very difficult indeed for the specialist to persuade him that his heart was quite normal.' Nevertheless, the exercise programme dramatically reduced the time spent in hospital and saved the authorities an estimated £50,000 a year.[49]

Lewis received a knighthood in 1921 from a grateful British government, but his 'Effort Syndrome' was still a *physiological* condition, accompanied, he claimed, by abnormalities in the blood and urine. The historian Alan Christophers has recently shown that ultimately none of this physiological evidence stood up. He argues that Thomas Lewis allowed himself to be swayed by the pressure of public opinion into believing in Effort Syndrome, ignoring psychological symptoms, the 'poorness of spirit' and 'lack of zeal' in his patients, because 'the thought of tens of thousands of malingerers [was] unacceptable. These [were] all brave soldiers.'[50]

By the end of the war, many psychiatrists had, in fact, come to believe that Disordered Action of the Heart was psychological, just another form of neurasthenia. 'It was pure chance,' one wrote later, 'whether a man was sent to my hospital as a neurotic . . . or to a heart hospital suffering from DAH.' The dominant American view was that these cases were suffering from a *cardiac neurosis* and American soldiers were treated in army psychiatric hospitals, but given the pseudo-organic label *neurocirculatory asthenia*.[51]

After the war, the British paid some 44,000 pensions for Effort Syndrome.[52]

The Army was given a free hand in its treatment of gas and heart disorders. But as the war went on there was increasing public concern about another issue – one which still aroused British public opinion eighty years later – the execution of soldiers suffering from shell-shock.

In 1993 a spate of stories about executions during the Great War began to appear in the British media, inspired by a campaign by a Member of Parliament to gain retrospective pardons for the 307 men shot for desertion, cowardice and other offences between 1914 and 1918. This campaign coincided with the final release, after a delay of 75 years, of the papers relating to the soldiers' courts martial. As when the issue was first raised in 1916, the argument in 1993 hinged on those cases where men were executed despite evidence that they were or had been suffering from shell-shock.[53]

In rejecting pleas for retrospective pardons, the British Prime Minister John Major made use of three arguments. Firstly, he said, it was wrong to try to rewrite history, by imposing modern judgements and values on the past. Secondly, the treatment of deserters had to be understood against the context of the 'bloodiest conflict ever' in which men were dying in their thousands every day and the authorities had felt that due punishment was necessary to maintain morale and discipline. Thirdly, said Major,

Shellshock did become recognised as a medical condition during World War One. And where medical evidence was available to the court, it was taken into account in sentencing and the recommendations on the final sentence made to the Commander-in-Chief. Most death sentences were commuted on the basis of medical evidence.[54]

In the light of this ex cathedra statement, it is worth pausing to examine how far medical knowledge about shell-shock *was* absorbed into the Army's judicial processes.

One of those disappointed by Mr Major's decision was Mrs Gertrude Farr, then aged 99. Her husband Harry Farr was executed in 1916 despite clear evidence that he was suffering from shell-shock.[55]

Harry Farr was then 25 and had been a soldier since enlisting in 1910. He went to France with the West Yorkshire regiment in November 1914 and was evacuated in May 1915 suffering from shell-shock; five months later he returned to the front. The facts in the case were not in dispute. On the evening of 16 September 1916, Private Farr's battalion went up to the line. The next morning, however, Farr reported to the Regimental Sergeant Major at his battalion transport lines claiming to be sick. He was sent to the nearest dressing station, but doctors there refused to treat him because he was not wounded and the sergeant sent him back up the line with a ration party that evening. When they arrived there was no sign of Private Farr.

Later that night he was found back in the transport lines standing near a brazier. Challenged by the RSM, he explained 'I can't stand it.' The sergeant, according to Farr, then replied, 'You are a fucking coward and you will go to the trenches. I give fuck all for my life and I give fuck all for yours and I'll get you fucking well shot.' An escort party tried to take Farr back to the line but after it had gone 500 yards he began to scream and struggle and, though threatened with a charge of cowardice, he refused to go any further.

During his court-martial Farr was asked why, after his arrest, he had not reported sick. He replied, 'Because being away from the shellfire I felt better.' A defence witness revealed that Farr had reported sick with nerves in about April 1916, being retained for a fortnight in the dressing station. He had reported again for the same cause on 22 July 1916 and had been kept in overnight. Unfortunately the doctor who had seen him then had since been wounded, and medical evidence was confined to a bald statement by the Battalion Medical Officer that Farr was 'fit to undergo the strain of trial'. Yet a lieutenant who had known him for six weeks testified that he had three times 'asked for leave to fall out and return to camp as he could not stand the noise of the artillery. He was trembling and did not appear in a fit state.'

Such was the evidence on which a man's life depended, and this was a great deal more detailed than most. What sentence would you as a junior-middle ranking officer in the latter stages of the Somme have imposed? The court's verdict was: death. The file then passed rapidly up the military chain of command. On 3 October the sentence was tersely endorsed by the Brigade Commander; the next day, by Division. On 6 October, the Earl of Cavan, commanding XIV Corps, also recommended execution. There was then a further medical examination; or rather, the Battalion Medical Officer wrote a second certificate confirming that he had carried out an examination *before* the trial.

Only at this point, on 7 October 1916, does the testimony of Harry Farr's company commander appear on the file. It was written at 9.45 p.m. 'in the field'.

This man came out with the 2nd Battalion West Yorkshire regiment 5.1.14 and was sent down to the base with shellshock 9.5.15. He joined the 1st Btn West Yorkshire Regt 20.10.15. He remained continuously with this Batn until his trial by FGCM. I cannot say what has destroyed this man's nerves but he has proved himself on many occasions incapable of keeping his head in action. Apart from his behaviour under fire, his *conduct* and *character* are *very good.*

But it was too late. Sir Douglas Haig confirmed the sentence. At 6 a.m. on 18 October 1916, Harry Farr was executed by shooting at Carnoy. 'Death,' says the standard note in the file, 'was instantaneous.'

Clearly by modern standards, Harry Farr had a raw deal. But did he, by the standards of October 1916 when, after all, the experts had only just begun to agree on what shell-shock was and Charles Myers was still trying to organise special hospitals for treating it? Let us, therefore, give the Army the benefit of the doubt and jump forward a year or so, to the later part of 1917 – a year in which no less than 94 British soldiers were shot. Was medical evidence being taken seriously then? What do the newly-opened records show?

First of all, they do not show the grounds on which dea commuted: the records of the 2,700-odd soldiers who were and then spared were destroyed 'sometime before 1947'. We whether John Major's claim that 'most death sentences wer basis of medical evidence' (rather than military convenience unlikely, though, because in many of the cases that do surviv of any kind is remarkable for its absence and when present is ... indeed.[56]

For example, 'of the 32 soldiers who were tried and executed for desertion between 20 July and 11 October 1917, only three appear to have undergone any form of medical examination in connection with their court martial or sentence.' Some of these cases were pretty straightforward acts of desertion, often after several previous offences, but others were more complicated. The records now open endorse the verdict of Judge Anthony Babington, on whose work much of the modern campaign is based:

The members of a field general court martial normally saw no documents relating to the prisoner they had convicted other than his conduct sheet and his personal pay book. During the last two years of the war a lot of men on trial for cowardice and desertion claimed to have been treated in hospital for shellshock. The corroborative medical records were never to hand.[57]

Captain Lawrence Gameson insisted on attending the court martial of a gunner from his battalion accused of cowardice in the face of the enemy in June 1917. The court was held 'at a little farmhouse in a low-ceilinged room with a stone floor' and an 'air of constrained embarrassment seemed to affect those who were taking part; amateurish embarrassment.' Having spent some hours with the prisoner before the trial, Gameson came to court with 'full data and a formidable case history' to argue that the gunner's 'undoubted failure should be imputed to those who had passed him as fit to serve in the Field Artillery'; 'his instability made him less fitted for such active service than a man who was deaf or had flat feet. My contention had the advantage of being patently true.' It obviously had some effect, for, though sentenced to death by the court, the boy was not shot.[58]

Gameson was an independent-minded man – a non-conformist and an Oxford graduate trained at the London Hospital. It was quite natural for him to 'shove myself into the picture' despite being 'ignorant in the thorny matter of mental states.' Although he got this man off, he thought that 'medical evidence . . . was not sought as matter of routine.'[59]

Public opinion in Britain was increasingly concerned that men who had suffered shell-shock were being executed without adequate steps being taken to assess their mental state. The Independent Labour MP Philip Snowden asked repeated questions in Parliament in 1916 and 1917 and, when fobbed off with general assurances, cited specific cases. These exchanges in Parliament have a completely unreal quality, particularly when read alongside the court martial records. As Babington has written, Ministers and MPs simply had no conception

reality of a Field Court Martial: 'the stilted brevity of the evidence, the
hazard presentation of the defence and the perfunctory enquiries which were
ually made into the character and record of a convicted soldier.' For example,
when on 14 December 1917, a Conservative backbencher inquired

Is it not a universal practice for a most complete and exhaustive report to be called for in
every case after a death sentence has been awarded and that, under those circumstances it
is practically impossible for any man to be executed who has suffered from shell-shock,
because the fact that he has so suffered is certain to be included in the report?

Mr Macpherson, the Under-Secretary for War, replied

I am assured of all these facts and in the cases personally brought to my notice the Court
had given them the most careful consideration.

Four days later, when pressed again, he asserted that when a prisoner on trial had
suffered from shell-shock that fact was always disclosed. Indeed, he had not come
across a single case 'where any soldier has been executed without being examined,
before trial, and before sentence, by a medical officer.'[60]
   Despite these assurances, the issue did not go away. There was, said one MP,
'no question among the people as a whole today upon which they feel more
concerned and more strongly than the carrying out of death sentences, not
because of anything said in the House but because of statements made by the men
who have to carry out these death sentences – the horror of them.' Mr
Macpherson gave his by now ritual assurance that he 'had not come across a single
case where a man was proved in the past to have suffered shell-shock, or was
proved to have been wounded, [had] suffered the death penalty.'[61]
   Then, in March 1918, there came a significant shift in tone. In a parliamentary
answer, Macpherson stated unequivocally that shell-shock was not the same thing
as cowardice: 'One has come across case after case of the most gallant fellows who
drew breath whose nerves are so badly shattered that only half of their whole
bodily strength and mental vigour remains.' He then quoted from a letter
recently received from Sir Douglas Haig himself.

When a man has been sentenced to death [Haig wrote] if at any time any doubt has been
raised as to his responsibility for his actions, or if the suggestion has been advanced that
he has suffered from neurasthenia or shell-shock, orders are issued for him to be examined
by a medical board which expresses an opinion as to his sanity, and as to whether he
should be held responsible for his actions. One of the members of the board is always a
medical officer of neurological experience. The sentence of death is not carried out in the
case of such a man unless the medical board expresses the positive opinion that he is to be
held responsible for his actions.[62]

Finally, in March of 1918, the Army had accepted shell-shock into its judicial
procedures. What lay behind this change of heart? Parliamentary pressure was
obviously important, especially when Liberals joined in, but there were other

factors as well. After the bloodletting and well-reported disasters at Passchendaele and Cambrai, Haig was fighting for his job and had to throw his chief of staff, head of intelligence and quartermaster-general to the wolves to hang on to it (the purge of Haig's cronies extended to the Medical chief, Sir Arthur Sloggett, who left France in March 1918). Also, for the first time in the war, Haig was worried about the morale of his Army. The autumn of 1917 had produced disturbances in the British Army (though nothing like the mutinies that swept the French Army in the summer) and the Bolshevik revolution of October 1917, in which disaffected soldiery had played an important part. In November 1917 Haig voiced concern that 'advanced socialistic and even anarchical views' were being expressed in the Army; lunching with King George V early in the new year, he spoke of the need, in the light of recent German peace initiatives, 'to tell the army in a few unambiguous sentences what we are fighting for. The Army is now composed of representatives of all classes of the Nation and many are most intelligent and think things out.' The change of policy on shell-shock and courts martial can, therefore, be seen as part of a wider sea-change in early 1918.[63]

Perhaps, though, it is wrong *always* to be cynical about official thinking – even in the Great War. There are signs that Haig had finally absorbed some of the realities of trench warfare; his handling of events in 1918 was to show a new level of skill. Culled of the 'mediocrities and conformists that he had always found so agreeable', the staff began to develop a new professionalism. There were now even staff officers with experience of the trenches. And, with the war over four years old, not only had practically every family in the land lost someone in France; it was also becoming abundantly clear that even the bravest man could break down.

Soon after Dr H. W. Hills became neurologist to Fourth Army early in 1918 – replacing Myers' protégé William Brown – the order came through that in future all prisoners were to be referred to the neurologist for a medical report. Hills found that many of his colleagues were unhappy at the change of policy: 'one "old stager" said, "If a man lets his comrades down he ought to be shot. If he's a loony, so much the better."' In the officers' mess, someone told Hills, 'We like you, but we don't like your circus. We think they ought to be shut up, or better still, shot.'[64]

Overall, though, the new system of boards seemed to tilt the balance of justice back towards the accused. In Hills' experience 'The court always gave prisoners the benefit of the doubt and many of them got off, not because of my arguments but because I was the doubt. In the seven months until the end of the war, there were no death sentences.' But this was only in Fourth Army. There were executions elsewhere on the Western Front, and although only thirteen soldiers were shot in the first half of the year, in the last four and a half months of the war no less than nineteen men were executed for desertion.[65]

HOME FIRES

Until the end of 1916, nearly all shell-shock cases were sent back to England for treatment. Even after special treatment centres were created in France, the worst cases continued to cross the Channel. Soon after his return from France in November 1917, Charles Myers was sent off by the War Office to find out how their treatment was going. He came back pretty depressed.[1]

The problems he found did not derive from any failure of official will or lack of public interest, and only in part from a lack of resources. Almost from the start shell-shock had caught the public imagination, featured in the newspapers and been debated in Parliament. The fact that many patients were officers helped to make it respectable; there was no talk of degenerates or weaklings. As early as August 1914, Dr Maurice Wright of the Psycho-Medical Society had urged the War Office to set up specialist hospitals. Lord Knutsford, the great hospital administrator and publicist, had taken up the cause and Lord Northcliffe's brother had offered his grand house in London as a hospital.[2]

The official response was equally prompt. By early 1915 – just as Charles Myers was being appointed 'shock specialist' in France – the Army medical supremo, Sir Alfred Keogh, had found 1,800 beds for shell-shock patients.[3]

But these resources proved inadequate to deal with the enormous numbers. According to one estimate, some 24,000 cases of shell-shock were sent back to England in the year to April 1916 – before the Somme battles turned the flood into a torrent. Even after special treatment centres were established in France in early 1917, the system in England was struggling to cope. Patients were supposed to pass through clearing hospitals and then be sent to specialist centres like the neurological hospital in Queen Square, but more than half ended up in general military hospitals, rarely accompanied by their 'notes'.[4]

It was hardly surprising that hard-pressed hospital doctors and nurses, with no psychiatric training were often dismayed and bewildered by a ward full of 'titubating shell-shockers', with their bizarre gaits and paralyses, stammers and tremors, nightmares and hallucinations, fits and shakings. One patient even had hair that stood on end: 'Nothing could make it lie down, not water or hair oil or anything'.[5]

The commonest symptom of all, a visiting American journalist observed, was 'a curious twitching of certain groups or most of his muscles, so that he cannot hold his head still, or walk or stand except with incessant jerkings and tremblings, while if he attempts to speak he stutters and stammers in the most appalling way.' All these jerkings and twitchings were increased by excitement. 'If, in a shell-shock ward you stop to look at one of the patients, instantly he begins to stammer and jerk, then the man across the aisle follows suit, and the infection spreads in ever widening circles until the whole ward is set jerking and twitching.' Yet all the movements and most of the spasmodic contractions ceased during sleep.[6]

Shell-shock patients were not like the wounded – meek, placid, manly and grateful. They moaned and complained and were difficult. They were also 'terrified of going back. They used to say, "I'm not going back to the front again, Sister. Will you tell the Major?"' They clung pathetically to their symptoms and wanted to justify themselves:

> Of course you've heard of shell-shock
> But I don't suppose you think
> What a wreck it leaves a chap
> After being in the pink
> What anguish we've to go through
> Or what pains we've to bear
> When we're thinking of our comrades
> Who are still doing their share.[7]

They envied the wounded's honour:

> Perhaps you're broke and paralysed
> Perhaps your memory goes
> But it's only just called shell-shock
> For you've nothing there that shows.[8]

Among well-meaning volunteer nurses and women visitors there was considerable sympathy for these patients. But doctors were adamant that this was a bad thing. 'Nothing retards recovery so much as the flying visits of unthinking, but kindly intentioned, philanthropic lady visitors,' said Sir John Collie. 'Aimless lounging, too many entertainments and relaxing recreations such as frequent motor rides' were also frowned on. An indulgent atmosphere not only made a return to the trenches less likely, it made it harder to face reality in general. Shell-shock cases were generally agreed to 'suffer from a disorder of will as well as of function'; it was therefore 'impossible to effect a cure if attention [was] directed to one at the expense of the other.' 'Shell-shock,' a prominent psychiatrist believed, produced 'a condition which is essentially childish and infantile in its nature. Rest in bed and simple encouragement is not enough to educate a child. Progressive daily achievement is the only way whereby manhood and self-respect can be regained.'[9]

Methods of treatment varied from hospital to hospital, ranging from discipline and physical exercise to the standard Weir Mitchell cure of isolation, rest, and a milk diet. There was also a good deal of unfocused massage and electrical stimulation of the muscles. Many patients were simply left to themselves. There was 'no more pathetic sight,' the American psychiatrist Thomas Salmon wrote, than the 'mismanaged nervous and mental cases' which crowded the wards of the British general military hospitals. They were 'exposed to misdirected harshness or to equally misdirected sympathy, dealt with at one time as malingerers and at another as sufferers from incurable organic nervous disease.' Frequently passed on from one hospital to another and finally discharged with pensions that could not subsequently be diminished, many 'enter[ed] the hospitals as "shell-shock cases" and c[a]me out as nervous wrecks.'[10]

One in six shell-shock cases was an officer, although at the front there were 30 men to an officer; officers and men went to different hospitals and got different levels of treatment. An anonymous soldier complained to the press in 1916 that while officers received 'all sorts of interesting methods', 'all that was done for nerve-shaken soldiers of the rank and file' was to place them 'in a block in a county asylum, and under the same management as the rest of the asylum, which is in use for certified lunatics'.[11]

Asylum doctors had experience of mental disorders, but Myers found them especially unhelpful – deeply conservative and lacking in intellectual curiosity. The dominant pre-war model of mental illness as something physical, hereditary and untreatable gave them a fatalism about shell-shock cases, who were seen as inferior people, bound to break down. There was no sense of dynamism, no expectation of cure. Asylum staff, according to another doctor, had 'no experience of the soldier' and were 'unsympathetic and ignorant of the soldier's trials, terrors and sufferings, which were the causes of the patient's condition . . . What was good enough for the pauper patients was thought sufficient for these wrecked soldiers.' There was also an eagerness to pitch as many cases as possible back into civilian life even if their symptoms were unresolved. One doctor said that 80% of his patients were 'boarded for discharge'.[12]

Discharge to what? As Tom Salmon said, 'to turn . . . adrift thousands of young men who developed the nervous disability through military service and can find in their home towns none of the facilities required for their cure was indeed a gross injustice.' Myers knew how vital it was to tackle the war neuroses quickly; given prompt and appropriate treatment, most men would get better. Left to rot and fester, they became convinced that they were genuinely ill; if left long enough, they became incapable of resuming normal life.[13]

Amid all this gloom, however, there were some rays of sunshine. By 1917, two important changes had occurred: the neurologists had recovered their nerve and new psychological methods of treatment were being developed.

*   *   *

If, in the early years of the war, the public had 'raised the psychoneuroses of war to the dignity of a new war disease before which doctors stood well nigh helpless', it was because most doctors at home *were* well-nigh helpless. There was no clear line from the leaders of the profession. In particular, the neurologists, the specialists in 'functional nervous disorders' occurring in the 'borderline' between outright mental illness and physical disorder, mostly kept silent, leaving it to Myers, an academic psychologist, and Mott, an asylum pathologist, to make the running. There were two reasons for this: firstly, the symptoms of shell-shock genuinely took everyone by surprise; secondly, most British neurologists, accustomed to look to Paris, waited for a line to emerge over the Channel.[14]

Then they began to find their feet. By the end of 1916, with the hospitals choked with cases of blindness, paralysis, deafness, and the rest, there appeared a group of people confidently prepared to act. At the National Hospital, Queen Square, two members of the wartime staff decided to try a more intensive method of treatment as described by the French. Edgar Douglas Adrian, future Nobel Laureate and Baron, was then scarcely out of medical school but had already done brilliant work in experimental physiology. Like many great men, he had an elemental, almost destructive, forcefulness of character. His colleague, Lewis Yealland, was the son of a Toronto newspaper editor and had worked briefly in Canadian asylums before coming to London. Though not intellectually on Adrian's level, he was a strong, self-confident man and a devout evangelical Christian.[15]

Their patients were nearly all of a particular type, of below average intelligence, suffering from hysterical disorders. Adrian and Yealland believed that 'the chief phenomena underlying the hysterical type of mind [were] weakness of the will and of the intellect, hyper-suggestibility and negativism':

. . . the patient has a fixed idea that he is dumb or paralysed and he resists all criticism of this idea, but outside he responds to external suggestions much more readily than a normal person. Indeed the fixed idea is developed as the result of autosuggestion acting on a mind enfeebled by fear and emotional tension and this autosuggestion becomes so strong that the patient resists all attempts to undermine his fixed belief.[16]

Although as a Cambridge undergraduate, Adrian had dabbled in psychoanalysis, he felt such methods would not be practical with these cases because 'the course of treatment may run to years if a serious attempt is made to purge the hysterical mind by curing it of the accumulated filth of a lifetime.' Instead, he and Yealland favoured 'a little plain speaking accompanied by strong faradic current.' Their method was to convince patients that they would get better and then to wheel on electrical equipment as a psychological prop to effect the cure. 'The therapeutic uses of the electricity,' Adrian wrote, 'are still mysterious enough to the layman and nearly every patient is willing to accept the suggestion that some form of electricity will cure him.' The electrodes became like a magic wand that brought function back into the patient's arm or leg. The current wasn't usually very strong, but, if the patient was inclined to resist, or had been unsuccessfully treated with electricity before, then higher voltage was used to enhance the doctor's authority:

The current can be made extremely painful if it is necessary to supply the disciplinary element which must be invoked if the patient is one of those who prefer not to recover, and it can be made strong enough to break down the unconscious barriers to sensation in the most profound functional anaesthesia.[17]

Adrian and Yealland claimed particular success with patients who were deaf, dumb or paralysed in one limb. As soon as the 'least sign of recovery' appeared, the patient was marched into 're-education':

The patient is given no time to collect his thoughts but is hurried along by a mixture of persuasion and command until the disordered function has recovered completely. The patient is not allowed any say in the matter. He is not asked whether he can raise his paralysed arm or not; he is ordered to raise it and told that he can do it perfectly if he tries. Rapidity and an authoritative manner are the chief factors in the re-education process.[18]

Some have described these methods as sadism. They certainly involved the 'triumph of a strong mind over a weak one'. For a dim, confused person to be confronted in a darkened room by Adrian and Yealland in full cry must have been an experience which, in itself, bordered on the traumatic. But it seemed to work in that it could remove the symptoms.

At the end of 1917, Adrian and Yealland parted company. Yealland then developed his technique further and wrote an extraordinary book giving blow-by-blow accounts of over a hundred successful 'cures'. His tone is quite different from Edgar Adrian's terse, detached, British cynicism; Yealland is fervent, sincere, over-dramatic. This is not just a doctor in action, but an evangelist grappling with evil, driving the devils from his patient's body.[19]

Yealland's patients were chronic cases of hysteria whose symptoms had persisted through various forms of treatment for over a year. One, for example, was a private soldier of 24, who had been in the war from the beginning. In July 1916, he had finally collapsed in intense heat in Salonica and been unconscious for five hours; when he awoke he was shaking all over and unable to speak. By the time Yealland saw this man, nine months later, he was the scarred veteran of much 'treatment':

He had been strapped in a chair for twenty minutes at a time while strong electricity was applied to his neck and throat; lighted cigarettes had been applied to the tip of his tongue and 'hot plates' had been placed at the back of his mouth. Hypnotism had also been tried.

To crack such a chronic case, Yealland pulled out every dramatic flourish: 'In the evening he was taken to the electrical room, the blinds drawn, the lights turned out, the keys removed. The only light perceptible was that from the resistance bulbs of the battery.' But his method was essentially the same – using electricity, 'the great sheet anchor of treatment', to bend the patient's will to his own. Yealland announced on arrival that neither of them would leave until the man was cured, and promptly gave him a burst of current at the back of the throat that made him jump backwards. After an hour of semi-continuous, but lighter electricity, the patient had been persuaded to say 'ah'. He was complemented on the improvement and assured he would soon be talking. After a further half an hour of electricity he could manage some vowels. He was then walked up and down the room and told he was ready for the next stage of treatment – 'the administration of strong shocks to the outside of the neck; these will be transmitted to your voice box and you will soon say anything you wish in a whisper.'[20]

And so it went on. A further slight improvement: a congratulatory lecture from Yealland. Even so it took 'shock and shock' to the back of the throat to get the soldier to repeat first sounds and then days of the week and numbers. An outburst of stammering led to yet more electricity and then, just when it seemed that recovery had finally been achieved, the patient developed a tremor in his left arm. This, too, was attacked by electricity: 'before it disappeared, it had to be chased from the left arm, the right arm, then from the left leg, and finally from the right leg, all those parts being treated similarly.'

Yealland's account concludes, 'He became quite excited and said "Doctor, doctor, I am champion," to which I replied "You are a hero." He then said "Why did they not send me to you nine months ago?"' After four hours' continuous treatment, the case was, it seems, 'cured'.[21]

For a while, Yealland enjoyed a great reputation. Doctors like Frederick Mott at the Maudsley sent him chronic cases they had failed with. But by the time his book detailing his methods came out, a new miracle worker had appeared.

Some things only moving pictures can show. To get a sense of the freakish, weird fascination of some shell-shock cases, one needs to look at a short film shot at two Army hospitals in England in 1917–18. Soldiers in hospital blues totter and sway towards the camera, their limbs shaking and flapping like dogs' tails. One man has an ear which twitches permanently; another's head constantly swivels on its neck; a third keeps diving under his hospital bed each time he hears the word 'bombs'. Young soldiers walk with the bent, contorted spines of old age, or move, without lifting their legs, by vibrating their limbs on the ground; numerous patients cannot walk or talk without a constant, involuntary 'nose-wiping' tic, bringing their arms up to their faces.[22]

Superficially these appear to be the symptoms of organic damage to the nervous system. In fact they were hysterical, and, as Dr Arthur Hurst proceeds to demonstrate in the film, could rapidly be 'cured'. The author of *Constipation and Allied Intestinal Disorders*, Hurst had made his name before the war by applying to the gastro-intestinal tract the new technique of X-raying a barium meal; but, of all English doctors, he was perhaps best equipped by experience and temperament to treat hysteria. In 1907, he had persuaded Guy's Hospital to let him open a neurology department, and gone off to Paris to see how it was done. As a result, he had seen the great French masters, Babinski, Dejerine and the rest, in action, while most other British doctors knew them only through their writings.[23]

Early in the war, Hurst worked on the sanitary disasters of Gallipoli and Salonica; it was not until the autumn of 1916, when some consensus about shell-shock was emerging, that he returned to England and took over neurological wards in Oxford. Then, after a spell at Netley Hospital, he managed, with remarkable sleight-of-hand, to set up his own shell-shock hospital in an Agricultural College at Seale Hayne, on the edge of Dartmoor. Hurst's background gave him rare confidence with hysterics – he was not afraid of these cases. Also, his own eager, enthusiastic temperament, and 'remarkable power of influencing younger men' empowered him. A small, frail man and a chronic sufferer from asthma, Hurst had always had a strong theatrical side to his nature, a flashiness some colleagues found unsound; one pupil remembered him as 'a great showman'.[24]

Even more than Adrian and Yealland, Hurst appreciated that an 'all-important preliminary is the creation of a proper atmosphere of cure.' Patients arriving at Seale Hayne would be carefully primed by the nurses, told of the doctor's miraculous record, shown other successful cases and the 'trophies in the shape of discarded splints and crutches' which lined the hospital's walls and given notice of when they would be 'cured'.[25]

By the following morning the patient is fully convinced that the hoped-for cure will take place: as the medical officer is equally convinced that he will cure the patient, the two essentials for recovery are present. The nature of the actual treatment is really immaterial [Hurst airily declared], but simple persuasion has the great advantage of making the patient take an active part in his own cure and it removes any suspicion of charlatanism from the proceedings.[26]

At first Hurst treated his patients either by suggestion under hypnosis and or by persuasion backed up by electricity. But by 1918 he had become convinced that most hysterical cases, even those of long duration, could be cured within twenty-four hours simply by talking to the patient. Electricity was unnecessary and often led to 'considerable emotional reaction'; hypnosis didn't seem to work very well and sometimes produced new symptoms. They were phased out, but the regime at Seale Hayne also included physiotherapy. Hysterical contractures, for example, were 'overcome by forcible manipulation, however much the patient may complain of pain, the movements being repeated until complete relaxation and the power to perform voluntary movements are restored.'[27]

Hurst's film shows that the pain was often quite considerable: several sequences in which a patient's head or ankle is wrenched round and round are as gruesome as a Chaplin comedy. But, being silent, the film reveals little about the critical ingredient, Hurst's own techniques of persuasion; we don't hear him talk to the patients.

Hurst claimed great success for his methods, and his film showed his patients, 'after' treatment, leaping around, feeding chickens, ploughing the fields at Seale Hayne and even having 'war games', re-creating the Western Front on Dartmoor. Hurst's friend, Sir William Osler, hailed techniques which 'intelligently followed

... should save the country thousands of pounds annually in pensions.' Others wondered whether it was quite that easy. Charles Myers, for one, doubted whether a 'quick showy cure' of the symptoms was enough. Other psychologists, while praising Hurst's work on cataloguing the symptoms of hysteria, felt he 'invested the subject with a spurious simplicity ... The removal of an obvious hysterical symptom was too often regarded as equivalent to the cure of the patient.' There was also muttering about relapses, cynics suggesting that many of Hurst's patients began to decline as soon as they left his charismatic presence and had usually developed new symptoms by the time the train away from Seale Hayne had reached Salisbury.[28]

Some neurologists came to share these doubts. After the war, Edgar Adrian looked back on his own experiences with hysterical patients.

You take a man who is paralysed in the legs: you assure him that all he needs is a little exercise, you force him to walk in spite of his protests and in half an hour he is apparently in perfect health again. Often he goes on his way rejoicing but sometimes you have not finished with him so easily for next morning although he walks well enough he speaks with a stammer that was not there before or he starts vomiting after every meal and he has to be treated all over again. Sometimes, though not very often, he does not develop any new bodily symptoms, but instead of this he becomes depressed, complains of headaches, insomnia, inability to concentrate his attention and so on although he was perfectly happy when his legs were paralysed. So that obviously there is still something wrong and the removal of his bodily symptom has not been enough.[29]

In a later talk Adrian explained why this was:

With the loss of the symptom which preserved their self-respect there would soon be a revival of anxiety and there was no certainty that the patient would not break down again if he went back to his unit.[30]

For this reason 'the miracle working methods soon palled' for Adrian. Instead, he and others turned their attention away from physical symptoms towards underlying psychological causes, influenced by the remarkable work going on in a hospital in the north of England.

*   *   *

Maghull is a small, gloomy village set in flat, wind-swept country just to the north of Liverpool, a mile or two inland from the links and sands of Formby. In 1911, Liverpool council laid out a large hospital for epileptics in the grounds of a mansion there. It lay unoccupied at the outbreak of war and was quickly commandeered by the War Office as a place to which 'borderline' and 'mental' cases could be sent without incurring the stigma of the asylum.

As hospitals went, Maghull was a cheerful place: two-storey, mock Georgian 'villas' clustered around squares of lawn, as yet untouched by the 'general atmosphere of apathy and neglect which broods over most lunatic asylums'.

There were also fields where patients could do remedial agricultural work. But it was the staff that made Maghull remarkable. Ronald Rows, the Medical Superintendent, was an obscure Lancashire pathologist who had come to prominence before the war as a researcher into organic mental disorders and as a passionate advocate of reform in mental hospitals. In 1914 Rows was Secretary to a committee recommending sweeping changes in the status and training of asylum doctors. But his belief in the need for out-patient psychiatric clinics to help 'borderline patients' before they reached the 'disaster of committal' had also led him to embrace the 'remarkable work' of Freud and Jung on the 'importance of psychogenic factors' in neurasthenia and hysteria.[31]

The war put the reformist agenda on hold but gave Rows 'not merely a new lease of life, but a new life', an 'opportunity to investigate a large number of those suffering from psychic disturbances during the early stages of the illness'; and the people to do it with. The Army's medical chief, Sir Alfred Keogh, was persuaded by the Medical Research Council to send to Maghull a 'brilliant band' of academic psychologists and doctors – the sort of Oxbridge heavyweights who normally shunned the drudgery of asylum work. Articulate, self-assured, not beholden to the state for their income, they were keen to try out the psychological ideas of Dejerine, Janet and Freud. Maghull's aura of self-belief and therapeutic optimism soon began to be expressed in articles and speeches.[32]

Whereas shell-shock cases aroused despair and hostility in general military hospitals and asylums, or were briskly dispatched by the neurologists, the 600 patients at Maghull – mostly soldiers suffering from neurasthenia – were greeted with sympathy and interest and encouraged to discuss their problems. 'I am doing real psychology here,' one doctor wrote in 1915. 'The work is extraordinarily interesting and instructive.' Maghull became a running symposium on the mind, 'a society in which the interpretation of dreams and the discussion of mental conflicts formed the staple subjects of conversation.' It was soon noticed, for example, that 'patients who when awake, joked, played cards and billiards [and] attended the dances,' also 'raved and sleep-walked at night,' thus 'giving the intelligent nurse the opportunity for revealing reports.'[33]

The effects of war on patients' conscious minds were also explored. Questions such as 'Why do I get these terrors? Why am I always seeing those things that happened in France? Why am I so irritable? Why do I get so upset?' were frequently heard from them, Dr Rows noted. 'In almost every instance,' he added, 'the memory of some disturbing past experience will be found acting as the cause.' Like Myers in France, the Maghull doctors were interested in memory; unlike Myers, they had the time and political protection to explore it.[34]

Not just memory, however, but also the 'emotional state' accompanying it. In a pioneering article in March 1916, Rows recorded the case of a soldier whose sweatings, stammerings and nightmares were caused by guilt at having accidentally shot a fellow Englishman in no-man's land. He showed, too, how the emotions produced by war experience often brought to the surface, and interacted with, previous emotional memories:

He and a comrade were carrying a pail of water to the trenches. It was very cold and they set down the pail in order to warm their hands. The comrade placed his hand against the cheek of the patient and said, 'That hand is cold'. At that moment he was shot dead.[35]

This incident was revived not only in dreams at night but if during the day he were quiet and closed his eyes he could feel the cold hand against his face. He was much distressed by the frequent revival of the incident in such a realistic manner.

But he was at the same time troubled by another dream, in which he ran down a narrow lane at the bottom of which there was a well. He dipped his hands into the water, but on withdrawing them he was horrified to find they were covered with blood. This dream was connected with a love affair in which his great friend interfered and angered him so much that he attacked him when next they met . . . he never heard whether the man he had attacked had died.[36]

Another patient was full of guilt because he had dreams which 'began with some terrible experience in the trenches and then turned to some sexual acts with women, usually his wife,' Rows noted. 'He would wake and find that he had "lost nature" [had a nocturnal emission]. Having for years believed that such "loss" would "affect [his] brain and drive [him] mad", he was very worried.' Rows did not pursue the implications of these cases, and made no reference to Freud. He simply endorsed Dejerine's view that the cause of all hysteria and neurasthenia lay in some previous emotional condition and recommended that the patient's history be carefully explored until the cause of the emotion was found, and that it should all then be plainly explained to him. Once he understood that he had no terrible disease, that no supernatural agency had been at work, he would start gently to recover.

The patient will understand that it will not be possible for him to banish the memory completely. But he can be induced to face the trouble, to reason about it and to recognize it simply as a memory of the past instead of allowing the emotional tone connected with it to dominate him until the condition of anxiety has been produced.[37]

We don't know what the patients made of all this; being soldiers not officers, they have left no recollections. They seem at first to have been 'highly appreciative of the attention paid to them'; but then 'the idea . . . got around that dreams were being used by medical officers as a means of testing whether their patients were to be sent back to France' and, after that, 'it was only rarely that [the doctor] was able to obtain more than the merest fragments of a dream.' This suggests that the men remained well aware of Maghull's role within the military apparatus of the war and, while flattered by the doctors' attention, were suspicious of their motives.[38]

Maghull was a military hospital, not a research establishment; its job, in theory, was to return men to the front. No War Office records survive and it is not clear what pressure was exerted, or whether the hospital was seen in Whitehall as a public relations showpiece. Doctors there initially had to put up with criticism from traditionalists and occasional inspections by 'the type of Brass Hat who professed to think that all the half-thousand patients were "skrimshankers" and malingerers' (Rows gave such visitors a good meal followed by 'a leisurely tour of mental defectives, schizophrenics and maniacs'). But, later on, the military authorities 'slowly and reluctantly' came to the conclusion that it was useless to return men with chronic neurosis to front-line duty. 'A medical general came almost secretly to the hospital,' a doctor recalled, 'and said would we please discharge as many from the army as possible, though we must not say he said so.'[39]

This would explain why, in the year to 30 June 1917, only around 160 of the 731 patients discharged from the hospital returned to military duty, while 65% went back to civilian life, 12% to other hospitals, and 1% to civilian mental hospitals. After the war, Rows acknowledged that 'the further the invalid soldier went from the front line the more difficult it was to get him back to it'; having crossed the Channel, he felt 'a sense of relief, a sense of safety, a feeling of escape from the terrible conditions on the other side, and quite naturally there arose a desire not to return.'[40]

It would be an oversimplification to say that the Maghull approach amounted simply to discharging the soldier from his military responsibility; but, equally, the leading academic psychologists who worked there at various times, like William Brown and William McDougall, were, one suspects, more interested in exploring theories of psychology than in the practice of military psychiatry. A visit to the hospital in late 1917 left Charles Myers with a lasting distaste for the 'wild and mutually antagonistic generalizations of the various schools'.[41]

The dominant personality at Maghull was not a psychologist at all, but the Australian-born anatomist and polymath Grafton Elliot Smith. It was probably thanks to Elliot Smith that William Rivers came to Maghull, in July 1915.

Rivers was then 51; a tall man, hunched, myopic, shy, with steel-rimmed glasses and a stammer; a strange combination of awkwardness and intellectual assurance. His medical knowledge, if slightly rusty, was profound: 'perhaps no man ever approached the investigation of the human mind by so many routes.' The son of a Kent clergyman, Rivers had been a medical student at St Bartholomew's, a general practitioner, a ships' doctor, house physician to Hughlings Jackson and Sir Victor Horsley at Queen Square, and a clinical assistant at the Bethlem Hospital – all before going to Cambridge to lecture in Psychology in 1893. Thereafter he had done important research into the physiology of colour vision and the effects of drugs on the brain and, with his friend Henry Head, carried out a famous experiment to establish the physiological basis of sensation. Every weekend for five years, in his rooms at St John's College, Rivers had severed the nerves in Head's arm and then observed the effects on its sensation.[42]

Rivers' own brain was too restless an instrument to be tied to a single discipline. When, in 1898, he and his pupils Charles Myers and William McDougall were invited to join the Cambridge expedition to the Torres Straits, a new passion, for anthropology and sea-travel, was aroused. In 1910 he handed the psychology department over to Myers, and devoted himself to producing immense scholarly works on the Toda tribesmen of India and the Melanesian islanders.

Two things stand out from this strange career. Firstly, Rivers' main interest as an anthropologist was in sorting out kinship patterns and social customs; his field-work trips therefore involved much patient questioning of tribesmen about their traditions and legends. On Murray Island in 1898, 'one never knew in what corner or retired spot one might not come upon the mysterious whispering of Rivers and his confidant. The questioning one overheard was mostly in this wise: "He married? What name wife belong him? Where he stop? What picaninny he got?"' This would prove ideal training for the wartime psychotherapist.[43]

Secondly, there was something odd and unresolved about Rivers himself. He was unmarried, lived in Cambridge as a recluse, concentrating on research, shunning all college or university life, and did not drink or smoke. He was a repressed and often unhappy man. Yet, in the Pacific – on a schooner, talking to missionaries and Melanesians – Rivers was a different person. Photographs taken in England show a tight, drawn reserved face with collar and tie; in the Pacific, a smiling, bare-footed hedonist.

Rivers came to Maghull still very preoccupied by anthropology and the theories about the diffusion of culture in the ancient world he was developing with Elliot Smith; their conversations in the evening mystified colleagues with 'references to stone seats, megaliths, rags hung on trees, dragons, cranial deformation, circumcision [and] mummification.' But by day they were involved in shell-shock – Elliot Smith writing a polemical attack on the mental health establishment, Rivers talking to patients and mugging up on Freud.[44]

Before the war, Rivers had taken some interest in Freud, but never tried to master his theory of dreams. Now, with *Die Traumdeutung* at last available in English, he saw at once that Freud might provide the key to understanding the dreams of the Maghull soldiers, of interpreting what lay in their unconscious minds. Freud's reading of his own highly complicated dreams may have seemed to Rivers 'forced and arbitrary'; its 'general method' so 'unscientific that it might be used to prove anything'. Yet clearly it aroused his intellectual appetite. 'Patients' dreams at Maghull,' Rivers wrote at this time, 'furnished confirmation of Freud's view that dreams have the fulfilment of a wish as their motive. Thus one soldier dreamt that he was sent back to the front, but directly he landed in France, peace was declared.' But Rivers was an academic: he needed complexity. He found it frustrating that the soldiers were often reluctant to reveal dreams or, if they did, that 'the dreams of uneducated persons are exceedingly simple and their meaning is often transparent.'[45]

Fellow of the Royal Society and friend of the tribesman, Rivers lacked the common touch with the ordinary Tommy and was itching to get back to his anthropological work. Only when he was transferred to Craiglockhart Hospital near Edinburgh, in October 1916, did he emerge as the most interesting of the shell-shock doctors.

* * *

Craiglockhart, one of six special hospitals for nerve-shattered officers set up by the War Office, was a large Italianate pile on the outskirts of Edinburgh; a 'monster hydro' built around 1880 as a hydropathic clinic offering rich invalids the water-cure amid bracing air and stirring landscape. Commercially, it had never fulfilled its builders' hopes and 'an air of genteel melancholy as pervasive as rising damp had entered the bones of the building long before the war.'[46]

The War Office took over Craiglockhart in the summer of 1916 and the Somme battles soon filled it with neurasthenic officers. Physical activity was always important at Craiglockhart and Rivers' arrival, as senior psychiatrist, did not change that. Patients continued to play billiards, badminton, bowls, croquet, cricket, golf, and tennis or have games of water polo in the hydro's heated pool; but, even more than at Maghull, a contrast emerged between the forced, communal, masculine gaiety, the 'energetic optimism', of the days, and the tortured, solitary agony of the nights – an antithesis wonderfully caught by one of Rivers' patients. 'Outwardly,' Siegfried Sassoon wrote, 'Craiglockhart was elaborately cheerful.'

Brisk amusements were encouraged, entertainments were got up, and serious cases were seldom sent downstairs . . .

The doctors did everything possible to counteract gloom, and the wrecked faces were outnumbered by those who were emerging from their nervous disorders. But the War Office had wasted no money on interior decoration; consequently the place had the melancholy atmosphere of a decayed hydro, redeemed only by its healthy situation and pleasant view of the Pentland Hills. By day the doctors dealt successfully with these disadvantages and [Craiglockhart], so to speak, 'made cheerful conversation'. But by night they lost control and the hospital became sepulchral and oppressive with saturations of war experience. One lay awake and listened to feet padding along passages which smelt of stale cigarette smoke . . . One became conscious that the place was full of men whose slumbers were morbid and terrifying – men muttering uneasily or suddenly crying out in their sleep. Around me was that underworld of dreams haunted by submerged memories of warfare and its intolerable shocks and self-lacerating failures to achieve the impossible.[47]

Rivers came to Craiglockhart in a state of internal uncertainty, his mind still preoccupied by anthropology, and at first he made little headway. The breakthrough came with a dream – one of his own, not a patient's – in which his repressed wish to get back to London and resume his academic career was expressed in slightly disguised form. This convinced him of 'the truth of the main lines of the Freudian position.' He at once re-read Freud on dreams and in March 1917 gave a lecture in Edinburgh arguing that Freud's ideas, though wrong in emphasising the sexual origins of mental problems, provided a valuable tool for understanding war neuroses.[48]

Rivers was not the first to go down this road. In 1916, the maverick English Freudian David Eder had published an interesting account of his work in a hospital on Malta with soldiers evacuated from Gallipoli. One of them, whose right hand remained locked in a hysterical contracture, was, said Eder, still clutching 'in the unconscious' the rifle with which he had defended himself against a group of Turks while being bayoneted fourteen times.[49]

Eder was the first person to adapt to warfare the Freudian idea that neurosis is produced by mental conflict. Thus he argued that a young Australian sniper had gone blind in his right eye after being nearly hit by sniper counter-fire as a result of a conflict between the 'ego instinct' and the 'gregarious or herd instinct' – a grandiose term for social instincts like duty and patriotism recently popularised by the British surgeon, Wilfred Trotter.

The unconscious [wrote Eder], acting on behalf of the ego sets the eye watering, forcing [the soldier] to relinquish his post. Then the soldier's instinct reasserts itself, the eye ceases to water and he returns to the loophole. But here the egocentric instinct, self-preservation, reasserts itself and the unconscious adopts a stronger attack. He is stricken blind in the shooting eye . . . He is now unable to carry out his conception of the soldier's duty and, without loss of self-respect is able to retire, his safety guaranteed.[50]

The mental conflict, Eder believed, was not between civilised codes of behaviour and the suppressed sexual needs of the unconscious (as with Freud and Breuer's patients), but between a sense of duty and an unconscious wish to survive.

A man of wide experience of life, Eder did not think it necessary, when treating a dramatic but simple case like this, to go back into the patient's childhood; using psychoanalysis on soldiers (many of them 'up-country Anzacs') would be 'to use a Nasmyth hammer to crack a nut.' Instead Eder relied mainly on hypnotic suggestion, for which his strong personality was well suited, and claimed to have cured 70 out of 100 patients in this way. However, in a few cases Eder did find sexual factors, which he analysed with a mixture of Freud and Jung which was not to readers' tastes in 1916. One man dreamt that he was

On a boat running out of A- Harbour, going down the River B. We went through a narrow passage which came gradually to a point and got stuck in the mud. Looking out of the porthole window I saw a Zeppelin in the distance. It was attacked by a fleet of balloons. One burst and all the bits came dropping through the air. One end of the Zeppelin was dropping but it rose and woke me with a start.

He was told by Eder that 'the narrow passage stood for the vagina and the mud was the anal region; that the boat coming down the passage (the vagina) was himself (c.f. the birth of Moses, or Ra, and other legendary heroes discovered in infancy floating in barks of water).' The balloon was identified as his mother's womb, the Zeppelin as his own phallus – 'his phallus (Zeppelin) is the prey of women (balloon) which will destroy his male power.' After further dream-analysis the patient discovered 'that his libido was still attached to his mother and that he must free himself therefrom before he can overcome his fear of sex.'[51]

Passages like this caused much alarm – 'the sooner that psychoanalysis of this kind ceases to be practised in England, the better it will be for all concerned,' wrote Arthur Hurst – and blinded other doctors to Eder's originality and good sense. Eder did not last long on Malta.[52]

By contrast, Rivers' article on Freud had a considerable impact on British medicine. It had a masterful tone of lofty academic detachment, holding the ring between 'the extravagance of Freud's adherents and the rancour of their opponents'; and it emphasised that Freud's theory that neurosis was produced by sexual factors had been decisively disproved by wartime experience.[53]

And yet, Rivers insisted, even though Freud was wrong about the underlying cause of the conflict in the mind, there was hardly a case which Freud's theory of the unconscious did not help us better to understand, 'not a day of clinical experience in which Freud's theory may not be of direct practical use in diagnosis and treatment.' Freud, Rivers argued, provided a 'working hypothesis', a 'theory of the mechanism by which . . . experience not directly accessible to consciousness, produces its effect'. Freud's principal merit lay in 'the importance he attached to forgetting' – his 'belief in a process of active suppression of unpleasant experience' (at first, Rivers avoided the word 'repression'). The idea that conflicts took place in the mind was not, in itself, new; what was original about Freud was his 'scheme of the nature of the opponents in the conflict, and of the mechanism by which the conflict is conducted.'

But although Rivers used Freudian concepts like repression and the unconsciousness, he was never a Freudian. His technique was very dependent on what he called 'the personality of the healer' and those who knew him best felt that his therapeutic power derived from his own personality – from what Freudians call a counter-transference: his patients got better because they wanted to please Rivers, to do what he wanted. (At least one of them had an elaborate dream about his relationship with Rivers.) Once at Craiglockhart, Rivers was dealing with his own class and was more able to form this emotional bond with his patients.[54]

Thus Rivers worked best with intelligent, educated patients, whom he led towards self-knowledge and self-analysis, a process he called *auto-gnosis*, a term borrowed by William Brown. How far this method was replicable in other hands, whether it could be put into 'language easily comprehensible to men of mediocre intelligence and education', was debatable.

The issue that brought Rivers' gifts as a therapist to the fore was a fundamental one. What advice should he give his patients about their horrible war experiences? Should they think about them or try to forget them? Most had been firmly told by friends, relatives or doctors to forget them ('Put it out of your mind, old Boy'), to 'lead their thoughts to other topics, to beautiful scenery and to other pleasant aspects of experience.' But, Rivers argued, it was not that easy. For example, one patient had been buried by a shell explosion in France, had remained on duty for several more months and had then collapsed after 'a very terrifying experience in which he had gone out to seek a fellow officer and found his body blown to pieces with head and limbs lying separated from his trunk.'[55]

From that time he had been haunted at night by the vision of his dead and mutilated friend. When he slept he had nightmares in which his friend appeared, sometimes as he had seen him mangled in the field, sometimes in the still more terrifying aspect of one whose limbs and features had been eaten away by leprosy. The mutilated or leprous officer of the dream would come nearer and nearer until the patient suddenly awoke pouring with sweat and in a state of utmost terror.

This man had tried to suppress his memories by day, 'only to bring them upon him with redoubled force and horror when he slept.' In treating him, Rivers had to find some way of letting the patient confront his memories that would also reduce the horror. The solution was to suggest to him that the friend's mangled body proved that he had been killed outright and thus spared the long-drawn out agony of dying of wounds. Whereupon, in Rivers' telling, the patient 'brightened at once' and agreed to try and think of the experience in that positive light. For several night he did not dream. Then

He dreamt that he went out into no-man's land to seek his friend, saw his mangled body just as in his other dreams, but without the horror that had always previously been present. He knelt beside his friend to save for the relatives any objects of value, a pious duty he had fulfilled in the actual scene, and as he was taking off the Sam Browne belt he woke with none of the horror and terror of the past, but weeping gently feeling only grief for the loss of a friend.

Some nights later he had another dream in which he met his friend still mangled, but no longer terrifying. They talked together and the patient told the story of his illness and how he was now able to speak to him in comfort and without horror or undue distress. This wasn't quite the end of it: the horrifying dream did recur occasionally, but, Rivers reported, he had left hospital and was 'regaining his normal health and strength'. This change, both in the subject matter and the 'affective' (emotional) character of the dream was, Rivers admitted, quite unexpected, but with experience he came to recognise it as one of the signs that a patient was improving. Realistic scenes of war, repeated in identical form night after night, would give way to other images, such as terrifying animals, and the accompanying emotion of fear would start to die down.

But there were obvious limits to what could be achieved by the simple lifting of repression. Sometimes a patient's experience was so 'horrible and disgusting' that Rivers could not offer him a positive way to confront it. For example, there was a young officer

. . . who was flung down by the explosion of a shell so that his face struck the distended abdomen of a German several days dead, the impact of his fall rupturing the swollen corpse. Before he lost consciousness, the patient had clearly realised his situation and knew that the substance which filled his mouth and produced the most horrible sensations of taste and smell was derived from the decomposed entrails of an enemy.[56]

By the time he reached Craiglockhart, this patient was 'striving by every means in his power to keep the disgusting and painful memory from his mind' and Rivers thought it best that he leave the Army and go off to the country where had previously found some peace of mind.

Rivers was still recording and analysing his own dreams; his posthumous book, *Conflict and Dream*, gives a revealing picture of his own mental state at this time. His growing conviction that dreams were not expressions of wish fulfilments – as Freud maintained and he himself had earlier believed – but ways of reconciling conflicts in the subconscious was confirmed by a series of vivid dreams expressing his uncertainty whether to stay in Edinburgh with his patients or to return to London and resume anthropology. As early as March 1917, the conflict between his increasingly strong pacifist beliefs and the fact that he was working for the Army and sending young men back to the front also seemed to be affecting his dreams. In the summer of 1917 this conflict came to a head after he had spent the evening talking to his interesting new patient, Lieutenant S. L. Sassoon.[57]

*   *   *

Rivers is today by far the best-known of the shell-shock doctors (and was featured in a novel and film in the 1990s) largely thanks to the skilful and loving portrait of him in Siegfried Sassoon's memoir *Sherston's Progress*. The story of their relationship is too well-known to need detailed retelling here – how Sassoon, the daring subaltern, denounced the war while recovering from wounds in London in 1917, was saved from court martial by influential friends and sent to Craiglockhart, to be treated by Rivers; how the two men became friends, their relationship coloured by Rivers' repressed homosexuality and Sassoon's increasingly confident avowal of his own; how, in the end, Rivers persuaded Sassoon to return to the war.[58]

Sassoon's wonderful account so dominates the lay literature of shell-shock, so completely shapes the modern idea of what that experience was like, that it seems almost churlish to point out that he was not a typical patient, any more than Rivers was a typical doctor or Craiglockhart a typical hospital. The majority of shell-shock patients were private soldiers, who, as we have seen, would be more likely to be lying neglected in a converted asylum in the depths of the country, or being given periodic baths and electric shock by a bored, unsympathetic hospital attendant.

Did Sassoon have shell-shock? *Sherston's Progress* is ambiguous, with Sassoon at once keen to distance himself from the condition and eloquent in ennobling it:

Shell-shock. How many a brief bombardment had its long-delayed after-effect in the minds of these survivors, many of whom had looked at their companions and laughed while inferno did its best to destroy them. Not then was their evil hour, but now; now, in the sweating suffocation of nightmare, in paralysis of limbs, in the stammering of dislocated speech. Worst of all, in the disintegration of those qualities through which they had been so gallant and selfless and uncomplaining – this, in the finer types of men, was the unspeakable tragedy of shell-shock.[59]

Sassoon evidently was suffering from more than 'an anti-war complex'; he had such symptoms as hallucinations; Rivers – in a private letter after Sassoon had returned to the war – called him exceptionally 'sensitive'. Above all, it is now clear how much Sassoon's mental conflicts, like his verse, were shaped by his homoerotic love of his men. In this, and his anti-war stance, he was certainly exceptional.[60]

Sassoon himself aroused mental conflicts in his doctor. Rivers' discomfort at being professionally obliged, as a uniformed RAMC psychiatrist, to 'cure [Sassoon] of his pacifist errors' and send him back to a war he was himself ceasing to believe in probably contributed to his decision to leave Craiglockhart and work in London on the physiological problems of flying.[61]

* * *

It is often assumed that, while at Craiglockhart, Rivers treated a more celebrated war poet and homosexual. He certainly had the opportunity: 'When a fresh convoy of patients arrived,' a member of the staff later recalled, 'Captain Rivers walked round them and took his pick. Nearly all the interesting patients floated his way.' But Rivers obviously found little of interest in Second Lieutenant W. E. S. Owen of the Manchester regiment, a 'quiet, round faced little man' with a rather absurd moustache, centrally parted hair and grammar school accent who reached Craiglockhart on 26 June 1917. He was put under the care of his colleague, Captain A. J. Brock RAMC.[62]

Wilfred Owen's case history as a shell-shock patient, researched in great detail by literary historians, makes an interesting contrast to Sassoon's. The treatment he received was quite different, yet notably successful, and had a dramatic effect on his development both as a poet and as a person.[63]

Whatever the arguments in Sassoon's case, Owen certainly was suffering from shell-shock, and for quite understandable reasons; in only a few weeks in the front line, he had lived through awful experiences. He had reached France at the end of 1916. Then, on 12 January 1917 he was sent with his platoon to hold a dug-out in no-man's land and stayed there for fifty hours in the face of intense German shelling. 'Those fifty hours,' he wrote home, 'were the agony of my happy life. I nearly broke down and let myself drown in the water that was slowly rising over my knees . . . One lad was blown up and, I am afraid, blinded.'

Then came two weeks in the line. In one place there were no dug-outs and he and his men had to lie in the snow and the wind.

I thought of you and Mary without a break all the time. I cannot say I felt any fear. We were all half-crazed by the buffeting of the High Explosions.[64]

This experience may have left its mark: at the end of January he was packed off on a 'course' – a common way of giving a break to officers showing signs of strain. He then injured himself falling down a well or cellar and it was not until early April 1917 that he re-joined his unit, which had been involved in heavy fighting. There followed '4 days and 4 nights (without relief) in the open and in the snow', a week's rest, and 'a Tornado of shells' as they moved back up to the line.

The various waves were all broken up and we carried on like a crowd moving off a cricket field. When I looked back and saw the ground all crawling and wormy with wounded bodies I felt no horror at all but only an immense exultation at having got through the barrage.[65]

As a reward for its courageous handling of this situation, the battalion was kept in the line for twelve days.

I think the worst incident was one wet night when we lay up against a railway embankment. A big shell lit on the top of the bank, just 2 yards from my head. Before I awoke, I was blown in the air right away from the bank. I passed most of the following days in a railway cutting, in a hole just big enough to lie in, and covered with corrugated iron. My brother officer of B Coy, 2/ Lt Graukroger lay opposite in a similar hole. But he was covered with earth, and no relief will ever relieve him, nor will his Rest be a 9 days-Rest.[66]

Ten days later, Owen's Commanding Officer noticed him behaving strangely and sent him to the Doctor, who found him to be 'shaky and tremulous and his memory confused'. He was sent down labelled 'neurasthenia', and wrote to reassure his mother: 'Do not for a moment suppose I have had a "breakdown". I am simply *avoiding* one.'[67]

The circumstances of Owen's shell-shock remain unclear. We do not know why he and his men had to stay in the line for such a long period, or why he remained in the hole for so long. Dominic Hibberd concludes that 'he may have been pinned down by enemy fire or he may have been helpless with shock, perhaps even unconscious for a while, because he later spoke of "coming-to after the Embankment Shell-Shock". Whatever the case, he can have been of little use to the men he was supposed to be leading.' Clearly, Owen felt he had failed his men, and the emotion of guilt was sharpened by whatever his Colonel said to him. Hibberd is surely right to suggest that these feelings of guilt partly explain his later actions and 'load his finest writing'.[68]

Owen was evacuated to the 'specialist centre' in France which Charles Myers had laboured to set up, and treated there by Myers' highly competent colleague, William Brown, perhaps under hypnosis. But Owen was too serious a case not to be sent back to England. Those who saw him in the summer found him stammering, shaky, 'nervy and highly strung' and 'liable to acute depression and self-distrust.'[69]

Owen had suffered nightmares before the war – a breakdown in 1911 produced 'phantasies', 'horrors' and 'phantasms'. Now, at Craiglockhart, they became so bad that he took to staying up late to cut down on his dreaming time. When he did fall asleep, he found himself re-enacting his worst moments in France – back with his platoon in the barrage, confined again in claustrophobic

holes and dug-outs, confronted once more by the accusing faces of men he had
seen gassed and blinded in front of him.[70]

> In all my dreams, before my helpless sight
> He plunges at me, guttering, choking drowning . . .[71]

> If in some smothering dreams you too could pace
> Behind the wagon that we flung him in,
> And watch the white eyes writhing in his face.[72]

> Eyeballs, huge-bulged like squids
> Watch my dreams still.[73]

References to 'Barrag'd nights' suggest that it was the experience of advancing
through a 'Tornado of Shells' which especially lingered. His letter to his brother,
talking of 'immense exultation at having got through the Barrage', had probably
not told the full story.

The phenomenon of the Battle Dream, the way that soldiers replayed their
wartime experiences in their dreams – first noticed at Maghull – had by this time
generated considerable medical interest. Battle dreams seemed to have a character
of their own. Unlike peacetime anxiety dreams, they were repetitive, the dreamer
usually returning night after night to the same scene of horror – though whether
it was a faithful repetition of an actual experience or a rendering of the affect, or
emotion, caused by it was a matter of argument. Ironically, though, Owen the
great war dreamer, found himself with a therapist, Arthur Brock, who wasn't
really interested in dreams; instead of talking about his dreams, Owen put them
into his poetry.[74]

Dr Brock was interested in activity. A 'lean, earnest man with deep-set eyes and
a nose like an axe-blade', a great talker and walker, a man of wide intellectual
interests, his approach to neurasthenia was a curious mixture of cloudy theory culled
from Bergson, Greek philosophy and the new discipline of sociology, together with
hard Scots common sense. 'The need for self-help,' Brock believed, took
'precedence over every other form of therapy.' If 'the essential thing for the patient
to do is to help himself,' the 'essential thing for the doctor to do – indeed the only
thing he can profitably do – is to help him to help himself.' The doctor must provide
an environment for the patient 'to exercise his faculties upon'. Ergotherapy, as Brock
called his treatment, meant, literally, 'the cure by functioning'. [75]

One aspect of ergotherapy was physical: the patient had to 'learn to do without
things' and 'impose a considerable amount of stoic discipline upon himself'.
Brock was keen on cold baths and swims; his practice of dragging patients out of
bed on dark cold mornings and marching them out for a walk before breakfast
led some to bolt themselves in lavatories and bathrooms. One officer 'boasted
that if he lay flat under his bed, so that the untidy bed clothes hid him, he
escaped.'[76]

But the crucial ingredient in Brock's regime was work.

When all is said and done, the essential ingredient of these patients resolves into 'finding them their job' – guiding them to it, keeping them at it, and only relinquishing them finally when their interests are sufficiently awakened to ensure that they will now 'carry on' of themselves.[77]

Brock may have been 'something of a crank', but his methods worked dramatically with Owen and had a decisive role in transforming him from a literary young man with a sense of failure into a major poet with his own distinctive voice – and a confident and determined young officer.

Once Owen had had a chance to settle at the hospital – and been re-united with his mother – the process of Re-Education began. First, Owen was sent off to write an essay on the Outlook Tower, a curious building erected by Brock's mentor, the Edinburgh polymath, Patrick Geddes. Then he was told to write a poem on the story of Antaeus, the mythological giant defeated by Hercules.[78]

Contact with Dr Brock was clearly doing Owen good; soon he spoke of 'a Greek feeling of energy and elemental life'. Brock encouraged him to experiment with new forms of rhyming and drew him into a welter of other activities – lecturing to the Craiglockhart Field Club, teaching at the Boys' Training Club, editing the Craiglockhart magazine *The Hydra*, and visiting the slums of Edinburgh with a socially conscious family. For 'little Owen', a lower middle-class grammar school boy who never made it to university, Brock was providing a 'free and easy Oxford'.[79]

And, on top of all this, came the famous moment, in the middle of August 1917, when Owen knocked on the door of the hospital's glamorous new patient, Siegfried Sassoon, and cautiously introduced himself as a fan of his work. After an awkward initial phase when Sassoon found his provincialness and poems 'embarrassing', they became friends and peers. Sassoon taught him how to write war poems and showed him 'how they could be based on a consistent, reasoned opposition to the war'. He probably also helped him to understand and draw creatively on his own homosexuality.

The effect of these stimuli was immediate. Within a fortnight Owen began to draft 'The Dead Beat', the poem that would usher in his *annus mirabilis*. He abandoned his flowery pre-war style in favour of Sassoon's hard, colloquial manner and used his own experience at the front. By the beginning of October, Owen was beginning to find his own voice, a mixture of wartime experience and elements of his pre-war work. For the first time, he began to confront his own private terrors, to draw on the imagery of his 'barrag'd nights'; as Brock later put it, 'to face the phantoms of the mind'.

> We dredged him up, for killed, until he whined
> 'O sir, my eyes – I'm blind, – I'm blind, I'm blind!'
> Coaxing, I held a flame against his lids
> And said if he could see the least blurred light
> He was not blind; in time he'd get all right.
> 'I can't,' he sobbed . . .[80]

Dominic Hibberd has shown how, in these poems, 'Owen is directly facing the central experience of his war dreams, the sight of a horrifying face which, Gorgon-like, renders him a "helpless, paralysed spectator". Yet, by the time he was writing these poems by day, his own nocturnal dreams had begun to evolve, in line with Rivers' theory. "I still have disastrous dreams," Owen reported early in September, 'but they are taking on a more civilian character, motor accidents and so on.'[81]

By late October, Owen was considered well enough to be sent – rather reluctantly – away from Craiglockhart, back to 'light duties' with his regiment in Scarborough and Ripon. His five months in the hospital had transformed him. 'I go out this year a poet,' he wrote to his mother late in 1917, 'as which I did not enter it . . . I am started. The tugs have left me; I feel the great swelling of the open sea taking my galleon.' Now self-consciously a poet of war, he set to work on his own and, in the spring of 1918, while training at Ripon, was able to polish the Craiglockhart poems and write half a dozen new ones. By May 1918 most of his best work was finished. But his relationship to his material began to change. 'I confess,' he wrote, 'I bring on what few war dreams I now have, entirely by willingly considering war of an evening. I do so because I have my duty to perform towards war.'[82]

That 'duty' was to tell the truth about the war to the public and to posterity; but it was a changing truth. In the preface to a possible collection which Owen wrote in May 1918, he arranged his poems by themes – Protest, Cheerfulness, Description, Grief, Philosophy – headings which roughly mirror the evolution of his own feelings since beginning to write. Owen was increasingly looking at the wider significance of the war; his main theme was now waste and pity, tinged with homoerotic yearning. When he returned to the subject matter of the past it was in a new manner.

His most famous poem 'Strange Meeting' *was* triggered by a nightmare – training at Ripon with 'the hideous faces of the Advancing Revolver targets' had brought his war dreams back. But this time Owen leads the reader, not into the concrete dug-out of the real battlefield, but into a 'profound dark tunnel' which, in turn, leads to the Underworld. We are in Dante's Inferno, not the Western Front, and, once more, the Gorgon eye is waiting.

> Then, as I probed them, one sprang up, and stared
> With piteous recognition in fixed eyes,
> Lifting distressful hands, as if to bless.
> And by his smile, I knew that sullen hall, –
> By his dead smile I knew we stood in Hell.

The later poems are far more accomplished than anything written at Craiglockhart, and, it seems to me, not nearly as powerful. The very success of Owen's recovery has made the real phantoms and horrors slip away, drained him of his unique voice.[83]

Owen's 'sudden convulsion into greatness' remains a mystery – an explosion in which many ingredients combusted. It was, though, the order and timing of experiences and influences which made 'Owen, the Poet': the brief exposure to the horrors in France, not long enough to dull the first impressions on a young mind; the months of convalescence during which this material gelled; the 'barrag'd nights' at Craiglockhart; the rigours of Brock's ergotherapy to train the will; the encounter with Sassoon to kick-start the poet; then, when he had begun to find his own voice, the time and comparative solitude of Ripon and Scarborough to hone and polish. It is almost as if circumstances conspired to make Owen a great war poet.[84]

The Army, for its part, had given Owen two years of training, medical treatment, psychotherapy, poetic instruction and writing room. On almost the last day of the war, it called in that debt.

EUROPEANS

I am so tired and feeble that I should like most to go to sleep and never wake up until peace has come, or never at all.

Dr Wilhelm Pfuhl, November 1916[1]

This is primarily a study of the war neuroses in the Anglo-Saxon countries. Even so, it is impossible not to follow the example of British doctors and have a look at how the French and Germans were coping.

There was enormous deference towards the Continentals. The French were the acknowledged experts on hysteria and pioneers of psychotherapy; the German psychiatric profession, with its well-funded university chairs and efficiently-run public clinics, was the envy of the world. Furthermore, neither in France nor Germany was there quite the split between psychiatry and neurology that had developed in Britain; most mental health doctors worked primarily for the state, treating patients of all social classes. Finally, the Germans had introduced back in the 1870s the sort of industrial insurance legislation that only came to Britain thirty years later and therefore had much greater experience of the medical issues surrounding claims for workers' compensation. For all these reasons, one might expect the French and Germans to deal more effectively with the problem of shell-shock than their British colleagues.[2]

A problem it certainly was: the Europeans were as astonished as the British by the scale of nervous casualties early in the war. 'Hysterical manifestations' were 'extremely common' the French neurologist Roussy wrote in February 1915, while 111,722 German soldiers, 'exhibiting the entire range of hysterical symptoms known at that time, passed through field and military hospitals' in the first year of the war. Both Paris and Berlin found it necessary to create specialist hospitals for nervous cases, though there was no European equivalent to the umbrella term 'shell-shock': German doctors spoke of *Nervenshock*, *Granatkontusion*, *Granaterschütterung* (shell disorder), *Granatexplosionslähmung* (shell explosion paralysis) and *Granatfernwirkung* (the indirect consequences or effects of a shell explosion); the French had a similar variety of terms. Nor was there the same early emphasis on breakdowns in officers as there was in Britain. Perhaps for this reason, nervous collapse never acquired in Paris and

Berlin the public respectability that it enjoyed, almost from the start, in London.[3]

Confronted with this unanticipated difficulty, the German Army turned to the prestigious and ideologically reliable psychiatric profession, which had already put itself at the military's disposal. Psychiatrists, their official spokesmen declared, would 'never forget that we physicians have now to put all our work in the service of one mission: to serve our army and our fatherland.'[4]

In France, too, the powerful Société de Neurologie was able quickly to mobilise medical opinion behind the state. As early as March 1915 it called for the creation of forward treatment centres in the army zone. By early 1916 they were functioning 'sufficiently well to draw the praise of the majority of neurologists' and to be visited by Charles Myers.[5]

Not that medical opinion in these countries was united. On the contrary, it was bitterly divided, along fault lines stretching back into the past. In Paris, the main division was between the rival power bases of Joseph Babinski at La Pitié hospital and Jules Dejerine at the Salpêtrière (Pierre Janet, an important influence on many British doctors, had no institutional power base and thus, ironically, carried no weight among his countrymen during the war). Babinski insisted that the symptoms appearing in soldiers were brought about not by the trauma of war itself but either by unintentional suggestion from doctors or by the patient's auto-suggestion and imitation. They could, therefore, be quickly removed by isolation and simple techniques of persuasion – the *traitement brusqué*. Against that, Dejerine, the pre-war pioneer of psychotherapy based on suggestion and emotional empathy with the patient, argued that hysterical symptoms in soldiers had emotional origins. But in 1914–15, his was almost a lone voice. Babinski's rougher, more masculine approach suited the wartime mood and won the support of his fellow doctors. 'We can understand how attractive it was to medical minds,' one of them wrote, 'when [Babinski] finally established a definition and limits to hysteria that were clear and neat and which contrasted favourably with the imprecise, cloudy and excessively extra-medical theories.'[6]

In Germany, the battle lines were at first slightly different. The war re-kindled a debate that had raged in the 1890s over the concept of 'traumatic neurosis' put forward by the Berlin neurologist Hermann Oppenheim. He had argued that the symptoms suffered by victims of railway and industrial accidents were caused by actual physical damage to the brain and nervous system – lesions too small to be detectable. In the 1890s, the opposite view, that the symptoms of railway brain were just hysterical and related to concerns over compensation, had, as in Britain, eventually prevailed. But early experience in the war prompted Oppenheim to revive his hypothesis and to argue, rather as Frederick Mott did in Britain, that shelling created microscopic lesions in the brain and nervous system, causing the bizarre paralyses and gaits from which men were suffering.[7]

By 1916, however, it had become apparent in Germany, too, that it was unusual for prisoners of war or the wounded to develop these symptoms, even if they had been exposed to heavy shellfire, whereas soldiers who had not been under shellfire often did. It was becoming clear, also, that most of these military cases could be 'cured' by hypnosis. Their disorder must therefore be psychological, 'hysterical', rather than physical in nature. In a celebrated debate in Munich in September 1916 Oppenheim was comprehensively routed.[8]

So by 1916 German doctors had arrived at what was then, roughly speaking, the dominant French and British view: that far from being anything very new, the soldiers' strange symptoms were just the 'functional disorders' or psychoneuroses of peacetime – hysteria and neurasthenia – dressed up in new guises. It was also becoming clear that their seemingly untreatable symptoms could be rapidly removed by skilful and confident therapists. Such 'miracle workers' were already beginning to appear, usually doctors with pre-war experience in treating hysteria with suggestion and persuasion.[9]

The most celebrated of these was the Hamburg neurologist, Max Nonne, who treated some 1,600 patients during the war. As a young man, Nonne had studied with the French masters of hysteria, Charcot in Paris and Bernheim in Nancy, eventually endorsing the Nancy school's emphasis on the role of suggestion. In October 1914, Nonne found himself treating a young lieutenant evacuated from Flanders to a Hamburg hospital unable to speak. Suspecting that the officer's dumbness was hysterical, Nonne falteringly tried on him the technique of hypnosis he had learnt many years before. To his astonishment, the lieutenant at once recovered his power of speech.[10]

Male hysteria was something Nonne had only previously seen in France. 'We used to say,' he recalled in his memoirs, '"That's something only the French get. In Germany there is no male hysteria". Now we saw it often in all forms.' Military distaste for hysteria as *unwürdig* (unworthy) of the German soldier, and medical distaste for the 'medieval mysticism' of hypnosis at first made Nonne hesitate before publicising his technique, but eventually its obvious effectiveness displaced all inhibitions.[11]

The three necessary prerequisites for successful treatment of soldiers, Nonne believed, were 'First, unfailing self-confidence; second, feelings of obedience on the patient's part; third, [the creation] of an atmosphere of healing.' Everything depended on Nonne's own mood, which varied according to the news from the war. Some patients were cured immediately; with others, Nonne had to 'slave away for hours' and found when he had removed their symptoms that he was himself shaking. Nonne's reputation as a *Zauberheiler*, or magical healer, was sealed by a film made in 1917. Against a plain, dark background a series of shuddering, juddering men, naked except for underpants, writhe and twitch tormentedly before the camera. Then, like a ghostly spectre, the doctor appears – tall, erect, a Teutonic high priest in a long white coat. Moving with hieratic authority, he places his hands on their pulsating limbs and stomachs, whispers in their ears or clicks his fingers and – pouf! – the symptoms disappear. The extraordinary expressionist effect – like a silent film by F. W. Murnau or Fritz Lang – is only a little diminished when one learns that Nonne had already cured these patients and then rehypnotised them for the camera.[12]

But few possessed Nonne's gifts. Most German doctors preferred to use simple authoritarian pressure to compel the patient to surrender his symptoms. Soldiers were kept in isolation, sent to lunatic asylums to 'give them a chance to reflect on their fate', given continuous baths, or made to do work therapy. But the main 'authoritarian' method was electrotherapy. In 1916, a neurologist called Kaufmann claimed great success at a hospital near Mannheim with an approach somewhat similar to that of Lewis Yealland at Queen Square. There was the same elaborate psychological build-up followed by electric therapy deliberately intended to cause pain, each shock lasting for between two and five minutes. However, from the first day in hospital, Kaufmann also insisted on 'the strict adherence to military forms' and gave instructions in the form of court orders or even military commands. Like Yealland, he was 'unflinchingly determined to force a cure in one session'. It was, he said, an *überrumpellungsmethode* or surprise-method – shock therapy ('the innervation brought out of line by a psychological shock is very often brought back on to the right path by another psychic shock'). Kaufmann emphasised how 'grateful' patients were for his treatment, though he admitted that it left them 'no longer suitable at all for service in the field' and was usually inappropriate for officers.[13]

One of his rare officer patients – suffering, unusually for his caste, from hysterical dumbness – wrote an account of the Kaufmann cure from the patient's angle.

The current was switched on. At first I had a prickly feeling, which suddenly burst into intense pain ... I heard someone yelling 'You must listen now,' and the doctor kept talking at me, 'Only uneducated people suffer from such conditions. How will you cope with your stutter in society?' The appeal was to my self-respect and my sense of honour. Nonetheless, when I stuttered again, the current hummed. The moment the doctor's suggestioning began, I felt like an object with no will of its own, being fought for by two opposing powers. Gradually my own will came into play, and took the side of the doctor, both as a result of my own reasoning and the doctor's means of domination. Ears and language braced themselves against the doctor's suggestioning and my will ... that I must be able to speak and understand. In these moments I felt myself to be two people. I held on to the doctor's scolding as a lifeline, clung to it tightly and pulled my nerves along with me. So the two of us pulled along until I could understand and speak.[14]

By 1916 this 'sadistic attack on the patient' had been accepted as the treatment model by many German doctors. There was, though, a contradiction in Kaufmann's writings between the idea of 'suggestive preparation' – that the cure would be brought by build-up followed by suggestion – and that of shock or surprise. Sometimes this deliberate re-traumatisation of the patient proved fatal, as some of Kaufmann's colleagues had warned it would. A certain Infantryman Heidenreich, of the 22 Bavarian Infantry Regiment, was admitted to the Catholic Sisters house at Zweibrücken because of a persistent paralysis of the left hand, and there treated by the assistant doctor, Dr Eggelhuber:

During the electrical treatment H suddenly stopped breathing and died soon afterwards of heart paralysis the onset of which could not be stopped by all suitable measures taken.

At least twenty patients died, others committed suicide; there may have been 'a serious revolt of the patients' in one hospital. The *überrumpellungsmethode* was, it seemed, a little too surprising.[15]

There was, evidently, increasing resistance by patients to 'active therapy'. Questions began being asked in the press and the provincial assemblies. Finally, in the summer of 1918, criticism was heard in the Reichstag itself. A prominent Centre Party deputy pleaded for the mood in neurosis stations to be kinder and more merciful, arguing that, for all their effectiveness in removing symptoms, the existing methods were undermining faith in Germany's doctors and giving ammunition to the political left. The head of the Army's medical services defended active methods, claiming that the discomforts suffered by a few individuals were vastly outweighed by the effective way that 90% of the 60–70,000 'neurotics' had been successfully treated and two-thirds had been made 'fully fit for work'.

However, by 1917 Kaufmann himself had admitted that his methods were not working and had turned to hypnosis.[16]

*   *   *

The British were quick to denounce the brutalities of the Kaufmann cure, which certainly conformed to their authoritarian stereotype of German medicine. All the more reason, then, to emphasise that in some ways the Germans' approach was kindlier than anyone else's. Their military courts sentenced some 150 soldiers to death during the war, of whom only 48 were subsequently executed; whereas the British handed out 3,080 death sentences, of which 307 were carried out and the French condemned some 2,000 men and executed about 700. The Germans were readier to evacuate soldiers from the front and quicker to provide specialised treatment for them at home; patients did not linger and fester in general military hospitals as they often did in Britain. They were also more willing to accept that men who had broken down would not be much use as soldiers again, and followed a deliberate policy, not simply of work therapy but of converting shell-shocked soldiers into farm or factory workers to fill labour shortages at home.[17]

Hence the paradox: German treatments, brutal as they were, did nothing to inhibit the flow of psychiatric casualties away from the front. 'Their number has grown and grown,' Dr Robert Gaupp reported in 1917. 'Scarcely is one nervous hospital opened than it fills up and space must be found somewhere else. We've now got to the point where nervous illness represents the most important medical category and in our province the nervous hospitals are practically the only ones that are always full.' Gaupp believed that the equivalent of several army corps had been lost from front and garrison duty.[18]

German practice at the front line has not yet been studied in detail. On the one hand, as Gaupp noticed, they were slow to grasp the advantages of retaining men in a military environment and did not clamp down on evacuation to the rear and introduce systematic front-line treatment until 1918. On the other hand, some effective front-line psychiatrists did emerge, such as Dr Edmund Forster who worked for four years with the Army in Flanders. Before the war, at the Charité Hospital in Berlin, Forster had 'taken hysteria to be mostly humbug and treated hysterics accordingly', shouting at them 'that they ought to be ashamed toward real sufferers'. Colleagues had been annoyed by 'his successes with such a method' and that 'those he "cured" should even remain devoted to him'. Now, with soldiers in Bruges, he used much the same method. 'Himself of an energetic and spirited disposition,' his chief reported in 1918, 'he made the treatment and cure of so-called war neurotics his special concern and, in many cases, went about it somewhat roughly in that he applied the standards of his own strength of will to others.' Forster would tell war neurotics that they were shirking, warn them that if they persisted they would be punished, and assure them that they were suffering not from any sickness but from a weak will that needed strengthening.[19]

For all its energy, the German approach was never as single-minded and ruthless as that of the French. The Germans rewarded hysterics by evacuating them away from the war; the French did not. In line with Babinski's belief that hysterical soldiers were indistinguishable from simulators and malingerers, they went to some lengths to unmask simulation and return soldiers to battle as soon as possible. Not only did they set up forward treatment centres near the front, they made sure that such cases as were evacuated remained within the military net; in November 1915 the Société de Neurologie asked the authorities to guarantee that no psychoneurotic patient should receive a discharge of any sort in order to 'dissuade "unconscious simulators" from thinking that they could escape their military duties from illness.' Thus the French soldier gained nothing from his hysteria. From the military's point of view, this approach seemed at first to work very well. 'All the neurotics whom we have had to treat, more than 600,' the French neurologist Pierre Léri wrote in December 1916, 'were cured through a simple and energetic psychotherapy and sent back to the front after a few days or at most a few weeks.' 'Since the creation of the army centres,' he continued, 'the neuroses transferred to the interior are becoming more and more rare. When we perfect this system of triage, they should cease to exist.'[20]

It never was perfected, however, and by 1917 complacency was increasingly giving way to doubt. For one thing, many soldiers evacuated to the interior for wounds were developing hysterical symptoms to prolong their stay in hospital and ward off the return to the front. Secondly, Babinski's simple formula began to seem inadequate to explain the increasingly intractable cases and symptoms which were appearing; also his insistence that hysterical symptoms only took hold during a 'meditative phase' in hospital was belied by evidence that in some cases they appeared at the time of collapse or soon after. 'As the pretence of an objective understanding of hysteria evaporated,' the historian Marc Ollivier Roudebush has argued, 'neurologists found themselves relating to hysterical soldiers according to the polarized conceptions of masculine identity that prevailed during the war. A patient was either a loyal, self-sacrificing wounded '*poilu*' or a cowardly, self-serving, simulating '*embusqué*', a victim or a villain.' Therapy in many cases became a simple battle of wills between doctor and patient, the function of the psychiatrist being to force the patient back to the war.[21]

And, just when Dr Kaufmann's 'cure' was emerging in Germany, France produced her own 'ruthless neurological matador', Dr Clovis Vincent of Tours. By adapting Babinski's *traitement brusqué*, Dr Vincent came up with the technique of *torpillage* – the 'torpedoing' of hysterical symptoms. Like Dr Kaufmann, Dr Vincent first showed the patient that his symptoms were not genuinely physical and then used a combination of electricity and vigorous persuasion to re-awake his sense of patriotism and masculine self-respect. For a time Dr Vincent's methods were *en vogue* and patients were sent from all over France to his clinic. Then came the case of Baptiste Deschamps.

A quarryman who became an infantryman in the French Army, Baptiste Deschamps was wounded in October 1914 and then passed through numerous military hospitals, acquiring, somewhere along the line, a deformation of the spine which made him stoop. By the time he arrived at Dr Vincent's neurological centre, in May 1916, he was fed up with army doctors and clearly expecting to be discharged. Instead, while awaiting his first meeting with the doctor, he heard something of his methods. 'I was terrified,' he said later. 'Some mates (*camarades*) told me that the "*Torpilles*" were extremely painful, and that some men had died because of them.'[22]

Two days later, he met Dr Vincent. After examining him, the doctor declared, 'It is nothing. I will cure you.' Then, according to press accounts, 'he rushed at Deschamps holding two electrodes in his right hand. Deschamps stood up straight and punched the doctor five or six times in the face.'[23]

Deschamps' trial in August 1916 for striking a superior officer became a *cause célèbre*. Dr Vincent's professional colleagues rallied to him, but press and popular sympathy lay largely with Deschamps presented as 'either a proud *poilu* or an innocent *blessé*'. More fundamental issues were also aired. A Dr Doyen, before the war an advocate of greater rights for patients, used the occasion to present what Roudebush has called 'a classically republican indictment of the tyrannical and dishonourable abuse of the helpless.' Doyen 'testified at length on the phenomenon of medical militarism, citing examples of incompetent surgeons abusing their power as officers and operating recklessly on unwilling subjects. Once a man was wounded, he had the same rights as any patient.' '*Torpillage*,' said Doyen, was the 'ultimate example of medical militarism'; he would have put Dr Vincent, not Deschamps, on trial. This provoked loud protests from uniformed doctors in court and noisy approval from members of the public. The court had to be cleared.[24]

Dr Vincent counterattacked by presenting himself as a decent man trying to combine his professional duty with his obligations to patients, giving honour back to those who had lost it. 'What,' he demanded to know, 'would be the inclination of the heroes of Verdun, if we showed them their comrades who were able but not willing to recover?' This, too, drew applause. In the end, public sympathy forced the tribunal to deal leniently with Deschamps. Though found guilty, as the military honour of France and the power of the scientific community demanded, he was given a suspended sentence of six months in prison. Morally, Deschamps had won.

Roudebush has argued that the Deschamps case revealed a deep divide between the French medico-military hierarchy and the world of ordinary soldiers and civilians, and 'demonstrated how little purchase the abstract discourse of self-sacrifice and unconditional obedience had with French men and women when they felt that enough had been asked of them.' He sees it not as an isolated incident but as part of a pattern of resistance to the French medico-military system which came to a head in the mutinies in the French Army the following year.[25]

The Deschamps trial generated so much bad publicity that French neurologists were forced to tone down their methods and retreat from their *offensive à l'outrance* (the strategy of unrelenting attack) against their patients. There had already been one important innovation, the admission by Joseph Babinski that there were some exceptions to his dictum that all *hystériques* were simply malingerers. There was, Babinski now conceded, a class of men suffering from 'reflex nervous disorders', disturbances of the autonomic nervous system, for which they were not responsible, even unconsciously, and which were beyond their will to cure; beyond, even, the will of the most macho therapist.[26]

The second innovation was the creation in 1917, at Salins in the Jura region, of a 'Centre for Psychoneuroses' using gentler and kinder methods adapted from the pre-war psychotherapy of Babinski's old rival, Dejerine (who had died in 1916). It was no holiday home, however; the emphasis was on returning men to combat by use of suggestion and electricity, relying heavily on ritual and medical authority. By 1918, the doctor in charge there was complaining that it was 'impossible for us to go on much longer like this. The patients we receive are more and more difficult . . . their treatment requires much time (I would even say wasted time), because most of them arrive in the worst frame of mind, determined to resist all treatment.'[27]

Thus far, French and German experience of shell-shock had followed roughly the same course as in Britain – from initial incomprehension to a realisation that the problems of war were largely those of peacetime in a more dramatic form. However, for nationalistic as well as intellectual reasons, the French stopped short of taking a further step in the psychological direction and did not adopt the methods of psychoanalysis associated with Sigmund Freud.

*   *   *

Freud had little directly to do with the war. He sat in Vienna with few patients, taking no direct part in hostilities, putting most of his energy into writing. According to Ernest Jones, 'He would glance through the newspaper, toss it aside with the condemnation *"scheusslich"* [horrible] and go on with his work.' Although he wrote (and did not publish) a paper on hysterical conversions in 1917, on the whole he did not address the issues raised by the conflict. It seems that, in private, he felt strong nationalist sympathies with the Austrian cause but felt it better to maintain a public stance of scientific neutrality and regret.[28]

Several of Freud's followers, however, did work directly with war neurotics.

Nor were they, at first, blessed with unique insight. In a vivid article in 1916, the Hungarian psychoanalyst Sándor Ferenczi recalled his puzzlement when confronted by a ward of 50 war neurotics, all of whom seemed seriously ill, many with 'peculiar gaits possible only to be reproduced by cinematography'. Ferenczi assumed their symptoms had been caused by organic injury to the brain or spinal cord and only gradually realised, by studying their behaviour in very close detail, that their symptoms were physical manifestations of psychoneuroses. Nor were Freudians necessarily less comfortable in the role of the military psychiatrist than other kinds of doctor. Most of them, Louise Hoffman has written, 'seem to have accepted patriotically the military demand that war neurotics be treated so as to enable their fastest return to the front lines.' But, as the war progressed, a definite psychoanalytic perspective did emerge.[29]

The Berlin physician Ernst Simmel was not a Freudian before the war. He began his career as a military doctor by trying to imitate Max Nonne's magical hypnotic methods with his soldiers and failing miserably. So Simmel, just like British doctors at Maghull and Craiglockhart, turned to psychotherapy – to investigating the underlying psychological cause of the symptoms. He didn't really know what he was doing – 'I did it intuitively,' he wrote in 1944. Like Rows, Simmel was sympathetic to his patients and, like Rivers, he found his attention drawn from the very beginning to 'the characteristic dream life' of his patients. Their recurring war dreams must, he thought, 'indicate a latent tendency at a self cure.'

Simmel began to develop a form of therapy that combined Freudian dream analysis with hypnotic abreaction.

I used dream contents in order to induce hypnotic repetitions of traumatic war scenes, or I asked the soldier to interpret his dream symbols himself, while under hypnosis. Sometimes I used post-hypnotic suggestions in that I asked the patient to supplement, by dreaming, certain fragments of memory which had come up in his hypnotic hallucinations.[30]

One example of this was a young lieutenant who, weeks after being blown up, was still swept by waves of rage and excitement that made him unable to read or count. Initial hypnosis led to a dream in which he beat to death a canal worker seen from the hospital window. Simmel then established in conversation that the innocent canal worker had the same features as an orderly who had detained the lieutenant in hospital and prevented him from going back to the front to avenge his recently-killed brother: 'the lieutenant had been fighting with fury and grief in order to avenge him when he was blown up.'

Simmel learnt that his own attitude towards the patient during hypnosis had an important bearing on how much the man could remember and how much trauma he could re-live. Simmel had to give him reassurance by suggestion that he was perfectly safe and need not fear physical annihilation or personal defamation. This was especially so with feelings of guilt, of which 'real, specific and complex conditioned war atrocities' were 'the inner kernel'.[31]

Simmel's function, he wrote as a Freudian elder statesman in 1944, was that of the benevolent super-ego, 'a representative of a good father who guaranteed him security and protection against his evil father.' If secure enough, the patient in hypnosis would 'not simply imagine his past experiences, as in a dream, but would act out his hallucinations . . . he would relieve himself of his mental pressure by discharging his aggressions into the outside world.' In the end Simmel found it necessary to 'introduce an actual enemy into the therapeutic situation' – a stuffed dummy placed in the treatment room as soon as the patient was under hypnosis. When 'the patient's initial fear of this dummy finally turned into rage, resulting in the dummy's partial mutilation or complete destruction', Simmel knew he was on the mend. 'In particular, depressive attitudes associated with pathological guilt complexes disappeared.'[32]

Simmel concluded his treatment by telling the patient, under hypnosis, that

he had killed his enemy in a dream and need not feel guilty about it. He could be proud and hold himself in high esteem for all he had done so far, and his good intentions in fulfilling his duties to the nation. In interviews under normal conditions I helped the patient to understand and to conquer intellectually what had happened to him under hypnosis, as well as in reality.[33]

Simmel, like Rivers, felt his patients were practically cured when their dream life 'appeared to change definitely by losing its tormenting character, so that sleep could fulfil its psycho-biological task of restoration and recreation.'

Clearly Simmel was a very skilful therapist, able to claim, in a pamphlet published early in 1918, impressive results with some 2,000 patients. His success, coupled with the work of other Freudians and the rejection of Kaufmann's electrical methods, aroused the interest of the military authorities, as keen to cut pensions, one suspects, as to get soldiers back to the front line. Official delegates of the German, Austrian, and Hungarian Army Command attended the Psycho-Analytic Congress in Budapest in September 1918 and for a moment it looked as if Freud's movement would gain from the military the endorsement it had hitherto been denied by the medical establishment. To achieve that goal, Freud was prepared to compromise, 'to alloy the pure gold of analysis freely with the copper of direct suggestion'; even to 'find a place for hypnosis'. It is not clear how seriously the military were flirting with psychoanalysis, but the sudden end of the war a month later brought their interest to an end. 'Our psychoanalysis has . . . had bad luck,' Freud complained. 'No sooner has it begun to interest the world because of the war neuroses than the war comes to an end.'[34]

But the problem of the war neuroses certainly dominated the discussions held in Budapest. On the one hand, Freud and his followers could feel vindicated. The war had confirmed all too graphically their view of the human mind 'as containing beneath the surface a body of imperfectly controlled and explosive forces which in their nature conflict with standards of civilisation.' It had shown that orthodox neurological explanations of mental disorder did not suffice, that it had a psychological basis. Experiences among war neurotics, said Sándor Ferenczi, had led neurologists very nearly to the discovery of psychoanalysis.[35]

But, at the same time, there was great defensiveness on the question of the libido theory. Karl Abraham and Sándor Ferenczi were adamant that wartime experience confirmed the sexual origin of neurosis. Ernst Simmel found that 'the unconscious meaning of the symptoms of the war neurotics was mostly of a non-sexual nature', but argued that a predisposition to neuroses could very well be connected to the 'psycho-sexual constellation of the particular person'. For example, many soldiers who had broken down 'solely under the pressure of discipline' showed quite clearly 'an attitude of father defiance in consequence of an infantile mother fixation as the subconscious condition of their need for opposition.'[36]

Freud, in his preface to the proceedings of the conference, kept his options open, conceding that the sexual theory had not been confirmed during the war, but pointing out that investigation had necessarily been rather superficial. He admitted that there had always been a difficulty in applying the theory of sexual origin to areas like schizophrenia, paranoia and, especially, trauma, but expressed confidence that the idea of a 'narcissistic' libido could be extended to cover the war neuroses. The British Freudian Ernest Jones had already had a go at doing this, arguing that in cases of external danger the threat to self-preservation was also a threat to self-love; the injury was to the individual's narcissism. Jones pointed to the evidence that victims of war neurosis, especially anxiety cases, seemed to show 'wounded self-love': 'the lack of sociability, the sexual impotence and lack of affection for relatives and friends, the feeling that their personality has been neglected or slighted, that their importance is not sufficiently recognised', were all, he argued, part of this.[37]

However, when Freud himself made a more thorough attempt to understand war neurosis he did not try to apply the sexual theory and came up with a radically different explanation. In *Beyond the Pleasure Principle*, published in 1920, Freud looked in particular at the effect of trauma on dreams; clearly the huge wartime literature on dreams had left its mark on him. Victims of traumatic neuroses had repetitive dreams, he suggested, because they were fixated to the trauma. They must, therefore, he admitted, 'be exceptions to the proposition that dreams are fulfilments of wishes.'

Then, to explain why this was, Freud suddenly wheeled on a completely new idea in his thinking, that of the *compulsion to repeat*. Certain events left behind in the mind a compulsion to repeat which could override the normal practice of remembering only that which was agreeable (to which Freud at this stage gave the confusing term 'the pleasure principle') and force a patient to remember unpleasant experiences. It was, said Freud, 'something that seems more primitive, more elementary than the pleasure principle which it overrides.' Indeed trauma, though sometimes described as similar to hysteria, was 'a far mor~ ~~~~~~~~ general enfeeblement of the mental faculties'.

Freud then went on to offer a crude model of what hap~ Normally, he said, the brain is protected by 'a shield against s outside world,' which makes sure that we only take in 'samples' of that world. We describe as traumatic, he went on,

any excitations from outside which are powerful enough to break through the protective shield. It seems to me that the concept of trauma necessarily implies a connection of this kind with a breach against an otherwise effective barrier against stimuli. Such an event as an external trauma is bound to provoke a disturbance on a large scale and set in motion every possible defensive measure.

At the same time, the pleasure principle is for the moment out of action. There is no longer any possibility of preventing the mental apparatus from being flooded with large amounts of stimulus, and another problem arises instead – the problem of mastering the amounts of stimulus which have broken in and binding them, in the physical sense so that they can be disposed of. [38]

Anyone unaware of Freud's neurological past would be surprised by how physical, how physiological, this all is. Freud admitted that it might seem that he was reverting to the 'old, naive idea of shock' as 'direct damage to the molecular structure or even to the histological structure of the elements of the nervous system'. In fact, what he was trying to understand was 'the effects produced on the organ of the mind by the breech of the shield against stimuli.'

The reason why patients returned in their dreams to these subjects, Freud argued, was that dreams were 'helping to carry out another task which must be accomplished before the dominance of the pleasure principle can even begin.' They were endeavouring to 'master the stimulus retrospectively, by developing the anxiety whose omission was the cause of the traumatic neurosis.' In other words, trauma only took place when there was surprise. If it was preceded by warning, and anxiety, there was no trauma. [39]

It is easy to point to the deficiencies of this model. Freud never explores his distinction between the neuroses of peace and war or between fear, fright, and anxiety. His ignorance of war cases is frequently apparent. His terms – such as 'compulsion to repeat' and 'organ of the mind' are grandly vague. His argument is taking him into the notoriously difficult area of instincts (with which much of *Beyond the Pleasure Principle* is concerned). But, by making plain that the actual, initial trauma is psycho-physiological and offering a simple model of its working, he helped to make explicit something inherent but seldom explicitly stated in the mass of Great War writing – that there are stages in the war neuroses: an initial, traumatic blow, followed by its psychological consequences.

He thus helped to clear the path for the most interesting of all writers about war neuroses, Abram Kardiner.

ARGUMENTS AND ENIGMAS, 1917–18

'SHELL SHOCK'
Invalided officers, suffering from nervous trouble, can receive a supply, free of charge, of the MULLER NUTRIENT, a concentrated nerve food restorative of the highest value in cases of nervous exhaustion and convalescence – Address, The Muller Laboratories . . .
Advertisement in *The Times*, 1 February 1917

'The orthodox medical reactionaries have been smashed . . . and psychology born,' wrote Dr Maurice Nicoll early in 1918. Shell-shock, it seemed, was forcing the British government to put its weight behind new ideas. The War Office had started a crash programme in psychological medicine at Maghull Hospital near Liverpool, the first 'school of clinical psycho-pathology'. A landmark in medical history was being erected – thanks to the ironies and opportunities of war, not by some tiny sect in Bloomsbury but by the British Army.[1]

To a Jungian like Dr Nicoll, this was a moment of great symbolic importance. Some historians, too, have tended to assume that the obvious success of psychological methods of treating shell-shock forced the medical establishment to accept the truths of psychoanalysis. The novelist Pat Barker would have us believe that by 1918 officer-patients in shell-shock hospitals were discussing the finer points of Freudian doctrine with each other. Yet while it is certainly true that the war revealed to many British doctors, especially the neurologists advising the War Office, the 'lamentable defects in [their] medical education' and forced them to recognise the 'psychogenic' factor in medicine, it is a huge oversimplification to assume that everyone shared Dr Nicoll's views or that psychotherapy suddenly became generally available. If anything the theoretical understanding of shell-shock evolved further at the end of the war, *away* from a simple psychological point of view.[2]

The thinking behind the War Office's decision was entirely practical. By the end of 1917 it had become clear that the treatment of shell-shock in Britain was being hampered by a shortage of specialist hospitals and a chronic lack of suitably trained doctors. The authorities were also increasingly alarmed by the numbers of 'uncured' patients being discharged from general hospitals back 'into the community' and drawing pensions. On the other hand, those sent to specialist hospitals like Maghull or Craiglockhart stood a reasonable chance of recovering and not being a drain on the state. Clearly more specialist hospitals and doctors were needed in a hurry; Maghull was by far the best established shell-shock hospital and seemed to get results, so it was common sense to use it as a training centre. The Army's medical chief, Sir Alfred Keogh, was cynical about theoretical medical arguments – 'you can always split the doctors', he once remarked to Charles Myers – and would not have endorsed Maghull methods had they not suited his own ruthlessly practical needs.[3]

The 67 medical officers who spent three months at Maghull immersed in a mixture of Dejerine, Janet, and Freud never made up more than a minority of the doctors treating shell-shock. By 1918 there were no less than 20 shell-shock hospitals in Britain, six for officers, fourteen for men, with over 6,000 beds, and numerous 'Homes for Recovery', offering a more traditional regimen of rest 'massage and electricity'.[4]

Nor did official endorsement of psychological methods resolve the disputes about shell-shock. The last year of the war saw renewed argument among the doctors. If anything, the mystery of 'shell-shock' deepened.

Early in the war, it had been hysterical cases that caught the attention – men with physical symptoms like paralysis or blindness. Now it was the other main category – the neurasthenics, men suffering from nervous exhaustion – that filled the doctors' case loads and posed the questions. 'As the war went on,' wrote Ronald Rows,

it was not infrequent to find men who had done one, two or three years hard service, but for whom the strain proved too great. Often in these cases there had occurred some other incident, such as illness or other serious occurrence at home which had acted as a disturbing agent, and then the strain had been felt more acutely. The fact that they had broken down was the cause of sincere distress to them; they were filled with shame and disgust with their condition.[5]

In July 1917, after visiting Maghull and Craiglockhart, the American psychiatrist John MacCurdy published a long article on the 'War Neuroses' (as shell-shock was now beginning to be called), placing heavy emphasis on *anxiety states* (the term increasingly replacing neurasthenics) and giving detailed case histories.[6]

MacCurdy's 'typical' anxiety case was an officer of 27, who had never been ill in his life, never shown any neurotic tendencies and been a 'normal mischievous boy'. He had gone to France in October 1914 as a private and had first undergone shellfire in February 1915. After a temporary reaction to it, he had become quite used to conditions at the front and functioned well as a soldier. At the end of 1915 he was invalided out with kidney trouble but, after convalescing, returned to France in June 1916, newly commissioned as an officer. He then went through four months of very heavy fighting on the Somme, 'during which time he developed no symptoms whatever', despite being buried three times by earth thrown up from shell explosions. But when, at the end of October 1916, he was sent to help with the burial of the dead in the Ypres sector, he eventually began to get depressed and to drink. His sleep grew poorer and 'scenes on the Som front were constantly in his mind'. At this stage, in late 1916, he began to ge nervous again and lost the ability to tell by its sound where each shell was going to land; now 'all of them seemed to be coming at him'. The 'horror that he had felt when first confronted with the bloodshed of battle' returned. The effort of hiding his mental state from his men made him more and more fatigued, he slept worse and drank more.

It was, though, not until he went on a raid in March 1917 that he finally collapsed. Seven men were killed around him and he was himself blown up and buried. Not even a doctor's 'pick-me-up' could keep him going. Recuperating in hospitals in France and England this patient had the classic nightmares of the 'anxiety state' – 'back on the Somme and being shelled mercilessly'. Nor, according to MacCurdy, did treatment help him. He became disheartened and hypochondriacal, 'quite convinced that he was physically and nervously a permanent wreck.'

What conclusions could you draw from a case like this? Did it show that shell-shock affected everyone – and thus finally destroyed all the old arguments that shell-shockers, like lunatics, were 'inferior' individuals? This was what Grafton Elliot Smith, the Australian anatomist working at Maghull, contended. An incorrigible polemicist, Elliot Smith wrote *Shellshock and its Lessons*, a racy manifesto for Maghull methods of treatment and a clarion call for the lessons of the war to be applied in peacetime psychiatry. The war, declared Smith and his co-author, T. H. Pear:

has shown us one indisputable fact, that a psychoneurosis may be produced in almost anyone if only his environment be made 'difficult' enough for him. It has warned us that the pessimistic, helpless appeal to heredity, so common in the case of insanity must [be abandoned] . . . In the causation of the psychoneuroses, heredity undoubtedly counts, but social and material environment count infinitely more.[7]

This was using shell-shock to re-open an old battle, the nature-nurture controversy, and to wave a red flag at the asylum doctors with their 'pessimistic, helpless appeal to heredity'. They were quick to respond. Heredity *was* a big factor in shell-shock, retorted Sir Robert Armstrong Jones, Superintendent of Claybury Asylum; there were few cases which 'did not inherit in their nervous system some [place of least resistance] which has tended towards a breakdown at some stage or other under the necessary stress.' Jones's colleague, Frederick Mott, author of numerous works on the hereditary origins of mental disorder, commissioned a study of 'The Pre-Disposing Factors of War Psycho-Neurosis' in 100 cases at the Maudsley Hospital, which found that the 'vast majority of the psycho-neurotic cases were among soldiers who had a neuropathic or psycho-pathic soil.' Seventy-four per cent had a 'positive family history' of 'neurotic or psychotic stigmata, including insanity, epilepsy, alcoholism, and nervousness' and 72% had a 'previous neuropathic constitution'.[8]

But, alongside this tired argument about 'predisposition', came a growing

e complex and fascinating ways in which *both* psychological and
ctors interacted in the 'war neuroses' over time. Many of the issues
ate modern research into Post-Traumatic Stress Disorder were
iled.

1917 Mott set out the odd cluster of symptoms from which
anxious (formerly 'neurasthenic') soldiers suffered: they had repetitive war
dreams; were startled by sounds or stimuli reminiscent of battle; were often
sexually impotent; sometimes had quasi-epileptic fits; and some had a disturbed
heart beat. Part of the explanation must be 'psychological' because wounded
men, as Wiltshire had shown in 1916, didn't usually have these symptoms; nor
did prisoners of war. Furthermore, it was perfectly possible to have some of these
neurasthenic symptoms without being blown up by a shell or going into action,
even without leaving England.[9]

What tied all these things together? Mott had a brave stab at some sort of
overall theory of shell-shock, trying to combine the hereditary theory of mental
disorder, the idea of neurasthenia as exhaustion of the nerves, Rivers' quasi-
Freudian idea of unconscious mental conflict and repression and Freud on
dreams. But he also added a new ingredient – recent American work on the effects
of emotion on the human endocrine system.

How does emotional shock act? [Mott asked] Very probably, the endocrine glands,
especially the adrenal and thyroid, are profoundly influenced by emotional shock, and the
persistence in the subconscious mind of memories of experiences associated with terror or
horror is revealed by the dreams of war experiences.[10]

The decade before the war had seen a considerable amount of medical research
into the relationship between the ductless glands and the nervous system: the
word 'hormone' (from the Greek *hormeo*, 'to excite') was coined in 1905 to
describe the chemical messengers that communicate between the nervous system
and the vital organs in the body; a new branch of medicine known as
'endocrinology' came into existence in 1913. But it was not until the Harvard
physiologist Walter Bradford Cannon published his classic book *Bodily Changes
in Pain, Hunger, Fear and Rage* in 1915, that the possible role of the endocrine
system in shell-shock became apparent. Cannon (and others) showed that
emotions like fear and rage do not just produce the surface manifestations we are
all familiar with – higher heart beat, sweating, trembling, hair on edge and so on.
They also set off profound changes deep within the body. In particular – by
bringing together a mass of earlier work with his own experiments on cats and
dogs – Cannon established that when an animal feels itself in danger its adrenal
glands (small ductless glands near the kidneys) play a vital role in mobilising the
body for *flight or fight* by directing blood from the stomach to the heart, lungs and
limbs. Sugar levels in the blood are raised, helping the muscles to revive
themselves, and the rate of breathing is increased. 'Adrenalin' had arrived.[11]

These mechanisms were designed by evolution to equip man also for 'flight or
fight' – to engage an enemy or run away from him; that is, to spend energy

violently, not to sit inertly under shellfire. In the static imprisonment of the Western Front, confined in a trench under artillery bombardment, he seldom did either of these things. How long, then, could the body sustain this state of mobilisation? What would the effect be of prolonged exposure to fear without the opportunity to 'work off' the various energising substances in the blood? Some doctors began to hypothesise that 'war-neurasthenia, the exhaustion, fatigue, loss of control' was 'due either to exhaustion or intoxication with the products of the ductless glands, which have been under constant stimulus, but whose products have not been properly metabolised by the actions they were intended to facilitate.'[12]

So, could the endocrine system also be the missing piece in the puzzle of shell-shock, the link between the 'psychological' and 'physical' sides of the question? No one was quite sure. Frederick Mott felt that 'instead of theories, we should seek . . . some biochemical or biophysical explanation why sudden emotional shock or continued emotional disturbance should produce an acquired emotivity in neuropotentially sound individuals, as it undoubtedly does . . . The dreams of soldiers exhibit in a striking manner how an incident of war associated with emotional shock is graven on the mind.' But he was not himself able to come up with such an explanation.

British psychologists paid lip service to Cannon's work but were not sure what its implications were. When, for example, William Brown returned to Britain in early 1918, to take over at Craiglockhart – and found he was unable to repeat with chronic patients there the almost miraculous results he had been achieving, with hypnosis and mild psychotherapy, on acute patients in France – he speculated that 'the far-reaching extent of the bodily changes, involving cardio-muscular and grandular activity in addition to that of the voluntary and involuntary musculature', might explain 'the intractableness of so many of these cases.'[13]

It was generally felt that the work of the endocrine researchers held out the possibility that, sometime in the future, a 'flood of light' would be thrown on the 'nature of the physical factors which play a part in the psychoneuroses, and in particular upon that vague but vastly important thing we call "consitutional predisposition".' It seemed possible that 'the physiologist and the psychologist [would] ultimately find a meeting place in which they could join hands and adjust their claims.' However, Brown, for one, didn't believe that psychotherapy should be replaced by new methods of treatment targeting the endocrine system.

If the originating cause was a mental disturbance, we may theoretically expect that psychotherapy may help to readjust the balance once more, even in such widespread physiological disturbances, and practical success, though slow and partial in many cases, seems to justify this expectation.[14]

*   *   *

The advances in medical thinking did nothing to help ordinary doctors with the thorniest problem that confronted them – distinguishing malingering from 'genuine' shell-shock. How was a doctor to tell a man who was pretending to be paralysed from another who had hysterical paralysis? Neither had any organic, neurological reason to be paralysed but the first was a malingerer and the second a patient.

Doctors repeatedly stressed that 'the dividing line between malingering and functional neurosis may be a very fine one'; occasionally they admitted that it was very arbitrarily drawn. 'The only difference between pure hysteria and malingering,' a prominent neurologist declared in March 1915, 'was probably a matter of the degree to which the "wilfulness" to be blind or deaf or mute was buried in the depth or flourished on the surface of consciousness.' He had a patient suffering from 'mutism after exposure to shell explosion' who was 'such a nice fellow' that no one would accuse him of malingering; yet 'his only successful attempt to speak for some time after his admission to hospital was when he blurted out his conviction that he would rather be dumb for the rest of his life than return to the Front.'[15]

There was, of course, a long and honourable tradition of malingering in the British Army – the old phrase 'swinging-the-lead' was of naval origin, whereas 'scrimshanking' was a more recent addition. In the First World War, according to John Brophy and Eric Partridge, the internal moral code of the men laid down strict rules about when you could and couldn't malinger. Overall, '"Swinging the lead" was a great source of pride with some soldiers and in certain circumstances – with all soldiers.' Within this overall code, though, there was a sharp distinction between 'a lead-swinger who let other men do work he was able to do, or who practised his craft when danger was threatened' who 'was beloved of no one', and the man 'who swung it successfully on experts, such as doctors in England or behind the line.' This kind of 'lead-swinger' 'received genuine admiration and kept up no pretence before his comrades.'[16]

On the Western Front this code acquired a further distinction – between those determined (in terms of their own private self-respect) to stick it out 'for the duration' and those who were considered, by themselves or their comrades, to have 'done their bit'. The idea that every man has his limit – what Lord Moran later called 'using up credit in the bank' – surfaced here and there and was widely applied by the officer class to itself, even if it was never officially accepted.[17]

The official view distinguished three classes of malingering. 'True' malingering – pretending to have shell-shock while in the field – was felt to be unusual; 'partial' malingering – exaggerating or prolonging hysterical symptoms once out of the line – was regarded as pretty common practice. Finally, there was 'quasi-malingering, scrimshanking, or skulking'. This third group were soldiers, in weaker units and at bad times in the war, who 'with little or no pretence decamped from the battle as opportunity arose, pleading "shell-shock" as the excuse for their evasion.' Their number was 'great', but 'for the most part they made but feeble if any attempt at deception and ultimately by persuasion or command returned to duty.' This sort of partial malingering occurred, it was admitted, 'in unprecedented proportions', particularly in the later months of 1916.[18]

The difficulty of sticking such labels on individuals c̄
fascinating personal narratives in the Imperial War Museun
and Edward Casey malingerers, genuine war neurotics or v

James Haygate Butlin came from a secure middle-class ba
minor public school and enlisted in January 1915 while st
then 19 years old. Three months later he was in France as a junior officer in the
Dorsetshire Regiment. His letters soon lost their initial jaunty and confident
tone: 'If only the people in England could see what I have seen they would be a
sadder and a wiser lot.'[19]

On 22 May 1915 he wrote with 'a profound sense of gratitude to my God that
I am still alive' after an episode in which he had ordered troops under his
command to fire on some surrendering Germans; none of them did. He had
given the order because German sniping was still continuing, but 'by this time
my nerves were shattered.'

A month later, he came home on leave – 'I hope I shall remain here for the rest
of the war' – but was soon was back in France. 'My nerves,' he wrote home, 'are
not what they were, I can tell you.' Then, in March 1916, an ear infection led to
his being invalided home.

I don't know how long I shall continue to remain in England, but you can take it from
me it will be as long as human ingenuity and cunning can continue. I've done 12 months
of it and that's enough in the infantry.
    [4 June 1916] I feel quite unable to face the trenches again.
    [6 November 1916] . . . in mortal funk of being passed fit for general service.

But he was, eventually, and in March 1917, was back in France again. He seems
to have done his best.

16 April 1917
    When we went over the top we came up against terrific shell and machine-gun fire; it
was perfect hell. A Coy was very lucky, however, and no man was hit. F Coy lost all its
officers. D had one left. B Coy was kept in reserve. We gained our objective and the
general was greatly braced with us.

But it was no good; after two short tours in the trenches he was back in Britain
suffering from neurasthenia. He was eventually sent to Craiglockhart, which he
considered a 'glorious loaf'; but his time there seems to have made no lasting
difference to his condition, for, following a further breakdown in January 1918,
he was pronounced 'permanently unfit for military service'. Butlin took no
further part in the fighting. After the war he returned to Oxford and took a
double first in Classics. He then worked for a publisher before, surprisingly,
rejoining the Army in 1939. He died at the age of 86 in 1982.
    Butlin clearly fits into category two – partial malingering – the exaggeration of
symptoms. But he also did his duty and suffered genuine psychological damage.

rious war record, but a perfectly decent and understandable one. No
n armchair warrior has the right to judge him.

Butlin writes with the fluency and evasion of the educated British middle
class, Edward Casey struggles to express himself at all. His rambling, picaresque
narrative 'The Misfit Soldier, A War Story 1914–1918', described by the
Imperial War Museum catalogue as 'illiterate and obscene', is also an honest
record of war as experienced not by a suffering poet or a tough artisan, but by
someone from the margins of society for whom laws and social codes mean little.
It also gives a rare glimpse of the psychiatrists from the soldier's angle.[20]

Casey was born in 1898, into a London Irish family and grew up, according to
Robert Ritchie, 'a scrawny, cocking, thieving, busking, truant turned odd jobs
man'. When the war broke out he was rubbing along selling matches and running
errands; 'the King's shilling seemed like a good offer'. Initially told he was 'too
thin and well under nourished, it's only your oversized boots that stops you
falling through the bars of the drains', he was eventually accepted and sent to
France.

Casey's approach to soldiering was from the start selective; he had no qualms
about deserting from a night patrol in no-man's land and waiting in a convenient
shellhole until the others returned. Some time in 1915, fairly soon after arriving
on the Western Front, he was sheltering from a German barrage in a dug-out
when a shell hit the roof. He woke up in hospital to be told by a doctor that he
was not wounded but 'badly shell-shocked and suffering from acute
neurasthenia.' To his delight, he was then evacuated to a hospital in England,
where 'titled ladies' brought him chocolates and picture books and a carriage took
the patients, dressed in hospital blues, off to 'Big Mansions'.

Three weeks later, though, Casey was back in the line. Badly frightened after a
night raid, he 'began to scheme as to how I could lose my memory again'
(evidently he had suffered genuine amnesia after being blown up). But his first
effort was a disaster. Although he simulated the symptoms acceptably, when
asked his name and number he automatically gave them. He then attempted to
desert, which resulted in five days' punishment. Clearly Casey was getting
desperate. At this point, however,

My chance came for my greatest malingering effort, there was talk of a big push and the
bombardment was raging along the whole front our section Ypres seem to get more than
its fair share . . . I was in a very bad shape, it was the worst shelling I had ever experienced
when it was over, the rest that were in the shell hole about left, I decided that I had had
enough and lay in the mud with my tunic covering my head.

Here, as elsewhere, Casey is both genuinely affected and consciously scheming to
get out of danger.

I was still shivering and shaking with fright and the lump on my head (how I got it God
knows). [I was] carried into a big tent . . . I was still in a state of shock. [But] my thoughts
were now on whether I can fool the doctors, the test came in a couple of days.

Casey had learnt by experience. This time, by simply saying 'I don't remember', he got his trip to England. But there he found a new obstacle to negotiate: a 'specialist in Hypnosis and Hypnotism' in Harley Street:

The first occasion I was told to lie on a Couch, the doctor held a dangling watch on a gold chain, telling me I would close my eyes and go to sleep. To myself I decided not to go to sleep, but I did altho I was asleep I could hear him talking, he opened his [my?] eyes with his fingers, then told me to raise my arm. The strange part about it, I did not want to obey him but my arm went up at his command.

I was able to answer his questions about my experience in the dug-out, I found out altho he had control of my body he could [not?] control my mind, and altho I experienced several seances he did not know my mind was not under his control. This doctor was a nice bloke, and explained as to why the shock of being buried in the dug-out affected my mind and to recover I had to experience another severe shock.

Casey was now seriously worried about the 'power of such new technique to find [him] out.'

Mermerism was then I'm told a medical rarity and not very often practised; Those medical blokes tell you nothing, for when they carried out all their tests, and found out I was malingering, I felt certain I would be for the Firing Squad, I would be fini.

Fortunately for him, while this was going on an air raid took place, which caused him to throw a (presumably genuine) epileptic fit. Eventually sent to Ireland, Casey went absent without leave and, to avoid punishment, volunteered for Salonica. Now came a bad blow: he found himself batman to a 'keen' officer who made him accompany him on patrols in no-man's land. He survived this ordeal, only to be 'bombed on his way to a brothel'. What happened next is a little unclear; it seems that Casey was taken to a hospital and tried his 'loss of memory' trick for a third time; but hastily regained it when he found himself in a mental ward. He was not returned to the line but sent back to England; at first, to a ward for 'nervous complaints':

a shattering experience, cases of shell shock, nerves shattered some in straight jackets, others walking around [like?] zombies, to tell the truth I was scared stiff, could not sleep, think, Christ I am not as sick as they were. If I stayed in here I might be like them. Oh Holy Jesus, Mother Mary, please don't let them keep me here and later send me to the mad house.

He was then sent to a convalescent home in the country, 'nearly as big as Buckingham Palace where the King lived', where he enjoyed croquet and more rides in aristocrats' carriages. Finally he came before a medical board of three doctors, who 'question[ed] me on my feelings, did I sleep well, was I frightened of going back to the front line, to that question I gave a firm No. I did not want to go again I have been there three times the thought of those guns, the shells dropping makes me feel bad.'

Edward Casey never returned to the front. His narrative makes clear that he probably should never have been chosen for the Army at all. He was physically slight, timid and fearful, and, because of his social background, quite without any sense of wider loyalty. When placed in an extreme situation he had no doubt about what to do – he simply ran away. He was therefore a liability to any unit and his fellow soldiers were probably glad to see the back of him. But because he never tried to contain his fear he may well have been less damaged than the many who spent years grappling with theirs.

*   *   *

Edward Casey was barely eighteen when he arrived on the Western Front. Most soldiers were in their teens and earlier twenties, half men, half boys. The very word 'infantry' means a collection of youths. Physically, they may have been mature, but emotionally they were not. Harold Macmillan, later the British Prime Minister, was wounded on the Somme in 1916. When he woke up in hospital he at once asked for his mother. Macmillan did have a particularly strong and dominating mother, but his response was quite normal and very common.[21]

Many of those who looked after shell-shocked soldiers noticed how under the strains of war they had reverted to childhood, or 'regressed'. Shell-shock, said Dr Hugh Crichton-Miller, produced a condition 'essentially childish and infantile in its nature'; the Oxford psychologist William McDougall felt towards his patients 'like the father of a multitude of helpless children, hopelessly stumbling on the brink of hell; they for the most part were very docile, dependent and grateful'. Having 'failed' as men, they wanted to be mothered and loved as boys.[22]

There were certainly some cases where the pressures of war brought to the surface long-hidden phobias and psychoses. Rivers had a patient whose boyhood claustrophobia (caused by having to sleep in enclosed bunk beds) was reactivated by the trenches and dug-outs of the front. Dr Henry Head treated 'a man, a regular officer, who went out to Gallipoli and went mad upon the beach.' He saw the whole beach covered with jewelled spiders of enormous size. 'They did not know what to do with the man so put him on one of the boats and as the barges came up with the wounded he saw his wife and child on a barge cut to pieces.'[23]

The image of the wife and child lying mutilated on the barge was easily explained: both had been ill when the officer was sent abroad and he was very worried about them. But the spider obsession proved very difficult to sort out. In the end, Head discovered that 'at the age of three he had had a psychosis, some nervous condition in which he saw a jewelled spider which his mother wore on her dress.' In the terrible strain of the Gallipoli landing, this old problem had re-surfaced.

The theme of regression was brilliantly seized on in one of the first 'shell-shock' novels, Rebecca West's *The Return of the Soldier* (1918). War, for her, is a kind of truth drug stripping away layers of falsehood to reveal emotional truths underneath. A young officer returns to his country mansion from the war suffering from amnesia and, rejecting both his trivial, fashionable wife and his adoring cousin, demands instead to be re-united with a plain working-class girl with whom (they learn to their horror) he spent a brief adolescent idyll. The officer has regressed, not to childhood, but to his late teens, when he 'turned to sex with a peculiar need'. Now, once more, he needs that kind of maternal love.

Regression, in *The Return of the Soldier*, is a neat, literary device, a mechanism for the book's real subject, feminine rivalry over a man. (While writing it, West was struggling to win H. G. Wells away from his wife.) Messier but far more remarkable are the cases of war-induced amnesia and regression written up in one of the great shell-shock texts, William McDougall's *Outline of Abnormal Psychology*.[24]

One of his patients, Private Meek, had been a basket-weaver before the war. During a heavy bombardment in 1916, he climbed out of his trench vowing to bring back the trench mortar that was shelling it, and was restrained and taken to a Casualty Clearing Station. By the time he got to England two weeks later he had developed tremors of the limbs and could not speak.

At Netley hospital, McDougall managed to communicate with him in writing but progress was so slow that he decided on hypnosis, an approach he had used only occasionally, 'as a method of exploration'. This revealed that Private Meek was visited every night by the ghost of a German he had killed on the Marne in 1914.

During the night the figure appears suddenly in the ward, points his rifle at P.M., says 'Now I've got you, you can't get away,' and fires point blank at him. P.M. hears the crack of the rifle, and sees the ghost sink to the ground. He takes this to be a real ghost come to take his revenge and every night he is terrified anew by this visitor.

McDougall explained this hallucination to the young man as fully as possible and expected him to get better. He stopped seeing the ghost, but did not otherwise improve; his twitching got worse, his muscles more rigid, and he could no longer even whisper.

In the autumn of 1916, McDougall was transferred to Oxford. The basket-weaver passed into the care of Dr Arthur Hurst, whose methods were rather different. Meek's limbs were now completely rigid and it was proposed to reduce this condition by severing some of his tendons. Perhaps because of terror at this prospect, perhaps because he had been abandoned by McDougall, Meek regressed completely into childhood, gave up all attempt to walk or speak and spent his time playing with dolls. He appears in Hurst's film *War Neuroses* – a hunched, cowering figure in a wheelchair, with a teddy bear in his lap, being petted by a nurse, 'completely unaware,' a title card announces, 'of the vigorous efforts to overcome the rigidity of his ankles.' A doctor then appears and wrenches violently at Meek's bare ankles, which do not move and remain fixed at a downward angle to his legs.[25]

He remained like that for almost a year. Then, one evening in November 1917 he 'had a headache and became excited in the evening.' His memory began to return during the night and he talked incessantly. He could now remember his experiences in France but not those in the hospital. It was not, however, till six months later that he could walk without assistance. The film shows him again in June 1918, moving awkwardly with a peculiar deformed gait; but, as he supervises other patients weaving baskets in the Devon sunshine, he is once more a responsible adult, a man reclaimed. How much the doctors helped (or hindered) his improvement is impossible to say, but by November 1918, Private Meek's recovery was complete: the film shows him for a last time running nimbly up and down steps and swinging his arms like mill-sails.[26]

Dramatic cases like these were quite rare. But were they suggestive of something broader? McDougall compared the process of regression in shell-shock to injury to a tree. Normally in a tree, the sap and vital energy tend towards the new growth at the top. But if the tree is injured by frost or fire, 'we may observe a new outburst of growth and vitality in the older, more primitive parts, namely we see buds growing out from these parts.' Similarly, in cases like that of Meek, the 'highest or more recently developed parts of the cerebral cortex represent the growing points of the upper branches of the tree. Arrest of these functions is followed by a new outburst of vital activity in the lower older parts.'[27]

One of McDougall's Netley colleagues thought that 'the idea of shock bringing out prehistoric and sometimes even embryonic activities' needed further thought. It was William Rivers, however, who really seized on this idea of regression. In his post-war book *Instinct and Unconscious*, Rivers, modifying his wartime position, argued that all the psychoneuroses of war – hysteria, anxiety neurosis and so on – were manifestations of regression, a reversion not just to childhood but to an earlier phase in human development. In this theory he attempted to reconcile the Freudian 'mental conflict' model he had explored at Craiglockhart with the neuro-physiological views he had acquired much earlier from his mentors John Hughlings Jackson and Henry Head.[28]

Living in the age of Darwin and Spencer, Hughlings Jackson's view of the brain and nervous system had been deeply coloured by a sense of their gradual development during human evolution. He saw mental disorder as a process in which the higher, more recently acquired functions of the brain – those handling matters like emotion and intelligence – went wrong, allowing older functions and more basic instincts, like sex, hunger, and self-preservation, to go unchecked (Jonathan Miller has called this idea 'the dog beneath the skin'). Rivers and Henry Head had taken this view a stage further and, in the famous 'arm' experiment they conducted in 1905, established to their own satisfaction the existence of two layers in the nervous system: a basic or 'protopathic' one, responsible for simple functions; and a 'higher', more complex one, the 'epicritic'. By 1920, though, several efforts to duplicate Head and Rivers' results had failed and doubts were beginning to be being raised about the epicritic/protopathic division. Rivers chose to ignore them.[29]

Psychoneuroses, Rivers argued, take place when the balance between the older, more primitive instincts (like sex and self-preservation) and the newer controlling 'forces' (like duty, fidelity, intelligence and religion) is disturbed by shock, strain, illness or fatigue. In civilian life it is usually the sexual instincts which are thus exposed; in war, those of self-preservation. Psychoneuroses, Rivers suggested, can be seen as attempts 'to restore the balance between instinctive and controlling forces.'

Hysteria was a way of escaping from this conflict rather than facing it, and usually the result of letting go of 'the modifying principle based on intelligence'. In hysteria, said Rivers, an 'ancient instinctive reaction' to danger – namely immobility – was reactivated, causing paralysis, dumbness, and insensitivity to stimuli. At the same time hysteria produced an extraordinary suggestibility, particularly in soldiers put through the rituals of military training. Hence the ease with which hysterics could be hypnotised or would start copying each others' symptoms.

The anxiety neuroses were also a form of regression, but of a less profound kind – a regression to childhood or the 'character of infancy'. The loss of emotional self-control was seen by Rivers as a return to the violent emotions of childhood. The war dreams of the anxiety patient were the same as childish night-terrors and were full of the same imagery, like terrifying animals (or, with one of Rivers' patients, Chinamen). There was the same failure to appreciate reality, to draw a line between your own imagination and external reality; in some patients this led to schizophrenia.

Rivers put forward this bold theory with clarity and conviction, and his book is still enormously suggestive. He was undoubtedly on to something. Unfortunately, though, the physiological keystone of his edifice – the idea of an 'epicritic/protopathic' division in the nervous system – already tottering in 1920, was soon afterwards demolished altogether by the neurologist Francis Walshe. Walshe was a pupil of Gordon Holmes at Queen Square and, like him, liked to destroy grand theories with inconvenient scientific facts. Head and Rivers' system, Walshe concluded after lengthy investigation, had only one flaw: 'that the anatomical pathways essential to the system as envisaged by them had not all been provided by nature.'[30]

'SKIRTING THE EDGES OF HELL'

If present plans go through, no class of men – military or civilian – will ever have had as prompt and as good attention in mental illness as the American soldiers in France.

Thomas W. Salmon, early 1918[1]

Given the close ties between British and American medicine, it was inevitable that the saga of shell-shock should be closely followed on the other side of the Atlantic. From the earliest days of the war, doctors in the United States had heard stories of 'strange new diseases apparently having their origin in the stress and special horrors of modern warfare', which seemed to present problems in treatment and prevention to the medical organisation of the British Army. The first published reports were eagerly read by American neurologists and psychiatrists who realised, even then, that the time might very soon come when they would be dealing with the same problems.

Oddly, the Americans drew hardly at all on their own rich writings in this field. They had, after all, some claim to be pioneers in the field, having produced during the Civil War a substantial literature on the effects of warfare on the nervous system. In the hospitals around Philadelphia to which the Army of the Union sent its terrible casualties, Da Costa had first observed 'soldier's heart', Silas Weir Mitchell had developed his cure and Charles Beard had begun to formulate 'neurasthenia'. The novelists Ambrose Bierce and Stephen Crane had made powerful use in their work of the after-effects of war – real in Bierce's case, both imagined and real in Crane's.[2]

But very little of this left much enduring institutional mark; anyway, by 1917, it was old stuff. The general view was that 'new conditions of war' – high explosives, trench warfare and gas – had ushered in a new world, taken things much further towards 'the saturation level of human nervous resistance'. The lessons of modern war needed to be learnt, and in May 1917 Dr Thomas W. Salmon was sent off to Europe to learn them.

Tom Salmon, then 41, was the Medical Director of the National Committee for Mental Hygiene, a lay body agitating for the reform of the American mental health system. He had not meant to be a psychiatrist. The son of an impecunious doctor in upstate New York, Salmon had lost his father, mother and only brother and failed as a country doctor himself, all before he was 25. With a young family to feed, he took a job as bacteriologist to the New York State Health Department and by 1904 was in charge of the psychiatric arrangements at Ellis Island, the teeming gateway to the American continent.[3]

Salmon's knowledge of psychiatry consisted of what he had picked up second-hand in a State hospital, which was probably just as well. Ellis Island in the 1900s was no place for academic theorisers; it was the university of life. In one year, 1907, over a million people entered America through the Port of New York; sometimes as many as 5,000 had to be psychiatrically assessed in a day. It was not done out of concern for their welfare: public opinion was deeply concerned that sound, native American stock was being diluted by 'degenerate' and 'feeble-minded' immigrants from Southern and Eastern Europe; the taxpayers of New York were tired of paying to keep immigrants in state institutions. Under such intense pressure, many people would have given way to despairing cynicism or detached official brutality. Salmon did not. He was that rare creature, a medical bureaucrat who cared. He was 'literally possessed by the need to help people, by the doctor's deep urge to relieve suffering – even if it meant neglecting his own family.'[4]

Salmon worked tirelessly to reform the system and improve facilities for those who made it to America and then broke down. 'I lack front and solemnity – two almost indispensable qualities,' he wrote once. 'What I have, though, is long experience in persuading people to do what they had not the slightest intention of doing.' Salmon's work brought him to the attention of Clifford Beers, a Yale graduate disgusted by the 'ignorant, brutal and incompetent' treatment he had received as a mental patient. In 1913 – with a relieved nudge from his former employers – Salmon moved to the National Committee for Mental Health, the body that Beers had created. Its mission was very similar to that advocated by Ronald Rows in England – to break down the barriers between sanity and insanity, to create out-patient clinics, to end the disaster of committal.[5]

Among other things, this meant surveying the condition of American mental health; for several years Salmon travelled the country seeing for himself and writing eloquent reports – 'Abandoned to filth and unbelievable misery lie the insane poor of this pleasant, fertile, prosperous American county,' begins his account of a Texas poor farm. It also meant cultivating public opinion and raising money from wealthy individuals, tasks at which Salmon excelled; his own salary was paid by the Rockefeller Foundation. By the time the Americans entered the war, the National Committee for Mental Hygiene was firmly established, and was the obvious body to assist the tiny medical corps of the United States Army in creating a psychiatric service. It trained military psychiatrists, opened wards in the United States and sent Salmon to England.[6]

Salmon spent two months there, spoke to all the great and the good, saw Hurst's *War Neuroses* film, and sent his assistant John MacCurdy to talk at length to the staff at Maghull and Craiglockhart. He then produced a masterly report on the British experience and its lessons.[7]

Salmon's approach was broad-brush, practical and based on common sense.

He recognised that there were undoubtedly *physical* elements in the war neuroses – the soldier' s endocrine system was disturbed; he might well suffer tiny injuries of his spinal cord; he often had irregular heartbeat – and Salmon noted shrewdly that there was still much to learn about the onset of these cases and just what happened in the first few days; he hoped that the Americans would be able to do more research in this area. But methods of treatment along the lines suggested by this physical data had 'thus far proved quite ineffective'; while *psychological* factors were 'too obvious and too important in these cases to be ignored'. Treating the war neuroses was 'essentially a problem of psychological medicine'. He thus came down firmly on the side of Maghull and not Mott.

Bravely, Salmon offered a broad sketch of how he saw the war neuroses develop in the mind. It makes no claim to originality, but as a clear, jargon-free statement of the view at this time, is worth quoting at length. 'The psychological basis of the war neuroses,' Salmon argued, was 'an elaboration, with endless variations, of one central theme':

Escape from an intolerable situation in real life to one made tolerable by the neurosis . . . Not only fear . . . but horror, revulsion against the ghastly duties which sometimes must be performed, emotional situations resulting from the interplay of personal conflicts and military conditions, all play their part in making an escape of some sort mandatory.

The most obvious form of escape, death, was not an option for most people. To flee or desert ran counter to the soldier's ideals of duty, patriotism and honour and his training. Malingering was a military crime and unthinkable to those with a sense of discipline and propriety. For many men, wounds resolved the conflict between honour and self-preservation most happily. For others,

The neurosis provides a means of escape so convenient that the real cause of wonder is not that it should play such an important part in military life but that so many men should find a satisfactory adjustment without its intervention. The constitutionally neurotic, having most readily at their disposal the mechanism of functional nervous disease, employ it most frequently. They constitute, therefore, a large proportion of all cases, but a very striking fact in the present war is the number of men of apparently normal make-up who develop war neuroses in the face of unprecedentedly terrible conditions to which they are exposed . . .
. . . Approached from the psychological point of view the symptoms in the war neuroses lose much of their weird and inexplicable character. Most of them can be summed up in the statement that the soldier loses function which either is necessary to continued military service or prevents his successful adaptation to war.[8]

Salmon was quite clear what the Americans should do. Firstly, rigidly exclude from their Army all 'insane, feeble-minded, psychopathic and neuropathic indi-viduals.' But that step would not, in itself, remove the problem. There would still be psychiatric casualties. Secondly, make sure that 'treatment by medical officers with special training in psychiatry [was] available just as near the front as military exigency will permit.' Salmon set out in detail the necessary organisational steps.

By contrast, he was vague about the form psychotherapy should take. Patients were to be 'reeducated in will, thought, feeling and function' by doctors who were 'strong, forceful, patient, sympathetic and tactful' as required. The 'resources to be employed' would include 'psychological analysis, persuasion, sympathy, discipline, hypnotism, ridicule, encouragement and severity'. If all this was done, he argued, the Americans could expect to reduce considerably the 'wastage' of men, have a more efficient army, and pay less in pensions.[9]

It was, of course, one thing for Tom Salmon and the National Committee to persuade the high-ups in Army Medicine of the need for psychiatric vetting of recruits, but quite another to carry it out on the ground. Psychiatrists arriving in the autumn of 1917 at remote, forbidding places like Camp Pike, Arkansas, had first to persuade their medical colleagues of the value of the exercise and then to conduct a fairly hasty examination. They 'went over each man, testing pupillary and tendon reflexes, co-ordination and station, looking for tremors and for scars suggestive of epilepsy, and asking a few questions as to heredity, environment, schooling, convulsions, or nervous breakdown, meanwhile noticing any peculiarities. Under the most favourable conditions . . . one examiner could make a fairly thorough preliminary survey of from 150 to 200 men a day.'[10]

Doubtful cases might get a further examination, but there was no point in being too thorough. The Army would only exclude men with 'obvious nervous or mental disturbances in which one could show the disorder in its early phases and point out how the disease influenced the soldiers' conduct and efficiency'; and, even with them, was reluctant to accept psychiatrists' recommendations. As a result, only 1,787 (1.05%) of the 170,000 soldiers seen in one camp were rejected. When the American Commander in France, General Pershing, complained in July 1918 of the 'prevalence of mental disorders' in American troops in France, it emerged that his overseas force contained no less than 3,000 epileptics, schizophrenics, 'general paretics, tabetics, psychoneurotics [and] imbeciles', whose discharge had been recommended by psychiatrists in America, but who had been taken anyway. After Pershing's letter, the psychiatrists' word carried more weight (the 'Pershing letter' was still a potent weapon in the early years of the Second World War).[11]

The work of the psychiatrists has, however, been completely overshadowed by a rival exercise conducted at the same time. America's psychologists, led by Robert M. Yerkes of Harvard, persuaded the War Department that testing the intelligence of recruits would help the Army to reduce mental casualties, even though many soldiers rightly suspected that Yerkes' true intention was to obtain data from the Army's recruits for his research on the relationship between race and intelligence.[12]

The psychologists hastily devised two procedures, the 'Alpha' written test for literate recruits and the 'Beta' for illiterates, both of which were heavily flawed by 'cultural bias' – a concept then in its infancy. Thus, literate recruits were asked such questions as whether Scrooge appeared in *Vanity Fair*, *A Christmas Carol*,

Romola or *Henry V,* and those unable to write were shown pictures of a camel without a hump and a tennis court without a net and asked what was missing. In all, over 1.6 million men and 42,000 officers were tested in this way, producing data from which Yerkes and his colleagues eventually concluded that the average American had a mental age of 13, 89% of 'Negroes' were 'morons' and 'older immigrants from Northern Europe were more intelligent than recent ones from the South and East.' These findings paved the way for tough new immigration laws in the 1920s, 'put psychology on the map in the United States' and gave a much-needed boost to Professor Yerkes' academic career.[13]

Yerkes' work has an important place in the history of 'racial science' and the 'measurement' of intelligence. Its impact on the war was less dramatic. Some 8,000 soldiers were recommended for discharge and the Army, alerted to the issue of intelligence, released a considerable number of other recruits during training on grounds of mental deficiency. The yardstick remained fairly crude – the standard of rejection was 'generally understood to be a mentality of or below that of a child of 8 years' – but, overall, the Americans were more successful in eliminating the mentally deficient than the British. There was less chance that someone who 'could not be counted on to take care of himself' would find himself in battle.[14]

Meanwhile, in France, Tom Salmon was trying to apply the second part of his scheme – forward psychiatry.

* * *

When the French General, Pétain, was asked in the autumn of 1917 what his strategy was, he replied 'We must wait for the Americans and the tanks.' It was to prove a long wait – only in August 1918 was the American Army established in Europe in real numbers. Tom Salmon, though, was in France by December 1917, his eye alive to incongruity:

War from behind the lines is a dizzying jumble. Revolving chairs, stuffy offices, dry as dust reports, blueprints one day and the next – with the help of a broken down Ford and a few gallons of gasoline – marching men with grimy faces and shining eyes, horses straining and plunging at guns, little white clouds drifting under the big ones and piles of bloody clothes and leggings lying outside the door of a field hospital. Everything which is dull and stupid and everything which yanks at your heartstrings, all mixed up together so that at the end of the week you can't quite remember whether you spent Tuesday going over the specifications for a portable laundry or skirting the edges of hell in an automobile.[15]

In July 1918, visiting the hospitals 'that catch the red tide that flows back', he was overcome by a sense of helplessness. 'Never did psychiatry seem such a useless branch of medicine,' he wrote. 'All I could do was . . . help a little in sorting.' He also saw for himself some of the strange effects of war on the mind.

One who thinks that cowardice is an essential ingredient should have seen [a group of cases he had examined]. One boy had volunteered to carry food to a detachment which had been cut off for many hours by shell fire. The three others who went with him were killed and he developed a distinctly psychoneurotic condition. Another brought in his comrade on his back under heavy fire. He developed his symptoms when he found his friend was dead. Another was in a dug-out when a shell entered it killing two and wounding several. He helped dig out and then brought out the wounded but became tremulous and mute a few minutes later when he saw his Lieutenant eviscerated by another shell.[16]

Although crumpled, untidy and long-haired, Colonel Salmon was an effective operator in the military machine, ceaselessly nagging and charming to get his piece of the action. 'All the time,' he complained to his wife in January 1918, 'I have to fight to get the mental cases what they need. Invariably they are over-looked and forgotten in planning new things unless I bring them to attention.' He also badgered his colleagues in the United States to provide more skilled doctors – 'When the grandchildren of famous neurologists and others sit on their respective knees and say "What did you in the great war?", I'm blest if I know what they will hear.'[17]

Salmon's letters show him veering between a confident faith that wartime work would blaze a trail of reform for post-war civil psychiatry and despair that opportunities were being missed because of lack of proper personnel and facilities. 'Day after day,' he wrote during the long drawn-out agony of the Argonne battle in October 1918, 'I have to witness here partial failures that could have been made conspicuously successful.'[18]

Tom Salmon was a complex, difficult man, a perfectionist with, his biographer notes, that 'certain temporary paranoia' which is 'part of all reformers'. After a while, he began to develop – as Charles Myers had – a 'Cinderella' complex about the way the Army treated psychiatric casualties. 'The best men and kind hearted men too,' spoke of the patients as 'nuts'; 'jokes about nut-pickers' (psychiatrists) wore thin. 'Folks don't like my patients,' he wrote, 'and sometimes I don't like them myself . . . shellshockers are pretty unattractive compared to the cheerful, patient wounded.' Outwardly, though, he kept up the facade.[19]

But events, in the shape of the German offensive in March 1918, blew all Salmon's well-laid plans aside. The Americans were flung in to help the French; with the front moving fast, the evacuation of casualties became chaotic and thousands of US soldiers were scattered in hospitals hundreds of miles behind the lines; few ever returned to the front. It was not until July, after the Germans had been held before Paris, that the Americans began to exist as a separate army; only at the end of August 'came the opportunity for putting into effect some American plans of work.' They were a definite advance on what the French and British had done and the model for everything thereafter, therefore worth describing in a little detail.[20]

Salmon created three tiers of psychiatry – at division, at 'Advanced Neuro-logical Hospitals', and at Base Hospital. The main innovation was the division psychiatrist, who divided his time between an advanced field hospital (usually a

large barn) about five miles behind the line and a treatment centre (usua
collection of tents) a few miles further back. His job was to sort, to 'cont
evacuation', to make sure that lightly affected cases of fatigue, concussion or very
mild neurosis were not sent miles back but kept near the lines until they had
recovered. He was there to prove that shell-shock, far from being complex and
dangerous, was 'relatively simple and recoverable'.

He had, of course, to contend with 'the natural instinct of a combat army' – to
'free itself of its sick and wounded in the quickest way possible' – by achieving
results. Treatment at this level was very basic: 'food, sleep, exercise and the
hopeful attitude of those who come into contact with them'.

Great care was taken never to mention the word 'shell-shock', for it was surprising to see
with what tenacity men clung to the diagnosis of 'shell-shock' or 'neurosis' even though
the tag had been made out by one of the enlisted sanitary personnel [medical orderlies,
not doctors]. Sometimes soldiers would wander into dressing stations and cheerfully
announce that they were 'shell-shocked'.[21]

Instead the Americans borrowed from the British the term 'NYD (Nervous)', felt
to deny soldiers 'something definite to cling to', something 'warranting treatment
in a hospital, thus honourably releasing them from combat duty'. And they did
their best to reinforce the sense of duty by 'suggestion' or, as we might put it,
emotional blackmail:

Constantly, and in every conceivable fashion were emphasized the glory and traditions of
the division, of the regiment, and of the company, and the very important part which each
soldier played in contributing his share. In the field with combat troops . . . an artificial
family instinct was often developed. This factor, too, could be utilized as a powerful
means of obtaining a healthy therapeutic atmosphere.

On the other hand, evacuation to the rear was painted in gloomy colours. The patient
came to realise that leaving the division or unit meant probably the opportunity forever
lost of having a part in its present victories and consequently in future honors and rewards.
It involved a total separation from the paternal officer, and brother soldier, and finally
becoming that most unhappy of mortals, the lone casualty. It was in a sense a desertion,
since it left comrades to 'carry on' alone.[22]

It takes skill and authority to urge a soldier to return to a battle you are yourself
keeping well out of. The American official history concedes that 'the intellectual
status of the patient' was significant and that the 'relatively ignorant soldier was
usually softer clay in the physician's hands than was the one in whom learning
and training had sharpened the habit of questioning, scrutinizing and weighing
in the balance.'

Salmon knew what he was doing; he had no illusions about the place of this
work in the wartime scheme. 'Many a scared kid,' he wrote privately, 'is being
saved (for future demolition) by a little rest and bucking up and good advice from
these men.' Similar dilemmas arose at the next tier of psychiatry – the Advanced
Neurological Hospital. There were three of these hospitals, a little bit further

line, designed to hold soldiers for two to three weeks within the
ighting and then get them back to their units. The men would
uddy, silent, trembling, tense, with drawn faces, and relaxed
resting places at once.' On admission, many presented 'coarse
and other hysterical symptoms.' It was soon learnt that 'much
uld be done immediately by simple suggestion and explanation
and reassurance . . . Hysterical symptoms which might require hours of treatment
in a base hospital could frequently be cleared up by suggestive therapy in a few
minutes in a fresh case.'[23]

Dr John Rhein, who ran two of these hospitals, also detected a condition that
he called 'hyperemotivity' (similar perhaps to British 'confusion'), in which
soldiers were

unable to carry on, felt weak, were dizzy and afraid . . . sought places of safety, desired to
run and hide, or stood still and shook; they lost their heads, they fell down from weakness
at the sound of exploding shells; they expressed themselves as afraid of shells and slept
poorly. This condition incapacitated the soldier and rendered him unfit for front line
duty. [24]

These men arrived in hospital with few symptoms, except evidence of great
fatigue, a slight general tremor, and terror that they might be sent back to face the
line.

They acknowledged that they could not stand the shells. There was no actual neurosis to
be recognized as such. The condition appeared to be an intense reaction to fear, an
exaggeration of the physiological response of this emotion.[25]

Cases like this were still fluid: they were very suggestible and could be easily
'cured'; but what did you do then? Rhein argued that the worst thing was to send
them to the base: 'in a base hospital situated a long distance from the front, the
horrors of the front are emphasized, and, as a result of the opportunity to
introspect, there develops a reaction which expresses itself in the creation of
symptoms or which incapacitates the individual for front line duty.'[26]

Nevertheless, with the hysteria and fear cases, staff at the Advanced Neurological Hospitals had also to decide whether it was wiser, from the standpoint of
the Army's efficiency, to send these men back to the front line on the chance that
they would carry on rather than send them to the Base Hospital to be reclassified
as labour troops. Despite the natural wish to send a 'plain case of fear' back up
the line, the chances were that they would not be individually dependable. The
American history concedes that there was 'a distinct absence of desire to return to
front line service', and nearly half of the hysteria and fear cases did not return to
front-line duty.[27]

A debate about methods of treatment at the Advanced Neurological Hospital
between Tom Salmon and his boss back in America, the neurologist Pearce
Bailey, came to a head after the latter visited the French in the summer of 1918.

Though a friend, Bailey evidently felt that Salmon inclined to a 'sentimental, introspective condition about such things which is decidedly opposed to satisfactory military operations'. Bailey was impressed by the hard-headedness of the French and noted approvingly that French neurologists used the threat of denying leave and solitary confinement as a way of combating the outbreak of hysterical symptoms. Also, even after the Deschamps trial,

Electricity with persuasion is used or the rougher quick method of suddenly turning on strong electric currents in the region of the part showing signs of defaulting function. By these various measures the French maintain that it is not necessary to send many functional cases back to the interior.[28]

Bailey argued that the Americans would develop neuroses 'to a greater degree than has occurred among the British' unless special steps were taken. 'French neurologists with whom I have talked,' he said, 'have spoken of the excessive nervousness of American soldiers.' Bailey put this down, in part, to the cultural differences:

The conditions of American life have been such that a young man suddenly taken from surroundings where he has more or less always had his way, where obedience was never necessary, where he was taught that he was the equal of everyone, suddenly taken from surroundings of that character and forced to obedience, forced also to face all this war has of horror, it would not be surprising if he showed his reaction to this change by developing a neurosis if he were given a chance.[29]

But the French approach favoured by Bailey, with solitary confinement, strong faradization and other such methods was alien to Salmon's whole philosophy. He fought back:

The young medical officers you saw working would be ashamed of themselves if they could not cure without resort to anything like punishment. The whole idea of punishment seems out of place in the treatment of any kind of sickness, functional or organic.[30]

But this did not mean that Salmon himself favoured anything very radical. Whatever the theory, the methods used were not too dissimilar to those of William Johnson and Gordon Holmes in the British Army.

Finally in the tier came Base Hospital 117, Salmon's particular pride and joy, which eventually came into existence in August 1918, in a pleasant setting in the Vosges, about fifty miles from what was then the front line. To it were sent very severe types of war neurosis. The Americans were determined to avoid what they saw as the worst mistake of the British – throwing men out of the Army with their disorders uncured; this hospital was meant to be the final net through which nobody fell. It was beautifully equipped and run with dedication and commitment; occupational therapy was raised to a new art. But, as the Americans conceded, 'nothing new or original can be said to have been discovered there.'

Like everyone else, they found that hysterical symptoms could quickly be removed by 'many methods of suggestive symptomatic treatment' – the sort of methods used by Hurst in England; and that 'anxiety neuroses' (as neurasthenia was now beginning to be called) were much more fundamental, and difficult to treat.[31]

Between the lines of the official account, it is clear that Salmon had problems. Perhaps it was the reluctance of the great men of medicine to come to France; perhaps it was the emphasis on facilities and equipment rather than on technique; perhaps the patients just needed to go home.

The decorations in the recreation huts were all planned to keep the military atmosphere in the minds of the soldiers through stirring posters and scenes of actual war conditions. The walls were covered by sketches drawn for the most part by patients, of men going over the top, artillery going into action, airplane fights etc.

Sympathy in the ordinary meaning of the term had little place in this hospital; intelligent insight and appreciation of the mechanism of the war neuroses in a measure took its place. The military necessity was accentuated and kept constantly in mind, but notwithstanding a certain grimness in the hospital's attitude to its patients, not the slightest suggestion of harshness or severity was ever permitted.[32]

It sounds a sad place.

It is difficult to judge the success or failure of Salmon's approach. The American involvement in the war was so brief and their elaborate psychiatric organisation came into final existence so late in the day – at a time when the tide of war had turned – that the American experience could be used to support almost any argument. After the war, one British doctor did not think, 'from experience of what did happen to the American troops,' that 'it did much good.' He doubted whether 'their casualties as far as "Shell-Shock" was concerned were much minimised by this elaborate preparation.'[33]

INQUESTS

On 9 November 1918, the German psychiatrist Karl Bonhoeffer walked as usual to his office in the Charité Hospital in Berlin. Along the way he met troop units marching in disarray, mixed with civilians carrying posters which read 'Do Not Shoot' – pale emaciated figures, covered in sweat, who gesticulated wildly and shouted at the soldiers. When Bonhoeffer tried to enter his psychiatric clinic, 'the porter confronted me in the stairs with a red cockade, apparently with the intention of barring my entry to my office, or at least to get into argument with me about it.' He was quickly deflected by a few stern words from the *Herr Professor Doktor*, but Bonhoeffer then found that a new regime prevailed in his hospital: valuable time now had to be spent discussing an eight-hour day for hospital employees and addressing other political demands. It was, Bonhoeffer later wrote, 'a dictatorship of the psychopaths'.[1]

This reversal of authority – which would prove shortlived – was brought about by the events of the previous few days. Germany had surrendered, her Kaiser had abdicated, the Imperial fleet had mutinied, and Socialist revolutions had broken out in Munich and Berlin. In both Germany and Austria, defeat and social upheaval dramatised the political role of the psychiatrists during the war in a way that never happened in Britain or France.

In Germany, the doctors' use of 'active' methods of treatment, causing the deaths of several patients, had earned them the hatred of working-class leaders. At the same time, the German patient, compared to the French or British, comes across in the literature as less a passive victim and more an active agent, using his symptoms to resist medical and military authority. By 1917, reports on home front morale complained that soldiers on leave and convalescing in hospitals were actively opposing the war and spreading subversive rumours; disabled soldiers were participating in protest marches. When a crowd marched on the town hall in Hof, near Bayreuth, in July 1918, demanding better rations and working conditions, officials noticed that 'a group of disabled veterans, including two so-called "shiverers" repeatedly simulated nervous attacks and thereby excited the women.' Another report talked about the 'disturbing nature of so-called "shiverers". The *Kriegszitterer* has become a freak, an actor exhibiting his symptoms in public.'[2]

There was another complicating factor. At the end of the war, the German

Army was still intact in the West; the Germans were 'brought down more by political collapse than by outright military defeat.' This led to the so-called 'stab in the back' legend, the belief that disloyalty at home, not defeat on the battlefield, had brought about Germany's downfall. Many psychiatrists blamed *Kriegszitterer* for this, seeing them as part of the huge tide of over a million wounded, disabled and discontented soldiers that choked the hospitals and lines of communication spreading alarm and despondency in the rear.[3]

The changed political situation seemed, however, to have a remarkable effect on many patients still in hospital. When rumours of the revolution swept into the neurosis station at Mergentheim, an hysterical soldier about to be examined by Dr Ernst Kretschmer at once 'ran to the town's market square and delivered a fiery political speech to an excited crowd.' Many of Max Nonne's neurotic patients suddenly shed their symptoms and became revolutionary leaders: 'In my ward, one refractory shaker, who had complained of being treated too roughly, took on the function of the soldiers' council, and was in high spirits, responsible for his "subordinates" from morning to evening.'[4]

During the first weeks of the German revolution, armed emissaries from soldiers' and workers' councils forced their way into the clinics of known war psychiatrists. Some doctors were threatened – Max Nonne had to escape through a back door at the Eppendorf Clinic from the 'mob' which was out to 'raid' it – and some unpopular treatments like the Kaufmann cure were forbidden.[5]

Most psychiatrists interpreted these events as a clinical disaster because they removed the military authority of the doctor and with it the possibility of making quick, magical cures. Others, though, argued that the ending of the war removed the threat of being sent back to the front and therefore made people better. Dr Kurt Singer of Berlin offered a much more sophisticated analysis, arguing that the revolution, by inverting the social system, had removed the social function of neurosis.[6]

The revolutionaries themselves were pathologised by the doctors, albeit with a bewildering range of diagnoses, being called everything from psychopaths to hysterics to manic depressives. There was general agreement among the doctors that four years of war had produced 'mass hysteria', which found an outlet in social upheaval. The shock of this episode left most German psychiatrists aligned with the political right long before Hitler came to power. Most importantly of all, however, German doctors vowed to pursue a much tougher and purely military policy towards war neurotics in any future war.

Many wartime currents flowed into the silent German cinema of the 1920s – a penumbral world of the supernatural and the unconscious, at once German/gothic and crudely Freudian, whose stories were often dominated by sinister psychiatrists or healers like Dr Caligari and Dr Mabuse (one of the scriptwriters of *Caligari* had been harshly treated by Army doctors).[7]

* * *

In Austria, too, military defeat and political upheaval brought a re-examination of what had gone on during the war. In 1920 the Provisional National Assembly in Vienna established a commission to investigate wartime misconduct by the military authorities, which soon turned to the methods used by psychiatrists working for the military. It was not a systematic investigation of their behaviour, just a two-day hearing of charges against a few doctors. But, in that raw atmosphere, the underlying moral issues of military psychiatry came closer to the surface than they ever did elsewhere, possibly because Sigmund Freud was involved in the hearings.[8]

In December 1918, the Vienna weekly *Der Freie Soldat* had revealed that the treatment of war neurotics was 'one of the most revolting chapters in the story of the Austrian army medical services.'

These pitiable victims of the refined methods of modern warfare were taken in hand in a most peculiar way. Since a complete cure demands time, trouble and good nursing, which the revered army command was not prepared to lavish on the 'common' soldier, the accommodating doctors found a way of clearing the neurological wards of their patients in a surprisingly short time. Electrical power currents were passed through the bodies of war neurotics causing them such excruciating pain that many died during treatment, but most of them escaped the torture by taking flight from the hospital – without, of course, having been cured. For, as first-class neurologists have declared over and over again, this electrical torture has cured nobody ... The score must be settled with these worthy doctors.[9]

Two months later, a second article described how at the Wagner-Jauregg clinic in Vienna 'our informant, an officer who had suffered concussion when a grenade exploded near him on the battlefield', had been kept locked in a padded cell for months, threatened with faradization, then 'made [to] watch wretched victims of electrical treatment twisting and howling with pain' – before finally being subjected to the agony himself. And all this just so that 'the Moloch of Militarism' might not have to miss one human sacrifice.[10]

Julius Wagner-Jauregg was the Professor of Psychiatry at Vienna and, as it happened, a member of the Commission of Enquiry into wartime misconduct. He immediately resigned from the commission and an investigation into events at his clinic began. Freud, as one of the few Viennese psychiatrists not directly involved, was called in as an expert witness. Wagner-Jauregg's main accuser (and the source of the newspaper articles) was a young Jewish journalist called Walter Kauders, who had volunteered for the war in 1914, been wounded in the head by a shell soon afterwards and spent some time in various hospitals before being discharged in 1916. He then went to work for the Berlin publishers, Ullstein. In 1917, as manpower became tight, he was recalled to be re-examined for medical service.[11]

His medical condition at that time was ambiguous; three years after being wounded, Kauders still had various problems (which Freud later thought were probably organic) and was very neurotic. But, in Vienna in 1917, Wagner-Jauregg had had no doubt that Kauders was a malingerer whose extraordinary way of walking with two canes, holding 'his head as though it were made of glass and as though he were afraid it might fall off and break', was put on: 'anyone who works for the Ullstein company can also do military duty.'[12]

Wagner-Jauregg, very busy and not much in the clinic, authorised his assistant Dr Kozlowski to give Kauders the necessary inducements to return to duty – isolation and electrical current. Kozlowski, a Pole specialising in dermatology and syphilis, was mainly interested in collaborating with Wagner-Jauregg on the programme of treating general paralytics with malaria (for which Jauregg later won the Nobel prize for medicine). Kozlowski had neither psychiatric nor neurological training and was clearly a sadist, sometimes applying electrical current to sensitive places like the testicles (though not in Kauders' case) and encouraging other patients to watch.[13]

By 1920, though, Kozlowski was back in Poland. Wagner-Jauregg, a tall, imposing man, a prominent figure in Viennese life, was a different matter. As he proudly told the court, he had given his services voluntarily, received no pay, treated many thousands of soldiers who had not complained; indeed many had thanked him. Electrical treatment was an old-established technique, the current used was mild and, in his experience, applied only on peripheral parts of the body. He accepted that his methods were 'disciplinary'. They had to be. The treatment had to 'act on the will'. Of course there were cases

in which these neuroses can be caused directly, without the conscious mind being involved, by some event's acting powerfully on the senses; for example, in people who had actually been at the front a severe fright caused by a grenade . . . In cases like this neurotic symptoms appear without the conscious mind being involved.[14]

But more often the neurosis developed away from the front or in training; symptoms were produced 'by a purpose'.

It happens like this. The thought can rise to the surface of consciousness that, if you were paralysed, you would not have to march, or to go to war. The thought can easily become a wish, and the wish a volition, and it depends only on how far the person in question is predisposed to remain conscious of this will, that is to say to go on working sub-consciously. If he is capable of this, then this is what we call hysteria. The idea is there and it subconsciously brings on the neurosis.[15]

It was, Wagner-Jauregg believed, the soldier's attitude to the war which determined whether he was disposed to contract neuroses or not, and it was interesting to see how the psychological attitudes of the different nationalities were quite different – a reminder that the Austro-Hungarian Army contained many nationalities. Czechs, for example, made it plain they this was 'not their war', and came down in their droves, whereas Germans had very few cases. In fact, Wagner-Jauregg went on, most of his patients were not German-speakers at all. Therefore hypnosis, let alone psychoanalysis – which took 'God knows how long' – was completely out of the question.[16]

This robust testimony clearly impressed the president of the commission, a Professor of Law. Kauders, on the other hand, did not. Freud, who spoke next, clearly found himself in something of a quandary. He deeply disagreed with much that Wagner-Jauregg had said, and must have known that as head of the hospital the professor was responsible for his deputies' behaviour; yet he respected Wagner-Jauregg personally and was reluctant to criticise a fellow psychiatrist before a lay Viennese audience. Politically, he was far too cautious to align himself with newspapers that exaggerated 'in an ugly manner out of a feeling of vengefulness against the old system'. And, of course, there were the needs of the psychoanalytic movement. So Freud, given a chance to speak up and denounce medical abuse, chose to tread carefully.

Overall, Freud saw the problem very clearly; the central dilemma of military psychiatry has never been better stated than in his written evidence to the Commission:

This therapeutic procedure . . . bore a stigma from the very first. It did not aim at the patient's recovery, or not in the first instance; it aimed above all at restoring his fitness for service. Here Medicine was serving purposes foreign to its essence. The physician himself was under military command and had his own personal dangers to fear – loss of seniority or a charge of neglecting his duty – if he allowed himself to be led by considerations other than those prescribed for him. The insoluble conflict between the claims of humanity, which normally carries decisive weight for a physician, and the demands of a national war was bound to confuse his activity.[17]

The war, he said in verbal evidence, had obliged doctors 'to play a role somewhat like that of a machine-gun behind the front line, that of driving back those who fled.' But then, resisting the logic of his own argument, he added that he was sure that in the case of *Hofrat* Wagner, whom he had known for 35 years, the motivating force of his treatment of his patients was his humaneness. Making no mention of the new theory of the war neuroses he would soon publish, he did his best to play down all theoretical differences between himself and Jauregg.

I would only venture the opinion that he draws the boundaries of simulation a little too broad . . . I would have seen fewer malingerers and more neuroses but that is not a difference of principle. I know, as he does, that all these neuroses are a flight from the conditions of war into illness.[18]

He would, therefore, have approached the case of Walter Kauders slightly differently – probably using the sort of psychoanalytic methods with which Simmel had had such success in Germany and which, but for the end of the war (this was Freud's plug and he made the most of it) would have been tried out by the Central Powers. But Freud repeatedly stopped short of criticising Wagner-Jauregg's methods. He agreed that it was not normal practice to use strong drugs on private patients because 'in private practice one tries not to be disagreeable; otherwise one is replaced by another colleague who is less so. Naturally, this motive does not operate for physicians employed by the government.' When asked outright by Kauders whether it was right for someone to be locked in a cell 'under the encroachment of madmen' for 77 days (as he had been), Freud replied that isolation of this sort was 'very unpleasant, but completely without risk.' At which point, Kauders later claimed, someone in the audience shouted back 'And that's said by a man who pursues a trouser-button back twelve generations!'[19]

Freud's strategy misfired: the following day, when he was no longer present, Wagner-Jauregg's colleagues launched violent attacks on psychoanalysis. Freud, said one, had suggested that 'these events are to some degree a punishment for those of us who have done this work because we have not practised psychoanalysis.' 'On the contrary,' the doctor argued,

I have done everything that can be considered as psychotherapy; I have set up a farm, orchestras, occupational therapy games; I have put together a library in all sorts of languages and given everyone the chance to work at his own trade; I have tried to distract their minds from their illness by entertainments and educational lectures. I have made myself unpopular enough with my physicians and my staff by insisting on cleanliness and order. The only deprivation which the patients had to suffer was the ban on alcohol.[20]

These doctors scorned Freud's claim that psychoanalysis had worked; it had never been tried; it could never be tried in wartime circumstances. How you could you psychoanalyse people with the staff ratios to be found in a wartime hospital? Freud, by presuming to judge them – however tentatively – brought down on his head all the pent-up frustrations of the past years:

We physicians who have tried hard to achieve the utmost in the war and have only had the bad luck to be decent, honourable and always helpful servants to our fellowmen, are now called torturers and are proclaimed as such to the whole world.[21]

After two days' deliberation, the commission exonerated Wagner-Jauregg from all blame, but rebuked Kozlowski for 'excessive zeal'. Kauders, on the face of it, lost badly.

*   *   *

In Britain, the winning of the war naturally led to a wish to close ranks and heal wounds, to move on and leave the past behind. Authority was not toppled and, though doctors might argue amongst themselves, the fact that the Army had won somehow legitimised most of its activities. Nonetheless, there were several inquests.

The most complete of these was into shell-shock itself. In April 1920, at a time when there was considerable pressure for an enquiry into the Army's wartime judicial record, the government agreed to a suggestion made by Lord Southborough, a former civil servant with considerable experience of high-level mediation, for a Committee to investigate the subject. A few months later, the Committee was formed with Southborough himself in the chair, along with seven representatives of the services, two MPs (one Liberal, one Labour), two mental hospital administrators, and Drs Frederick Mott, Maurice Craig and Aldren Turner. Few of these worthies, Dr Charles Wilson sourly pointed out in

The Times, had served in France. Stung by this criticism, the Committee spread its net wide, taking evidence from a number of battle-scarred officers and doctors, as well as rounding up the usual medical suspects: Henry Head, William Rivers, Arthur Hurst, William Brown, Gordon Holmes and Ronald Rows.[22]

But Charles Myers refused to testify. He said later that to have appeared there (or to have helped in the writing of the official medical history of the war) would have been 'too painful'. Certainly, to appear before Sir Frederick Mott and Dr Aldren Turner and admit being the father of that now abandoned orphan 'shell-shock' would have been more than his pride could bear. Furthermore, a man of his scruples would have found it hard to rewrite history.[23]

Perhaps he need not have worried, for neither the War Office nor the doctors on the Committee wished to go back over the entire saga apportioning blame. Mott probably had more words to eat than anyone; yet here he was, newly knighted, sitting in judgement. As witness after witness agreed that the term shell-shock was a misnomer and should never have been used, you might have wondered why, if there was such unanimity on this point, it ever *had* been used. Nor, with one exception, were the embarrassments of 1914–16, such as the Army Council's adoption of the label 'Shell-shock Wounded', explored. Neither Sir Arthur Sloggett nor Sir Alfred Keogh, the men ultimately responsible for the Army's handling of shell-shock, gave evidence. The issue of shell-shock in courts martial was barely touched on and an assertion by the Deputy Adjutant-General, Sir Wyndham Childs, that prisoners routinely received examination by experts in nervous disorders, though, as we have seen, completely untrue, went unchallenged.[24]

However, in three ways the Southborough Committee did gather valuable evidence. Firstly, a succession of doctors testified to the chaos and confusion that had attended the recruitment process in 1914. Their evidence brought home the folly of accepting men as soldiers without getting some idea, however rudimentary, of their mental state. Secondly, a number of Regimental Medical Officers who had been on the 'sharp end' explained, without jargon or self-justification, something of what really went on at the front. There was Dr Dunn of the Royal Welch Fusiliers, a hero to Robert Graves, but very hard in his handling of men, with sharp anti-Semitic views; there was the warm, humane, and occasionally tough Colonel Rogers of the Black Watch, whose earthy realism shines through. 'Without the rum ration,' he said, 'we would have lost the war.' Above all, there was Billy Tyrrell, the Ulster athlete and doctor, who had broken down in 1915 after several months in the Ypres salient. Tyrrell prepared assiduously for his appearance, and spoke with an eloquence no other witness matched.

Shell shock is born of fear. Its grandparents are self-preservation and the fear of being found afraid. Any emotion which has to be repressed or concealed demands an unrestricted but well-controlled output of nervous energy. Craven fear is the most extravagant prodigal of nervous energy known. Under its stimulus, a man squanders nervous energy recklessly in order to suppress his hideous and pent-up emotion, and mask and camouflage that which if revealed will call down ignominy upon him and disgrace him in the eyes of his fellows. He must save his self-respect and self-esteem at all costs.[25]

Tyrrell appeared in the first instance as a doctor who had tried to control shell-shock in troops about to crack. But he also began to speak as a victim himself. The Committee members were so impressed by Tyrrell that they asked him to describe fully, under cover of anonymity, his own breakdown. It became the centrepiece of their report.

It was quite a thing, in the service culture of that day, for men to stand up and admit that they had been afraid. There was still 'an idea among young soldiers especially, that there should not be such a thing as fear' and, according to another witness, this 'fear of being thought afraid was often a cause of trouble.' But Tyrrell admitted he 'was in an awful funk the whole time' during the war and thought most people were. Other similar testimonies followed. A submariner who had won the VC said he used to

feel in an awful funk at times. It is absurd to say you do not. I have yet to meet the fellow who will lie in his ship at the bottom of the sea, and be depth-charged and not suffer from cold feet.[26]

This was a significant change in public attitude, but a limited one; for, although these men had felt fear, they had mastered it. Tyrrell had cracked, under intolerable strain, but had returned, after six months out of the line, and served again; he now held a high position in the RAF. His story was thus a good model of shell-shock as the War Office would like it perceived – the triumph of a man who had felt fear, as anyone would, struggled with it, been briefly broken by it, but had managed nonetheless by force of character and determination to get back to duty. Tyrrell had taken responsibility for his condition. He showed that any-one could break, even an athletic hero, but also that anyone could get themselves back into the line.

Tyrrell fitted easily into the overall message of the report. 'Shell-shock', it was agreed, was a meaningless word because 90–95% of 'shell-shocked' soldiers were suffering not from shock caused by an exploding shell but from a nervous breakdown brought about by fear, fatigue, and horrific experiences. Everyone feels fear. True courage consists in recognising your fear and overcoming it (or, to put it another way, every soldier experiences a mental conflict between the instinct of self-preservation and the sense of duty). The crucial force in tipping the balance towards duty is morale. Morale is determined by leadership, training and esprit de corps. Regular soldiers, it was argued, do not suffer breakdowns because they are so well led and trained; poorly led troops are much more vulnerable. At the same time, as Colonel Rogers said, 'a man has only so much endurance' and under certain pressures any man will break.[27]

The Committee's recommendations were straightforward. In any future war, steps should be taken to prevent unsuitable men coming into the Army (though quite what steps, was not spelt out); the term 'shell-shock' should be avoided;

doctors on the front line should keep a close eye on their men and treat them as soon as possible but with very simple methods. On the crucial question of how you distinguish between malingering and genuine breakdown, the Committee came to no clear conclusions.

The second, and related, set of inquests carried out by the British related to the issue of the death penalty and the fairness of the legal procedures in Army courts martial. In spite of the Army's acceptance of shell-shock into its judicial procedures in March 1918, wartime concern continued in peacetime. It was a matter that refused to go away. In 1919, the writer A. P. Herbert published *The Secret Battle*, a fictionalised account of one wartime trial, while at Westminster the Labour MP Ernest Thurtle continued to press for an enquiry into wartime executions. The War Office's response was finally to release the figures of those executed and to establish official committees in 1920 and 1925. These, in the hallowed tradition of British whitewashing, ruled that there had been no miscarriages of justice but refused to discuss particular cases or to publish the evidence on which their conclusion was based. Some amendments to courtroom procedures were introduced, but the past remained a closed book. The official line was, and would long remain, that to reopen these cases would only cause distress to the relatives of the men executed. By means of this ploy, the Army was able, as we have seen, to hide the details of the cases – and the extent of official lying – until the 1990s, by which time all those directly involved were long gone.[28]

But concern in public and in Parliament did have an important impact in the 1920s. A small group of Labour backbenchers made sure that the annual debate on Army estimates was marked by attempts to confine and limit the military's use of the death penalty. Their pressure eventually told, for in 1928 Baldwin's Conservative government (while refusing to return to the events of the war) removed the death penalty for eight offences such as sleeping on post, disobedience and striking a superior officer. Two years later, the process was carried further by the Labour administration when it was proposed that cowardice and leaving a post or guard without orders should also cease to be capital offences. This last step went well beyond military thinking and provoked outspoken opposition from the Army Council and from retired soldiers like Field-Marshal Allenby. Only the knowledge that he would die 'a death which is dishonourable and shameful,' Allenby told the House of Lords, would deter a man from putting his comrades' lives at risk to save his own.[29]

Heeding his words, the Lords did throw out the measure. But this was hardly an issue on which to force a constitutional crisis and the bill returned to the Commons and became law. Twelve years after the war, the only military crimes still carrying the death penalty in the British Army were treachery and mutiny.

The third kind of inquest was more general and open-ended and related to the overall conduct of the war. The official version was the first to appear, in the immediate aftermath of victory, with the Army riding high. Modern stereotypes of the Great War – mud, slaughter, 'lions led by donkeys' – are so well rooted that it needs to be emphasised that the British Army had, in the last year of the war, kept going where the French, Italian, and Russian Armies had wavered, belatedly acquired the professionalism and sophistication so lacking in 1916 and 1917 and achieved, after August 1918, one of the greatest sustained feats of arms in its history. In the euphoria of victory, a grateful nation gave its generals peerages and large sums of money – Haig received £100,000, a fortune in 1919. But even in their days of glory, Haig and his colleagues were aware of the need to safeguard their reputations for posterity by massaging the historical record to show the successes of 1918 as stemming from the disasters of the earlier years. Although Haig did not write his memoirs, he made sure that his record was defended and, by the time of his death in January 1928, had 'established a literary legacy which had been deployed in the defence of his reputation and that of the British High Command.'[30]

The counterattack was long delayed but, when it came, devastating. Books like Graves' *Good-bye to All That*, Remarque's *All Quiet On the Western Front* (both 1929) and Vera Brittain's *Testament of Youth* (1933) spoke directly from front-line experience of the war and shattered literary and social convention by revealing the horrible realities of trench warfare. The inadequacy of the wartime leadership, particularly at the Somme and Passchendaele, was ruthlessly exposed. This literature of 'disenchantment' would have far-reaching consequences. Twenty years later, as another war loomed, every educated person in Britain had preconceived ideas of 'the bestiality of modern war' and 'the incompetence of British generals.'[31]

'WILL PEACE BRING PEACE?'

Old Etonian (twenty-seven) married and suffering from neurasthenia, but in no way incapacitated in urgent need of outdoor work. Would be glad to accept post of head gamekeeper at nominal salary.

Times personal column, 1919[1]

The children's writer Roald Dahl was sent to boarding-school, aged nine, in the autumn of 1925. The staff at his new school, in the seedy resort town of Weston-Super-Mare, included a Captain Hardcastle, a thin, wiry man, with bright orange hair parted down the middle and a moustache of the same colour. There was something very odd about Captain Hardcastle. He was 'never still. His orange head twitched and jerked perpetually from side to side in the most alarming fashion, and each twitch was accompanied by a little grunt that came out of the nostrils.' Dahl soon learnt that this 'constant twitching and jumping' was the result of war service, caused by 'something called shell shock'. The boys weren't sure what that was, but 'took it to mean that an explosive object had gone off very close to him with such an explosive bang that it had made him jump high in the air and he hadn't stopped jumping since.'[2]

There were many Captain Hardcastles around in the 1920s, damaged ex-servicemen struggling to readjust to civilian life. The disenchanted veteran was nothing new in Western society, but the scale of the problem after the First World War was unparalleled, reaching into nearly into every home in the land and leaving its mark for generations. It was perhaps inevitable that Lloyd George, the British Prime Minister, should say in 1919, 'The world is suffering from shell-shock.'[3]

The historian's problem is that 'to calculate the effect of mental and bodily suffering, not on a man but on a whole generation of men' is an impossible task. He can make broad assertions about the mental legacy of the Great War: that it left France powerless to resist the Germans in 1940; undermined for ever the confident will to govern of the British ruling elite, making the dissolution of the Empire after 1945 inevitable; and destroyed the confident certainties of Victorian authority and morality, ushering in modern doubts and hesitations. He can argue that the fragmented minds of shell-shock herald the dissociations and dislocations of modern art, and that Germany, the most traumatised nation of all between the wars, regained its self-esteem and will by turning for leadership to a shell-shock victim (Hitler), and by submitting herself to a course of his brutal shock therapy

Or he can parade the statistics. By 1939, some 120,000 British ex-servicemen had received final awards for primary psychiatric disability or were still drawing pensions – about 15% of all pensioned disabilities – and another 44,000 or so, as we have seen, were getting pensions for 'soldier's heart' or Effort Syndrome. There is, though, much that statistics do not show, because in terms of psychiatric effects, pensioners were just the tip of a huge iceberg.[4]

Once the excitement of peace was over, everyone faced a long and difficult process of returning to life at home. The readjustment, after years of idealising home and its comforts, was often very difficult. The war correspondent Philip Gibbs quickly saw that

Something was wrong. They put on civilian clothes again and looked to their mothers and wives very much like the young men who had gone to business in the peaceful days before August 1914. But they had not come back the same men. Something had altered in them. They were subject to sudden moods and queer tempers, fits of profound depression alternating with a restless desire for pleasure. Many were easily moved to passion where they lost control of themselves, many were bitter in their speech, violent in opinion, frightening.[5]

There was at first some alarm in official circles that returning soldiers would provide a violent, revolutionary paramilitary force (as they had in the Bolshevik and other revolutions in Eastern Europe), but, by demobilising soldiers singly and drawing skilfully on the residual loyalty of old soldiers to the figurehead of Haig, the British coaxed their ex-servicemen into a single, non-political, multi-denominational body, the British Legion. Anyway, Robert Graves thought, most people were in too great a state of 'nervous instability' to muck about with revolution. They just wanted quietly to sort themselves out. 'In most cases the blood was not running pure again for four or five years: and in numerous cases, men who had managed to avoid a nervous breakdown during the war collapsed badly in 1921 or '22.'[6]

Most people, says Denis Winter, required 'a period of quietness, a second adolescence as it were, to shed the past and get back into life at a lower key than they were used to.' The period of adjustment varied in length, from a year to ten years – to never. Ford Madox Ford, blown up by a shell in December 1916 and a passenger for the rest of the war, finally 'got over the nerve-tangle of war' in 1923, after 'hibernating' in the Sussex countryside with a sympathetic woman and gently writing his way through his wartime experiences.[7]

This process of gradual mental self-repair is movingly described in one of the rare accounts of shell-shock by a working-class patient. *Shellshock, Neurasthenia and the new Life* by Joseph S. Milne, published in Newcastle in 1918, may bear 'all the signs of its neurasthenic authorship', but it is the authentic voice of the sufferer. Milne tells little of his own history or military service, but his medical treatment had evidently included both electricity ('my whole body became very blue each time') and cold baths ('the boxed in strain became worse through the cold shock'). The hospital attendant, he says feelingly, should be 'a companion and not a warder'. Probably discharged uncured, Milne developed his own form of self-therapy, consisting of stooping exercises, gentle walking, warm baths and mental games. Milne believed that his brain had been 'very low down in my head' and must have been 'torn down from behind almost to the forehead', thus producing the poor vision and other symptoms he suffered. Alongside this anatomical absurdity is some acute self-analysis:

You can understand what you see, but you cannot think; your head is in awful agony, and you feel as though you were 'boxed in' and wanted relief for your head, and the more you struggle, the more you feel madness creeping over you.[8]

Milne urged his readers to stay calm in the face of the threat of madness and to follow his daily regimen, gradually building up their minds by gentle mental exercise.

Both Ford and Milne came back from the war minus some of their memory – suffering partial amnesia. Milne described how this felt for the sufferer:

A struggle is going on within his brain to hold out, and . . . an effort is being made with the power he has left; but he cannot get the brain or mind to work, and so he is governed by his feelings. The brain won't work, therefore he cannot think or recall anything except when prompted.[9]

Joseph Milne devised a series of ways to train the memory. The patient, he explained, should use 'his mind's eye', not only to 'regain the use of memory, but to establish the power of recalling what has been seen or said' – a process somewhat similar to that used by Dr Brock with Wilfred Owen. Milne was confident that by consciously training his memory, the patient could not only begin to function again but find a new life.

I don't ask what you feel like, but I tell you and I can do so because I have been like you, and although I have been just as ill as you have got better. I tell and teach you how to get better. Oh try and keep on trying what I tell you and you will.[10]

*　*　*

The effect of shell-shock on relations between the sexes is perhaps the most fascinating area of the subject and the most hidden; for, in that reticent age, it was not thought proper to wash dirty linen in public. What little we know mostly derives, as always, from garrulous literary folk, and how far they represent a wider reality remains to be seen. There is the further complication that, while men were away at the war, many women's lives at home were transformed by new employment opportunities and greater social freedom. Modern historians like Eric Leed, Sandra Gilbert and Elaine Showalter would have us believe that the British soldier returned from the war, crushed, alienated, and un-manned by the horrors of trench warfare – nerves shattered, penis flaccid – only to find waiting for him not the meek, obedient creature he had left behind but a new breed of waged, emancipated and sexually demanding woman. The shell-shocked veteran in Dorothy L. Sayers' *The Unpleasantness at the Bellona Club* (1928), who declares

No wonder a man can't get a decent job these days with these hard-mouthed cigarette-smoking females all over the place pretending they're geniuses and business women and all the rest of it

is voicing not just his own frustration at being kept by his wife, but a wider male *angst* at the decisive shift in sexual power brought by the war.[11]

Sandra Gilbert has gone on to assert that the 'sexual gloom expressed by so many men as well as the sexual glee experienced by so many women ultimately triggered profound feelings of guilt in a number of women . . . a half-conscious fear that the woman might be in an inexplicable way a perpetrator of some unspeakable crime. [As a result] the invigorating sense of revolution, release, re-union and revision with which the war paradoxically imbued so many women eventually darkened into reactions of anxiety and self-doubt.' Or, to put it another way, men regained some of their lost power by dragging everyone else down to their own neurasthenic level – by stopping their wives having fun. This neat dichotomy between men's 'sexual gloom' and women's 'sexual glee', like much modern feminist writing, is derived from a few literary models.[12]

This huge topic can only be summarily dealt with here. The experience of war, especially of combat, creates an unbridgeable gap between those who have been there, done the business, looked into the face of death, been through the fire – and those who have not; between the *Frontkampfer* – and *everyone* else: the general in his château, the doctor in his hospital, the corporal servicing tanks, and the girl in the ammunition factory just as much as the profiteer and the armchair propagandist at home. It is, though, within sexual relationships that this chasm has most effect. A sensitive woman like Vera Brittain realised, soon after her fiancé Roland went off to France, that the war was creating 'a barrier of indescribable experience between men and the women whom they loved . . . Quite early I realised the possibility of a permanent impediment to under-standing.'[13]

Brittain understood that shared experience of battle creates between men a bond that can never be severed, a relationship unlike any other. 'Friendships between soldiers during the war were a real and beautiful and unique relationship which has now entirely vanished,' wrote Richard Aldington in *Death of a Hero* (1929), adding quickly, 'Let me at once disabuse the eager-eyed Sodomites among my readers by stating emphatically once and for all that there was nothing sodomitical in these friendships . . . It was just a human relation, a comradeship, an undemonstrative exchange of sympathies between ordinary men racked to extremity under a great common strain in a great common danger. There was nothing dramatic about it.'[14]

There *were* homosexuals on the Western Front. On one occasion Eric Hiscock 'awoke from an uneasy sleep to find [one] pressed up close to me and that his hand was undoing my fly-buttons.' He 'groaned inwardly. Another bugger.' But they were the exception not the rule. Similarly, efforts to argue that the British Army led a life of monkish all-male seclusion, only occasionally encountering a prostitute, French or Belgian peasant or VAD nurse are not borne out in memoirs of all ranks or by the VD statistics.

The most believable account of sexual matters during the war – among officers anyway – is in Charles Carrington's *Soldier From The Wars Returning*. His picture is of an Army pursuing sex whenever the opportunity arose, and finding compensation for 'sex starvation' in endless bawdy jokes and rhymes. But, having got used to the 'all-male society of the regiment, with its acceptance of death and bloodshed as commonplace events, and its uninhibited approach to women', Carrington found it hard to readjust during his home leaves to the 'quiet respectability of [his] family with its unaltered moral standards'. By 1918, he no longer returned home but chose to masquerade as a private soldier and spend his time in the East End with his men's friends. His way of handling the strain of the war was to form a strongly dependent (though not physically sexual) relationship with his men; having devised this *modus operandi* he found the strain of reverting to his home persona too great. He paid a price for this, however:

I used to think that knowledge of adult problems had been forced upon me too young and that, at twenty-two I was mature. I now think quite the contrary. The 1916 fixation had caught me and stunted my mental growth, so that even ten years later I was retarded and adolescent. I could not escape from the comradeship of the trenches, which had become a mental internment camp or should I say a soldier's home. I might as well have been in Chelsea Hospital.[15]

What about the women they left behind? There had certainly been some big changes. The female workforce rose by 50% and by the end of the war some 700,000 women had taken the place of men. The surge of satisfaction with which they did so was noted at the time; and, scanning the Imperial War Museum's photographs of 'Women at War' seventy years later, Sandra Gilbert noticed how, 'liberated from parlours and petticoats alike, trousered "war girls" beam as they shovel coal, shoe horses, light fires, drive buses, chop down trees, make shells, dig graves'. Had this improved their health? The *Daily Mail* – no friend to feminism, then or now – had no doubts. In July 1918, it recorded the extraordinary effect of the war on 'Women and Nerves'. One woman who before the war had had two rest cures a month was now running the kitchen of a hospital: 'she does not know what rest is, and in spite of it all she looks years younger and worlds happier.' Another, whose hysteria used to be 'spoken of with awe in the house' had 'found herself now she had three boys in the Army.' A third, 'whose headaches were a domestic institution', was now 'bustling away at the Red Cross'. Young girls, too, were 'better in every way since they took to hospital work, or war work or business.'[16]

Some of these girls were also having opportunities for sexual self-discovery. 'Women in particular,' we are told, 'reacted to the war experience with a powerful increase of libido' – a fact again registered in the VD statistics. Partly it was the greater social mobility, partly the charged atmosphere of the times. 'Life was cheap,' one later recalled, 'it was thrown away.'

The religious teaching that the body was the temple of the Holy Ghost could mean little or nothing to those who saw it mutilated and destroyed in millions by Christian nations engaged in war . . . Little wonder that the old ideas of chastity and self-control in sex were, for many, also lost . . . How and why refuse appeals, backed up by the beating of your own heart, which were put with passion or pathos by a hero here today and gone tomorrow?[17]

There were nuances to this, however. Vera Brittain felt 'almost adoring gratitude . . . for the knowledge of masculine functions' she acquired from the men she nursed and thanked them for her 'early release from . . . sex-inhibitions' – not because she slept with them; simply because the enormous pre-war geographical and psychological barrier between the sexes had been broken down.

Given the general dislocation of relationships, resuming them could be a complicated and difficult business for men who had been shell-shocked. Some had an additional complication: impotence was one of the principal side-effects of shell-shock. 'Almost all' the patients in the neurological section of the hospital in Budapest complained 'about their entirely damned up, or very strongly retarded sexual libido and potency' and a German doctor on the Western Front found that 'in the field not a few officers and men of previously sound nerves complained that at the beginning of their leave an erection was either completely lacking or very often extremely defective.' 'It is a dreadful thing,' an Australian wrote to Dr Marie Stopes, 'to walk about feeling your vigour has gone. Will you help me please?' 'I'm so sorry, I can't be more encouraging!' she replied. 'So many men have had their vitality sapped by the war and their wives have just to put up with affection minus *coitus*.'[18]

Did impotence last? In 1923 a Ministry of Pensions doctor declared that 'all war anxiety neurotics are either completely sexually impotent or almost so . . . the degree of sex potency . . . varies inversely as the intensity of his neurosis.' Physiological research made clear that, in these cases of 'chronic suppressed fear', the adrenalin was still switched on and the blood too busy elsewhere to make itself available for sexual purposes; but, the doctor emphasised, it was 'mind treating the man needs and not body treatment.'[19]

The convenient historical cliché about this period, fathered by Lawrence and Hemingway, is that a kind of collective impotence descended on the Western male; like Clifford Chatterley and Jake Barnes in *The Sun Also Rises*, he looked on with helpless yearnings as his women turned for satisfaction to younger, coarser partners – a gamekeeper, a Spanish matador. For Lawrence sexual impotence is a metaphor for cultural decadence, for a class system that has lost its authority, for a dead civilisation. But the 'impotence' stereotype (which conflicts with another cliché of the 1920s as a time of wild promiscuity) does not begin to do justice to the full complexity of the relationship between the shell-shocked soldier and the women around him. Sometimes he was met with contempt, and branded a coward or a lunatic. Quite often, though, a renewal of sexuality provided the pathway back to sanity and a normal life.[20]

The real point about shell-shock – in the culture of the 1920s – was that it undermined men's authority, and with it the traditional roles of the sexes in the family: men, supposed to be strong, self-controlled, the providers to the household, were reduced to being weak, self-pitying, dependent creatures. Women, hitherto the main sufferers from mental illness, now became carers. For both sexes that was hard to handle.

If the wife lost her traditional husband, the rest of the family lost its traditional father. Talking to people who had known her father as a young bank clerk before the war, Doris Lessing heard them speak of his 'high spirits, his energy, his enjoyment of life.'

Also of his kindness, his compassion and – a word that keeps recurring – his wisdom . . . I do not think these people would have easily recognised the ill, irritable, abstracted, hypochondriac man I knew.[21]

* * *

The returning veteran had to relate not just to his partner and family, but to the wider society as well. If shell-shocked, he might, like Roald Dahl's schoolmaster, have to overcome the suspicions his own weirdness might arouse. Dr Millais Culpin, an experienced and sympathetic shell-shock doctor, wrote in 1921, 'I must confess I have often looked at a patient and thought that I should not care to employ him myself.'[22]

Reviewing social attitudes in 1925, the American psychiatrist Norman Fenton found that sheer ignorance of the realities of shell-shock remained a problem. The average American, while sympathetic with the war neurotic, regarded him with something of the fear of the unknown. 'The very name itself,' the Harvard psychiatrist E. E. Southard wrote in 1918, 'has within it a good deal of the essence of mob-psychology; in another age we should have had the same mob fear of it that now invests such things as insanity, syphilis, cancer, leprosy.' Shell-shock, Fenton found, was 'associated with queerness, with twitchings, forgetfulness, eccentricity and the like'. Mystery writers like Agatha Christie and Dorothy Sayers were quick to exploit the possibilities of shell-shocked characters who behaved in wild and unpredictable ways or, like the killer in Christie's *ABC Murders,* carried out crimes in a state of hypnotic suggestion.[23]

Testifying in 1916 on behalf of a former medical student accused of bouncing cheques, an Army doctor said that 'in the case of a good many officers affected by shell-shock their moral character was entirely altered.' He claimed to have seen numerous cases where 'men were deprived of the sense of distinguishing between right and wrong even where they had enjoyed excellent characters previously.' Even Millais Culpin believed that 'neurasthenics are peculiarly unreliable; in some of them the deterioration has affected their social sense to such an extent that they are definitely dishonest.'[24]

None of this made it any easier to find a job. 'I'd like to re-employ you,' one of Fenton's patients was told, 'but I'm afraid you'd get to breaking things and hugging the girls etcetera.' The tragedy was that work, absorbing fulfilling work, was probably the best therapy they could have had. But anyone who grew up in Britain between the wars remembers 'utterly unemployable human derelicts, some of them with Mons medals and decorations for valour, begging on the streets of London.'[25]

*   *   *

Most doctors expected the end of the war to bring an end to the war neuroses. Within a day of the Armistice, a senior American doctor told Congress, 2,100 of the 2,500 shell-shock patients awaiting return to the United States had been 'restored to normal'. 'The certainty of being safe from the bullet,' the German writer Emil Weiss wrote, 'performed more cures . . . than any doctor could have achieved.'[26]

One type of case did recover quickly. The 'grosser manifestations of hysteria', like blindness, deafness, paralysis and fits did not persist for any time after the war. Many cases recovered spontaneously; others responded to the official effort to 'reclaim' uncured patients, begun in Britain in 1917 with the opening of ten convalescent 'Homes of Recovery', and redoubled after the war. In January 1920 the Ministry of Pensions appealed to general practitioners to bring forward any remaining cases without further delay for treatment in its out-patient clinics, then being set up all over Britain. Though no overall figures survive, the clinic in Edinburgh treated 2,000 patients between 1920 and 1922.[27]

Undoubtedly, many cases were belatedly recognised as 'psychological' and cured. A note of optimism could still be heard as late as July 1921; one doctor felt that Pensions Board clinics 'were doing a great deal of good'. But others weren't so sure; cases where treatment had been long delayed, another doctor felt, 'made no great progress' and were 'the most difficult to treat'. A new distinction – between acute and chronic cases of war neurosis – was emerging. 'Few of us,' Millais Culpin wrote in 1921, 'expected a large number of men to be disabled by mental symptoms which would persist indefinitely after the war had ceased. Yet that is what is happening.'[28]

Efforts were made to discover why. Soon a consensus emerged about the type of patient still unrecovered: it wasn't necessarily those who had had the toughest time and been through the worst experiences in the trenches who became chronic war neurotics after the war. Culpin himself found that people who had broken down *quickly* (perhaps without even going to the front) were the hardest to treat after the war. Indeed, he thought 'the amount of stress endured before break-down is a measure of the man's original stamina and hence of his likely response to treatment.' From this view, widely held amongst doctors, emerged a distinction between 'false' and 'true' war neuroses. British official historians defined 'true' war neuroses as 'those manifested in men with a minimal pre-disposition'. The symptoms in these cases, it was agreed, 'rapidly disappeared on the cessation of exposure to war conditions.' In contrast, 'false' war neuroses were those occurring in those with a 'fairly well-marked predisposition'. They were 'false' war neuroses not because they were feigned, but because they had not been caused uniquely by the war. These cases, it was noted, only recovered 'if the circumstances were favourable, and the men were able to obtain suitable employment.' But the post-war environment was not, by and large, very favourable. Times were hard and jobs not easily come by, especially after 1929.[29]

For the most part [the British official history continues] these men could not in any case have made successful adaptation to the conditions of Post-War life, and there can be little doubt that, even if there had been no war, these men would sooner or later, and from one cause or another, have been likely to break down under the stress of everyday life.[30]

Those left, all this suggests, were not 'war neurotics', just neurotics and mental weaklings who probably would have broken down with or without the war. Increasingly, a moralistic, judgemental tone emerged. Those still ill, it was even suggested, lacked the will and guts to pull themselves together; they didn't *want* to get better. In Britain, the pre-war rhetoric of degeneration, mostly forgotten during the war, began to return. Unrecovered pensioners bore the 'congenital stigmata of degeneration' and were 'constitutional psychopathic inferiors', doctors in the Ministry of Pensions declared in 1928. Furthermore, they started asking whether, if a man's problems were pre-war in origin, or had been brought on not by experiences in battle but just by the everyday pressures of army life, he deserved a pension?[31]

Behind all the theorising lay a hard practical imperative – to reduce the vast pension bill.

The whole world of compensatory pensions has always been a nightmare of complexity and calculation – this was Franz Kafka's line of work. Something about the process of expressing human disablement and suffering in quantifiable financial terms leads inevitably to bizarre and unreal outcomes – particularly when the rigid formulae of English law are applied to the murky truths of mental illness. Furthermore, although it was generally agreed in Britain that the state had a clear moral duty to help men left mentally damaged by service to their country, evidence was emerging that giving them a pension might not be the best way to do that. In fact, it was suggested, pensions actually hindered recovery.

The effect of pensions and allowances on war neurotics had already been noticed during the war. 'The whole therapy was so vitiated by the pension system', the respected British psychotherapist, T. A. Ross wrote of his work between 1917 and 1921, 'that it was impossible to gauge the value of any form of treatment.' Ross found that, as men got better, the thought of losing their allowance (and with it a guaranteed livelihood) would cause their hysterical symptoms to return or new symptoms to appear. He described how, on one occasion, the prospect of a visit to his hospital of a famous specialist renowned for removing symptoms aroused such anxiety that each patient in succession was 'seized with epileptiform fits, so that the healer was obliged to leave.'[32]

Other liberal-minded doctors agreed. Bernard Hart warned that it was very dangerous for there to be a relationship between symptoms and pensions. Consciously or not, as long as a pension depended on the existence of symptoms, recovery would be impeded.[33]

The French took this approach to its logical conclusion and paid no pensions at all to psychoneurotic cases – a policy even Charles Myers thought right and 'therapeutically valuable'. The Germans paid them until 1926 when the burden on Weimar's finances proved unsupportable (whereupon, according to the doctors, all the *Kriegszitterer* abruptly lost their symptoms and could function again). In Britain and the United States, the strength of public opinion made sure that pensions were given, but subject to many a slip and proviso.[34]

British Ministry of Pensions files record some of the bureaucratic Catch-22s that arose. In 1923 officials tied themselves in knots over 'a certain residuum of nerve cases which [had] not responded at all to medical treatment' and were showing no tendency to improve. Experts advised that 'in many of these cases treatment can do no good because the man fears that if he gets better he will lose his pension. Anxiety about the pension is sufficient to counteract benefits of treatment.' The answer appeared to be to give the man some final pension and so relieve him of his pension anxiety. But what if this *worked*? What if the award of a final pension *did* make a man recover? Then the cash-strapped Ministry, horrified officials realised, would be paying out pensions to *healthy* people.[35]

At the same time a different and contradictory picture was emerging. The official line – that the only people who continued to suffer were those predisposed to mental weakness or neurotically paralysed by pensions – was belied by the observation of many doctors. For, waiting for them in their clinics, were patients who had certainly 'done their best', yet had not been able to function properly; men who had attacked the challenges of peace with admirable strength and determination, only to be struck down by forces within them. Some of them had come through the war unscathed only to break down after demobilisation.

In many cases the eventual outcome was a messy compromise. Donald Cameron, the hero of A. G. McDonnell's satirical *England Their England*, is blown up at Passchendaele and it is not until 1920 that his doctor judges him ready to face the outside world. On leaving he is given a document,

which said that he would only be forty-hundredths of a normal man for the next seven years . . . but that on expiration of the seven years he would, unaccountably, become once again hundred per cent citizen with no further claim on the finances of the country. Such was the mathematical exactitude of prophecy with which the Ministry of Pensions was endowed in those years that immediately followed the War. To this document was attached a statement that the missing sixty-hundredths of Lieutenant Donald Cameron was worth £85 a year . . . to be paid in half-yearly instalments and . . . subject to income tax.[36]

* * *

The American post-war experience is historically the most important because of the parallels with events since Vietnam. In the United States, as in Britain, there was a long delay in creating the machinery to treat ex-servicemen with psychiatric problems; little was done while Tom Salmon was away in France. When it became clear, at the end of 1919, that mental and nervous cases constituted over 38% of all hospitalised veterans, responsibility was still divided between four government agencies. It was not till August 1921 that a single body, the Veterans' Bureau (later Administration) was created; only by late 1922 was the political will to do something for psychiatric cases mobilised. Unfortunately, to overcome official inertia, Tom Salmon had had to use shameless rhetoric to dramatise the issue, calling on 'the voice of public opinion' to 'take up the protests of the mothers of our insane soldiers'.[37]

It didn't help either that the Veterans' Bureau's first director, like several members of the Harding administration, was jailed for corruption. Finally, though, the Bureau began to establish itself. Hospitals were built, and staff were trained; by 1925 the Bureau was producing its own *Medical Bulletin*.[38]

By then, however, another dynamic had kicked in – the long American tradition of generosity to veterans. Ever since the Civil War the political muscle of the ex-service lobby had resulted in very generous benefits, often given regardless of a man's service record. Some historians have even argued that the lavish welfare provided for war veterans and its association with 'patronage democracy' may have helped to discredit in the minds of progressive American opinion the kind of 'welfare state' by then emerging in Europe. The medical service of the Veterans' Bureau became, in effect, an enclave of publicly-funded medicine within a private health service in which the extent to which a man's problems related to his war service was increasingly ignored.[39]

The net effect of this combination of delay, muddle, Tom Salmon's dramatisation of shell-shock, and, finally, the provision of lavish facilities and pensions was, in most doctors' opinion, disastrous. Far from healing men, it turned them into chronic neurotics. The system offered the veteran no incentive to get better, allowed patients to reject treatment and change doctors, and forced doctors who had once been able to rely on 'control and authority' in the Army now to 'beg' for the 'co-operation' of their patients. Public sympathy made it easy for undeserving men to get generous benefits. One doctor believed that most conditions would be cured 'almost overnight' if Congress simply prohibited the Veterans' Bureau from paying any compensation. He cited the case of a recently discharged soldier 'who never knew that he had any nerves' who was turned into a thoroughgoing neurotic by a combination of unemployment, doctors' attention and 'introspection'.[40]

* * *

Yet from this wrong-headed muddle and confusion came the single most important attempt to understand the chronic war neurotic. In 1922 a young doctor, Abram Kardiner started work at No. 81 Veterans' Bureau Hospital in the Bronx, New York City. An intense and complicated man, Kardiner's long medical education had included a personal analysis with Sigmund Freud immediately after the war.[41]

Over a four-year period, Kardiner saw over 1,000 patients with neurotic disturbances connected to the war. About 700 of them had what he called 'traumatic neuroses', and of this group he tried to help about 150, with a third of these being intensively treated for anything between several months to two years. Eventually he wrote up and published some 24 cases.

Looking back, he found the experience the 'most instructive and the most dramatic' of his career, but also very depressing. Nothing in the medical literature had prepared him for the 'tortures and discomforts' these men and those who lived with them underwent in their daily lives. Six or seven years after the war, a man would find that he had a phobia that prevented him from riding the New York subway; a tailor could no longer hold a needle; men were unable to concentrate at work or found themselves suddenly fainting in the street. There were funny gaits, disturbed hearts, tremors and paralyses.[42]

Many of the cases seemed to show the same curious picture. For example, there was a patient who during the war had had the horribly unpleasant experience of being gassed while asleep. Some years later, he began to have spells: his heart would beat violently, he would vomit and then lose consciousness. It emerged that these attacks 'usually followed exposure to certain odours from volatile oils – perfume, lemon oil, banana oil, or ether.' The man worked in a butcher's shop frequented by fashionable women, many of whom came heavily perfumed, and 'when they would enter the butcher shop . . . the patient would become dizzy and lose consciousness.' 'The flushing, the rapid pulse, the dizziness and the vomiting,' Kardiner decided, were 'a repetition of the original traumatic event which overtook him in sleep.' Another man, who noticed that certain smells gave him spells of vertigo, even changed his job, only to find that working for a taxi cab company, the smell of gasoline would produce attacks. These men's loss of consciousness was being triggered by 'external factors which prove under close examination to be exactly the same factors causing the original loss of consciousness on the battlefield'. 'In short', Kardiner concluded, 'we have here a typical conditioned reflex.'[43]

Some patients Kardiner was able to help. A man who had been in a plane that plunged to the ground during training in Texas suffered from convulsive seizures and losses of consciousness. But by explaining patiently that these were 'repetitions of reactions which began with the traumatic experience' and then demonstrating that the therapist could bring on any of the symptoms at will, Kardiner somehow shook the log jam loose. The patient began to sleep, his nightmares ceased, he was able to work and had no more convulsions. Treatment had taken some fifteen months.

Such successes, though, were rare. More typical was 'T', who had fought in France with exceptional courage, being blown up and buried four times. After the last experience he had been left mute, deaf, blind, and 'without body sense'.

Body feeling returned within six months [Kardiner noted], and it took another six months for the sensory organs to regain their function. It was more than a year before he could read or write, and it is interesting to note that the latter ability was the last of all to return.[44]

In 1924 'T' still suffered from repetitive war dreams and was exceptionally sensitive to loud noises, 'especially unexpected ones, which would often cause him to lose consciousness.' This, wrote Kardiner later, 'was no epileptic convulsion but a reviving of the last shelling.' 'T' was seen over and over again, talked to sympathetically and taken endlessly back to the traumatic incident from which his symptoms flowed. But nothing seemed to work and, in the end, Kardiner gave up, convinced it was just too late. Perhaps if he could have treated this man sooner, within the first few months, he could have achieved something.

When it came to interpreting these cases, however, Kardiner developed a form of paralysis himself. He was a Freudian, touched by the hand of the master himself and, by 1929, was becoming prominent in American Freudian circles. Yet the more he struggled to apply to his war veterans the Freudian apparatus of interpretation – 'the concepts of the libido theory, which are based on instinctual energies, phylogenetically programmed stages of development and a predetermined Oedipus complex' – the less relevant it seemed. If anything, his material – with its recurrent motif of the man paralysed or rendered unconscious by a sensory stimulus – pointed in a different direction altogether, towards the work of the Russian psychologist Pavlov and of Pavlov's American affiliates, the behavioural psychiatrists. Human behaviour, according to Pavlov, is the product not of thought but of *conditioning*. 'We are biological machines and do not consciously act; rather we react to stimuli.' Was this not what Kardiner had noticed and called 'a conditioned reflex'? But, rather than acknowledge this, Kardiner abandoned his work on veterans' problems and it was not until a decade later that he returned to the subject, having by then devised a new angle of attack.[45]

The 1930s were an era of big social issues – Depression, Fascism, collectivisation and purges in the Soviet Union. The preoccupations of individual psychopathology – sitting in a consulting room on Park Avenue listening to the problems of rich neurotics – came to seem an irrelevant luxury and many psychoanalysts ventured into social issues. Kardiner, reviving an old interest, collaborated with anthropologists at Columbia University in studies of the effects of different social customs and child-rearing practices on personality. These soon showed him that Freud's vision of human development just didn't work with primitive societies: by 1938 Kardiner was obliged to abandon 'the libido theory's assumption that most human development was propelled by certain inborn energies and occurred under a certain pre-ordained order', substituting instead a more environmental approach to development. Because of his special ties to Freud, he found this particularly hard to do.[46]

When in 1940, Kardiner was asked to write something on the current topic, the 'War Neuroses', he finally managed, 'after several attempts', to come up with a 'plausible hypothesis'. The war neuroses, he said, rest on a simple principle: 'an activity which fails or causes pain tends to become inhibited.' This was a reaction found throughout nature and on which all adaptation and integration to environment rested. Someone who almost drowned was left with a distaste for swimming, someone who had fallen from a horse might not want to ride again.[47]

What you usually see in these cases, Kardiner argued, is not the inhibition itself but its effect on the man's general capacity to adapt to a new environment. If that ability to react becomes blocked, but the person continues to have the same drives and needs, crises will take place – disturbances of the nervous system, fits, outbursts of rage and so on. Furthermore, this change in the man's capacity to absorb and relate to stimuli in the outside world would soon affect his whole conception of himself, leading him to adopt neurotic or antisocial behaviour; or, in many cases, to limit his contact to the world to a few situations that he could cope with, usually by becoming dependent on others.

Kardiner believed that the doctor's task was to intervene before the 'defensive reaction' had become consolidated and 'a new adaptation established on the ruins of what remains of the uninhibited personality'. There was 'reason for haste in diagnosis and treatment. It is a race against time.'[48]

Kardiner's was by far the most sophisticated interpretation of the war neuroses yet offered, managing to integrate the physiological side with the psychological and to bring together the two strands in a two-tier model, for which he coined the term a 'physio-neurosis'. His account was also rooted in hard clinical reality over a long period in a way that few previous studies had been. It was still not perfect, of course: Kardiner had only studied chronic cases, years after the war. He knew very little about the processes that operate in the heat of battle and did not, for example, explain why soldiers who serve in units with high morale and good discipline do not succumb in circumstances where poorer soldiers do.[49]

This may help to explain the paradox – which suits Kardiner's dark and paranoid personality – that his book *The Traumatic Neuroses of War*, though finally published in 1941 when its subject was intensely topical, nonetheless had little influence on practice in the forthcoming war. The long delay in completion left little time for his ideas to be absorbed into the medical bloodstream before hostilities began, and the book was not easy to read. Above all, Kardiner did not offer the simple maxims and easy answers both the military and psychiatrists were looking for as they geared up for war. His message was grim, almost determinist – that war inevitably damaged men and unless they were treated effectively very soon after their breakdowns their cases were hopeless. No one wanted to be told that in 1941. In the United States, the book had some influence within the analytic coterie, but there are few contemporary references to it in Britain.[50]

And yet, ultimately, Kardiner would prove the most influential writer on the war neuroses. In the 1970s, when American medicine was confronted by an epidemic of mental disorders in Vietnam veterans, his book was a bible, almost the only thing the psychiatrist could turn to.

* * *

No survey of the mental after-effects of the Great War, however broad, could be complete without some mention of another class of patients, those suffering from serious mental disorder or psychosis. Men like the 33-year-old private in the Royal West Surreys evacuated from France to Netley Hospital, Southampton on 21 September 1918. He had been 'normal' until 6 weeks previously, when he 'heard his mother had thrown herself out of a window'. Now he said there was 'some sort of electricity wireless' in his head. Nine months later, 'still very delusional', he was committed to an asylum.[51]

Almost from the start of the war, this issue aroused strong public feeling in Britain. It was felt to be inappropriate that soldiers who went insane should be treated as 'pauper lunatics'. As a result, although the Army followed its usual custom of sending insane soldiers to civilian mental hospitals, the Lunacy Board of Control was obliged in 1916 to meet public concern by creating a new class of 'service patients' who enjoyed special privileges, such as grey felt uniforms, were spared the stigma of 'certification' (being legally committed under the Lunacy laws) and were kept quite separate from 'pauper' patients.[52]

The publicity given to the new methods of treating shell-shock further aroused public expectations. In 1920, a doctor at Wakefield Asylum complained that relatives were now constantly demanding to know why his patients had not been given 'methods of treatment to which prominence has lately been given by the Press'; he was fed up with explaining to them that 'suggestion, psycho-therapeutic conversations, hypnotism and psychoanalysis' would not help these men. The media even began to investigate asylums. In 1920, the magazine *Truth* ran an extended exposé of the 'obscene methods of torture', 'general atmosphere of brutality', overcrowding, and poor facilities in military mental hospitals.[53]

Mental wards in wartime hospitals were clearly not pleasant places, and were crowded and understaffed. Yet they were a huge improvement on most pre-war asylums, not least because many military patients got better – 56% in one hospital. A doctor treating psychotic soldiers in the Lord Derby War Hospital proudly revealed that, instead of a 'mere visit of the medical officer to the wards and the official walk round', there were now 'private rooms' in which doctors could have 'confidential chats' with the patients. This was clearly a big innovation.[54]

By the early 1920s, however, it was felt that those who were going to recover had done so, and that those who were left were hopeless cases, doomed by heredity or bad habits. Of the 11,600 servicemen who had 'passed the border and been certified in the asylum system', about 1,500 had died by 1922 and some 3,800 (exactly a third) had recovered, leaving a hard core of some 6,000 psychotics. Men who showed no signs of recovering after nine months were eventually put into ordinary asylums, though with the privileges of 'private patients', paid for by the Ministry of Pensions.[55]

They were joined over the years by a small but significant number who developed psychoses after the war: in 1929 the British government paid out more pensions for illnesses like schizophrenia and dementia than had been granted in the four years immediately after the war. The historian Eric Leed has argued that many of these were men who had 'stuck it' at the front, having too much self-control to escape into illness by becoming 'neurotics', and then paid the price years later.

While the war was going on it appeared that the large number of neuroses had a great deal to do with the surprisingly few psychoses of combat. In peacetime this ratio was reversed . . . There are numerous examples of men coming home either 'normal' or with slight hysteria to end up, four years later, as schizophrenics.[56]

Most British doctors thought these were men who would probably have broken down with or without a war, but they resisted Treasury pressure to distinguish between cases of insanity caused by the war and those not. Instead, official stinginess was felt most by patients' families. According to a recent study, 'the family of a paraplegic received roughly 60% more in allowances than the family of a lunatic.'[57]

An avalanche of requests to visit and inspect mental hospitals testifies to the unhappiness of ex-service organisations with the way their old comrades were being looked after. These groups wanted separate Ministry of Pensions hospitals for service cases – like those set up by the Veteran' Administration in the United States – an idea always vetoed as too expensive. Public pressure did, however, ensure that service patients retained some of their separate and more privileged status, 'personalised underwear and nightwear' for example. In November 1927, the Ex-Service Mental Welfare Society (a private charity) was arranging for service patients to be treated as voluntary boarders 'in a beautiful villa' in the grounds of one of the leading London mental hospitals, free from stigma and not herded in with paupers. Several thousand less severe cases were housed in homes run by the Society, where they did light work.[58]

Had the war sent these people mad? The difficulties in establishing causation are shown in one well-documented case, that of the composer and poet Ivor Gurney. Gurney was a sensitive, gentle man with a pre-war history of 'neurasthenia and dyspepsia' and a troubled family background – precisely the 'imaginative, artistic' type many thought most vulnerable to war. Yet at first the structure of Army life helped him to function better, and, if he hated shellfire as much as anyone, he was also proud to have 'the name for being extremely cool' under it.[59]

Gurney was wounded in April 1917 and gassed at Passchendaele in August the same year; but only lightly. He was then evacuated to an Edinburgh hospital and kept on because skilful piano players were few, though he disliked having to play 'ragtime' on demand. 'Doing nothing and eating too much' and 'staying in bed' put Gurney into 'the devil of a temper' and made him 'a bundle of oppressed nerves'. By October 1917, though, he had discovered the kindness of his nurses and began to fear the front because 'life is so pleasant here'; he was lucky to be sent to the regimental Depot – 'owing to slight indigestion (presumably due to gas; wink, wink!).' By this time his indigestion had become his alibi.[60]

Gurney had also fallen in love with one of the nurses, Annie Drummond, '30 years old and most perfectly enchanting'. Visiting her for a weekend, 'for the first time I felt Joy in me; a clear fountain of music and light. By God, I forgot I had a body – and you know what height of living that meant to me.' It was 'a hot pain leaving her'. 'To get her and settle down,' he wrote, 'would make a solid rock foundation for me to build on – a home and tower of light.'[61]

But Annie Drummond rejected him and the effect is dramatically shown in Gurney's letters. A period back home in Gloucester, 'little by little . . . gain[ing] happiness and health', was followed by a return to hospital in Newcastle, 'my inside having been a little extra troublesome lately . . . stomach trouble caused by gas'. By the end of March 1918 he was writing that he had 'never felt well' in France, and had 'had continual digestive and general nervous trouble' out there. He was also comparing his doctors to prostitutes.[62]

A steep decline followed. After being found talking to Beethoven – 'it was Ludwig van all right' – he was sent to the infamous 1,000-bed hospital for psychotic soldiers in Warrington, an experience he described as 'trying'. A few days after being discharged he wrote a suicide note – 'I am afraid of slipping down and becoming a mere wreck' – but lost courage and could not do it. Then, thanks perhaps to 'some very nice people' he met in a soldier's home in Warrington, Gurney slowly recovered and by August 1918 was once more writing poetry and trying to get the doctors at Napsbury Hospital, St Albans, to provide a piano for him to play. A month later he was allowed to go home.[63]

'Will the Peace bring peace?' Gurney had asked back in 1915. For him, it did not; his post-war history was again a switchback of achievement and decline. A volume of poems in 1919 and efforts to revive his musical career were followed by a more complete breakdown. He entered an asylum in Gloucester in 1922 and died in the City of London Mental Hospital in 1937. Words continued to pour out of him – letters, poems, appeals – but 'with a degenerating coherence quite dreadful to observe.' In his later years he developed an increasing sense of paranoia that his war service had not been properly recognised or a full pension paid. This suggests that his underlying problem may have been a 'sense of guilt', to which he refers in one of his letters in 1918. Overall, though, his letters suggest that as much as the horrors of the front, it was his time in hospitals and the failure of the love affair that did for him.[64]

* * *

In 1936, at a meeting of the Ex-Services Mental Welfare Society, doctors discussed the chronic cases still left. 'The commonest later forms of war neurosis,' said Edward Mapother, 'was either still anxiety or perhaps nowadays a condition of depression and ready exhaustion.' Dr Nattrass of Newcastle agreed that the vast majority of the current patients presented the picture of neurasthenia – an anxiety state which did not seem to improve with the passage of years. War neurotics, he added, were not now capable of improvement and should be cared for by the state, to give them some of the happiness that was their due.[65]

In November 1998, a reporter from the *Mail on Sunday* went to the Stratheden Hospital in Fife, Scotland, to interview David Ireland, a former private in the Black Watch. Mr Ireland had been admitted to the hospital in 1924 suffering from 'delusory psychosis'. He had never left it.[66]

THE LESSONS OF SHELL-SHOCK

Many of those who toiled in shell-shock hospitals were sustained by the hope that wartime experience would usher in a new, more enlightened era of mental health care. 'The war,' Grafton Elliot Smith and T. H. Pear wrote in 1917, 'has forced upon this country a rational and enlightened method of caring and treating disorders among its soldiers. Are those signs of progress merely temporary? Are such successful measures to be limited to the duration of the war and to be restricted to the army?' Such people wanted the barriers between sanity and insanity to be lowered, 'early' treatment to be made available in out-patient clinics, the stigma of mental illness to go and medical students to be taught something about psychological medicine.[1]

Their hopes were by and large fulfilled. In the decades after the war, great changes did come about. By 1939 there were 187 out-patient clinics in Britain treating psychological problems, a solid core of doctors applying wartime experience of psychotherapy to civilian problems and a torrent of publications popularising the 'new' psychology. Younger doctors came to recognise the need for psychological training – though in Britain, as Rivers had predicted, Freudian ideas proved more popular with writers and artists than with most medical people.

At an institutional level, the lessons of the war took longer to be absorbed; economy drives and the 'rapid evaporation of post-war idealism' slowed the pace. It was not until the Mental Treatment Act of 1930 that some of the old rigidities of certification, the links with the Poor Law and the term 'asylum' were finally swept away.[2]

It is a sad fact of history that the high hopes of wartime are usually destined to be forgotten in peace. A cynical modern reader will see enshrined in Elliot Smith's plea for 'progress' towards 'rational and enlightened methods' all the illusions of endless medical advancement which recent experience (and the writings of such as Foucault) have made most suspect. Yet out of the experience of shell-shock were born two institutions which have been unequivocal forces for good in British life – the Cassel Hospital and the Tavistock Clinic.[3]

The Cassel was the brainchild of Alfred Keogh's advisers at the War Office, Dr Maurice Craig and the neurologists Henry Head and Farquhar Buzzard. They felt that 'all that had been learned in the bitter experience of wartime might be used in dealing with neuroses among the civilian population', and persuaded the banker and philanthropist, Sir Ernest Cassel, to give £212,000 to make that possible (in selling the idea, Craig shrewdly took Sir Ernest to Arthur Hurst's clinic at Seale Hayne rather than to Maghull; 'showy cures' in rural Devon were more likely to attract sponsors than the hard grind of psychotherapy on the windy Mersey). For many years the Cassel remained the only hospital of its kind.[4]

The Tavistock Square Clinic opened its doors in a 'depressing, gloomy, tall old house' in Bloomsbury in 1920. It was a dramatic sign of the change of attitude brought by the war that its patrons included the former Warlords, Haig and Beatty. The 'Tavi' was created by a former shell-shock doctor, Hugh Crichton-Miller, to give ordinary people the sort of help with their everyday psychological problems that had been so hard to get before the war. Although it owed 'most of its conceptual basis' to the 'then still much-feared and suspect psycho-analytic school', it was from the start cheerfully undogmatic and eclectic in its staff and its teachings. Crichton-Miller, like many of his colleagues, was a 'son of the Manse' (the Tavistock was sometimes derisively known as 'the parson's clinic'), and combined strong religious feelings with a potpourri of Freud, Jung, Adler and 'the developing sciences of biochemistry and endocrinology'.[5]

From the start, though, the Tavistock had a rival. In 1923, the hospital endowed by the Victorian psychiatrist Henry Maudsley to 'break down the unfortunate isolation from general medical knowledge and research in which the study and treatment of insanity remains' finally opened its doors to civilian patients. The Maudsley was a hospital not an asylum; it took voluntary rather than certified cases, and it provided research and teaching facilities and an out-patient clinic. Under the doughty leadership of a formidable Anglo-Irishman, Edward Mapother, it finally gave British psychiatry something of the rigour and scientific weight enjoyed by German clinics since earlier in the century. It became part of London University, trained most of the younger psychiatrists and rapidly established an international reputation.[6]

The Maudsley looked for inspiration not to Vienna, but to Baltimore – to the Phipps Clinic at Johns Hopkins University, which became, under the steward-ship of the Swiss-American Adolf Meyer (1913–1940), the finishing school for English-speaking mainstream psychiatrists. Meyer's approach, known as 'psycho-biology', was a half-way house between psychoanalysis and traditional psychiatry. Meyer believed that a wide range of factors lay behind mental illness: 'Each person was mainly a product of social forces and other life experiences, and heredity was relatively less important'. The psychiatrist's job was, therefore, to 'understand his patients as individuals by studying their biographies – it was not enough to assign them to diagnostic categories'. Meyer's emphasis on the individual patient, insistence on drawing on a wide range of scientific procedures in investigating illness, 'common sense' approach and rejection of the specialist vocabulary of psychoanalysis were all greatly to the British taste. The standard British textbook between the wars was written by two pupils of Meyer. Within the US itself, Meyer's was the dominant voice throughout this period.[7]

However, the arrival of the Maudsley and the Tavistock eroded only g̲
the role of neurologists in British mental medicine. Socially, they remained
dogs. Most well-heeled private patients with mental problems would usually b
referred to a Harley Street specialist who was a neurologist at one of the big
teaching hospitals and probably had a rather rudimentary approach to psychiatry.

They conceived their function as that of making a careful physical examination and
excluding organic disease. Having done this, and having diagnosed 'neurasthenia' or
'hysteria' they returned the patient to his general practitioner for the bromide therapy.
The patient was only sent to see a psychiatrist . . . if he was thought seriously mad and
might have to be put under a 'certificate'.

Dr Gordon Holmes, whose distaste for neurotics was legendary, continued to see
neurotic patients during the 1930s, his brusque manner frequently leaving female
patients in a shattered and tearful condition.[8]

The awkward, inhibited approach of the neurologists suited many patients,
especially male ones, who continued to take a 'robust' view of mental illness and
of psychiatrists. 'The majority of men, especially in this country,' an Army officer
wrote in the 1940s, 'are healthily devoid of any interest in psychiatry . . . [which]
is regarded as a queer interest for queer people.' There was, too, a 'revulsion
against the invasion of mental privacy which is unavoidable in prolonged
psychiatric investigation.'[9]

*   *   *

Sigmund Freud died in exile in London, in September 1939, in W. H. Auden's
words, 'no more a person now but a whole climate of opinion'. The previous two
decades had seen an extraordinary flowering of Freudian ideas among the
Western intelligentsia and the application of psychoanalytic ideas across the
cultural spectrum Yet Freud's influence on mainstream medicine was much more
complicated and patchy.[10]

Even among those affected by Freud, different groupings emerged. The older
British psychologists – like the shell-shock doctors Bernard Hart, William Brown
and William McDougall – used and adapted many Freudian ideas, particularly
the unconscious and repression, but retained their original orientation. Many in
the younger generation took up Freud more wholeheartedly. But which Freud?
Between the wars, the splits and splinters endemic to psychoanalysis continued
and Freudian ideas underwent profound changes. Many of these new psychoanalytic ideas would be tested in the coming war.[11]

In the 1920s, Freud began to construct a theory of the personality, to write
about the normal, rather than the pathological, mind and to look at human
interactions in groups. In 1923 came a new emphasis in Freudian psychoanalysis,
on the development of the mind of the child. Indeed, the analyst Adam Phillips
has recently argued, by the 1930s, the place of the unconscious begins to be
usurped by a new figure called the child. 'The child was, as it were, the

ou could see it in action. It had been found: in fact you could
[12]

ed, others followed. By the time of his death in 1939 – to
plex process – there had begun to emerge two main schools of
, one of which has come to be labelled 'ego psychology', the
tions theory'. According the analyst John Padel, ego psychology
followed .... dency in Freud's later work which invested a new importance
in the development of the rational ego and emphasised the growth of the ego and
self-awareness and relates the stages of libidinal development described by Freud
to the emergence of a sense of identity.' It was particularly associated with Freud's
daughter Anna, whose book *The Ego and the Mechanisms of Defence*, published in
1936, had a profound influence in America, where her emphasis on the
'psychology of the normal' was particularly welcomed.[13]

By contrast, 'object-relations' came to dominate psychoanalysis in Britain. Its
ideas derived from the work of Freud's one-time favourite, Sandor Ferenczi –
whom Peter Fuller has called 'the first analyst to grasp the clinical and theoretical
importance of the primary relationship between the mother and the child' – and
of Ferenczi's pupil, Melanie Klein, who came to England in 1925 and rapidly
became the *monstre sacrée* of the British Psycho-Analytical Society. Ferenczi and
Klein emphasised the developing child's emotional dependence on the people
('objects') around it, most notably its mother. For them, weaning – and the
'separation anxiety' that attended the child's gradual removal from its mother's
breast – were the dominant motifs in psychological life.[14]

Psychoanalysis was a time-consuming, expensive business, a luxury few could
afford, or wanted. 'To be encouraged by a doctor to talk about oneself in the most
prattling detail was,' wrote Robert Graves, 'a new and grand experience,
especially for moneyed and lonely women who had had "nervous breakdowns".'
Psychoanalysts were still figures of fun, depicted in movies as bearded, heavily-
accented, and Jewish/foreign. But the ideas of psychoanalysis cast a wider shadow
and were absorbed, unconsciously, in the agony columns of women's magazines
(in wartime novels, the role of mothers in creating personality is emphasised).
And, paradoxically, while in Britain the Freudians were the only group not
invited to contribute to wartime psychiatry, they provided many of the ideas and
the interpretative tools on which it would rest. The idea of emotional maturity –
of someone progressing through the various stages of Freudian development,
becoming emotionally independent of his mother and acquiring 'ego strength' –
would underpin much of American wartime work; its British equivalent,
'separation anxiety', was similarly omnipresent.[15]

Also drawn on would be the newly-fashionable field of psychosomatic
medicine. The idea that mind and body interact in illness was as old as medicine
itself, but had been given fresh impetus by the work of W. B. Cannon and Ivan
Pavlov on the effects of emotions such as fear on the workings of the body's
systems – the heart, the stomach, and the nervous system – and by the Freudian
idea of 'unconscious emotion'. Although, as we have seen, Cannon's work was
known to doctors during the First World War, the 'psychosomatic era in

medicine truly got under way' in Germany in the 1920s when psychiatrists began to apply it to the study of emotional stress in chronic organic diseases. Much of the running was made by maverick Freudians like Wilhelm Reich or Georg Groddeck – who went so far as to argue that organic diseases were just the expressions of unconscious mental conflicts – but the psychosomatic approach gained fresh respectability when some eminent psychiatrists began to suggest that most duodenal ulcers had a neurotic origin.[16]

This German approach was brought to America by Freud's pupil, Franz Alexander, who began to develop psychoanalytic treatment techniques for patients suffering gastrointestinal problems like ulcers or constipation in Chicago in the 1930s. Studies appeared to show that patients with certain personality types developed particular disorders; there was an 'ulcer personality', a 'coronary personality' and 'arthritic personality'.[17]

The British properly discovered psychosomatic medicine just before the war; Tavistock researchers investigated psychological aspects of peptic ulcer, cardiac pain, colitis and asthma and concluded that 95% of ulcer patients had worrying, tense personalities, as compared to 30% of hernia patients. This new medical fashion would be reflected in wartime diagnoses: whereas in the first 15 months of the First World War, only 709 British soldiers were discharged for gastritis and peptic ulcer, in the first 27 months of the Second, no less than 25,374 soldiers were discharged for peptic ulcer alone.[18]

The overall effects of these changes was to create a generational divide within medicine, as a shrewd outsider noticed. 'There are two types of medical man,' General Sir Ronald Adam wrote in 1942. 'The older school dislike psychologists and psychiatrists intensely and will do anything to stop their use. The younger school, on the other hand, are mostly psychiatrists themselves to some extent.'[19]

* * *

The Second World War, unlike the First, could be seen coming. Hitler had scarcely come to power before the Germans began discussing what to do about war neuroses in the next conflict. In Britain, the Munich crisis in the autumn of 1938 concentrated minds and provoked a rash of books and articles about war neurosis. But the debate that determined policy took place in camera, in Whitehall, and was initiated not by the services but by the Ministry of Pensions.

It is not hard to see why. In 1939, there were still some 40,000 people in Britain receiving pensions for mental disorders derived from the last war and a further 80,000 cases had been settled. Determined not to incur such a bill again, the Ministry set in motion yet another post-mortem designed to lock the medical policy machine into a very restrictive definition of war neurosis.

As a first step, the Ministry's psychiatric expert, Dr Francis Prideaux, wrote a memorandum setting out the lessons of the last war and his recommendations for the next. Prideaux drew not only on the 1922 War Office Committee on Shell-shock but detailed investigations of cases of 'neurasthenia' he had carried out between the wars. These showed, he argued, that the great mistakes made in

1914–18 had been, firstly, to assume that most cases of neurosis were caused by traumatic experience in war and, secondly, to allow men to leave the Army and to receive pensions on the grounds of neurosis. Taken together, this policy had amounted to an open invitation to soldiers to develop and maintain neurotic symptoms. In fact, his research showed that most (57%) of the men still drawing pensions for neurosis had not been near the front line and a further 20% had served there only very briefly. The only constant factor in the great majority of these cases, said Prideaux, was a 'constitutional predisposition, either inborn or acquired early in life' to nervous illness.[20]

What was more, said Prideaux, any claim for 'delayed shell-shock' made after seven years was clearly bogus. Nor was there any evidence at all that the war had increased the incidence of epilepsy or psychosis. The 6,000 psychotic patients for whom the Ministry was paying would have been mental patients even if there had been no war. To avoid repeating past mistakes, it must therefore be made clear from the start of any future war that no one would get out of the Services because of psychoneurosis and that no pensions would be paid to cases of neurosis.

Prideaux's memorandum was circulated to a small group of eminent neurologists and psychiatrists and then discussed at a meeting in July 1939. Those canvassed included many of the Grand Old Men of shell-shock doctoring – Bernard Hart, Hugh Crichton-Miller, Aldren Turner, Farquhar Buzzard, Gordon Holmes and Edward Mapother. However, word of the exercise obviously got about because, not long afterwards, the Ministry of Pensions also received a long and unsolicited memorandum from four other shell-shock doctors of a more independent-minded and 'psychological' persuasion – Charles Myers, the psychiatrist T. A. Ross, the psychologist J. T. MacCurdy and the neurologist George Riddoch. This second group were very much the inheritors of Rivers' mantle; three had been close friends of his.[21]

These 1939 discussions are fascinating and important for two reasons. Firstly, they show, much more clearly than the report of the 1922 Committee, how the 'shell-shock' episode was perceived in retrospect by most of the surviving major players. Secondly, they reveal a surprising amount of unanimity between the 'hard' and 'soft' schools. Indeed, many of the strongest statements can be found in the 'psychologists'' memorandum. A soldier's personality, they declared, not the level of trauma to which he was exposed, usually determined whether he got better. Nobody questioned Prideaux's account of what had gone wrong: that medical mismanagement, as much as the war, had done the damage by allowing soldiers to think that they had an actual disorder, and all agreed that quasi-medical names like 'shell-shock' should not be used. Everyone endorsed Bernard Hart's view (first given to the 1922 Committee) that all necessary steps must be taken to fight the 'subconscious motive lying behind the psychoneuroses of war' by eliminating any prospect of reward: nobody should get out of the Army through neurosis and no pensions should be paid.

It was the psychologists who declared:

There should be no excuse given for the establishment of a belief that a functional nervous

disability constitutes a right to compensation. This is a hard saying. It m
those whose sufferings are real, whose illness has been brought on by
very likely in the course of patriotic service, should be treated wi
callousness. But there can be no doubt that in an overwhelming proport
patients succumb to 'shock' because they get something out of it. T
reward is not ultimately a benefit to them because it encourages the wea
their character. The nation cannot call on its citizens for courage and sa.......and, at the
same time, state by implication that an unconscious cowardice or an unconscious
dishonesty will be rewarded.[22]

There was, too, general agreement that methods of treatment should be much
more basic – that in the Great War psychotherapy had often made people *worse*
not better. For all the mythology about psychology in the Great War, these
doctors knew from experience what had worked best with acute cases in wartime.
'It is hoped to avoid elaborate psychotherapy such as was usual in the last war,'
wrote Edward Mapother of the Maudsley, 'and substitute common sense
methods of restoring morale.' At the outbreak of war, T. A. Ross visited hospitals
in North London, 'having talks with the medical staff and nurses asking them not
to make frightened people into cases of neurosis.'[23]

However, while there was general agreement about the importance of these
preventive steps, there was disagreement on two specific issues – the question of
predisposition and the role of selection. In the light of their experience between
the war, Prideaux and the Ministry of Pensions considered those who broke
down to be 'constitutional neuropaths' – people with hereditary or acquired
weaknesses of the nervous system or lacking in the moral strength of character
needed to honour their social obligations. This view was sharply criticised by
Edward Mapother, the most powerful and respected man in English psychiatry
and certainly no weak-kneed liberal. Mapother resisted any idea of branding
everyone who broke down as a weakling. He also wanted pensions to be paid to a
small minority of 'true war neuroses'; that is, people of previous good character.

There were a number of cases [he declared] which arise solely from war service and showed
no indication of previous abnormality. Justice required that adequate provision be made
for such men. To label a man as a constitutional neurotic though you could trace no
evidence of it in his past history was unjustifiable.[24]

But how could you discourage the many from breaking down, yet compensate
the few who deserved pensions? It was the central dilemma in the handling of the
war neuroses. The solution eventually adopted in 1939, after two meetings, was
a compromise: no pensions would be paid for war-related psychoneurosis while
the war was going on but once it was over there would be a review and pensions
would be awarded to deserving cases. Service representatives at the meetings
wondered whether this was 'practical politics'; in fact, political pressure would
lead to amendments during the war.

The second area of disagreement involved selection. Here the 'psychologists'
like Myers and MacCurdy went much further in asserting the need to avoid any

...tion of 1914–18 by making sure that weak and vulnerable people never got to the front line. In theory, the necessity for such vetting of recruits to the forces had been accepted since 1922 but to implement it in practice posed many organisational and bureaucratic problems, including overcoming the opposition and inertia of the services. Nothing was done before the war came.

What did emerge from these discussions, a month into the war, was a memorandum known as 'Neurosis in War Time', which was sent to every doctor. It emphasised the need for simple, early treatment; and the importance of not letting the patient think he was seriously ill.

* * *

This overall framework, designed to prevent or discourage neurosis, set the context for the war. But policy was determined also by alliances between the British armed services and the different factions in British mental medicine. In the late 1930s, in Pall Mall clubs, over dinners in Harley Street, enquiries were made and overtures extended; eventually, marriages were consummated. There was a crude logic in these matches, each service getting into bed with the species of doctor it felt most at home with. The Royal Air Force, the most exclusive and snobbish of the services, engaged a neurologist and psychiatrist from Guy's Hospital. The Royal Navy acquired a group from St George's hospital. This left the least glamorous bride, the Army, to the struggling poor relation of psychological medicine, the Tavistock Clinic, where the old Great War traditions of psychotherapy co-existed with a mild, British version of Freud. It was run by Dr J. R. Rees. The Freudians, who held themselves apart from the psychiatric mainstream, got nothing, though they offered their services; Ernest Jones later complained that advertising men had more influence on the running of the war. But, as we shall see, one or two individual Freudians were to make important contributions.[25]

The story of the war neuroses in 1914–18 is a drama almost Aristotelian in its simplicity of character and setting. Events between 1939 and 1945 were equally dramatic but more diffuse; more like a film, made up different sequences set in different locations, collectively telling a story. The following account is not comprehensive; that would be wearisome and repetitive. Instead, it looks at some of the main themes that unfolded – attempts to choose men for the forces and the impact of new drugs and social theories on methods of treatment – within a roughly chronological narrative.

13

DUNKIRK, THE BLITZ AND THE BLUE

Don't worry if your man screams at night or throws himself down when a plane flies over the back garden.

Army advice to soldiers' wives after Dunkirk[1]

At the end of May 1940, the British Army was back in Flanders and fighting for its life. Only three weeks earlier the Wehrmacht's panzers had attacked in the Ardennes. Now the British Expeditionary Force found itself driven back to the Channel coast and a quarter of a million men were crammed into a tiny salient round the port of Dunkirk. While British and French units held up the Germans on the perimeter, the Royal Navy, together with an improvised armada of small craft, attempted to get the men off. Whenever the weather allowed, the Luftwaffe's Stuka dive-bombers would appear like angry hornets, swooping down to attack with their hideous, unnatural screams.

The town of Dunkirk was a carnival of war; a huge pall of smoke from burning oil tanks hung in the air and the streets were littered with abandoned vehicles, weapons and possessions. In the cellars, drunken British, French and Senegalese troops sang, wept, and screamed, 'the catcalls and babbling of the drunkards soon form[ing] a curious and rather sinister accompaniment to the shrieks, whistles and bangs that went on outside'. Groups of men, deserted by their officers, prowled the town in a mood of savage violence. Outside a brothel, soldiers queued patiently for service.[2]

North of Dunkirk, the beaches and dunes were crowded with tired, anxious soldiers waiting and hoping for deliverance. For many of them, the past week had been a long sleepless nightmare of exhaustion, hunger and fear: staggering like zombies along roads crammed with refugees, with the fabric of command shredding all the time. Many had seen civilians machine-gunned from the air or wounded comrades abandoned. Now, defenceless against the Stukas, some cracked under the weight of fear. One man stripped to his underclothes and proclaimed himself to be Mahatma Gandhi. Another lay flat in the sand for hours, not stirring. An officer cringed in the dunes clutching a champagne cork, a second lay paralysed with terror, his hands hovering over an imaginary basket of eggs. A soldier ran through the sand crying 'Lord have mercy on us, Christ have mercy on us!' One group of men roamed around clutching Teddy Bears, another quietly feasted with imaginary knives and forks.[3]

Long queues stretched to the water's edge and beyond, waiting for rowing boats to come and ferry them to ships. But every time a boat appeared, panic threatened to break out, with men rushing forward and grabbing the side. A major was shot dead by another officer to prevent him capsizing an already overflowing rowing boat. A corporal of the Guards kept order in his boat, filled with fear-crazed troops, by threatening to shoot the first one who disobeyed him. Every so often a German bomber would appear, machine-gunning the queues or straddling the ships out to sea with bombs.[4]

Yet, underneath it all, 'some sort of order' survived. Thanks to nine days of calm sea ('the real miracle of Dunkirk'), firm and decisive leadership by the Navy, and the interminable humdrum heroism of sailors, almost 338,000 British and French troops were brought back across the Channel. The sight of the Navy, clean, cheerful and impeccably dressed, raised spirits:

As soon as our Cockney boys met the sailors a verbal battle started and the jokes were cracked in good taste and bad language. 'Blimey chum, what about a trip round the light house?' 'Bye, bye china, where's yer little boat?' Anyway these sailors were very brave and unperturbed, they were an inspiration to us war weary stragglers.[5]

The worst cases were sedated by naval doctors. Getting on board a ship was not necessarily the end of the ordeal, however; there might well be further air attacks to contend with as well. Six destroyers and 108 other craft were sunk during the evacuation. *HMS Wakeful* went down in 15 seconds and when the old Thames paddle-steamer, *Crested Eagle*, was hit, onlookers saw 'men on fire from head to toe, dancing like dervishes, their faces contorted, leap screaming into the sea.' Some unfortunates had ships sunk from under them two or three times.[6]

The sailors at least had something to do and 'that sense of mutual support which is present in the closely knit comradeship of a ship's crew'. But, as the operation came towards its end, men who had had no sleep for sixty hours began to behave oddly. Stokers 'running amok with strain' had to be 'carried from their engine rooms laced in strait-jackets'. When the minesweeper *Hebe* was bombed on 1 June, no one on board had slept for five days and nights.

One young officer suddenly had an attack of hysterical epilepsy on the bridge. Some 30 members of the ship's company now became similarly affected with generalized [spasms] and incoherent mumbling. The Medical Officer who had to deal with these cases himself finally succumbed to this mass suggestion.[7]

These kinds of breakdowns usually took place once the ship was out of action. On *HMS Hussar*, once the mission was over, 'men became hyper-emotional and broke down and wept when given an order.' 'The legacy of psychological trauma,' says the official British naval history, 'was probably limited only by the number of men who were present.'[8]

*   *   *

Nor was morale much better when the 'miracle of Dunkirk' had been completed. As trains drew away from Dover many men threw their rifles through the windows in disgust. The theatre director Basil Dean found a pub on the south coast crammed with 'seething soldiery' from Dunkirk, 'dismayed men, savagely wounded in their pride ... seeking relief in bitter criticism of those set over them.'[9]

By the early days of June 1940, streams of patients from Dunkirk were beginning to reach hospitals near London, 'slouching along ... in tin hats and filthy uniforms'. A doctor was shocked by the numbers of men in states of 'total and abject neurotic collapse'.

What the papers termed a great British achievement seemed to us [he later wrote] nothing better than a defeated and defeatist rout. Men swarmed into the hospital, some raging mutinously at their officers for having deserted them in a panic, and others swearing that they would never fight again. So complete a loss of morale in some was scaring to witness.[10]

Many of the men were too old to be soldiers, Territorials who had joined their regiments for the sake of a summer holiday or to mollify patriotic employers. Now, numbers of them were 'suffering from acute hysteria, reactive depression, functional loss of memory or the use of their limbs, and a variety of other psychiatric symptoms'. Men arrived at a hospital in Wiltshire 'in all states'. A doctor was struck by the numbers of 'awfully poor chaps, some subnormal, poor intelligence' and noticed how easily 'the weaker, dumber ones went off into hysterical states.'[11]

Soon hospitals in the South of England were full, and patients were sent up North. At the Fazakerly hospital, Liverpool, their arrival provoked a crisis among the staff. It was clear to two young psychiatrists, John Bowlby and Kenneth Soddy, that many of the men were mentally ill, suffering from anxiety and depression brought about by 'the loss of close friends or horror at the treatment of refugees'; they needed sedation and psychotherapy. But, to their astonishment, the hospital's director William Johnson – the neurologist who had run the Army's treatment centres at Passchendaele in 1917 – refused to allow this. Psychotherapy, he told Bowlby and Soddy, had been the cause of much neurosis in the last war and he would only permit very brief treatment. The men were not ill, apart from the few who were exhausted, concussed or psychotic. What they needed, Johnson insisted, was discipline and somewhat forceful 'encouragement'; they should be sent back to their units as soon as possible.[12]

The young psychiatrists were so incensed by the way that Johnson kept referring to the patients as 'scrimshankers' that they appealed over his head to his superiors in the Emergency Medical Service. The consultant psychiatrist was unavailable, so the matter was dealt with by the Consultant Neurologist, Charles Myers' old adversary and Johnson's old boss, Dr Gordon Holmes. The years had not mellowed Holmes' manner; he came up to Liverpool, tore a strip off Bowlby and Soddy and inspected the patients, making it clear that he regarded them as cowards. For Bowlby and Soddy this was the last straw. They resigned at once from the Emergency Medical Service and joined the Army.[13]

For the second time in a generation, British doctors were confronting the effects of war on the human system, and disagreeing about how to treat them. The arguments in Liverpool – like much that followed – were shaped by wider changes in social attitudes.[14]

*   *   *

It is the logic of our times
No subject for immortal verse
That we who lived by honest dreams
Defend the bad against the worse.[15]
                    C. Day-Lewis, 1941

No one went to war in 1939 with exultant heart, full of romantic dreams. There were no crowds in the streets, no rush to volunteer. Even in Berlin the mood was subdued; memories of the past were too strong. The 'enthusiasm and easy conviction', the innocent illusions of the previous war had gone forever. This war was 'a bad job that had to be got through'.[16]

The nation going reluctantly to war in 1939 was profoundly different from that which had flocked to the recruiting offices in 1914. 'Probably at no time in [British history] had the quality of life changed so rapidly, and generally so much for the better, as in the decades between the wars,' the historian R. K. Webb has argued. The British male was now taller, better fed, and much healthier. Seventy per cent of recruits were found to be 'perfectly fit and healthy', compared to 36% in the last war. The 'immense improvement in the health and muscular development in the young men', their 'real beauty both in features and appearances' sent an elderly medical officer examining recruits in 1940 into raptures.[17]

But soldiers need mental more than physical toughness; on that score, Britain's generals were unimpressed. 'We are not anything like as tough as we were in the last war,' complained Sir Alan Brooke. 'There has been far too much luxury ... Our one idea is to look after our comforts and avoid being hurt in any way.' There was 'definitely a decrease in the spirit of pugnacity', an Australian surgeon agreed. The 'pioneer spirit of the people had evaporated', leaving a 'deplorable tendency for young men to claim as their sports bicycle-riding and lawn tennis.' The population was indeed much more urbanised and office-bound, but large numbers still earned a hard living, as labourers, miners or farmers. Many aspects of life remained primitive by modern standards – working-class women still gave birth at home, with newspaper between their teeth (to stop their cries of pain reaching the menfolk downstairs) and most dentists still extracted teeth without an anaesthetic.[18]

But life had become more precious as rising living standards brought smaller families. By the 1920s, the British birth rate was roughly half that of the 1870s and it continued to fall. Whether it brought with it a softer, more indulgent approach to child-rearing is, however, debatable. Evidence from child manuals (mainly read by the neurotic middle-class) suggests that between the wars child-rearing practices became, if anything, tougher. The heyday of the indulgent mother was just before the First World War but between the wars there was a reaction back to a more disciplined and masculine approach, associated particularly with the behaviourism of J. B. Watson and the military precision of Dr Truby King's regular feeding and harsh potty-training.[19]

Other less visible changes, for example in attitudes to authority, were equally important. Britain in 1939 maintained the structures of 1914 – monarchy, church, Army, Empire, public schools – but no longer had such tremendous sureties. At Marlborough School in the 1920s, the poet Louis MacNeice belonged to a circle of friends dominated by a boy called Anthony Blunt, with a 'precocious knowledge of art and an habitual contempt for conservative authorities'. For them, 'the only real values were aesthetic. Moral values were a delusion and politics and religion a waste of time' and 'all persons who had any religious faith were regarded as museum pieces'. 'Freud having taught my generation that sex repression is immoral, fornication had become a virtue'. 'Our generation,' MacNeice concluded, 'attached the greatest importance to personal relationships and saw the war, when it came, as "just power politics".'[20]

These views, wildly untypical even of Marlborough, represented in extreme form a wider reaction against the First World War – a shift in values away from Character, bedrock of the Victorian Public School system, towards the new gospel of Intelligence. The growing influence of the 'intelligentsia' – a term coined in 1920 in Bolshevik Russia and quickly taken up in the West – was noticed and decried by traditionalists. 'In the last thirty years,' wrote Dr Herbert Moran in 1946, 'there has been more and more a tendency to put the emphasis on intelligence. Morals, the progressive ladies and gentlemen say, morals, there are no such thing: they are simply the mores of a people for a time being.' Dr Moran disagreed. 'In warfare,' he wrote, 'character is all.'[21]

Like many of his generation and class, General Brooke attributed this new mood to the loss of 'natural leaders' on the Western Front; others, on the left, argued that the governing class had forfeited its right to lead by its incompetence and betrayal of trust during the Great War. Equally important were the political divisions and social changes between the wars: having lived through the General Strike, the 1931 crisis, mass unemployment, the Means Test and the 'Munich betrayal', conscripted soldiers of 1939 were bound to be more independent and more politically aware.[22]

There was also a strong collective sense that the working man, having given unstintingly in 1914–18, had been betrayed when the promised 'homes fit for heroes' had failed to materialise; that the governing classes had not kept their side of the bargain. One of the most disturbing things about his men, an officer in the Welsh Guards found in 1943, was their 'complete distrust of their leaders'.

They are all convinced that they will be forgotten after the war as they were after the last. I have even got to the stage of telling them the war is worth fighting even if they are completely forgotten afterwards.[23]

Patriotism and duty were still powerful forces: millions volunteered for the Home Guard in 1940, while only a few thousand registered as conscientious objectors, showing George Orwell 'how vast is the strength of traditional loyalties compared with new ones'. But this patriotism was now often conditional, qualified. 'I've done my bit. Now it's somebody else's turn' was to be a common cry. When an armoured division returned from the desert late in 1943, to prepare for the invasion of Europe, several of its senior NCOs, with 'splendid records of gallantry and devotion to duty as tank commanders', applied for 'transfer to units less likely to be in the front line again'. They were, an officer wrote, 'undoubtedly influenced by their wives from whom they had been separated for several years and who resented their husbands going into the heat of battle again, when so many others who had been in Britain all that time had not risked their lives in action.'[24]

In place of the excitement of 1914, for many the mood in 1939 was one of dread. Scarcely had the Prime Minister, Neville Chamberlain, told the nation in his reedy voice that a state of war existed, than the air-raid sirens began to sound. It seemed that the worst fears of the previous decade were being realised.[25]

The idea that 'the bomber will always get through' – that civilians were powerless against aerial bombardment – had become embedded in the popular imagination in the 1930s. First developed by military theorists like Emilio Douhet, who argued that air power offered a way of avoiding the stalemate of trench warfare, it was then fanned into a mass phobia by sensationalist books, apocalyptic movies (like Korda's version of H. G. Wells' *Things to Come*), and self-serving Air Marshals and aircraft manufacturers. It was even endorsed by major political figures and reputable scientists. Winston Churchill, in a series of speeches in 1934, painted a blood-curdling picture of what would happen if London were bombed; four years later the geneticist J. B. S. Haldane wrote an alarmist book on the subject.[26]

Doom-laden scenarios of air attack were not confined to public pundits. They also influenced secret official preparations for a coming war, which began in the late 1930s. With little past experience of bombing to go on, civil servants turned to the 1917 Zeppelin raids on London and, by misinterpreting data, came up with the formula of 50 casualties per ton of bombs dropped. Projected forward to the era of Hitler's Luftwaffe, this produced terrifying secret estimates of the death toll from aerial bombardment (35,000 per day according to one). Simply to provide coffins to bury such casualties would, the Home Office worked out, require 20 million square feet of timber; it began to draw up secret plans for mass graves and burial by lime.[27]

The aerial holocaust, it was assumed, would not only kill civilians; it would also send them mad. There would be panic and hysteria, a danger of civil disorder; the planners 'accepted almost as a matter of course that widespread neurosis and panic would ensue'. Perhaps, in forming this view, they were guided by a 'deeply ingrained contempt for the civilian masses', and a feeling that the 'proletariat were bound to crack, panic, and even go mad, lacking the courage and discipline of their masters and those regimented in the forces'; but they were also following the advice of eighteen eminent psychiatrists who privately warned in 1938 that in the coming war three psychiatric casualties could be expected for every one physical. This 'would have meant, on the basis of the Government's estimates of killed and wounded, some 3–4 million cases of acute panic, hysteria and other neurotic conditions during the first six months of air attack.'[28]

The years of 'vague, holocaustic visions' explain the extraordinary 'moral landslide' which took place in London during the Munich crisis of 1938. 'Trenches were being feverishly scratched open,' noted Wilfred Trotter. 'Many of those who could afford it were openly running away, and people of whose nerves better might have been expected confessed to an uncontrollable alarm. It was generally believed that a first-class air-raid might kill 50,000 and wound 300,000 more, that there was no real defence, and that an attack might occur at any moment.' Nor did reports from the war in Spain, suggesting that the effects of aerial bombardment had been exaggerated, allay fears. The horror of Guernica, rather than the disciplined response of the people of Madrid and Barcelona to air raids, stayed in the public imagination.[29]

When war broke out, the British authorities took prompt steps to avoid the 'impending catastrophe'. The mass of vulnerable civilians was evacuated from the cities and large psychiatric hospitals were established on the edges of major conurbations, where the expected 'trembling hordes' could be treated. Within a few weeks, some three and a half million people had left the cities of Britain, to seek refuge in the countryside, of whom about a million-and-a-half were schoolchildren or mothers with young children.

There were enormous difficulties in assimilating such numbers; country people were appalled by the filthy, verminous condition of some town-dwellers, their foul language and fondness for the pub. Slum kids were unnerved by the 'open space and the quietness', the 'privies at the end of a dark garden path'. When no bombs fell, most evacuees returned to their homes. Conceived from the best of motives, the evacuation of children was probably the single most psychologically damaging act of public policy of the war. Many children were miserably unhappy; they wet their beds, soiled their pants and were rebuked by their foster parents. One bed-wetter remembers coming home from school and being hauled into the 'front room of the house where the mattress was drying in front of the fire. The lady of the house thrust my nose into the mattress and said, "How do you like that, you little pig?"'[30]

Evacuation was quickly recognised as a mistake. 'The effects of separation from parents,' declares the 1950 edition of the standard British psychiatric textbook, 'are much more pernicious than the effects of exposure to danger.' Wartime experience eventually led to a new emphasis on not separating children from their parents, for example when entering hospital.[31]

Meanwhile, in 1939, there were no air-raids and, for almost two months, no patients – 'the hospital beds and poised psychiatrists waited, unemployed.' Then the hospitals began to fill up with 'neurotics' who had been drafted into the Army and quickly broken down. With no one else to treat, the high-powered psychiatrists soon produced a vast literature on 'neurosis' and a team at Mill Hill Hospital finally established that Effort Syndrome – the mysterious heart condition men developed in the Army – was a manifestation of fear and anxiety.[32]

On 7 September 1940, more than a year into the war, 247 German bombers carried out the first heavy raid on London, dropping over 10,000 tons of high explosive and many tons of incendiaries on the Docks and East End. They were to return to London every night until 2 November, when the attack was switched to other industrial towns. This second phase of the Blitz lasted until 16 May 1941, when the Luftwaffe began preparing for the invasion of Russia.[33]

The first air-raids produced some scenes of panic and hysteria. Celia Fremlin, an ARP warden who worked for Mass Observation, remembered the atmosphere in a street shelter in the East End of London:

At the beginning, when nobody was used to it, the women got absolutely hysterical. They were screaming and saying 'I can't stand it, I'm going to die, I can't stand it'. And there was usually one who was saying 'Calm down, calm down'. Sometimes the women would be really hysterical, crying and falling on the floor. I only once saw it as bad as that, in a shelter. The next time I went there, four nights later, they were all much calmer, they'd brought stools to sit on, and there was even a bit of community singing. Because, once you've been through three nights of bombing, you can't help feeling safe the fourth time. So the only real panic I saw was then.[34]

One important stage of the process of adjustment was the 'near miss', the close personal experience of bombing on your house, street, or neighbourhood. A young woman caught outside during a raid on 9 September 1940 remembered hearing a sound 'as if someone was scratching the sky with a broken finger nail', followed by 'the most God awful crash' and the 'earth juddering under me'. Running towards her house, it was 'as if the whole air had fallen apart, quite suddenly' and when she entered the kitchen, 'there seemed to be waves buffeting me, one after another, like bathing in a rough sea.' A bomb had hit the house and brought down the ceiling. Other people were shouting and screaming; for a time chaos reigned. Eventually neighbours appeared to help, and were appalled to find everyone 'smothered in white plaster all over and streaks of blood from the glass'. The girl was taken off and given blankets and a hot water bottle 'for the shock' and 'delayed shock'. But she did not feel shock, only exhilaration and relief, like a soldier baptised by fire.[35]

Pretty soon, though, the novelty wore off. People tried to adjust to this new way of life. Some abandoned their homes and 'trekked' towards safer places – to Epping Forest and the countryside or to the West End; about a quarter of London's population spontaneously evacuated itself. Others stayed, but devised ways of surviving. Lack of sleep, it was quickly discovered, was the worst problem and the most important priority was to create an environment in which some rest was possible. Despite the folklore, only some 4% of Londoners took refuge in the Underground, with a further 9% going to public shelters and about a quarter sleeping in their own shelters. Over half the population, though, stayed in their homes.[36]

Novels about the Blitz convey a febrile, unreal world of excitement, alcohol, and violent sexual activity, tinged with panic and horror, and behaviour a layman would describe as hysterical. The novelist Mary Wesley recalls 'an atmosphere of terror and exhilaration and parties, parties, parties,' in which 'people did things they wouldn't have done otherwise, and were frivolous as well as desperate.' This is the experience of the well-off, middle-class young. Mass Observation's diarists record a more prosaic world of 'distress and minor misery' in which people struggle to keep their underlying values and routines alive – a mother manages, after a long evening of tension and near-panic, to get her children into a shelter in a West End store; families quarrel bitterly as strain brings repressed hostilities alive.[37]

The impression is that everyone lived on their nerves and kept going by accumulating debts – to the liver, to the nervous system, to their spouses. For many, the debts began to be called in later in the war, when overwhelming weariness took over and by the time the V-Weapons arrived in 1944 many had had enough.

Quite early on – from the moment when American correspondents reported that 'London can take it' – the Blitz began to generate a self-congratulatory glow, which the government exploited cleverly in the media. The inevitable revisionist backlash against this mythology has brought a few skeletons to light and now, alongside the familiar newsreel tableaux of Londoners doggedly going to work through shattered streets and cheerful cockney camaraderie in the Underground shelters, there are darker images of frailty and wickedness. Nicholas Monsarrat recorded the first thing that firemen and rescue squads saw when they arrived at the cellar ballroom of the Café de Paris in London, after a direct hit on 8 March 1941:

As their torches poked through the gloom and the smoke and the bloody pit which had lately been the most chic cellar in London [there] was a frieze of other shadowy men, night-creatures who had scuttled within as soon as the echoes ceased, crouching over any dead or wounded woman, any soignee corpse they could find, and ripping off its necklace, or earrings or brooch: rifling its handbag, scooping up its loose change.[38]

More importantly, it is now clear that there were isolated moments of panic and short-term breakdown. Arriving in the Midlands industrial town of Coventry soon after the devastating German raid of 14 November 1940, Mass Observation's team found 'more open signs of hysteria, terror, neurosis, than during the whole of the previous two months together in all areas. Women were seen to cry, to scream, to tremble all over, to faint in the street, to attack a fireman, and so on.' The Coventry raid had come as a complete surprise and the official response had been feeble. Survivors, instead of being comforted, given soup, re-housed, or taken to hospital, were 'left to themselves'. By the evening after the German attack there was a 'feeling of utter helplessness. The tremendous impact of the previous night had left people practically speechless in many cases. And it made them feel impotent. There was no role for the civilian. Ordinary people had no idea what they should do. And this helplessness and impotence only accelerated depression. There were several signs of suppressed panic as darkness approached.'[39]

That night there was a stampede into the countryside before the Luftwaffe returned. 'If there had been another attack,' Mass Observation's Report continued, 'the effects in terms of human behaviour would have been much more striking and terrible'. But there was not another attack, at least not immediately. Coventry had a chance to recover. Five days later, industrial production was back to normal and by the end of the month, Mass Observation was noticing a return of 'purposeful demeanour'. 'Smiles and laughter were still noticeably sparse, but a thankfulness nearer to joy was quite strong. "It's a miracle anybody's still living" people said.'[40]

These signs of panic or disorder, however, do not alter the overall historical truth that – as Angus Calder was forced to admit after a sustained attempt to debunk the 'Myth of the Blitz' – 'the British were bombed and endured it.'[41]

The Blitz killed some 40,000 people, a terrifying figure but tiny when put alongside the pre-war predictions. And it did not produce an epidemic of mental illness. It soon became clear that the expected torrent of psychiatric cases was failing to appear; with monotonous regularity, doctors reported that the incidence of 'bomb neuroses' was 'astonishingly small'. Indeed there were some signs that aerial bombardment was actually improving the mental health of the population: suicides and drunkenness fell, though juvenile delinquency rose.[42]

Why were experts' predictions so hopelessly wrong? Of course the Germans' attack in 1940 was never quite the overwhelming blow dreamt of by military theorists. The Luftwaffe was not designed for serious strategic bombing and the way in which the attacks developed helped the population to come to terms with them. Hardest hit were a few provincial towns like Coventry which, without having had the opportunity to acclimatise to bombing, had the heart torn out of them in a single night, usually because fire-fighting techniques in 1940–1 had not yet learned to cope with incendiary bombs. But because the Luftwaffe did not usually return night after night they had a chance to draw breath. London's experience was quite the opposite; it was bombed 69 times over this period but its vast size and the slow build-up of attacks gave the population a chance to adjust and work out ways of coping.[43]

But if the doom-laded pre-war forecasts now seem ridiculous, some of the wartime psychiatric reports also arouse disbelief. Were there really so few cases of traumatic neurosis? Photographs of people being pulled from the rubble and reports of conditions after some raids do make one wonder whether psychiatrists, having reflected the psycho-panic of 1938, were now affected by the 'Britain can take it' mood of 1940–1. That was certainly the view of the prominent Freudian Edward Glover, who warned in 1942 that the pre-war mass neurosis myth was being replaced by 'the opposite myth that no neurotic reactions are produced by air raids, which is equally fallacious.'[44]

A closer look at the medical literature bears this out to a certain extent. 'My general impression,' wrote a psychiatrist from Coventry, 'is that the number of neurotic disturbances is considerably higher than we realise, but that the cases just do not get treatment; that is not to say that the majority of them do not make a spontaneous recovery.' After raids the emphasis was on the physical cleaning up of cities – the Coventry blitz attracted fire-fighters from all over the country, but no extra social workers were drafted in. Until 1941 the general social backup was, by modern standards, basic and inhumane and carried the grudging stigma of the old Poor Law tradition – 'to be bombed out was to be treated as if you were a pauper in the workhouse.' Secret government reports on the effects of bombing in Hull and Birmingham showed that 'having one's house demolished is most damaging to morale. People seem to mind it more than having their friends or even relatives killed.'[45]

All in all, it was not an environment that encouraged you to come forward to your doctor – let alone be referred to a psychiatric hospital – unless your symptoms were extreme. 'The chief psychiatric problem after a big raid,' according to the Coventry doctor, was in 'coping with early senile cases who had become maladjusted and mental defectives who should long ago have been institutionalised.' Meanwhile, the emphasis in the press and political speeches was on 'carrying on normally'.[46]

People were affected by the experience. There were certainly many cases of minor emotional shock – 'hysterical screaming and weeping, or trembling and incoherent speech' – that did not reach the First Aid posts and recovered in a few days when given rest, sympathy and reassurance. There were also people who seemed numbed by events and showed signs of mild depression, 'characterised by apathy, lethargy, retreat from social activities and pessimistic attitudes'.

Some persons were seen in the East End of London who, upon viewing the destruction of their homes became speechless for a time; they were unable to eat and wandered about in an aimless and apathetic way, returning every now and then to the ruins of their home or street.[47]

There were also people who kept on doing their jobs and running their families though suffering sporadic symptoms like stammering, trembling or frequent crying-spells.

Concerns about absenteeism in industry caused by neurotic illness, especially among women workers, led to the creation of a 'neurosis survey' – an official 'investigation of the extent of neurosis and allied states', which finally reported in 1946. Like most attempts to quantify the unquantifiable, it proved unable even to define what neurosis was, let alone to measure its incidence, and it became a blueprint for the psychiatric organisation needed under a National Health Service. But it did find that more than half of the directors of psychiatric out-patient clinics thought that much of the population was carrying latent neurosis that might emerge after the war.[48]

While the raids seemed to cheer a lot of people up, a number of groups who had functioned reasonably well in peacetime reacted badly to comparatively little strain. Psychiatrists became familiar with certain vulnerable types: women in their thirties in loveless marriages; menopausal women plunged into confusion or florid psychosis, like the lady who denounced her neighbours as the Gestapo; old soldiers whose dormant shell-shock was reawakened; refugees from occupied Europe, often friendless and already carrying bad memories; and, surprisingly often, men with feelings of guilt related to masturbation.[49]

Yet, the psychiatrists found, most people were very resilient and it took a situation of extreme severity or a culmination of horrors to bring on a psycho-neurosis. Firemen and emergency salvage workers might break down if unused to horrible sights, like shelters or Tube stations that had received direct hits. Air-raid victims had short-term reactions. A girl of seventeen, for example, had been in a pub when it was hit, killing everyone except herself and her epileptic friend, who had begun to fit. The patient suffered for headaches for several weeks and was then given a dose of the drug evipan, under which she described vividly the scene of horror which had precipitated her condition: 'There is a man's head under the piano – I can't see where the body is. It's horrible. I'm going mad,' she was quoted as saying. But, having got this experience out, she apparently 'recovered well'.[50]

In an effort to understand why the mass outbreak of hysterical neurosis predicted before the war had not materialised, officialdom commissioned surveys of the mental health of the British people. One answer, given by Home Intelligence during the war, was that whereas the soldier could escape by breaking down the civilian had no choice but to keep going. 'The refuges from bombing (the country and the deep shelter) are reached, not by having a breakdown, but by having sufficient determination to get there.'[51]

After the war, the sociologist Richard Titmuss put it differently: civilians were freer to adjust, better able to assert their own needs and find their own safety valves – by evacuating themselves from danger, going to a public shelter, or 'trekking' into the countryside at night, they made sure they got sleep. It was significant that both the occupation of the London Tubes as shelters and the practice of 'trekking' off to sleep in the countryside when raids were expected were spontaneous public acts, at first disapproved of then reluctantly accepted by the authorities. Soldiers would never have been allowed to 'desert their posts' in the same way. If the civilians felt happiest drinking all night in a pub or dancing in the Dorchester they could. Secondly, the war offered many people a new sense of solidarity and purpose. The unemployed now had something to do, the elderly were no longer lonely. There was a sense of common effort and sacrifice (the novelist Julian Symons remembered London in the Blitz as 'more nearly an egalitarian city than it ever has been . . . for a few months we lived in the possibility of a different kind of history'). Finally and probably most important of all, civilians were able to keep around them their family and home, their friends and community, the bastions of their emotional security.[52]

The psychiatrist T. A. Ross, on the other hand, believed that it was largely the no-nonsense approach of the doctors responsible that led to the surprising paucity of cases of neurosis.

*   *   *

Pre-war concern that German air raids might produce 'one vast raving Bedlam' among the civilian population had led the Ministry of Health to consult, on the advice of the Royal College of Physicians, two veterans of the Great War, the neurologist Dr Gordon Holmes and the psychiatrist Dr Bernard Hart.

Gordon Holmes – Charles Myers' old nemesis – was notorious for his contempt for psychotherapy and neurosis, while Hart, once the evangelist of Freud and Janet, was now a 'cynical old man' who had lost faith in psychiatry. Both shared Edward Mapother's view that in 1914–18 medical mismanagement had done as much damage as the horrors of battle. They produced an elaborate, quasi-military, pyramidal structure for evacuating casualties, and laid on courses in neurology and psychiatry for the doctors likely to be providing initial treatment which emphasised the need to 'guard constantly against the danger of prolonging the individual case and increasing the number of cases.'

Thus a paradox developed. Psychiatric policy towards civilians was being run by tough-minded veterans of the First World War, determined not in any way to encourage neurosis, whereas policy towards soldiers was run by younger, quasi-Freudian analysts from the Tavistock. The individual soldier was 'permitted to be a psychiatric casualty' but, one doctor noted sardonically, the 'non-combatant civilian is not permitted to be so diagnosed.'[53]

As a result of this approach, acute psychiatric cases from air raids were pretty briskly dealt with. At the London hospital, for example, patients

were all told that their reaction was due to fear, that that fear was one they shared with all other patients and with the first-aid workers, and that it was important that they should return to their normal work and resist the temptation to exaggerate the experiences through which they had passed.[54]

According to Dr T. A. Ross, acute cases from the Blitz

were given warmth externally and internally with hot tea. If they did not respond immediately they were given a strong sedative and kept in bed or lying on mattresses for ten or twelve hours. They were then reassured about their condition, and in almost every instance they could be sent home and back to their work in twenty-four hours.[55]

In one respect, however, Holmes and Hart got it wrong. Because – like all shell-shock doctors – they were obsessed with hysteria and 'malingering', their Ministry of Health memoranda laid great emphasis on the need to deal promptly with hysterical symptoms, in line with Great War experience, 'by showing the patient that a powerless limb is not paralysed or anaesthetic, or by making a speechless patient phonate.' This emphasis seemed to one young psychiatrist both ridiculous and inappropriate. It meant

that a terrified, tremulous and tottering patient, who has narrowly escaped death by bombing should be marched up and down to show him that his legs work still, then told to relax, pull himself together and go home. All he really needs is sleep and encouragement. Intensive symptomatic treatment has never been necessary . . . so long as amnesia is prevented and [the patients] were allowed to sleep.[56]

Tough measures seemed particularly inappropriate when it became clear that civilians were not developing hysterical conversions on anything like the scale that soldiers had during the First World War.

It has been suggested that admission to hospital is the worst thing that could happen to a patient suffering from emotional shock, as the patient comes to regard himself as an invalid and the condition as perpetuated. This has not been our experience. The patients admitted have all improved rapidly in the comparative security of hospital. They want to get well, and there is no such motive for invalidism as there was in shell-shocked soldiers in the last war. As soon as their minds are rested they recover.[57]

Official policy, however, remained unchanged.

*   *   *

For two years after Dunkirk, the only theatre of war to see much fighting was the Western Desert. 'The Blue' aroused in a few men 'awe and an inexpressible affinity'; but to most it was a hostile and alien place, a world of heat, sand, and flies.[58]

In the early days, the desert war had a romantic, addictive quality, a return, in a machine age, to the knightly duelling of the past. It was war purged of inessentials like civilians, an expression of masculine courage and sporting endeavour with operations given code-names like 'Woodcock', 'Snipe', or 'Grouse'. For the tank men, especially, there was great exhilaration in being able to operate independently and to charge enemy Panzers. But romantic indiscipline took its toll; by 1942, British tanks had been so frequently outgunned or ambushed by German 88 guns that a collective loss of nerve had descended, a reluctance to take risks.[59]

First-hand accounts of desert tank battles convey a life of stark essentials, warfare pared down to a test of will and courage in the face of exhaustion and fear. Confined in a tank most of the time, with perhaps four hours' sleep a night, living on tea, bully beef and biscuits, knowing that the Germans were better armed and led, the crew of a tank lived in intimate, shared danger for weeks at a time. 'No man could hide his fears and weaknesses for long' and, in the passions and terrors of battle, 'something of the fundamental qualities of each member of the crew was revealed to the others.' Cyril Joly, a tank commander between 1940 and 1943, found that when 'closely engaged' the 'intense concentration and the exhilaration of fear . . . made us live entirely in the moment of battle and oblivious of time.' But the strain of sustained fighting soon wore people down. Joly learned to switch off by detaching his mind and concentrating on 'thoughts of leave, or my home in Somerset, or anything else that was pleasant', while on one occasion two members of his crew 'fell to the turret floor good-naturedly wrestling with each other.'[60]

With everyone under such strain, there was little sympathy to spare for weaker brethren. Joly describes how one tank commander, gradually losing his nerve – 'almost desperate with anxiety and a fear which grew every day and fed on any incident or word' – is ignored by his colleagues, even when his wireless operator is killed in front of him. He still has 'enough pride to prevent him putting his troubles' to senior officers or doctors and keeps going till finally his tank is crippled in battle and the others hear over their radios 'the most unnerving sound of all, the wailing, uncontrolled moans and sobs which denoted [his] complete breakdown.'[61]

The sight and sound of another tank's death throes as it 'brewed up' was not something easily put behind you. For Robin Maugham watching two Cruiser tanks burning was 'the bitterest moment of my life': he had felt great affection for their commanders. Days later he 'could [still] hear the screamings of men trapped to death.' Even more awful was the decision, sometimes forced on a tank commander, to abandon his own crew, the men he had lived with so intimately, to their fiery fate inside a doomed tank; riding in the turret, he could get out and they could not. That left a nasty aftertaste and, for some, terrible incapacitating depression.[62]

There were different techniques for coping, usually involving visits to Cairo. Others made their own arrangements. The psychiatric consultant to Middle East force

came across transvestism practised by a considerable group in a unit in 1940. It could not have been entirely harmless as officers, sergeants and other ranks were involved. The military work of the unit was at a high level and there was very little drinking. The 'girls' and their partners were particularly contented people though the opportunities to dress up became increasingly difficult and this created unhappiness and irritation. The moving spirit was an officer with a splendid fighting record and the group was left alone as very few people knew of its activities which took place under the guise of 'rehearsals for a play.'[63]

As a young doctor, 'Jimmy' James had served through Loos, the Somme, Passchendaele, and the long retreat of March 1918, winning the Military Cross twice. He was a cynical, clubbable man with a taste for geopolitics and Shavian aphorism; a realist and a pragmatist among psychiatrists. Already 54 in 1940, James was not pleased to leave wife and children and return to the wars; nor to find, on arriving at the 'Army of the Nile' in September 1940, everything so depressingly familiar – the same sense of strain and lack of preparation that had existed in the last war, a painful shortage of equipment and 'lots of dummies constructed with great ingenuity and skill . . . dummies of ships, of guns, of depots and camps.' Nor was there, in all the vast area served by Middle East Force, anywhere where a soldier could be 'treated on modern lines for psychiatric breakdown', indeed Army doctors 'appeared to have no conception of breakdown in war and its treatment, though many of them had served in the 1914–18 war.'[64]

James had no administrative powers; he could only advise. But gradually he acquired the means to treat soldiers evacuated from the desert back to the Nile delta. His methods were simplicity itself, summarised by the text: 'Fluid, food, sleep, and stool', a recognition of the fact that 'men who broke down in battle came down to their distant psychiatric centres dehydrated, remarkably constipated and very often sleepless.' The first psychiatric hospital was opened in 1942 but it was only in the summer of that year – just before Alamein – that specialist psychiatric help was available at the front. Until then it was down to the ordinary doctors.[65]

Only about 35% of psychiatric casualties were the result of battle. Perhaps in the competitive masculine world described by Joly and other writers, it took a brave man indeed to take his 'troubles' to the doctor. Perhaps, as Dr James thought, the pared-down intensity of desert warfare – the absence of physical obstacles or civilians to get in the way – made it less destructive psychologically. The tank engagements themselves were usually quite short and most of the troops of very high morale; given a little sedation and rest at the front or a chance to tear up Cairo on leave, they were usually once more raring to go.[66]

The incidence of breakdown, James found, was much higher among support troops, the vast 'tail' which serviced a modern army's fighting 'head'. Driving great distances in the desert, frequently dive-bombed by the Luftwaffe, yet without the pride and exhilaration of the fighting troops, they tended to crack sooner. They were also more vulnerable to the particular pressures of the desert in 1940–1 – the lack of news from home and the worry that relatives were being bombed. The 'tail' was also more likely to contain the 'useless and ill-trained men', who, it sometimes seemed, were deliberately sent to the Middle East by the authorities at home.[67]

British fortunes ebbed and flowed several times during the desert war – from the exhilarating defeat of the Italians in 1940, to the disasters and distractions of 1941 and the long, desperate defence of Egypt against Rommel that culminated in the Alamein battles. Visiting the troops in July 1941, James found 'more frequently than before evidence of battle nerves . . . men would show tremors or a stammer or comrades would tell of disturbed nights, of shouting during sleep, sometimes even of attacks on others in a somnambulistic state. Yet, as a rule, men would object to leaving their units and going into hospital.' A year later, after the very hard fighting around the Knightsbridge 'Box' which preceded the withdrawal to the Alamein line, he felt that the 'war-torn soldier' was becoming a considerable anxiety. The men, he reported, had 'got tired of fighting', become 'somewhat apprehensive of the German power and leadership' and were 'fed up' with the desert. Montgomery's great achievement was somehow to lift them at this point.[68]

There were, James felt, very definite limits to what soldiers could take. Troops subjected to 'dive bombing or other disliked enemy action' would crack after four or five days. Officers and NCOs should not do more than a year in unrelieved operational work; men could probably manage two years. At the same time, he constantly emphasised the part played in the desert by physical factors and by morale. After examining some fifty psychiatric casualties in July 1942 he found that most of them just needed rest. Henceforward, the standard psychiatric diagnosis was 'physical exhaustion' rather than the old 'NYDN', unless more serious problems were found. James also agitated to improve the rather basic amenities for British soldiers in the desert, especially the mail from home.[69]

Perhaps the worst cases James came across were among Royal Engineers who had to clear the minefields before the Battle of Alamein. Although they had been thoroughly trained, and had rehearsed their technique a few nights before – picking up bully tins buried in the ground by other Engineers – it was a shock when, on the morning of 23 October 1942, they were called together and addressed by an officer:

Well, lads tonight at 9.45 pm you Sappers are going to open the minefields that Jerry has laid, and you won't find any bully tins there. In fact, I know I'm speaking to young men only about 20 or 21 years old, but I have to give it to you straight: right behind you is a whole division relying on you Sappers to open the lanes for the tanks and infantry to pass through. Also behind you are a thousand guns. They will put up a terrific barrage as you Sappers go in. Some of you will be killed, or lose an arm or leg, because Jerry will be trying to stop you. There will be mortaring, Stuka dive bombing and the rest.[70]

The listeners were, therefore, well aware of the danger. One remembers, 'I must have smoked about twenty cigarettes in about ten minutes. I was shaking, saying my prayers and wishing it was only a dream.' By this stage of the war, an electronic detector had been invented which reliably picked out the German 'teller' and 'S' mines, though some units also used the old technique of probing with a bayonet. If anything, the detector required even more courage, for the sapper had to stand upright, 'moving the detector arm backwards and forwards over the desert surface, listening for the whining noise that located the buried mine.' The 'rottenest job', however, was actually lifting the mine out, 'because of the booby-traps that were fitted or the cunning anti-handling devices.' Because of the strain, they worked in half-hour shifts: 'any longer than that and we lost our concentration and became careless.'[71]

General Montgomery's assumption that the Engineers would be able to clear a narrow corridor of eight feet through the minefield at the rate of 100 yards per three minutes proved completely unrealistic: 'for hour after hour the work went on. The teams were relieved at half-hourly intervals and many of the mentally exhausted Engineers lay where they were and fell instantly asleep, oblivious to the gunfire, the bombs and the bullets.'[72]

'Sapper A' saw his closest pal blown up by a mine. He collapsed and was evacuated, unable to speak, to a psychiatric centre. From there, he was transferred to the psychiatric hospital in Cairo for narcosis treatment, 'tremulous, dazed, tearful, show[ing] the startle reflex'. Most of the patients there 'had severe battle dreams and were restless and inclined to scream in their sleep.'[73]

In ten days, though, they were symptom free and anxious to return to their units, which was not permitted. Sapper A was in hospital for 28 days, at a convalescent home in Palestine for 21 days and then returned to Eighth Army. He fought in Sicily and Italy. By 1946, living with his wife and two children in one room in a London suburb, he sent his wife (who had been very shaken by bombing) to see Dr James. She reported that he was 'well employed but inclined to rush out of doors when the children are noisy.'[74]

'WE CAN SAVE THOSE BOYS FROM HORROR'

There is no accurate method of forecasting who will break under prolonged physical and mental strain.

J. R. Rees, 24 November 1942[1]

If there was one lesson British doctors took away from their experiences in the Great War, it was the need for 'selection'. There must not, in any future war, be a repeat of the chaotic scenes and 'indiscriminate enrolment' in 1914. Vulnerable people like 'misfits' and 'congenital defectives' must be kept away from the battlefield by 'efficient examination of recruits'.

However, when it came to putting this aspiration into practice, problems at once arose. What criteria should be used to assess whether a man had what it took to be a soldier? Should an Army officer, a military doctor or a civilian psychologist make the judgement? These questions, posed but not answered by the Shell-shock Committee in 1922, hung in the air for two decades. Apart from a brief experiment with testing in the 1920s, the British Army made little attempt to address them. 'Physical fitness,' the consultant physician said in 1936, 'should be a good guide.' When Dr J. R. Rees of the Tavistock Clinic proposed early in 1939 that the Army introduce into its recruitment procedures some of the psychological tests then being developed in industry, the idea was rejected.[2]

As a result, for the first two years of the war no systematic attempt was made to screen recruits to the British Army. The medical examination, carried out by civilian Medical Boards working for the Ministry of Labour, was much more thorough than the farcical procedures of 1914. But there still wasn't the time – 'at most 6½ minutes' – to give each candidate much more than the standard checks and to take his medical history. The doctors on the Boards, who were often elderly, patriotically-minded GPs, tended to give the Army the benefit of the doubt, weeding out obviously mentally unstable recruits but paying no great attention to intelligence. Like most of their generation, they believed that 'men who were a bit slow, but well-muscled and fit' were 'just the stuff for the Army'. A considerable number of what were then called 'dullards' – men with an IQ of between 70 and 90 – were let in.[3]

In the Great War, many soldiers had passed through training and come under fire before their inadequacy became apparent, often when they developed hysterical symptoms. Two different issues had thus been jumbled up together and never really separated – the relationship between stress and mental disorder and that between mental deficiency and mental disorder. In Hitler's war, the long lulls in fighting made it much easier to eliminate those who were struggling before they were sent into battle. Just being in the Army, without fighting at all – 'mooching disconsolately around training camps and air bases, shuttling to and fro on leave in ... cumbrous equipment in cold, ill lit, overcrowded trains, crowding into dance halls at week-ends' – was enough to send many men 'off their heads'. By 1941, psychiatrists were treating thousand of 'neurotics in the forces'. 'Many more [soldiers],' the *Lancet* complained, 'have broken down with neurotic disorders under the trivial strains of army life and separation from the family than under the stresses of violent action.' Thirteen hundred psychoneurotics a month were being discharged from the Army; many more were being dumped on other units by their officers, or sent to the Western Desert or Singapore.[4]

The British response to this problem emerged from an alliance forged between elements in the Army and psychiatrists from the Tavistock Clinic.

The Army, reeling from Dunkirk, was desperate to show critics like the *Daily Mirror* that it was no longer blimpish, chinless, class-bound, incompetent and stupid. The Tavistock psychiatrists brought to the war effort the convictions of the intellectual left, above all the belief in a modern, meritocratic democracy. Their partnership was largely based on the relationship that developed in Leeds in 1940 between Ronald Hargreaves, a sharp and self-confident researcher at the Tavistock, and General Sir Ronald Adam, a highly competent artilleryman who had commanded a Corps at Dunkirk.[5]

Intelligence testing was the instrument that both solved the Army's manpower problems and gave it a more democratic sheen. Ronald Hargreaves first used testing – on his own initiative and at his own expense – to eliminate 'unsuitable and inadequate men' whom research showed to be much more inclined to pose disciplinary problems, to desert, and to have high rates of venereal disease. He quickly established that, of the tests developed by psychologists before the war, one called Progressive Matrices worked best under Army conditions and gave a reasonably reliable quick test of intelligence. Hearing of Hargreaves' work, General Adam demanded to be shown the test and, to the psychiatrists' amazement, did the '40-minute version' in 12 minutes and 'got every one right'.[6]

The attraction of Progressive Matrices was that it used science to repair the injustices of the British education system: it tested not scholastic knowledge or acquired skill, but creative mental activity, 'the rate and clearness with which a person was able to learn from his immediate experiences'. A soldier would be shown a design with part of it left out and then be asked to choose, from a group of alternatives below, a piece which completed it. A series of designs followed, each presenting a 'matrix of relations from which it is possible to deduce the nature of the missing figure'. In all there would be perhaps 60 such problems.[7]

When in 1941 General Adam became Adjutant-General to the Forces, responsible for all questions of medicine and morale, Tavistock psychiatrists like J. R. Rees and Ronald Hargreaves became, in effect, psychological consultants to the Army. To the fury of their medical rivals, they established a medical division of their own in Whitehall, 'AMD11', advising on a range of issues that went well beyond usual definitions of psychiatry. From this secure power base, they were able to make numerous bold policy initiatives – and enemies.[8]

Adam and Hargreaves shared a vision of 'personnel selection' that went beyond weeding out 'dullards' and 'misfits'. They were out to create a new kind of Army altogether: mechanised, technocratic and specialised, an aspiration widely shared at the time. The panzer crews of the Wehrmacht carving their way across Europe had been 'carefully hand picked' 'by 200 fully-trained Army psychiatrists'. The Luftwaffe, spreading terror from the skies, owed its sudden revival, it was thought, to the skill with which its personnel were selected. Highly-trained parachute troops, 'heavily drugged, fearless and beserk', were taking out key objectives behind the lines. War now seemed to involve brains and special technical skills as much as brawn and physical fitness.[9]

Much of this was exaggerated. Many of the instruments of blitzkrieg – tanks, Stukas, and parachutists – would later prove militarily very vulnerable; nor were the Germans' methods of selection as 'scientific' as they first appeared. But in 1940 they combined to provide an extraordinary psychological coup. The British, having just managed to escape this scorching flame, were shocked into a mentality of self-conscious toughness which the psychiatrists faithfully mirrored, determined, like the smart young officer in Michael Powell's film *Life and Death of Colonel Blimp*, to sweep aside the old fustian ways of the Army and force it to become modern. Intelligence was the weapon with which they would do it. The long-standing problem of how to predict who would break in battle was therefore obscured by the new drive to create an intelligent army.

After June 1942, all recruits to the British Army were given intelligence and aptitude tests during their six weeks of basic training, and assigned accordingly to one of the seven categories into which Army jobs had been classified – Driving, Mechanical Maintenance, Signalling, Practical and Constructional, Clerical, Storeman, General Combatant and Labouring. There were to be no more square pegs in round holes, in theory, anyway. The system even became computerised in a rudimentary way, with each candidate's details being punched on a card and fed into an electromechanical device known as a Hollerith machine, from which information could be retrieved. The 'dramatic moment when we gathered round and saw it begin rapidly to print out lists of men' symbolised, for the psychiatrists, the triumph of modern rationality over old school ties. For traditionalists like Evelyn Waugh, however, this 'Electronic Personnel Selector' embodied all they hated about the war: 'We don't have any electronic personnel' a character in *Sword of Honour* remarks sarcastically.[10]

Of course there was a political sub-text to this exercise. Modern-minded, leftward-leaning psychiatrists took a certain pleasure in getting the Army to alter its old class-ridden ways in 'identifying young men whose high innate intelligence had been concealed by poor upbringing or lack of educational opportunities'. But the shrewder of the Tavistock group learnt to tread warily. Ronald Hargreaves flattered obstructive generals by quoting from Fortescue's mighty *History of the British Army*; John Bowlby managed tactfully to persuade a cavalry regiment belatedly converting to tanks that they could not 'afford the risk of retaining hard-working and pleasant dullards' arguing that 'one really couldn't expect' a man who scored below 43 on the Raven's matrices to be 'an effective gunner or trainer or wireless operator'. But on one occasion Wilfred Bion, the most abrasive and complex of the Tavistock group (and a former tank officer himself), was driven to ask a cavalry officer if his regiment 'having lost its horses, was now unwilling to lose its other dumb friends.'[11]

Personnel Selection did have its detractors. One doctor ridiculed the 'reliance placed on aptitude tests carried out in numbers of a hundred, often under the control of NCOs, half-baked in their knowledge even of the most elementary procedures.' A more important objection was that it assumed 'that the war would always be fought by modern, mechanised forces. Accordingly, personnel selection officers channelled the most qualified men to armoured, gunner and other specialist corps, leaving the infantry too often as the depository of the less educated, the less motivated and sometimes even the less physically fit'. When, however, terrain and logistics dictated that a campaign be fought mainly by the infantry – as they did in Italy – this could cause problems.[12]

Personnel Selection performed one vital function: it kept 'dull men' out of harm's way. Ideally, they should have been discharged from the Army altogether, but the chronic manpower shortage made this difficult. Instead many were sent to the new Pioneer Corps to do the labouring jobs that had been such a trial to the fighting soldier in the Great War; the conventional wisdom was that 'the worst soldiers were often the best diggers'. The Pioneers tended to be a dustbin for criminals and malingerers, but, if 'dullards' were to stay in the Army, it was the obvious place for them; unarmed companies of Pioneers were made up from men 'incapable of absorbing Army training at the speed at which wartime pressures demanded and who therefore were not equipped with lethal weapons.' There is some evidence that 'living and working together with men of like capability' and with some special assistance, they adjusted better to the Army environment, but, the psychiatrists realised, it was not a satisfactory solution. Pioneer units continued to give more than their share of trouble. But at least these men were not exposed to battle.[13]

At the same time the psychiatrists were involved in another campaign, over the selection of officers.

When R. C. Sherriff, the future author of *Journey's End* and *The Dam Busters*, volunteered for the British Army in 1914, he was rejected out of hand as a potential officer on the grounds that he had not attended a public (i.e. private) school. At the time, Sherriff found his treatment humiliating and unfair, but when he came to recall this incident in the 1960s, he could see 'common sense and reason' behind it. The easiest way for the Army, in the face of desperate emergency, to create a new, cohesive officer class overnight, was to accept only those who already shared its set of values. A generation later, facing once more the problem of expanding the officer class, the Army could not revert to the nakedly class-prejudiced procedures of 1914. Instead, it came up with a variant more suited to the spirit of the times. Would-be officers now had to start off in the ranks, and if they caught the eye of the commanding officer of their unit, they would then be given a brief and not particularly searching interview by three officers.[14]

By 1941, this system seemed to be breaking down. Alarming numbers of officer cadets were failing to complete their training, and able people seemed reluctant to come forward. The general view was that army interviewers, having exhausted the pool of talent in their own class, 'found themselves rather at sea' with candidates 'whose personality and background were quite alien', and were giving commissions to articulate but unsuitable middle-class candidates like Evelyn Waugh and Randolph Churchill, while denying worthier men of working-class origin.[15]

Something had to be done. General Adam commissioned a small group of psychologists and psychiatrists – working with regular Army officers – to come up with an alternative. They began by looking at records of the Wehrmacht's procedures and tests, obtained from American attachés in Berlin or captured in the desert. Judging from their performance in the war, all agreed the Germans certainly knew how to pick an officer.

The Germans had had no choice. The Treaty of Versailles, by limiting the size of their army, had forced them to think hard about how best to choose officers. Back in the 1920s they had begun using psychologists on a considerable scale to devise ways of finding the right material, their approach differing in important ways from those developed by industrial psychologists in Britain and America. German psychologists believed that it was not enough simply to analyse the job, identify the abilities, character traits and temperament it required, and then devise tests to pick out men with those particular qualities. That was to disrupt the 'total personality' of the candidate, which was what they believed counted in an officer. Instead, what was needed were situations in which the candidate's behaviour could be observed and a 'holistic' appraisal of his suitability made. In short, they 'recognised that the assessment of character was difficult but had to be attempted'.[16]

To that end they devised a battery of new test situations, what J. R. Rees called 'elaborate, thoroughly teutonic tests of personality'. Some certainly lent them-selves to mockery, such as the test in which the recruit had to pull a strong metal spring as hard as he could, sending an increasingly powerful electric current through his body, while a hidden camera recorded his facial expression. But others of their innovations, such as the Command Task (*Führerprobe*) and Leaderless Group Discussion (*Rundgespräch*) were to have huge influence on the armies of post-war Europe.[17]

The British rejected the German tests as too ponderous and mechanistic for their army, but tried to come up with their own 'holistic' methods. A group of serving officers were examined and an experimental Officer Selection Board set up. The most celebrated innovation was the 'Leaderless Group', devised by the psychiatrist Wilfred Bion as a way of bringing together the diverse selection procedures of military officers and the 'technical side' (the psychologists and psychiatrists). Candidates were given a task – such as building a bridge over a river; or escaping from a POW camp – to do as a group, under the observation of all the Board personnel. Bion had won the DSO and Legion D'Honneur as an 'overgrown schoolboy of 19' and knew from experience that a wartime officer needed a 'capacity for maintaining personal relationships in a situation of strain that tempted him to disregard the interest of his fellows for the sake of his own.' Trying to build a bridge across a stream might lack the full emotional tension of battle, but in the context of the Board would be stressful enough to test 'the quality of the man's relationship with his fellows'. The important thing was not how well a group did any given task, but the way in which a man's capacity for personal relationships stood up to the strains.[18]

Leaderless Groups, the military historian Shelford Bidwell has argued, did as much to win the war as the invention of the Bailey Bridge; the procedure is still in use in the British Army today. Psychologists, though, regard 'the exercise as to a large extent a diversion which could be used to keep their uniformed colleagues busy while the psychologists got down to the real business of assessment using tests and interview.' The Leaderless Group procedure did have what psychologists call 'face validity': those who took part in it could see the point of it. It aroused considerable enthusiasm in officers who witnessed it in Scotland in 1941, and did much to gain military approval for the new War Office Selection Board (WOSB) procedure introduced by the Adjutant-General in 1942. Over three days officer candidates underwent three intelligence tests, three 'personality tests' and three 'military tests' of which the leaderless group was one. The board was presided over by a Regular officer, but contained a psychiatrist and a psychologist.[19]

Interviewed in 1990, John Bowlby was adamant that these new procedures had completely restored soldiers' faith in selection and identified 'a hell of a lot of officers', especially among sergeants in the Territorials. They also enabled the Army finally to shake off the charge of being Blimpish and class-based and contributed to the increasing professionalism of the Army by the end of the war.[20]

But the new methods were not universally popular. The idea that psychiatrists – specialists in the study of abnormal mental behaviour, many with no experience of war – should help determine a man's suitability to be an officer touched a deep nerve in the British Army. Personality testing was a particular source of ridicule. At first, the British experimented with the 'ink-blot' test devised by the Swiss psychiatrist, Hermann Rorschach – a *projective* technique, intended to stimulate the candidate into revealing something of himself and his latent emotional state. But to the 1940s' English male interpreting a grown man's response to inkblot patterns seemed plain daft – an act of Middle-European absurdity, on a par with kindergartens, Rudolf Steiner, herbal teas, and foreign plumbing. The Rorschach test was quickly dropped.[21]

Instead, the psychologists persevered with two other personality tests, strikingly different from those of the Germans. Word Association Tests, first devised by C. J. Jung, rest on the theory that 'if a person is given a word and told to reply with the first thought that comes into his head, it is possible to tap the "unconscious level"', and get 'valuable clues to personality'. Candidates were shown a series of cards in rapid succession, each with a word on it, and asked to write down their immediate reactions. The 'answers to certain key words such as Mother, Afraid, Home, Worry' enabled the psychiatrist to 'distinguish the anxious, spoiled, homesick youth from the stable, well-balanced man'. Significance was also attached to words capable of being interpreted both in a 'war or non-war sense' – Butt, Barrel, Desert, Arm, Front – 'the man with drive who is war-minded tend[ing] to seize on the military meaning and reject the other.'[22]

In Thematic Apperception Tests, 'candidates were shown certain pictures and invited to write a three-minute story about each picture, the theory being that they would 'expose unwittingly their own relations with their home'. Thus, the reaction to a slide showing 'an elderly woman standing with her back turned to a young man who is fingering his hat, both of them looking depressed, would reveal whether there was still parental dependence or whether the subject was independent'. According to one psychiatrist

If all the stories end happily, with the hero overcoming his difficulties, it is likely that the writer is well balanced and energetic. On the other hand where the hero is helpless, victim of circumstances and passive, there is a strong suspicion that the writer himself is an ineffectual person with little drive.[23]

Intelligent candidates did their best to subvert these procedures – many 'arrived with ready-made stories to fit the pictures'. The playwright Peter Ustinov, noticing that one of the 'pictures of a vaguely troubled nature' flashed on a screen in front of him depicted a Goyaesque scene of a man leaving a besieged city, suggested:

This is perhaps a Spanish insurgent contained in the fastness of Zaragoza during the Peninsular War, making good his escape with some vital information from General Palafox to the advancing troops of Sir Arthur Wellesley.[24]

His paper was returned with the words 'This is perhaps' 'under-lined with no less than three red pencil marks, accompanied by the single word "indecision".' Ustinov failed to become an officer.

Most controversial aspect of all, however, was the psychiatric interview, originally given to all candidates, then, because of staff shortages, to those whose 'personality pointer' had raised doubts. The psychiatrists saw this as 'the heart of the sandwich' – their chance to provide a real counterweight to the judgements of the military and to clear up anything dubious which had emerged in the tests. They alone, they argued, were trained to spot certain unsuitable types – 'the anxious and worrying', the 'schizoid', the 'hypomanic', the obsessive self-driver – not just the mentally unstable but also 'those who habitually evade their difficulties', 'the selfish individual who would spare no thought for the welfare of his men', 'the aloof, solitary, isolated man', 'the feeble ineffective individual'. They could 'see through the bluster of the showman and the bully'.[25]

The psychiatrists' approach was, of course, based on assumptions derived from their epoch and culture about what made a successful officer: he had to be emotionally mature, intelligent, adaptable, and generous to his men, with a MATCOP (a mature co-operative or objective personality) rather than a IMAG (immature-aggressive personality) or an IMDEP (immature-dependent personality). These assumptions are open to reasoned objection. The most notable problem was, as one psychiatrist conceded after the war, that there was 'no adequate test of courage'. But objections arose for much simpler reasons: candidates were being asked about sex. 'Have you ever had a woman?' was the third question one remembers being asked. This was inevitable if a candidate's emotional maturity was to be tested, but some psychiatrists evidently did so over-enthusiastically or tactlessly, violating a social taboo still very strong in the 1940s. At the same time, many senior officers disagreed with their judgement and felt worthy candidates had been wrongly excluded; relatives of important people were grilled too hard or turned down. Stories began to circulate, and were seized on by the psychiatrists' enemies, prominent medical figures like Lord Horder and the Prime Minister's physician, Lord Moran.[26]

In June 1942, the War Cabinet discussed the matter and decided that 'there might be a tendency to use the psycho-analytic tendency too extensively [which] . . . if unwisely handled . . . might encourage the very tendencies it was hoped to combat.' The Lord Privy Seal, Sir Stafford Cripps, was asked to look into the matter. Intense manoeuvring in Whitehall followed. Cripps, newly back from a mission to India and busy with other matters, suggested that the situation be assessed by an 'independent medical man'. General Adam, rightly suspecting that this might prove to be Lord Moran, who, far from being independent, was 'certainly completely biased' against the psychiatrists, slyly suggested that Cripps should instead 'ma[k]e up his own mind about the situation,' adding tactfully, 'We are all sceptics about psychiatry and have only adopted any particular methods after great trial and experiment.'[27]

This proved a masterstroke. 'A brilliant barrister of unstable outlook', Cripps came from the same pious, idealist, high-minded background as many of the psychiatrists. 'By temperament Cripps had always been both a technician and a moralist'; he 'loved expertise of almost every kind: political, social, economic'; and had campaigned throughout 1942 for a more 'scientific' and 'modern' approach to the war. Persuaded to visit a War Office Selection Board, he was at once fascinated by the work being done there, ate in the mess with candidates and staff – 'since he was a vegetarian, special quantities of carrots were provided for his meals' – and 'participated fully in a group'. At the end of his three days, Cripps declared himself 'completely satisfied and . . . surprised at what he had learned.' His subsequent report concluded that 'there was no substance in the criticisms . . . made of psychiatrists and psychologists in the Army', but suggested that steps be taken to co-ordinate their work.[28]

This posed a new threat. An Expert Committee was to be set up, giving the psychiatrists' medical enemies a fresh opportunity. 'I view this committee with the greatest gloom,' wrote General Adam. 'The whole of the psychologists are up in arms as they consider this an attempt to place psychology under the doctors.' Who would sit on the Committee? Adam warned against some of the suggested names. The Cambridge psychologist F. C. Bartlett was 'regarded with the greatest suspicion by all the services'; Dr Aubrey Lewis of the Maudsley was 'the great rival of our consultant in psychology, Colonel Rees'. After hard lobbying, the committee was suitably packed with friendly figures and its report – published secretly in 1943 – proved anodyne and uncontroversial.[29]

Then another threat appeared. Soon after Alamein, his position now secure, Churchill ejected from the War Cabinet that thorn in his side, Sir Stafford Cripps, who became Minister of Aircraft Production and gave up responsibility for the work of service psychiatrists. Churchill took the opportunity to lash out angrily at them. 'I am sure,' he wrote, in a long memorandum to Cripps' replacement in December 1942,

. . . it would be sensible to restrict as much as possible the work of these gentlemen, who are capable of doing an immense amount of harm with what may very easily degenerate into charlatanry. The tightest hand should be kept over them and they should not be allowed to quarter themselves upon the Fighting services at the public expense. There are, no doubt, easily recognizable cases which may benefit from treatment of this kind, but it is very wrong to disturb large numbers of healthy, normal men and women by asking the kind of odd questions in which the psychiatrists specialise. There are quite enough hangers-on and camp followers already.[30]

As this paper circulated in Whitehall, 'gloom and utter despair' settled on the psychiatrists. The inevitable clampdown came in April 1943 when Grigg, the Secretary of State for War, took steps to 'review and limit' the 'somewhat dominating position which psychiatric examination had attained in the Army selection machinery'. Thereafter, the psychiatrists only examined such officer candidates if they were referred to them and anyone rejected on psychiatric advice had the right of appeal. But Churchill's attempt to banish General Adam to Gibraltar in January 1944 was, fortunately for the psychiatrists, vetoed by Adam's friend, the Chief of the Imperial General Staff, Sir Alan Brooke. Adam remained in post till the end of the war.[31]

* * *

Ironically, while all this effort went into choosing potential soldiers, the people doing most of the fighting were not selected at all; they were volunteers.

Frogmen, parachutists, commandos, rangers, chindits, marauders, irregulars, guerrillas: the years between 1940 and 1944 were the heyday of 'special forces', irregular units operating in small groups, carrying out 'deep penetration' behind enemy lines; and of clandestine, 'cloak and dagger' units with mysterious acronyms – SOE, SIS, OSS and so on.

These organisations needed men (and sometimes women) of exceptional courage, character, and physical fortitude. They might therefore have been expected to use meticulous psychological testing in selecting personnel. Yet very few did, most preferring to recruit through patronage and social networks. One obvious reason for this was the need for secrecy. Another was that many of these organisations – in a way which belied talk of modern warfare and harked back to the trained bands and privateering ships of the past – derived their existence and character from the personality, initiative or social connections of a single charismatic individual. Colonel John Durnford-Slater, for example, 'raised' No. 3 Commando 'to go raiding' as a way of 'getting back to something not unlike pig-sticking' which he had known and loved in India; Lieutenant David Stirling, 'still to all appearances an unremarkable subaltern of twenty-five', managed to persuade General Auchinleck to set up the Special Air Service brigade to disrupt German communications in the desert. Two friends of John Verney's 'formed a small hush-hush unit, a private army of their own, in which they wore odd clothes, lived at GHQ's expense at a Cairo hotel, and disappeared for a few nights every now and again by aeroplane or submarine to the Greek islands.' It was natural for such leaders to surround themselves with their social acquaintances, the extreme example being No. 8 Commando, whose officers mostly came from White's Club and the Brigade of Guards and included at least three members of the peerage.[32]

Motives for joining the 'special shows' varied from boredom, rejection in love or a thirst for adventure to a simple adolescent wish to break the rules. In its early days, SAS was dominated by Paddy Mayne, a 'large and formidable Ulsterman', who 'possessed a total disregard of danger and a genuine love of fighting for fighting's sake which can rarely have been equalled.' He was believed to have destroyed over a hundred enemy aircraft on the ground 'with his own hands' in a year. By contrast, John Verney, an artist in civilian life, hoped to find in such a unit 'a pleasant, if hazardous, solution to the problem of being a soldier . . . the war without the Army.'

Officers normally volunteered, and were interviewed, without quite knowing what lay ahead. The initial interview was 'a formula of circumlocution', which made its way into cinematic cliché.

'I can't tell you what you've come here for,' said Colonel Guy Tamplin [of the SOE] to one captain, 'except to say that it's very secret and it involves a good deal of danger and isolation. If on reflection, you have second thoughts, nobody will think the worse of you, and you can go back to the regiment as if nothing had happened.[33]

The British tended to operate their usual double standards towards special forces:

while 'eccentrics might make good officers in this sort of unit', the men had to be 'first-class soldiers by ordinary standards'. Early in the war, such material was quite easy to come by – Commando recruits in June 1940 were 'well-trained, keen, professional soldiers in the prime of life. They knew their weapons, had seen some fighting and wanted more.' Similarly, in the early days of the SAS, 'every man in the unit had been picked by [Stirling] personally.' Later on, however, it was not so easy to skim off the cream, for 'commanding officers grew cunning and learned to keep back their volunteers or to clear their prisons.' For his first Chindit expedition, in 1942–3, GHQ Delhi gave Orde Wingate a mixture of Gurkhas, men of the Burma Rifles and a battalion of the King's Liverpool regiment, mostly in their thirties, 'which had been deployed on coastal defence duties in Britain before being sent to India.' Wingate was 'appalled' by their 'low standard' and 'almost complete absence of esprit de corps'. Many had low medical categories and 'showed a marked lack of enthusiasm' for the task in hand, a far cry from the elite volunteers requested originally by Wingate.[34]

* * *

If the British only turned to personnel selection reluctantly and in the face of the obvious failure of existing procedures, the Americans had the opposite experience. They began the war with a strong faith in the value of pre-selection and finished it with doubts about the worth of any selection.[35]

The starting point, as in Britain, was an awareness of the cost of past mistakes. Between the wars, the United States government had spent almost a billion dollars on the psychiatric problems of veterans, and nearly $42m in the year 1940 alone. Every psychiatric casualty, it was estimated, had cost the taxpayer some $30,000.[36]

Could you, American medical opinion began asking in 1940, avoid paying such a bill again by screening Army recruits? Some argued that the potential psychiatric casualty could be identified in advance, provided the interviewer was given adequate time (about 15 minutes each) to assess him and enough background information on his case. Others doubted whether you could predict a man's behaviour in battle. 'I should hesitate to offer any criteria that can be used to predict that a given candidate will have a traumatic neurosis,' wrote Abram Kardiner, who probably had as much experience of the aftermath of war as anyone in America; indeed, he had found that war sometimes helped severely neurotic people to get better. He would therefore only rule out men with a history of fits, stammering and other nervous disorders.[37]

The negative voice of experience is often at a disadvantage against the siren voice of hope. So it proved on this occasion. The more ambitious approach carried the day in Washington and Dr Harry Stack Sullivan was made psychiatric consultant to the draft, instituted in November 1940.

It was an interesting appointment. Sullivan was the *enfant terrible* of American psychiatry, a man whose career had been based on ambitious innovation and impractical dreams. 'Passionate, immature, and emotionally confused', homosexual, a socialist with a taste for wild extravagance and a history of break-downs and financial embarrassments, Sullivan had won a national reputation with the 'ward milieu program' he initiated with male schizophrenics at the Sheppard hospital, Baltimore. This had laid emphasis not on interviews to explore the past life of the patient, nor on research into the biological origins of his condition, but on 'interpersonal' relations; a regime in which trained hospital staff gradually created healthy patterns of thinking and feeling in the patient. In Washington in the 1930s, Sullivan had pioneered collaboration between psychiatrists and social scientists, believing that medicine could no longer remain politically uncommitted or ignore the obvious connection (first noticed by Freudians like Wilhelm Reich) between the problems of the individual per-sonality and political movements like Fascism, which fed on fear and paranoia. His concern about events in Europe led him, while many of his colleagues were still oblivious or isolationist, to think hard about how America was to be mobilised for war.[38]

Professional ambition played a part in this: Sullivan and his collaborators saw a way of finally establishing, after the ambiguous experience in 1917–18, that psychiatrists had a 'scientific ability to predict mental breakdown'. But his ambitious, humanitarian vision of an Army containing only young men who would not be 'broken down by *any* [italics added] strains or stresses' also appealed to politicians trying to persuade a sceptical and isolationist nation that the United States should once again involve itself in Europe's wars. For example, the powerful Mayor of New York, Fiorello la Guardia, told Senators in July 1940 that medical science could now 'easily discover' the 'boy that just cannot face it'.

. . . we did not know much about those things during the World War. But with the progress in medical science today you can discover those things . . . We can save those boys from horror.[39]

As adviser to the draft, Sullivan set about organising psychiatric screening with energy and passion. He realised that to convert talk in Washington into action across the country would take some doing; there were, after all, only 2,500 psychiatrists in the whole of America (mostly in the big cities) and some 600 medical boards. Much of the work of weeding out unsuitable men would therefore have to be done by ordinary doctors who knew little or nothing of psychiatry. In the middle of 1941 Sullivan and his team organised a crash programme of nine two-day seminars on military psychiatry across the country.[40]

Having himself developed great skill in interviewing, Sullivan felt confident that a 15-minute interview, if conducted in a spirit of 'straightforward professional enquiry coupled with real respect for the registrant's personality and due consideration for his feelings', plus some background information, would provide an adequate guide to a man's 'ego strength'. The man's body language, Sullivan believed, also provided valuable clues. Once the recruit came into view, the psychiatrist should not waste a second. He had to learn to observe the way that the patient seats himself, what he does with his body, with his posture, his restlessness, his statuesque quietude, his relaxation, his rigidity: and . . . what he does with his eyes.[41]

Often, by the time he arrived at the psychiatrist, the man was naked. But, if still clothed, said Sullivan, he should be asked to undress, for the 'observation of his process of disrobing' gave further important clues about his personality.

All sorts of things about the patient and his body are important, the posture, the gross posture of the body, taking it naturally or finding it a matter of continuous interruption when you ask questions during the process.[42]

How innocent it all was in those days. It's easy to mock Sullivan as a gay doctor rationalising his own wish to look at a lot of guys' bodies. But Sullivan firmly believed that the ability to coexist easily with other men, to adjust successfully to male groups (and not in any explicitly sexual way) was a vital ingredient of the successful soldier. Anyone who felt inhibited undressing in front of a psychiatrist didn't have what it took; and if he couldn't disrobe and answer Sullivan's questions at the same time, he clearly didn't have much intellectual grasp.[43]

By what criteria should men be judged? At this stage, in early 1941, the War Department wanted quality rather than quantity of manpower; the psychiatrists believed that they should eliminate not just 'marked feeble-mindedness and clear-cut psychoses', but also those 'thought to have a predisposition to mental disease'. Far from believing that military service 'made a man' out of weaklings, the dominant philosophy was that 'great emotional stability' was required of the soldier. The list of types not wanted for the Army included 'low-grade morons', 'psychopaths', 'the eccentric, the leader in subversive activities, the emotionally unstable, the sexually perverse, those with inadequate personalities that do not adapt readily and those who are resentful of discipline.' Neither the aggressive nor the passive was suitable. The general attitude was 'when in doubt, reject'.[44]

The result was dramatic. One out of four white registers for the draft was rejected because of a nervous or mental condition, often one they were previously unaware of – a shattering blow to individual self-esteem and the national psyche. 'Where does that leave America if she is to win the war?' asked General Lewis B. Hershey on a 1942 newsreel. Particularly startling were the high levels of rejections among the youngest group, many of whom seemed to lack the required maturity.[45]

Although seen by the press as an 'inclusive look at the mental and physical state of [America's] young manhood', the draft boards were often, in practice, nothing of the kind. As last physician in an examining line, past whom an unending stream of young men passed, the psychiatrist often had only three minutes – rather than the planned fifteen – to make his assessment; time only to ask a few basic questions such as 'What do you think about the war', 'Have you had a nervous breakdown?' or, most famously, 'Do you like girls?' Many of the examiners were not psychiatrists at all, but physicians drafted in. Some had odd methods; one doctor's 'consisted of suddenly approaching the nude man before him and slapping him very hard in the abdomen; he then purported to assess the man's emotional state on the basis of how high he jumped.' A group of Harvard physicians believed they could easily tell those who would hack it in battle from those who wouldn't: normal, masculine, men had flat, angular bodies, narrow hips and pubic hair running towards the navel, whereas cowards had soft bodies, wider hips, and pubic hair that spread laterally.[46]

All attempts to get hold of background detail on recruits proved administratively impossible. So it often came down to a snap judgement, based on hunch or prejudice and, at its worst, the system descended into sub-Freudian farce, with any admission of masturbation being grounds for rejection, and interviewers taking a particularly dim view of nail-biters.[47]

Sullivan was a man of ideas, with none of Tom Salmon's practical experience. A more seasoned hand might have seen the enormous social risk in imposing the values of metropolitan psychiatrists on a society that still saw mental illness in terms of horror and stigma. Men who had functioned quite satisfactorily as neurotics now found themselves branded '4F' (rejected for psychiatric reasons) and cold-shouldered as 'nuts' by employers. Others learned from their medical records – until they were made confidential – that they were 'idiots', 'imbeciles', 'sexual psychopaths' or 'Peeping Toms'. Far from being grateful that their menfolk were to be released from military service, many communities were deeply offended, accusing urban psychiatrists of failing to understand black or Southern white culture. 'Rural farm boys who looked withdrawn and autistic were often diagnosed schizophrenic with no reference to their taciturn cultural pattern', and psychiatrists operating in Oklahoma were accused of being 'too much influenced by John Steinbeck's The Grapes of Wrath.'[48]

After Pearl Harbor and America's entry into the war there was a new mood of urgency and a clamour for American armies to be committed abroad as soon as possible. General Lewis Hershey who took over the draft (and ran it till 1972) wanted quantity not quality. 'Supermen' were no longer in fashion. There was also growing evidence that the system lent itself to abuse and, with fathers now being called up, there was growing public resentment of 'disloyal' 4Fs. Besides, psychiatric screening didn't seem to work: large numbers of men who had been screened were still breaking down and getting 'nut discharges' from the Army; and when American forces went into action in 1942 in Guadalcanal and Tunisia, a very high percentage of their casualties were psychiatric.[49]

At the end of 1941, an attempt by General Hershey to curtail the psychiatric interview provoked the inevitable trial of strength with H. S. Sullivan. Soon afterwards, Sullivan was fired as adviser to the draft; but the policy of selection he had initiated was not at first reversed. If anything it was intensified: selection procedures were made both stricter and more consistent. Finally, to counter the barrage of public criticism, the psychiatrists brought in the Medical Survey Program, an ambitious attempt to pull together the criminal, medical and educational records of recruits (a dramatic invasion, in the name of medicine, of their civil rights). In the end, in what can now be seen as a rehearsal for the

McCarthyite witch-hunt of the 1950s, over 9,000 field agents hunted up the school and hospital records of some 3 million registrants for the draft.[50]

In 1943, attempts were also made to introduce personality tests. The most important of them, devised by a groups of Cornell psychologists, consisted of a questionnaire to the recruit designed to elicit his self-confidence, range of interests, decisiveness, and sexual abnormalities. Scattered through the list were 'stop questions', a positive answer to which would trigger a major psychiatric examination. These tests had some advantages over the interview: they were more 'scientific' than Sullivan's highly subjective method. But there were severe disadvantages as well, such as an inherent bias towards the more literate draftee and the better-educated sectors of the population, which meant that their verdict usually needed to be corroborated in an interview. As a result, they did not simplify the induction process, but complicated it. The great beauty of British intelligence testing, that the tests could be given by semi-trained sergeants leaving the psychiatrists free to concentrate on the lower-scoring recruits, did not apply.[51]

But neither the Medical Survey Program nor the various Tests could avert the crisis that overtook US Army psychiatry.

By the middle of 1943, it was becoming clear that by concentrating on selection, the United States Army and the psychiatrists had ignored the lessons of the past. Selection, however thorough and expert, could only address one of the several variables which went into a man's experience of battle. 'The psychiatrist in the induction centre,' a post-war account pointed out, 'had no possible way of evaluating the four most important factors of influence upon the adjustment of soldier: the nature of the leadership that would be provided for him; the degree of motivation that he had to do his job or that could be instilled into him; the type of job to which he might be assigned; and the degree of stress which might confront him.'[52]

While emphasising selection, the Americans had ignored the lessons of Tom Salmon's work in the First World War and sent their armies into battle without a coherent framework of forward psychiatry. But at the same time, enormous numbers of men were breaking down and being discharged in the continental United States. The scale of the problem was worrying. In September 1943, the Army lost 112,500 enlisted men and inducted 118,600. 'At this rate,' it was pointed out, 'the Army had to induct 100 men to secure a net increase of five enlisted men.' With concern mounting in Congress, the Army Chief of Staff, the great and good General George C. Marshall, demanded to know 'how such a thing could come about?' Following a report by his staff, he then produced a memorandum in December 1943. He did not mince his words. Psychiatric disorders, unlike physical problems, Marshall pointed out, were, 'for the most part invisible, and their detection rests with [the] professional ability and experience of neuro-psychiatrists.' These, he said, had been 'either over-enthusiastic or over-cautious', or too limited in number or too inexperienced to cope.

To the specialists, the psychoneurotic is a hospital patient. To the average line officer, he is a malingerer. Actually he is a man who is either unwilling, unable or slow to adjust himself to some or all phases of military life, and in consequence he develops an imaginary ailment which in time becomes so fixed in his mind as to bring about mental pain and sickness. In a sense, this might be considered as shirking, yet among the thousands of psychiatric cases in the Army no record exists of any psychoneurotic ever having been convicted for malingering. This is because no doctor is either willing or able to state under oath that the pain complained of by the psychoneurotic is nonexistent. [As a result] laymen or uninitiated line officers incline to the belief that a medical officer's diagnosis of psychoneurosis is either wrong or else that the doctor is influenced by a hyperconsiderate professional attitude.[53]

Marshall then cited instances where the impending visits of inspectors to hospitals and rumours of a new tough regime had produced remarkable relapses in symptoms. The fact that thousands of hospital beds were being occupied by psychoneurotic cases was also, however, due to the way in which officers were using psychiatric channels to get rid of men they were too lazy to train. Once a man got into hospital he was militarily useless, learning from other patients the 'symptoms most likely to perplex the doctors.'

He wears the clothes of an invalid [Marshall continued]. His food is brought to him. He is catered to by 'gray ladies,' and, above all, he escapes from those duties which he seeks to evade. He cannot be punished for malingering; therefore, the worst that can happen is to be sent back to his organization where he can and will start the same process all over again. In the meantime he enjoys a life of leisure with one great goal ahead: to wit, a discharge for physical disability, a comparatively highly paid job as a civilian, a discharge bonus, and eventually a pension from the Veterans Administration Bureau.[54]

Marshall blamed the 'spread of psychoneurotics in our Army' on 'the Nation's educational programme and environmental background since 1920'. At the same time, he took steps drastically to curtail discharges and to issue tougher new instructions.

Marshall's report was, for the Americans, a defining moment in the psychiatry of the war. With his immense prestige and authority, he was pulling the psychiatrists up straight, telling them bluntly that they were out of touch with the real world and must reset their compasses, that 'when put to the acid test, the American psychiatric conceptual framework was not consonant with the needs of its culture.'

This formidable broadside might have sunk completely the cause of Army psychiatry. That it not only survived this setback but prospered, was due to the arrival in Washington, at about this time, of Dr William C. Menninger.

Will Menninger, then 44, came from a remarkable German-American dynasty, founded by his father, a gentle, scholarly, 'horse and buggy' doctor in Kansas, but dominated by his ambitious, money-minded mother, an able woman confined by

Victorian gender roles. His brother Karl Menninger had introduced the 'new psychiatry' of Freud and Janet, of clinics and psychoneuroses (instead of the 'old psychiatry' of hereditary mental disorder and vast custodial asylums) to the American mid-west and become one of the intellectual leaders of American psychiatry. Will was the capable manager who had made the Menninger Clinic a success.[55]

Will Menninger was an intellectual lightweight compared to Harry Stack Sullivan, his theoretical approach to psychiatry an eclectic compôte of old-fashioned 'moral therapy', Adolf Meyer's psychobiology and bits of Freud. But he was an able administrator with great skill in handling people. Operating in the corn belt, the Menningers were even more aware than Adolf Meyer in Baltimore of the social politics of psychiatry – of the need to carry, rather than offend, local opinion, to turn the truths of psychoanalysis to the American grain. These skills proved useful in Washington, too. At one of his first meetings with the military, Will Menninger broke the ice by telling a dirty joke learnt from the Rotarians back in Topeka, something Sullivan could never have done. Soon afterwards, he played the piano at the Surgeon-General's party. 'Personable and convivial', Will showed a 'remarkable capacity to inspire confidence among military officers.' His first task, once he had won the trust of the Army, was to try to discover what had gone so badly wrong at the front line.[56]

FRONT-LINE PSYCHIATRY

'Trick cyclists' they were to begin with; till the High Command took them up in a big way. Now it's the thing. 'This psychiatry business, old boy . . . the General's very keen on it.'

Fred Majdalany, *Patrol*[1]

The treatment of soldiers breaking down on or near the battlefield in the Second World War might have been expected to be a straightforward matter of reapplying lessons painfully learned in 1914–17 and enshrined in the 1922 Shell-shock Committee's report and Tom Salmon's writing.

In practice, it was not simple at all. For one thing, the relationship between the military and the psychiatrists had lapsed since 1918 and now had to be rebuilt. For another, warfare was this time both more intermittent and much more diverse geographically: every theatre of war had its own military hierarchy, invariably ignoring the psychiatrists until forced to use them. The immense 'shell-shock' literature dealt mainly with chronic cases seen at base hospitals in England, not with soldiers immediately after they had broken down; the basics of 'forward' psychiatry had therefore to be re-learnt from scratch. Furthermore, medical fashions had changed and a young generation of psychiatrists brought new assumptions to the battlefield. Finally, there were 'turf wars' between doctors fighting to establish 'priority' for new treatment techniques.

The tone for much that followed was set in June 1940 when one of the first soldiers to be evacuated from the beach at Dunkirk arrived at the Belmont Hospital near London. He was completely unable to speak and his hands shook violently, like those of a Parkinson's patient. He had not urinated for days and his enlarged bladder had blown up his lower body like a pumpkin. He was in a 'pitiable state of terror'.[2]

A young doctor at the Belmont, William Sargant, had with him supplies of sodium amytal, a fast-acting barbiturate drug, which he thought might be useful in sedating hysterical air-raid victims. Dr Sargant gave the man from Dunkirk sodium amytal. It seemed that a new, pharmacological, era in military psychiatry had arrived.

* * *

Little was said about drugs during the debates about shell-shock because it was not then fashionable to use them. The Great War was fought in an era of 'therapeutic nihilism' when the normal medical practice was to avoid using medication – other than anaesthetics and sedatives – if at all possible. This minimalist approach, spearheaded in the 1890s by the Canadian physician Sir William Osler, was itself a reaction against a previous kind of medicine practised in the early nineteenth century, captured in the novels of Wilkie Collins, in which 'anything that happened to pop into the doctor's mind was tried out for the treatment of illness'. Osler and his colleagues at Johns Hopkins University believed that drugs like arsenic and laudanum did more harm than good and that the body often fought disease better if left alone than when bombarded with medication. They set out to cleanse and purify medicine, insisting that the doctor rely only on 'a small number of genuine therapeutic drugs – digitalis and morphine the best of all'. His function was not to bombard his patient with medicines, but to diagnose his illness and help him, with encouragement and good sense, to overcome it.[3]

The spirit of Osler still ruled over medical schools in the 1930s. But by then a revolution was in the offing, as decades of work into the mechanisms of infection and disease began to bear dramatic fruit. In the 1920s, the new barbiturate drugs began to be widely used; in the following decade the first sulphanamides appeared, soon to be followed by the first antibiotic, penicillin. The new drugs would ultimately bring about another dramatic *bouleversement* of medical orthodoxy, replacing Osler's nihilism with the pharmacological optimism of 'modern medicine'.[4]

This spirit infected even the despised Cinderella of medicine, psychiatry. In the new climate, psychiatrists welcomed dramatic but unproven techniques that seemed to offer hope to patients otherwise condemned to years of asylum twilight. The Viennese psychiatrist Julius Wagner-Jauregg showed the way by using malarial infection to arrest the spread of General Paralysis of the Insane; in the 1930s other 'physical' methods of treatment followed. Another Viennese, Manfred Sakel, treated schizophrenics by giving them large doses of insulin to put them into a coma; a Hungarian by the name of von Meduna became convinced that there was an antagonism between epilepsy and schizophrenia and began inducing epileptic fits in schizophrenic patients. To overcome practical problems with the convulsive drug cardiazol, two Italian doctors developed a technique using an electrical current applied to the frontal lobes of the brain to induce fits – they had noticed that animals in a Rome slaughter-house had epileptic seizures after being given electric shocks to the head. Electro Shock Therapy – or Electro Convulsive Therapy (ECT) as it came to be known – had arrived.[5]

These new treatments culminated, just before the war, in the psychosurgical procedure known as leucotomy (lobotomy in the United States), which involved severing the connection between the prefrontal cortex and the rest of the brain. Developed by the Portuguese neurologist Egaz Moniz just before the war, it was taken up with great enthusiasm by Walter Freeman, an American neurologist.[6]

This climate of activism also affected psychiatry's philosophy towards the use of drugs. Although it was still standard practice in the 1930s to sedate long-term mental patients with bromides, researchers also tried out a bewildering variety of drugs – some forty substances ranging from cocaine, hashish and mescalin to alcohol and medinine – on every sort of mental disorder. Despite 'a general lack of uniformity as to technique, duration and drug use', it was agreed that the most promising medications were those belonging to the barbiturate family.[7]

Barbituric acid, first discovered by Adolph von Bayer in 1864, remained 'only a laboratory curiosity' until 1903 when the first barbiturate drug 'veronal' was registered by the Bayer company. A further refinement, 'Luminal' (pheno-barbitone), appeared in 1911, and proved to be an effective anti-convulsant. The British Army made some use of barbiturates at the end of the First World War, but their real impact came in the 1920s. While older doctors warned that barbiturates were addictive and dangerous to the liver, psychiatrists soon began to try them out. In 1929 Dr William Bleckwenn administered sodium amytal, a barbiturate developed in the Indianapolis laboratories of the Eli Lilly company, to catatonic schizophrenics at an asylum in Wisconsin. A few years later Erich Lindemann gave it to students in Boston who reported 'a desire to communicate and a willingness to speak about personal problems usually not spoken of to strangers.' The drug's attraction for psychiatrists trying to 'reach' difficult patients or speed up psychotherapy was obvious.[8]

In 1936 a rash of American newspaper stories hailing the newly-marketed Pentothal as a 'truth drug' prompted the British psychiatrist J. S. Horsley to reveal that he had been experimenting with a wide variety of drugs as an aid to analysis – a method he christened 'narco-analysis'– and had found Nembutal the most effective in producing sedation with the minimum of confusion. It enabled the physician to obtain in an hour 'a quantity of relevant information which he would not have obtained in a month by ordinary methods.' A true hypnotic state was induced, making suggestion possible, which had to be given 'with great care and forethought', primarily to 'restore the contact of the patient with the realities of his life and environment.'[9]

Horsley was using drugs as a substitute for hypnosis and a pathway to psychotherapy, a 'practical substitute for the economically unavailable, if desirable, method of psycho-analysis'. But another school of thought, associated with the Zurich clinic, the Burgholzi, thought that the drugs themselves were the therapeutic agents. The Swiss also developed a technique known as 'Deep-sleep Therapy' or continuous narcosis, which aimed to 'produce as many hours of sleep as are consistent with the safety of the patient, over a period of between ten days and a fortnight', the rationale being that, by switching the patient's mind off completely, deep-sleep broke the 'faulty habit of thought into which the psychotic patient had fallen.' An exhaustive analysis of the literature concluded in 1937 that while there were enormous practical problems and dangers with 'deep-sleep', it was a valuable method of treatment for 'both the milder and more severe forms of mental disorder.'[10]

Thus, by the time war came, there was a variety of new drugs and techniques available and a new generation of doctors prepared to use them. It was hardly surprising that William Sargant should have a supply of sodium amytal on hand for he was an ambitious, headstrong young man determined to make a name for himself. Taken on by Edward Mapother at the Maudsley Hospital, Sargant had eagerly embraced the new 'physical' methods of treatment. He had visited the lobotomist Freeman while on a visit to the United States and during the London Blitz of 1940, 'unblushingly resorted to every trick that would help by-pass heartless medical authoritarianism to overcome the London County Council's resistance to the introduction of leucotomy.' 'It is into the hands of bold experimenters that success has fallen', he wrote in 1944; and his ardent belief in medical progress and willingness to cut corners to achieve it have about them something of eighteenth-century medicine, the era of the body-snatchers.[11]

The shot of sodium amytal William Sargant gave to his Dunkirk patient had an immediate and dramatic effect: 'His bladder suddenly emptied, his speech returned, his hands stopped trembling, and he became intelligent, articulate and comparatively normal, at least until the effects of the injection wore off.' Encouraged by this, Sargant began to give the drug to other patients. Soon he noticed its strange side effects. Soldiers suddenly regained suppressed memories of the horrible experiences that had 'caused or hastened [their] breakdown' and would start to relive them before the doctors. After venting their pent-up terror or hostility to their officers, they seemed suddenly to improve.[12]

One of these patients had come in trembling all over, unable to remember anything of the recent past and with his right hand paralysed. An injection of sodium amytal 'cured the tremor and restored the use of his hand and his lost memory; but only after a frightening emotional release.'

He described, with dramatic gestures, how during the retreat he had come across his own brother lying by the roadside with a severe abdominal wound. At his brother's earnest plea he had dragged him into a field and put him out of his misery with a rifle shot. It was the hand that pulled the trigger that had suddenly become paralysed.

After his confession of grief and guilt this hand worked again.[13]

These dramatic results seemed to suggest that it was possible, by the timely use of drugs, to avoid the psychiatric disasters of the past – the long drawn-out hysterical cases, the war pensions, the wasted lives. Sargant and his collaborator hastily published an article in the *Lancet*. Though cautiously worded, its effect was dramatic. The popular press seized on the case of the man who had shot his brother and Sargant was forced to send the patient off to the country to protect his anonymity. More importantly, this first serious account of 'real' war neuroses in the Hitler War seemed to herald a new and exciting era in treatment. It was widely read in Britain and America.[14]

Sargant was not in the British Army, however, but attached to the Emergency Medical Services, waiting for civilian casualties. The Battle of Britain and the London Blitz brought him more patients, but of a slightly different type – people who had 'broken down after weeks or months of useful service' in Civil Defence units. Most had not experienced such strain as the Dunkirk patients, had less stamina, responded less dramatically to treatment and were much harder to get back to duty.[15]

At the end of 1942, having treated some 3,000 patients, Sargant set out some of the principles of the new 'physical methods' of treatment. Drugs had both sedative and abreactive uses, but it was especially the sedative ones he commended. 'Immediate first-aid treatment of the acute neurosis' – i.e. knocking the patient out immediately with intravenous barbiturate – would prevent 'conditioned fears from becoming ingrained in the personality' and stop 'neurotic behaviour patterns that were primarily released under severe stress from recurring whenever the individual is again exposed to the slightest danger.' If, however, severe anxiety or hysterical symptoms continued for more than a week, then the next line of defence, deep-sleep treatment, was necessary to 'destroy' the conditioned fears. Sargant and his colleagues were now able to keep patients asleep under drugs for up to three weeks 'after which they would wake up greatly refreshed.'[16]

Nor did that exhaust the battery of treatments. Patients suffering from physical exhaustion and loss of weight could be given 'modified insulin coma', in which they were made semi-comatose by insulin and then fed on mashed potatoes (sugar being rationed). This technique had not worked with depressives, but, Sargant claimed, it produced good results in patients suffering from anxiety or hysteria. It was, he recognised, a return to Weir Mitchell's idea of a 'cure' fattening up the body and nervous system. Finally, for a minority of patients suffering from feelings of guilt and depression, there were the new (electro) convulsive therapies.

But what about the mind, amidst all this attention to the body? Sargant had little faith in psychotherapy ('talk, talk, talk'), which anyway was not easy in the crowded, chaotic conditions of war – the Belmont Hospital was itself bombed several times. His model of the 'war neuroses' was physiological, Pavlovian, almost mechanistic; he talked of patients becoming 'conditioned' to neurotic behaviour and of the need to switch off their brains and nervous systems before they had become maladjusted. Yet many of his patients clearly had symptoms that needed psychological as well as physical attention – 144 of his first 1,000 suffered from amnesia. Though Sargant and his colleagues 'found it best not to ignore the amnesiac symptoms, to explore the gaps in memory', they were noticeably uncomfortable with these cases. They treated amnesiac patients with barbiturates, which 'made it easier to establish a semi-hypnotic contact', but warned that 'the information gained will often be a mixture of truth and fantasy.'[17]

This raised important questions. Was abreaction under barbiturate – the 'amytal interview', as it was now sometimes called – just 'hypnosis without the need for a skilled hypnotist', 'safe rapid, sure', or was it an altogether new technique for exploring the subconscious? In the summer of 1942, doctors voiced their disagreements in the *British Medical Journal.* Dr J. F. Wilde found that 'if an impasse was reached in which a patient, though trying his best, simply could not remember the painful matters that were repressed,' and if all efforts to get at the repression through psychotherapy had failed, 'then one resorts to narco-analysis.' He cited the case of a soldier who was suffering from nightmares and had complete amnesia for the period of 36 hours after he had been exposed to bomb blast. Under Pentothal this man became 'euphoric and excessively loquacious . . . He recalled the bombing and recounted how he was thrown down violently and covered with mud . . . He made an immediate improvement.'[18]

Another doctor, J. L. Clegg, disagreed completely. He didn't believe that using drugs produced any more information from the patient than was available from ordinary conversation, provided one departed from the usual type of interview and met the patient half way. Patients usually responded to simple sympathy with an emotional reaction and tears. It was sometimes worth using Pentothal if the patient's anxiety stopped him relating to the doctor, but once the effects of the drug wore off he might well relapse to his former hostility. All in all, Pentothal was a weapon of last resort, not a 'reliable means of effecting a transference. [Or] gaining access to deeply repressed material.'[19]

Charles Burns, a third psychiatrist, introduced a note of greater complexity. Of course Pentothal wasn't the 'royal road to the unconscious'; it was, he argued, a 'crude mental enema'. But it had its uses in revealing personality and could save a lot of time. Perhaps, he speculated, 'different methods such as narco-analysis and shock treatment . . . may lay open different portals of the mind.'[20]

Even as this debate rumbled on, the war was moving into a new phase. Whatever the theoretical issues, psychiatrists were about to be confronted by the hard practical issues of looking after men in the line. Would drugs make a difference? Would they make it possible, as William Sargant hoped, to eliminate 'war neuroses' altogether? It was not until November 1942, when the Allies invaded North Africa, that these questions were really put to the test.

*   *   *

Even three years into the war, parts of the British Army refused to accept that psychiatric casualties were inevitable. The medical planning for Operation Torch, the invasion of Algeria and Morocco, made no provision at all for psychiatry. Security was tight and space on landing craft limited, but the British medical chief – Sir Ernest Cowell, a surgeon always known as 'Two Gun Pete' because of his keen Territorial activities – also felt that 'psychiatry in British theatres of operation [was] being over-emphasized.' On the American side, too, doctors admitted that 'little thought was given and no special plans made for the handling of psychiatric cases that might be expected to occur in the combat zone

... none of us had any appreciation of [such] psychiatric problems.' Tom Salmon's labours had left no mark on US Army medicine.[21]

By the time two British psychiatrists, John Wishart and Colman Kenton, finally arrived in North Africa in January 1943, having been torpedoed on the way, a 'frightful mess' was developing and 'Two-Gun Pete' had been flown to Cairo for a hasty tutorial in psychiatry from 'Jimmy' James.[22]

The Allied plan was that the Anglo-American First Army would advance eastwards from Algiers while Montgomery's victorious Eighth Army drove the Germans and Italians westwards, trapping the Axis army between them. At first all went well. Within three weeks of landing, First Army had advanced over four hundred miles and stood within artillery range of Tunis. Then problems developed. Heavy rain transformed Tunisia into a quagmire. The Germans decided to reinforce Tunis and quickly massing troops and armour, began to counterattack, preferring the newly arrived First Army rather than the seasoned veterans of the Eighth. Thinly stretched over the stony hillsides and cornfields of Tunisia, green, inexperienced soldiers met the full force of the Afrika Korps and the Luftwaffe.[23]

Some British units fought well, showing 'a professionalism and vigour which exorcised the recollection of Dunkirk'. Yet when Dr John Wishart was sent forward he found many examples of psychiatric collapse. In one engagement in January 1943, there was a 'generalized panic' of a brigade of the Royal Ulsters new to this kind of fighting, especially to the deadly German mortars. The brigade had lost many officers and NCOs and had been three days without sleep. But Wishart also found that the unit contained a considerable number of 'dull and backward men and neurotics', including a former asylum patient of his from before the war. His boss 'was amazed that this chap had ever got into the army.'[24]

Wishart was initially very unwelcome and was told he was 'the most unwanted man in North Africa.' The Corps commander 'was afraid that, since he had a psychiatrist, discipline ... would be ruined. A man who was under arrest for some breach of discipline, it was thought, had only to see a psychiatrist, tell a tale of his mother being frightened before he was born or some such plausible tale, and he would be let off any punishment.'[25]

Meanwhile, in Algiers the other British psychiatrist, Colman Kenton, was struggling to cope with the torrent of casualties arriving from the front. Matters were not helped by the fact that his patients 'took a long time to reach him' and 'travelled, without sedation, by slow stages along the winding valley routes from the front. In turn they were bullied, ignored and mollycoddled.' The ward in Algiers, Wishart later recalled, was 'like a cage of monkeys'. He had never seen 'so many hysterical gaits, hysterical aphonias and all sorts of things' and remembered thinking, 'Thank God, I'm not in charge here.' Kenton put it more technically: 'It was as if the ego defences to anxiety were overwhelmed in greater or lesser degree, producing clinical pictures of stupor, confusional states, uncontrolled primitive behaviour, psychotic pictures often of a bizarre character, childishness, apparent idiocy, and, in some exceptional cases, simian behaviour.'[26]

A calm, business-like man, Kenton did what he could for the psychotics and began experimenting with treatments on the others. He had got as far as finding that 'prolonged narcosis' – knocking them out with barbiturates for a long time – didn't seem to work when his ward was suddenly flooded with American patients.[27]

The scale of American psychiatric casualties was already causing alarm when on 19 February 1943, Rommel (briefly back in command of the Afrika Korps) attacked American units near the Kasserine Pass. He quickly exposed a very raw nerve. In modern warfare against seasoned troops, American soldiers showed the same weaknesses as the British in France and Singapore; their leadership and training were, if anything, worse. Although the German attack was at first held, the American forces were soon swept by 'rumours of disaster that inflamed the fires of panic.' Units began to pull back before receiving the order to do so; the available roads soon became jammed with a 'dense mass of churning traffic', a mechanised rout.[28]

There were understandable reasons for this: night fighting was a terrifying novelty; a gradual and ordered withdrawal is a difficult military manoeuvre at the best of times. In addition, according to historian Martin Blumeson:

The harrowing events of three days of defeat had exhausted many soldiers, morally and physically. Uncertain and nervous, fatigued and confused, hemmed in by widespread firing that seemed to be all around them . . . demoralised by their piecemeal commitment and the intermingling of small units, no longer possessing a firm sense of belonging to a strong and self-contained organization, and numbed by a pervading sense of weariness and bewilderment, many men lost their confidence and self discipline.[29]

These were, in terms of David Eder's old formula, men whose instinct for self-preservation was not being controlled by any sense of duty or obligation. In one engagement, American tank crews were overwhelmed by German Panzers. Jumping out of their tanks, they ran.

Like a herd of frightened animals, they stampeded up the dry watercourses, stumbling over boulders, tripping over rocks, sliding in the loose shale in a nightmare of tearing gasps of breath and blind panic.[30]

The Americans also confronted for the first time the horrors of war – mortared, dive-bombed by Stukas, forced to go days without water in the mountains of Tunisia with no means of transport except mules. About a third of all non-fatal casualties were psychiatric. They came to the hospitals of Algiers 'terror-stricken, mute and tremulous'. There, waiting to treat them, were Colman Kenton and Roy R. Grinker.

Roy Grinker was a medical aristocrat. The son of a famous neurologist, he had trained in Chicago, Zurich and London and written the standard neurological textbook while still in his early thirties. Then, finding neurology increasingly dominated by brain surgery and 'no longer fun or exciting', he had turned to psychiatry. Consulting the works of Freud (kept in a locked case in the University of Chicago), he became excited by the resemblance between psychoanalysis and classic Hughlings Jackson neurology and persuaded the Rockefeller Foundation to send him to be analysed by Freud himself.[31]

Grinker did not enjoy his time in Vienna. Several aspects of the Freud ménage were unsettling to this burly, self-confident mid-western Jew. There was the 'great big wolfhound' which, when Grinker rang the door of Freud's waiting room, 'would attack me with its snout at the same level as my genitals. So I entered Freud's office with a high level of castration anxiety.' There was a second 'damn dog', apt to jump on top of Grinker as he lay 'emoting with a great deal of vigour' on the professor's couch. There was Freud's passion for geography, which led him, on one occasion during the analysis, to cross the room to consult an atlas and trip over an electric wire, cutting himself badly and bringing the session to an abrupt end. Finally, there was Freud's habit, at moments of analytic breakthrough, of leaning over his patient and dribbling on him.[32]

There were more fundamental problems: Freud's deep-seated hostility to Americans; Grinker's grounding in neurology which made him resistant to such Freudian ideas as transference; and Grinker's dominating temperament which made him unhappy in the role of the confessing patient. For all that, he was delighted to be told by Freud when they parted, 'Your psycho-analysis was one of my few last remaining pleasures'. Grinker returned to Chicago in 1935 not exactly a Freudian, but no longer a conventional neurologist.[33]

With the coming of war, he approached the Army Air Force and, in his usual masterful way, negotiated the rank of Major and a job running a psychiatric treatment centre in Northern Ireland. But the fortunes of war dictated otherwise. 'When he got to the dock,' the story goes, 'they miss-read his ticket and put him on a boat to North Africa instead of North Ireland.' So 'for the first time in his whole life, he arrived at a place where nobody had ever heard of him.' He spent his first nights in North Africa in an olive orchard in Oran in a sleeping bag.[34]

This setback was only momentary. Very soon, Major Grinker had fixed himself up as Psychiatric Consultant to the 12th Army Air Force, found an apartment in the Rue Michelet (the handsome main street of Algiers) and arranged for his chief resident in Chicago, Dr John P. Spiegel, to join him (Spiegel turned out to be only 300 miles away, on a forward airfield in Tunisia). Finding the staff of the American hospital in Algiers unsympathetic, Grinker arranged to work alongside Colman Kenton at the large British hospital, to which many American casualties were being sent. There he and Spiegel treated many of the soldiers from Kasserine Pass as well as a number of airmen. Working with great intensity, they wrote up their experiences in a book, which came out before the year was over.[35]

War Neuroses in North Africa is a descriptive masterpiece, alive with shock and wonder at the extraordinary symptoms of acute war neurosis: the 'weird, wobbly, disorganized gait' of the hysterical conversion states; the soldier so riven with terror that he 'resembles a frightened, inarticulate child, with only a few islands of his past well-organized behaviour'; the patient lying in bed dreaming, shouting out to his battlefield companions, and trying to dig a hole through the bed to escape shell-fire. Precisely because the authors had so little experience, their horror and excitement were all the greater.[36]

But these symptoms were familiar enough. What was superficially new was Grinker and Spiegel's method of treatment. John Spiegel, after reading Sargant's article about treating Dunkirk patients, had begun experimenting with Pentothal at the forward airfield in Tunisia, using supplies liberated from the medical stations in the area. He found the drug 'extremely effective' in treating patients. In Algiers, Roy Grinker called this technique 'narcosynthesis' because, Spiegel recalled, 'under the influence of a narcotic substance the patient was able to synthesize the experiences he'd had, to put it together in his memory, to digest it, and to get himself back in a relatively normal state with the help of the therapist standing by his side and giving him reassurance that things were going to be alright.' Thus pre-war 'narco-analysis' was subtly rebranded and appropriated by Grinker.[37]

In Grinker's highly dramatic account, the patient arrives shocked, tremulous, mute, or amnesiac, unable to say what has happened to him or perhaps who he is. He is isolated in a semi-darkened room, told he will receive an injection that will make him sleepy, and given pentothal. There then follows a short period while the patient is brought to the right level of coma. Some begin to talk at once, but most require a bit of stimulation to get them going.

The patient is told in a matter of fact manner that he is on the battlefield, in the front line. Depending upon the amount of known history, specific details are added . . .[38]

If patients resist, the stimulation is made 'more dramatic and realistic:

The therapist plays the role of a fellow soldier, calling out to the patient in an alarmed voice, to duck as the shells come over, or asking him to help with a wounded comrade. Persistence is rewarded in almost every case by an account of the scene in progress.[39]

Some patients simply told their story; others acted it out, leaping out of bed and rushing about the room. But usually they re-experienced the original emotions.

The terror exhibited in the moments of supreme danger, such as the imminent explosion of shells, the death of a friend before the patient's eyes, the absence of cover under a heavy dive-bombing attack, is electrifying to watch. The body becomes increasingly tense and rigid; the eyes widen and the pupils dilate, while the skin becomes covered with fine per-spiration. Breathing becomes incredibly rapid and shallow. The intensity of the emotion sometimes becomes more than they can bear; and frequently at the height of the reaction, there is a collapse and the patient falls back in bed and remains quiet for a few minutes.[40]

When these intense emotions were re-experienced the patient frequently threw himself into the arms of the doctor sitting beside the bed, 'as if seeking forgiveness and consolation from a kindly parent.' This was often the moment when Grinker would try to move the situation forward by absolving him of guilt or assuaging his anger.[41]

It might take several sessions to extract all the repressed material. A soldier mortared in the Kairouan Pass could, at first, simply remember two buddies being killed; himself standing up and saying 'Never mind, I'll get even' and then going off to look for 'Steve'. A second dose of pentothal a day later brought back his own name, the fact that his wife was pregnant (and he had been worrying about her) and a good deal of gruesome battlefield detail. After witnessing his comrades' terrible wounds, he had seen a gunflash giving away the position of the German mortars and was on his way to tell 'Steve' in the Command Post to bring artillery down on it (and so avenge his dead buddies) when three shells had burst near him. There was no physical damage but, in his emotional state, they were enough to finish him off.

Having remembered all this, though, the soldier now had guilt and depression about having been a 'baby' and abandoned his comrades without getting wounded. Because he clearly had strong 'dependent needs', Grinker felt he had no choice but to send him home.[42]

Grinker and Spiegel argued that it was 'impossible to estimate from the clinical state the amount of underlying repressed anxiety without giving the patient the pentothal treatment': pentothal abreaction thus became their central therapeutic tool. This view was widely disseminated – some 45,000 copies of their book were produced and distributed within the medical community – and for a couple of years 'Grinker and Spiegel' was the Bible of every new military psychiatrist – modern, up to date, American. But in North Africa there was almost immediately a reaction against their methods.[43]

There turned out to be both clinical and military problems with pentothal. Clinically, it wasn't just the chemical functions of the drug that mattered; you also had to have Grinker and Spiegel's theatrical commitment to the whole exercise. Inexpert use of pentothal made later treatment difficult, producing 'pentothal-resistant' patients. Even enthusiasts like Colman Kenton found with experience that 'prolonged treatment, after the initial improvement by abreactive short-term psychotherapy was difficult, such factors as secondary gain, imperfect transference, and resolution of guilt feelings playing a part.' There was growing evidence that the pentothal interview left patients more anxious. It just wasn't that easy.[44]

The military's objection was simpler: pentothal abreaction didn't get anyone back into combat. Indeed it encouraged soldiers *not* to return. By opening up fundamental clefts and chasms in the personality, it effectively removed the last vestiges of military discipline and, in effect, gave the psychiatrist the power to free the soldier from his military obligations – a power Grinker did not hesitate to exercise. Indeed, its greatest danger, from the Army's point of view, was that it made the therapist too sympathetic.

The patients pleaded or insisted that they should not be sent back into combat. As the therapist participated with the patient in the dramatic reliving of battle scenes, he almost invariably identified with the distress and needs of the patient and was therefore impelled to promise relief from future battle trauma.[45]

* * *

Even while Grinker and Spiegel were composing their book, a quite different model of treatment was being developed in North Africa by a young neurologist, Frederick R. Hanson. An American working in Montreal, Hanson had gone to England with the Canadian Army in 1940, and, after taking part in the disastrous Dieppe Raid and a few torpedo-boat excursions to France, become interested in 'emotional reactions to combat'. He transferred to the American Army but was not sent to North Africa until March 1943, just when the panic there was at its height. Hanson plunged in, arranging to treat psychiatric casualties not 500 miles back in Algiers, but at a corps clearing station just behind the front line.[46]

Experience led Hanson to believe that sheer physical exhaustion was the major factor behind most acute war neurosis.

They walked dispiritedly from the ambulance to the receiving tent, with drooping shoulders and bowed heads. Once in the tent they sat on the benches or the ground silent and almost motionless. Their faces were expressionless, their eyes blank and unseeing, and they tended to go to sleep where they were. The sick, injured, lightly wounded, and psychiatric cases were usually indistinguishable on the basis of their appearance . . . these men were fatigued to the point of exhaustion.[47]

Physical fatigue didn't just wear the soldier out; it lowered his resistance to emotional strain. But for that very reason, many of his symptoms, alarming though they seemed, were only superficial. 'The effect is a transient one and produces no lasting alteration of the personality and when the effects of fatigue have been counteracted the ability to withstand the emotional stress of combat returns to its former level.'[48]

Hanson rejected Sargant and Grinker's assumption that catharsis and abreaction of traumatic experiences were needed to treat the soldier. Most cases just needed rest and reassurance near the front line and, after a few days, gentle persuasion would be enough to get them back to duty. His method of doing this was well described by Roy Grinker:

Each man was interviewed in the open ward. Only when highly personal matters were discussed was the conversation inaudible to others. The convincing reassurances that the psychiatrist had no doubt of the patient's ability to go back, the pseudo-physiological explanations of anxiety, discussions of the universality of fear and the leading question 'You want to go back and try again, don't you?' were all loudly given so the entire ward heard the same procedure repetitively.[49]

Grinker was contemptuous of these primitive techniques and their use of social pressure. But crude though they were, Hanson's methods were highly effective from the Army's point of view. By 'using brief periods of rest along with techniques of suggestion and ventilation', an official history records, he was able to get 30% of psychiatric casualties back to combat duty within 30 hours; and during the battles of Maknassy and El Guettar returned 'more than 70% of 494 neuropsychiatric casualties to combat after 48 hours of treatment.' The remainder were sufficiently improved to be capable of duties at the base. By then, of course, the campaign had lost some of its ferocity.[50]

Hanson was clever, energetic, and handsome, a slim figure in dark glasses and well cut uniform. His bravery – 'personally placing himself in difficult combat situations' – 'impressed both line and medical superiors with his realistic understanding of battle-induced psychiatric casualties'; and his habit of turning up unannounced on the front line won him the nickname 'Phantom Freddy'. He knew how to handle the Brass, too; and was quite prepared, if necessary, to fake data to get his point across. 'You have to have a graph when you go to see a general,' Hanson told a battalion surgeon before going off to argue the case for giving the troops more rest.[51]

Thanks to Hanson, General Omar N. Bradley laid down at the end of April 1943 that the term 'exhaustion' would for the first time be the initial diagnosis in all psychiatric cases in the US Army. By the end of the Tunisian campaign, it seemed that the Americans were beginning to rediscover the principles of military psychiatry.[52]

At the other end of Africa, Montgomery's Eighth Army had been slowly pushing the Axis armies westwards – and beginning to incur significant psychological casualties again, too. These had been low overall during the Battle of Alamein and in the pursuit that followed, when morale was fairly high. But by the end of 1942, in the 'rocky, wooded and built over' areas of Tunisia, the neurosis rate was rising fast, thanks to the accumulated strain of so much fighting, the tougher terrain and the rough weather.

When the Libyan capital Tripoli was captured in January 1943, a new forward psychiatric unit was set up there to avoid having to send men 1,300 miles back to Cairo. To run it, 'Jimmy' James installed Major Harold Palmer, a tough no-nonsense Northerner, formidably well-trained in general medicine and 'physical' methods, and strongly against psychoanalysis. Palmer was someone you either loved or hated. To some, he was a 'saint' – whose 'driving force and heightened sense of mission' drew devoted service from every nurse and orderly; a man who courageously took on any challenge, and carried the world on his shoulders. Yet he had a genius for rubbing people up the wrong way, and was disliked by many psychiatrists because of the dogmatic and grandiose claims he made for his work.[53]

Palmer was short but powerfully built, 'a rugged-looking man with a broken nose' and a 'great hairy chest the nurses used to swing on' in the swimming pool in Tripoli'. Psychiatric colleagues respected his energy, but were wary of his 'rather dramatic, very simplistic ideas', the way he talked about 'cowardice'.[54]

In his papers, Palmer often strikes a tough note. The psychoneurotic casualty was 'a menace to the morale of fighting troops'. Men who broke down in warfare had 'failed in their job as soldiers' and 'dissolved their comradeship in arms'. Why should they get special treatment?[55]

The soldier's comrades may well ask 'Why should the neurotic be safe-guarded against the nervous breakdown, any more than the ordinary soldier is safe-guarded against the risk of wounding or death?' A community at war has as much right to demand that a soldier gives his 'nerves' for his country, as in principle it exercises the right to demand that a soldier gives his eyes, limbs or even his life for his country.[56]

Palmer claimed to have brought about a new kind of military psychiatry in which the doctor, instead of dealing with the patient's underlying psycho-neurotic conflicts, simply attacked his superficial problems in functioning as a soldier. But in many ways, he was a throw-back to the First World War and the world of Gordon Holmes and William Johnson. Like them, he believed strongly that breakdowns usually occurred 'in men who possess[ed] a hereditary constitutional predisposition, in whom previous emotional trauma [had] occurred' and used words like 'neuropathic' and 'dissociated' which more fashionable colleagues had discarded. His emphasis on maintaining a military atmosphere and determination not to create in the patient's mind 'the concept that he is a sick man and therefore unable to fight' is reminiscent of much post-1917 forward psychiatry. At the same time, Palmer developed a sophisticated repertoire of treatments tailored to the different kinds of case among the 12,000-odd soldiers he treated. A third of patients, he suggested, could be successfully managed with 'commonsense restorative measures such as sleep, hot meals, showers and a change of kit.' More serious cases would receive a mixture of sedation, ether abreaction and 'intense persuasion prosecuted with vigour'. Crucially, Palmer was careful to maintain – and to play on – the soldier's sense of loyalty to his comrades, unlike Grinker, who often at this point liberated him from the bonds of the 'superego'. But his ether abreaction was broadly similar to Grinker's methods.[57]

On the face of it, Palmer achieved very impressive results – 93% back to full duty within a month, 98% within two months. In fact, only 30% of those soldiers returned to their units, the others being posted elsewhere within Eighth Army. Nor is it clear how many of this third had had severe problems or were simply exhausted. Psychiatrists like Palmer knew full well that statistics of this kind were of limited meaning. Yet, politically, they were vital: 'the higher command', as one American put it, being 'apparently composed of men impressed by figures and much too busy to look behind them and inquire into their meaning.' Palmer's results were seized on by the Adjutant-General in London, to rebut 'people who are inclined to regard Army Psychiatry as a species of black magic . . . invented during this war by a certain type of doctor, who has succeeded in imposing new and untried theories upon the Army.' The psychiatrists' value, General Adam wrote in a circular in December 1943, could best be judged from their work to *prevent unnecessary wastage* overseas. Palmer's success, treating men within two days of leaving the front line, when compared with the poor results being achieved in Algiers, showed 'that if the psychiatrists' assistance is sought quickly, the permanent loss from battle exhaustion will be negligible.'[58]

But it was one thing to lay down this principle in London or Washington, quite another to apply it in every theatre of war. When the Allies invaded Sicily in July 1943, it was not possible to treat American psychiatric casualties on the island. Instead, they were evacuated back to North Africa and treated there by young doctors fresh from medical school, who had read Freud, were excited by Grinker and Spiegel's 'narcosynthesis' and had no experience of war. They assumed that every soldier's symptoms sprang from deep-seated personality problems stretching back to his childhood which must disqualify him from any further fighting. They asked men about 'their childhood, whether they wet the bed, whether their fathers drank.' 'We were too inflexible,' one later admitted, 'and insisted that in all such reactions one must postulate of nipple dependency or father hostility or some other type of bunkum.' Having heard the soldier's tales of battle, they seldom had the heart to send him back to it; only 3% of psychiatric casualties returned to Sicily.[59]

The psychiatric 'wastage' on Sicily helps to explain the famous incident on 3 August 1943, when the American commander on the island, Lt-General George S. Patton Jr., visited a hospital near Palermo. After talking to several wounded men he stopped beside the bed of a young private seemingly untouched by war. 'What's wrong with you, soldier?' he asked. The man replied that he was a psychiatric casualty. Patton then slapped him across the face with his glove and said, 'You're just a goddamned coward.' A week later, at a second hospital, Patton threatened another soldier with his pistol and punched him on the head. It has been suggested that 'Old Blood and Guts' was himself overwrought at the time; or that he was, beneath all the braggadocio, a sensitive man who had only conquered his own fears by a supreme effort of will. But Patton, who was largely responsible for the transformation in American morale after the disasters in Tunisia, may simply have been exasperated by the drain on manpower.[60]

The uproar caused by the 'slapping incident' forced Patton to make a public apology and lost him his command. It also brought the problem of psychiatric casualties to public attention and forced the US military finally to address it. When Italy was invaded in September 1943, arrangements for forward psychiatry were finally sorted out and something similar to Salmon's plan in 1918 recreated.

Battlefield medicine has always involved crude triage – dividing the wounded in three classes, and giving the most effort to those who can fight again while ignoring the dying. From the point of view of the Allied military command in 1943, psychiatric casualties, too, fell into three simple categories: men capable of returning to battlefield duty; men finished as fighting soldiers but worth retaining in the theatre of war in auxiliary roles; and men with no military future, to be sent home for treatment or discharge. The Italian campaign – a slow advance up a long, thin country – lent itself to tidy administration and both Armies evolved similar three-tier arrangements. First of all, there was forward treatment near the front line for soldiers capable of further fighting after two to five days of rest and simple treatment – at the Corps level in the British case, Division for the Americans. Then, further back up the lines of communication, there would be a hospital of 300–400 beds where 10–14 days of more sophisticated treatment was offered. Finally, for serious cases, a Base Psychiatric Centre was established.[61]

A vivid glimpse of acute battlefield casualties arriving at the first of these levels survives in a fragment of film shot at the British XIII Corps 'Exhaustion Centre' at Piccilli, south of Rome, on 21 May 1944. The fourth battle of Cassino was then a week old and the Allied High Command, having failed three times to take the monastery, was mustering everything for a final effort. XIII Corps had just spent 'three hellish days' – and suffered nearly 4,000 casualties – establishing a bridgehead across the Rapido and Gari rivers against Germans who 'fought with fury'. General Mark Clark, the Fifth Army commander, had decried its lack of progress.[62]

A lorry arrives at an arbitrary collection of tents in an anonymous Italian landscape. From it emerge soldiers fresh from the battlefield, some huddled in blankets. Two types are at once apparent: boys, with cocky, almost cheerful faces, who have broken down almost at once; and men, some of them regulars – great rocks of men, with austere 1940s haircuts, their faces etched with shame, grief, and weariness. Most combine dignity and distress; one is 'agitated' by the noise and presence of the camera.

In a reception tent, they talk individually to a psychiatrist. Apart from that, they sleep. The third day of treatment consists of lolling around in deckchairs, reading and dozing. Finally, two of the mild anxiety cases are seen after treatment, looking completely recovered, on their way back to the front.

Those who did not benefit from this simple regime were sent further back. The future comedian Spike Milligan broke down near Cassino in January 1944, and was given tea, sedatives, sleep and a pep talk at the Exhaustion Centre – a psychiatrist with a 'small, almost pencil-thin moustache' told him that it took 100,000 German shells to kill a British soldier, and (in a louder voice) that he would get better before being sent back to his regiment.' But although Milligan did return to the front three days later, another week of crying, stammering and distress at the noise of the guns made it clear that his battlefield days were over. It was, Milligan later recorded, 'one of the saddest days of my life.'

I got up very early. I didn't say goodbye to anyone. I got into the truck . . . as I drove back down that muddy mountain road, with the morning mists filling the valleys, I felt as though I was being taken across the Styx. I've never got over that feeling.[63]

This time he was sent back to the next tier, the Military Hospital in Caserta near Naples, where he was given a shot of sodium amytal that put him out for three days: 'In moments of consciousness one was on a sort of high. I remember asking an Italian cleaning lady to marry me.' After days of lying in bed reading poetry, he finally saw Harold Palmer (of whose boxing exploits he had heard) who sympathised with his wish to be occupied. 'A lot of the bastards like to malinger here as long as they can,' Palmer told him. Milligan was then informed that he was an 'anxiety state chronic' and would never return to his beloved Battery. Instead he was sent off in a lorry to a Rehabilitation Camp at the Base to work as a psychiatric clerk. There were some thousand men there under the command of a 'loony' officer called Captain Peters, who had been 'been blown up on the Volturno and blown down again at Cassino.' He was 'tall and thin, [with a] large horse-like face, pale blue eyes with a rapid blink and a twitch of the head; all done with a strange noise at the back of the nose that goes "phnut".' Evidently well-meaning, Captain Peters improved the food and allowed some of the men out for the evening.

But the effect of alcohol on some of the loonies who were on tranquillizers was alarming. It was something to see the guard commander and his men holding down a half naked, shit-covered, wine-stained loony alternately being sick, screaming and singing. Some loonies tried to climb Vesuvius. God knows how many fell in. A resident psychiatrist arrived. He immediately dished out drugs that zombified most of the inmates, who walked around the camp starry-eyed and saying 'Hello' to trees.[64]

An air of despair, failure and self-hatred hung over these establishments.

* * *

In the more settled conditions of the Italian campaign, it finally became possible for young American psychiatrists to visit the front line. There, they were amazed to discover that nearly all the troops, even soldiers singled out as functioning effectively, had most of the same symptoms as the patients they had been treating back in North Africa. They 'had the shakes, had nightmares, had sweats, were frightened, had many of the same symptoms as those who'd broken down'; but kept going out of pride or determination. For many of the psychiatrists this marked a further stage in the getting of wisdom, in realising the differences between military and civilian psychiatry.[65]

Even as the psychiatrists were becoming more 'military-minded', so Command was losing some of its suspicions and seeing their uses. By the end of 1943 'trick-cyclists' had become accepted as a necessary part of modern warfare in most areas of Allied Forces abroad. They weren't usually regarded with great enthusiasm and ranked somewhere with VD doctors in status, but they had their role. In the campaigns in the Far East, geography enhanced their importance.

In Burma, because 'human problems abounded' among the British troops, Command was more welcoming. To fight in Burma was to inhabit every Western schoolchild's nightmare – thick jungle, murderous climate, fanatical oriental enemy. The early campaigns, like that in the Arakan in 1942–3, produced enormous casualty lists with entire units succumbing to neurosis. There was said to be no point in counting psychiatric cases in 14th Indian Division when it returned from the Arakan; the entire division 'was for practical purposes a psychiatric casualty'. Thereafter, it functioned only as a training unit. Visiting a hospital in India later that year, the Supreme Allied Commander, Lord Louis Mountbatten, was startled to find five consecutive patients who had not even got as far as the front line before collapsing with neurotic complaints. 'I could not imagine anyone getting shell-shocked until they had been shelled,' he remarked.[66]

The psychiatrists' job in Burma was to prevent evacuation syndromes developing. In the early days, patients who broke down in action had been labelled 'NYD Mental' by Regimental Medical Officers ignorant of psychiatry and evacuated back to India; a 'substantial wastage in manpower had taken place and was taking place every day.' To stem this tide, psychiatrists were poured into the sub-continent; the 'Indian Army' which had six psychiatrists before the war, none of them full-time, had almost a hundred by 1945, an expansion engineered by E. A. Bennet, a Tavistock stalwart, Jungian and capable organiser, sent to Delhi in October 1942. The very different worlds it brought into contact are evoked by a scene in Paul Scott's novel *The Towers of Silence*, when starchy Memsahibs of the Raj encounter a 'Jew-boy trick-cyclist' at a party, start questioning him about psychoanalysis and are appalled when he explains to the company Wilhelm Reich's views on the function of the orgasm.[67]

The terrain and manner of warfare in Burma made the evacuation of casualties difficult; to have any effect, psychiatrists had therefore to work well forward. By November 1943, they were being sent to the Divisional level, and co-operating unusually closely with the military. In the two terrible battles in the spring of 1944 which broke the Japanese threat to India, psychiatrists attached to all British and Indian Divisions were able to return a high percentage of casualties to combat. In the retreat to Imphal, a psychiatrist attached to 20th (Indian) Division worked right in the 'Boxes' or defensive positions. 'Cover from shelling,' his reports tersely states, was 'secured by digging in, but there was no head cover'. Not surprisingly, 'dealing with psychiatric cases was complex', but he managed to get 50% of them back into action within three days. More attention was given to British than the Indian casualties.[68]

At Kohima, Captain Paul Davis of 2nd Division began treating soldiers at a dressing station just a few miles behind the front line, but found that the noise of artillery firing made patients panicky and alarmed and hard to sedate. He then retreated to a converted goat shed some eighteen miles from the fighting, giving soldiers 'little more than the most superficial therapy' consisting of 'simple explanation, reassurance and encouragement.' 'Persuasion,' Davis acknowledged, also played an important role. 'In a formation in which morale and pride of Unit stand high it is profitable and, I consider, justifiable to play on those aspects in treatment and to use them as levers with which to boost up the patient's natural recuperative powers.' On the other hand, he did not consider Pentothal abreaction 'a particularly useful procedure'.[69]

Davis' work was thought 'worth its weight in gold' and earned him one of the few decorations ever given to a British psychiatrist. He had sent 112 soldiers back to duty, a success he attributed not to any great clinical insight but to his long military experience, knowledge of the practical difficulties and problems of the soldier and skill in mixing with officers 'using every art of diplomacy and tact.'[70]

How much of the credit for Davis' success belonged with General Slim in fostering higher morale and a belief in the possibility of victory within Fourteenth Army it is impossible to say.

*   *   *

In the Pacific the Americans had psychiatric problems right from the start. Understandably so, for the first campaigns against the Japanese were amongst the toughest of the war. The 17,000 Marines landed on the island of Guadalcanal in the Solomons in August 1942 found themselves more or less abandoned when a disastrous naval battle gave the initiative back to the enemy; for four months they received inadequate supplies and reinforcements, while enduring poor food, tropical diseases, sleeplessness and unceasing attack from land and air. Hanging over everything was a sense of being isolated and forgotten; that they, doomed to a terrible death, were fighting the war alone while the higher command bickered and the folks back home paid no attention. Guadalcanal, Samuel Eliot Morison later wrote, 'is not a name but an emotion, recalling desperate fights in the air, desperate night naval battles, frantic work at supply and construction, savage fighting in the sodden jungle, nights broken by screaming bombs and deafening explosions of naval shells.' By the time the Marines were relieved by Army units, some '95% of the original landing force was hors de combat, mostly by fever.'[71]

Marines evacuated to a hospital on Fiji were 'bedraggled and emaciated youths with frozen expressions on their aged faces and a far-off stare in their eyes', suffering from anxiety and depression; 'the only patient who appeared moderately happy was obviously manic.' Their conditioned reflexes were so overdeveloped that 'a sudden loud noise would bring the entire ward to their feet, prepared to dash for a slit trench.'[72]

During the day, these men engaged in 'constant chatter about the fighting filled with criticism of the weapons, the strategy, the command, the lack of relief from the army.' 'Killing, grousing, self-protection, shouting, cursing, waiting for death, distrust of the night, abandonment of hope had become ingrained,' Dr Theodore Lidz wrote later. 'Life had so long consisted of waiting in the jungle hoping and longing for relief that it was a slow process for more social trends to return into the pattern of behaviour.'[73]

Psychiatric casualties had no more been planned for in the Pacific than in North Africa. When men broke down, facilities had quickly to be improvised. On Guadalcanal, a Divisional surgeon found himself mugging up on psychiatric texts his wife sent him from the United States while struggling to persuade the Army commander not to court-martial his patients. General Alexander Patch did eventually accept that men could receive medical treatment, but insisted on administrative punishment for officers, forcing the doctor to label them as 'blast concussion' cases.[74]

Given the primitive forward facilities, most nervous patients were evacuated back to hospitals in Australia, New Zealand, Hawaii or even San Francisco, and once gone, few returned to the front. As always, 'wastage' – the impact of psychiatric casualties on manpower – forced the official mind to overcome its distaste for the whole subject and send for the psychiatrists. The scale of the problem was revealed by the militarily unimportant campaign in New Georgia in July 1943 when psychiatric casualties were 'alarmingly high', and there were signs of 'mass' outbreaks in some units. Dr Lidz's hospital back on Fiji was once again 'overwhelmed'.[75]

In October 1943, a prominent Freudian, Dr Moses Ralph Kaufman, was sent to the Pacific as Consultant Psychiatrist; having read Grinker and Spiegel on their Tunisian experiences, he took with him all the sodium pentothal and benzedrine he could carry. 'Moe' Kaufman was a 'greying, chunky dynamo of a man', forty-three, who had spent a year in Vienna in analysis with the then highly regarded young Freudian Wilhelm Reich, and had built up a reputation as a respected clinical psychiatrist and teacher in Boston. He was a man of authority and charm, with a quick wit and ever-present cigar. 'Ambitious, a leader, dangerous,' was one assessment.[76]

Kaufman never had any problem with accepting his military role; he was 'able to work effectively with the command.' He reversed the evacuation policy, making it plain during the Bougainville campaign that casualties would not be evacuated off the island. His message was not altogether welcome. Theodore Lidz recalls: 'Moe came fresh from the States and went round telling the troops that no one would go home till the war was over . . . At that time we had captured two small islands in two years.' Dr Lidz's hospital on Fiji was 'flooded by depressed patients who did not yet know that all battles would not be like Guadalcanal and New Georgia.'[77]

But Kaufman was not just doing command's bidding. He came genuinely to believe that it was often better for the soldier himself if he was not evacuated but sent back into combat. 'From a long-term point of view,' he wrote after the war, 'one did not always do a soldier a favour by evacuating him from the combat zones.' The soldier was of course removed from stress, but at the price of being turned into an invalid.

There were feelings of guilt and a need for constant justification for having run out 'without any wound' or organic illness to show as the 'Red Badge of Courage'. The loss of self-respect was also a factor that made for the necessity to continue neurotic symptoms into civilian life in many instances. In terms of the future of the individual, the gain in self-respect at being able to overcome the neurotic difficulties and to return to combat or duty was of inestimable value. There was a pride in being able to say 'I went through such and such a campaign,' rather than 'I had to be evacuated.'[78]

Kaufman's experiences on Bougainville convinced him that psychiatric treatment should take place as far forward as possible, 'in the combat zone . . . within the sound of artillery', where 'morale factors' could still operate. There may have been an element of projection in this for, like Fred Hanson, Kaufman enjoyed the drama of war, was personally fearless and brave and took a masculine pleasure in being near the front line. But it also acknowledged the enormous psychological impact of letting a man leave the battle zone during the Pacific campaigns. As for the treatment itself, Kaufman rejected the use of sodium pentothal. Firstly, he claimed, it messed up the patients and, far from calming them, often made them more confused, sometimes adding to their amnesia (Sargant, it will be recalled, had described barbiturates magically *removing* amnesia). 'It was no uncommon sight,' wrote Kaufman, 'to see patients stagger about as if drunk on barbiturates, confused and with an amnesia that was fixed by the drugs.' Secondly, it got in the way. Chemical sedation prevented the establishment of 'that interpersonal relationship which is one of the most essential relationships in therapy . . . [the] sort of parent-child (doctor-patient, officer-man) relationship on the first contact with the patient.' On the other hand, 'reassurance, a kindly but firm approach and the technique of hypnosis' made such a relationship possible. Finally, barbiturates were simply unnecessary with highly suggestible front-line patients. Kaufman found this out one day on Bougainville when he 'filled up a syringe and, before I had the opportunity to push the plunger (I still don't know how to find a vein), the patient was already reacting as if I'd given him the sodium pentothal. So I said, "To hell with this, what do I have to waste sodium pentothal for?" So I started to use hypnosis.'[79]

Kaufman only had the opportunity to carry out this approach once, during the Okinawa campaign in April 1945. At the staging area for the invasion, at Leyte in the Philippines, he announced to his 'somewhat astounded' team that in the forthcoming battle they would be using hypnosis, not pentothal, both as a sedative and as an aid to abreaction. He had not previously made this clear, he explained, because 'with the general attitude of medical and line officers to the use of hypnotic therapy, the mere mention of hypnosis might jeopardize the whole treatment program.' None of the doctors had any experience of hypnosis and were 'somewhat apprehensive' but Kaufman assured them of its simplicity.[80]

Film shot on Okinawa shows a succession of sad, twitching men brought to a field hospital – a few tents a couple of miles from the front line – and there hypnotised with calm authority by Kaufman and his colleagues. The soldier is laid out like a corpse on a slab on a simple trestle table set up under the sun, in the open ground between two tents. Kaufman bends over him and with pent-up energy, touches his head. The patient goes off to sleep, or he is taken back over the events which produced his present condition:

One soldier grasps at his backpack under hypnosis and is unable to find the shovel with which he would have been able to dig a foxhole, re-enacting this with the terror that went with it.[81]

Afterwards the soldier is told what he has remembered and given the inevitable cigarette. Then for the next day or two he is with other men who have had similar experiences and spontaneous group psychotherapy takes place. He also receives warm food and clean clothes.

How far did Kaufman's team go in their psychotherapy? Did they simply concentrate on rest and crude abreaction, a sort of vomiting out of traumatic material, which would hopefully take away the symptoms? Or did they attempt to deal with the whole underlying personality of the man? Like William Brown in 1917, the Americans on Okinawa were trying to achieve a half-way house between two extremes, to serve both Army and individual. Their account acknowledges that there was 'a danger of producing personality fragmentation through too quick a liberation of primitive defenses.'

Though the aim was indeed to bring about an immediate recovery of military usefulness, through dealing with the immediate psychic trauma, there was an awareness of the pre-combat personality of the soldier and a concern for his future personal, as well as military, stability.[82]

Proximity to the line and Kaufman's bravery in facing danger infused the proceedings with urgency; psychiatrists felt the 'excitement of battle'. Nobody visiting this hospital could feel, as Harvey Cushing did at Passchendaele, that none of the doctors knew or cared about psychiatry.

Did this method work? As always, figures for men returned to the line provide the only, inadequate, yardstick. These were very high to begin with – some 83%; and even after things on Okinawa began to get tougher they were still respectable – about 57% returned to duty. But by June 1945, with the campaign into its ninth week, weariness set in and the figure for returns began to sink, to an average of 38.32%. Only a third of men were going back into battle, pretty much the standard figure. Moe Kaufman's energy and determination had made some difference, but not that much.[83]

*   *   *

Overall, the pattern in front-line psychiatry was of a gradual loss of faith in chemical abreaction and a return to the simpler methods used in 1917–18. In terms of keeping a man fighting, a good night's sleep near the battlefield probably helped more than elaborate psychotherapy. Many of the more complicated procedures also proved impractical; the insulin-coma method, for example, required a huge investment of nursing time and could be dangerous in hot countries like Egypt.

But no central orthodoxy emerged. One British psychiatrist could declare in 1944 that 'psychocatharsis and analytic methods in general serve[d] no useful purpose and indeed constitute[d] a menace and often a disaster.' Yet, at the same time William Sargant was treating a group of thirty patients with deep-sleep treatment and modified insulin therapy *combined* – something he admitted he would never do in peacetime. He also adopted Harold Palmer's technique of abreacting patients with ether, claiming that it was more effective than sodium amytal in provoking *emotion* rather than simple recall. Indeed, in the end Sargant decided that the memory recalled didn't need to have been *correct* so long as there was emotion associated with it.[84]

Sargant's most assiduous disciples turned out to be a group of American psychiatrists based in England. They treated Air Force pilots and Army casualties with insulin coma and deep sleep, sometimes in harness, together with group psychotherapy and, where it was felt to be appropriate, Pentothal abreaction. According to one account, it was 'the practice to hustle practically all patients off into bed and for a period of ten days, in the hushed atmosphere of a darkened ward, where whispers and muffled footsteps only enhanced the drama of the scene, to administer routinely a narcosis-insulin regime'.[85]

This enthusiasm for drug treatments fitted in, one critic argued, with the mechanistic mood of 'a global war in which accomplishment depends so much on mass production methods in all spheres.' 'The need of the hour' was for 'wholesale, conveyor-belt systems of output,' rather than for slow patient psychotherapy; drugs could be applied with the minimum of effort and time and without benefit of trained personnel. It was inevitable that they would 'supplant more individualized approaches'. The danger was that in its enthusiasm for drugs and 'external agents', the hierarchy tended to forget the need for individual psychiatric attention. Dr William Needles – despite his name analytically-oriented – doubted the wisdom of 'the indiscriminate application of pharmacological therapy in medical installations far removed from the front lines where less acute cases are received, in whom the factors of physical exhaustion have long subsided and psychological factors provide the basis for symptoms.'[86]

This sort of critical note is rare in the literature and it is hard to know whether psychiatrists were happy to serve the Army rather than their patients. Usually, it depended on the military situation and how close the doctor was to operational conditions. Dr Philip S. Wagner, who served in Normandy, made no bones about the need for the psychiatrist to 'set aside [the] traditional primary aim of making the experience of living desirable to his patient. He had to find himself able to extend instead *an invitation to death*' (italics added). Wagner frankly described the techniques of manipulation necessary:

One would pound the table, shout with admiration, and lean towards a colleague to say, 'Hey, Major, here's a real soldier for you. Forty days on the line, knocked off his can by an "88" and he wants to go back and give the bastards more!' Whereupon all the psychiatrists would turn around, beam, and shout approval. Or another would shout, 'What an outfit the X-regiment is, keep them on their feet long enough and they'll take the Goddam German Army themselves,' whereupon a chorus of approbation and solemn nods would prevail throughout the receiving tent.[87]

Whereas, to Dr Needles, working in a hospital back in England, it was 'appalling to reflect how frequent the miscarriage of psychiatry must have been. To one who was obliged to listen in while a dynamic, chest-thumping psychiatrist, who had never been exposed to anything more than a toy pistol, embarked on "pep talk number three" and harangued a combat-ridden soldier about the necessity of "standing up like a man" it was a memorable experience. One was led to wonder what incentives spurred on these stethoscopic heroes and whether they were solving their own difficulties by projecting their impulses on to the unfortunate patients who fell into their hands.'[88]

16

NEW WAYS OF WAR

The cry during the last three years has been 'We know what we are fighting against – but what are we fighting for?'

Captain David Elliott to his sister, 1943[1]

Charles Upham was not a regular soldier. Before the war he was a farm manager, mustering sheep on the high country of Christ Church, New Zealand. It was a tough life, which helped to form his austere, self-reliant character. When hostilities began he volunteered immediately: 'I couldn't get there quickly enough and I hated the Germans because they had killed a lot of my relations in the first war.'

In May 1941, defending Maleme airfield on Crete from German paratroopers, Upham revealed fighting skills of Old Testament dimensions. Although 'racked by severe dysentery', he destroyed, virtually single-handed, two German machine-gun posts, using his 'remarkable stalking skills' to 'make himself invisible in the *garrigue* of the Cretan hillside until the moment he burst from cover.'

A year later, in the Western Desert, his unit found itself completely surrounded by the Germans and 'broke out at bayonet point'. 'Upham himself, unseen in the darkness of night, ran from one German vehicle to the next, lobbing in grenades to clear a path to let the New Zealanders through.' Soon after, at the first battle of Alamein, he led his company in an assault on a German formation, personally destroying a tank, four machine-guns and a number of trucks.

Observers of his performance have since described him as being possessed of an almost divinely inspired rage against the enemy as he strode forward destroying everything in his path.

Later that day, heavily wounded, Upham was taken prisoner and, despite several attempts to escape, spent the rest of the war behind barbed war. In 1945 he married, returned to New Zealand and became a farmer. By then he had twice been awarded the Victoria Cross. Charles Upham 'had in full measure that quality which is the hallmark of the best fighting troops – a relentless desire to get to grips with the enemy.'[2]

But such men are rare except on the movie screen. Most soldiers are more like Roy Farrant – whose tank was shot up by aircraft on Crete:

I lost my head. I was so afraid that I could have buried into the ground. And so I ran . . . crashing through the undergrowth, tumbling into ditches and all the time looking up at the sky at the black crosses on the aeroplanes.[3]

In the early campaigns of the war, the normal emotion of fear was exaggerated by the sense of German and Japanese omnipotence, a feeling that the Allies had nothing to fight back with. A doctor on Crete noticed the paralysing effect of a new factor in war – German air superiority:

The feeling was seldom that of animal fear. Rather did it go beyond reason, the sensation of an animal, trapped and helpless, sufficient to numb the stoutest heart. Men felt it whose courage was never in question, men who continued to give orders and to fight with no thought of surrender or withdrawal. What had changed in them was their spontaneity and their power of decision. A lethargy gripped them. They spoke in low monotones, and replied to questions in sudden feeble irritation. They became unrecognisable to their friends. . . . It was as though the enemy had enlisted in his support the powers of the supernatural.[4]

The central question confronting both the British and the Americans between 1940 and 1944 was: *How do we get them to fight?* How, in a democratic age, without the traditional weapons of punishment and execution, were men to be got to risk their lives in battle? Would drill, discipline and tradition still be enough? What would men fight *for?* Could the new mental sciences like psychology and psychiatry, yoked perhaps to the persuasive power of the mass media, help to motivate them?

The answers came to revolve around questions of ideology, motivation, leadership and tactics – matters which in the First World War had mostly been left to the Regular Army. This time, however, outsiders were telling the generals their business right from the start.

*   *   *

The disaster of Dunkirk, while not quite bringing down the British state, created a vacuum of political and moral authority into which stepped what Correlli Barnett has called 'a stage army of philanthropists and social engineers and . . . anti-appeasement Conservatives,' people for whom the war was as much about creating a new Jerusalem as about defeating Hitler. Churchill's coalition government was forced to widen its support – the liberal intelligentsia was for the first time given limited access to the mass media and official propaganda, hitherto full of the bombastic certainties of the newsreels, now stretched to poetic documentaries, even, for a while, to the folksy socialism of the writer J. B.

Priestley. Subjects like unemployment and fascism, censored in the 1930s, could now in wartime be tackled in the cinema and on the radio (though colonialism remained taboo).[5]

The British Army faced a particular crisis of legitimacy in 1940–1. Buffeted by Blitzkrieg in France, Norway and Crete, it was lampooned in the press as a bastion of blimpish incompetence, incapable of modern warfare. How could it be modernised and mechanised? How could its unenthusiastic recruits ever be a match for the Wehrmacht? Only, said many people in 1940, by creating a new kind of Army altogether, an Army fuelled by ideology, an Army that (in Oliver Cromwell's then much-quoted words) 'knows what it is fighting for and loves what it knows'. Looking to the Parliamentary Army of the seventeenth century and the People's Militias of the Spanish Civil War, left-wing intellectuals like George Orwell dreamed of turning the Home Guard into a 'quasi-revolutionary People's Army' and of replacing Britain's 'class army' with a modern, rational, thinking-person's army in which intelligent, well-motivated soldiers were led by educated and rational-minded officers who knew exactly what they were fighting for. Fear, instead of being repressed, hidden in a cloak of taboo and irrational masculine ritual, would be acknowledged, addressed and vaccinated against. This would be an army of well-adjusted adults able to handle the emotional stresses of war.[6]

In *New Ways of War*, Tom Wintringham, the leader of the British brigade in Spain, argued that for Hitler to be defeated 'men must be persuaded, made to understand, given the enthusiasm that will change their discipline from an acceptance of orders to an eager use of all their powers in pursuit of a common aim.' They had to be made to feel that their own contributions had value and were accepted, 'that the war is their war'. Wintringham argued that this 'could only be done on a political basis'.[7]

The logic of such remarks was that the British should introduce into their Army political commissars on the Soviet model. In the middle years of the war, when the Russians were offering the only meaningful resistance to Hitler, naive idealism for 'our gallant Soviet ally' was widespread. 'The common expression among soldiers when some foolish order has been given,' 'Captain X' reveals in his book *A Soldier Looks Ahead* (1944), is ' "What would Joe say?" '. This does not, he explains, 'signify an ideological acceptance of Marxism, but it does mean that many soldiers look upon Marshal Stalin as the embodiment of goodness and common sense and as a sort of patron saint of Tommy Atkinses all over the world.'[8]

The British Army never went that far. But, faced by a crisis in morale in 1941, the Adjutant-General, Sir Ronald Adam, took steps to give the Army a more democratic ethos. Most notably, he created the Army Bureau of Current Affairs (ABCA), run by a former director of Penguin Books and the Workers' Educational Authority, which was intended to organise discussion of current affairs in the Army. ABCA was heartily disliked by Churchill (who tried to kill it off), denounced by conservatives as an instrument of socialist indoctrination and earned General Adam a reputation among his colleagues as 'a serious menace both to morale and discipline'. Soldiers' memories of the weekly ABCA debates on such topics as 'food in war' or 'Our Ally Russia' are more cynical. The average British soldier, Fred Majdalany later wrote, 'never gave democracy a thought'. It was soon clear that such political education could never solve the Army's main headache – finding a way to defeat the Wehrmacht. Only training could do that.[9]

The disasters of 1940–2 and the inevitable resultant loss of public confidence eventually forced the British Army to rethink its traditional ways. 'Exasperated by the endless retreats before Germans and Japanese, who seemed to have got hold of something new by way of battle procedure,' Peter Ustinov recalled, it 'was determined that a new, more aggressive fighting man should rise like a khaki phoenix from the fires of abandoned supplies and gutted citadels.' This 'new toughness' often involved the mortification of other people's flesh – General Montgomery, commanding a division in England, made his officers run seven miles a week – but its most important manifestation were the 'Battle Schools', which sprang up in 1941. These training grounds attempted to inject 'more realism into the weapon and tactical training of British infantry to enable them to meet the formidably efficient Germans with greater confidence.' Live ammunition was used and attempts made to develop new methods of infantry attack.[10]

'Battle drill' was now derived from an analysis of German practice in France in 1940 and of the tactics and techniques of German *sturmtruppen* in the Great War. The thinking was that, for all the attention given to the Luftwaffe and the Panzers, Blitzkrieg had in fact owed much of its success to the remarkable ability of German infantry to fight and win 'hundreds of LITTLE battles'. Wehrmacht infantry tactics assumed the rapid deployment of fire – 'infantrymen using their own initiative and weapons to fight themselves forward', usually by first pinning the enemy down in a fire fight, then blinding him with smoke and explosive, before moving closer to finish him off in close combat. It was decided that British infantry, too, needed to be taught to adopt set procedures in battle.[11]

For many pupils, however, the primary function of the Battle School was psychological: to counter the idea of an inevitable German victory by creating, from the opening address, an ethos that was self-consciously radical and hostile to the staid ways of the old Army. One of them remembers his 'state of exaltation' after hearing 'the first positive and credible assessment of the British Army's task since I had become a soldier'. He and others 'willingly ran and crawled and jumped and climbed, fasting and thirsting from dawn to dusk, and found a certain stern joy in the harsh yet not entirely grim routine of their life in Ashdown Forest.'[12]

Some Battle School instructors went further, trying to motivate their pupils with a positive ideology. Major Lionel Wigram – a successful solicitor before the war – delivered a philippic against the Germans as 'politically evil, socially vile, their leaders with characters gross and distorted, power-mad, brutal and sadistic,

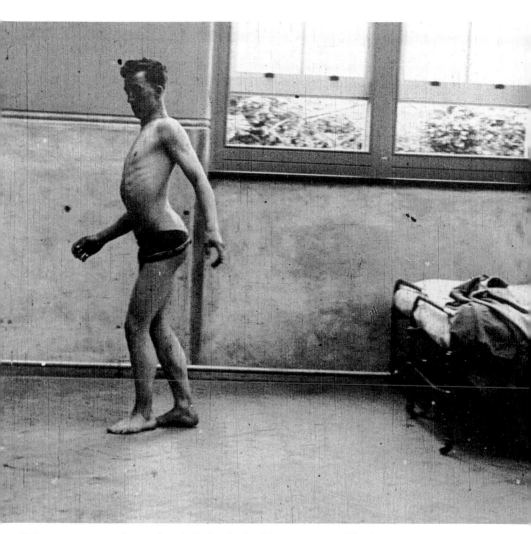

'You never saw such gaits.' A shell-shocked soldier showing off his hysterical symptoms, Netley Hospital, Southampton, 1917.

'A formidable antagonist': Dr Gordon Holmes.
A silhouette taken in Boulogne, 1916.

Charles Myers.
A studio portrait in Folkestone, 1915.

The Duchess of Westminster's Hospital, in the Casino at le Touquet,
where Myers first described 'shell-shock'.

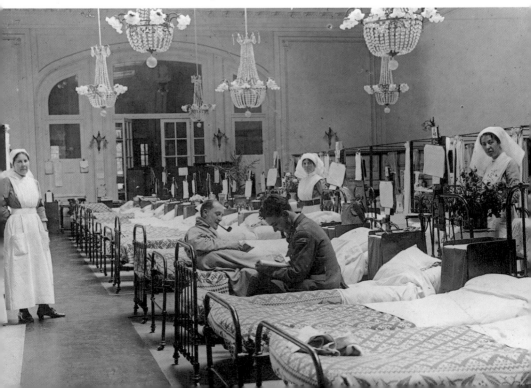

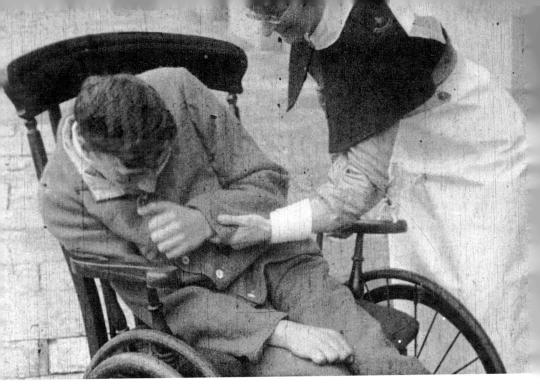

'His mind was that of a year-old child.' Private Meek at Netley Hospital, February 1917, after unsuccessful hypnosis by William McDougall and further treatment by A.F. Hurst.

November 1918. Private Meek, an adult once more, teaches his pre-war trade of basket-making at Seale Hayne, Devon.

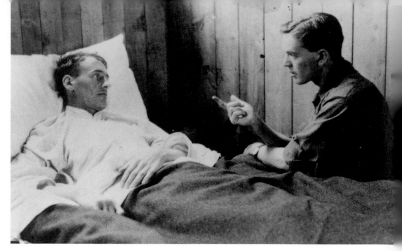

An American
doctor hypnotising
a soldier, France,
1918.

The 'Kaufman cure'.
An Austrian cartoon.

(*Below left*) Thomas W. Salmon in his office,
Neufchateau, France, 1918.

(*Below right*) William Brown, W.H.R. Rivers
and Grafton Elliot Smith at Maghull
Military Hospital, Liverpool in 1915.

'Phantom Freddy': Frederick R. Hanson
in Tunisia, May 1943.

Moe Kaufman, without a cigar,
Okinawa, April 1945.

Roy R. Grinker in his office at the Don Cesar, Florida, 1945.
A publicity still for his book *Men Under Stress*.

The British Freudian John Rickman interviewing an officer candidate, 1944

Officer candidates taking a Thematic Aperception Test, England 1944.
Peter Ustinov's interpretation of this slide cost him a commission.

(*Facing page*) The pain of defeat. A German soldier, Frankfurt, 1946.

The strain of bombardment. German troops at Cassino, 1944.

'Psychiatric casualties are lower than in any previous war.' An American patrol in Vietnam, 1965.

they stood for all a decent democratic community loathed and despised'. Attempts were also made to employ experimental psychological techniques in motivation, the most important being the tragi-comic episode known as 'Hate Training'.

On 27 April 1942, a month after the loss of Singapore, the BBC carried a talk on a 'New British Battle School', whose commandant was a Lieutenant-Colonel aged only 21.[13]

He was thin and always on the move – he never walked, always ran . . . His job was to teach men . . . how to hate the enemy and how to use that hate.

The School's intensive four-day course for officers and NCOs began with 'a lecture on hate'

delivered in the Hate Room, which was hung with photographs from occupied Europe of starving people and sick people and dead people in ones and in heaps. The Commandant explained that you kill your enemy more quickly and efficiently if you hate him, and it saves time if the men go on the battlefield already hating, if they have pictures in their minds of the things he's done, ready to be remembered.

This was followed by realistic battle training, with live ammunition and simulated booby-traps, while instructors and loudspeakers yelled 'On, on, kill, kill'. All the time, a 'chant of hate' superimposed on the sound track of the German film *Sieg im Westen*, blared out.

When the men finished their course, listeners were told, they would not be surprised by the noise of battle, they would know that quick ingenuity would get them past every obstacle and they would not be 'so shocked as they might, by blood and flesh and death', having gone 'to watch animals being killed in the slaughter-house, for this reason . . . And at the back of their minds they'll have this hate, this natural mainspring of relentless attack against the enemy.'

The broadcast provoked a storm of public outrage. Church leaders demanded that such immoral methods of training be stopped at once; a retired general warned that 'a new stage of hysteria has developed . . . which, if not checked, may develop and do much harm.' Within the Army, similar views were expressed by General Montgomery. Dr Tom Main, the psychiatrist attached to the Battle Schools, discovered that some of their best students – the 'prize alumni of hate training' – became depressed, thought of themselves as killers, and lost all interest in soldiering and fighting. Hate training produced guilt; whereas, Main said later, 'If you have a positive cause to fight for, an ideal, then you make a good soldier, not a killer'. On 25 May 1942 it was announced that 'blood lust tactics' were to cease. Such an attitude of hate, said General Paget, was 'foreign to our British temperament and any attempt to produce it by artificial stimulation was bound to fail, as it did in the last war.' But he would not want to dampen down the enthusiasm which had given rise to them.[14]

Some attempt was also made at 'battle inoculation', principally by getting recruits used to the sounds of battle, by using live ammunition and, in some cases, recordings of battle noise. The psychiatrists' main contribution seems to have been to persuade the Army to do it in small doses rather than by total immersion.

The most contentious question of all was how to handle fear; the views of soldiers and doctors usually dividing along generational lines. For example, when the Germans began systematically to bombard Malta in 1942, British medical opinion on the island was split between 'representatives of the "Tough school" which holds that the expression of fear in any form is a display of cowardice and should be treated as such' and

representatives of the 'compassionate' school that holds that fear is a normal healthy and reasonable reaction to danger, that it should not be suppressed, that in the intelligent and educated individual it can be diminished and controlled through the proffering of sympathetic, understanding, prophylactic help of a skilled kind and to regard anxiety as a form of cowardice and of military crime is not only useless but thoroughly mistaken.[15]

The decisive voice on Malta, the chief medical officer, Brigadier Morrison, was very much of the 'tough' school and relied on 'that combination of empirical knowledge and prejudice which guided the soldiers of his day'. He refused to allow a psychiatrist sent by the War Office even to land on Malta and, to make sure the troops clearly understood the situation, had notices posted in all gun sites which declared, with a forcefulness bordering on the obsessive:

Fear is the weapon which the enemy employs to sabotage morale.
    Anxiety neurosis is the term used by the medical profession to commercialise fear.
    Anxiety neurosis is a misnomer which makes 'cold feet' appear respectable.
    To give way to fear is to surrender to the enemy attack on your morale.
    To admit an anxiety neurosis is to admit to a state of fear which is either unreasonable or has no origin in your conception of duty as a soldier.
    If you are a man you will not permit your self-respect to admit an anxiety neurosis or to show fear . . .[16]

This 'tough' line worked: the guns kept firing and Malta fought heroically on until the siege was lifted in November 1942. But the human cost was high. By the end of March 1942 at least a quarter of the garrison were showing 'a pathological degree of response' to aerial attack and a month later things were even worse. Yet these men got only 'rest, sedation and reassurance'. When specialist psychiatric help was finally brought on the island in June 1943, a special hospital had to be set up to deal with the enormous backlog of cases.[17]

    Malta was exceptional; it was unusual in the Second World War for the issues to be spelt out so clearly. Most of the time, in both British and American Armies, the 'compassionate' line prevailed; fear was seen as a normal and natural human response to the strain and horror of war, which could be controlled. The

Americans were particularly direct about it. 'YOU'LL BE SCARED,' the handbook issued to all recruits declared:

Sure you'll be scared. Before you go into battle, you'll be frightened at the uncertainty, at the thought of being killed. Will it hurt? Will you know what to do? If you say you're not scared, you'll be a cocky fool. Don't let anyone tell you you're a coward if you admit being scared. Fear before you're actually in the battle is a normal emotional reaction. It's the last step of preparation, the not-knowing, in spite of all you've learned. After you've become used to the picture and the sensations of the battlefield, you will change. All the things you were taught in training will come back to you. This is the answer. This is where you will prove that you're a good soldier. That first fight – that fight with yourself – will have gone. Then you will be ready to fight the enemy.[18]

Could ways be found, then, to control fear by applying the insights of science? In the Battle Schools, 'the instinctive motions of fear were examined – bending double, protecting the eyes, diarrhoea. Methods of coping were discussed – how to counteract and pre-empt fear by building up the collective courage bank, and by the judicious use of alcohol, never forgetting the importance of a hot meal and a dash of cold water on the face.' American antidotes to fear included keeping busy with tasks involving detail and engaging in roll-calls and castings-off in order to emphasise the proximity of buddies, both as support and as audience. There were also many specific tactical manoeuvres to take in particular situations – under air attack, when ambushed by mortar fire and so on.[19]

But what if you couldn't control your fear, however well prepared? Attitudes varied enormously. The Americans were generally much more permissive than the British and some believed they had many fewer psychiatric cases as a result. 'The men,' wrote Grinker and Spiegel, 'as a rule feel that they have not too much to lose if they admit their anxiety since it will be understood and accepted, as long as they continue to make a firm effort to control it. The teachings of psychiatrists and the enlightened attitude of the Army leadership are responsible for permeation of this tolerance throughout the service.'[20] 'Enlisted men with combat experience,' declares *The American Soldier*, 'adopted a permissive attitude toward fear in combat . . . the majority of men regarded men who crack up mentally in combat as genuine medical casualties rather than as cowards and . . . the majority of troops showed little tendency to deny having experienced emotional reactions to combat but rather appear to have been willing to admit readily that they experienced fear and anxiety.'

American doctors claimed, too, that the permissive attitude to fear had been a major factor in avoiding neurotic and hysterical complications. American troops were on the whole strikingly free of the sort of symptoms seen in the First World War, but in units like the Airborne, where the prevailing group culture did not allow the expression of anxiety, men's fear would express itself in weakness or paralysis of the legs.[21]

Much that was written about fear smelt more of the campus than the battlefield. 'This upper and remote-echelon hope that fear can be turned, by argument and reasoning, into something with the appearance of courage,' one combat soldier later wrote, 'illustrates the overlap between the implausible persuasions of advertising and those of modern military motivators.' By 1943, however, it was becoming possible to study fear in the field.

* * *

In November 1943, Major Samuel Lyman Marshall was taking part in the American landings on the Pacific Islands of Makin and Kwajalein. 'Slam' Marshall was a short, stocky man who had served briefly in the Great War, done twenty years as a newspaperman in El Paso and Detroit, and – on the strength of two quick books on the European war – joined the staff of the US Army's historical division. The years as a reporter had not been wasted: he soon carved out a unique role as analyst of the Army's operations and devised what he claimed was a new kind of military history. After one dramatic night battle on Makin, Marshall spent four days interviewing participants to find out what really had happened. He claimed that by slowly putting together the different pieces of the jigsaw, 'every fact of the fight was procurable'. The fog of war – the fact that nobody ever knows what is happening in a battle – was magically lifted.[22]

For example, Marshall was asked to find out why, when an advancing line of infantry ran into enemy fire, there was always a delay of between forty-five and sixty minutes before any further movement took place. The answer, he discovered, was that 'when men go to ground under circumstances where they cannot see one another, the moral disintegration of that line is for the moment complete. All organizatonal unity vanishes temporarily. What has been a force becomes a scattering of individuals . . .while erect they feel the presence of others; when they go down this feeling is lost.' Cut off from one another, the men no longer felt social pressure to fight and became paralysed by fear and inertia until regrouped and roused by their leaders.

Fear is general among men [but] men commonly are loath that their fear will be expressed in specific acts which their comrades will recognize as cowardice. The majority are unwilling to take extraordinary risks and do not aspire to a hero's role, but they are equally unwilling that they should be considered the least worthy among those present . . . Social pressure, more than military training, is the base of military discipline, and . . . when social pressure is lifted, battle discipline disintegrates . . . Personal honour is the one thing valued more than life itself by the majority of the men.[23]

About three-quarters of soldiers, Marshall claimed, didn't actually fire their weapons at all. Why didn't they? Because the American soldier is 'what his home, his religion, his moral code and the ideals of his society have made him . . . he comes from a civilization in which aggression, connected with the taking of life is prohibited and unacceptable.'[24]

The situation was not helped, Marshall added, by the Army's methods of training. The emphasis on drill and discipline, designed to make men act together, ignored the fact that 'the advent of the rifle ended the days of close order formations'. Every modern battlefield was a loose, amorphous affair with units spread out and frequently out of touch with each other. What was needed was not parade ground precision, nor some general screaming down the telephone from behind, but troops motivated and intelligent enough to seize the initiative on their own. This new philosophy of military discipline had to 'free the mind of man – enlarge his appreciation of his personal worth as a unit in battle . . . stimulate him to express his individual power within limits that are for the good of all.' It was no good pumping the soldier full of propaganda, 'men do not fight for a cause but because they do not want to let their comrades down', Marshall postulated. His answer was to recognise up front that only a few had what it took and organise the fighting around them. Those who were 'no good' should be removed or given another role.[25]

Historians have recently cast doubt on whether Marshall actually carried out the interviews on which his statistics purported to rest; he was, they say, carried away by his journalistic sense of a story. It is also true that his work had more influence after the war than during it. But observing the behaviour of Eighth Army units in Sicily in 1943, a British officer came to remarkably similar conclusions. The main reason for the low German and high Allied casualties on Sicily, concluded Colonel Lionel Wigram, the *wunderkind* of the Battle School movement, was the crude tactics used by the British. Even with artillery support, frontal assaults on German positions were bound to be costly; what was needed were new tactics for infiltrating German positions, as the Japanese had done so successfully in Malaya. And it was the way those frontal assaults were delivered that took such toll of life and limb. After a preliminary artillery barrage, the British would move towards a German position.

Enemy Machine Guns open fire, the whole Platoon [about 22 men] lie down except the Platoon Commander and three or four gutful men. Five or six men start making tracks for home, meanwhile the gutful men under the Platoon Commander dash straight into the enemy position without any covering fire and always succeed in taking the position. In some instances some positions are taken by as few as two men, and every Battalion Commander will confirm that it is always the same group of nine or ten who are there first and on whom the battle depends.[26]

Like Marshall, Wigram suggested that instead of assuming that every man is brave enough and experienced enough to do as he is told, the Army should frankly accept that in the average twenty-man platoon there would be

Six gutful men who will go anywhere and do anything, 12 'sheep', who will follow a short distance behind if they are well led, 4–6 who will run away.[27]

To substantiate his figures, Wigram matter-of-factly referred to one of the Army's most taboo subjects, 'the number of Court-Martials for running away that follow every Campaign. Every battalion [of about 2,000] has between forty to sixty and there are of course, many others who aren't caught.' Wigram proposed two major changes. Firstly, it should be openly recognised that there were some men, here and there, who would 'lose complete control and start to clear out' when shelling and mortaring start. These men were invariably known beforehand; their actions often had the 'most demoralising effect on the whole platoon'. He had once thought 'it was right to make chaps like this go into battle and take their medicine like everyone else', but experience in battle had shown they were too dangerous and could do too much harm. Officers should be able to have such people removed from the front line as unsuitable (Wigram was unaware that, unofficially, this was already a widespread practice). Secondly, he made a number of specific suggestions for improving training and organisation so as to bind the 'gutful' men more effectively to the 'sheep'.[28]

Wigram's insights were not appreciated by General Montgomery. Sicily had not been his finest hour and he took Wigram's suggestions as criticisms of Eighth Army and of himself. With extraordinary vindictiveness, Wigram was demoted in rank and sent to command a company, where he was killed – leading a frontal assault.[29]

Not that Montgomery was himself under any illusions about British soldiers' behaviour. He simply preferred different methods. 'The difficulties, dangers and discomforts inseparable from the battlefield,' Montgomery wrote after the war, 'make men cry out for the leadership they can do without in peace. At such moments men are too weak to stand alone: they find the burdens too great to bear and their own selves unequal to the task'. Only discipline could conquer fear. 'Discipline can help a man to lose his own identity and become part of a larger and stronger unit. It is in this way that discipline will conquer fear. This corporate sense which discipline creates helps man to face the unknown.'[30]

Montgomery was scathing about the left's 'rhetorical statements' asserting that the soldier 'must know what he fights for and love what he knows'. 'The fact is,' he wrote, 'that the soldier, instead of having a "fire in his belly", advances into battle with a cold feeling inside him'.

Nor was tradition that important. 'It is not devotion to some ancient regimental story which steels men in the crisis; it is devotion to the comrades who are with them and the comrades who are in front of them.' Far from believing the British should emulate the Germans and train soldiers to think for themselves, 'Montgomery's tactics and strategy were determined by his perception of the limited capacity of the troops under his command.' He was, Michael Howard has written, 'concerned to keep everything simple by the greatest possible amount of preparation before the battle as he did not expect the units under his command to take any bold initiatives during or after the breakthrough. He was in fact a very good First World War general, and he did not regard his troops as capable of any higher performance.'[31]

There was, however, one important difference between the two wars. The British no longer shot soldiers for desertion.

*　*　*

In the Western Desert in early 1942, when Rommel was seemingly unstoppable, desertion was a very serious problem; one unofficial estimate puts the number of men who 'stole away from their units and lay low in the delta' then as high as 25,000. General Auchinleck repeatedly asked the War Office in London to bring back the death penalty for desertion in the face of the enemy. He argued that there was nothing 'undemocratic' about shooting 'those who shirk their duty and abandon their comrades and their arms' and was convinced that most soldiers would thoroughly approve of such a policy. The alarming figures he produced convinced the Adjutant-General and the Secretary for War that 'the British soldier is inclined to surrender rather than to fight it out'. They agreed to reopen the issue.[32]

However, they soon ran into snags and complications. The Eighth Army might approve of executing deserters, but would public opinion at home? Moreover, introducing the appropriate legislation in wartime would be tantamount to admitting you were losing the war. In a memo to Churchill, Sir James Grigg spelled out the Catch-22 involved: 'If legislation is necessary, the facts and figures must be serious. But if they are serious, we can't afford to tell them either to our friends or our enemies.'[33]

So nothing was done and, with the Afrika Korps in retreat, the problem momentarily went away. The deserters, nearly all private soldiers, did not wait to be picked up and punished but quickly returned to their units where, in most cases, they were 'greeted with sardonic amusement by their fellows and were subjected to little more than black looks from the sergeants and spells of extremely hard work.' NCOs were usually stripped of their rank, though they could regain their stripes by exceptional service. A few officer-deserters were taken on as troopers by elite units like the SAS and Long Range Desert Group, on the understanding that they might be able to earn redemption, and have their records doctored, if they really excelled themselves.[34]

Once the Allies invaded the European mainland, however, the problem of desertion returned. While enduring German shelling in the Sabine Hills south of Rome, in May 1944, Private Alex Bowlby noticed out of the corner of one eye that Corporal Baker, one of the NCOs in his rifle company, was remonstrating with another soldier, Private Coke.

'No one's going to fuck off from my section!' he shouted. 'Get that into your napper.'[35]

But when the company came to attack a village the following day, Private Coke (and another man called Cooper) were nowhere to be found. A couple of days later, when the attack was over, Coke and Cooper reappeared, looking shamefaced, having been 'let off with a warning, along with some other part-time deserters'. Nonetheless, soon afterwards Coke deserted again and this time was caught and threatened with a court martial. In the meantime, he was returned to his unit and boasted to them that he had told his CO 'I 'ad a feeling I shouldn't go up no more hills.'

We tittered. Baker was furious. 'You'll get three years!' he roared.

Coke grinned. 'And I'll be 'ere when you're pushing up the daisies.'

Baker grabbed him by the throat. 'Say that again and I'll shoot you me fucking self!'

Coke went white. 'I got me rights as a prisoner,' he muttered.[36]

This was not an isolated incident; in Italy, desertion was commonplace. The scale of the problem led British generals to call again for the re-introduction of the death penalty. The numbers 'on the trot' were so great that 'commanders and staff were alarmed . . . quite apart from the effect upon operations, the difficulty of providing accommodation for deserters in detention barracks was becoming acute.'[37]

Italy in summer, with its friendly European population and reasonable quantities of food and wine, inevitably seemed more attractive to some soldiers than taking part in yet another badly conceived frontal assault on a German-held mountain. In mid-1944, 'the grapevine reported that there were thirty thousand men in Italy on the trot.' Even in the Italian winter, desertion had its attractions, as the end of the war neared and the futility of the campaign grew ever more obvious. 'They were lads who'd been right up Italy,' a sergeant in the Durham Light Infantry later recalled. 'They'd had a bellyfull . . . and at the first real thump a lot of them would disappear.' According to official figures, 70% of all desertions in Italy took place in the winter of 1944–5; British deserters and absentees were then running at about 1,000 a month while in the American Army, 'each division psychiatrist saw literally hundreds of such offenders.'[38]

There were thought to be three kinds of deserter: the man who shouldn't really have been in the army at all; the man who'd been through it all and couldn't take any more; and the 'Whole Skinner', the 'deliberate' deserter who 'would rather do periods of imprisonment than go into battle'. The general British view in Italy was that the third type – of which Private Coke was a good example – 'forms a useful subject and should be shot'. There was, however, much argument about the relative numbers of each type of deserter. John Sparrow, sent out to Italy by the War Office in 1944, concluded after talking to the relevant people, including psychiatrists, that most desertion was 'involuntary' and could be prevented by prompt treatment at exhaustion centres. Most men, he thought, would take the chance to redeem themselves, if given one.[39]

This may well have been an over-optimistic view, but it was shared by an unpublished Eighth Army Report. 'Some men,' it conceded 'were genuine cowards – men who deliberately set out to avoid action; their number, however, was probably no greater relatively than in any other campaign'. The most serious aspect of the problem in Italy, however, 'was the number of soldiers with good records who eventually broke down under the strain of prolonged action.'

One of the principal causes of such collapse was the need to return men again and again to the line after evacuation for wounds or exhaustion. Men felt that they would go on being sent back into the line until they were killed, totally incapacitated by wounds, or broke down or deserted. The absence of any prospect of home leave and the long period of overseas service greatly strengthened the feeling, to which many succumbed, that it would be better to spend the time in the safety and comparative comfort of a military prison rather than to return to the line with so little hope of final relief.[40]

General Alexander failed to get the death penalty restored in 1944, just as Auchinleck had in 1942. Instead, deserters were given between three and five years' penal servitude. Nearly all sentences, however, were reviewed after six months and, in the light of the chronic manpower shortage, suspended, allowing the man to return to his unit (though their officers were not keen to have them back). This fact soon became common knowledge and by the end of the war court-martial sentences for desertion were 'regarded by the courts, and indeed by the fighting officers, as part of an inflated and debased currency'. Courts would pass sentences of seven or ten years, which Army Commanders would then reduce to three, and after about six months the sentence would be suspended.[41]

Eventually, in an attempt to restore some teeth, it was announced that anyone convicted of desertion in action after 1 February 1945 would lose all entitlement to early demobilisation. But this failed completely to provide any deterrent and the numbers deserting continued to rise.[42]

The debate about First World War executions has given the issue of desertion during the Second World War fresh topicality. Defenders of the British Army's record in 1914–18 have pointed to what happened in North Africa, Italy and north-west Europe between 1942 and 1945 as an illustration of the importance of having the death penalty and the folly of its removal. Certainly, as we have seen, it was the general view of many British officers in these theatres of war that the execution of a few 'deliberate deserters' like Private Coke would have made a huge difference to morale and efficiency.

But this view should not go entirely unchallenged. Firstly, experience in 1939–45 demolished the claims made in 1930 by the military Jeremiahs that without the death penalty there could be no discipline at all – 'abolish the death penalty and you might as well abolish the Army', Sir Nevil Macready had said. Secondly, calls to bring back the death penalty tended to be an alibi for failure, coming from generals looking for scapegoats to cover their own poor leadership. A few executions in the desert in early 1942 and Italy 1944–5, even if they had improved discipline, would not have removed the fundamental problems, which lay at the top. Private Coke's remark about 'no more hills' perfectly illustrated the folly of fighting your way up Italy from the south. Thirdly, the War Office itself found that the death penalty was not an effective deterrent: the 1914–18 desertion rate, at 10.26 per thousand per annum, was in fact considerably higher than the 6.89 in 1939–45. Finally, it was recognised that the difficulty in deciding when desertions were deliberate or involuntary, of drawing the line between the legal and the medical, would inevitably lead to injustices, as it had in the First World War.[43]

But at the same time, the situation that arose in Italy in 1944 and in north-west Europe in 1945 was unsatisfactory. Because troops were, in effect, allowed to think that desertion and cowardice were 'not regarded a very serious offences', large numbers of men were able to leave their comrades in the lurch; it was hardly surprising that they felt very angry about it. Indulgence towards those who removed themselves was in effect cruelty to those who *did* stick it, increasing their load and weighting further the odds against survival. But, as Colonel Wigram's studies made clear, that was the general tendency of modern warfare anyway.[44]

* * *

Alongside desertion, Italy highlighted another problem for the psychiatrists, that of homesickness. Soldiers have always yearned for home. In 1678, a Swiss doctor coined the term 'nostalgia' to describe a complaint found in young soldiers from country districts who had spent too long away from home. A century later, there were epidemics of *nostalgie* among the peasants conscripted under the Napoleonic *levée en masse* and a surgeon in the American Civil War believed that 'homesickness, the most pitiless monster that ever hung about a human heart', 'killed as many in our army as did the bullets of the enemy.' 'Nostalgia' was the second commonest medical diagnosis among Union doctors in the 1860s and was thought to affect two kinds of soldier: 'young men of feeble will, highly developed imaginative faculties, and strong sexual desires'; and newly married soldiers separated from their families for the first time. The symptoms were officially described as 'disordered digestion; increased sensibility; palpitations; illusions; a succession of morbid feelings which appeared to stimulate the greater part of the disease; panics; and exaggerated uneasiness of various kinds, chiefly in regard to health.' Soldiers quickly became aware of its uses. At the Battle of Shiloh in 1862, 'it was found impossible to prevent the flocking on board [Union ships] of many whose only complaint was nostalgia'; and the evacuation of the wounded had to be suspended. In the later years of the war, the incidence of the disorder declined, probably because 'claims of nostalgia after battles came to be viewed as malingering or weakness.' Little is said about nostalgia in the medical literature of the Great War – by then 'neurasthenia' had absorbed most of its symptoms. But songs, poems and letters contain little else.[45]

For several reasons, nostalgia returned with a vengeance between 1939 and 1945. Firstly, the sheer numbers of people taken from their homes and sent off to far-away places amounted to one of the great disruptions in history. Secondly, standards of marital fidelity were not what they had been. Finally, psychiatry, influenced, as we have seen, by Freudian object relations theories, had rediscovered the importance of ties to home.

The British writer Ronald Blythe has argued that in the First World War homesickness 'was expressed more in terms of places than of people' whereas in the Second, 'the mood of these longings for home shifted from landscape to the family and its circle'. This may be true in poetry, but World War Two psychiatrists found men homesick for both places and people. Among British troops in the Western Desert, the local paper from home was 'treasured perhaps beyond anything else . . . Men did not want to read *The Times* or the well-known weekly or monthly journals. What they craved for was the local *Gazette*, *Star* or

Post describing events in their home town.'[46]

Alongside this went a yearning for people, an emotion strongest at times of crisis. Dr Tom Main found the 51st Highland Division, resting on Cyprus after Alamein, 'in a state of deep mourning', compounded by 'problems of being overseas and lonely for their home.' The men's letters home , 'caricatured a bit but not too much,' he said later, 'read "Dear Mum, I am fine. I have had a spot on my bum a week ago but it's all right now. Sleeping all right. Grub good. Your loving son." That's what mothers were for – food, sleep, illness. It came out so crudely, so nakedly. It was quite clear these chaps were lonely for mother.'[47]

But you didn't have to have won the battle of Alamein to suffer homesickness. Working in British hospitals in 1942, the analyst Ronald Fairbairn concluded that 'Not only is separation-anxiety invariably present but it is the only single symptom that is universally present. This symptom must accordingly be regarded as the great common measure of all forms of war neurosis.' The official British view was that there was a time limit. 'The psychological effect of prolonged absence from home began to be apparent in most men after two years' absence,' says a War Office Report on Morale, and it was generally agreed that three years was the longest period that men should be kept overseas in all but exceptional cases.

The effect was most marked in those who had left a wife or 'girl' at home. Moreover, it was found that it was usually after from two to three years of separation that the woman's fidelity broke down. The number of wives and fiancées who were unfaithful to soldiers serving overseas almost defies belief: every month the censor's reports contained a large crop of stories of unfaithfulness on the part of women at home, which were heartbreaking in their effect on the soldiers concerned. Nothing did more to lower the morale of troops serving overseas than news of female infidelity, or the suspicion of it and no disease was more infectious than the anxiety and depression arising from bad news or the absence of reassuring news on this topic.[48]

* * *

The Americans, more than anyone, faced problems in motivating their troops. 'Can our boys, rushing into battle after one year, and sometimes two of high-gear training, outsoldier German troops slowly schooled since 1933 to panzer and Stuka formations?' asked a newspaper in January 1943. Their national situation was quite different to that of the British or the French, let alone the Russians. As the United States was not being threatened by the Germans, it was not immediately obvious, even after Pearl Harbor, why Americans should risk their lives in out-of-the-way places no one had ever heard of, like Tunisia or New Guinea or how slogging up a mountain in Italy contributed to the defeat of Hitler.

At first the Pentagon put its faith in selection and indoctrination: careful screening of draftees would weed out the weaklings, leaving an Army of soldiers with the emotional strength not to break down, while Hollywood was commissioned to explain to the troops *Why We Fight*. Its answer, essentially, was that America fought to fend off a threat of Nazi subversion of the Western hemisphere – which was nonsense – and to defend freedom and democracy against fascism and slavery – which was pretty abstract stuff.[49]

Selection and indoctrination, it soon emerged, were not enough. If all the weaklings had been left behind, why were so many soldiers breaking down in Tunisia and Guadalcanal? Why were veteran combat troops cracking much more readily than fresh, inexperienced soldiers? Was it that anyone, no matter how normal, will crack with sufficient exposure to unfavourable conditions? As for ideology, the liberal pieties of *Why We Fight* meant nothing to most GIs; they did not 'feel like romantic heroes who had charged forth in the face of danger to rid the world of evil forces'. What really concerned them was their own immediate unit, their buddies, and their home towns. The basic truths of military psychology were rediscovered – and clothed in the Common Man rhetoric of the New Deal – by the war correspondent Ernie Pyle, the cartoonist Bill Mauldin and by Dr Herbert Spiegel, a psychiatrist who served as a front-line doctor during the Tunisian campaign. 'If abstract ideas, hate, and the desire to kill did not dominate the men, what did?' asked Spiegel.

What enabled them to attack and attack and attack, week after week in mud, rain, dust and heat? It seemed to me that the answer lay not in any negative drive but in a positive one. It was love more than hate that propelled these men. This love was manifested in a number of ways: in regard to their comrades who shared the same dangers; in respect for their platoon leader or company commander who led them well and supported them with everything he had; in concern for their reputation with their leaders; and in the urge to contribute to the success of their group.[50]

Their fundamental loyalty, Spiegel saw, was to *the group*. Meanwhile, other psychiatrists working far behind the lines saw the same thing in reverse: that once the man was withdrawn from the front and from the ties which bound him to his buddies – as casualties from Sicily were when they were evacuated to North Africa – the urge to go back to the line was gone and was hard to recover.

Having decided that loyalty to his primary group was the main thing motivating the soldier, American psychiatrists began to ask how that bond could be reinforced, and perhaps used as a tool to prevent him breaking down.

This was probably their most important contribution to the war. Unfortunately, it came up against the managerial dogmatism of the Pentagon. In tackling the problem of expanding their tiny peacetime force, the planners in Washington had drawn up a scheme for the United States to have an Army of ninety divisions, serviced by mechanisms to keep them up to strength. The system was highly efficient and provided units with almost immediate replacements for their wounded and sick. But it also meant, firstly, that a man often joined his combat outfit as an isolated individual: in Tunisia, Herbert Spiegel recalls, 'they would send up reinforcements at night time to start fighting the next morning. These guys were going into combat without even knowing the name of the guy next to them.' Such men proved especially likely to break down because they had had no time to develop ties to the a group and therefore had no sense of pride and self-respect towards it. But the replacement system meant, also, that divisions were never rested en bloc and soldiers who did not break down were kept constantly in the line.[51]

In the spring of 1944, John Appel, a psychiatrist on Menninger's staff in Washington, spent six weeks at an 'exhaustion center' near the Cassino and Anzio battlefields. He then produced a strongly-worded report which called attention to the 'psychiatric problem'. 'The danger of being killed or maimed,' Appel wrote, 'imposes a strain so great that it causes men to break down.' All men, sooner or later. There was no such thing as 'getting used to combat' and experience showed that 'practically all men in rifle battalions who were not otherwise disabled ultimately became psychiatric casualties.'[52]

Just as an average truck wears out after a certain number of miles, it appears that the doughboy wore out, either developing an acute incapacitating neurosis or else becoming hypersensitive to shell fire, so overly cautious and jittery that he was ineffective and demoralizing to the newer men.

Appel reckoned the average man could last between 200 and 240 combat days before becoming ineffective as a soldier – though only 7% actually lasted that long without getting wounded or killed. The soldier was at his peak in the first ninety days and, if exposed to battles like Cassino or the Rapido River crossing, wore out sooner. The British, he said, reckoned to keep their men effective for about twice as long – 400 regimental combat days – by pulling them out of the line every twelve days or less for some four days' rest.

Appel proposed that the Army set a specific limit, a 'tour of duty', of 210 days, giving the soldier something to look forward to and take steps to bolster the morale of infantrymen by improving the replacement system.

Appel was right about the replacement system: everyone now agrees it 'was one of the dumbest things the Army did,' as Stephen Ambrose has written. But although the 1944 report was endorsed in Washington and copies of it sent to Generals Eisenhower and Clark in Europe and to MacArthur in the Pacific, it had little real impact on the war, apart from producing greater use of rotation – pulling weary units out of the line to have a chance to rest. But the replacement policy, two American medical historians conclude, 'interacted with the stresses of the European fighting to produce a large and, in substantial part, probably preventable burden of neuropsychiatric casualties ... The same units were committed to battle, month after month, by a theater that possessed a huge support system but few reserve combat troops. The result was extremely wearing on the men who bore the brunt of the fighting'.[53]

In the longer term, one of Appel's ideas – that everyone wears out in the end – would prove very influential, providing part of the justification for the one-year tour of duty served by American soldiers in Vietnam. But his more important principle, that group loyalty must be sustained, was to be disastrously ignored.

D-DAY AND AFTER

By the end of 1943 it was becoming clear that after almost two years of planning and postponement, 'Overlord', the Allied invasion of north-western Europe, was finally imminent. On 6 December 1943, three weeks before General Montgomery was given operational command of the invading force, the British Army's psychiatrists put in their bid for a piece of the action.[1]

This time, they argued, the Army must not wait for a crisis to develop and then send for the psychiatrists to sort it out, as it had done in the Middle East and North Africa. It must accept from the start that men would inevitably break down, and build into the medical planning a 'psychiatric organization' to deal with any casualties and reduce wastage. This argument prevailed and on 26 January 1944 the doctor responsible for the British invasion force, the Director of Medical Services 21 Army Group, was introduced to his Psychiatric Adviser.[2]

This was the job every psychiatrist involved with the war coveted. Had his personality been less abrasive, it might have gone to Harold Palmer, who had successfully treated thousands of men in North Africa and Italy; it nearly did go to Palmer's administrative head in Italy, Stephen MacKeith, who had a good record of working with the Army authorities. Instead, J. R. Rees decided to ignore these two men with field experience and turn to the outstanding man in Britain, Dr T. F. Main.[3]

Tom Main had had a good war. The son of a colliery manager, 'a grammar school type', he was twenty-eight when it began, a promising but unknown asylum doctor in the north-east of England. Then he found himself working in Leeds for the brightest of the Tavistock doctors, Ronald Hargreaves. and was dazzled and awed by the calibre of the Tavistock people and generals like Ronald Adam. They, in turn, were impressed by his charm, charisma, drive and adaptability. Somewhere along the line Main had acquired his greatest gift, the ability to explain psychiatry – even subjects he barely understood himself – in everyday language of wonderful clarity. He was also tall, athletic, with a huge RAF moustache; 'so good looking he could get away with things'. By 1942, without ever having heard a shot fired in anger, Main was an acknowledged expert on leadership and morale. Officers attending Battle Schools had heard him lecture with authority and conviction on *esprit de corps* and how to foster it, the foundations of morale and how 'battle inoculation' could be used to build up response to stress.[4]

From this evolved a position as psychiatric trouble-shooter to the Army. He was called out to the Middle East to advise on problems of morale in the Parachute Regiment and characteristically he insisted on getting Wings himself. He studied the effects of different weapons on the troops, finding that they were terrified of the German 88mm gun but would happily charge the equally lethal MG34 machine-gun with fixed bayonets. He also persuaded BBC producers to use women announcers and replace some of their more high-flown broadcasts with simpler fare designed to feed the troops' need for a sense of everyday life at home.[5]

This was important work. Main's underlying concern was that a man should somehow, through the whole dreadful business of war, the atrocity of killing and seeing others killed, keep his sense of being loved, his feeling of his own worth, and emerge from the moral poison of the battlefield still whole and good. But in spite of his experience in the Battle Schools and the Middle East, by the beginning of 1944 Main had seen little of the hard business of forward psychiatry: of sending back into battle men who would rather not be there; of working alongside and winning the trust of an army in the field as it fought and suffered.

For their part, the inner core of staff and medical officers preparing for the invasion still believed that psychiatry was 'a new form of witchcraft, to be treated with deep suspicion.' Tom Main only met General Montgomery once, a few weeks before D-Day. He was summoned into the presence and stood there, at attention, wondering what rocket from above he was to receive. But Montgomery simply said, 'You can go now. I just wanted to know what a psychiatrist looks like.'[6]

The Field Marshal's impressions of his psychiatric adviser have not survived. In any event, Main was never admitted to his inner circle or consulted about an important amendment to the 'Overlord' plan – Montgomery's decision to 'stiffen' the invasion force by adding to it 'seasoned' troops from the Eighth Army, including 51st Highland Division. More generally, there was a reluctance to commit resources to the treatment of 'exhaustion' cases.

The 'psychiatric organization' for D-Day, serving a British Army of 150,000, consisted of exactly four men, one of whom, Colonel Main himself, remained back at 21 Army Group Headquarters in London. The three Anglo-Canadian Corps each had a psychiatric adviser attached to them. These scant resources were to be augmented, when conditions allowed – D + 18 onwards – by one psychiatrist in every general hospital in the beachhead and finally – D + 48 – by a specialist psychiatric hospital with 600 beds. The numbers of cases would, it was assumed, allow 'forward psychiatry' – the actual handling of men on the battlefield – to be done by regimental medical officers suitably trained for the job. This was certainly 'a considerable advance on the planning for any previous campaign', but whether it would be enough would depend on the number of 'exhaustion' cases.[7]

British medical planners reckoned to treat some 7,000 casualties in the first three days of the assault, but there is no record of how many soldiers they expected to break down. This is hardly surprising. Any such figure would obviously rest on assumptions about the morale, training and leadership of the Army which were bound, in the eve-of-battle mood of spring 1944, to be highly contentious and unwelcome. Tom Main, his daughter believes, was several times nearly accused of sedition and of branding British soldiers as cowards because his estimates of psychiatric casualties were thought to be too high. On the other hand, the Canadian historian Terry Copp has argued that Main shared 'the prevailing view that "battle exhaustion" would not be a major problem in the British Liberation Army' and 'firmly believed that a carefully screened division would develop few psychiatric casualties.'[8]

Main never argued, as Harry Stack Sullivan had in 1941, that you could predict in advance the man likely to crack in battle simply by assessing his mental state in a short interview, but he did see in 'Overlord' an opportunity for the British Army finally to put into the field a force both carefully weeded and properly trained – and so to avoid some of the predictable casualties of the desert and North African campaigns. Perhaps in his public utterances his buoyant optimism – and need to justify psychiatry to the Army – led him to promise too much; but it is unlikely that he thought screening would eliminate, rather than simply reduce, casualties.[9]

He must, anyway, have known that screening was patchy. There was rigorous selection in some units; for example, 3rd Canadian Division, after extensive weeding during its long period of assault training, lost a further 150 men (including three officers and one NCO) just before D-Day. But a British colleague of Main wrote that while 'all troops [were] psychiatrically vetted, large-scale changes [were] impracticable', mainly because of the looming manpower shortage (the War Office expected to run out of Infantry altogether in September 1944). Dr John Wishart, who had despaired of the quality of some of the men he treated in North Africa, remembers joining XXX Corps at Newmarket and examining men considered doubtful by their regimental and medical officers, mainly 'mental defectives and obvious misfits'. His recollection was that when the invasion came 'we'd done our very best, we'd reduced them by all the weeding but we were prepared to have heavy [psychiatric] casualties.'[10]

At the last minute, Wishart learnt that one of the doctors due to go in on D-Day had decided that, 'having done previous landings, he couldn't face another'. Wishart took his place, joining the thousands of others waiting apprehensively for the invasion.

*   *   *

No operation in military history had been as elaborately planned or long anticipated as D-Day. The operational planning document alone was two feet thick. The troops received pep talks and leaflets from presidents and prime ministers and every level of officer. They were told they were liberating Europe, that the fortunes of freedom rested on their shoulders.[11]

Men faced the forthcoming ordeal in different spirits. 'None of us had ever seen action before,' a British paratrooper recalled, 'and all of us were excited about the big day that was approaching. I didn't see any sign of nerves among the men; all I saw was great enthusiasm.' Private Joe Minogue of 7th Armoured Division, however, remembers men bleating like sheep when the roll was called as light relief from the tension.

We were all edgy and getting a bit nervous about the invasion. One day when we were waterproofing the tanks, the divisional commander Percy Hobart popped his head under a tank and said, 'We're expecting 70% casualties, you know, but if any of you chaps get there I'll see you after D-Day . . .'

. . . we used to have these long discussions with each other about the kinds of things that might happen, you know, whether we'd ever get off the beach alive and all the rest of it. I wouldn't say we were cowards as such . . . I think everybody who was involved in the invasion was afraid. Later one learned that basically this is what war is about; it's really two groups of very frightened men facing each other.[12]

The real thing, when it came, was terrifying and unforgettable: the long tense wait before embarkation; the rough weather in the channel; the awkward mid-Channel transfer down nets and ladders to landing craft; the agonising hour-long run into the beaches, decks sloshing with fear and vomit; the first faltering steps towards the beach. Again and again in soldiers' tales the same motifs recur: the spectacle of the 16-inch guns of the battleships firing into a continent; the screaming pyrotechnics of the rocketships; the men who sank like stones into the sea as they left the landing craft and never came up; the mines and obstacles in the surf; the odd, incongruous sights on the beach – beachmasters with dogs. But only the Americans on Omaha Beach met serious resistance.

As at the Somme and Gallipoli, the actual assault produced few psychiatric casualties. Then, a week or two after D-Day, the numbers began to mount, for two main reasons. 'Units [were] attempting to throw their black sheep through medical channels', while psychiatric evacuation 'provided an easy means of escape' for 'men of poor personality unwilling to serve'. Several Corps Exhaustion Centres had, as planned, been opened, but they were so overwhelmed with cases that there was scarcely time to examine, let alone to treat them. And with pressure from above not to keep 'exhausted soldiers' for longer than 48 hours, the psychiatrist could only hang on to very mild cases who only needed a couple of nights' rest. The rest had to be evacuated back across the Channel.

During rush periods, when as many as 50 a day supposedly A1 men were being evacuated to the UK, a feeling of disquietude arose [one psychiatrist admitted]. Was one becoming party to a racket? The apprehension became more marked when one was criticised by older officers – 'we had nothing like this in the last war, they had to fight on, frightened or not'. The loss of manpower was certainly staggering but I am convinced that few would have been of any use to their units in the near future, the facilities available were such that we had no recourse but to send them home.[13]

Although the 'exhaustion rate' (about 10%) was only about half of what some psychiatrists had privately expected, fear of an 'evacuation syndrome' caused alarm in high places. 'Psychiatry is getting out of hand,' a senior officer reported after a visit to the beachhead. Something had to be done to tighten things up. Tom Main – on 25 June still in London supervising the making of a film on 'Psychiatry for the Field Medical Officer' – was sent to France to sort things out. In fact, his highly capable deputy, Donald Watterson, had already taken steps to reduce 'wastage', skilfully persuading the Army to reverse its policy and to improvise more adequate psychiatric arrangements in France.[14]

And so, at the end of June, the policy was reversed. Now, conservation, not evacuation, was the priority. Regimental medical officers were warned not to send mild cases back from the line; extra psychiatric staff and hospitals were made available in the bridgehead to treat men in France; and up at the front itself doctors began to improvise 'forward' psychiatry at division level.

It had taken the British Liberation Army a month to rediscover the truths about military psychiatry. It was none too soon, as it proved, for at the end of June 1944, General Montgomery launched a series of full-scale offensives designed to break out of the Normandy bridgehead, committing his Army to the wholehearted engagement with the Wehrmacht it had spent the last four years avoiding. This precipitated a real 'battle exhaustion' crisis.

The Allies enjoyed a huge overall superiority in Normandy. They had complete command of the air, three times as many tanks as the Germans and were much stronger in artillery. But in infantry the two sides were about equal, and in some kinds of weaponry – tanks, anti-tank guns, mortars – the Germans were qualitatively much better off. The Normandy *bocage*, 'a maze of narrow, sunken roads and high, thick, almost impenetrable hedgerows dividing the myriads of small fields', favoured the defenders, making it impossible for any attacking force to mass in strength across a wide front and offering innumerable strong points where small pockets of Germans could remain unseen with machine-guns and anti-tank weapons.[15]

The Germans made the most of the situation, showing, a British history concedes, 'individual determination and fieldcraft of the highest order'. The long years of fighting against huge odds on the Eastern Front had given them a mastery of sophisticated infantry tactics. They had learnt, for example, 'to hold fire until almost point-blank range so that the first shots would obtain a kill. Then, before the British artillery could range in and bombard the position, to choose a new location and open fire from a new direction.'[16]

Quite early on in the campaign, bogey weapons began to emerge, notably the 'Tiger' tank and the German mortars. This was the first time the British had come up against the giant, 70-ton Tigers and the discovery that 'the armour-piercing shells of Allied 17-pounder guns would pounce harmlessly off a Tiger tank even at close range' induced, says David Holbrook, 'hysterical fear'. Although there were only about thirty-six Tigers on the whole Normandy front, 'the legend of their invulnerability was paralysing', and, of course, every tank became a 'Tiger'. Holbrook describes an occasion when an English Churchill tank retreating from the battle is mistaken for a Tiger and immediately drilled by every available gun.

There was a note of obscene despair on the radio.
'Cunts!'
And then silence, as the now familiar flames and hideous smoke-rings soared from the machine, their own brother weapon destroyed by themselves . . . Two of the Churchill's crew had scrambled out of the turret, exhausted, maimed things no longer men, riddled internally by a hundred fragments, their legs shattered. They lay in the smoke and died, only a few yards from the North Countrymen who had killed them in their panic, pointlessly.[17]

For the infantry, though, the real bogey was the mortar:

a soft siffle, high in the air, like a distant lark, or a small penny whistle, faint and elf-like, falling. But then, with a spiral, pulsing flutter, it grew to a hissing whirr . . . The mortar bombs landed with ferocious blasts, followed by a whine of fragments which cut into the trees, driving deep white scars into their trunks and filling the air with torn shreds of tree foliage whirled about in clouds of blue-black smoke.[18]

In the first few weeks of June, Allied progress had been disappointing. Now, with Montgomery committing his forces to all-out attack, a note of genuine alarm emerged. Psychiatric casualties were dangerously high. 'By mid-July, the small infantry component of 21 Army Group, less than 15% of the total manpower in the bridgehead, had suffered enormous casualties. On average one in every four of these casualties was due to exhaustion'. When 51st (Highland) Division attacked near Caen on 23 June and was subsequently counterattacked by 21 Panzer Division, something like every third casualty was 'exhausted' rather than wounded. The Highland Division, despite its illustrious record, was showing signs of being profoundly war-weary. Nor did 49th (West Riding) Division fare any better. A territorial unit, none of its men had seen action before. In its first encounter with the Germans – 12th SS Panzer Youth and Panzer Lehr – one of its battalions ran away, leaving the unfortunate medical officer to retrieve discarded rifles and ammunition on his bicycle, 'pedalling along like a small-time arms salesman' to the mocking laughter of other soldiers. A subsequent attempt to restore morale had to be abandoned 'so completely had some junior officers' nerves gone to pieces.' Throughout July of 1944, 49th Division had a very high exhaustion rate; towards the end of the month the commander of one battalion, 6/Duke of Wellington's, felt it necessary to warn his superiors that morale and efficiency were 'in tatters'.[19]

75% of the men react adversely to enemy shelling and are 'jumpy'. There have been 5 cases in 3 days of self-inflicted wounds . . . Each time men are killed or wounded a number of men become casualties through shell shock or hysteria. In addition to genuine hysteria a large number of men have left their positions under one pretext or another and gone to the rear until sent back by the Medical Officer or myself. The new drafts have become affected and 3 young soldiers became casualties with hysteria after hearing our own guns.[20]

Other British Infantry Divisions reported similar rates of exhaustion and things were, if anything, worse among the Canadians. In a few cases those breaking down were weak or inadequate men who should have been eliminated from the Army. Soldiers from 1/5 Welsh Regt admitted for treatment on 17 July 'were very poor personality types, chronic neurotics, men of low average intelligence etc. [who] should obviously have been eliminated from the regiment long ago'. However, it was absurd for Canadian psychiatrists to diagnose as 'psychopathic personalities' 197 men whose unit had recently been flung into 'a frontal attack on a position which the Germans were steadily reinforcing'; they were clinging perversely to the idea of individual predisposition (or using a powerful label to get men evacuated).[21]

The real explanation was bad leadership. 'The number of cases coming from a given unit,' said Donald Watterson, 'is an index to that unit's quality of men and of its well-being and morale.' Major Phillips, psychiatrist to VIII Corps, reckoned he could tell from a man's behaviour which unit he belonged to. 'The general morale seen from cases from 43 [Wessex] Div. was low,' he reported. 'Very few indeed' of these men 'showed any desire to return to their units' and it was 'apparent, from the number of cases arriving in groups . . . often accompanied by NCOs or even officers, that not only had individual morale gone, but group morale as well.'[22]

He was evidently right. According to Max Hastings, 'it was a matter of astonishment to officers of other units that 43rd Division still retained any morale at all. Its commanding officer, Major General Thomas, was a ruthless, driving soldier for whose determination Monty was grateful but who had earned the nickname "Butcher" for his supposed insensitivity to losses'. By contrast, soldiers from 15th (Scottish) Division were keen to rejoin their units and their doctors came to inquire about their well-being.[23]

Military analysts saw the problem in Normandy slightly differently. They noticed a lack of initiative in British infantry troops, and considered that it was caused by a leadership vacuum at the junior level. Because the good non-commissioned officers had by now mostly been promoted to officers, junior officers were forced to lead by example, in the traditional First World War way. 'Men lie down in such country,' a New Zealand observer wrote, 'and are only urged forward by the personal example of their officers.' British troops needed 'continued pressure of immediate leadership' and their officers, 'easily seen by their map boards with talc coverings that flash in the sun' were easy prey to snipers. When officers were killed, men tended to become disheartened and attacks would peter out.[24]

Psychiatrists noticed that 'a sudden influx of cases following the death or wounding of the commanding officer' was a 'common story'. A dip into the archives provides vivid confirmation of this. Over half the British exhaustion cases in the week preceding 17 July 1944 came from a single Division, 43rd

(Wessex); and a sizeable percentage from a single unit, the 7th Hampshires, whose War Diary shows the battalion involved in a fairly classic Normandy action – advancing on the village of Maltot on the morning of 10 July only to undergo an immediate German counterattack.

3 Tiger Tanks reported coming into village . . . the enemy was seen infiltrating through the village, orchards, and cornfields, while our position was being mortared and shelled by 88mm.[25]

For several hours the Commanding Officer was 'agitating' for defensive artillery fire, but the Royal Artillery had 'other commitments'. Just when the position was about to fall, the Germans were stopped by a very accurate artillery barrage 'just forward of the line of the hedge we were in'. The 7th Hampshires were withdrawn that evening, but were back in the front line two days later.[26]

    The real giveaway, though, is that over the course of four days the 7th Hampshires lost its commanding officer (twice), plus its second in command, medical officer, forward observation officer and numerous other officers. Even as the battalion was forming up, two more officers were wounded and

had to be left on the battlefield as all attempts to get them back to Regimental Aid Post were sniped. Battalion support troops under Captain Terry and Lt Evans *did not deploy* as they were incessantly mortared. Both officers were killed in action.[27]

The Canadians had an especially traumatic time in Normandy. Appalling leadership, bad staff-work, inadequate training and the troops' feeling that their sacrifices were not being shared across the nation, all combined to produce a succession of disasters, often in comparatively minor or unnecessary engagements. Five battalions of Canadians, with massive artillery support, were kept at bay by only 50 Panzer Grenadiers at Carpiquet airport on 4 July 1944. During Operation 'Goodwood', 2nd Canadian Division was ordered into 'the final stages of an operation which had already failed'. The decision to commit two 'green' infantry brigades to a frontal attack on a position which the Germans were steadily reinforcing was not a wise one and 149 men were killed and 900 wounded in its first operation on 25 July, 'one of the blackest days in the history of the Canadian army'. Another 450 dead and 1,000 wounded were lost in Operation 'Spring'. Each time, the tally of exhaustion casualties was enormous – the ratio well above 30%.[28]

    These were men the Allied armies could not afford to lose and the psychiatrists were left in no doubt that it was their job to stem this wastage. Like Myers on the Somme in 1916, they suddenly found themselves in great demand, no longer the mocked pariahs of medicine. The doctors with 2nd Canadian Division, who before going to France had declared, 'We will have no psychiatric casualties' and had refused to integrate the psychiatric service into the corps or divisional medical system, now rushed to offer the tiny psychiatric staff any help he could. All over

Normandy, in late July and August of 1944, they set to reverse the trend.[29]

Impromptu front-line treatment centres had already been created in several British divisions. Donald Watterson, the senior psychiatrist on the ground, 'welcomed this initiative and moved to encourage divisional psychiatry without psychiatrists' at Field Ambulances in the other divisions. Under this scheme men were given basic treatment by the medical officer under loose supervision from psychiatrists. It assumed that most men were suffering from simple exhaustion rather than anything more complex, and 'every effort . . . made to prevent them feeling that they were ill or . . . patients in the true sense of the word'. On arrival at the Field Dressing Station, the exhausted man would be told to wash himself, be put into pyjamas, sedated with a light dose of barbiturate and left to sleep on a stretcher for a day or two. After waking up he was transferred to another tent and given a day to recover from sedation and sort himself out. Finally, he went to a third tent where he became 'a soldier once more', with 'morning parade for inspection, PT, organized recreation, educational lectures, baths and, if possible, a visit to the cinema.' The average stay in the Field Dressing Station was five to six days, after which a man was usually fit to rejoin his unit. This improvised forward treatment produced a dramatic improvement in rates of men returned to units – from 10% to 65%.[30]

What really brought the battle exhaustion crisis under control, however, was the dramatic transformation in the military situation, following the break-out of General Patton's Third Army at the end of July. British and American 'exhaustion' rates fell dramatically in August, though they remained high for the luckless Canadians, whose failure to seal the Falaise gap prevented the capture of the entire German Army. As it was, thousands of German tanks and soldiers were destroyed in the Falaise pocket, mainly by artillery and air strikes. By 20 August, Montgomery's armies were across the Seine. Nevertheless, this was not the end of the 'exhaustion' problem in north-west Europe. It had come to be accepted that about 10% of casualties were psychiatric and whenever there was serious fighting, the numbers of 'exhausted' soldiers shot up.[31]

Somewhere along the line, Tom Main, the psychiatric adviser to 21 Army Group and the blue-eyed boy of Army psychiatry, faded from the picture. He visited the beachhead in July and reported to the medical chiefs on the step taken to cut down evacuations from France. But thereafter, apart from a long memo in late August in which he asked for more staff, he disappears from the records. He seems to have been marginalised by Watterson's quiet competence and rapport with the military on the ground. On 17 October 1944, following a visit by the Top Brass of Army Psychiatry to Brussels, now Montgomery's headquarters, Donald Watterson was made Psychiatrist to 21 Army Group. Tom Main returned to England to work at the Army's large psychiatric hospital in Birmingham, which was proving a hatching ground for new techniques of treatment. There, as we shall see, he performed interesting work.[32]

A TALE OF TWO HOSPITALS

Everything we do here is treatment.
Northfield patients' magazine[1]

Meeting a boatload of returning casualties in Southampton Harbour in 1944, a psychiatrist was astonished to discover that every soldier on board had pinned to his lapel his medical diagnosis. Some patients had travelled a third of the way round the world with labels like 'psychopathic personality with abnormal sexual trends' stuck on them. Not surprisingly, when asked what their problem was, they would proudly reel off the official tag.[2]

In the Second World War, most patients with serious psychological problems were evacuated back to Britain or the United States for more extensive treatment. Working with these more complex cases, though not as glamorous as front-line work, consumed a vast amount of psychiatrists' time and generated an enormous literature. Far from relying on the methods of Rivers and his contemporaries, psychiatrists developed an extraordinary range of techniques drawing on a variety of intellectual, social and political influences. Some of the methods used are well illustrated in the work of two famous hospitals through which thousands of soldiers passed – Northfield near Birmingham, in England; and Mason General, on Long Island, near New York City.

Northfield was the military's name for the old Hollywell Mental Hospital, the municipal asylum for Britain's second city: a 'huge Victorian bin', an immense, antiquated, jerry-built pile of red brick surmounted by a huge copper water tower visible miles away. In April 1942, the British Army turned it into the largest military hospital in the country, bringing together there all the psychoneurotic cases thought capable of further military service. Two and a half years of war had produced many 'military misfits' – people who hated the Army and clung to their medical symptoms as a way of 'working their ticket', getting out of the service. But anyone who hoped to find at Northfield a refuge from Army life was in for a nasty surprise.[3]

The patient arriving at the hospital . . . had a five-mile journey from Birmingham on a rickety tram before walking nearly a mile uphill with his kit . . . standing at the end of the drive, [Northfield] presented a forbidding institutional appearance. Once inside, the hospital was as uncomfortable as the approach to it and its appearance would suggest – echoing stone corridors and enormous barely furnished wards.[4]

Northfield was no rural idyll; it was overlooked by barrage balloons and throughout the day rang to the sound of automatic weapons chattering 'at different speeds and in different voices on a testing range' at the Austin works across the valley.

As originally established, the hospital was rigidly divided into Medical and Military zones. You started off in the Hospital Wing of two hundred beds, wearing comfortable blue uniforms, looked after by a psychiatrist and allowed to do as you pleased; then, as you recovered, you moved to the Training Wing (600 men), wore the hated military khaki and were subject to Army discipline under regular Army officers. This arrangement could hardly have been better designed to deter men from getting better. The new arrival at the hospital – usually a reluctant soldier with a long record of trouble in the Army – quickly saw that 'the key to the "pearly gates" into civilian life was the patient's neurotic symptom.'

If he had nothing dramatic to show when he set out from his unit for the hospital, by the time he had reached the top of the drive and had a chance to talk to some of the other patients he was well equipped with agents for promoting his civilian freedom which he would use in the battle with his psychiatrist to come . . . his first target [was] to remain sufficiently ill and unserviceable to the army to avoid his transfer to khaki and the Training Wing.[5]

Enuresis – wetting the bed – was a particularly useful and negotiable symptom which, correctly handled, could get you discharged. Those who were sent to the Training Wing became resentful, ill-disciplined and untidy, determined to prove that they had no future in the Army.

To this slough of despond, the War Office sent two of the intellectual heavyweights of British psychoanalytic psychiatry, John Rickman and Wilfred Bion. They were an odd couple, both tall and very large, spreading out of their khaki uniforms. Rickman was probably the most psychoanalytically literate man in England. A pupil of Rivers at Cambridge, he had then been psychoanalysed by Freud, Ferenczi and Melanie Klein. He was also a Quaker, had served with the Friends' Ambulance in Russia in 1920 and had a life-long romantic attachment to the collectivist traditions of the Russian *mir* or village. A skilful writer, Rickman had done much to apply Freudian ideas to social questions like child-raising. Something of an intellectual snob, he also had a selfless, maternal, self-denying side and liked to put others into the spotlight. One of his first actions on arriving at the Northfield was to begin experimenting with group therapy in the Hospital Wing.[6]

Things really began to happen, however, when Wilfred Bion was put in charge of the Training Wing early in 1943. Bion was as close to a man of action as a psychiatrist can be, always determined and committed; his resolve, if anything, stiffened by the slights he had received from the Army medical hierarchy. Finding that the main treatment was 'sedative: sedative for doctors and patients alike', Bion took a bold step. Instead of trying to arrest the chaos and indiscipline he found in the Training Wing, he deliberately let it continue, allowing things to get so bad that the collective neurosis would be displayed and dramatised to the point where the men themselves would be driven, in terms of their own self-respect, to organise ways of controlling it. Within a few days, the patients began to complain that the wards (hitherto always spotless) were dirty. Beds were wet, drunkenness and absence without leave were going unchecked, and 'the whole hospital staff was alarmed and angry'.[7]

Some of his patients came to Bion demanding that he take action; but he refused. Instead, he held a daily parade of all the wards, at which progress was reviewed, insisted that all men should join a group of some kind and offered advice on how to run these groups. Meanwhile he watched.

The main group to emerge was of men who wanted to set up a dancing class, which Bion interpreted as a way of testing his own 'sincerity in promising facilities for group activity' and evidence of 'the pathetic sense of inferiority towards women [felt] by men taking no part in fighting.' But he took the proposal seriously and allowed the men to organise dancing lessons 'at the end of a day's work'. Bion clearly thought this was the start of something. After a month, he began to find the daily meetings 'business-like, constructive and lively'. 'An unmistakable *esprit de corps*,' he claimed, 'showed itself in the smartness with which men came to attention when officers entered the room at the 12.10 meetings . . . a subtle but unmistakable sense that the officers and men alike were engaged on a worthwhile but important task even though the men had not yet grasped quite fully the nature of the task on which they were engaged.' Alas, no records have survived of what patients made of Major Bion with his daring ideas and public school manner.[8]

In a remarkable article written in 1943, Bion explained that he had decided what was needed at Northfield 'was the sort of discipline achieved in a theatre of war by an experienced officer in command of a rather scallywag battalion.' This rested, firstly, on the presence of a common enemy and, secondly, on an intelligent and flexible officer. The job of a psychiatrist in charge of a rehabilitation wing was not to think 'that patients are potential cannon-fodder, to be returned as such to their units'; it was to produce 'self-respecting men socially adjusted to the community and therefore willing to accept its responsibilities whether in peace or war.' 'Only thus,' Bion added revealingly, 'will he [the psychiatrist] be free from deep feelings of guilt which effectively stultify any efforts he may otherwise make towards treatment.' There was, he continued, no great mystery about the common danger facing everyone in the Training Wing – it was their collective neurosis; and once it had been displayed to the group it was for the group, with his help, to sort it out itself.[9]

The theory was daring and imaginative. In effect he was throwing the hospital into the heightened, purposeful mood of battle. It was war as therapy. Unfortunately Bion and Rickman committed the fatal mistake of plunging into their experiment without carrying with them, or even informing, their medical colleagues in the hospital and the War Office. Many of the other psychiatrists felt threatened and excluded by what Bion and Rickman had unilaterally embarked on. Soon, alarmist noises began to reach Whitehall and, frightened that Bion's approach might 'lead to anarchy and chaos', War Office officials paid a lightning visit one night. 'The chaos in the hospital cinema hall, with newspapers and condom-strewn floors, resulted in the immediate termination of the project.' The 'First Northfield Experiment' had lasted a bare six weeks. Bion and Rickman were hastily posted elsewhere.[10]

With their departure, Northfield returned to its former gloom and inertia, well conveyed in Rayner Heppenstall's novel, *The Lesser Infortune.* A minor writer and friend of George Orwell, Heppenstall had served in the ranks for two miserable years before being arrested for smoking in an Army vehicle in Northern Ireland; to avoid punishment, he asked to see the psychiatrist.[11]

Heppenstall's medical report described him as an 'asocial, disgruntled type, of first-class intelligence and ability' who had 'failed to adjust to the Army' and become 'bitter and sulky and passive in his attitude'. He clearly had a deep, all-pervading anxiety about everything to do with the war, a childish dependence on women and a violent, phobic dislike of his fellow men. The petty horrors of Army life – the sanitary orderly 'collapsed across his bed in a pool of vomit'; the 'tea urn and its attendant slut'; the simple-minded ATS girl available for sex in a broom cupboard to anyone with a pound of margarine; the lavatory seats covered in urine – all reduced him to misanthropic frenzy. Serving in the ranks, he had no romantic illusions about the working classes, who sang or made love 'to ease themselves. They used a wife or a local whore as if they were lavatories.' Although claiming to have no objection to 'the idea of battle', he thought that 'going into action is rather an intimate business' and 'the idea of dying or lying wounded or even feeling afraid' surrounded by 'the animal cries of his companions and superiors' appalled him.[12]

Northfield, to Heppenstall, is a tired, defeated, ugly place. The psychiatrists have given up, yawn constantly, and are not even familiar with the Freudian terms he uses to describe his own problems. The patients go through the motions but spend most of their time playing cards, watching film shows or sitting in a nearby café smoking – waiting for the war to end. There is a hospital magazine, which literary types like Heppenstall (and his more glamorous friend, the literary dandy Julian Maclaren-Ross) help to produce as a way of getting out of less congenial tasks. The only unsettling influence is the arrival late in 1943 of a 'large new intake of men from the Eighth Army'.[13]

Full of guilt at his own failure to make it into battle, Heppenstall watches with envy and fascination the new arrivals, who lie awake at night, hide under beds in thunderstorms and twitch or drag their feet. Some of them are 'smug', forming themselves into 'little Eighth Army enclaves' and ignoring their fellow patients.

What they had been through was really something. They could not see what the rest of us had to be neurotic about. These were the privileged neurotics, the snobs and bores of pain.

Heppenstall is quietly confident that, after a year or two of 'the drip of Army routine at home', these men too will sink into silence and self-defeat.[14]

He was wrong. In fact, the 'sense of emergency throughout the country created by the imminent Second Front' helped to shake Northfield out of its slumbers and force it into 'greater contact with realities'. In December 1943, the Army decided to send to Northfield only men who had a realistic chance of becoming fighting soldiers: malingerers and professional neurotics like Heppenstall were no longer to be bothered with. Then, after June 1944, 'young active soldiers who had seen battle' began to arrive in large numbers. In questionnaires, some of which have survived, they vividly expressed their feelings.[15]

Trooper S, for example, had been near a petrol dump in Holland when it blew up, and now had attacks of depression and palpitations brought on by brooding. He was 24, and very close to his mother (his father had died when he was four). 'Going into the second front,' he had 'braced up' as he had many times before in the desert and in Italy. But this time the strain, tension and worry about his mother had been too much. 'I'm hoping,' he concludes, 'to be home soon so that I can be in the normal surroundings and feel the great benefit that goes with home and loved ones and friends and my pet hobby is music and I long to be taking part in singing and "playing" as it all helps to give me confidence again and forget a lot of what I've been through.'

Private H's DUKW amphibious vehicle had been hit by a shell at Arnhem and 'did about eight somersaults before landing upside down'; he was pinned underneath and lost consciousness. He was now depressed, irritable and suicidal: 'I sometimes get in a mood that I want to kill myself or somebody who has said something I dislike, it has only been since I came back from the front line, my life before I came into the army was uneventful but full of childish dreams.'

Gunner M, 20, shy and studious, had been wounded at the end of June 1944. Returning to action, he found he 'could not stick it. I had great difficulty in forcing myself out of my slit trench to go on duty. Even when things were quiet I could not relax and felt all tensed up as though waiting for something to happen.' He now had insomnia and 'a strange sensation as though I were falling and involuntarily my whole body jerks as though to save myself'; he also had terrible dreams from which he awoke sweating. He was rather apologetic: 'some chaps have had a few years of it out East, but I just can't help myself.'

By contrast, Corporal M from Liverpool had served in Italy and France and felt he had done his bit. He put his case with simple eloquence:

I am quiet (sic) normal and healthy and I cannot bear being away from England. I have been in the front line so long, seen many things which has shaken me up . . . I have a wife and 2 kiddies which I adore and I cannot bear to be away from them. I think I have done enough for my country . . . I have seen my wife 28 days in 3 years. My best friend was killed by the side of me in France. I thought the six months I was back in England [before

D-Day] my nerves were better but as soon as I was back in action I felt I was wrong. In fact they were worse than I had them in Sicily. Each time it gets worse and I have been so bad that I have been on my knees praying to God to let me live and pull through it. And it plays on my mind what would happen to my family if anything happened to me.[16]

You had to respect what these men had been through. Northfield became a more purposeful place and the barriers between medicine and the Army, between psychiatrists and regular officers, began to come down. And, at the end of 1944, a second 'experiment' began there.

This time the initiative came from the top, from the psychiatrists at the War Office. Visiting Northfield, J. R. Rees and his colleagues had noticed one ward where small-scale group therapy was being done by a German expatriate called S. H. Foulkes; morale there seemed to be higher than in the rest of the hospital. At the same time they were keen to extend the work on the 'psychology of groups' – group discussions, group projects – which had been developed in Officer Selection Boards. It says much for the relationship Rees and Ronald Hargreaves had forged with the Adjutant-General, Sir Ronald Adam, that they were able to introduce these highly experimental techniques in a military hospital supposedly intended to return men to the front line at a time of acute manpower shortage in the forces. But, unlike Bion and Rickman in 1943, they prepared the ground with great care and did not move until almost a year had been spent squaring the military authorities. Whether they promised to send more men back to duty is not clear.[17]

One day in 1944, Ronald Hargreaves discussed with Dr Foulkes 'the experiment of running the hospital fully and uncompromisingly as a therapeutic unit'. Foulkes would carry on giving therapy to small groups (and teach his methods to sympathetic young psychiatrists who were to be brought in), while Major Harold Bridger, an experienced Officer Selection Board instructor, would take over 'rehabilitation'. Clearly much of Bion and Rickman's spirit had survived, albeit reworked by the managerially-minded Hargreaves. There was from the start, though, a tension inherent in this second 'experiment' between the two meanings of the term 'group therapy': between those, like Foulkes, who saw group therapy as the treatment of a number of individuals assembled in a group; and those with experience in the Army, who saw it as a 'planned endeavour to develop in a group the forces that lead to smoothly running co-operative activity.'[18]

Siegfried Heinrich Fuchs – always known as Michael Foulkes – was one of the first German psychoanalysts to emigrate to Britain. He had fought in the Kaiser's Army and undergone a long medical apprenticeship in Vienna, Munich and Frankfurt, being influenced by the neurologist Kurt Goldstein and the 'Frankfurt school' of sociologists, as well as by Freud himself. Foulkes had been experimenting, in his own practice in Exeter in 1940, with the idea of getting groups of his patients together to hear each others' problems, 'to become aware of the part which social conditions play in their troublesome conditions.' At Northfield he had begun having weekly meetings at which patients he was seeing individually were encouraged to talk to each other.[19]

Foulkes was a small, compactly-built man, with a large Jewish nose, sharp grey-blue eyes and a strong German accent. His professional rival Tom Main later described him – unjustly – as 'a funny little refugee whom no-one could understand, a nobody'. But to the young psychiatrists at Northfield he was an inspiration. 'A feeling of intense excitement,' one later recalled, 'surrounded his whole personality'; he 'seemed to transcend the conditions of those oppressive days and sparked off in those associated with him an enduring inspiration and enthusiasm.' To such people, Foulkes had 'the charisma of an original and creative thinker' and 'a mind that far exceeded in depth anything we had come across before.' Foulkes gradually built up around him a devoted circle of pupils.[20]

There was, however, evidently some 'resistance' from patients bewildered by Foulkes' German accent and 'groping habit of speech' which included 'inexplicable hesitations', 'mental detours', 'sudden truncation of sentences', 'often enlarged syntax', 'tapering of the thought processes that left you floating in the air' and 'numinous nebulousness'. Soldiers reported back that Foulkes was 'too clever for them, they think that he must talk sense, but they [did] not understand him', and that 'they were afraid of his attacking them. When you begin you don't know where he'll make it lead.'[21]

When his colleague Martin James announced to one group of patients (on 5 December 1944) that Foulkes was away on leave, the news was greeted with cheers, weeks of tension suddenly lifted and 'there was a free and active discussion immediately involving all but two members of the group'. Foulkes, Dr James reported,

was thought to exert a sinister influence and there was general agreement that the atmosphere improved when he was not present. His piercing glance was singled out particularly and deep material was produced about hypnosis and the power of the human eye and the idea of hypnosis as a relationship of the type Superior-Inferior Adult-Child.[22]

When some Americans visited Northfield a fortnight later, Foulkes did not attend the group session 'as it was considered that his presence might result in resistances which would interfere with the visitors' impression'.[23]

Foulkes, though, had such inner confidence that he was not put off by experiences like this and continued to evolve and develop his ideas, nursing and coaching the younger psychiatrists as they struggled with groups. They responded to 'his calm, his patience, and his ability to tolerate uncertainty and confusion'. Whereas Bion was naturally rather challenging in his handling of groups – and probably communicated some of his own inner tensions – Foulkes was more democratic, gentler; 'his therapy was like his tennis – he let the opponent do most of the work.'[24]

Foulkes' method was to gather men in groups of about eight. He wasn't too particular about marrying up those with similar war experience or problems, though he did try to avoid too wide a scatter of intelligence or education. Having sat down in a circle the group were then invited to talk about anything, with Foulkes only intervening after very long silences or to bring in group members who had not been involved in the talk. In one session – of which Foulkes later published a partial transcript – eight soldiers begin by discussing the work they are doing at the hospital, talk about the disruption the war has brought to their family lives and careers and then plunge abruptly into an attack on the behaviour of English women in the war – 'If their wives had been straight they wouldn't be here now.'[25]

In later meetings, this group moved on from such general discussions to talk frankly about their own problems and, says Foulkes, 'developed very well with a degree of individual treatment as appropriate'.

Group therapy, Foulkes argued, was not only a more efficient use of the psychiatrist's time than individual interviews, it was also in some ways clinically superior. Group therapy allowed the psychiatrist to observe his patients, not in the artificial atmosphere of the consulting room, but in a quasi-social environment. Patients with difficulty in interacting with their fellows would be gently led into contact with the group. Above all, what Foulkes saw as the central core of the 'war neuroses', getting patients to take responsibility for themselves, could be addressed. If the group became responsible for its own actions, gradually its individual members would, too.[26]

Privately, though, Foulkes accepted that the length of stay of the military patient was usually so short that it was 'wiser to avoid becoming too involved in the deeper levels'. He also hinted that group sessions did not always go as easily as this and warned of the challenge they posed to the therapist. In getting the group 'engaged and in a state of spontaneous participation':

the Therapist's measure will be taken . . . he must prove his worth . . . he will be found out for what he really is for good or bad. He will be taxed mercilessly and there will be no chance of escape. It will be discovered then whether he has a genuine right to stand in front of other people and claim to guide them to a better way of dealing with their problems and difficulties. If he passes this test he can proudly say to himself: 'I am a human being'. He will find no difficulty in being truly modest and in feeling, genuinely: 'Here we are together, facing reality and the basic problems of human existence. I am one of you, not more and not less.'

The note of exultant triumph is unmistakable; whatever else Foulkes achieved at Northfield, he had – like William McDougall in 1917 and Harold Palmer in 1943 – attained the state of exhausted self-fulfilment which comes from intensive contact with the war neuroses.[27]

Later accounts say little about another form of therapy tried out at Northfield. 'Psychodrama' was a technique recently developed by the Viennese psychiatrist, Jacob Moreno, in which the patient acted out his conflicts and problems, with other people playing different aspects of his personality. The theory, as with abreaction, was that the process of re-enacting the traumatic events would have a cathartic effect on the individual and allow him to get rid of a lot of repressed material.[28]

Michael Foulkes saw drama as a natural extension of his group sessions, and a special 'Moreno stage' was built at the hospital by the patients. But the technique must have taken some selling to the ordinary British soldier. One of Foulkes' therapeutic groups, after watching a drama in action, 'showed great concern lest they might be asked to act themselves'. They were, he says, 'terrified of this and the analysis of their different reactions proved a great stimulus'.[29]

In May 1945 doctors described how a corporal recently evacuated from the front in Holland was asked to relive his experiences again and to show what had happened: 'Two others acted with him, the rest were wiping brows and sweating.' Some sort of battlefield horror was then re-enacted, which provoked at the next group meeting a discussion on cowardice 'which got very heated – far more emotional than the psychodrama. Abreaction came out in the form of aggression against each other, cowardice and the country.' Following this, two members left this group because they were reluctant to re-live their experiences in public.[30]

Looking back, many doctors doubted the value of psychodrama. Dr Millicent Dewar felt it 'allowed people not just to fantasise, but to act out their fantasies, which might be dangerous.' Her main memory was of a man who was 'an actor manqué so to speak, who was absolutely superb. He was a crook – he'd been in the Army, but he was a crook – and he was absolutely *superb* . . . It was terribly funny [but] it *increased* his problem rather than diminished it.'[31]

Meanwhile, even more important developments were taking place in the old Training Wing of the hospital, now under the control of Major Harold Bridger.

Bridger was not a psychiatrist. Before the war, he had taught mathematics at Rugby 'public' school, and between 1940 and 1943 had commanded an Anti-Aircraft battery. Transferred to the Officer Selection Boards, he had shown such skill in 'handling group discussions and drawing inferences from them' that he was chosen by Ronald Hargreaves to take over from Bion at Northfield. Bridger's lack of psychiatric experience made him hesitate, but he was given many months to prepare himself – by visiting other military hospitals, talking at length to Bion and reading a recently-published book on the 'Peckham Experiment', an episode in the 1930s when a group of biologists and physiologists had set up a scheme to monitor a group of residents in a poor area of South London; by offering the free use of a swimming pool as a 'lure' to attract subjects, they had inadvertently sparked off a community initiative 'with a life of its own.'[32]

With Hargreaves' support, Bridger persuaded the Commanding Officer at Northfield to abolish the Training Wing with its military discipline and turn it into 'an organization for promoting activities of all sorts'. He also proposed an important change in lay-out. A large ward in the centre of the hospital was cleared, designated 'the Hospital Club', then left empty with its purpose unspecified while Bridger waited for the patients to react to its presence. After some weeks, they responded not with a proposal for its use, but with a protest meeting (to which Bridger and the hospital's Commanding Officer were summoned) demanding to know why 'public money and space' were being wasted in wartime. The hospital commander was horrified. 'Do you realise we have got a mutiny?' he asked Bridger. But Bridger was delighted: 'I thought, My God, this is wonderful! Fancy thinking of the war . . . They were supposed to be ill and here they are saying, my God, the war!' Having got them involved, Bridger then helped them to create a social club which, though 'frequently damaged, despoiled and even smashed up on occasion', became a focus for the men's activities.[33]

At the same time, Bridger and his staff began to foster social and recreational groups and to draw the patients into the running of the hospital. Like any good teacher, Bridger wanted to bring out the 'spontaneously felt desires and urges of the patients'. Instead of the 'kindergarten level' occupational therapy provided in the past, the patients could now choose what they wanted to do and try their hand at almost anything – painting, writing, learning a skill at the Austin Motor Company, farming at the local agricultural college. Many men chose an activity that would 'test' their psychiatrist and social therapist or 'test themselves in a real or fantasy role'. This was particularly true of the growing number of returning prisoners of war, who dreamed of having a 'farm', a 'cottage in the country' or of 'help[ing] to look after horses'.[34]

Gradually, too, the patients became involved in their mutual care, helping to induct new arrivals at the hospital and producing a substantial pamphlet Introducing You to Northfield:

We have been sent here because our health has been impaired. There may be many reasons for this. It may be due either to the way a man is constituted or to the experience that he has been through at various times during his life . . . Everything we do here is treatment . . . Your activity can be changed at any time by having a talk with your Psychiatrist about it.[35]

The 1940s mania for meetings reached its acme at Northfield. In addition to group therapy sessions organised by Foulkes, there were meetings of activity groups, weekly ward meetings, and, on Fridays, ward committee meetings (the 'House of Commons level') at which questions concerning the whole hospital were discussed. In addition, the staff held weekly seminars to review progress. With Foulkes' enthusiastic co-operation, Bridger broke down the barriers between psychiatrists and the rest of the staff; psychiatrists, as well as seeing patients in wards, now helped them in all their various activities.[36]

According to Foulkes, the 'increased spontaneity' fostered by letting the patients run things for themselves 'changed the whole atmosphere of the hospital'. The patients' sharing in hospital management caused them to be much more engaged with hospital affairs, which they now saw as their own interests; the meetings and common work gave increased opportunity for contact between all who were involved. Instead of clinging to their symptoms and staying as long as possible in the blue uniform of the Hospital Wing, patients now resented being in blue (which marked them outside as 'mental cases') and clamoured to wear khaki. For both Foulkes and Bridger, the excitement was enormous. Increasingly, visitors came to see what was going on at Northfield.[37]

Beneath the triumphant surface, however, 'tremendous tensions' developed. The growing rivalry, both personal and ideological, between the Bridger and Foulkes camps is evident at a staff meeting in August 1945. One ardent Bridgerite demanded that the hospital recognise that 'the most important contribution being made to the patients is in Major Bridger's department. Much more should be done along those lines.'

Why is this much more realistic psychiatry than the actual thing we are taught in text books? In what ways can you make it more effective and in a way eliminate the psychiatrist?[38]

Patrick de Maré, a protégé of Foulkes, countered by saying that they were dealing with two types of patient. A man who had blackouts and headaches after war service had to be treated personally – as well as 'socially'.

There is the social field and the psychiatric field and they overlap but they both have their own field of reference. One is an individual problem and the other is a social problem. However many groups you have, you won't be able to clear up a person who has had symptoms of a traumatic incident.[39]

Bridger then intervened to calm both sides down, calling the 'attempt to create a dichotomy between social and individual psychiatry' futile. He was, though, very annoyed when soon afterwards Foulkes went off to give a 'rather glamorised' talk about Northfield to the Psycho-Analytical Society in London, claiming credit for developments really initiated by Bridger and using Northfield to advance his own standing in the psychoanalytic community. When a lady in the audience stood up and asked 'Do they ever riot?', Bridger, irritated by Foulkes' bland answer to the question, intervened and said, yes, there were always riots of one kind or another going on, of which Foulkes perhaps was not aware.[40]

Certainly, when Tom Main, late of 21 Army Group, arrived at Northfield early in 1945 he found 'much indiscipline' in the troops there and the military hierarchy very unhappy at the state of things and resentful of the way patients were being allowed by psychiatrists to question orders. Although Bridger's experiment was supposed to involve the whole hospital and not just one wing (like Bion's), in practice the non-psychiatric staff felt excluded and annoyed by what they saw as the indulgence shown to patients. Eventually, in an effort to overcome this problem, Dr Main tried to create a 'therapeutic community', in which a 'total culture of enquiry' would involve everyone at the hospital.

It became ordinary for orderly room clerks, staff sergeants, Matron's staff, secretaries,

military cooks and orderlies and night staff – yes and sometimes my commanding officer
and his adjutant – to be seen in groups alongside patients and psychiatrists.[41]

After the war the phrase 'therapeutic community' became a stale cliché of
psychiatry, a label which many differing spirits tried to pin on their attempts to
redefine the old 'medical' model of treating mental illness. One Northfield
psychiatrist, Millicent Dewar, felt in retrospect that it was all a bit of a nonsense:
'[Tom Main] made it so that one couldn't do anything without asking the nurse's
permission. I didn't, by the way, adhere to this. Being a woman, I think, was
important. But the men had great difficulties ... I agree tremendously that
doctors had far too much power and nurses were subservient. But it *aint any good
to put it round the other way.*'[42]

Main himself later acknowledged that his initiative was unpopular with some
psychiatrists as well as with the military. Breaking down all barriers would remain
a dream. 'Every community,' he told an interviewer in 1984, 'requires and in
subtle ways gets certain people to act as containers for its conservative wishes on
the one hand and its progressive wishes on the other, and tends to require, create,
and maintain various split-off sectors of itself into which it can variously project
evil, disorder, financial discipline, illness, inefficiency, health, and insensitivity
and to encourage these in subtle fashion to create trouble. Thus internal personal
conflicts are socially externalised.'[43]

Ideologically, Main belonged in the Bion/Bridger camp, and was critical of the
cult Foulkes had created. But he also recognised that for all the excitement about
groups, there was still a need for individual therapy. Certain people didn't do very
well in groups, particularly those 'recognizably preoccupied with intrapersonal
problems; mourning lost comrades, for example.

A number of new forms of individual treatment were now available. Pentothal
was used at Northfield with rather mixed results, and Tom Main developed an
extraordinary technique with one group of patients – tank commanders who had
several times lost their crews, become depressed, and refused to fight. He found
these men still had the elite self-respect of the tank corps and were 'very snobbish,
very standoffish' and wouldn't talk to him. Deciding that what they needed was
a period of compulsory mourning, he drew on his authority as a Lt-Colonel and
had them shut up in darkened cells for three days with only bread and water and
an hour of daylight and an hour of electric light. He believed that this method,
however authoritarian, did work because it 'sanctioned the sadness', gave them
the opportunity, within the masculine, disciplined world of the Army, to express
their grief, but without going in for all the mumbo-jumbo of therapy which they
equated with feminine weakness. 'The problem was to get rid of the bloody
mindedness behind the depression, the rage at the Army and the loss of their
crews,' Main said later. He believed some these patients had even gone back to
commanding tanks.[44]

But Main's colleague, Millicent Dewar, disagreed strongly. 'I thought it was
cruel and I told him so,' she later recalled. 'I do not think "compulsory
mourning" is ethical – can I use that word – because it's *phoney*... One mourns,

one doesn't *compulsorily* mourn. . . . I loved Tom, but he had very strange ideas sometimes.'[45]

Another Northfield technique was designed to deal with the problem of 'imported temporary regression' which sometimes followed continuous drug narcosis treatment – in layman's terms, patients knocked out with drugs for long periods sometimes behaved like babies when they came to. The rationale, Tom Main explained to American visitors in 1945, was that

The patients were allowed and encouraged to regress to infantile acts and attitudes. They were fed when they seemed to want it, with their heads on nurses' shoulders. When sucking movements occurred they were allowed to take milk from a bottle. One patient emptied 17 small bottles before this oral drive was appeased. Nursery rhymes were recited or sung to the patients on request. The return to full consciousness was treated as a weaning experience, through which they were allowed to pass slowly.[46]

Interviewed in the 1980s, Main conceded that although 'the patients loved it and so did the nurses', the treatment 'had no effect at all'. The patients 'wanted to go on being like babies'. It was a 'kind of forced regression in a medical sense' and an 'absolute waste of time'.[47]

*   *   *

Once, during a group psychotherapy session at Northfield, it emerged that the psychiatrist, Dr Martin James, was the only person present who had consistently had a bed to himself from childhood. No doubt, like psychiatrists in wartime training films, he also talked with clipped vowels and a plummy Hampstead accent. Similarly, patients in the hospital addressed the three women doctors, who all had voices like cut glass, as 'ma'am'.[48]

The issue of class is never explicitly mentioned in the millions of words about Northfield, but its presence is not hard to detect. One advantage of group psychotherapy was that it bridged the class divide and turned the process of talking about your fears and feelings – seen in the culture of the time by working-class men as weak and feminine – into something carried out with masculine peers. One former patient at the hospital, interviewed many years later, recalled that 'all this therapy stuff' had been 'a great help'. He had 'improved con-siderably' at Northfield. 'It completely rested me, I felt much more relaxed, much calmer.' But the treatment he remembered was the 'Jungle Juice' he was given on arrival at Northfield, which sedated him for his first three weeks in the hospital. He recalled trusting his doctors – 'You had to do what they said because they were the learned ones.' He had, though, sometimes thought that 'they hadn't been what we'd been through, but we still had to do what they said because we were in the Army.' Few other patients remember taking part in group psychotherapy, which they did not regard as 'proper' treatment.[49]

The Northfield psychiatrists were trying to create a democratic, non-authoritarian group psychology, fusing Freud and ideas of group dynamics, as an alternative to the authoritarian methods of the Army. But there is some evidence that patients, far from being empowered by these anti-authoritarian procedures, were in fact bewildered and unsettled by them. It seems they were aware of the internal contradictions of a regime based on 'spontaneity' and self-expression operating within the framework of the Army. Repeatedly the patients posed the simple question that was never addressed by the psychiatrists. What was Northfield for? If it was to keep people in the Army and not let them work their ticket, why did its methods, a sergeant demanded to know, 'bring his personal problems to the forefront of his mind'? Why was he being de-militarised, 'drained of unit spirit'? Other patients had the same complaint. Foulkes thought they were blaming the hospital for their own guilt at abandoning their units, but admitted that 'from the point of view of getting better results we might do better by [returning them to their units]. We could close the hospital and perhaps do better than we know.'[50]

In July 1945 the men of one ward demanded (after an impeccably democratic meeting) that an unpopular ward sister be dismissed. The doctors were plunged into discord. Some were for removing the nurse; women doctors wanted solidarity with their female colleague; the more senior officers worried about discipline. In the end the nurse stayed.[51]

After VJ Day in August 1945, the question of the hospital's purpose was posed afresh by the patients themselves in their newspaper, *The Mercury*. An angry front page editorial demanded that Northfield 'make up its mind between being a Military institution re-habilitating a man back to the Army or a hospital for resurrecting an abnormal Army man back to a normal civilian.' After reminding the psychiatrists that 'Indecision, together with lack of clear thinking and control, is a symptom of neurosis yet, this hospital, our supposed salvation, exhibits exactly the same troubles,' it suggested that the hospital should be run as a civilian resettlement unit. Patients should have civvy suits and proper pay: 'a reasonable amount in one's pocket gives independence, confidence and security . . . at the moment we are like marionettes trying to be humanised at a Fancy Dress Ball.'[52]

In response, Foulkes, by now 'activities officer', set up a 'Co-Ordinating group' drawn from the brightest patients, as an elite body to keep the hospital on its toes (a Jewish refugee from Germany, Foulkes consistently showed himself a 'realist' about power). But, by the end of 1945 most of the important psychiatrists were impatient to get back to civilian life themselves and the group feeling among the doctors that had sustained Northfield began to subside. One by one, Foulkes, Main and Bridger returned to civvy street, their professional names now made. The hospital continued to function for several more years but by early 1946 what John Rickman called 'one of the biggest costliest experiments in psychodynamics' was over. When the poet Vernon Scannell arrived at Northfield in 1948, he found the atmosphere there just as described by Heppenstall in 1943. An overworked psychiatrist advised him to get out as soon as possible.[53]

By then, however, Northfield was part of psychiatric folklore. 'The brilliant success of this experiment,' a breathless article declared, 'was due to the cooperation of many eminent and experienced psychiatrists. Their wisdom, learning and deep knowledge of humanity provided a co-operative force in which patients and staff, both professional and administrative, contributed to the socialization of the unsociable, disappointed and unhappy neurotic.' Yet in all the vast Northfield literature something is lacking – a strong sense of the individual patient.[54]

In November 1945 the Northfield doctors held an inquest over a group that had broken up. One of the psychiatrists, Ronald Markillie, warned of the need to make patients feel secure before experimenting on them:

I have often thought that [those] bringing up children progressively often have their failures, not because the methods used were bad, but because the experimental attitude is insecurity producing. Here there is a tremendous spirit of enquiry going on into the various ways of dealing with patients and that in itself can be insecurity producing.[55]

It was a wise remark. Over and over again in the Northfield notes what comes through is how uncomfortable, embarrassed or ill-at-ease the patients are, preferring individual therapy to group, not wanting to act out their neuroses, either wishing to retain their military identity or to get out of the Army. But Foulkes, Main and Bridger were all in the grip of a big idea, and remained strangely blind to this.

*   *   *

It is impossible to make a direct comparison between the regime at Northfield and that of its main American equivalent, Mason General Hospital. Apart from divergences in function, the two hospitals have survived in very different ways. What we know about Northfield derives from the papers S. H. Foulkes kept with Germanic thoroughness, whereas the main source on Mason General is a 'lost' masterpiece of the cinema that was shot there.

John Huston's documentary, *Let There Be Light*, was intended by the United States Army to be a public relations exercise to reassure the American public. In 1945, General William Menninger, the Army's chief psychiatric adviser, had begun receiving irate letters from the mothers of recently discharged soldiers. 'My boy was brought home last week,' went one. 'They told me he was all right. But he doesn't seem to know what he is doing.'

Why did the Army doctors send my boy home? Why didn't they do something for him? The Army caused this . . . He was all right before he joined up. Why doesn't the Army keep him till he gets well?[56]

These letters reflected a revolution in public attitudes since 1918 and a debate on 'the returning veteran' then sweeping through the American media, putting a powerful spotlight on the Army's psychiatric work. No longer content meekly to take back their boys as shattered hopeless parcels dumped on their doorsteps, mothers now demanded them back good as new, having been told by the media that the expertise and resources existed to do just that.[57]

Until the spring of 1944, Menninger later wrote, 'the official point of view of the Army toward psychiatric illnesses [had been] a mixture of fatalism and disinterest.' It had not felt obliged to provide 'definitive treatment' for psychoneurotics deemed incapable of further military service and had discharged them 'uncured', the medical responsibility of the Veterans' Administration. Faltering steps had been taken to change this policy when in December 1944 President Roosevelt, with a politician's instincts for a shift in public mood, swung his weight behind the campaign and urged that 'the ultimate' be done to return disabled men returning from the war to useful citizens. No overseas casualty was to be discharged until he had received 'the maximum benefits of hospitalization and convalescent facilities,' which 'must also include physical and psychological rehabilitation, vocational guidance, prevocational training and resocialization.' Secretary of War Stimson assured him no soldier would be sent home without every such effort being made. If in 1943 the policy had been no treatment, now it was treatment unlimited.[58]

Menninger (a skilful exponent of public relations) commissioned the Hollywood director John Huston, who had just made two fine documentaries for the US Signal Corps, to show that 'the ultimate' was indeed being done for these men. After visiting several Army hospitals, Huston quickly settled on Mason General, near New York – the main treatment centre for the East Coast. Huston had scripted the medical biopic *Dr Ehrlich's Magic Bullet* but his knowledge of psychiatry went no further than 'a superficial acquaintance with the ideas of Freud, Jung and Adler'; he was astonished by what he saw at the hospital. Eventually, by shooting 300,000 feet of 35-mm film (at a cost of $350,000) he was able to capture more of the excitement and drama of military psychiatry than anyone before or since. He also romanticised what was going on at Mason General.[59]

Let There Be Light opens with shots of a hospital ship returning from abroad and wounded and limbless soldiers coming down the gangplank. Over solemn music, the narration sets the tone.[60]

The guns are quiet now.

The papers of peace have been signed.

The oceans of the earth are filled with ships coming home.

In far away places men dreamed of this moment, but for some men the moment is very different from the dream.

Here is human salvage, the final result of all that metal and fire can do to violate mortal flesh.

Some wear the badges of their pain, the crutches, the bandages, the splints.

Others show no outward signs.

Yet they too are wounded.

Then we see ambulances arriving at a vast, multi-storey modern building – Mason General Hospital – and a group of men being admitted.

These are the casualties of the spirit, the troubled in mind, men who are damaged emotionally.

Born and bred in peace, educated to hate war, they were overnight plunged into sudden and terrible situations.

Every man has his breaking point and these, in the fulfilment of their duties as soldiers, were forced beyond the limit of human endurance.

The film follows one such group (of seventy-five men) over the eight weeks they spend in the hospital. First, each is interviewed by a psychiatrist – by shooting miles of film with several cameras and live sound recording, Huston made these scenes very real. The men are incoherent and muddled, the psychiatrists brisk and brutally matter of fact. There is the usual cross-section of cases: one lost his buddy, 'the last one of the original boys that were with me'; a second dreamt of his brother (killed on Guadalcanal) while serving on Minandao; a third saw the rest of his patrol blown up by a Panzerfaust in the Hartstein forest. There is a stutterer, a man who trembles, another who cannot sleep. But the most interesting case is a very respectable, middle-class black soldier, who has not been in action at all but was overcome by homesickness when he got a picture from his girl back home, 'the one person that gave me a sense of importance'. His suffering has a terrible poignant dignity.

In its humanistic focus on each man's suffering, *Let There Be Light* transcends propaganda and becomes both a powerful work of art and a quasi-documentary record of psychiatric practice. Huston's spendthrift perfectionism enabled him to capture the 'extraordinary and completely unpredictable exchanges that sometimes occurred' and to provide the first visual record of the 'seemingly miraculous' 'cures' of symptoms with hypnosis and drugs hitherto known only in the literature. Putting it more cynically, his was probably the first film to exploit for dramatic purposes the voyeuristic potential of emotional catharsis.

Huston was fortunate that one of the doctors at Mason General, Colonel Benjamin Simon, was a virtuoso of hypnotic and chemical abreaction. For instance, in one dramatic sequence, a patient is brought in with hysterical paralysis in both legs, given sodium amytal and then taken back over the events which have caused this hysterical conversion (they involve conflicts at home between his mother and father). By suggestion under the drug, Simon is able to restore the power to walk.

Another man cannot remember his own name; 'a shell-burst in Okinawa', we are told, 'wiped out his memory. The experience was unendurable to his conscious mind which rejected it and along with it his entire past.' He is briskly hypnotised by Simon, standing 'face to face with the subject' and speaking in 'short, measured sentences'.

'Now, clasp your hands in front of you. Clasp them tight, tight, tight, tight, tight. They're getting tighter and tighter and tighter and as they get tighter you're falling asleep. As they get tighter, you're falling asleep. Your eyes are getting heavy, heavy. Now your hands are locked tight, they're locked tight, they're locked tight. You can't let go, they're locked tight. You can't let go. When I snap my fingers you'll be able to let go. When I snap my fingers you'll be able to let go and then you'll get sleepier. And your eyes are getting heavier. Now your eyes are getting heavier, heavier, heavier, heavier . . . You're going into a deep, deep sleep. You're going into a deep, deep sleep . . . deeper sleep, far asleep. Eyes now closed tight, closed tight. Going into a deep, deep sleep deeply relaxed – far asleep. You're far asleep. You're fast asleep. Now you're in a deep sleep. You have no fear, no anxiety. Now you're in a deep, deep sleep . . .'

and taken back to the battlefield

'. . . We're going back. We're going back now, going back to Okinawa, going back to Okinawa. You can talk. You can talk. You can remember – everything. You can remember – everything. You're back on Okinawa. Tell me what you see, tell me. Speak . . .'
    'I'm in the battery area.'
    'You're in the battery area. Go on. Tell me what's going on.'
    'Getting fire missions.'
    'You're getting fire missions. Go on. You see everything now – clearly.'
    'We're getting shells thrown at us.'
    'You're getting shells thrown at you. From where?'
    'Japs.'
    'Japs. Go on. Yes. Keep on. You'll remember it all now. Every bit of it coming back.'
    'Japs getting near us to get our position.'
    'Japs getting near to you to get your position. Go on.'
    'Told us to get cover.'
    'Who told you to get cover?'
    'VC.'
    'VC? Go on.'
    'They spotted me. One of the boys get hurt.'
    'One of the boys got hurt.'
    'Took him away . . .'
    'Yes. Go on, you remember it now. Tell me. It's all right now, but you can tell me. You can tell me.'
    [shuddering] 'Explosion.'
    'Yes. You remember the explosion now. All right. Go on.'
    'They're carrying me.'
    'They're carrying you. Who's carrying you?'
    [pause]
    'Where are they taking you?'
    'Carrying me across the field.'
    'Across the field? Go on.'
    'Put me in a stretcher.'
    'Yes. Yes. Go on'
    'They're still trapped, they're still . . . still . . .'
    'Yes. Can you hear them? You see them?'
    'No.'
    'All right. Where they taking you now?'
    [pause]
    'Why are you fearful now?'
    'I don't want any more of it.' [Shudders]

'You don't want any more? You want to forget it? But you're going to remember it because it's gone now. It's gone. You're back here now. You're away from Okinawa. You've forgotten it. But you remember who you are now. Who are you?'

[music]

'That's right. Full name now.'

'Dominic Dolley.'

'You know your mother's name?'

'Isobel.'

'That's right. Father's?'

Colonel Simon was careful to re-integrate the hypnotic memories into the conscious mind, so that the soldier could 'regard the experience in its true perspective as a thing of the past which no longer threaten[ed] his safety.'

'That's right. You know who they all are now . . . All right now you're coming back with us. This is going to stay with you. You are going to remember it all.'

[Groans]

'You're going to remember about Okinawa. You are going to remember about the shells and the bombs. But they're gone. At ease, relaxed. No fear, no anxiety . . . when I wake you up you will be comfortable, relaxed. No pains and no aches. But you will remember all that I've told you, all that you've remembered. You can wake now.'

[music. Boy wakes up]

'Well, how are you?'

'Pretty good.'

Cases such as these are very moving, but not at all typical of what went on at Mason General. In an article in 1946, Colonel Simon stressed that the sheer number of cases and shortage of trained staff made it impossible to offer much individual therapy there; most men could only get a 'broad program of treatment directed at large masses and groups'. This lasted up to two months, was designed to stabilise rather than to cure their disorders and was, he conceded, based on an 'oversimplification' of their problem. Most men, the rationale went, had come to terms with unbearable anxiety by developing symptoms which served the function of isolating them as individuals from others, and thus releasing them from their social obligations to others. If, therefore, you could get them to re-engage with their fellows, to 'break down the barrier of self-imposed isolation', they would begin to get better again.[61]

Clearly this has something in common with British 'social psychiatry', but Simon's methods, instead of relying on 'spontaneity' and 'self-expression', were quite authoritarian, with a strong behaviourist tang. The 'groundwork pattern' for treatment is called reconditioning, and the aim is 'ceaseless stimulation towards an increased participation with larger and larger groups', by means of a variety of rewards and incentives. At each step, attempts are made to lure the patient into a community of interest with others.

As Huston's film shows, there was great deal of group therapy at Mason General, but most of it was quite different and much more structured than at

Northfield. Psychiatric social workers held weekly discussion groups (of whole wards) on topical subjects like 'The GI Bill of Rights', and doctors had weekly sessions to discuss patients' symptoms, relying very much on 'the commonality of experiences seen in these discussions' to 'break down the self-imposed isolation of the patient'. Finally, a small number of patients with 'similarity of background, experience and function' – such as battle dreams – were given treatment in small groups.

Let There Be Light shows one such session, in which a psychiatrist tries to help a group of men 'to understand something of the basic causes of [their] distress' and that their 'inner conflicts are, with variations, common to all men.' A small man with a thin moustache, he speaks with fluent authority:

We want to get you out of your own feeling of isolation, to get you to feel that you are like other people. In order to get to that we have to use knowledge as one thing; and something else which has to be added. And that is an experience of safety. You could say it is almost the core of all our treatment methods – development of knowledge of oneself with the accompanying safety it brings.

Then, under his encouragement, the men talk about their own childhoods – how they handled fear, how they related to their parents, how economic conditions create insecurity because 'mother and father arguing in the home pass that on to the children'. The middle-class black soldier reveals that his mother wouldn't let him play with other kids unless 'their parents had the equivalent of what our parents had.'

But none of these men is offered more than a few words of general reassurance; the purpose remains to create a sense of common experience – what Simon called the 'ceaseless stimulation towards an increased participation with larger and larger groups'. Rewards and privileges within the hospital are skilfully used to 'lure the patient into a community of interest with others'.

In Huston's film the therapy is shown to work: after a few weeks 'the shock and stress of war are starting to wear off'. The men, 'blessed with the natural regenerative power of youth', are now 'living less in the past and more in the future' and thinking about what to do back in civilian life. They play baseball, even the boy whose limbs were paralysed; they craft wooden dolls, strum the guitar, chat to visitors,

the people they are coming back to, whose lives are bound up with theirs. Without their understanding, all that has been accomplished in the last weeks can be torn down. With it, their return to life can be doubly swift and sure.

Now, in their group sessions, the men worry about going back into society; the social worker reassures them that an educational programme has been changing public attitudes. They must feel proud to have withstood 'stresses that civilians are rarely subjected to'. They need have no shame and must be honest with employers about their pasts.

Towards the end of the film, the second psychiatrist delivers his final pep talk. The theme again is emotional security and, interestingly, he makes some of the same points as Dr Ronald Markillie in the discussion at Northfield. But the language is more accessible:

You know in The Bible where it says, 'Man does not live by bread alone'? Children don't grow up well without safety and confidence. If that wasn't in one's childhood in growing up, you could say now there was something missing during all that time. And the next question is, how to supply it – and it does need to be supplied. Not all of the learning in all of the books is half as valuable in getting over nervousness as to find someone that you esteem, that you can learn to feel safe with, where you can get a feeling of getting accepted, and cherished, where you get a feeling that you are worthwhile and that you are important to someone. You could say the feeling that you didn't get – that something more than bread – when you were little – you still need to get it. You still need to be fed . . . to get acceptance, and to find the safety. In other words, knowledge alone . . . is not enough.

And, after a final parade, at which an officer tells them 'on your shoulders fall much of the responsibility of the post-war world', it's on to the bus and jauntily back into civilian life to the strains of 'Johnny Comes Marching Home'.

Let There Be Light conjures up today a lost world of New Deal idealism, confidence and hope. There is a moving sense of common enterprise, an assumption that the gifted, the intelligent and the strong are helping their fellow men in a spirit of purpose and authority. There is order and self-belief – as well as light. The psychiatrists are full of firm, confident authority. At the time, though, the issues were different. Herbert Spiegel, an experienced front-line psychiatrist who worked at Mason General, remembers feeling that Huston had 'slobbered over the men. He encouraged them to act like cry-babies. He wanted to sentimentalise how the poor boys suffered.' Spiegel was uncomfortable with the way that Huston 'conveyed the feeling that we had a lot of weak-willed namby-pambies. That was not the picture of the men I saw in combat . . . Many of [the patients in the film] were not combat casualties.' This view was shared by the US War Department which suppressed the film, on the pretext that it violated patient confidentiality. The real reason, Huston felt, was that 'they wanted to maintain the "warrior" myth which said that our American soldiers went to war and came back all the stronger for the experience, standing tall and proud for having served their country well. Only a few weaklings fell by the way.'[62]

Clearly *Let There Be Light* does gives a distorted picture; it says nothing, for example, about the closed psychotic wards at Mason General where a 'high percentage' of schizophrenics and catatonics received shock therapy – from twelve to sixteen sessions of ECT. It doesn't mention the chronic shortage of trained nurses which meant that most of the nursing at Mason General was done by psychiatric technicians who regarded the men as 'goldbricks' (malingerers) and often treated them brutally. Like the media of the day, it dramatises and oversimplifies the complexities of abreactive treatment and drapes inadequate men in the cloak of the battle casualty. Huston puts a warm, Irish, humanistic gloss on what was in reality a tough and authoritarian regime. But in conveying a sense of optimism and purpose, I do not believe he misrepresented the overall truth.[63]

Ultimately, though, perhaps what occurred in these hospitals mattered less than what happened in the wider society to which their patients returned.

THE HELMETED AIRMAN

The Romance of the Air – war's last beauty parlour.

E. M. Forster, 1944[1]

In August 1943, the Allied bombing campaign against Germany was at its height.

On the night of 23 August, Bomber Command of the Royal Air Force attacked Berlin. Crews were briefed on the target in the late afternoon and the first of 719 aircraft took off at 7.36 p.m. The Dutch coast was crossed at 10 p.m., and the bomber force arrived at Berlin at about 11.45. By then, about 77 aircraft had turned back with mechanical and other troubles and sixteen had been shot down. On this occasion, however, the RAF had temporarily managed to knock out the German radar with its 'Window' device and most of the Luftwaffe's night fighters had been sent on to Berlin (correctly guessed to be the target) to operate there visually. Conditions favoured the defenders: the moon was clear, searchlights 'were doing a good job' and 31 aircraft were shot down over the city.

Meanwhile, the rest of the bombers tried to carry out the plan. It was intended that the target would initially be marked by Pathfinders using electronic navigation aids, and then periodically re-marked by Back-Up Pathfinders as successive waves of aircraft went in. For the first time a 'Master Bomber' was to circle the target, guiding and encouraging the crews. But this was not a night to linger over Berlin and 'bombing discipline' soon wavered. It turned out later that only a quarter of the force bombed 'the vulnerable area of Berlin and that most of the remainder bombed lightly built-up suburban areas' – though 854 people were killed.

At about 40 minutes past midnight the last bombers left the target area. The return trip involved a long dog-leg over the Baltic, during which four more bombers were lost and two landed in Sweden. On the last leg, six more were shot down over and three crashed into the North Sea. Finally, in the early hours of the next morning, as the bombers returned, another four machines were lost on landing (two Halifaxes collided in mid-air). Three members of the crew of a Lancaster which had been badly damaged refused to fly again.

Its night's work had cost Bomber Command 62 aircraft and their crews, but its commander, Sir Arthur Harris, continued to believe that he could wreck

Berlin and perhaps end the war. He sent his force back to the German capital eighteen times in the course of the winter. Tactics grew ever more sophisticated and some nights Bomber Command had a success, but the operation as a whole was 'more than a failure. It was a defeat.'[2]

Six days earlier, on 17 August 1943, the Americans had carried out one of the most famous operations of the war: a daring raid on 'strategic' targets deep inside Germany – the Messerschmitt factory at Regensburg and the ball-bearings works at Schweinfurt. The original idea was for both forces to fly together, with the Regensburg aircraft then flying on to North Africa while the Schweinfurt bombers returned to England. This would have minimised the exposure to German fighter attack. At the appointed hour of 5.45 a.m., however, all American airbases in Britain were covered in cloud, posing a serious risk of collision as the vast fleet of planes took off. Yet the weather over Europe was perfect, and the need of the Regensburg bombers to reach North Africa before darkness fell meant that any delay could scupper the mission. Confronted by this dilemma, the American commander took what turned out to be the wrong decision. He sent the Regensburg force off at 7.15, but kept the Schweinfurt aircraft back till 11.20 when conditions were better. There were no collisions on take-off, but the German day-fighters got two bites of the cherry.

The Regensburg force was escorted by American fighters as far as the Belgian border. Then it was on its own against the German fighters; by the time it reached Regensburg, fourteen of its 139 aircraft had been shot down and another three were in trouble. Nevertheless, the Americans carried out the complicated and terrifying procedure of the bombing run, flying in formation straight and level over the target and releasing their bombs on the lead bombardier's command. Regensburg was accurately and effectively hit. By 12.08 (British time) they were on their way to North Africa five hours and 900 miles away. After a long and stressful flight, 119 planes were able to land in Algeria.

Meanwhile, the men who were to fly to Schweinfurt had undergone the agony of delay. After some four hours' sleep, they had been awake since about 2 a.m, being briefed for several hours, breakfasting and then waiting by their aircraft. When they did finally take to the air, the Luftwaffe, alerted by the Regensburg mission, was waiting for them; the German air controllers had had time to mass huge numbers of fighters in western Germany. The moment the American fighter escorts were forced to return to base, the Germans fell on the bombers like angry bees, attacking from the front in line abreast. For the next hour or so it was 'just pandemonium', an extraordinary aerial battle as the vast Flying Fortresses clung to their tight formations and the gunners thundered out their 50mm fire, while some 200 German fighters attacked in wave after wave with a ferocity and determination they had never previously shown.

The American philosopher Glenn Gray has written of the 'lust of the eye' that warfare can sometimes arouse. Even in the heat and terror of combat, some of the American aircrew were aware of a spectacle around them that 'even Hollywood could never match' – the German fighters flying straight at the Fortresses and veering off at the last minute, the 'din and smell of ammo' as the gunners flailed impotently away at their targets, 'aircraft stalling, slow-rolling, wings disintegrating, chutes on fire'. The sheer intensity with which the battle raged left people breathless.

At about 3 p.m. some 195 (out of the original 230) Flying Fortresses arrived over Schweinfurt and began dropping their bombs. Not surprisingly, the formation had become rather confused and there was some 'hit and run' bombing. 'If the lead bombardier was shaking as much as I was,' a pilot later recalled, 'he had reason to miss.' Bombs fell over a wide area and although over twenty people and many farm animals were killed, the damage to the ball-bearings factories was only slight.

More aircraft were lost on the return trip, but the Luftwaffe was itself rather exhausted by its exertions and the Americans were able to achieve a surprise by bringing their fighter escorts fifteen miles further east than ever before. By 8.20 that evening the last of the Schweinfurt bombers had landed in England. Of the 230 that left, 32 did not return. The two raids had cost the lives of 109 men and another 392 had been captured.[3]

*   *   *

Flying aircraft in war has always been a stressful business. 'All war pilots would inevitably break down in time if not relieved,' the Royal Air Force's medical chief told the Southborough Committee in 1922. In the Battle of Britain, a stage was reached when it became clear that pilots would end up 'Crackers or Coffins'; thereafter, their time in the air was rationed. But it was in the bombing offensive against Germany that the most serious problems of morale and discipline arose.[4]

Between 1942 and 1944 bombing was seen as the principal means of 'striking back at the Germans', and the Bomber barons were given the cream of British and American manpower and industrial production to do it with. The British soon ran up against 'operational factors', when early attempts to bomb Germany by day – in line with pre-war training – proved suicidal, and to survive as a fighting force the RAF was obliged to switch to night bombing. New navigational aids were developed and 'precision' attacks abandoned in favour of 'area' attacks on cities. Yet it remained a hugely difficult task for a large force of aircraft to find a target like Berlin in darkness. The Germans quickly developed ways of guiding night fighter aircraft towards the bombers, using ground and air based radar; which the British, in their turn, attempted to neutralise with electronic countermeasures.[5]

There were occasions when the RAF overwhelmed or outwitted the defences – Cologne in 1942, Hamburg in 1943 and Dresden in 1945 – but these were quite rare. The cold actuarial truth which emerged after the war (to the fury of the Air Marshals) was that until late in 1944 the Bomber offensive did more damage to the RAF than it did to Germany. At the time, in the bunkers of Bomber Command, belligerent optimism and bureaucratic conformity silenced all doubts.[6]

The Americans had illusions of their own. The United States Army Air Force arrived in Europe in 1942 convinced that it could succeed where the RAF had failed. Its vast, heavily-armed B-17 Flying Fortress aircraft, flying in tight geometric formations, would see off the German fighters by day; its unique Norden bomb-sight would enable it to hit targets with pin-point accuracy while flying high above the German flak. Translated from California to the murky skies of Northern Europe, none of this proved to be true – the Germans quickly devised tactics for attacking formations from their vulnerable angle, the front – but the air generals stuck obstinately to their guns. It was not until the Mustang fighter was introduced in 1944, enabling bombers to be escorted all the way to Germany and back, that the Luftwaffe was defeated and the bombing offensive began to achieve significant results.[7]

These are the facts. But history consists also of *mentalités* – states of mind which dictate how men interpret and respond to events – and to understand the bombing of Germany several distinct states of mind have to be resurrected. There is the mind-set of the Bomber barons, men who had spent their entire careers absorbing the ideology of Air Power, and, in the American case, had still not achieved an Air Force independent of the Army. With so much yet to prove, they were hardly likely to be deflected from their set course by what they saw as temporary and local reverses. In a time of doubt, they had the strength of faith and instilled it in those they led. Like Haig in 1916, they were blind to evidence and saw only what they wished to see.

Then there is the public mood. In Britain especially, bombing was the only way of getting back at Hitler; the only way for Churchill to show Stalin and Roosevelt he was doing something. Only a tiny minority questioned the morality of what was done; after all, the Germans had started it, by bombing civilians at Rotterdam and Coventry. 'They have sown the wind,' 'Bomber' Harris told the newsreels in 1942. 'They will reap the whirlwind.' No one bayed louder for German blood than the media: 'Is it really necessary for the BBC to gloat so much?' a correspondent to *The Times* asked two weeks after the RAF had reduced the medieval town of Lübeck to ashes.[8]

And, finally there are the 'bomber boys'. Their strange mixture of bravado, public school exuberance, understatement and irony is very hard to recover today, after decades of parody and mockery. Perhaps it survives best in Eric Partridge's *Dictionary of RAF Slang*, a few entries of which read:

Crump Dump, the The Ruhr
Depth charge A prune. In the Services, prunes are provided as a mild and not unpleasant laxative
Frozen on the stick Paralysed with fear
Black-outs A pair of WAAF knickers
Twilights A WAAF's pair of summer-weight knickers.[9]

Theirs was an odd, novel way of fighting a war: living a life of ease and privilege on an airfield in eastern England, with good food, plenty to drink and access to women – all the things the Poor Bloody Infantry dreamt of. And then, every so often when the weather allowed, flying hundreds of miles over Europe in a cold, rattling aeroplane, shot at by flak and fighter, to drop a cargo of incendiaries and high-explosive on the enemy's cities. It was all unreal. 'How could you fight a war and be able to walk through the Backs at Cambridge the next day?' But you could.[10]

The two operations in August 1943 were worse than average; Schweinfurt, much worse. But they were not unique. The attrition rate in the bomber fleets was appalling: life expectancy compared unfavourably to that on the Western Front in 1916. In 1942–3, American crews 'had little chance of survival and only a small proportion did survive', and the RAF estimated that there was a 'one in five chance of surviving two tours in a heavy or medium bomber, which compared favourably with those in a light bomber. For the less statistically minded, the 'empty bunks and the new replacements told the story more bitterly than the steady disappearance of familiar aircraft.'[11]

The German Air Force placed no limit on the flying a pilot did; he simply kept going till he was killed, disabled or captured. But the British and Americans eventually recognised that in the interests of morale, it was wiser to set a term on the flying expected of airmen. The RAF tour of duty, as finalised in 1943, was 30 operations, followed by a period of training and a second tour of a further 20, which, supposedly, gave you a 50/50 chance of survival. In the USAAF a crew flew 25 missions. In both air forces, 'the tour of operations with its definite promise of relief' was, as John Terraine says, the 'sheet anchor of morale. It made the unbelievable endurable.'[12]

All aircrew were volunteers, the elite of an elite, carefully chosen and put through a training costing 'some £10,000 for each man – enough,' said 'Bomber' Harris, 'to send ten men to Oxford and Cambridge for three years.' Yet despite a 'selection process far more rigorous and realistic than anything the psychologists could devise' you still couldn't predict before a man had his first taste of combat flying whether he could hack it; some experienced pilots with hours to their credit broke down straightaway.[13]

They fell into the first broad category of breakdown the psychiatrists noticed: people who cracked in the first few missions, unable – when they found out what was involved – to control their fear,

watching close-in and constant enemy fighter attacks, flying through seemingly impenetrable walls of flak, seeing neighbouring planes go out of control and at times explode in mid-air, returning with dead or wounded on board.[14]

These men were felt to be fundamentally unsuitable for combat flying and impossible to treat medically.

But even 'fundamentally sound individuals' who had managed to control their fear might start to fall apart by about their fifteenth mission as they 'began to show the exhausting effects of chronic tension and anxiety, frequent briefings, real and practice missions'. Having had plenty of experience these men knew what to expect: the night before a mission 'they see the wing on fire, or their blood spattered over the cockpit window, or their crew freezing in a dinghy in the North Sea or drifting down on a parachute into a German field.' The worst bit was 'immediate anticipation', between briefing and take-off. A long delay – as before Schweinfurt – took a terrible toll. 'No one who has seen the mask of age which mantles the faces of these young men after a period of continued standing by punctuated by inevitable false alarms, is likely to forget it,' wrote an RAF doctor, David Stafford-Clark.

Their pallor, the hollows in their cheeks and beneath their eyes, and the utter fatigue with which they loll listlessly in chairs about the base, are eloquent of the exhaustion and frustration which they feel. In ten hours they may seem to have aged as many years. After a long and exacting operational flight similar evidence of fatigue both of body and mind may display itself. But in this case there is no element of frustration; the emotional hangover is far less; and because tension has dissolved in action, sound sleep may be expected to restore resilience in all but those who are already in need of medical assistance.[15]

In battle, there were some men who would become paralysed with fear, throw up or faint during moments of danger. But in general it was remarkable how most people seemed to keep functioning, 'outwardly calm, precise in thought and rapid in action' while hell raged around them.[16]

The strain of living with fear and anxiety could produce the sorts of symptoms seen on the Western Front – tremors, twitching, depression, nightmares, sweating, irritation – and eventually make a man incapable of continuing. But, because much of the problem was simple exhaustion and underlying morale was usually quite good, rest and appropriate drug treatment ('flak leave') got quite a lot of them back flying again.[17]

Finally, there was the man who had been through an experience so traumatic that his whole underlying mechanism of control, his whole faith that the aeroplane would stay in the sky, had snapped. These horrors came in many forms and often left the man with a phobia, an almost physical inability to get back into the plane.[18]

Of course aircrew who did not crack up and managed to keep going still went through troughs and peaks of morale over the tour of operations. Initially, the novelty and excitement of the experience would make them very cocky and self-confident, but after about five missions the full immensity of what lay ahead began to lie heavy in their minds. The airman was now 'passing through the critical phase of his . . . tour'; he had 'probably never been so close to death in his life before'. But if he managed to keep going his morale would improve as the end neared until, perhaps five missions from the end, he began to worry again. The last trip was usually very fraught.[19]

How did aircrew keep flying in the face of the mathematical certainty of death? Some were capable of existential toughness. To keep sane, Robert Kee wrote in his diary, 'you have to treat death lightly'. An American airman remembers with gratitude a colonel who gave him 'a little clue how to fight this war – make believe you're dead already; the rest comes easy.'[20]

More common, though, was the Calvinist approach, the belief that you alone had been singled out for survival. Most aircrew, an RAF officer wrote, were 'simple and to a certain extent selfish', preferring to 'boost up their morale by the simple but often effective saying "It won't happen to me".' He thought 'this somewhat unintelligent outlook was far more comforting while on the job than the saner course of taking a mathematical view of one's chances.' Not surprisingly, a young scientist visiting a RAF base in 1944 found 'the subject of survival rates was taboo. The whole weight of Air Force tradition and authority was designed to discourage the individual airman from figuring the odds.'[21]

To bolster faith in survival, extraordinary rituals and superstitions arose. Scarves or chains associated with good luck were faithfully preserved; to lose such a talisman was tantamount to signing your own death warrant. John Steinbeck once watched an American bomber station grind to a halt as everyone searched for a tail gunner's lost medallion and an RAF staff officer noticed after a raid that a tired bomber crew waiting to be de-briefed automatically sat their golliwog mascot in one chair beside them: 'Golly had been on every trip and had never missed an interrogation.'[22]

Bomber crews often went to great lengths to appease fate. Part of the attraction of Bomber Command was the easy access to girls it offered, but if a WAAF had gone out with a succession of men who had later gone missing or 'got the chop', she became known as a 'chop-girl' and no one would touch her. Similarly, certain aspects of the job, such as flying with a trainee pilot, were traditionally unlucky and therefore unpopular.[23]

Some men did lose their faith and plunged into a spiral of despair. 'Fear of death,' says the Canadian pilot Doug Harvey, 'was so strong in some of the aircrew that no form of discipline was effective. These were the ones who had convinced themselves they would be killed and everything else was therefore trivial.' One such man became the 'mess drunk'.[24]

Leadership was crucial, leadership within the squadron. Much of it had a talismanic quality: someone who had survived hitherto obviously had luck on his side; the more operations a squadron commander or wing leader went on, the more extraordinary the fact of his survival became, the more his authority was enhanced. But it rested also on professionalism and skill, on showing his aircrews that he was prepared to go to any lengths to minimise the chances of their death. The best leaders were not just perfectionists, they worked tirelessly to improve the flying technique and safety of their crews, flew on dangerous raids and created a spirit of camaraderie between aircrew and ground staff.[25]

Within each aircraft, the pilot set the tone. Miles Tripp's great memoir, *The Eighth Passenger*, is an extended tribute to 'Dig', his Australian skipper, whose maturity, strength of character and flying skill carried his seven-man Lancaster crew through a bombing tour. He was, says Tripp, 'a father to us all'. Dig was a tough, limited, philistine man, with two catch phrases, 'It's a great life if you don't weaken' and 'You'd whinge if your arse was on fire'. In the early days his loyalty and support helped meld seven disparate individuals into a crew; thereafter, his determination kept them going. Long after the war, Dig revealed that he had been constantly afraid himself, but a sense of duty instilled in him by his father – who had served throughout the previous war, winning the MC – and a wish 'to help in time of trouble' had driven him on.[26]

* * *

Flying has always posed special problems of military discipline. Whereas in the Army or Navy there was a 'disciplinary hierarchy to hold a man to his duty if necessary', in the Air Force one man (in a single-seater fighter) or a crew of six or ten (in a bomber) had to be entrusted with valuable and expensive technology and let loose in the air. How could you be sure that a pilot had done his best, really had reached the target and dropped his bombs where he said he had? To a large extent there had to be trust. The crew's discipline had, as John Terraine says, 'to come from within'. Nevertheless the staff was constantly trying to find ways to reinforce aircrews' sense of duty. In the First World War, British fighter pilots were simply not issued with parachutes lest they be tempted to bale out prematurely. A generation later, when such purblind crassness was no longer acceptable, cameras were mounted on bombers as much to check on crews' stories as to record damage to targets. At times of great strain a battle of wills would develop between the aircrews and the staff, with the crews trying to cut corners and stay alive and the staff attempting to keep the attack going. From early on in the war, the RAF felt it necessary to have up its sleeve an ultimate sanction, a moral weapon, some procedure for dealing with cases of 'flying personnel who will not face operational risks'. It was known as LMF or 'Lack of Moral Fibre'.[27]

Arthur Smith 'went LMF' after his twentieth 'op'. The target that night was the well-defended Ruhr and the weather was awful. Even before the aircraft crossed the English coast, he had lost control of his fear; his 'courage snapped and terror took over'. 'I couldn't do anything at all,' he later recalled. 'I became almost immobile, hardly able to move a muscle or speak.' Thinking he was ill, the crew turned back, but the station MO could find nothing physically wrong with him and when Smith said, 'I don't want to fly any more', 'that was it'. After a severe dressing-down from his commanding officer, he was bundled off the station without the chance to say goodbye to his crew.

Smith remembered being driven to another station, where a kindly psychiatrist listened to his life story and then explained what would happen to him. 'I'd be stripped of my rank, lose my flying pay, be sent away to another station to do a menial job. Everyone would know what I had done. My family would know and I realised that I'd be branded a coward for the rest of my life.' Smith was so horrified at the thought of this that he opted for the alternative now being offered – to go back to his squadron and finish his tour of operations (his crew had agreed to have him back). He managed to complete his tour, at great strain, and was badly burned on his final operation when the aircraft crashed on landing.[28]

Smith was an NCO. For officers, LMF involved loss of rank, dismissal from the service, and removal of flying wings. It was tantamount to loss of self-respect, of manhood. A deterrent of this sort was felt to be essential if discipline, morale, and the elite status of the service were to be preserved particularly as LMF was thought to be 'dangerously contagious'. At the same time, the staff and the politicians realised that some aspects of the policy would be 'quite indefensible in Parliament'. As little was said as possible and for many years the subject, like 'shell-shock', remained shrouded in official secrecy. In the 1970s, the authorities remained 'implacably hostile' to historians' enquiries and the heavily weeded official files now available leave many questions unanswered.[29]

How many men were declared LMF? Was it less than 0.3% of the total aircrew in 1943–44, as suggested by an internal memorandum quoted by John Terraine? Was it 416 out of 2,919 cases of 'psychological disorder' seen in the year to 9 February 1943? Or was 'around one man in seven lost to operational aircrew' at some point between the end of training and the completion as an operational tour 'for morale or medical reasons' as Max Hastings concluded, after talking to over a hundred veterans? Was it common knowledge inside Bomber Command headquarters in 1944 that 'the number transferred out of squadrons before the end of their tour was roughly equal to the number completing the full tour' as Freeman Dyson has claimed? There will never be a definitive answer, but the American historian Mark Wells concludes that Bomber Command's six-year war produced about 6,000 emotional casualties and about 200 cases of LMF per year, somewhere between 1,000 and 1,200 in all.[30]

Certainly, LMF was an important issue during Bomber Command's severest trial, the Battle of Berlin: the thirty-five or so heavy raids against Germany in the winter of 1943–44 (sixteen against the German capital), conceived by Harris as an 'all out' assault that would 'bring Germany to her knees'. He was driven not simply by over-optimism but by a determination that the Air Force should win the war on its own before the Allied landing in Northern Europe scheduled for May/June 1944.

The Battle of Berlin, John Terraine has argued, was Harris' Passchendaele, his prolonged exercise in futility. It was also, a Group Commander in Bomber Command believed, the second time in the war that 'aircrews balked at the jump'. As the winter of 1943 wore on, the symptoms of 'lack of enthusiasm' were increasingly clear: planes returning to base with minor mechanical defects ('early returns'); bombs 'wasted en route in an effort to increase aircraft performance'; 'fringe merchants' dropping their bombs on the edge of the target, away from the worst hazards, confident that cloudy skies would conceal the photographic evidence. The bombing run was generally agreed to be the worst moment of the flight; anything you could do to abbreviate that moment of supreme vulnerability, to lighten the aircraft and allow it to get out of danger, would increase your chances of survival.[31]

As one would expect, 'enthusiasm' was lowest in units with the worst casualties (and flying the most vulnerable aircraft) and in those with the weakest ties to the ideology of the RAF. Talking to over 300 veterans, Martin Middlebrook found that morale held up well among the Pathfinder force – who had the worst losses but were conscious of being an elite – but was not so good among the Canadians and in British units flying the more vulnerable Halifax bomber. 'Crews were weary and angry, strained and more fearful for their next trip than usual, cursing "Butch" Harris for his unrelenting demands and his apparently uncaring attitude towards his own men', according to a Canadian veteran. He and several others recalled the stigma of LMF being ruthlessly used to keep men flying who should have been rested. Some of these men had died soon after or gone mad in the air. A wireless operator described how Station Medical officers had instructions to 'keep aircrew off the sick list'. He himself had developed bad boils 'under the crotch and on the buttocks' after a disastrous raid on Berlin in February 1944, flown on another raid in some discomfort and then had the boils lanced by a doctor. This rather savage treatment made him faint, but the next day he was passed fit to fly: 'Bomber Command was terrified of too many people going sick and reducing the available force and that other crew might catch the "don't want to fly" bug.'[32]

Yet a pilot with a Lancaster squadron could recall no morale problems on his unit. Young, unattached, their faith in authority unassailed by the media, they had been 'united in our belief in the cause and in giving unquestioning support to those in authority'. A former flight engineer in the Pathfinders who had gone through no less than seventeen raids on Berlin as a 'mere lad of nineteen', remembered being 'more concerned about whether the local pub would run out of beer and if a certain WAAF would be there.'[33]

Eventually Harris, like Haig, got the message. Early in 1944, he pulled the Halifaxes out of the front line and switched his emphasis away from Berlin to the cities of southern Germany.

What is interesting, however, is the numbers who did *not* break down, for it is generally agreed that Bomber Command, unlike the US Eighth Air Force, never faced a crisis in morale during the war. There was nothing comparable in the RAF to what happened on some American air bases in late 1943 where 'aircrew [were] heard openly saying that they don't intend to fly to Berlin again or do any more difficult sorties.' Nor did anything like as many British as American aircraft 'crash-land' in Switzerland or Sweden on the way back from Germany.[34]

RAF crews kept going, but was that in spite of or because of the policy of LMF? Did LMF keep 'up to the collar' many men who would otherwise have faltered? Or was it insulting to the men, unnecessary and cruel? On these fundamental questions, the RAF's own doctors disagreed.

*　　*　　*

Dr Charles Symonds held the title of Consultant Neurologist to the RAF. A pupil of Gordon Holmes (at the National Hospital, Queen Square) and of Arthur Hurst (at Guy's), Symonds was the coming man of British neurology; he had also spent time studying psychiatry at Adolf Meyer's clinic in Baltimore.[35]

Symonds knew about war. As a young dispatch rider and regimental doctor on the Western Front, he had had his share of shells and bombs, watched with contempt as medical staff officers offered 'expert' advice on a front line they never visited and had written bitter letters home. Witnessing the aftermath of battle for the first time, he had 'simply felt [he] wanted to weep'. His experiences at Passchendaele gave him nightmares for the rest of his life.[36]

Yet, even as a front-line doctor, Symonds had had steel in him. 'War could not go on at all,' he wrote in 1917, 'unless there were men at the back sufficiently protected against intimate knowledge of its realities to be detached, and to drive the fighting man on from behind.' The freakish death of his young bride in a cycling accident in 1919 and an unhappy second marriage further hardened his heart. Having mastered his own misfortunes, he expected others to do the same. Though widely respected, Symonds had a reputation as a cold, unlovable man.

The Consultant Psychiatrist, R. D. Gillespie, was a very different character: at the parties given by the Child Guidance Clinic at Guy's before the war, the Physician in Psychological Medicine to the Hospital, would play 'nuts in may' with gusto, 'egged on by cries of "Ow be a sport!"', a bunch of children hanging round his waist and spurring him on to greater efforts. 'Very tall and thin, with a slightly quizzical expression, and a boyish, rather diffident, smile and laugh', Gillespie had a 'shy, self-conscious, sensitive disposition', which made him seem aloof or cynical. In reality, he was a kind and gentle man 'who would not intentionally have harmed anyone'. Intensely learned and scholarly, in a rather unworldly way, he was capable, on a winter's day when the hospital's heating system had packed up, of sitting at his desk, 'his hands blue with cold, his long legs stretched characteristically out in front of him, discoursing philosophically upon psychological types to a half-frozen ward-clerk who was longing for an overcoat and wishing that psychiatry was a less sedentary subject.'[37]

A Scot, Gillespie came to Guy's at the age of 29 after a meteoric career that had included a scholarship to Adolf Meyer's clinic in Baltimore and co-authorship of the standard British textbook of psychiatry. He was seen as brilliant but 'sound', impressing colleagues by his 'common sense' and immaculate dress. Charles Symonds, then Consultant neurologist at Guy's, was a particular patron. During the 1930s, however, Gillespie's interests moved, if not towards the Freudians, then towards a greater emphasis on the effects of the environment (rather than heredity) on behaviour; and on the psychiatric problems of young children. Gillespie 'gathered round him a team of workers, medical and lay . . . all inspired by his enthusiasm' and just before the war, a private donation enabled him to plan a complete psychiatric clinic with 40 beds within the hospital.[38]

This provoked his first row with Symonds. Having worked so hard to win a place for psychiatry in the hospital, Gillespie saw no reason to include neurology in his grand new plans. Symonds, who saw himself as a benign protector and 'thought that all psychiatry was only applied neurology', was very angry to find himself excluded. The two men observed the formalities and 'were perfectly polite to each other', but never took combined rounds as other physicians did. Only a month before the war, they traded blows publicly in the pages of the *Lancet*. Symonds said that there was no essential difference, except of degree, between a neurosis and a psychosis; a week later, Gillespie attacked this 'quantitative' approach. They disagreed, too, about whether psychotherapy required expert training (Gillespie) or was something that could be supplied by any doctor (Symonds).[39]

Given all this bad blood, it seems extraordinary that they should have joined the Air Force together, but they did. If, before the war, Gillespie had been ahead on points, now Symonds wiped the floor. The Air Force judged a doctor by his war record, his sympathy to their point of view and his social manner. Symonds had fought in the war and won the *Médaille Militaire* whereas 'nobody seemed to know what Gillespie had done in the First World War, if anything' (he'd been a student during the war; but had worked on psychotic shell-shock patients after it). Symonds was a commanding, confident figure in uniform, at ease in the mess and an excellent public speaker. Gillespie was uncomfortable in uniform – tall, lanky, round-shouldered – and there was something shifty about him. 'Although Gillespie was a psychiatrist and had a lot of empathy, he wasn't very good at conveying it. So people often got the impression that Gillespie was dodging issues, whereas Symonds came out and said what he said.'[40]

Symonds not only fitted easily into the grand style of the RAF. He also shared the Air Force view that war was essentially a test of character. His own war experiences had left him pessimistic about human nature, concerned to shut any medical 'back doors' which might enable men to shirk their duty. One of his first acts was to remove the category of 'flying stress', current in Air Medicine since the First World War, which he considered as dangerous to morale as 'shell-shock'. Symonds insisted that the term 'flying stress' should only be used to describe the external strains imposed by flying-duties; 'if, as the result of over-loading or temperamental handicap, a neurosis developed, the diagnosis should be made in terms of recognized psychiatric headings, e.g. anxiety, hysteria etc.'[41]

Symonds was unhappy with the phrase 'Lack of Moral Fibre' and repeatedly urged administrative modifications to its use; but he agreed completely with the principle of using a diagnostic label as a weapon of deterrence – his preferred term 'lack of courage' was, if anything, even more judgemental. Believing that in warfare 'scientific standards . . . must give way to standards of practical necessity', Symonds made no bones about medicine serving the needs of the military situation. There would often be no clear dividing line between an anxiety neurosis and a normal emotional reaction to stress, yet 'in the interests of morale a line must always be drawn'. Inevitably, in making the 'arbitrary' decision where to draw that line, doctors would be guided by 'the group attitude toward danger.'

> In the distinction between anxiety neurosis and cowardice expediency usually in the end counts more than scientific judgment. This should surprise no one who has reflected upon the part played by group opinion in deciding when individual behaviour should be regarded as pathological.[42]

Symonds was an energetic researcher, carrying out numerous studies of the pressures on aircrew, which emphasised the role of fear and anxiety. But unlike many of his contemporaries, he ignored the role of group dynamics, ideology or military context in motivating men. To him, it was a simple matter of individual character. His own behaviour towards crewmen who broke down was unsympathetic. Medical colleagues recall him berating flyers as 'cowards' and ignoring pleas that pilots who had developed phobias – against night flying, for example – should be allowed to continue in the job in less exposed capacities. He was, he told them, looking not just at the individual patient, but at his 'place in the war effort'.[43]

Confronted by this alliance between the Air Staff and Symonds, there was little that Gillespie could do. Lunching with him in 1941, a former student found him 'sad because he was being asked to do something he had never envisaged doing – being part of a machine that sent young men to their death.' Medical *amour propre* played a part in Gillespie's discomfort, as it had in Myers' in 1916: his professional pride was hurt by the way Symonds invaded his territory and stole the loyalties of his pupils. But his conscience also troubled him. 'He felt this whole concept of lack of moral fibre was wrong . . . that more gentleness and kindness should be shown . . . that more trouble and more doctors and more time should be devoted to trying to help men who became afraid of going on flying.'[44]

Gillespie tried to bring in a more modern-minded approach. He argued, for example, that selection procedures should be amended: Symonds' own studies repeatedly showed that many of the men who were breaking down were unstable types predisposed to fail. But the RAF, by far the most unresponsive of the services to every kind of civilian expertise, refused to allow psychiatrists to play a part in choosing aircrew. Gillespie did manage to set up and run a convalescent home for aircrew who were resting, at Matlock in Derbyshire, but when the Americans began to appear in England, he turned hopefully to them for moral support. He had worked in America, given a set on lectures in war neurosis in New York in 1941, and had many American admirers.[45]

*   *   *

The culture in the United States Army Air Force was much more relaxed and democratic than that of the RAF. If the British tried to maintain the atmosphere of the regular service, the Americans frankly acknowledged that they were civilians in uniform. One aspect of this was a much greater readiness to acknowledge fear and to talk about it. Having been told in training films that 'everybody going into battle is always afraid', the men were 'not generally afraid to admit a certain amount of anxiety'. Terms like 'flak happy' or 'Focke-Wulf jitters' were used openly.[46]

The dominant philosophy among USAAF psychiatrists was also both much more easy-going and sophisticated than that of their RAF equivalents. Having placed such faith in predisposition early in the war and then lost it, the Americans did not by 1943 share the RAF's view of the importance of individual 'character'. They believed rather that the strains of operational flying gradually wore everyone down, but that psychodynamic forces such as leadership or group loyalty might create defences against breakdown.

In dealing with disciplinary problems, the Americans were less draconian than the British but much less consistent. Their greater reserves of manpower certainly meant that they could accept greater wastage, but even within the European

Theatre of Operations, there was no uniform policy. Clearly there were enormous and prolonged battles on this question between the psychiatrists (who tended to be more 'permissive'), the flight surgeons and the Air Force officers. But psychiatrists tended to be held at arm's length and were seldom directly involved with the pilots. It was the flight surgeon that the crews saw day-by-day.

In Joseph Heller's masterpiece it is the flight surgeon, Doc Daneeka, who first tells Bombardier Yossarian, 'There's a catch . . . Catch 22 . . . Anyone who wants to get out of combat duty isn't really crazy'. Doc Daneeka is a one-time abortionist who hates flying and does what he is told by Command lest they transfer him 'to the Pacific'. He obviously wasn't that untypical because the American official history concedes that many flight surgeons knew little about aviation medicine and were incapable of the intellectual effort needed to practise even basic psychiatry. But, at his best, the flight surgeon was, like Colonel Rogers in the First World War, a man who combined a little medicine with a good deal of character and common sense to keep men fighting.[47]

According to the official history, the 'common tacit policy' of flight surgeons was 'to help the men carry on to the limit of their capacity, and then perhaps fly a few more missions'. Although psychiatrists warned of dire consequences, the 'unwritten plan worked magnificently . . . Twelve years after the end of the war one fails to see the grave psychic consequences of pushing men to – and beyond – what many then considered the breaking point.'[48]

The Air War placed an enormous burden on young, middle-ranking officers: wing commanders and below bore the daily strain of operational command and quite frequently found themselves torn between loyalty to their men and orders from above. Just as subalterns on the Western Front raged at the High Command's ignorance of conditions in the trenches, so impatient young airmen sounded off at 'key commanders [who] took little or no active part in warlike operations and were, therefore, out of practical touch with the air war over Germany'.[49]

The bomber ace Leonard Cheshire questioned the normal Bomber Command method of planning an attack in which 'everything was wound up and pre-set like an alarm clock hundreds of miles from a target, as if all the unknown factors could be predetermined infallibly and the raid conducted by the remote control of unseen experts.' The system often went wrong and he felt in his 'wilder moments that if it meant building an enormous aircraft for an Air Marshal and his staff we should have someone on the spot. Flexibility of tactics is as essential in an air as in a land or sea attack.' Beneath the surface, there were also generational overtones to this resentment.[50]

In the American air forces, the gulf between the Brass and the flyers was never as great, not least because fairly senior commanders such as Curtis le May regularly flew on missions and shared their men's risks. But there were periods of great tension, especially in 1942–3, when the whole philosophy of daylight bombing was being thrown into doubt by horrifying casualty rates. The mood of that time is well caught in the film *Twelve O'Clock High*, in which a staff officer takes command of a Bomb Group reeling after a period of heavy losses and succeeds, by ruthlessly imposing discipline, in turning its morale round, only for the strain of command to paralyse him as he is about to fly on his first mission over Germany.[51]

This is not just fictional exaggeration. Guy Gibson, the 'dam-buster', the 'Boy Emperor' of Bomber Command, ignored medical advice to fly on the Dams Raid in 1943; the strain of planning the operation had given him gout and throughout the long operation he was in pain. Gibson had assumed the 'crushing responsibilities of command' while still 'scarcely older than an undergraduate', driven by fierce ambition and an 'almost manic intensity of enthusiasm for war and blood-brotherhood.' According to his biographer, he became 'addicted to stress', finding it 'increasingly difficult to relax or disengage, appearing restless or truculent at one moment, cheerful or charming the next.' Unable to confide in his wife, who remained outside the 'bomber world', he developed a platonic relationship with a young WAAF who found him, the day after a difficult sortie to Berlin, waiting in his car, 'staring forward through the windscreen and gnawing obsessively on the stem of his unlit pipe.'

He was shaking uncontrollably. At length he pleaded, 'Please hold me.' Margaret reached out and hugged him. Gradually the tremors subsided and after half an hour Gibson had recovered his composure. 'Ops last night?' asked Margaret. He never referred to the incident again and their next meeting his customary ebullience seemed restored.[52]

In Gibson's case, a new factor in war – the corrupting effects of Public Relations – combined with the strains of command to bring nemesis. After the Dams Raid he did not fly at all for over a year, touring America as a war hero and writing *Enemy Coast Ahead* for the Air Ministry. Rumours began to circulate that he 'spent more time in bed with other chaps' wives than he ever did in the air.' Then, spurred on by the prospect of the war ending, through 'frustration and fear of marginalization, rather than simple self-regard', he returned to operations. The victim of his own publicity, he broke all the rules by appointing himself master bomber on a complicated and much-revised operation over a German target, using a Mosquito, an aircraft he scarcely knew. Flying low over Holland on the return flight, Gibson and his navigator perished.[53]

Gibson may have been driven to his doom by rivalry with his successor at the elite 617 squadron, Leonard Cheshire. Cheshire was also consumed by the war, but in a different way. His war hinged on a day in September 1943, when he went to see the RAF's expert in 'flying stress', Dr Charles Symonds. Cheshire was then twenty-five years old, and had already served two full tours as a pilot in Bomber Command, winning great distinction, numerous decorations and the command of a squadron; he was married, the youngest Group Captain in the RAF, and was being groomed for the staff. Instead, he asked Symonds to help him return to operational flying.[54]

Cheshire sought to persuade Dr Symonds that although pilots usually developed anxiety neurosis from doing too much flying, he had developed anxiety neurosis through doing too *little* flying. Symonds, says Cheshire's biographer, 'was completely satisfied that this extraordinary young man would go on eating his heart out like a caged swallow until he was released again.'[55]

And so he was released. Cheshire took over 617 Squadron at a time of tactical rethink and strategic reorientation. Neither high-level mass attacks using Pathfinders to lay flares nor low-level attacks by small elite forces seemed to be working. A new technique, with the mass of the force bombing from high altitude under the orchestration of a master bomber flying low over the target, was being developed. Using the fast, manoeuvrable Mosquito as his command platform, Cheshire was able to carve out for himself a new role: that of the master bomber who lingered over the target and directed operations over the radio-telephone – the local commander he had always believed was necessary.

These tactics were often very costly, but Cheshire's performance earned him a legendary position in RAF mythology. His presence over any target was, the official historians wrote, 'rightly recognised . . . to be a factor of incalculable advantage.' After a breathtaking roof-level marking of Munich in April 1944, he was awarded the Victoria Cross, the only person in the war to win it not for a single act of bravery but for his behaviour over years, 'placing himself invariably in the forefront of battle'. But on 6 July 1944, after he had completed his hundredth operation, his Group Commander took him aside and grounded him. Air Marshal Cochrane 'had noticed a tell-tale sign of the prolonged strain. Now and then Cheshire's right eye flickered as though he had a nervous tic.' Cheshire served on the staff in the Far East and in America and was sent to observe the dropping of the atomic bomb on Nagasaki, but he never flew operationally again.[56]

Charles Symonds never had the slightest doubt that he had done the right thing in helping Cheshire to go back to the war. Cheshire, he said later, was 90% fearless and only 10% courageous.

Normally, it's the introspective man who knows the sweat of apprehension before an attack and has to summon all his powers of will to carry on. Cheshire, though an acutely sensitive and introspective man, seemed as completely immune from apprehension as the most phlegmatic and unimaginative types, with whom the stolid quality of fearlessness is invariably associated. He had the heart of a lion and the incisive brain of the practical planner, so that risks appeared to him as impersonal obstacles made to be overcome.[57]

Cheshire, it came to be believed, was 'a man different from the rest of us in ways that cannot be fathomed.' Fearless or not, Cheshire paid a terrible price for his deeds. In 1945 he was treated at an RAF hospital for bouts of deep depression and a year later discharged with a disability pension for psychoneurosis. His post-war career was punctuated by long intervals of nervous collapse and when he tried to rejoin the RAF in 1947, he found the door barred by Symonds himself. The war had taken something out of Cheshire that was never restored.[58]

It is unlikely that Symonds, given his medical orientation and pressure of work, investigated Cheshire's background in any detail. Had he done so, he might have found a number of clues to his patient's record. Before the war, as an Oxford undergraduate, Cheshire had been a renowned daredevil, fantasist, and publicity seeker, known for such exploits as climbing steeples and jumping out of the way of cars in the High. He held 'the record from Hyde Park Corner to Magdalen Bridge in an Alfa Romeo for which he could not pay.' But he was more than just a tearaway; he had 'an ostrich-like gift of burrowing his head comfortably in the nearest patch of sand, blithely cheerful and blind to realities' and, like Orde Wingate, the famous Chindit commander, seemed to impose his own reality on his world, often with disastrous financial consequences.[59]

Then there was his wife. In 1941, while on a promotional trip to the USA, Cheshire married Constance Binney, an American actress of independent wealth who was twice his age. Just another piece of wartime folly? He was apparently seduced by her wealth and celebrity, but photographs show a plain, homely woman of considerable bulk, inevitably prompting suggestions that Cheshire was marrying his mother or, as a young pilot, needed a mother close to hand. In fact, he soon tired of Constance and although she followed him faithfully around the bleak, ill-heated air stations of eastern England, one of his motives in returning to operations in September 1943 was to escape the inevitable crisis in his marriage. Constance was eventually abandoned and suffered a nervous breakdown in November 1944.

These are dark waters. Cheshire's medical record has not been made public, probably never will be, and it would be foolish to engage in amateur psychology. The scale of his achievements will always silence denigrators. And yet, one can't help wondering what would have happened had Cheshire been to see, on that day in September 1943, not Dr Charles Symonds but Dr Douglas D. Bond, the Psychiatric Adviser to the United States Army Air Force in Britain. Bond was one of the few full-blooded Freudian analysts to operate as a military psychiatrist and his post-war book *The Love and Fear of Flying* combines wildly overheated passages with fascinating insights into the psyche of the flyer.

To Bond it was clear that flying provided a 'lift, thrill, and relief'. Many flyers derived from flying an intense gratification. Their behaviour, when grounded, was 'akin to that of a frustrated lover . . . restless and unhappy . . . build[ing] up a tension that only flying can relieve.'[60]

Aware that flying had 'long been known to symbolize sexual intercourse in the unconscious', Bond worked out the mechanisms involved. At first glance it would seem that the aircraft was a 'symbol for a feminine figure'; and aircrews spoke of their craft in feminine terms and festooned them with busty pinups and feminine names like 'Violent Virgin' or 'My Angel'. But on closer analysis, Bond argued, it became clear that separate unconscious fantasies surrounded flight and the aircraft. Flight was the sexual act itself; the aeroplane, the instrument, was the phallus, while the firmament of the air was the feminine element to be penetrated. The aircraft was in fact, *masculine*. 'Unconsciously, the combat aircraft, most purely the fighter, fulfils childhood desires for an exaggerated phallic power.' The love which flying generated was not love of 'another person or object' but rather 'narcissistic love for one's own body', which was why many pilots felt castrated when forced to stop flying. Because they were narcissists, flyers found it difficult to give to others and their marriages were 'notoriously casual'. But their narcissism also protected them:

Perhaps it is precisely this narcissistic quality of the fantasy that provides the protection against trauma so noticeable in devoted airmen. For when there is a close blend of flyer and plane, there may be no room for the insertion of a traumatic factor that might separate them.[61]

Bond speculated, too, on other strange aspects of flyers' behaviour: their need constantly to prove themselves by death-defying stunts; their attitude to death. Stunting, he thought, was reminiscent of the 'excess of pleasure which some men feel in doing forbidden things', or the perverse thrill which some men got from having sex in 'dangerous' circumstances; whereas flyers saw death rather as naughty children view a parent – as 'a living threatening father who dwells appropriately in the sky'. Bond quoted from John Magee's famous poem 'High Flight' – that begins 'Oh I have slipped the surly bonds of Earth' – in which the young Canadian airman talked of how he dared to 'touch the face of God' and 'got by' with it.[62]

Bond frankly acknowledged that many men enjoy war. The 'unbridled expression of aggression', he thought,

forms one of the greatest satisfactions in combat and becomes, therefore, one of the strongest motivations. A conspiracy of silence seems to have developed around these gratifications, although they are common knowledge to all those who have taken part in combat. There has been a pretence that battle consists only of tragedy and hardship. Unfortunately, however, such is not the case.[63]

These feelings were at their strongest with fighter pilots, whose 'frank pleasure . . . following a heavy killing is shocking to outsiders'. But bomber crewmen got their kicks, too. A bombardier would 'jump up and down in his seat like a happy child' when he watched his bombs dropping (the Freudian Bond noted that 'the dropping of bombs is commonly linked to excretory processes or birth in Air Force slang').

War gave men a chance to give full expression to their 'pleasurable childhood fantasies' of violence, but such expression of aggression could also revive childhood fears of punishment, 'to fill the minds of men in a haunting and confusing way.' The 'image of the angry father' would now be 'projected on to the aircraft, making it the instrument of the father's wrath' and 'destructive to the flyer'.[64]

Douglas D. Bond came over to England in 1943. He was one of the American psychiatrists whom R. D. Gillespie visited on his tour of Eighth Air Force bases when, increasingly detached from his colleagues in the RAF, he was hoping to find allies in the Americans. At a personal level they liked him; as a Scot, Gillespie had none of the snobbishness of his colleague, Charles Symonds. Professionally, too, most of the Americans were on his psychodyanmic wavelength. But they quickly saw that Symonds had power and Gillespie did not. Like his former pupils at Guy's, they deserted him.[65]

By late 1944, Gillespie was unwell, suffering from that classic psychosomatic symptom, a 'peptic' ulcer. A colleague was distressed to witness 'the steady deterioration in his physical and mental health. A bottle of milk and a beaker were always to be seen on his desk [for the ulcer]. But it was his deepening depression that was most distressing.' Early in 1945, ill-health compelled him to resign from the Air Force.[66]

Gillespie's problems were, in part, domestic: his wife and daughter were in Canada, and he was desperately lonely. But it is clear from an article published soon afterwards that he also felt intense guilt and frustration at what he had been part of. With the war still going on, Gillespie voiced doubts whether 'we know all we should about psychiatric disabilities after flying accidents and terrifying experiences in combat'. Did we, he asked, 'do less than justice from the medical aspect in some cases in which disciplinary problems arise?' The RAF's doctors were deliberately choosing to ignore evidence that some men who had been in traumatic accidents were unable, because of conditioned fears, to return to flying. Why then should they be punished?[67]

Gillespie returned to Guy's Hospital and continued his work there. On 30 October 1945 he took his own life. Eight days later, a Memorial Service was held at Guy's chapel. Air Vice-Marshal Symonds did not attend.[68]

In 1946, a knighthood was bestowed on Symonds.

Who was the better military psychiatrist, Symonds or Gillespie? Perhaps the last word should lie with Dr Noble Frankland, co-author of the magnificent official history of strategic bombing and himself a former Lancaster navigator. Frankland does not believe that 'there was much useful room for psychiatrists in Bomber Command'. 'The needs and rigours of the campaign,' he has written, 'were such that it would be unrealistic to expect that aircrews could have been afforded the sympathy and psychiatric treatment which, in normal circumstances, would be anyone's due. The aircrews had to be used to, and often beyond, the limit of endurance. Otherwise, coupled with the conventional casualties, the withdrawal rate would have produced a front line of green novices.'[69]

LEARNING FROM THE GERMANS?

From the German military standpoint, the First World War can be seen as a badly run general rehearsal for the Second World War.

Hans Binneveld[1]

In August 1946, the British analyst John Rickman went to the rubble of Berlin to re-establish contact with his German colleagues. He found one Berlin Freudian more interested in 'coal and extra food' than recent developments in psychoanalysis. Another was so embarrassed that he could not look Rickman in the face and spent most of the interview 'with his head in a cupboard or down on his knees looking for a book which turned out not to be there.' Then, suddenly counterattacking, he demanded to know if Rickman 'as an Englishman, could explain why it was the German women despised the British troops. They were cold and frigid sexually and hadn't the spunk of the Americans, and were altogether a queer lot.'[2]

By then, de-briefing Germans had become something of an industry. Quite apart from the war crimes investigations, sociologists were interviewing German prisoners of war and producing long, jargon-filled analyses of 'the German character' while the British military historian, Basil Liddell Hart, was being flattered by German generals into endorsing their sanitised, apolitical account of the war. One of the first people to talk at length to German military psychiatrists was Lothar B. Kalinowsky, a Berlin-born doctor who had emigrated to the United States in 1939. In an important article in 1950, Kalinowsky contrasted the very high rates of psychiatric casualties suffered by the Americans (who had had a comparatively easy war) with the very low rates suffered by the German Army (which had had a very tough war indeed).[3]

The reason for this disparity was quite simple, said Kalinowsky. The Germans had absorbed and understood the lesson of the First World War – that the war neuroses are caused not by war experience as such, but by secondary psychological mechanisms. Unlike the British, who had eventually given in to popular pressure, the Germans had applied this lesson consistently, by treating psychiatric casualties as purely disciplinary cases and making sure that the soldier gained nothing by developing psychological problems. As a result, they had had very few such cases. What was more, there was nothing particularly Nazi about the German policy. It was 'based on concepts developed shortly after the First World War and therefore not dictated by the Nazi regime . . . and accepted by practically all German psychiatrists.'

Kalinowsky thought the Allies had something to learn from the Germans, as did prominent people in the British Army. At a hospital in Normandy in 1944, the Consultant Physician to 21 Army Group was 'much struck' by the 'apparently few cases of psychoneurosis' among German prisoners of war. He wondered whether it was because German doctors did 'not recognise the condition in the same way as ours do and . . . men showing symptoms of fear or panic are not dealt with by the medical service.' Or was it just that 'fifteen years of Nazism may be a much better preparation for war than our own pre-war philosophy.'[4]

Throughout the war, British generals privately expressed admiration for the fighting qualities of the Germans. Brooke in 1940 called them 'the most wonderful soldiers'; to Alexander in 1944, they were 'the best soldiers in the world – what men!' They admired them for their tenacity; their capacity to go on fighting when a situation seemed hopeless, to counterattack immediately a position was taken, to escape from pockets which were surrounded and for their flexibility – the ability of even small groups of soldiers to adapt to situations and think for themselves.[5]

After the war, many attributed the Wehrmacht's superior performance to its harsher code of discipline. 'The German soldier,' the British general Sir David Fraser has written, 'suffered rough, even brutal initial training: he was expected in and out of battle, to show discipline in its most formal expressions of saluting, rigid position of attention when reporting and so forth [and] suffered draconian punishment, instantly meted out, for disobedience and failure.' Yet, says Fraser, 'he enjoyed, on the whole, a very high *esprit de corps*, a strong camaraderie' and although 'it was customary to mock the German army and to extol the milder systems of the British', 'the military performance of the Wehrmacht throughout the war was seldom equalled and only on rare occasions surpassed.' Fraser's almost envious tone reflects the private feeling of some British commanders that if they could have shot a few fainthearts, as the Germans did, they could have had an Army like theirs.[6]

Admiration for the Wehrmacht's performance reached its apogee in *Fighting Power*, Martin van Creveld's influential 1983 study of German and American fighting effectiveness, which argued that harsh discipline and a no-nonsense approach to psychiatric casualties were important ingredients in the superb professionalism of the German Army. More recently, however, this picture has been drastically redrawn. The opening of archival records, the end of the Cold War and a more critical examination of the German medical past have transformed our sense both of the German Army's role in the Second World War and of German psychiatry under the Nazis. While much of the traditional view derived from study of the German Army's role in the West, the revisionist case is largely based on work on the Ostfront and the Holocaust.[7]

The German Army, once seen as the last bastion of Prussian correctness and decency, is now depicted as a very political organisation, killing Soviet prisoners and condoning the Holocaust. Similarly, it is now accepted that the involvement of the German medical profession went far beyond the few 'Nuremberg doctors' prosecuted after the war. The Nazi regime, historians argue, was a 'biocracy', a state in which 'major social and political issues like the "Jewish question", ethnicity, gender, poverty, crime, "asocial" behaviour and sexual deviance, were transformed into and reduced to biological and medical problems, for which there were apparently medical solutions.' If military psychiatry is an inversion of ordinary psychiatry – with the doctor's primary loyalty to the state not the individual – then all psychiatry in the Third Reich was military: carrying out a crude triage of the population between the biologically worthy, the socially deviant and the doomed 'failures of nature'; and providing, respectively, a modern welfare state, the concentration camp, and medical euthanasia for each grouping. Thus any simple comparison between the narrow details of organisational practices is meaningless, as are statistics. The only comparison which makes any sense is between the whole ethos, the whole *Weltanschauung*.[8]

*   *   *

The central tradition in German psychiatry had always been biological and hereditarian, dominated by physical interpretations of mental illness and 'firmly based in the principles of biological thought and investigation'. Well before the First World War, the liberal emphasis on the doctor's overriding obligations to the individual patient was giving way to 'viewpoints which stressed such collectivities as "society" and "the race".'[9]

Medicine in general, and psychiatry in particular, were further politicised and polarised by the extraordinary series of upheavals through which the country passed. By the 1920s, a sharp divide had emerged between two different paradigms. For a few years, under the Weimar Republic, the minority view briefly prevailed and the Germans pioneered the political left's version of eugenics – a kind of social medicine, embracing family guidance, health care, sexual advice and birth control. But, with Hitler's arrival in power in 1933 came the rapid exclusion of Jews from the practice of medicine and the exiling of radicals; the balance tilted back towards the racial dogmatists. The Nazis were able to appropriate 'a coercive system of medical thinking which placed the health of the social whole and of future generations above that of individuals' and to use it for their own ends. The reaction of the psychiatrists ranged from a small minority who enthusiastically embraced the psychopathology of the regime, advising the Gestapo on methods of torture, through figures like Ernst Kretschmer, who went into internal academic exile for the duration, to a single individual, John Ritmeester, who was hung for political opposition. The great bulk of the profession, however, collaborated.[10]

The complexities of the situation are perhaps best demonstrated by the case of

Karl Bonhoeffer. The leading psychiatrist in Berlin for twenty-five years, Bonhoeffer lost one son in the First World War and two more to the Nazis, was widely respected for his 'common sense and incorruptibility' and comes across, in biographies of his son Dietrich, as the embodiment of decency and strength. Yet he was a member of the Prussian Committee for Racial Hygiene in 1920, denounced homosexuality as 'psychopathic' and in the 1930s gave lectures to those responsible for carrying out the Nazis' policies of compulsory sterilisation. He was also one of the first to lecture on the war neuroses to the newly-rearmed German Army.[11]

Orthodox German psychiatrists like Bonhoeffer were strongly opposed to Freudian psychoanalysis and Freud himself was routinely denounced as a Jew by the Nazis; yet there was also a strong German psychotherapeutic tradition, combining many of the basic tenets of psychoanalysis with a distinctively Teutonic emphasis, which not only survived but thrived under the Nazis. Its proponents shared some common ground with Freud's former disciple, C. G. Jung, who claimed in an article in 1934 that the Jewish race possessed 'an unconscious which can be compared with the Aryan only with reserve' and that it had been a great mistake to try to apply Jewish categories to Germans. 'The Germanic consciousness,' Jung wrote, 'contains tensions and potentialities which medical psychology must consider in its evaluation of the unconscious. Its business is not with neuroses but with human beings – that is, in fact, the grand privilege of medical psychology: to treat the whole man and not the artificially segregated function.'[12]

This emphasis on the 'whole man' was echoed by Wehrmacht psychologists in the 1930s and by German psychotherapists, who embraced 'holistic medicine' and 'nature therapy'; a so-called 'new German therapy' began to emerge which laid great emphasis on sport, a healthy diet, and ideas of air, light, and sun. In 1936, most of its practitioners came together to form an institute headed by Dr Matthias Heinrich Göring, a cousin of Reichsmarschall Hermann Göring; thanks to the protection of his name, it enjoyed access to some areas of the Nazi power structure.[13]

*   *   *

Nazi Germany was a society preparing for war. As part of that process, as early as 1935 German doctors began to consider their policy towards future war neurotics. This was not, for them, some minor, subordinate issue of medical policy: it was what had cost them the last war. Slack and inappropriate discipline was generally believed to have contributed to the epidemic of 'war neuroses' that helped to bring about the shameful defeat of 1918 – the 'stab in the back'. In 1917–18, malingerers, cowards and 'left psychopaths' from the German Army, instead of being shot (or at any rate disciplined) had been sent back to Germany for treatment and there had poisoned the Home Front, infecting civilian morale with their degeneracy and defeatism. Then 'at the stroke of the armistice, tens of thousands of psychopaths were cured as if by magic and became active and noisy revolutionaries'. Thus – according to the legend – the comparative moderation shown by German military courts and military doctors had not simply let down the armed forces; it had brought about the destruction of the old Empire.[14]

Psychiatrists knew that they must not let that happen again. Nor could they allow another epidemic of 'war shakers', those uncontrollably shaking men whose rifles fell from their hands in the fight, found in large numbers near the front in 1914–18. It came to be believed in hindsight that these men had been neither physically nor mentally ill; they had simply had 'abnormal psychological reactions' which would have gone away if they had known they would be returned to the front. This time around, soldiers must know that such symptoms would gain them nothing. This sternness was reinforced by the apparent lessons of inter-war pension policy; the decision in 1926 to stop paying pensions to neuropsychiatric discharges from the Army had, it was generally agreed, caused 'the shell-shock cases with shaking, paralysis, mutism, Ganser syndrome and so on', to 'disappear almost entirely.'[15]

There was thus general agreement by both military and psychiatrists that the war neuroses would be treated primarily as a problem of military discipline, enforced under the much tougher code introduced into the Army after 1933. Psychiatrists would assist in treatment but remain well in the background. At meetings with the military in the late 1930s, German psychiatrists outbid each other with demands that 'dangerous elements should be kept away from the Home Front, either by being kept at the front or by being sent to concentration camps.' If British psychiatry's pre-war nightmare was that aerial warfare would provoke the mass breakdown of civilians, their German colleagues were obsessed by fears that the Home Front would be undermined by 'left psychopaths' from the Army. How far this fear was genuine, how far conformist public rhetoric to bolster their professional position, is unclear.[16]

There was, however, nothing rhetorical about another strand to the social psychiatry of the war. In October 1939, at a villa in Berlin, plans were secretly made to set in motion the murder of mental patients in asylums. This was a logical part of clearing the decks for action, designed, the head of the Nazi party Chancellery explained, 'not only to continue the struggle against genetic disease but also to free up hospital beds and personnel for the coming war.'[17]

*   *   *

The military culture in which German psychiatrists worked was in several ways different from that of the Allies. The Germans had a long soldiering tradition, especially in Prussia, and a genius for the details of administration and staff-work. Having always taken war with 'a seriousness with which only sport is treated by the English', they were able, with the small Army forced on them by the Treaty of Versailles, to refine and modernise the principles of military organisation. The rapid expansion of the Wehrmacht in the 1930s produced a formidable war-making machine.[18]

Compared, say, to the American Army, the Wehrmacht was a lean, mean, and curiously antiquated organisation. It was designed to fight and everything about its structure and culture – pay, decorations, promotion – favoured the field soldier over the desk wallah. Administration was kept to a minimum. Internal statistical monitoring, for example, was very crude by American standards, no mechanical models being employed. The overriding principles were simplicity, trust and decentralisation.[19]

Their tradition accorded great respect to regimental spirit and to regional loyalty – Germany had, after all, only been a united country since 1870. 'The fighting spirit of the German Army,' says John Keegan, 'derived ultimately from its own character.'

Unlike the American or even the British, which for all its parade of territorial titles was quite lax in matching them to the regional origins of the soldiers, the German Army had always taken the greatest care to see that its units were formed of men from the same province or city, that replacements for casualties also came from the same places and that returned wounded went back to the units with which they started.[20]

German generals often make the same point in their memoirs. Von Senger und Etterlin, for example, attributes the skilful defence of Italy to the traditional military principles of good leadership, unit cohesion, thorough training and choosing the right units for the job. He never claims that all German troops were wonderful: if the elite parachute troops at Cassino were 'beyond praise', the units he commanded in late 1944, flung together from different groups, were 'mostly third rate'. Senger reminds us, too, that there was more than Prussian efficiency in the German military tradition. In his eulogy of General Baade, the heroic commander at Cassino, he reaches back to a knightly, pre-industrial spirit. Baade, a famous show-jumper before the war, wore 'over his riding breeches . . . a Scottish khaki kilt. In the place of the large leather sporran worn by Scotsmen he had a large pistol, suspended in a holster from his neck.'[21]

Education was another important factor in the Wehrmacht's success. The average Wehrmacht corporal was better educated than his Allied equivalents and 'all ranks in the German army were well trained in leadership, for with us this was a tradition'. In pre-war manoeuvres, junior officers were forced to take independent decisions – to the amazement of a British observer.[22]

Alongside such traditional virtues came the effects of '13 years of Nazi rule'. A soldier aged 20 in 1940 had passed through adolescence in a society that glorified and prepared for war, championed the warrior ethos and inculcated masculine rather than feminine values. Indeed the conditioning of young minds was one of the regime's priorities, great care being taken at the various stages – when joining the *Jungvolk* at ten, the Hitler Youth at fourteen or the Wehrmacht or *Arbeitdienst* at eighteen – to emphasise physical culture and disciplined teamwork. The Nazis, like Stalin's Russia or Mao's China, showed great skill in 'mobilising the rebellious spirit of the young against their parents and teachers, providing them instead with military trappings, power over their elders and an opportunity to sacrifice themselves for a good cause.'[23]

In Nazi Germany the mythology of war and in particular of the First World War was quite different from that in the democracies. While pacifism and disenchantment captured the minds of the educated young (especially in Britain), in Germany Hitler and Ernst Jünger's ecstatic vision of the war had prevailed over the waste, horror and militarism of Remarque's *All Quiet On the Western Front.* It had thus become an article of general faith that the German Army had not been defeated on the battlefield in 1918 and had only collapsed because the morale and discipline of its soldiers had been fatally undermined by Socialists, Democrats and Jews at home. The war experience took on a rich glow of nostalgia, as a time of *Kampfgemeinschaft,* a 'community of warriors in which all social and material distinctions had allegedly disappeared under the impact of a shattering *Fronterlebnis.*' In wanting to return to this world of fellowship and shared suffering, Hitler was by no means unique.[24]

Letters written by German soldiers show that they genuinely believed they were fighting for a new world order. The younger men, who had grown up in the Third Reich, accepted Hitler's view of reality, seeing the Russians as an Asiatic horde led by Jewish Bolsheviks and believing in the Führer as a quasi-religious leader. As Omer Bartov has written, 'The regime won the loyalty of Germany's children and youths by entrusting them with tremendous destructive powers. Far from jettisoning this view when the war began to go wrong, most of them clung to it ever more strongly and were only released from it by Hitler's death.'[25]

All of this was reinforced by ferocious discipline. In contrast to the First World War, when only 48 soldiers were shot, during the Second World War the German Army executed thousands of its own soldiers – 10,000 by the end of 1944 and probably another 5,000 in 1945. Most were executed for desertion or for the offence of *Wehrkraftversetzung,* 'attempting to subvert the will of the people to fight' – usually defeatist talk in public places; but some soldiers found guilty of theft also faced the firing squad when an example needed to be made. In addition, in the last year of the war an unknown number of soldiers were summarily executed on the spot while attempting to desert or flee. Furthermore, the Germans, like the Russians, made use of punishment battalions for particularly dangerous missions.[26]

There was, however, one important proviso to the Wehrmacht's harsh code of discipline – on the Eastern Front a blind eye was turned to most atrocities and crimes of property against Russians, Jews and gypsies. Omer Bartov has argued that in this way the Wehrmacht 'created a mechanism that allowed the increasingly brutalized soldiers to vent their anger and frustration at targets other than their superiors and then tied them to each other with terror of the enemy's vengeance in case of defeat.' It is generally agreed that this tough disciplinary code contributed greatly to the Wehrmacht's survival, and to its ability to continue fighting to the bitter end. But the more important question, in terms of the argument of this book, is whether the Germans' policy of making the war neuroses a matter entirely of military discipline succeeded in stamping them out.[27]

It certainly did if the psychiatrists themselves are to be believed. 'In this war there are no more neurotics,' the rabidly pro-Nazi Carl Schneider declared. 'That has been taken care of by the political education of the people.' His more temperate namesake Kurt Schneider agreed there were only 'about 1% of the number of neurotics we saw in the last war', but when interviewed in 1945 attributed the decline rather to 'a united medical front against neurosis . . . formed from the very beginning', in contrast to the divisions and debates of 1914–16. Kurt Schneider's united front 'included all medical echelons' but its most effective element was the regimental surgeon 'who could nip neurosis in the bud by encouragement and by controlling evacuation to the rear.' German psychiatrists were still making similar claims in the 1970s. In fact, things were much more complicated.[28]

As one might expect, there were few problems in the early Blitzkrieg years, as the Wehrmacht swept through Europe in brief, intense campaigns. Of course, not even the Germans were quite the supermen of their own propaganda and, seen from the inside, none of these campaigns was as triumphant as films like *Sieg im Westen* made out. For example, the parachutists dropped on Crete wore uniforms specially designed for Arctic temperatures and, for all their training, were still, as they queued up inside their Ju-52 before jumping into battle, 'gripped by a strange unrest'. During the fighting that followed, one German 'lost his nerve and ran amok . . . [rushing] forward, shouting and firing his pistol towards the British lines'. A company commander has described how, fighting on Crete, he 'suddenly felt fear crawling into [his] heart'.

It literally crawled, I could feel it rising from my stomach to my heart. It quickened the heartbeats, then seemed to stop them altogether. In vain I set my teeth to try and steady myself. I clutched the earth, pressing my body against it, seeking protection from it as a mother would cling to its mother's breast.[29]

But these acute short-term reactions passed. The expected epidemic of shaking and quaking was nowhere to be seen, though doctors were mystified by the number of disturbances of the stomach and gastrointestinal tract which appeared. 'There were practically no tremblers,' Dr Eduard Beck told the Americans in 1945. 'In this war the stomach was everything.' As a doctor in the trenches, Beck had experienced trembling himself and then seen it seized on by 'neurotic personalities' as the nucleus of symptoms; whereas, 'in a war of movement, due to the inevitable irregularity, shortcomings of preparation, lack of balance of hastily consumed cold meals, everyone – even the strongest and bravest – developed at many periods various degrees of gastric upset,' so the stomach became the 'symptom choice' of the neurotics.[30]

After the invasion of Russia in June 1941, the situation changed. Only five weeks into the campaign, long before the Russian counterattack outside Moscow, a prolonged Soviet counterattack against the 18th Panzer's motorcycle battalion – 'ten days of defensive trench warfare under constant Soviet artillery barrages, and infantry assaults, highly reminiscent of the Great War' – led its doctor to report 'a complete state of exhaustion . . . among all men of the battalion . . . as a result of a far too great mental and nervous strain. The troops have been under a great barrage of heavy artillery for six days ... The men are completely indifferent and apathetic, partly suffering from fits of crying, and are not to be cheered up by this or that phrase. Food is being eaten only in disproportionately small quantities.'[31]

Hitler's failure to take Moscow in late 1941 and General Zhukov's successful counterattack were followed by the long Russian winter, for which the German Army was poorly prepared. For the six Wehrmacht divisions cut off in the Demyansk 'pocket' south of Leningrad, the first months of 1942 meant 'living in damp, dark bunkers, badly ventilated and cramped, almost impossible to heat and thus offering little opportunity to rest from action'. In April 1942, the men of one infantry regiment were described by their doctor as 'greatly over-strung':

This is becoming more visible every day, in loss of strength, loss of weight and increasing nervousness, and has a progressively negative effect on battle performance with the accompanying appearance of friction, breakdowns and failures on the part of commanders and men as a result of over-fatigue and over strain of the nerves.[32]

For the ordinary German soldier, the *Landser*, the 'vast alien areas' of the Russian theatre meant interminable marching on foot and long sleepless hours manning a huge, inadequately-held front line. Soviet partisan activity further promoted a state of nervousness and insecurity. Even in 1941, when the Wehrmacht was triumphant, the Germans had felt disbelief at the Soviets' capacity to go on fighting long after logic dictated that they surrender. By the time of Stalingrad their letters demonstrate how deeply disturbed they were as a result of stress from the apparent lack of logic in the warfare in which they found themselves. This was the Wehrmacht's Achilles heel. It is hardly surprising that former German soldiers, when interviewed today, strike a note of self-pity.[33]

Yet the Germans seem on the face of it to have been strikingly successful in preventing these strains manifesting themselves in psychiatric casualties, the numbers of which remained small. Of the half a million soldiers in Army Group South in the period March–June 1943, only 844 men came to the Consultant Psychiatrist's attention. Many of these had been wounded and then developed secondary psychiatric problems or had 'organic' neurological problems. Only 121 cases were thought to be 'psychogenic' and 91% of them were either older men of 'wormly character' who were resisting discipline or slightly retarded men who had difficulty fitting in to their units – what the British called 'military misfits'. This left only eleven men, out of half a million, suffering from 'primary fear neurosis following enemy action' and even then, the 'majority' of these eleven were said to be 'unstable and neuropathic characters'. Other reports emphasise that psychiatric cases tended to be soldiers recently arrived at the front who had not had time to forge the bonds of *Kampfgemeinschaft* or *Volksdeutsche* whose poor command of German often left them isolated.[34]

These figures – in four months fighting, only eleven out of half a million – must, however, be heavily qualified. First of all, this was a period of intense shock, chaos and fear for Army Group South and many of those who cracked up were dealt with summarily (one report from this time talks of 364 executions in eight days). Furthermore, the German refusal to recognise psychological manifestations of stress encouraged soldiers to develop physiological symptoms instead, while physicians at the front 'always tried to prove the existence of an organic disease because the diagnosis of neurosis was discriminating.' The British doctor who visited German prisoners in Normandy in 1944 noticed that 'many psychoneurotics were masquerading under a diagnosis of organic disease such as commotio cerebri, heart disease, gastric disease, etc.' After 1942, the incidence of suicide and self-inflicted wounds also grew alarmingly, especially on the Eastern Front; one estimate is that during the war some 23,000 soldiers tried to 'escape' the war in this way. On top of that, men admitted to hospital for wounds tended to develop 'emotional reactions', obliging the authorities to crack down on misplaced 'sympathy'.[35]

In fact, despite all these measures, the classic war hysterias did return in the defensive battles on the Eastern Front, which brought a manner of warfare if anything, more brutal, more basic and more callous than the trenches of World War One.

Man becomes an animal [a German officer later wrote]. He must destroy, in order to live. There is nothing heroic on this battlefield. The battle returns here to its most primeval, animal-like form; whoever does not see well, fires too slowly, fails to hear the crawling on the ground in front of him as the enemy approaches, he will be sent under . . . The battle here is no assault with 'hurrah' cries over a field of flowers.

During the intense fighting at Kursk in July 1943, 'soldiers with abnormal reactions' made up some 14% of the admissions to one front-line hospital. Serious trembling conditions and shivering fits were particularly common, but cases of soldiers 'hysterically mute, deaf, blind, stuttering, hoarse, paralysed and stuporous' were also reported. Despite the official dogma that only 'inferior persons' suffered from psychological disorders, the psychiatrist reported that 'most of these soldiers were not abnormal characters or outstanding psychasthenics. Amongst them were a number of people with decorations for bravery as well as several young officers.'[36]

The German authorities became increasingly concerned about war neuroses as the war progressed and took steps to improve the recognition and treatment of these conditions. The German system of treatment was structured in the standard way. At a field hospital close to the front, the soldier was talked to 'in a firm but comradely way' and dosed with sedatives, and then, after about a week, put through a programme of 'strict military exercises'. Finally there was a short convalescence. Most, we are told, went back to their units 'completely recovered'.[37]

For more serious cases, there was a military hospital in the theatre of war and, for a tiny minority, treatment back in Germany (though well away from the patient's home town and relatives). Most of these hospitals employed traditional techniques derived from the First World War – suggestion backed up by electric shocks, baths and sedation. In one hospital patients with 'war shakes' (*Kriegszitterer*) were apparently 'given each day a larger dose of castor oil until the patient asked to go back to the front, at which time regardless of his condition, the request was granted.'[38]

The star German psychiatrist, featured in a film made for Hitler's office in 1943, was the consultant to the Cologne military district, Professor Friedrich Panse. Experienced in handling military cases in the 1920s, Panse had also been one of the first psychiatrists to carry out hereditary-biological surveys of Germany's mentally ill (on which the sterilisation and euthanasia programmes were based) and one of the 'experts' who had filled in questionnaires on mental patients suitable for euthanasia, receiving five pfennigs per patient. With military cases, Panse used a version of the old First War 'Kaufmann cure' electrical technique, modified to avoid the nerve ends and thus avoid deaths by heart failure. As with Kaufmann, Panse used electricity as an aid to suggestion. The patient would be told something like 'You are going to notice that your numb arm is going to become red and hot. But this is the first step to your healing', and then given galvanic current 'for as long as necessary until a noteworthy improvement or healing had come about'. It sounds similar to Lewis Yealland's technique in London in 1917.[39]

While the electricity was there mainly as an aid to suggestion, it was both powerful and very painful, a current of 300 milliAmps. A medical colleague who tried it for himself found it 'unbearably painful' at 30 mA, but nonetheless recommended the full dose. Soldiers, according to one account, were 'filled with such terror that they would risk anything rather than be exposed to it again' and another doctor called it 'pure unadulterated sadism'. Indeed, when the Panse method was first announced in 1941, the Chief Psychiatrist to the Wehrmacht, Otto Wuth, worried that it might be used on Nazi party members, denounced it as 'brutal and unacceptable'. The dramatic increase in numbers of those discharged from the Army soon led Wuth to change his stance.[40]

The reader will by now be aware that a soldier who submits, in a consulting room in London or Cologne, to the all-powerful will of Dr Panse (or Dr Yealland or Dr Hurst), will not necessarily be much good for further soldiering by the time he has got back to the front, hundreds of miles away. One of Panse's colleagues, Dr Oswald Bumke, told his American interrogators that, while the problem of the neurotic had been handled well in the German Army, 'in that it was prevented from playing a great practical numerical role . . . due to the policy of retaining neurotics at the front in whatever limited capacity was possible', the Kaufmann type of electrical treatment 'had freed people of their symptoms' without 'making good soldiers or more stable human beings out of them.' This suggests that one should be fairly sceptical of Panse's claims to have returned 85% to the front.[41]

It has become an historical cliché to say that, behind the monolithic facade, power in the Third Reich was arbitrarily divided between the competing personal empires of Göring, Himmler and Bormann – what the historian Trevor-Roper called satrapies. At the same time, the various different mental health professionals – the psychologists, psychiatrists and psychotherapists – were themselves competing for access and influence. It is unnecessary to chart the ramifications of these turf wars here, but one detail conveys something of the bizarre professional rivalries that arose. By 1942 the psychiatrists began to worry that the very success of the euthanasia programme was undermining their professional *raison d'être*. 'The danger to German psychiatry,' Dr Otto Wuth believed, lay 'in the fact that on the one hand the psychologists and on the other the psychotherapists claim the whole field of psychopathy, "neuroses" etc. for themselves, while the mentally ill fall under euthanasia.' It would, he thought, 'be bad for our successors if the field is cut up like this.'[42]

Wuth's fears were a little exaggerated: as we have seen, treatment of the war neuroses in the Army remained the province of the psychiatrists. The Luftwaffe, however, though by far the most Nazified of the services, was more 'advanced' in its approach, partly because of the family connection between Göring and the psychotherapeutic institute run by Dr M. H. Göring, and partly because air crew, being better educated and more highly trained, could not easily be driven back to work by the sort of brutal methods employed by Dr Panse. For a while, the Luftwaffe made use of 'psychotherapy, autogenic training, hypnosis, physical therapy, exercise, hydrotherapy, and relaxation' to coax its airmen back into the skies, and for a brief period Dr Ernst Göring (son of M. H. Göring) was even able to offer 'riding therapy' to *abgeflogene* ('Flown-out') night fighter pilots.[43]

By early 1943, however, Blitzkrieg was over and Goebbels was announcing that *totale Krieg* had arrived. Measures like riding therapy began to seem a luxury. Ernst Göring was sent to the Eastern Front as a front-line doctor, the Wehrmacht abruptly shed its Psychological Selection Service and the Luftwaffe closed down its psychological research services. In a time of 'total war', doctors were urgently needed to tend the wounded, and the battlefield was providing surer tests than could be devised in any laboratory. Total war, Geoffrey Cocks has written, 'created a climate in which incapacity would be interpreted as a lack of will – a failing subject not to the intervention of a psychotherapist but to that of a firing squad or a hanging party.'[44]

Labelling is always crucial to the practical administration of a mass medical problem like 'war neurosis'. In June 1944, in an effort to clamp down in this area and to reclaim it from the doctors, the High Command of the Wehrmacht issued an order banning the use of the word 'neurosis' in diagnosis and laying down instead a variety of acceptable alternative terms such as 'abnormal mental reactions' or even 'psychogenic (experience conditioned) functional disruptions'.[45]

The system of military discipline became much tougher and, in the end, arbitrary. It became commoner for commanders to take summary action in the field without bothering with the distraction of a trial; the German Commander in Sicily, General Hube, ordered in August 1943 that 'anyone showing panic or indiscipline during the evacuation of [the island] was to be clubbed or shot'. After the failed *attentat* of 21 July 1944, the niceties of military justice were further abbreviated, with Himmler taking charge of all security and arbitrary actions by the SS going unchecked. While there are no reliable statistics for military executions in the last year of the war, a German historian talks of a 'depraved orgy of coercion' and an 'explosion of executions'. Commanders like Model and Schörner earned terrible reputations as 'bloodhounds' while, in the last few weeks of the war, Himmler issued an order allowing any soldier to shoot any other soldier found 'out of earshot of battle' – something of an absurdity since, as Heinrich Böll later pointed out, 'the one doing the finding would himself have to be "out of earshot of battle".'[46]

The interesting question is whether the savagery of the Germans' methods helped or hindered their capacity to go on fighting. Given the state of the evidence, the answers given tend to reflect historians' prejudices. Several recent studies have argued that the measures taken were actually counter-productive. 'The Nazis' repressive new directive,' argues Geoffrey Cocks, 'only contributed to a noticeable upswing in psychological stress and breakdown in the military.' Robert Schneider finds 'a kind of evacuation syndrome' beginning to emerge by the middle of 1944, 'as it offered an honourable way out of the war.' According to an information sheet he quotes, in 1944 'unnecessarily and in dangerous amounts, cases [were] multiplying where officers and soldiers [were] delaying their recoveries from illness, wounds and accidents for a long period of time.' Finally, Karl-Heinz Roth has estimated that, whereas until the beginning of 1944, there were 'about 20–30,000 classical "war neurotics", in all branches of the service, by the end of the year 1944/45 their numbers were "around the 100,000 mark",' an escalation he attributes to 'the sharp increase in terror by military justice'.[47]

I suspect that the likes of Keitel and Jodl, were they still around to join in the argument, would give this line pretty short shrift. The fundamental point, they would say, is that the German Army collapsed in 1918, but did not in 1945. Therefore, from the High Command's point of view, the draconian discipline did work. However, although the Germans fought to the bitter end on both Eastern and Western Fronts, they fought much more savagely against the Russians in order to cover the retreat westwards of the civilian German population. Had a separate peace with the Anglo-Saxons been on offer, Himmler (for one) might well have settled for it. For this reason my own view is that fear and hatred of the Russians, simple lack of choice, and the tight grip which Goebbels maintained on the Home Front (by contrast to his predecessors in 1918), explain the continued resistance of the Germans (with continuing loyalty to the *Führer* and his ideology an also-ran).[48]

* * *

In April 1945, after visiting a small town in Western Germany recently captured by the Americans, the American journalist Martha Gellhorn wrote, with heavy irony:

No one is a Nazi. No one ever was. There may have been some Nazis in the next village, and as a matter of fact, that town twenty kilometers away was a veritable hotbed of Nazidom. To tell you the truth, confidentially there were a lot of Communists here.

It should be set to music, she thought: 'Then the Germans could sing this refrain and that would make it even better.'[49]

These were just simple villagers. Higher up the social scale, the evidence was more difficult to hide, but the paintwork infinitely more accomplished. During the war, some Allied psychiatrists had fantasised that after the defeat of Germany its population should be made to undergo some kind of collective therapy; William Brown had talked of 'psycho-catharsis'. Such dreams soon gave way to the practical problems of administering the country and the logic of the Cold War. De-nazification was particularly skimpy in the medical profession, doctors proving skilful in airbrushing their past – all 10,000 copies of a report on the Nuremberg Doctors Trial in 1946–7 were bought up and pulped by the German Medical Association.[50]

Some of the leading psychiatrists committed suicide or were prosecuted, but Dr Friedrich Panse became a full professor and ran the psychiatric hospital in Frankfurt in the 1950s. On his death in 1973 the clinic's journal declared that 'a life of work for the service of suffering humanity is ended.'[51]

PRISONERS OF WAR

'Oh God,' wrote Signaller Cyril Coombs in his diary on Good Friday, 1943. 'What have I done to deserve this?' He was then in a remote part of Thailand, building a railway line for the Japanese. 'I have never been so depressed in all my life,' he went on. 'We are working from dawn to dusk with 15 minutes for tiffin and continual beatings from the Nipps. My shoulders are raw with carrying heavy articles. I put one box down and nearly burst into tears.'

Written in ink on scraps of lavatory paper, Coombs' diary is a cry from the heart, artlessly expressing the sense of outrage, violation and sheer disbelief of a soldier pitchforked by war into the medieval horror of a Japanese prison camp. A cry from the stomach, too; for many of the entries concern food, and whenever Coombs has eaten well he lists the menu:

Oh what a dinner. Nazi Goring with a duff of fruit and custard . . .
    Tiffin. Dirty rice, some kind of gravy with an onion flavour, mincemeat and onion, and a small pancake affair with gula malhalca on it, sweet tea . . .

And it is a romantic epic, the yearnings of a young soldier for the girl he left behind at home. Muriel is ever present in his dreams, and thoughts of being reunited with her keep him going. They even drive him to improve his mechanical skills 'in readiness for when we get our Morris 8'. On bad nights, Coombs dreams that Muriel has left him and the singing of Salvation Army songs in the prison camp brings back memories of the Sundays he spent with her.[1]

More than thirty million people shared Signaller Coombs' predicament during the Second World War. The more mobile warfare made it possible for armies to cut off the enemy's forces in their thousands, like counters in a strategy board game. Twenty thousand men were captured at Dunkirk, 12,000 in Crete, more than 130,000 at Singapore. The Germans lost 110,000 at Stalingrad and an astonishing 275,000 Axis soldiers surrendered in Tunisia in 1943, while the British offensive in North Africa in 1940 trapped 130,000 Italians in its net. The figures for the Eastern Front are in a league of their own. Between 1941 and 1945 an estimated 3.4 million Axis soldiers and civilians were captured by the Red Army, 0.5 million of whom never reappeared, while about 60% of the three million Russians captured by the Wehrmacht died in captivity. By 1945, there were some quarter of a million British, 100,000 American and countless millions of other nationalities in the bag.[2]

In August 1942, Dr A. T. Macbeth Wilson, one of the Tavistock group of psychiatrists attached to the War Office, went to talk to people who had worked with returning prisoners after the First World War. He learned that, at that time, very little official energy had been directed at these men's needs and that many of them, on returning to England, had found themselves unemployed and indeed unemployable. Some had turned to crime and a good number had never succeeded in re-entering the civilian world. Wilson was determined it would be different this time.[3]

His concerns were shared by many of the doctors from German POW camps who by 1943 had returned to England. In a stream of papers and letters to the medical press, they warned that the country would soon be flooded by hundreds of thousands of people with a 'Prisoner-of-War mentality' and that, unless the medical profession took steps to understand it, it would not be able to help them. The prisoner of war, it was explained, had been through a complex series of psychological processes, like a deep-sea diver descending through different levels of atmospheric pressure. He had known, first, the shock of surrender and had felt the 'complex poison of guilt, shame and dishonour' enter his system. This was very hard for any well-trained fighting soldier, particularly if there had been a military disaster. After the Cretan débâcle of 1941, men who a few days before had been strong, well-disciplined soldiers seemed stunned by the experience of defeat and capture. They hadn't just been bombed, starved of sleep and 'seen their fill of sudden death'; their morale had collapsed so completely that they 'honestly believed that the Higher Command were dithering incompetent idiots'. A doctor who tried to help them was told to 'fuck off'.[4]

After capture, many soldiers passed through a second stage – of chaos, disorganisation and starvation. American troops in the Philippines had to undergo the Bataan 'death march' that killed a third of them. British soldiers on Crete spent five months in an overcrowded and insanitary transit camp in Salonica. During that time, some of them never properly regained the will to live and function and died fairly quickly; others behaved in bizarre ways or collaborated with the Germans.[5]

Eventually, though, most Allied prisoners in Europe reached a properly-run prisoner of war camp, with basic sanitation and access to Red Cross food parcels, which lifted their diet above the starvation level. This was the third stage in the POW's descent into darkness – an alien environment, but a stable one where a man could start to readjust, 'convalesce', and come to terms with his lot. There would be a rediscovery of purpose; men would devise plans and schemes, get mail from home, and plot their escape.

The prisoner [wrote Dr Philip Newman in 1944], having reached the depth of his depression, gradually reawakens to the life around him. He licks himself and his wounded pride, opens his eyes, and finds that away on the horizon there is still a ray of sunshine left. Now he begins to shave, to undress when going to bed, to talk intelligently, to plan and to organize his life. He grasps at the small things which give him pleasure and builds his life around them . . . he gathers together what little personal belongings remain to him. . . . the possibility of a reason or object for living gradually emerges and forms itself from the all-enveloping fog of shattered values.[6]

The doctors acknowledged that, even at this stage, life was frequently intolerable. The overcrowding, the lack of privacy, the 'atmosphere of irritability', the uncertainty as to the length of the sentence, all took their toll, even on the tough-minded. They wrote eloquently, too, about the 'outstanding reaction of POW life' and the main topic of conversation and thought – food. One doctor had dreamt of omelettes and treacle pudding on consecutive nights and thought that every prisoner developed a 'food-fear complex' – feelings of anxiety that there would not be enough to eat, manifested in petty squabbling over the rations.[7]

Sexual matters, too, were discussed with a frankness unthinkable a generation before. There were thought to be two sides to this: the emotional need for company and love and the biological need of young men for sexual outlets. The experience of being a 'kriegie', Dr Newman argued, aroused in men a 'longing for home, security, female society, and above all for sympathy. This suppressed longing for sympathy remains and is stored up until the day of repatriation.' Newman was a surgeon, not a psychoanalyst, and did not talk about a need to return to the mother's breast; but in his way he made the same point.

In [the] broader sense of lack of affection, sexual deprivation is not only a fundamental but the fundamental factor in the formation of the prisoner-of-war attitude. Deep within the prisoner, but seldom expressed, there lies the fear of becoming a forgotten man.[8]

He recalled an episode in 1941 when a talk about the war by a recently-captured RAF officer had been heard with polite interest, but his final, throwaway remark – 'And, chaps, the girls still love you' – had sent an 'acute emotional reaction' through his audience. In the same way, the receipt of news that a prisoner's wife was seeking divorce would plunge the whole camp into gloom.

Many soldiers had been away from home for years before being captured. With the passing of time, the whole world of relations with women had become more and more remote; for some the image of the loved ones themselves began to fade and 'it became increasingly difficult to conjure up a picture of them as we had known them.'

Very soon, as the men became adjusted to life in the cages and camps, women played less and less part in their thoughts and conversations, until they came to live in the end an almost asexual existence, where even the desire to contemplate desire could not be evoked. This, in the circumstances, fortunate state was most abruptly shattered whenever a woman, or even woman's apparel, appeared on the scene and much mental anguish was undergone for some time after such brief reminders of the existence of the other sex.[9]

One such reminder came when some of the prisoners from a camp at Piacenza in Italy put on a show in which one young man was 'made up as a rather fast piece of female goods'. Reviewing the show the following day, the editor of the camp journal remarked that 'Private Jones gave an excellent representation of flowering womanhood; so excellent in fact that it made you want to go to the lavatory and think.'[10]

The poor diet dulled sexual desire, but did not extinguish it altogether. There was much merriment at the Italian belief that sexual abstinence lead to mental illness, but it was an equally 'commonly held belief among the ordinary British soldiery that a man might lose his sexual potency through lack of intercourse.' The soldiery were in this regard more fortunate than their officers: leaving the camps to go out to work, they might, if determined and courageous enough, find sexual partners among civilians. A tobacco factory near Stalag IX saw brisk trade. There was also, the doctors thought, a fair amount of homosexuality of various forms; not so much 'actual sodomy' – the lack of privacy made that difficult – as 'friendship' and transvestism.[11]

For obvious reasons, the wartime medical literature says little about the subject that dominated later accounts of POW life – escape. In fact only a small percentage of prisoners of war – rare people who 'lived for action' and found captivity unendurable – made persistent attempts to escape; 'sooner or later the majority accept[ed] captivity and tr[ied] to endure it with as much cheerfulness as possible.' Escaping was also, among the British, a class-defined activity; very few other ranks ever escaped – why risk your life to return to the Army? Whereas officers, especially Air Force officers, found themselves in a quasi-public school culture in which escaping, or being seen to try to escape, was expected of you, like 'house spirit'. In fact, the main function of attempting to escape was psychological, it kept people busy: 'In building a tunnel, making clothes, forging papers or preparing maps,' wrote Aidan Crawley, 'men took part in a common effort and once again got the feeling of serving a community.' After the war, Robert Kee brilliantly described the fantasies of escape, the 'personal romanticising in bed at night', the 'stimulus of a mild sense of danger' while working in a tunnel. Many people, he wrote, 'took this game of make-believe to fantastic lengths and went through the whole elaborate business of preparation for escape without the slightest real intention of ever carrying it out.' Often, after months of effort, a scheme would collapse – to everyone's silent relief. Then another would take its place.[12]

What alarmed officialdom about the 'POW mentality', however, was not so much the pattern of deviancy or dysfunction in the camps, as the evident difficulty men were having in readjusting to life back home. Philip Newman described how most 'kriegies' had built up, over the years of boredom and inactivity, a 'high pitch of exaggerated optimism and false hope' about the life they had left behind, expectations which were often dashed when they returned home. Nor did the returning POWs take kindly to any re-assertion of Army authority and bull, not least because the Germans had put officers and men into separate camps. They showed 'restlessness, irritability, disrespect for discipline and authority, irresponsibility, and even dishonesty'. Many also suffered from a fear of enclosed spaces or crowds and 'cynicism, embarrassment in society, rebellious views against any code which tends to restrict the repatriate's activities and tendency to quick and violent tempers.' The two main problem areas, then, were relationships with women and attitudes to authority.[13]

Precisely because the POW was like a deep-sea diver returning to the surface, Newman argued, he needed a decompression chamber, a half-way house between camp and civilian life, in which to acclimatise himself to his new environment.

The extended public discussion forced the War Office to accept its responsibility for these men and strengthened the hand of those in Whitehall arguing for some sort of 'rehabilitation scheme' for prisoners of war. The psychiatrist Tommy Wilson and his team were clever and energetic. They talked to men who had been prisoners of war a generation before and read up the 1914–18 literature on 'barbed-wire disease'. They also did follow-up studies of returned prisoners from the current war, which quickly revealed that 18 months after returning a third of former POWs still had serious problems. They also showed that difficulties usually developed a few weeks or even months after the homecoming, when the initial elation had worn off. What was therefore needed was some kind of facility available to the POW after he had had a chance to touch base, which would help him to talk through his problems and find a job.[14]

To achieve anything, Wilson had to fight hard on two fronts. He had to force the Army bureaucracy to accept that there was a potential problem that needed a scheme of some kind, and he had to get inside the mind of the POWs themselves, to find out how they could best be helped to help themselves. Most POWs, it became clear from an experiment in 1944, denied having any problems and resented any suggestion that they were psychiatric patients. For any scheme to work, therefore, it would have to be voluntary, and employers and families would need to be 'educated' and staff carefully trained.[15]

The outcome was the Civil Resettlement Units scheme. Some 20 communities were set up in the spring of 1945 in large houses around the country, which returning POWs could join, if they wished (60% did). Each unit took some 250 repatriated POWs for an average of about four or five weeks and gave them a period of temporary security, during which they could gradually resume responsibility for job and home life and regain some sense of their own worth and identity. The emphasis was very much on 'social therapy', and instead of army discipline, which POWs loathed, there was a loose, democratic structure intended to encourage men to 'develop the self-control necessary for life in a civilised community'. Psychiatrists were involved, but mainly to orchestrate group discussions among the POWs; any suggestion that the POW had psychiatric problems or should seek psychiatric help was deliberately played down. At the same time, Wilson insisted that the staff be large enough to allow the inmates to be waited on at table, because research had shown that queuing for food aroused anxiety in ex-prisoners.[16]

The American writer Paul Goodman once said that most good therapy is a combination of a whorehouse and an employment agency. The CRU scheme was outstandingly successful in re-integrating POWs into the labour force with retraining, 'job rehearsals' and vocational guidance. So far as one can tell, it also helped them emotionally: the medical literature paints a picture of men arriving like 'hurt and lost children' with the 'dependent attitudes and primitive reactions of childhood' – suspicious, insecure, irritable, full of guilt and resentment – and leaving a month later their confidence, self-respect and maturity regained. Doctors marvelled at the speed with which patients learnt to relate once more to women and to authority, like a limbless man learning to walk again. One man who had once seen 'the social intimacies of the dance' as 'an unbearable provocation' gradually developed the 'capacity to derive pleasure from it'.[17]

The psychiatrists attached most importance, however, to 'the resocialisation of the individual' in the CRUs: by taking part in group discussions, men would help each other in the various activities of the unit and be encouraged gradually to take social responsibility for each other. Doctors proudly described how at one unit a group of fifteen men who had refused to co-operate in communal activities and 'were using the CRU as an easy-going hotel from which they could enjoy the neighbouring night life' were persuaded by their fellow patients to stop making trouble – to replace 'the external authority of military life with the self-discipline necessary in the civilian.'[18]

No doubt much of this writing was rather starry-eyed – the atmosphere in the men-only camps in Germany had been much more tribal and less 'democratic' than idealists like Dr Wilson believed. But for all that, the CRUs were perceived to be a success, a verdict confirmed by a small-scale follow-up study which found that graduates of CRUs readjusted more quickly than POWs who did not attend them.[19]

By the spring of 1945, thoughts began to turn to the other prisoners, those held by the Japanese in Burma, Malaya, and the Dutch Indies. Their needs were not so easy to assess. There were no books to lift off the shelf, for the psychological literature of torture and degradation, so extensive today, was then very slender. Only a 1943 article by Bruno Bettelheim, describing his experiences in Dachau, gave some sense of what might be going on; few British doctors read it, and it would have taken some temerity to suggest that the servile and infantile behaviour Bettelheim had observed in German civilians was any guide to that of British soldiers.[20]

Then again, no one had escaped from the Japanese camps and no prisoners been exchanged, so no first-hand accounts were available until September 1944, when the Americans torpedoed a Japanese troopship containing prisoners of war and the survivors were able to provide information. But they were not doctors. The British government, fearful of upsetting prisoners' relatives and jeopardising the safety of the 140,000 people still in Japanese hands, refused to release details to the press. By contrast with the frank examination of the psychology of being a

German prisoner, there was no public discussion of the Far Eastern prisoner of war's 'mentality'. Parliament was simply told that morale had remained high and that British prisoners had 'been true to the highest traditions of our race'.[21]

Behind the scenes, it was decided to provide short-term medical care in the Far East and get the men home as quickly as possible. The Civil Resettlement system, which was working so well with German prisoners, would be available to help with any problems in readjustment. At the same time leaflets instructing relatives how to behave were prepared. Official concern was partly allayed by the optimistic impressions of T. F. Rodger, the psychiatrist on Mountbatten's South East Asia Command. In June 1945, Rodger reported to London that 'British Prisoners of War recovered from Japanese hands showed *fewer psychiatric symptoms and a much more stable and satisfactory reaction to their captivity* than POWs from German hands' (italics added). Dr Rodger 'considered this to be due in large measure to the contempt which British soldiers were able to feel for the Japanese and the absence of any feeling that the enemy was a man of similar outlook and cultural background to themselves.'[22]

This will seem an extraordinary statement to a modern reader. How could Rodger have missed so much? We know from countless memoirs that these men had endured years of starvation and mistreatment in almost complete isolation from the outside world and had been plunged into a world of Biblical horror, a tapestry of sadism and dysentery. They had watched friends die, lying in their own filth on makeshift hospital floors or beaten up by Korean guards; they had had to suppress all emotion, kowtow to the Japanese, steal food, and lie in order to survive. Now they were full of hatred, anger, grief and despair, and were 'cursed with the gifts of deviousness, prevarication and impassivity' which had been essential during their captivity.[23]

Yet Rodger, a solid, reliable team-player among the Tavistock group, was simply reflecting the general view at the time. The Pacific war was an explicitly racial conflict on both sides, with the Japanese doing their best to reverse decades of European condescension by inflicting degradation and misery on their captives. The latter, in their turn, drew strength from racial pride and hatred of their gaolers, whom they saw as low, bestial animals. Other factors, too, seemed to justify Rodger's optimism. In most Japanese camps, British troops had not (until late in the war) been separated from their officers, as they had in the German *Stalags*, and so *esprit de corps*, the backbone of military morale, had remained intact (Rodger would not have known that while many individual officers did provide heroic leadership, there was also resentment at the better food and freedom from manual work which officers enjoyed). Finally, it was thought that the very horrors the prisoners had endured had winnowed out the weak and the vulnerable among them, with only the fittest surviving. Visiting liberated camps in August 1945, Dr Rodger spoke of the 'fitness and happiness' of the men. There was, he added, 'no doubt that the group was proud of itself: "We are the best".'[24]

This optimistic picture was not questioned by the doctors who had worked in the Japanese camps with such heroism and devotion; on the contrary, they reinforced it. 'We have shown we could take it, and we still can,' one wrote defiantly. The great Australian surgeon, 'Weary' Dunlop, stressed that mental disorders had been 'surprisingly infrequent and neurosis uncommon among Anglo-Saxon prisoners'. The men themselves were equally proud to have survived: of 60,000 prisoners released from the camps only 60 were admitted to psychiatric units in the Far East. Any mental problems were overshadowed, anyway, by the numerous physical disorders the men presented after three years of starvation and ill-treatment. The disorders of tropical disease and the relationship between vitamin deficiency and the nervous system, rather than the psychological consequences of maltreatment, dominated the medical press in 1946.[25]

Considering the abrupt end of the war, the logistics of repatriating over 37,000 people half-way round the world were tackled with commendable efficiency. In their memoirs, survivors record the abrupt transformation of their lives in August 1945: their bewilderment when the Japanese began to behave well to them; the arrival of their liberators, often surreally marked by planes flying overhead dropping cans of food and spruce, well-fed British officers floating down on parachutes. They describe too the waystations along the road home, the WVS women who gave them peaches and cream at Rangoon; the slow sea voyage, with plenty to drink and frequent ENSA entertainments; and the final agonising approach to a home port, marked for some by a cable announcing that their wives had found other partners. Signaller Coombs' diary concludes with a flourish:

FINALE.
   17 October [1945]
   Good Old England.
   First glance of coastline of Anglesey and the Great Orne at Llandudno. What a sight after 5 years. Landing at L'pool amid cheering throng of relatives. Marvellous! Splendid! Wonderful! Thank God for everything He has done for me and for having brought me back safely to the shores of the Grandest Country in the World.[26]

And after that? How did men cope with all the cultural and social changes that had taken place while they were away? How did their stomachs readjust to a 'civilised' diet; and their wives and children relate to the prematurely aged figure that arrived home, instead of the smiling youth of the mantelpiece snapshot?

To generalise about the emotional state of 37,000 individuals is hazardous, but some broad points are clear. Firstly, only a minority of former Japanese prisoners attended the Civil Resettlement Units, about 4,500 people; most preferred to stay with their families. Secondly, there was a general, officially orchestrated repression of the 'unpleasantness' in the Far East, born of a very British combination of concern for relatives' feelings and obtuse official secretiveness. Leaflets warned prisoners to 'guard their tongues' and not to talk to the 'more sensational press'. But the reticence went far beyond keeping the details out of the papers. Ex-prisoners were told not to upset their relatives by talking about their experiences to them, and their next-of-kin were instructed in official pamphlets not to ask about them.[27]

Thirdly, there was a disappointing lack of recognition for what these men had been through. There were no special services or parades. The civilian population, themselves bombed, rationed, uprooted, had little sympathy to spare, while the attitude of the War Office seems to have been coloured by memories of the humiliating loss of Singapore, a feeling that the soldiers had brought their misfortunes on themselves by surrendering to a smaller Japanese force. The Ministry of Pensions was determined to avoid paying out for psychoneuroses, as it had in the 1920s. One former prisoner remembers being dismissed 'after the quickest and rudest interview' he had ever had; another, tortured in Burma, was given a brief medical examination in Edinburgh in November 1945: 'I could walk across the room, was warm to the touch and had no incurable diseases, so they turned me loose.'[28]

For some, the system did work well. One satisfied customer was Ian Watt, a young officer who had been at Changi and on the Burma Railway (and probably owed his survival to a bout of malaria at a crucial moment). Back in England in September 1945, Watt found that he and his fellows 'tended to pooh-pooh the idea that anything in particular had happened to us'. Not only was it difficult to talk; he found it hard to function without the social system he had got used to in the camp and, contrary to his expectations, sought out the 'old gang' and went to a Civil Resettlement Unit. Watt believed that two experiences in particular helped him to put the camp behind him. One was an intense performance of Chekhov's play *Uncle Vanya*:

by the end of the first act, I was weeping, or trying to force myself not to, so violently that I got a cramp in my throat. It was terrible to feel there was an uncontrollable force within.[29]

Then, a few days later, Watt went to a film show organised by a CRU, a compilation of wartime newreels designed to fill the men in on what had happened while they had been away and give them more common ground with the rest of the population.

I didn't enjoy the battle scenes much, but when they came to the pictures of the relief of Stalingrad and one saw two endless lines of muffled people slowly advancing to greet each other across the waste of snow, I found that awful crying had started again; and here was I in uniform, and with men who'd been prisoners with me. Just then – horror of horrors – the film stopped, and the lights went up for an interval: and I saw that a lot of others were ashamedly wiping off their tears.[30]

Watt felt that the psychiatrists who had organised the programme at the CRU 'knew something that we didn't know':

that as prisoners we had been forced to build up a total block against expressing, or even allowing ourselves to feel, our deepest emotions; it would have been too dangerous for us to realise how sorry for ourselves we were. They knew, too, that this habit of repression had to be broken: and that the best way of doing it was to show us that it was there – in all of us.[31]

Watt gained further insight and perspective on his time in the Far East from a talk on the psychology of imprisonment by a former prisoner. He later recalled how one day, on a train back from London passing through beautiful Kent countryside, he suddenly had 'a moment of positive rejoicing, of letting my feelings for the first time accept home fully . . . As I looked out of the window I gradually became intensely exhilarated.'[32]

Watt was an intelligent and articulate man; when he wrote his graceful memoir in 1956, he was an English Professor at Cambridge. He said himself that his case was probably not representative. Evidence on how others less gifted or more marked by the camps adapted is inevitably much harder to come by: as the policy was not to draw attention to the Far Eastern prisoners of war (FEPOWs), but to treat them like everyone else, no follow-up surveys were made. By 1948, social workers were reporting that although it had been surprisingly easy to place returning prisoners of war in jobs, 'a significant number [of Far Eastern prisoners] developed depressive reactions after arrival in the United Kingdom.' About a year after returning home, many – it is impossible to say how many – FEPOWs had had a crisis of some kind. There were suicides, accidental deaths, cirrhosis of the liver, and a good deal of depression.[33]

For some, the sense of a separate identity remained. They 'not only harboured residual bitterness towards their captors and to their fellow countrymen,' a doctor later wrote, 'but also retained feelings of isolation and guilt. They felt that they are not as other men.' In that spirit, some FEPOWS began, in the late 1940s, to form their own clubs and associations 'to keep going the spirit that kept us going'.[34]

Other formal supports had by then been withdrawn. The Civil Resettlement Units were closed down in June 1946; they were very expensive to run at a time of public austerity. Besides, a War Office spokesman explained, 'the majority of chaps were back at work. The last thing they wanted was to be reminded they were old POWs. There weren't sufficient of them to fill the centres.' Some FEPOWs were treated at Northfield, some at Belmont, and many attended the tropical diseases clinics. Nearly half the 4,684 patients seen at one such clinic near London between 1946 and 1968 had psychiatric problems and the hospital's tropical physician became for some of them a kind of camp commandant, the stern paternal figure without which they could not function.[35]

Mostly, though, the problems remained within the family; a generation of women carried the burden. In one case, a group of young, newly-qualified nurses sent to a hospital near Leeds found themselves treating men horrifyingly tortured by the Japanese and some, moved by their suffering, married their patients, only to spend a lifetime as unpaid caregivers to men emotionally crippled by their experiences. In another case, a girl married an unknown man she had written to in the camps. In 1995, their daughter wrote of the 'daily drama played out within our family home, and perhaps replicated up and down the country, [which] meant that we as children also bore the scars of war.'

The culture of the time [she continued] did not provide assistance to those with emotional scars. It was not manly to admit you had been frightened during the war, or that you were having problems adjusting to normal life. Perhaps the only way to ease the pain was for the victim to regain his lost power by becoming the persecutor . . . [Her father had become] a tyrant venting his frustrations on those closest to him. As children we lived in constant fear of his rage and temper and periods of black depression. We hated Sundays because with all of us together, the rows were constant.[36]

In the late 1970s, when the social climate had changed completely, British doctors belatedly offered all FEPOWs the full medical examination they had not received in the 1940s. This exercise showed that many still had tropical diseases and that something like a third had significant psychological problems, particularly irritability, depression and recurring nightmares.

Final judgement on this episode is difficult. Clearly, mistakes were made and some FEPOWs got a raw deal. In theory the 'social psychiatry' pioneered at Northfield was inappropriate; individual psychotherapy would have worked better. But could much more have been done and would it have made a great difference? One doctor who has worked with FEPOWs doubts whether it would have been feasible to have offered all 37,000 more elaborate 'de-briefing', especially as they themselves did not want it at the time – 'if anyone had offered me "counselling" in 1945 I'd have been insulted,' recalls one. In many ways, it was precisely the old buttoned-up British tradition of suppressing emotion which got people through the wartime experience; switching off the anger and hatred could not be done quickly.[37]

A GOOD WAR?

In May 1940 a young airman sent his mother a letter to be opened if he did not return. 'Today,' Flying Officer Vivian Rosewarne had written, 'we are faced with the greatest organized challenge to Christianity and civilization that the world has ever seen, and I count myself lucky and honoured to be the right age and fully trained to throw my weight into the scale.' More recently, the historian Sir Michael Howard said much the same thing more plainly: 'for most of those who took part in it, the Second World War had a great deal of point.' Whatever the murky obscurities of its beginning, the war's apocalyptic ending – the liberation of the concentration camps, Hitler's death pyre in Berlin, the Nuremberg trials – gave it for many the character of a moral crusade.[1]

However, that is not the view of the American war veteran and literary critic, Paul Fussell. With increasing stridency, Fussell has argued that 'there has been too much talk about the Good War, the Justified War, the Necessary War and the like. It was war and nothing else, and thus stupid and sad.' Fussell believes that 'because the Second World War was fought against palpable evil, and thus was a sort of moral triumph, we have been reluctant to probe very deeply into its murderous requirements.' A similar ambiguity hangs over the role of psychiatry in the years 1939–45. Psychiatrists had a 'good' war in the sense that they raised their profession's status, but how much 'good' did they actually do?[2]

The psychiatrists themselves had few doubts that their work had enabled the services to make more efficient use of manpower, ushered in a more humane way of fighting (using selection to keep vulnerable individuals out of the firing line), provided skilled medical attention for those who broke down and helped countless individuals to readjust from war to peace. What was more, they believed, the war had taught them lessons that could usefully be applied in civilian life. Their peacetime role needed, therefore, to be widened.

Numerous critics were equally sure that 'trick-cycling' had been given too much rope during the war and must now be reined in. By 1946 a sharp backlash had begun in the British Army; psychiatrists were widely seen as naive, inexperienced, ignorant of military realities and overdogmatic; and accused of wasting a great deal of manpower. The objection was partly to the more democratic culture they had attempted to introduce. The strength of feeling obliged Sir Ronald Adam's successor as Adjutant-General severely to reduce psychiatrists' role in selection procedures and their status in the Army. They became, once again, lowly creatures.[3]

In the United States, psychiatrists were accused of putting too much faith in selection and needlessly turning thousands of exhausted or disheartened soldiers into chronic cases. William Menninger and his naval counterpart Francis Braceland admitted that their doctors had not at first been properly trained to understand 'the specific needs of the military, in which one must accept the group aim . . . as of paramount importance, instead of the individual'; and had 'entered the military service with insufficient knowledge of the vicissitudes of everyday life, and the slight deviations of young adults under stress, and thus . . . were unprepared for most of the situations which they were to encounter'; but they argued that early errors had been outweighed by solid achievements later in the war.[4]

Where, then, does the balance lie? Judgement must come in two stages. Firstly, whether the military got its money's worth out of the psychiatrists or whether the war would have been better waged without them. Secondly, whether society as a whole was well served. Although in so slippery a subject statistics are of limited value, that is where one has to start. The figures suggest, first, that 'preventive' psychiatry did not prevent psychiatric casualties. They remained consistently high: 10–15% of all British battle casualties during the active phase of the Battle of France in 1940, 10–20% during the first ten days of the Normandy battle and 20% during the two following months, 7–10% in the Middle East in the middle of 1942 and 11% in the first two months of the Italian campaign. American figures tell much the same story. 'In the US ground forces alone . . . 504,000 men were permanently lost to the fighting effort for psychiatric reasons – enough manpower to outfit fifty combat divisions.' Indeed, the sheer scale of manpower loss in the Army led Eisenhower to commission a post-war enquiry into 'the lost divisions'.[5]

Behind the statistics, there were wide divergences. One of the few hard statistics comes from the British. During the campaign in north-western Europe 'about one third of all exhaustion cases treated eventually remained at full duties. This represents 4,400 men saved for further battles at a time when the manpower situation was the most critical.' When you consider that 'the total annual cost of the comprehensive psychiatric services of the British Army equalled the cost of running the war for an hour and twenty minutes' that sounds like value for the Army's money. How many of these soldiers would have recovered spontaneously, one cannot say.

The Americans underwent a marked change of view, switching from their initial belief that 'a clear cut distinction [could] be made among men as between the "weak" and the "strong",' to the view that 'every man has his breaking point'. As their psychiatrists' knowledge of wartime realities grew, so they began to take account of factors like unit morale, leadership, news from home and the political situation as well as of the personality of the man. 'Motivation' was felt to be crucial, enabling some men to keep going where others faltered.

The incidence of psychiatric breakdown in the United States Army was two to three times higher in World War Two than in World War One. Dr John Appel believed this was not so much because war had become more terrifying, but because attitudes had changed from enthusiasm and an 'emotional conviction that they were fighting the war to end all wars' to a spirit of resignation.[6]

In Britain, the Second World War did not produce an epidemic of mental disorders, as the Great War had and as Vietnam has in the United States. There are, of course, many possible explanations for this – it was a war of movement, not static trench warfare; leadership was better and men better trained. Fear was now accepted and the death penalty for cowardice abolished. Men had fewer illusions; there was less of a gulf between romantic stereotypes of war and the horrible reality. The war was socially sanctioned, a good war; veterans were honoured and feted when they returned (though not for long). The doctors knew what to expect and perhaps had better techniques with drugs enabling them to nip neurosis in the bud. Finally, a much greater percentage of vulnerable and 'slow' recruits were, eventually, weeded out.

Somewhere in this list one must place the main legacy of the First World War, an official determination that quasi-medical words like 'shell-shock' should never be used, that the whole question of psychoneuroses should be both recognised and played down and that few pensions should be paid.

Turning to the impact of the psychiatrists' efforts on the wider society, the difficulties of judgement become even greater and much of what follows here is inevitably impressionistic. The British and the Americans pursued sharply differing approaches and while it would seem that the British method was more successful, this may simply reflect the gulf in data.

Apart from the efforts made to help prisoners of war in Civil Resettlement Units, British society in the 1940s did not place great emphasis on the problems of the returning ex-serviceman; there wasn't the time, money or energy to spare. The soldier was given a 'demob' suit, a victory parade perhaps, and expected to muck in to help rebuild a country physically shattered by war and struggling to survive economically. The pensions regime was very mean – the husband of the crime-writer P. D. James, a doctor, went off to the war perfectly sane and came back five years later severely disturbed. He was hospitalised for the rest of his life, but received no pension, his case not being considered service-related. His wife became the family breadwinner.[7]

Nor was the military pensioner favoured in Britain's workplaces, as he had been in 1919; the trade unions, now represented in the Cabinet by Ernest Bevin, made sure there was no positive discrimination. There was, of course, a network of 'welfare' and voluntary bodies like the National Marriage Guidance Council, to help couples whose marriages had been threatened by the years of wartime separation, and the National Association of Mental Health, which provided psychiatric social workers at the local level. And there was a 'National Health Service' of a sort which had not existed after the Great War. The main difference, however – and it was a crucial one – was that for two and a half decades after the war there was full employment. A great deal of official time and energy went into finding jobs for ex-servicemen. It may be, as some have argued, that it was too readily assumed that simply getting a man a job solved all his problems but the therapeutic importance of work cannot be underestimated.[8]

Was British post-war policy a success, then? The only yardstick of measurement, the number of pensions paid for continuing psychiatric disorders, is as much a barometer of political and medical fashion as of objective clinical need. However, if the standard view of the Great War as a psychiatric disaster is based on such statistics as the 120,000 pensions paid for psychiatric disorders and the 6,000 hospitalised psychotics, then the fact that many fewer pensions were paid after the Second World War must also have some significance. It is clear from many sources that the post-1945 figures were considerably lower than the post-1919 ones, but unfortunately all efforts to prise precise numbers out of the British War Pensions Agency have proved fruitless. All one can say is that between September 1939 and August 1945 some 109,000 cases were discharged from the British Army (there are no comparable figures for the Royal Navy or Air Force), and that 'mental disorders' accounted for some 40% of discharges from the forces over that period.[9]

Putting it another way, I believe British policy during the Second World War was fairly successful, combining the overall 'preventive' framework laid down at the 1939 conference with quite effective psychiatric treatment. 'Avoidable' war neurosis was, so far as possible, prevented from developing; 'real', unavoidable, war neurosis was treated by a battery of therapies. Because the civil population was itself exposed to traumatic experiences, great care was taken not to pay too much public attention to the question of war neurosis. The evidence for these judgements is, however, largely anecdotal, because successive British governments have withheld from public scrutiny the statistics which would support it.

Nor does this mean that numerous individuals did not have difficulties after the war. In 1947, a psychiatrist described treating some 44 patients, all of whom had undergone troubling experiences: a former member of the Special Air Service still felt guilt at having accidentally killed his jeep driver in a battle in France in 1944; a tank officer still suffered from claustrophobia; a former prisoner of war was irritable and prone to mood swings; a woman had nightmares about being trapped under the ruins of her house. Abreacted with chloroform and ether, one man re-enacted strangling a Japanese sentry, an air gunner flew back to Berlin, a fireman pulled corpses from buildings.[10]

But, overall, British post-war policy was very low-key and, by modern standards, tough, whereas American policy was more ambitious, even tender. Firstly, there was money: the way home was 'paved with every comeback aid the nation could provide'. The buoyant American economy combined with the long political tradition of generosity to returning soldiers and the power of the veterans' lobby to produce the GI Bill of Rights, which provided $50m in low-interest loans, gave 7.8 million men job re-training and sent 2.2 million to college, effectively creating 'a new ex-service middle class' (by 1970 the Veterans' Administration reckoned that GI education had boosted incomes so much that the increased tax yield had paid back the programme's cost).[11]

Secondly, there was work. Despite fears that '16 million Americans would be returning to an economy that was not ready for them', the post-war consumer-led boom produced plenty of jobs. Thirdly, the psychological problems of 'the returning veteran' were explicitly discussed in innumerable novels, magazine articles, movies and radio plays. It was generally agreed that women had a 'primary role in the social aspects of demobilization' and an army of 'experts' and commentators told them how to play it. Wives should rebuild their husbands' egos by giving them 'lavish and undemanding affection' while expecting 'no immediate return'; be tolerant of wartime infidelity; and surrender 'some of their newly found competence and economic independence'. A generation of American women was happy to comply. 'Women as well as men,' the feminist Betty Friedan later wrote, 'sought the comforting reality of home and children . . . a pent-up hunger for marriage, home, and children was felt simultaneously by several different generations, for the girls [the lonely years during the war] added an extra urgency to their search for love . . . when the men came back there was a headlong rush into marriage.' The Americans also provided, in full measure, recognition for their warriors – bands, parades, tickertape.[12]

American veterans of World War Two are generally regarded as the most fortunate in history. But the American approach had its downside. The endless emphasis on emotional problems eventually drove *Stars and Stripes* to protest that most returning soldiers would be quite normal. 'We will be happy to sit in front of fireplaces, and let our wives and sweethearts fetch us Old Fashioneds,' the soldiers' newspaper wrote. 'But not, please God, with the look of a trapped and frightened doe, waiting for the blow to fall.' Advice literature to wives and mothers, said Marine Sergeant David Dempsey, was 'in danger of turning them into kitchen psychologists determined to "cure" the veteran – even at the cost of his sanity'; all most returnees needed was 'some guidance' and 'a little pre-Freudian love and understanding from their wives'.[13]

What especially distinguished the American approach from the British, however, was the lavish psychiatric treatment provided. The United States had ended the war on a high tide of optimistic faith in material progress allied to an economic boom; never in history had the belief that human problems could be solved by throwing money at them been so combined with the money to do it with. 'In a period when medical research had just produced the yellow magic of penicillin only to have it promptly topped by streptomycin,' the historian Eric Goldman later recalled, 'it did not seem utopian to talk of conquering tuber-culosis, infantile paralysis, and even cancer.' It was 'a "can-do" era which focused, as during the war, on accomplishing a mission and clearing up the details later.' In this spirit, President Truman sent America's outstanding wartime administrator, General Omar N. Bradley to the Veterans' Administration, charged with providing veterans with the best medical care. Boasting that 'we spend as much in nine months as the atom bomb cost to develop', Bradley hired some 4,000 physicians in six months and encouraged his medical chief, Paul Hawley, to embark on the largest hospital-building programme in American history. Naturally, psychiatry played an important part in this – 60% of VA patients were psychiatric.[14]

This is the background against which the plentiful American statistics need to be read. In June 1947, a total of 475,397 patients with neuropsychiatric disabilities from World War Two were receiving pensions from the VA, of whom 286,000 were classed as having a 'functional' illness, the rest as having 'organic disorders'. In addition, there were 50,662 World War Two neuropsychiatric veterans in VA hospitals in 1945. A quarter of a century later, in 1972, there were still 44,000 such patients occupying beds in VA hospitals.[15]

The 'follow-up literature' on World War Two veterans is nearly all American. A Veterans' Administration study of some 800–900 former patients, published in 1951, found that most of them continued to have symptoms, but that 67% had made a 'satisfactory occupational adjustment', 74% a 'satisfactory economic adjustment' and 67% had reached 'satisfactory family adjustment'. The investigators considered only 56% to have 'socially acceptable behaviour and mores', but the vast majority – some 70% – were not considered to have any psychiatric disability. This study, like Salmon and Fenton's in the 1920s, 'revealed a marked tendency for significant improvement among psychiatrically troubled veterans five years since discharge from the service'. At about the same time, a study of schizophrenic patients found that most had recovered, but one-fifth were still severely disabled by the symptoms after five or more years. 'The most important factors in promoting a good readjustment were a warm, tolerant, helpful attitude on the part of a wife or other family member, satisfactory work situation, and success in school and social contacts.'[16]

Other studies, using much smaller numbers, found that fresh cases of traumatic war neurosis were developing in men who had not previously sought treatment since the war. They commonly suffered from intense anxiety, recurrent combat-related dreams, startle reactions, depression, guilt and tendency to sudden, violent, behaviour. Secondary symptoms included a tendency to avoid people, fear of criticism, difficulty in making decisions and various sleep disturbances.[17]

So, the follow-ups tend to show that most neuropsychiatric cases had satisfactorily readjusted. But they also show that there was a substantial number of people who had not.

*   *   *

The Second World War left a profound mark on psychiatry, but in a very different way than the Great War. For example, there was little new writing about the effects of trauma on the individual. The history of the Tavistock Clinic says, with refreshing honesty, 'we made scarcely any major new contribution to the treatment of traumatic neuroses' during the war. Indeed, much of the theoretical writing was produced by doctors who played a fairly marginal role in the war. A lengthy period of sick leave allowed the British psychiatrist William Sargant to read Ivan Pavlov's account of the effects of traumatic experiences on dogs and come up with a theory of war neurosis as a conditioned response, elements of which had been anticipated by Abram Kardiner.[18]

In the United States, the major theoretical figure was Roy Grinker. After working in Tunisia in 1942, this 'arch wangler' was sent to the Don Cesar, a palatial hotel in Florida, once the playground of Scott Fitzgerald and numerous gangsters, now being used as a convalescent home by the United States Army Air Force. There he was joined by his assistant, John Spiegel, and for the rest of the war they treated returning flyers. In 1945 Grinker and Spiegel published *Men Under Stress*, a bulky and ambitious tome, garlanded with classical references and psychiatric erudition, setting out to be the definitive work on the psychological problems of flyers. Its first half, however, is simply an elaboration of the authors' earlier *War Neuroses in North Africa* while the second is an extended variation on one simple, almost simplistic theme. The key to the war neuroses, for Grinker and Spiegel, is regression – but regression of a 1940s Freudian kind. A soldier or airman, they argue, subsumes his own ego into the military 'superego' and in so doing, 'regresses to a less mature, more dependent level'. But the strains of combat often then break the ties between him and this superego – the Army lets him down in some way (for example, he is shelled by his own side); or the officer or buddy on whom he depended is killed – and the soldier is then left bereft, in a 'passive dependent state', needing to be mothered and cosseted. Many of Grinker and Spiegel's patients were 'immature boys' but, they argued, the pressures of battle could also produce regression in previously mature men.[19]

Suffering from 'psychic bankruptcy', these men needed 'replenishing affection, consideration and attention, as a small child needs to be praised and comforted after a particularly strenuous and exhausting activity'. Clearly, in the luxurious comforts of the Don Cesar, they got just that. The doctor–patient ratio of 1 to 35 allowed a considerable amount of time and attention to be given to each patient, with frequent use of the barbiturate narcosynthesis which Grinker and Spiegel had made their hallmark. It was possible, too, to explore the relationship between present and past in some detail. Many of the patients' problems are traced back to the psychodynamics of their childhood and upbringing: a man blamed himself unnecessarily for his buddy's death because his disapproving father had given him a sense of low self-regard. One airman's feelings over the loss of his comrades 'revived the old conflict over the loss of his mother when she had faithlessly had another baby, to whom she was more attentive.'[20]

Grinker and Spiegel were, of course, dealing with men who had nearly all been home and seen their families before developing psychiatric difficulties, men whose wartime experiences were intermingled with old difficulties and recent domestic troubles. Perhaps for this reason, *Men Under Stress* lacks the vividness of much American airforce literature. Nor does it give much of a feel of the atmosphere at Don Cesar – there is a solitary reference to a patient who feels better because he met a girl on the beach outside the hospital.

Oddly enough, the most influential wartime writing about trauma came from a civilian disaster, a fire in the Cocoanut Grove nightclub in Boston on the night of 28 November 1942. Four hundred and ninety-one people were killed and hundreds of casualties taken to two Boston hospitals which, by this stage of the war, were 'catastrophe-minded' and had large teams waiting. Penicillin was used on civilians for the first time. Several psychiatrists, notably Dr Erich Lindemann at Massachusetts General Hospital, were already interested in the physiological and psychological aspects of acute grief because of its perceived role in producing psychosomatic symptoms such as colitis. They were brought in a few days after the tragedy, when patients began breaking down on learning that they had lost relatives, and were able to make detailed studies of the normal stages through which acute grief passes and the ways in which morbid reactions can set in. They found that recovery was usually inhibited by emotional complication such as guilt – in one case a young man had abandoned his pregnant wife. However, what distinguishes these papers from the much more hurried British literature on the Blitz is that the Americans say nothing about the role of social pressure and assume an explicit role in the process of recovery for individual psychotherapy.[21]

*   *   *

Much more influential than the writing on individual trauma, however, was the literature on 'social psychiatry'. The war produced not just a new confidence in the effects of psychiatry but a completely new sense of the social role of the psychiatrist. It 'marked a watershed in the history of mental health policy and the evolution of American psychiatry' says Gerald Grob.

Wartime service appeared to show that psychiatric problems were much more widespread than previously imagined, that environmental factors like the stresses of battle were a main contributory factor, and that early and purposeful treatment in noninstitutional settings produced favourable outcomes. If, therefore, the successful wartime model could be applied in peacetime, with early identification and treatment of symptoms in the community, much serious mental illness and confinement in asylums could be prevented.[22]

The war also produced an immense expansion in the size of the profession, particularly in America. In 1940, there were 2,423 psychiatrists in the United States; a decade later, 5,856 – many now psychoanalytically inclined. 'Before the war,' the joke went, 'the analysts chased the patients; after the war, the patients chased the analysts.' In the United States, a new awareness of the problem of mental health happened to coincide with bountiful resources and the optimistic assumptions of 'the year when man mastered the atom' to produce the National Mental Health Act of 1946, which pumped money into ambitious new programmes.[23]

It might seem paradoxical that American psychiatry should have emerged from the war with its reputation enhanced when its wartime record was so poor. But that is to misunderstand the situation. The changed role of psychiatry sprang from several factors. For one thing, the profession had a higher profile during the war; the services needed thousands of psychiatrists and so they were trained in a hurry, mostly by Moe Kaufman at Atlanta. Secondly, the methods of treatment developed at this time, whether Grinker and Spiegel's narcosynthesis or Moreno's psychodrama, were intensely dramatic and Menninger's genius for publicity made sure that they were well covered. The American public could see in numerous images that a psychiatrist, even a Freudian analyst, was not a foreigner with a beard and a funny accent but young, virile, all-American. Finally, psychiatry became in wartime a vehicle for the hopes and fears of the whole society – for its anxiety that young men would be damaged by war, its hope that they return well and sound, its feelings about the war.[24]

In depicting war neurosis to the public, Menninger and the press overcame the problem of censorship and of the inherently downbeat nature of a subject which 'went against the conventions of war reporting which typically celebrate the heroic'. They managed to establish 'saving stereotypes'; 'psychoneurotic patients', as Nathan Hale has written, 'were heroes – big apparently tough men, with long weeks of continuous fighting against the Japanese on Guadalcanal or months of combat against the Germans in Europe or North Africa.' 'I fought the Jerry on more than a dozen missions,' one of them told the *Woman's Home Companion*. 'I fought until most of my outfit was killed, until I lost my ability to sleep, until hollows deepened under my eyes and my weight melted away.' The message, as Hale says, was that 'anyone could become a psychoneurotic patient, and everyone, even the strongest, had his breaking point. Because of the special horrors of modern warfare, that breaking point could be reached more quickly than ever before.'[25]

These popularisations projected a heroic picture of military psychiatry, emphasising to the full the dramatic potential of abreactive catharsis and dream analysis – techniques that were not proving uniformly successful. They included, as Hale has shown, 'little or no discussions of theory. They were dramatic stories designed to entertain and raise morale. Little of the psychoanalytic ego psychiatry that informed some of the psychiatric discussions surfaces in these popularisations. The psychoanalytic model seemed much like the one Freud [developed in the 1900s] ... the sense of often inappropriate guilt from a punishing conscience was perhaps the one new element.'[26]

The most interesting retrospective judgement on the wartime changes came almost half a century later from the analyst, Robert Michels. During the war, he said, psychoanalytic training was 'seen as the most potent and scientific strategy' for transforming ordinary doctors into military psychiatrists. These doctors,

learned a little about psychoanalytic thinking and then went to the battlefield and saw soldiers who were in acute mental distress due to the trauma of war. They used their newly learned theory to treat their patients and were astonishingly successful, in great part because they were treating people with an excellent prognosis. If persons who are acutely distressed and have had a traumatic experience are separated from the trauma and treated nicely, they will get better.

Michels then described how these doctors came back to the United States 'excited and enthusiastic about the new psychiatric theory they had learned and eager to use it for all kinds of psychiatric illnesses'.

There was great excitement and enthusiasm for this new treatment that was going to revolutionize American psychiatry. It didn't work, or, to be more precise, what worked on the battlefield with acute shellshock was useless in the state hospitals with chronic, seriously mentally ill patients.[27]

In Britain, as we have seen, there were never the same resources. Energies went rather into finding a role within the new National Health Service. But the wartime spirit lingered on in an aspiration towards a role as social engineers, a feeling that psychiatrists could fulfil in peacetime the function they had played in the Army, could somehow 'evolve a pattern of society which would enhance the personality of man and diminish his social ills.'[28]

The war had given the Tavistock psychiatrists a taste of real power and a vision of a better world; it had taken them 'from the then narrow and secluded life of the pre-war mental hospital or from the consulting room and the couch, deeply concerned with only a few individuals . . . to assume great responsibilities.'

Through their experience of Officer selection and the application of group techniques and through having studied the effects on morale and sickness rates of good and bad Army communities, they were able to think in new dimensions . . . They were now fully aware of the potentialities of a psychiatrist as a social therapist and a social scientist. They knew where they had to go and what they had to do to promote community mental health services.[29]

Even the normally level-headed J. R. Rees was infected by this mood. Lecturing in New York in 1944, at a time when the Beveridge Report had thrown the British post-war social order up for discussion, Rees day-dreamed about a future in which 'progressive scientific and health activities [would] pay a positive dividend,' and saw psychiatrists as Platonic Guardians of a Brave New World, vetting politicians for their emotional stability and solving the 'problem of household help' by 'an organisation of women into groups or a service.' Some of Rees' ideas were unpleasantly tinged with the eugenic mood of his Edwardian youth ('dullards in service labour corps'); others were foolishly fellow-travelling: it took some naivety still to believe that 'the change in social structure in the Soviet Republics ha[d] led to a marked diminution of the amount of neurosis.'[30]

Such hubris did not go unnoticed. The acerbic Freudian analyst Edward Glover warned in a wartime interview that the techniques of personnel testing used in the Army might well be applied in peace. 'Not only will it suit employers and the state to aim at 100% efficiency in their workers,' said Glover, 'but army psychiatrists have developed swollen heads over the use of selection tests and are therefore likely to push for their development in peacetime.' The best safeguard, Glover thought, would be to 'submit all Army psychiatrists to a course of "rehabilitation" (as it is called when applied to others) in order that they may regain a proper perspective regarding the rights of citizens'. Otherwise, the system might have the seeds of Nazism in it, whatever the experts said.[31]

Certainly, industry seemed the obvious place to apply wartime lessons. Soon after the war, Ronald Hargreaves, the ablest member of the Tavistock group, joined the Unilever company as its chief industrial medical officer, hopeful of using psychological methods to enhance productivity and harmony. He was quickly disillusioned. In practice, Unilever had no interest in applying his ambitious preventive techniques. 'It was like going back to the Boer War,' Hargreaves told a friend. He realised that his experience with the 'well-defined population of the Army' had led to an 'overoptimistic view of what was possible in the political and social complexities' of civilian life. Both Hargreaves and Rees tried also to carry the wartime spirit to the new United Nations agencies. But for Hargeaves, 'Some of the optimism he had carried through the years of the war and afterwards had gone.'[32]

A more enduring wartime legacy was 'the therapeutic community', the idea of organising institutions in a non-authoritarian way and so helping patients or inmates to help themselves. Immediately after the war, when the mood was still favourable, Dr Maxwell Jones, who had developed methods of group psychotherapy while running the Effort Syndrome unit at Mill Hill and run a conversion centre for prisoners of war, persuaded the British Ministry of Labour to set up an Industrial Neurosis Unit at Belmont Hospital. Here patients with long-standing neuroses and character disorders and employment difficulties were sent. It continued to exist until 1959 and aroused much interest within psychiatry, and distrust in the hospital to which it was attached; its results were debatable. A charismatic but wilful man, Jones was one of the spoilt children of British psychiatry, indulged by a few powerful patrons (R. D. Laing would be another). He became something of a cult figure, but had little mainstream influence. The ideal of the 'therapeutic community' was much buffeted by the turbulent winds of the 1960s, but survives.[33]

* * *

The war veteran of the 1940s was returning to a very different world than his equivalent twenty years earlier and, if he needed psychiatric help, might find himself given radically different treatment. This happened to Harold Smith.[34]

Thirty-six years old in 1946, Harold Smith had led a perfectly ordinary life. He had been one of eight children, all quite normal, though perhaps he was the most sensitive. Average at school, he had enjoyed sports and after a seven-year apprenticeship had started regular work as a printer before volunteering for the British Army in 1942. His wife described him as 'happy, good-natured, hard-working and certainly not nervous'.

He went ashore with the first wave of tanks in Normandy and was in the thick of heavy tank fighting for the next six months. 'Many of his friends were gradually either killed or burnt to death in their tanks and the patient expected every day to be his last.' On two occasions he was himself in a tank which received a direct hit and although he managed to escape, he felt 'mounting tension and aggression'. By November 1944 he was back in England, in hospital for wounds to his legs; his wife found him 'obviously changed as a result of his battle experiences'. Though his foot soon recovered, Harold 'gradually became nervously worse in hospital' and, after spending some time in a military nervous centre, was discharged from the Army on a small pension.

He went back to work in August 1945 but soon began to take time off, plagued by pains in the legs, lethargy, headaches and irritability. He slept badly and his marriage and financial situation soon deteriorated. A year later he was back in hospital for nine months of psychotherapy, including a dozen sessions of drug-induced abreaction. 'Many traumatic incidents were gone over, accompanied by a release of great emotion, but with little effect except to relieve some of his headaches.' Electro convulsion treatment only made him worse and had to be stopped. Nothing seemed to work. Harold grew more and more irritable, demanding that the doctors *do* something. And so, with his and his wife's full consent, they performed a leucotomy on him.

During the war, while attention was focused on the 'war neuroses', psychiatry's treatment of serious mental disorders like depression and schizophrenia had been transformed as the new treatments developed in the 1930s came into general use. For example, Electro Convulsive Therapy, only introduced in 1939, had by 1945 become the routine treatment for depression; in remote parts of the world, Army psychiatrists ingeniously devised equipment for giving electric shocks to their patients and in the huge base hospitals in Britain and the United States, ECT was being used on an enormous, but unquantifiable scale. In the understaffed and overcrowded civilian asylums, too, the new methods quickly gained control. When the psychoanalyst Donald Winnicott condemned ECT in 1943 as 'a short cut to psychotherapy and a wonderful way of doing psychiatry without having to know anything about human nature', he found most of British psychiatry lined up against him.[35]

The psychosurgical procedure known as leucotomy (lobotomy in the United States), had also become established in wartime, largely thanks to the publication in 1942 of the book *Psychosurgery* by Freeman and Watts, the American neurologist and neurosurgeon who had taken up and considerably refined the technique. Their book was widely read on both sides of the Atlantic and was felt to have 'brought some order to a confused and chaotic subject'. 'It hit us like a bomb,' one British surgeon later recalled. 'It seemed to answer all our questions.'[36]

Freeman and Watts offered a more sophisticated rationale than had Moniz (the pioneer of leucotomy) for what was now a subtler operation: severing the nerve fibres which connected the frontal lobes of the brain to the thalamus. Psychosurgery, they argued, separated the 'thinking brain' from the 'feeling brain' and thus removed 'the sting' from any psychosis. They freely conceded that the operation resulted in personality changes and that they had had failures but claimed that, on balance, it was worthwhile in certain intractable cases.[37]

Not all psychiatrists were convinced, psychoanalysts least of all. 'The psycho-surgeon,' one declared in 1949, 'is indeed treading on dangerous ground when he decides that a patient without a soul is happier than a patient with a sick soul.' But because such critics could offer no practical alternative methods for treating the huge numbers of seemingly incurable patients in the public asylums, their views were largely ignored. The media eagerly endorsed the new techniques and patients' relatives clamoured for treatment on their behalf.[38]

In this climate, there was a dramatic surge in leucotomies in the United States. The number conducted rose from only 150 in 1945 to 5,074 in 1949, most of the operations being carried out on long-stay patients in state mental institutions. The Veterans' Administration was initially very cautious about using leucotomy on its patients, perhaps because the introduction of antibiotic sulphur drugs on the battlefield meant that many more head injury cases were now surviving than in previous wars and VA surgeons, 'just learning to partially alleviate the scarring caused by head wounds, were understandably reluctant to purposely damage the brain.' But by 1948 some 48 operations a month were being carried out in VA hospitals and some 12% of the 18,000 leucotomies carried out in America between 1936 and 1951 were in VA hospitals.[39]

British doctors, discussing leucotomy at a meeting in April 1946, were cautiously in favour. By then, some 1,000 operations had taken place in Britain by then and, said one doctor, 'the scepticism with which the operation was originally regarded [had] given way to tempered enthusiasm.' Once again, most of the patients targeted were from long-stay mental wards: cases of depression, schizophrenia or obsessive/compulsive disorder, some of whom 'posed an unending nursing problem' to the staff. There was also, however, a group of psychiatrists, of whom Dr William Sargant stood out for his missionary zeal, who advocated the use of leucotomies on neurotic patients who had not been confined to asylums but who suffered from 'mental tension' or obsessions. Sargant argued that continued refinements in surgical technique were reducing the risk and enhancing the potential of the operation, making it possible for 'the minimum of brain tissue . . . [to] be destroyed that will produce the desired clinical effect.' He worked frequently with the surgeon Wyllie McKissock who, by 1947, had done some 500 leucotomies.[40]

It was Sargant who persuaded Harold Smith to undergo a leucotomy and McKissock who carried out the operation, at Belmont Hospital on 5 June 1947. The procedure was very quick. Once the patient was anaesthetised, the surgeon drilled a small hole in the front of the skull, into which he inserted a small, blunt needle which he carefully moved laterally in order to sever the connection between the lobes of the brain. The surgery took a mere six minutes. Half an hour later, Harold Smith was back in the ward.[41]

Six months later, Sargant reported that the operation had produced an immediate lessening of Harold's symptoms; within six weeks he was asking to return to work. His pains seemed to have gone and he was once again 'kind, considerate, cheerful, good-tempered and less sensitive.' In November 1947 he was back at his old job and both work and home life were reported as satisfactory, with an increased restoration of his old energy.[42]

But six months is quite a short interval after such an operation. Early in 1949 Dr Sargant and his social worker did a further follow-up study of all their leucotomy patients, the files for which survive. Several patients wrote in, describing in grateful, deferential tones their roller-coaster voyages through hope and despair. A man who in 1945 had offered Sargant 'heart-felt gratitude' for his 'great brilliance in recommending the pre-frontal leucotomy . . . for me . . . It has made me much better as regards the appearance problem I had', was now 'sorry to say', four years on, that he was 'by no means well, as I have recently had a return of my old complaint, whereby I am worried about my appearance.' By contrast, an estate agent was 'pleased to say I am going strong . . . We shall never forget what [Sargant] did for me'; and a woman operated on in 1947 was 'much better since having the operation . . . and grateful for having had it', despite having to go to the lavatory five times a night.[43]

Harold Smith was part of the survey, referred to as 'a service patient'. The file records that on a particular day he was 'seeing Dr Sargant at St Thomas's [Hospital]', rather than being visited by the social worker. After that there is no further mention of him. It is unclear whether he turned up or not. Nor is there any mention of Smith in a notably up-beat review of his work which Sargant published in 1953. It may be relevant, however, that soon after the operation on Harold Smith both Sargant and McKissock began to experiment with much more limited surgical techniques, some of which were specifically aimed at obsessional neurotic patients. By 1953 Sargant himself had concluded that 'it is wrong to subject the ordinary run of neurotic patients, and many psychotic patients, to a routine full standard operation, till modified procedures have been tried first', and McKissock had published an account of his new modified 'rostral' technique.[44]

Perhaps Harold Smith was lucky. Perhaps his was one of those dramatic cases which for so long blinded doctors to the dreadful after-effects of leucotomy. Perhaps he never needed to see the doctor again and was able to lead a happy and contented life.

Nineteen forty-nine turned out to be the highwater mark for leucotomies. That year, Egaz Moniz, the inventor of the procedure, was awarded the Nobel Prize for medicine. He received it in a wheelchair, having for some years been paralysed after being shot in the spine by a patient he had leucotomised.

The numbers of leucotomies had already gone into decline when, in the spring of 1954, the arrival of anti-psychotic drugs caused the procedure effectively to be abandoned.[45]

VIETNAM DOCTORS

Corporal A was helicoptered to a hospital near Saigon, one day in November 1967. A 20-year-old infantryman who had been serving with the American Army in Vietnam for five months, he was seen on arrival to be 'mute, grunting incomprehensibly, and posturing'. He was also 'quite disorganized, could not communicate with his examiners, was easily startled by noises and walked with a slow, shuffling gait. When he sat in a chair, he rocked with his eyes closed and occasionally mumbled "Mama".' A physical examination found no other abnormalities.

Corporal A was sent to the hospital's psychiatric unit, where he was given a shower, reassured and 'put to sleep' with the drug chlorpromazine. Eighteen hours later, when he awoke seemingly 'alert, coherent, and rational', he was issued with a fresh uniform, inducted into the quasi-military routine in the ward, and 'told that he was recovering from overexposure to combat and could expect to be returned to his military unit soon.' He then took part in a group therapy meeting.

Corporal A emotionally described how he had been serving as fire team leader when six of his friends were killed and mutilated by enemy fire; he had become agitated and began screaming while loading their bodies into a helicopter. He talked despondently of his revulsion at the killing and was regretful that he had 'gone to pieces'. He felt torn because he always sought to be 'good' and wanted to be a good soldier, but it just wasn't in his 'makeup' to kill. He said he could not return to the field.

Ignoring this, the psychiatric staff assured him there was nothing wrong with him and gave him 'ego support of his duty and mission' – a pep talk, presumably. That night he was informed that he would be returning to his unit the following day and given more chlorpromazine.

Because of his rapid improvement and lack of a past psychiatric history, Corporal A was discharged back to his unit with the diagnosis of 'combat exhaustion' and the recommendation that he be re-examined by his division psychiatrist if his symptoms recurred.[1]

The case of Corporal A was routine; the psychiatrists treating him simply doing the job they were trained to do: keeping up the fighting strength. But the Vietnam War inverted traditional values and wisdoms and called into question the role of military psychiatry. The 'routine' case of Corporal A would be remembered and nearly two decades later would form the centrepiece of a long and anguished re-examination of the role of psychiatry in Vietnam. Perhaps, also, cases like that of Corporal A shed light on one of the great mysteries about the Vietnam War – the extraordinary contrast between the way it was perceived at the time and its later psychological legacy.

The Vietnam conundrum can most easily be understood if we invert chronology. Consider, first, a report published in 1990, authorised by Congress and costing some $9m, which concluded that no less than 480,000 out of the 3.15 million Americans (15%) who had served in Vietnam were still, fifteen years after the end of the war, suffering from war-related psychological problems – or Post-Traumatic Stress Disorder, as it was by then called. In addition, it was concluded that over 960,000 men and 1,900 women, between a quarter and a third of all who served in Vietnam, had at one time or another had the full-blown disorder.[2]

Yet if we then do a fast rewind back to 1967, we find a very different picture. That year, a leading Army psychiatrist declares that 'the incidence of neuropsychiatric illness in US troops in Vietnam is lower than any recorded in any previous conflicts.' Admittedly, that was early on in the war, when things were still going relatively well. But as late as 1970, the respected medical researcher Dr Peter Bourne was writing that the Vietnam experience was yielding new information about how some people are more vulnerable in combat than others, and that 'command', by making use of this new research, had been able significantly to enhance the adaptive capacity of most men. In fact, said Dr Bourne, 'there is reason to be optimistic that psychiatric casualties need never again become a major cause of attrition in the Unites States military in a combat zone.'[3]

I've chosen extremes at either end to accentuate the contrast, but neither the 1990 study nor Dr Bourne's 1970 research are one-off aberrations. They reflect an extraordinary contrast in perception, in understanding of what was going on in Vietnam, which has still not been adequately explained. What did do the damage in Vietnam and why was it not noticed at the time?

*　　*　　*

The main outlines of the Vietnam War are too familiar from memoirs, 'oral' histories and movies to need more than brief redrawing here. Vietnam was a different war, that's the first thing everyone says. Different because, instead of being a full-blooded war of national survival, Vietnam was, for the Americans, a guerrilla war, an insurgent war, fought without clear military objectives and no front line, with some constraints on freedom of military action. Furthermore, it was fought by soldiers on year-long tours of duty, a third of them conscripts; and it was a war fought amidst a civilian population, some of whom were friendly and some of whom were not. It was a foul, vicious, technologically overwhelming war, but one in which most of the fighting took place at night, in small-scale actions where the enemy was seldom seen, in hostile, impenetrable jungle.[4]

Medically, too, Vietnam was different. Most Americans wounded in the field there would be in a hospital within an hour; on an operating table in Japan within two. Those same helicopters flew in breakfast and dinner for soldiers operating in the field. It was also different in another way. There was military psychiatry from the start, not from the point where things began to go wrong; it was different because this time the military saw the need for psychiatrists and psychiatrists understood their function in the military, so there didn't have to be all that manoeuvring and neglect before the programme came into effect.[5]

Korea had seen to that. The Korean War came as a terrible shock to the United States. Hastily responding to the communist invasion in June 1950, Washington sent to Korea 'one of the least professional, least motivated armies America had ever put into the field', which at first proved incapable of standing up to advancing waves of North Korean and then Chinese troops. 'There was just mass hysteria in the position,' one American soldier later recalled of a Chinese attack. 'It was every man for himself. The shooting was terrific, there were Chinese shouting everywhere. I didn't know which way to go. In the end, I just ran with the crowd. We just ran and ran until the bugles grew fainter.' 'This is a sight which hasn't been seen for hundreds of years,' an officer remarked at the time. 'Men of the whole United States Army fleeing from a battlefield, abandoning the wounded, running for their lives.'[6]

Had General Mathew Ridgeway not been sent out to take command at the end of 1950, and had Ridgeway not quickly restored morale by firm and effective leadership, the Truman administration might have been tempted to heed the pleas of the military and to use the newly-developed tactical nuclear weapons to keep the communists at bay. As it was, a stalemate developed. Talk of peace began as early as June 1951, but it was not until two years later that an armistice was finally signed. For soldiers, that meant two years of static trench warfare on World War One lines – a mixture of cold, boredom, bad food, fear and endless patrolling. Korea was an unattractive place to the American soldier, its people barbarous and without charm. Understandably, the GIs' attitude was 'How soon can we get t'hell out of this goddam country?'[7]

Army doctors only hinted at the morale problem they faced in Korea. The modern young man, two psychiatrists wrote, had 'only vicarious experience in the stern business of sacrifice for the sake of duty [and] little call to live dangerously'. He had been 'pretty well conditioned to regard aggressiveness as an unwonted, dangerous thing.' It was difficult to 'raise an Army when almost everyone feels he should contribute in some way other than by functioning as a rifleman'. And, to make it worse, Americans grew up to believe 'that illness relieves a man from obligation and responsibility'. The doctors found that these 'cultural self-serving, self-deceiving concepts' came together in the oft-repeated statement, '"Why sure,

Doc, I want to return to duty, I want to fight for my country, but you'll have to cure my back first".'[8]

At first the Army in Korea ignored the lessons of the World Wars and tried to do without psychiatrists altogether; but the level of evacuation from the front soon reached alarming levels. With the arrival in the Far East of Colonel Albert J. Glass, one of Fred Hanson's lieutenants in the Mediterranean in 1943–4, things changed. Glass didn't just reinstate the World War Two arrangements, he improved on them. He put psychiatrists in at the division level, but also began an energetic programme to teach medical officers nearer the front, at regimental and battalion level, how to treat potential casualties as soon as possible. Aware of the disastrous mistakes his colleagues had made in North Africa and Sicily because of their initial ignorance of combat conditions and reluctance to send men back into battle, Glass made a point of immersing psychiatrists in front line realities from the start, so that they could understand the needs of the Army as a whole and not 'overidentify' with individual patients. 'With this change,' he wrote, 'the psychiatrist lost anxiety and guilt when making decisions because he became convinced that it is in the best interest of the individual to rejoin his combat unit, for in no other way can the individual regain confidence and mastery of the situation and prevent chronic tension and guilt.'[9]

Korean experience reinforced Moe Kaufman's observations in the Pacific: that the interests of the individual and of the military were one and the same. Any psychiatrist finding it 'easier to send a frightened young soldier who reminds one of one's own self or of one's own son, to the rear, than to return him to combat duty' should realise that medically to evacuate a patient who had 'not yet performed with the degree of honour required of him by both his superego and the community as he sees it' was 'the greatest possible psychiatric mishandling, and the greatest possible unkindness', for it aided him to 'burn his bridges behind him' and made his guilt irrevocable. The soldier must be denied any possibility of 'gain' from his illness and must never be allowed even to hope for evacuation. The doctor had to be 'firm, decisive, fair, moderate and brief in his statements'. There was no need for 'uncovering therapies' – like abreaction or narcosynthesis – with or without drugs.[10]

The literature on Korea is thin and was written now by Army professionals with records to protect, more inclined to put service loyalty before scientific truth. Yet the available evidence suggests that the very tough psychiatric programme in Korea was a success. After the first three months, levels of psychiatric casualties fell to almost nothing, a development helped, it was thought, by the introduction of a policy of 'rotation' whereby soldiers were removed from the line after nine months. For the Americans, then, Korea became a successful application of experience, an example of what could be achieved by applying 'well-known principles of combat psychiatric management, without having to learn it all over again, the hard way'.[11]

Its success in Korea firmly established military psychiatry as a separate branch of American medicine. The Army now had full-time psychiatrists, who began for the first time to write about their history. Over and over they repeated the same story: how the basic principles of military psychiatry were formulated by Tom Salmon in the Great War, forgotten and rediscovered in 1941–4 and then reapplied in Korea. They also reduced the lessons of the past to a simple, pat instructor's formula – PIE: Proximity, Immediacy, Expectancy. Psychiatric casualties should be treated near to the line (Proximity), as soon as possible (Immediacy), in an atmosphere that encouraged men to return to their units (Expectancy). Any medical student could get hold of that.[12]

Psychiatrists were now accepted by the Army. In a speech in 1962, General William C. Westmoreland, then Superintendent of West Point and soon to take command in Vietnam, declared that although some generals and many soldiers were still 'leery of ... "Head Shrinking",' he had found psychiatrists to be 'ordinary fellows' with 'specialised skills and knowledge', 'conscientiously trying to do their job and contribute to the conservation and effective utilization of manpower.' In January 1966, there were no less than 274 'shrinks' working for the United States Army, 227 clinically active, 47 in training. Sixty-two were regulars, the rest held reserve status. Twenty-nine were stationed in Germany, and only eleven in Vietnam itself, though a further thirteen were working in Okinawa, Japan, and Hawaii. A year or two later the number in Vietnam had risen, but it never exceeded 20. No one of the calibre of Tom Salmon, Roy Grinker or Fred Hanson emerged.[13]

* * *

The writings of psychiatrists in Vietnam often reveal more about their own dilemmas and states of mind than those of the men they were serving. They also faithfully chart the emotional trajectory of the war, from high confidence to despair.

Early reports are matter of fact, optimistic and rather dull. The Divisional Psychiatrist to the Tropical Lighting Division between 1965 and 1966, when the war was still 'limited' and there were only 200,000 US troops in Vietnam, reported high morale, good food, and very few psychiatric cases, which were nearly always among drunken support troops at the enormous American base at Chu Chi, not among combat soldiers. He had so little to do that he volunteered to join a medical team helping the local Vietnamese village.[14]

Equally upbeat was Dr Spencer Bloch, who reported applying the principles of proximity, immediacy and expectancy in one of the two main treatment centres at which 'psychiatrically sophisticated treatment' was attempted between August 1967 and July 1968. He told, in tones of modest self-congratulation, how he had reduced the evacuation rate by a half. Again, very few of his patients were combat soldiers, who were usually treated much closer to the front line.[15]

By then, however, the mood was changing. The North Vietnamese showed in the Tet Offensive of 1968 that they would be harder to defeat than the Pentagon had believed; thereafter, the American media took a more sceptical tone towards the war. Back in the United States, generational conflicts were coming to the boil.

* * *

Anyone who lived through the 1960s remembers the extraordinary way social values changed in that decade. 'Up until 1964,' one Vietnam veteran later recalled, 'I was told to obey my parents, obey my teachers, go to college, plan my life. By September 1965, it was "Do anything you want to do. It's okay". I recall it as a time of enormous freedom. Everything changed. All attitudes toward power figures, authority figures. Respect for authority truly broke down. In college we were just against everything.' The war in Asia became unpopular among many middle-class young men who might be sent to fight in it; they took steps to avoid it. 'The draft,' Lawrence Baskir and William Strauss have argued, 'worked as an instrument of Darwinian social policy. The "fittest" – those with background, wit or money – managed to escape. Through an elaborate structure of deferments, exemptions, legal technicalities and non-combatant military alternatives, the draft rewarded those who manipulated the system to their advantage.'[16]

If manipulating the system didn't work, you could try cheating in your medical. In the classic account, a group of well-fed Harvard men persuade medical examiners they are unfit to serve and then watch guiltily as a busload of draftees from the poorer districts of Boston arrives to fill the Army's quota. Psychiatry helped to emphasise the social divide. On the one hand, it gave the more educated a useful shield: 'a reputable psychiatrist's letter works wonders with draft boards,' readers of *How to Beat the Draft* (1968) were told, and one New York analyst was said to have written 75 letters a week, at $250 a time, certifying men as 'emotionally unfit for military duties', though Selective Service doctors claimed to ignore them. Those seeking to avoid the draft were, one psychiatrist wrote, usually 'passive-aggressive, father- and authority-hating men, who tended to identify with their mothers.'[17]

On the other hand, psychiatry failed to discharge its most basic function: it did not eliminate the vulnerable. Because of the failure of Harry Stack Sullivan's over-ambitious programme in World War Two, 'routine screening of all inductees was abandoned' and 'only persons with gross psychiatric disability were rejected' in the Vietnam era. What was more, the Pentagon – in a move dressed up as part of President Johnson's Great Society programme, bringing opportunity to the disadvantaged – relaxed the standards relating to recruits' intelligence in order to meet its manpower needs. It accepted people with an IQ as low as 62, who were then cruelly called 'MacNamara's Morons' (after Secretary of Defense Robert MacNamara). Officially known as 'Project 100,000' the scheme ultimately took in some 350,000 recruits, of whom 40% were African-Americans. Some 140,000 of these troops were trained for combat.[18]

Vietnam was a 'class war': the burden of the fighting was unfairly borne by ethnic minorities and the poor, though some historians have since conducted a 'bitter and slippery methodological dispute' in an attempt to prove otherwise. In 1965, the Pentagon grew concerned that a quarter of those dying in Vietnam were African-American and took steps to reduce the figure. Overall, 12.5% of the dead were black, but 'discrimination against the young, the under-educated and the poor' continued. It was 'not an equal opportunity war'.[19]

Psychiatrists were overwhelmingly white. The ethnic factor was another reason why, in Vietnam, the ethical conflicts which lie at the heart of military psychiatry came into the open:

Is the military psychiatrist justified in rapidly treating combat fatigue? Is the physician ethical in using his patient's guilt about deserting his comrades and his identification with his unit in order to have him quickly returned to combat, where he might soon be killed? Should not the psychiatrist help the soldier to rationalise that he was in fact fighting in a wicked war? Should not the psychiatrist affirm that all wars are wicked, that the patient's own self-interest lay in expunging all sense of guilt or obligation to others and in seeing, in a clear-eyed way, what is best for him?[20]

Dr Ransom Arthur, an experienced US Navy physician, believed that such 'Hamlet-like dilemma[s]' only 'became a serious concern within the context of an affluent society in the midst of a distant and unpopular war in which national survival was not in jeopardy'. Such 'ethical fastidiousness' was a luxury enjoyed only by pampered baby boomers. 'Most people,' he thought, 'through one mental process or another, manage to reconcile their duties as citizens, physicians, and organizational members without serious moral repugnance.'[21]

Some younger doctors didn't see it that way. Take, for example, Major Gordon Livingston – a product of West Point, the elite 82nd Airborne Division and Johns Hopkins medical school – who arrived in Vietnam in November 1968. Livingston was sent as regimental surgeon to the Eleventh Armoured Cavalry regiment, commanded by Colonel George S. Patton junior, son of old 'Blood and Guts', and found himself as a member of the staff eating at his table and attending his nightly briefings. Before leaving the States, Livingston had attended an intensive State Department course on the politics, culture and religion of South Vietnam. Now, in Bien Hoa, he quickly discovered that 'most Americans simply [did] not care about the Vietnamese . . . the attitude of our people on the ground, military and civilian [was] one of nearly universal contempt.' Livingston was appalled by the callousness shown to the Vietnamese – women on bicycles being deliberately run down by a helicopter, soldiers driving their vehicles through rice fields and showering villagers with filth while they were eating. His fellow Americans, he felt, were blind to the pride and identity of a sensitive and intelligent people.[22]

To him, the real battle was political; yet the military ignored this, concentrating on their own professional self-interest in war and destruction. Colonel Patton 'received numerous decorations while pursuing unrelentingly the one major criterion by which a commander's performance is judged: the body count'. The regimental chaplain prayed for 'the wisdom to find the bastards and strength to pile it on'. Livingston's efforts to bring medicine to the local people were completely irrelevant. He was also 'confronted by cases of combat neurosis who told me that they saw nothing in what they were doing that justified the risks they were being asked to take'. 'In effect,' he wrote, 'they had seen enough of death to know that they preferred life. What was I to do with deviant behaviour like that?

They were given a brief respite and returned to their units; the fighting strength was conserved.'

Eventually Dr Livingston decided to protest. On Easter Sunday 1969, a change of command ceremony was held for Colonel Patton, attended by the American commander in South Vietnam, General Abrams. It was 'a true dance of death with Patton recounting his successes and Abrams awarding him the Legion of Merit'. At the climax of the proceedings, the chaplain's blessing, Livingston moved through the congregation distributing copies of a prayer he had written:

God our heavenly father, hear our prayer. We acknowledge our shortcomings and ask Thy help in being better soldiers for Thee. Grant us, O Lord, those things we need to do Thy work more effectively. Give us this day a gun that will fire 10,000 rounds a second, a napalm which will burn for a week. Help us to bring death and destruction wherever we go, for we do it in Thy name and therefore it is meet and just. We thank Thee for this war fully mindful that while it is not the best of all wars, it is better than no war at all. We remember that Christ said, 'I came not to send peace, but a sword,' and we pledge ourselves in all our works to be like Him. Forget not the least of our children as they hide from us in the jungles; bring them under our merciful hand so that we may end their suffering. In all things, O God, assist us, so we can do our noble work in the knowledge that only with Thy help can we avoid the catastrophe of peace which threatens us ever. All of which we ask in the name of Thy son, George Patton. Amen.

Livingston was immediately relieved of his duties and a month later sent back to the US as 'an embarrassment to the command'. He was not court-martialled but allowed to resign from the service. By July 1969, a civilian again, he was active in work against the war.

Few went as far as Livingston. Serving in Vietnam at the same time, Dr Edward Colbach 'decided not to be a wave making hero and . . . [to] go along with the program as best as I could. If I had a major ethic at that time,' he later wrote, 'it was that of survival.' A Catholic from a middle-American household, recently qualified, with a wife, child and sick parents, he desperately wanted *not* to be sent to Vietnam. Having been told in training that the duty of the military psychiatrist was to 'conserve the fighting strength', he did his best to carry out that order; but was tormented by doubts about his position and role in the war.[23]

Most of the patients Colbach saw in his ten months as chief psychiatrist to a hospital at Qui Nhon on the South China Sea were support, not combat, troops; their problems related more to fitting into an Army they did not want to be part of than to fighting the Viet Cong. There was Danny, a young black kid (part of Project 100,000) who had been having troubles with a white sergeant and really should have been drafted out. But, because the 'evacuation quota' had been used up, Danny was retained in the hospital, where he shot himself – badly – with an M-16 rifle and eventually died. There was Todd, a troublesome young white kid in a support unit. The authorities did the easy thing and transferred him to a combat unit where he was immediately killed.

Colbach describes, with painful honesty, many traditional problems of military psychiatry. 'I didn't look very deeply [at patients]. I just tried to get rid of the symptom and then tried to bring about as much peer pressure as possible on the fellow to return to duty. So what if he was suffering? Wasn't everyone?' He talks frankly about his failures, like the bed-wetter he hypnotised, thought he'd cured, and sent back to his unit. This man returned soon afterwards, 'screaming my name and as psychotic as anyone could be', and had to be evacuated to Japan.[24]

Psychiatrists were supposed to get out and visit the front. Colbach admits he was too frightened to do so very often. He was also very uncomfortable with black soldiers. He particularly hated the way 'command used him as essentially . . . a rubber stamp to get rid of a troublesome fellow'; the way 'Mental Hygiene was "the rectum of the army", eliminating unwanted wastes.' But, in the end, Colbach learned to cope by acquiring a certain toughness and even began to get a sort of excitement from being in or near the war: 'for my own survival I was trying to accept the values of the military in Vietnam. I didn't like what I was doing and most of the soldiers I met didn't like what they were doing either. But so what? It wasn't a happiness factory over there. If Joe didn't do his job, Jim would have to come over from the United States to do it for him.'[25]

Colbach acknowledges that most of the work with combat troops was done not by psychiatrists, but by 'psychiatric technicians', 'usually college-educated young men who had been given a very intensive course in Army mental health.' He thought they were 'very talented and ingenious fellows . . . more easily able to identify with the enlisted men than we were'; but few have written about their work. Both psychiatrists and technicians made generous use of powerful new drugs, like the 'major tranquillizer', Thorazine. 'We used the major tranquillizers,' writes Colbach, 'not only for psychoses but all kinds of anxiety and psychosomatic states.' Many soldiers, he says, 'went into the field with Thorazine or Mellaril in their pockets.'

Among ourselves we debated whether this was really a good idea. Obviously the medication made people less alert. At the same time, though, excessive anxiety could be very harmful to functioning. In civilian life no one would ever operate a motor vehicle while on such medication. In Vietnam they regularly did. Our job was to keep the Army functioning.[26]

By the time Dr Norman Camp went to Vietnam in 1970, opposition to the war had developed further; anti-war demonstrations were sweeping Washington as he completed his training at Walter Reed hospital nearby. Camp had his own doubts about the war but felt it was his duty to go (though he noticed that many of his fellow Army psychiatrists managed not to). Arriving in Vietnam, he was surprised to be put in command of the psychiatric section of a hospital at Da Nang. He soon learnt that the entire mental health team in the hospital had recently been disbanded after carrying on an agitation against the war; it was hoped that he, as a recent graduate of Walter Reed, would be more loyal. The hospital itself was in a state of undeclared war. Patients threatened doctors whose diagnosis they disliked, the neurologist on Camp's team was nowhere to be seen, hiding from a soldier trying to kill him and the barracks of the hospital 'had become the exclusive territory of the "brothers"'(black enlisted soldiers).

The pervasive despair was glaringly evident with practically every encounter with a service member, almost regardless of rank. Especially noticeable were the intentionally provocative behaviours of the black soldiers.[27]

A few days later, an unexploded grenade was found on the officer's volley-ball court – an example of the practice of 'fragging' (GIs trying to kill their officers), then becoming widespread. To cap it all, a heroin epidemic had begun. Little wonder that one account of psychiatry in Vietnam at this time is subtitled: 'Portrait of anarchy'.[28]

By now, military psychiatrists in Vietnam were coming under attack from their own profession. The old formula that you helped the individual by helping the military was now dismissed. 'By acting to "conserve the fighting strength" in this war of boundless immorality', they were, said one critic, 'partak[ing] of the passive complicity which is the mark of guilt in our time'. 'Managerial technicism,' said another, was taking 'reasonably decent practitioners' into 'ethical corruption'. Comparisons were made with the Nazi doctors. In May 1971, the American Psychiatric Association passed a motion 'add[ing] its voice to the great masses of the American people who have so firmly expressed their agony concerning the war in South East Asia' and voiced concerns about its 'grave effects on morale and on the rate of alienation, dehumanization and divisiveness among the American people'.[29]

The anguished and divided mood of the times began to pervade the clinical literature. 'As I finish the final draft of this paper,' a veteran turned psycho-therapist wrote on 28 April 1975, 'President Minh announces the surrender of the Saigon government. It is over. I am in tears with pain and bitterness.'[30]

*　*　*

In 1966 two Pentagon doctors had reported that psychiatric casualties in Vietnam were lower than in any previous war. The reasons for this, they said, were quite clear: no one served in that theatre of war for longer than a year; there was plenty of rest and recreation during the tour of duty; battles were short; soldiers had to endure few major artillery barrages; and their morale was high. The major psychological bogeys of the past, especially combat exhaustion, had been overcome. There was 'not the sense of hopelessness that prevailed in previous conflicts, where death, injury and peace became the only possible ways in which the soldier could find himself extricated from conflict.' Four years later, a divisional psychiatrist in Vietnam was still reeling off the traditional tale, how psychiatric casualties had fallen from a high of 101 per 1,000 troops in World War Two to 37 per 1,000 in Korea, to 12 per 1,000 in Vietnam.[31]

Official accounts at this time saw Vietnam very much as a continuation of previous wars, with the 'accumulated knowledge' of the past being successfully applied. They did, however, recognise one new element: the role of 'stress'. As a word, 'stress' was nothing new and had turned up frequently in earlier wars, used in a loose metaphorical way. Akin to 'distress', 'stress' meant 'a strain upon endurance', but it was also used in a more specialist way by engineers to denote the external pressures on a structure – the effects of 'stress' within the structure being known as 'strain'. Then in 1935 the Czech-Canadian physiologist Hans Selye began to promote 'stress' as a medical term, denoting the body's response to general external pressures (he later admitted that, new to the English language, he had picked the wrong word; 'strain' was what he had meant). Academic physiologists regarded the concept of stress as too vague to be scientifically useful, but Selye's determined self-promotion, coupled with the upheaval and distress brought by the war to many millions of ordinary people, popularised the term.[32]

By the time of Vietnam, 'stress' had become a well-established part of military medicine, thought to be a valuable tool in reducing 'wastage'. In the military context, it was an extension of the work done at the end of the First World War on the long-term effects of fear and other emotions on the human system and seemed to address the underlying problem of soldiers, the continuous long drawn-out strain, rather than just the moment of trauma or horror which precipitated a collapse. 'Stress,' writes the historian Russell Viner, 'was pictured as a weapon, to be used in the waging of psychological warfare against the enemy, and Stress research as a shield or vaccination against the contagious germ of fear.' Not only did the one-year tour of duty make sense in terms of 'stress'; Army physicians in Vietnam also spent much time measuring the effects on the heart, blood, urine and endocrine system of such 'stressful' activities as piloting combat helicopters.[33]

*   *   *

The psychiatrists on the ground in Vietnam were young, inexperienced and, on the whole, anxious to keep their heads down. They had also been taught that 'combat fatigue' was the main problem in war and that they must keep up the fighting strength. But they were not blind. Some saw that things were not quite as they seemed and that Vietnam was not the same as previous wars.

For one thing, the policy of twelve-month rotation undermined unit cohesion among the troops. Every soldier's internal life was now ruled by his calendar, his private clock, his sense of waiting for his own year-long term to be up. 'Every man knows the exact number of days he has left to serve in the country, and as a result he sees himself as fighting directly for his own survival.' One consequence of this was 'Short-Termer's Syndrome', the reluctance of soldiers to risk their lives when their year in Asia was nearly up.

As a person's tour . . . nears its end, the individual begins to withdraw that part of his emotional energy which has been tied up in his group there. This is done in preparation for investing it all again in the relationships back home.[34]

Secondly, official statistics began to be questioned. The classic psychiatric casualties were indeed low, but the incidence of 'character disorders' was high and, as the conscript element in the American force increased in the late 1960s, growing. Yet, because the Army did not consider such behaviour 'psychiatric diseases', these cases were not usually seen by psychiatrists. Instead, they were discharged through 'administrative channels' and did not appear in the statistics. By 1970, the phrase 'acting out' was beginning to be used: 'contemporary youth,' it was said, expressed its 'emotional maladjustment' by 'acting out behaviour rather than by internalization or somatization'. They 'let it all hang out'. Could it be, psychiatrists wondered, that, just as symptoms had taken the form of shell-shock in World War One and combat exhaustion in World War Two, so 'behaviour disorders' were the typical symptoms of Vietnam?[35]

'Acting out', some psychiatrists argued, reflected the soldier's alienation from the war, his 'confrontation with the tragic absurdity of risking his life or of killing other human beings in this meaningless military exercise', his wish to extract himself from the situation. Traditionalists like Dr Bloch disagreed. It was nonsense to say that the typical psychiatric casualty in Vietnam wanted to get out of the war for moral reasons. Men were just frightened or homesick; those who claimed to have moral scruples about the war were rationalising their guilt at abandoning buddies.[36]

Amidst all the jargon, telling details stand out: signs of indiscipline, like the unit in which 'an enlisted man's acceptance by his peer group was in part dependent on his contracting gonorrhoea'; and signs of racial tension. One black enlisted man was described as 'uncooperative, hostile, provocative, disrespectful and incapable of soldiering'. Investigation revealed a tense situation in the soldier's unit in which 'expressions of Black Pride and "brotherhood" were being interpreted by some cadre members as threatening.'[37]

All these concerns came together in the issue of drugs

Soldiers have always used drugs, mainly alcohol. By the mid-1960s, the drug culture had arrived in the United States and, with marijuana freely available in Vietnam, it was natural that American soldiers should smoke it there. Support troops were the heaviest users, but combat units turned to it between episodes in battle. It was felt by some to be 'a relaxant of tension and a way of bonding with peers'. Its 'sedative and tranquilizing properties helped reduce anxiety and blunt the hyperarousal state so frequently seen between periods of combat'. 'Many men,' it was argued, 'may actually have been helped in their attempts to cope with a tremendously stressful situation.' In Vietnam, where 'peer group ties assumed heightened importance', two psychiatrists wrote in 1975, 'marijuana often became the sacrament which bound a group together. Its tranquilizing and euphorgenic properties allowed combat losses to be temporarily forgotten while new relationships were solidified.' But marijuana was an illegal drug and the Army brass got very exercised about its use.[38]

Despite repeated efforts to stop it, the smoking of marijuana continued through the war. But by the middle of 1970 a heroin epidemic was also well underway; any visitor to Vietnam 'would have seen soldiers intoxicated on "skag" and heard the crunch of empty plastic vials splintering beneath his feet.' At this time, heroin was still very much a drug taken by urban blacks in the United States; the number of white users quite small. But in Vietnam heroin that was 90 to 96% pure and very cheap became widely available: 'nearly every barracks maid and taxi driver can now furnish a hit, and Vietnamese children barely out of infancy loll along the truck routes and major highways to make quick fortunes as long convoys rumble by.' Heroin became the drug of choice because of its 'potency, availability and difficulty of detection.' By late 1970 one-fifth of the Army was thought to be 'addicted to narcotics' and the following year more soldiers were being evacuated from Vietnam for drug use than for wounds.[39]

Heroin was taken partly because of the Army's heavy-handed crackdown on the milder but more easily detectable marijuana and partly because greedy South Vietnamese drug barons made it available. But a young Chicago doctor working in Saigon in 1971 also thought heroin use was just 'the visible tip of an iceberg of despair', and doubted 'if we can rid ourselves of heroin unless we can melt the iceberg of despair' – made up of boredom, harassment and a sense of futility. Heroin was a 'way to turn the place off', a 'highly practical escape route in the short run, since it provides a reduction in tension without, if undetected, anyone knowing the soldier has "escaped".'[40]

The scale of the drug epidemic forced psychiatrists to look beneath the surface. They found that soldiers in Vietnam did not simply count the days till their return but saw their time in Asia as a limbo till they could return to 'the world'. Drugs, they began to realise, defined the whole culture of some soldiers:

Initiation of heroin use tended to occur early in the tour – usually in the first three or four months. The usual source of the drug on this first occasion was another soldier. The drug was taken in an informal social context established by a 'head' group. In Vietnam, a 'head' was a person who 'did' either dew (marijuana) or skag (heroin) in an appropriate group context. In Vietnam the consumption of marijuana was a group-validated activity which could be indulged in either alone or with others of the group. Several soldiers would get together in the evening to 'blow pot' and to attend such gatherings was to identify oneself as a 'head'. The heroin-using population was a smaller sub-set of this 'head' group, which was protected as having the right 'to do their thing' (heroin).[41]

It turned out that in most company-sized units there was a 'stable group of men organised around consumption of marijuana, heroin or other drugs. Group members would act together to ensure supply, initiate new members, protect users from detection and 'maintain a particular set of values'. Usually, members were both black and white and the more fundamental antagonism was between them and regular soldiers ('lifers') and drinkers of alcohol ('juicers').

In fact, some later argued, the kind of 'primary groups' found in the Second World War were reconstellated in Vietnam around drugs and alcohol. 'The juicers and the heads became primary group identities and provided ideologies that affect the way the men perceived what happened to them day-to-day, and the way they evaluate the purpose of American military presence in Vietnam . . . Beer symbolized the juicers' solidarity around the enlisted men's club, whorehouse raids, gang rapes, arson, shooting civilians and fights with blacks . . . the men were ideologically and behaviourally transformed into compliers with military rules and discipline and noncompliers.'[42]

Precisely because it had such deep social roots, the drug problem proved very difficult to treat. In many ways, the Army didn't want to know about it. 'Command was hysterical,' Dr Camp recalls, 'eager to get these people out of their hair.' His hospital was flooded with drug cases and he and his colleagues fought a losing battle to keep beds for psychiatric patients. The soldiers themselves were keen to get evacuated out of Vietnam as medical cases and did all they could to maximise their symptoms. Meanwhile, in some parts of the military, an amnesty programme was in force, offering freedom from prosecution to soldiers who came forward for treatment.[43]

The situation was further complicated when the public and the politicians heard about the heroin problem. In June 1971 President Nixon announced a 'war against drug abuse', the main effect of which was the introduction of urine testing at the end of the tour of duty. It was called 'Operation Golden Flow'. No one would get on a plane home if his urine was 'dirty'. Random urine sampling was also introduced. The effect of these measures, the Army believed, was to 'effectively reverse a heroin epidemic', but statistics failed to pick up the numbers of people who gave up heroin a week or so before the final test and underwent 'cold turkey' (known as 'Jonesing') on their own. Working at the Amnesty Centre in Saigon, Dr Robert Ratner estimated that about a third of lower ranking enlisted men were regular heroin users, yet the official figures showed a detection rate of only some 5%.[44]

Did Vietnam turn a generation into junkies? Many doctors doubt that it did, accepting the men's assurances that it was only in Vietnam that they took drugs. 'Back in the world', confronted by the disapproval of friends and family, the stigma of being a 'junkie', it would be different. That is still Dr Camp's view: 'these guys were not addicted, just habituated'. Smoking pure heroin, rather than mainlining the version of the drug sold on the streets back home, they did not have physical dependency. 'They were healthy individuals,' he said in 1994. Others were more sceptical. 'Their expressed intention,' Dr Harry Holloway wrote in 1974, 'was to leave their habits behind them in Vietnam. Whether this jejune prediction was correct is unknown.'[45]

Although it would be easy to exaggerate the scale of the problem, there certainly was an enormous amount of drug taking in Vietnam. What is much more difficult to assess is the *effect* of drug use, which requires subjective judgement. Several authors assert that marijuana and heroin were not used by troops in combat and did not affect their military effectiveness. Against that, a substantial body of anecdotal evidence suggests that drug use did hamper the efficiency of the army.

If, however, we return to the substantive question – what did the damage in Vietnam – then clearly drugs *are* important, both in themselves and for what they reveal about the climate of moral numbness and the sub-culture of alienation among soldiers serving in Vietnam. It has also been suggested that the widespread availability of tranquillisers like chlorpromazine and drugs like heroin may have made it more difficult for soldiers to 'process' what they were feeling at the time and to 'express or "abreact" their emotional responses' later on.[46]

In 1975, the year the war ended, two psychiatrists speculated on the prospects for veterans. 'One may predict,' they wrote, 'that, after a latency period characterized by relief and relatively good functioning, typical stress response symptoms may appear ... We are predicting general and delayed stress response syndromes . . .'[47]

FROM POST-VIETNAM SYNDROME TO POST-TRAUMATIC STRESS DISORDER

There is no trauma field without advocacy.
Dr Arthur S. Blank, Jr.[1]

More than any other war in the twentieth century, Vietnam redefined the social role of psychiatry and society's perception of mental health. Five years after the fall of Saigon, a new psychiatric term was devised, tailored to the needs of veterans. Psychiatric counselling was made available on an unparalleled scale, paid for by the United States government. Even more significantly, Vietnam helped to create a new 'consciousness of trauma' in Western society.

Some see this train of events as a triumph, a 'self-help success story', in which 'informed public opinion prevailed' and a group of victims fought for their rights. To others, it is a tragedy, a disastrous incursion of politics into medicine, the hijacking of traditional values by a small minority of activists, the elevation of the pathological into the mainstream.[2]

It is certainly a complex tale, into which many social, political and medical strands were woven; a story which cannot be understood without some sense of the fevered, divided mood of the United States in the early 1970s. Four main elements contributed: the acrid political aftermath of a lost war; the politics of veterans' affairs; a revolution in American psychiatry; and the legacy of the Nazi Holocaust.

The story begins in the late 1960s – when a small group in New York formed an organisation called Vietnam Veterans Against the War. Its membership remained tiny but, because they were all veterans, VVAW had a status denied to more powerful anti-war groups. After news of a massacre by American troops at the village of My Lai appeared in the press late in 1969, VVAW began to use the issue of atrocities to undermine support for the war and held a widely-publicised series of hearings into the behaviour of American forces in Vietnam at which many soldiers testified to having witnessed or committed atrocities.[3]

VVAW also organised 'rap groups' – meetings at which members talked together about their own experiences during the war and their feelings about them. These rough stabs at psychotherapy brought them into contact with the psychiatric community. In 1970, a New York analyst called Chaim Shatan was approached at a university mass meeting on 'My Lai and Kent State' by a number of veterans who told him they were 'hurting'. They either didn't want to go to the Veterans' Administration for help or they were 'ineligible'. Shatan and another prominent analyst and opponent of the war, Robert Jay Lifton of Yale, agreed to work with the groups, helping them to organise their sessions: 'They said shrinks could join provided that we joined as peers. They knew more about the war than we did, and we knew more about what makes people tick.'[4]

At one rap session Shatan attended, the men sat 'on packing cases, filing cabinets and radiators in a ramshackle downtown office building' in Manhattan. The group that day included Bob, a former Marine still seized by 'unpredictable episodes of disorientation and panic' in public places; Phil, avoiding enemy snipers six years after leaving Vietnam; Bob, a former helicopter doorgunner, only able to forget his 'pleasure in killing [his] first 16-year-old Commie for Christ' by hurtling along freeways at night on his bike; and Don, who had watched his friend die for four days in Vietnam and was ashamed of being alive when his buddy was dead.[5]

The veterans' groups also organised workshops on the themes which obsessed them, 'The John Wayne image', 'When Do we stop being Vets?' and, inevitably, 'Women and Sex'. Hallowed institutions like the Marine Corps were also questioned. Earlier generations had joined the Marines in a spirit of 'blazing patriotism' and endured the sadistic abuse of its drill instructors as a necessary price for the glory of Tarawa; every boy in America had wanted to be like John Wayne in *The Sands of Iwo Jima*. Now it was said that Marine Corps basic training – during which recruits were routinely taunted by a litany of 'You dirty faggot' and 'Can't hack it, little girl?' – produced a degraded masculinity. Recruits were whipped up into a state of quasi-sexual excitement, which had traditionally found an outlet in the short, climactic battles that won the Corps its honours. But in Vietnam there were no pitched battles, no great release of aggression and energy, just a year of tense, inconclusive, unresolved patrolling, during which the enemy was seldom seen, let alone vanquished. The ordinary Marine, whipped up to pitch of sexual frenzy, never 'got his gun off'. Consequently, many men sought an outlet in atrocities and in brutal, sadistic sex with Vietnamese women.[6]

One member of the early rap groups remembers that they helped him to understand why he felt as he did. 'We had these shrinks but we weren't really in therapy,' Jack Smith, a former Marine, said in 1988. 'We were trying to understand what we were feeling about the war . . . it was a safe place to talk . . .We weren't thinking of ourselves as victims, but rather thinking, "How are we going to get our act together so we're not undone by our feelings about what's going on, and how are we going to convey what's going on to the general public?"' 'The vets who came to the early rap groups,' Arthur Egendorf recalled, 'brought with them, as an overwhelming residue from the war, a deep demoralization and loss of trust in their leaders, in the cause, and in the person they were before going in.' 'When I went to Vietnam,' said one, 'I believed both in Jesus Christ and John Wayne. After Vietnam, both went down the tubes. It didn't mean nothing.' The poet Robert Bly later wrote that 'when the Vietnam veteran arrived home, he found a large hole in himself where his values were.'[7]

One way for members of VVAW to rediscover a sense of values was through political activism. The high point of the movement, for many, was a demonstration in Washington in April 1971 when veterans staged a 'medal turn-in' ceremony. Jack Smith found it 'probably the most powerful moment of my life'. It was 'enormously cathartic,' another veteran agreed: '[For] all of us who did [it], it was as if we had a device for throwing our sins away.' But, with the scaling down of the American presence in Vietnam – the last soldier came home in 1973 – political opposition to the war became muted and Vietnam Veterans Against the War 'splintered into warring regional and ideological factions.'[8]

However, from these beginnings emerged a more broadly-based movement, the National Veterans Resource Project, bringing together veterans, psychiatrists and members of religious groups, which aimed to get the needs of Vietnam veterans across to the public, politicians and psychiatrists. For, increasingly, it came to be felt that the war had left a psychological aftermath on all who fought in it; that there was a 'Post-Vietnam Syndrome'.

* * *

The aftermath of Vietnam first really claimed public attention on 30 April 1971, the day that Sergeant Johnson was shot.

In Vietnam, Sergeant Dwight Johnson had won the Medal of Honour, the United States' highest decoration for valour, for single-handedly knocking out twenty enemy soldiers during a raid on his position. He had then served with distinction for another two years, but on returning home, found difficulty in readjusting to civilian life. He became convinced that the Army exploited all black soldiers and made no effort to help them afterwards; Army psychiatrists did not change this view. His frustrations grew until he decided to deploy in his rundown Chicago neighbourhood the skills he had shown in Vietnam. He was robbing a liquor store when he was killed.[9]

The fact that a heavily decorated soldier could behave in this way shocked public opinion and put veterans' issues on the map. A year later, the *New York Times* carried an article by Dr Shatan on the 'Post-Vietnam Syndrome', a term veterans detested and psychiatrists were uneasy with, yet whose 'evocative quality' and 'availability as catchall' made it 'widely used by almost everyone'. According to Shatan, Post-Vietnam Syndrome often set in nine to thirty months after the return from Asia. Men would notice, often for the first time, 'growing apathy, cynicism, alienation, depression, mistrust and expectation of betrayal, as well as an inability to concentrate, insomnia, nightmares, restlessness, uprootedness, and impatience with almost any job or course of study.' They were suffering, he said, from 'delayed massive trauma', guilt feelings and self-punishment, the feeling of being scapegoated, rage, psychic numbing and alienation from their feelings – in short, from 'impacted grief'.

The so-called Post-Vietnam Syndrome confronts us with the unconsummated grief of soldiers – impacted grief, in which an encapsulated, never-ending past deprives the present of meaning. Their sorrow is unspent, the grief of their wounds is untold, their guilt is unexpiated. Much of what passes for cynicism is really the veterans' numbed apathy from a surfeit of bereavement and death.[10]

This was powerful and eloquent, but also vague and hyperbolic. Army psychiatrists hit back, accusing Shatan and Lifton of making politically-motivated generalisations from a tiny sample. Just because the small group of anti-war veterans they had worked with had these problems didn't mean *all* Vietnam veterans were similarly maladjusted. This was a telling point; but, in making it, the military doctors relied on data derived from small samples of Vietnam veterans still in the Army, in garrisons in the United States; no follow-ups had been done on veterans back in civilian life. The Army's studies tended to show that *all* soldiers were miserable and taking drugs, whether they had been in Vietnam or not. The more intelligent Army psychiatrists were also aware that much more should have been done to ease the process of readjustment to civilian life by providing 'reorientation programs' to soldiers while they were still in the Army. The contrast between the imaginative, confident leadership shown by Menninger in 1945 and the feeble buck-passing thirty years later pained them.[11]

The truth – which, in a less charged atmosphere, would have been acknowledged – was that many Vietnamese veterans *were* having troubles readjusting to civilian life, as all returning veterans do, both practical and emotional problems. Like earlier generations, they had built up unrealistic fantasies about their home lives, received 'Dear John' letters, developed 'passive-dependent' needs of the kind described by Roy Grinker in the 1940s, and were having to adapt to changes in their absence. But there were also elements about Vietnam that aggravated the usual difficulties. For all the technological wizardry of the war, no thought seems to have gone into understanding the basic dynamics of 're-entry'. Soldiers usually returned home from Asia abruptly, by aeroplane, and as individuals (where their World War Two equivalents had sailed slowly home with other members of their units). They were not welcomed as heroes; indeed the opposition to the war meant that some were reviled:

The day I arrived home a woman of my own age walked up to me with several of her friends, while I was waiting for a bus, at the Newark New Jersey Airport and asked me if I had been in Vietnam. When I responded that this was my first day home she spat in my face and the group let loose with a barrage of insults. I don't think that she knew then that her spit would forever stain my face. It is not possible to wipe that spittle clean. It is on my face today.[12]

Not only were there 'no victory parades', there were fewer jobs: the great post-war economic boom was over and full employment a thing of the past, especially in the sectors of society from which many veterans came. The therapeutic power of work was not automatically available, as it had been in 1945. Relations between the sexes, too, were changing. The arrival of feminism and the unpopularity of the war left middle-class women reluctant to provide the mothering they had so readily given in the 1940s; the warm, supportive, female embrace was no longer as easily available.

All these issues, though, were poisoned by political divisions. The Nixon administration was trying to end the war while pursuing and harassing its domestic opponents, including Shatan and Lifton, whose links to Vietnam Veterans Against the War led to their mail being tampered with. In August 1971, following the publication of the *Pentagon Papers*, the President himself authorised a break-in at the offices of Dr Daniel Ellsberg's psychiatrist; eleven months later, on 17 June 1972, the five 'Watergate' burglars were arrested. In this climate of polarisation, it was probably inevitable that battle lines should be drawn, with one side denying that the war had had any effects at all and the other overstating its consequences.[13]

The mood of those times has been evoked by one of the moving spirits in the veterans' movement. 'In the mid-1970s,' the psychologist Charles R. Figley has written, 'the mental health professions barely recognized the plight of the emotionally disabled Vietnam veteran.' There was a division between hawks and doves. 'Hawkish' psychiatrists maintained that the psychiatrists' dictionary of mental disorders did not recognise combat fatigue or any other stress disorder originating from a catastrophic event. Whereas, continues Figley, 'Perhaps with some overreaction, "dovish" psychiatrists and other practitioners believed that emotional disorders among returning veterans could reach epidemic proportions. The post-Vietnam syndrome became a frightening buzz word among clinicians and journalists, but in fact was a thinly veiled position of opposition to the war: stop the war or more young killers will be released to terrorize the population.'[14]

The 'doves' were influenced, too, by the growing psychiatric literature on two terrible episodes in the recent past, the Holocaust and Hiroshima.

Nowadays, we routinely talk about 'the Holocaust'. There are Holocaust Museums around the world, Holocaust days, and – it must be said – something of an Holocaust industry. Yet little of this existed in 1970. Similarly, the emotional after-effects of the Nazis' Final Solution on those of its victims who survived took time to reveal themselves. Immediately after the war, everyone had wanted to forget, to get on with building new lives. A few doctors and psychoanalysts had lingered on what the camps had revealed about human behaviour, but most people wanted to move on.[15]

In the late 1950s, however, two things happened. Doctors in Scandinavia began to study the Holocaust survivor population there – which was small enough to trace and monitor – and found that many of its members were having problems. Secondly, the issue of compensation arose. The West German government offered reparations to camp victims, but only if a causal link could be established between their current ill-health and the traumatic experiences they had undergone. A number of German 'experts' then testified in the German courts that it was 'common knowledge that all psychic traumata, of whatever degree or duration, lose their effects when the psychologically traumatizing event ceases to operate'. One German psychiatrist even stated that a man who had spent most of his early childhood hiding in a cellar, being stifled or even choked into silence in case he revealed his parents' hiding place, could not have been damaged because 'he was quite young at the time of the war and would have forgotten it all.'[16]

The gauntlet was thus thrown down – to all psychiatrists outside Germany, but doubly to Jewish psychoanalysts – to prove that the effects of that experience *were* prolonged. Whereas most medical work on veterans had hitherto been carried out by doctors institutionally inclined to minimise the effects of trauma, now it was being done by doctors inclined – for understandable and laudable reasons – to stress them, to get justice for their patients. Holocaust survivors were examined by doctors all over the United States. In 1961, after seeing some 800 people, Dr William Niederland, an analyst in New York City, coined the phrase 'survivor syndrome'.[17]

Massive psychic trauma, said Niederland, caused 'irreversible changes' in the personality. Death camp survivors, who had been 'selected' to live by the SS and seen others (including, often, their own families) selected to die, were crippled by 'survivor guilt'. They were prematurely aged, often confusing the present with the past. Having learned to function in a world without morality and humanity, they now found it difficult to relate to ordinary people, to have ordinary feelings. They suffered from depression, anxiety, and nightmares.[18]

Some have since argued that Niederland and his colleagues exaggerated and overgeneralised. The distinguished Israeli psychiatrist, Shamai Davidson, for example, believed that 'the somewhat stereotyped diagnostic construct' of the survivor syndrome was both too sweeping and too pessimistic, that Holocaust survivors *could* be helped considerably by sympathetic therapy. Besides, he pointed out, the vast majority of the large survivor population in Israel had not become psychiatric patients. Davidson thought the blanket label 'survivor syndrome' had, by 'focusing solely on the pathological consequences of trauma,' 'obscured the remarkable potential for new adaptation, recovery and reintegration throughout the life span.' It also lumped everyone together:

Each survivor is unique in the individual nature and meaning of his experiences and responses to these experiences . . . this uniqueness may be obscured by the shared events and common behaviour patterns. Experiencing similar events in the same situation often had entirely different meanings for different survivors.[19]

The cases seen by Dr Niederland in New York were also, by their very nature, 'self-reporting': people claiming compensation.

The point, however, is not whether the concept of survivor syndrome was right or wrong, helpful or unhelpful, in the lives of Holocaust survivors; rather that in the late 1960s the post-Holocaust literature had a considerable influence on psychiatrists working with Vietnam veterans. It created a new professional model: the psychiatrist as patients' advocate, helping a group of wronged victims to win reparation. It also popularised the idea of a general, loosely-defined 'syndrome' among a group of patients, made the idea of *delayed* emotional after-effects of trauma respectable and put guilt, especially *survivor guilt*, on the agenda. Thus the balance was shifted between trauma and victim, putting much greater emphasis on victimhood than on endurance.

To the lay mind it may seem perverse, even obscene, to equate the experience of those who were victims of terror – at Auschwitz, say – with that of perpetrators of it – for example at My Lai. Was not the Holocaust experience unique in its effects on the personality, not least because of the removal of all social supports? Niederland himself was ambivalent on this point. Chaim Shatan, though, was very struck by the resemblance between the emotional after-effects of extensive Vietnam combat experience, the 'homecoming syndromes' of prisoners of war and the 'survivor syndromes' of living concentration camp inmates. In 1972, he invited Niederland to give a workshop presentation on 'The Guilt and Grief of Vietnam veterans and Concentration Camp Survivors' and the shadow of the Holocaust was seldom absent from his work.[20]

For Robert Lifton, however, Hiroshima was 'the main encounter'. His work with survivors of the atom bomb, described in his 1968 book *Death in Life*, left him with a vision of modern history as 'immersion in death'. He felt that American veterans who opposed the Vietnam War made up, together with Holocaust survivors, Hiroshima victims and some of the scientists responsible for the Hiroshima weapon, 'a special contemporary group of "prophetic survivors" whose "inspiration" derives not from the Divinity, but from the holocausts they survived . . . who have managed to emerge from their holocaust with special regenerative insight.'[21]

A powerful and persuasive writer and an important figure in American intellectual life, Lifton was also in a self-promoting tradition (to which Benjamin Spock and Bruno Bettelheim also belonged). He brought a grandiose, rhetorical quality to everything. 'No theory, unless it is probing and one-sided,' he once told an interviewer, 'amounts to anything. The trick is to have one-sidedness in creative tension with a certain amount of balance and fairness. But it has got to be one-sided.' The overstatements of the Vietnam era came easily to Lifton.[22]

If some of the 'doves' saw Vietnam veterans through distorting lenses, the 'hawks', too, had baggage of their own. This was especially true of the 'iron triangle' in Washington that controlled the powerful ex-service lobby: the Veterans' Administration, the traditional veterans' organisations (like the Veterans of Foreign Wars) and the Congressional committees concerned with veterans' affairs. By the 1970s, the Veterans' Administration had become a vast federal bureaucracy, the single most important health care provider in the country, run by and for the 'class of '46'; its primary purpose to provide free medical care to 12 million veterans of the Second World War (one of its hospitals was said to be 'essentially . . . a place for World War Two guys to die from alcoholism'). Any attempt to remodel this system and to redirect its benefits towards Vietnam veterans would inevitably arouse resistance from the politically very powerful veterans' organisations, worried that their main constituency, the World War vintage, would lose out.[23]

There were several further complications. Many Vietnam veterans viewed the VA with suspicion as another bureaucratic arm of the government they loathed; yet, if they needed help, they could only get it for free through the VA. The VA's leadership saw that it needed to become more user-friendly to the Vietnam generation but was constrained by politics, some veterans' opposition to the war having aroused the wrath of President Nixon and his circle.[24]

In this divided national mood, readjustment after Vietnam inevitably became a highly political issue. The 'doves' argued that the 'post-Vietnam syndrome' was made worse because veterans rejected authority and mistrusted institutions and therefore only went to the VA when they were desperate. Then, it was suggested, the VA doctors frequently failed to understand that the symptoms these men complained of – aggression, combat flashbacks – were caused by stressful war experiences. As a result, the VA doctors were misdiagnosing them as schizophrenics and giving them massive doses of anti-psychotic drugs. What was needed, therefore, was a way of providing psychotherapy or 'readjustment counselling' for these veterans.[25]

The 'hawks', on the other hand, denied there was such a problem. They accused Shatan, Lifton and their allies of feeding public hysteria with overstated claims – for example about the numbers of veterans to have committed suicide – and saw no reason to make further resources available. If Vietnam veterans had problems, they were the problems of American society at large. This view prevailed in Congress throughout the 1970s.[26]

Gradually, however, ways of breaking the deadlock, and of bridging the gulf of suspicion between the veterans and the VA, began to emerge. In 1974, staff at the VA hospital in Brentwood, California, began offering Vietnam veterans treatment at 'storefront' out-patient clinics in the community; they brought in a maverick Vietnam veteran, Shad Meshad, to run it. The success of this 'Outreach' model formed the basis for several bills that were introduced into Congress throughout the 1970s and defeated thanks to the opposition of the traditional veterans groups and their political allies. In 1979, however, nearly ten years after most veterans had returned, both Houses of Congress voted for a general Outreach programme. The bill's passage, the historian Wilbur Scott has written, was 'due not to widespread public support but to a handful of Vietnam veterans who had by that time either been elected to Congress or had risen to influential positions in the VA and traditional veterans' lobbies.'[27]

By that time, however, the veterans' advocates were fighting another campaign, to persuade the American Psychiatric Association to create a new terminology reflecting the veterans' psychiatric problems. For, by 1974 it had become clear that, on top of everything else, American psychiatry was undergoing a revolution.

*   *   *

There is a recurring tension in medicine between the general and the particular, between the illness and the patient, especially in psychiatry, which concerns itself with the human spirit rather than the body. How can human souls, each separately formed, the product of a complex interaction between personality and environment, be lumped together in categories? Yet as soon as medicine is practised on any scale and taught in medical schools, once public money is spent, standardisation becomes inevitable, and with it, quantification. In modern society, many forces outside medicine pull in this direction: as governments have acquired bureaucrats, so their hunger for statistics, and skill in manipulating them, has grown. It was the Bureau of Census that in 1880 first persuaded America's mental hospitals to put their patients into different categories. More recently, the advent of computing has given further impetus to quantifiers and further removed many doctors from their patients.[28]

The greatest classifier of mental disorders was the German physician Emil Kraepelin, a sinister figure to historians of racist ideas, yet a colossus within his own profession, the man whose 'nosology' – or system of classification – created modern psychiatry. 'The Kraepelinian classification of the psychoses,' a recent work states, 'governs twentieth century psychiatric thinking.' Yet even Kraepelin has had to be adapted over the years, for, as Edward Shorter says, 'a naming system incorporates the dominant philosophy of the day'.[29]

For example, the labelling system American psychiatrists were supposed to use during the Second World War derived from experience in large mental institutions; for much of the time, it simply didn't describe the mental disorders of soldiers on the battlefield. As a result, it was largely ignored and numerous fresh terms invented instead. In 1952, the American Psychiatric Association attempted to resolve the ensuing shambles by publishing a standardised system of classification, *The Diagnostic and Statistical Manual of Mental Disorders*, generally known as *DSM-I*[30]

Both *DSM-I* and its 1968 successor *DSM-II* reflected the dominance which psychoanalysis then enjoyed in American psychiatry. By the 1970s, however, the pendulum was swinging the other way, with the Freudians now in retreat as a 'biological' counter-revolution swept through psychiatry. This was set off by a new wave of pharmacological breakthroughs. Chlorpromazine (or largactil), 'the drug that changed the face of psychiatry', was first used by a French naval surgeon in 1951 as a pre-anaesthetic sedative and then quickly taken up by Parisian psychiatrists. By May, 1953, 'the atmosphere of the disturbed wards of mental hospitals in Paris was transformed: straitjackets . . . were things of the past'. Later that year, a psychiatrist in French Canada reported on 'the remarkable effects' of the drug in calming 'restless, excited, overactive patients without oversedating them to the level where they could not function'. A successful drug trial at the Maclean Hospital, Boston was followed by energetic selling by the Smith, Kline company – a brash newcomer to the field. Many state hospitals were soon persuaded of the drug's merits, especially in saving them money. Chlorpromazine was presented 'as the first drug in psychiatry to abolish the symptoms of psychosis though not necessarily to cure the underlying brain disorder'. In Edward Shorter's judgement, it 'initiated a revolution in psychiatry, comparable to the introduction of penicillin in general medicine.'[31]

Chlorpromazine, which worked best on schizophrenics, was quickly adopted by psychiatry. By contrast, the effects on manic patients of the natural substance, lithium, though first observed by the Australian John Cade in 1949, were not generally appreciated in the United States until the 1970s. By then, a third major disorder, depression, had also been tamed, by the 'tricyclic' anti-depressant, imipramine, developed by the Swiss Geigy company. From quite early on, it was apparent that these miraculous new drugs had side-effects. But for psychiatrists who had spent centuries grappling with psychoses, the new treatments were indeed marvellous, making it 'relatively easy to remove symptoms'. They also made it possible to clear the asylums. In 1955, there were some 559,000 patients in state and county mental hospitals in the United States. By 1970 the figure had fallen to 338,000, by 1988 to 107,000.[32]

Most of the running in this swing back towards 'biological' psychiatry was made by the drug companies: theory trailed some way behind clinical practice. Nonetheless, there was a group of psychiatrists at Washington University, St Louis, interested in the chemistry of the brain and in devising standard procedures and criteria for doctors to follow when diagnosing patients. Just as in economic theory the free market group in Chicago associated with Milton Friedman suddenly went from being wacky, marginal irritants to the ruling Keynesian orthodoxy to being the dominant school themselves, so, in psychiatry, the St Louis group went from being obscure provincial mavericks to the new masters of the universe.[33]

The swing towards biological psychiatry was one factor behind mounting pressure in the early 1970s for a further revision of the classification system, the DSM. Another was that newly assertive gay groups were unhappy that homosexuality was still listed as a psychiatric disorder; a third, that insurance companies wanted the vague parameters of Freudian psychoanalysis replaced by a much more tightly defined system of classification based on symptoms, rather than presumed underlying causes. Drug-based treatments were creating a more biological climate. The American Psychiatric Association decided to go with the flow; it entrusted the revision of DSM to a 'task force' dominated by 'biological' psychiatrists. This group did its best to produce a 'scientific' document, with elaborate field trials to establish the effectiveness of each diagnosis, but in practice was open to lobbying and pressure.

As has been said, all naming systems embody the values and experiences of their time. DSM-I, written in 1952 in the aftermath of war, contained a category known as 'gross stress reaction', a reaction thought to occur even in emotionally sound soldiers on the battlefield, which then usually went away and which was quite different from a neurosis or a psychosis. DSM-I made no reference to delayed after-effects. By the time that system was revised in 1968, however, few psychiatrists with first-hand experience of warfare were still around and, as a result, the new system of classification, DSM-II, no longer had a specific listing for psychiatric disorders produced by battle. It was suggested instead that the symptoms associated with 'gross stress reaction' should now be classified under the catchall term 'adjustment reaction to adult life'.[34]

The result was that by the 1970s, as Wilbur Scott has written, 'mental health professionals across the country . . . assessed Vietnam veterans using a diagnostic nomenclature that contained no specific entries for war-related trauma. In hospitals, insurance companies and the courts, the *DSM-II* nomenclature was important because it provided the official diagnoses for categorising sicknesses. It was also the biggest barrier to getting appropriate help from the Veterans' Administration. For that reason, the psychiatrists agitating for proper help for veterans believed it was vital to make sure that the new nomenclature, *DSM-III*, currently in the works, *did* acknowledge the role of war-related stress. Yet in June 1974 Robert Lifton, Chaim Shatan and their allies heard that it was not planned to 'reinstate stress reactions associated with combat'. The group appointed by the American Psychiatric Association to produce *DSM-III* – mostly, as we have seen, apostles of the new 'biological' psychiatry – did not feel 'a separate classification was necessary in diagnosing the problems of Vietnam veterans'. Lifton, Shatan and their allies were not put off, however. In a two-pronged offensive, they took their message to the American media and public and, at the same time, lobbied and organised within the psychiatric profession.[35]

In 1974 radio station WBAI in New York City was persuaded to stage an all-day marathon broadcast on Vietnam veterans. Listeners from all over New England called in with comments and questions and the station's lobby was invaded by veterans. The broadcast had a huge impact and won awards.[36]

Ever since the early 1970s there had been press stories about the problems of Vietnam veterans – their drug addiction, high crime rate, homelessness, propensity to violence and suicide. Whereas, after World War Two, 'the symbol of the vet was GI Joe, the lovable, typical young American, the veteran who came home from Vietnam was perceived as something sinister, disturbing, frightening'. Now this was redoubled. 'Vietnam Veterans called Time Bombs' went a *Baltimore Sun* headline in January 1975. Four months later, the prominent *New York Times* columnist Tom Wicker told the story of a Vietnam veteran who slept with a gun under his pillow and had shot his wife during a nightmare, 'only one example,' wrote Wicker, 'of the serious but largely unnoticed problem of "post-Vietnam syndrome", or PVS, the label by which the extraordinary psychological difficulties of hundreds of thousands of Vietnam veterans have come to be identified.' Wicker quoted statistics from *Penthouse* magazine showing that 38% of those who were married before they went to Vietnam had separated or got divorced within six months of their return, that 500,000 veterans had attempted suicide since leaving the service and that some 175,000 had 'probably' used heroin since returning to civilian life.[37]

The media image of the Vietnam veteran as a 'trip-wire killer' reached its apotheosis in the hands of Hollywood. In Martin Scorsese's *Taxi Driver* (1976), Robert de Niro is unable to distinguish between the New York present and the 'Nam' past and kills accordingly; in *Rambo; First Blood* (1982) Sylvester Stallone is driven by isolation and frustration to turn hunter. 'Hollywood finally caught up with the image of dysfunctional vet created first by the antiwar movement and veterans' advocates and added its own mythic twist: Vietnam vet as dysfunctional superman.'[38]

The media, then, was fertile ground for those wishing to highlight the plight of the Vietnam veterans. But how bad *was* the problem? Even among those committed to the veterans' cause, estimates of the size of the problem varied sharply. Chaim Shatan argued in 1974 that there were probably one to one and a half million men suffering from 'post-combat syndrome'. In 1978, John Wilson put the number of 'veterans suffering from adjustment problems' at 250,000 whereas, four years later Arthur Egendorf (using looser criteria) made it over two million, a figure almost ten times as great. Another article in 1982 declared that 500,000–700,000 veterans were 'in need of emotional help at the present time'.[39]

Yet a *Los Angeles Times* survey of veterans in 1975 concluded that, overall, 'there is ample evidence to suggest that the vast majority of Vietnam veterans have melted back into society as successfully as any soldier from any war.' Vietnam veterans were joining the traditional veterans' organisations, using the GI Bill for education in greater numbers than any previous generation and successfully getting off heroin. Only 2% of Vietnam veterans used narcotics in civilian life. The LA *Times* quoted a VA psychiatrist: 'Our society was scared by the image of the Vietnam veteran coming home and shooting up the community, of being a junkie. It was a distorted image that the veteran is still paying for.' There was, he believed, 'no evidence that Vietnam has produced a dispro-portionate share of people who are maladjusted to society and no evidence that the primary contributor to that maladjustment was military service.'[40]

Why then did the negative stereotype persist? Eric Dean has argued that although, objectively, the difficulties of the Vietnam veteran were over by the late 1970s, there was at that time a renewed emphasis on the uniqueness and difficulties of the Vietnam veteran, focusing especially on 'delayed stress syndrome', Agent Orange, and a supposedly high suicide rate in veterans.[41]

For Shafton, Lifton and their allies, mobilising the media was important in helping to create a climate of emotional pressure. But skilful lobbying of fellow psychiatrists had the more immediate effect. The psychiatrists working with veterans managed to shake off the impression of being a special interest group by creating a wider category of trauma and shrewdly presenting their case in a way designed to appeal to the new psychiatry.

The contact between the psychiatrists working with Vietnam veterans and doctors working with concentration camp victims led Shatan, Lifton and their associates 'to think of the diagnostic category as a more generalised phenomenon of which post-combat disorder was but a single example'. Then they started to review the literature of catastrophes in general, and to make contact with fellow doctors who had worked with victims of civilian disasters, including burns victims.

Lifton and Shatan were both outside the psychiatric mainstream – psycho-analysts in New York – but they used allies within the profession to put their case

in a series of presentations at conferences and meetings wit[ ]
looking into Reactive Disorders in *DSM-III*. They also adap[ ]
new mindset, with its emphasis on hard quantifiable data, a[ ]
on some 700 cases, mainly Vietnam veterans. While they fa[ ]
researchers at St Louis, who continued to argue that 'the [ ]
categories of depression, schizophrenia and alcoholism adeq[ ]
veterans' symptoms, they did eventually persuade the drafters [ ]
case. Shatan and Lifton wanted a category called 'catastrophic stress disorder',
divided into acute, chronic and delayed manifestations. They also 'argued that
the only significant predisposition for catastrophic stress disorders was the
traumatic event itself, and stated that the symptoms' course and treatment
differed by the cause and onset of the disorder.'[42]

An important role in getting the concept of post-trauma stress accepted by the
psychiatric world was played by the San Francisco psychiatrist, Mardi J.
Horowitz. A tireless builder of intellectual structures, Horowitz was thoroughly
steeped in the literature of civilian and military trauma and the discourse of
modern psychology. He had also made a close study of the responses of patients
to trauma and systematised their course. In his book *Stress Response Syndromes*
(1976), Horowitz drew on the writings of Freud, Janet, Kardiner, Grinker and
Spiegel and on Erich Lindemann's work with the Cocoanut Grove fire victims to
provide a coherent framework within which to understand the pattern of
responses to trauma. Although called, with a nod towards modern experimental
psychology, an information-processing model, it dealt in fact more with the
processing of emotion. Everything was factored into Horowitz's equation –
except experience with military cases and an awareness of the role of social
culture. The building bricks of his model were intellectual, not practical. In the
battle between the consulting room and the laboratory, the field hospital and the
study, the intellectuals had triumphed.[42]

Opinion is divided as to whether Horowitz really came up with something new
or just dressed up old ideas in new garb. But in his hands, Shatan's vague and
emotive 'post-Vietnam syndrome' acquired real intellectual authority. A bridge
was forged between 'war neurosis' and the victims of civilian trauma that had
never really existed before. Mardi Horowitz, along with Shatan and Lifton,
helped to create a new, unitary kind of 'trauma'.[43]

What finally emerged from the APA's committee in 1980 was the term Post-
Traumatic Stress Disorder. According to Wilbur Scott, 'PTSD is in *DSM-III*
because a core of psychiatrists and veterans worked consciously and deliberately
for years to put it there. They ultimately succeeded because they were better
organized, more politically active and enjoyed more lucky breaks than their
opposition.'[44]

In 1981 the psychologist Charles Figley looked back over the battles of the 1970s.
'Since those days,' he wrote, 'there have been dramatic and precedent-setting
changes that have depoliticised the debate over the mental health of Vietnam

erful and prestigious bodies have deliberated the issues and concluded a group the VN combat vet is neither a walking time bomb nor an incible robot; that the vast majority of the survivors of the war are leading productive lives and are more emotionally stable than the general population. However, the catastrophic stress of combat leaves its marks on the psyche that require both time and confrontation to erase; and a small but significant minority of combat veterans are suffering from the frightening and debilitating aftershock of VN and should be helped. They are getting that help now.'

One reason for Figley's optimism was the new public mood of acceptance, symbolised by 'Vietnam Veterans Week' in 1979, when President Carter told a gathering of some 200 of them in the White House that 'the nation ha[d] not done enough to respect, to honour, to recognise and to reward their special heroism'. The unveiling of the Vietnam Wall in Washington and the 'surge of patriotic feeling' generated by the Iran Hostage Crisis in 1981 all seemed to set the seal on the process of healing. 'The Strangers,' Figley wrote, 'have been welcomed home'.[45] On 10 November 1982 the Vietnam Wall in Washington was dedicated.

'WHEN THE PATIENT REPORTS ATROCITIES . . .'

Is there a danger that the increasingly standard perception that we live in a 'sick society' also carries with it the idea that nothing is anyone's fault any longer?

H. Stuart Hughes, 1969[1]

In September 1969, soon after taking her master's degree, Sarah Haley reported for her first job – as a psychiatric social worker at the Boston branch of the Veterans' Administration. She was the daughter of a World War Two veteran, an alcoholic who had, a friend wrote, 'not only caused her pain, but taught her a great deal about the relationship between the VA and war veterans'. But, although brought up on soldiers' tales, she had not served in the military or in Vietnam.[2]

On her first day at work, she interviewed a new patient, very anxious and agitated, who told her that his company had killed women and children at a village called My Lai. He had not fired any shots himself, but had been threatened by the other soldiers. He thought they were now coming to kill him.

At this stage, Sarah Haley was unaware of the story then beginning to break in the media. On 16 March 1968, a company of the American Division had killed more than 400 women, children and old men at My Lai; but the story had been hushed up by the Army until a soldier-photographer sold pictures to the press on his return to the United States. She accepted the veteran's account at face value but found that her colleagues were unmoved by it, insisting that the patient was 'obviously delusional, obviously in full-blown psychosis'.

I argued [she recalled in 1988] that there were no other signs of this if one took his story seriously. I was laughed out of the room. I was told that it was my first day and just didn't understand how things worked . . . I was aghast. These professionals denying the reality of combat! This clouded their clinical judgment. They were calling reality insanity! I knew from my father's stories that [this man was] not crazy. That encounter became typical.[3]

This was to be the first of many variations on the same tale. By 1974 Haley had seen 130 patients, of whom 40 reported responsibility for atrocious acts; by 1978 she had handled 500 patients and had learnt to tell, sometimes in advance, when a patient was going to begin to describe an atrocity, something which caused 'a dread and foreboding and a stealing oneself against it, along with a sense that it is absolutely imperative to hear what is going to be described. Then, as the horror of the act emerges, the therapist is thrown back; "This cannot be! He is a monster, an animal! No human could have done that".'[4]

In a famous article in 1973, Haley wrote up the cases of 'John' who had killed prisoners after entreating them to surrender and murdered civilians without provocation; 'Bob', a former Marine had refused 'R & R' because he was 'too into killing'; and Bill who had watched his comrades commit atrocities, though avoided them himself. These were not isolated cases. The clinical literature of this period suppurates with horrible details – prisoners thrown from helicopters, old men mutilated, terrible things done to women. The scope which war offers to the 'beast in man' is amply demonstrated:

Bill had dreamed that a combat buddy was kicking the heads of dead Vietnamese like soccer balls. In actuality, Bill had once shot off the heads of dead Vietnamese and his friend had kicked them . . .

Gary . . . described a pattern of uncontrolled violence that involved raping, killing and cutting up bodies of South Vietnamese women along the highway.

Ray . . . was in charge of a South Vietnamese Army team that regularly tortured, mutilated and killed villagers . . . he was increasingly excited watching it and soon became actively involved.[5]

Many of the worst atrocities were committed by the other side; the sight of American soldiers with their genitalia in their mouths recurs in the war dreams of veterans.

Atrocities occur in all wars – even 'good' ones. Between 1914 and 1918, prisoners were frequently shot in hot and cold blood and German soldiers only began to surrender in large numbers in 1918 when they felt they could be confident of surviving. 'What kind of war do civilians suppose we fought anyway?' a journalist asked in *Atlantic Monthly* in 1946. 'We shot prisoners in cold blood, wiped out hospitals, strafed lifeboats, killed or mistreated enemy civilians, finished off enemy wounded, tossed the dying into a hole for dead, and boiled the flesh off enemy skulls to make table ornaments for sweethearts.' Eugene Sledge, James Jones and Norman Mailer all show that in the war against the Japanese mutilation of, and disrespect for, enemy dead was commonplace; many soldiers got a thrill from such practices as urinating in the mouths of corpses.[6]

There were, however, aspects of the Vietnam War that encouraged this behaviour. The enemy was everywhere, yet impossible to identify. They were not perceived as 'human'. The pattern of fighting put a heavy responsibility on junior officers who frequently lacked the authority or experience to control their men. At the same time, the frustrations of the war created a pressure to act, to do something; and often gave dominance within the unit to individuals prepared to shoot first and ask questions later. Finally, young, poorly trained soldiers were given terrible firepower.[7]

It is futile to attempt to quantify the scale of atrocities in Vietnam, though historians have tried. We do better to heed the words of the most eloquent apologist for what went on there. Philip Caputo was the sensitive, bookish son of a middle-class Chicago household who came to find himself facing court martial for the cold-blooded murder of two innocent Vietnamese civilians. 'The aspect of the Vietnam war which distinguished it from other American conflicts,' Caputo wrote, was 'its absolute savagery. I mean the savagery that prompted so many American fighting men – the good solid kids from Iowa farms – to kill civilians and prisoners.' Caputo thought there had been a great deal of exaggeration about US atrocities in Vietnam, 'exaggeration not about their extent but about their causes'. He dismissed both the theory that Americans were racist and the idea that they were schooled in violence by their frontier-heritage. Both contained an element of truth, but they ignored the barbarous treatment the Viet Cong and the South Vietnamese army often inflicted on their own people:

The evil was inherent not in the men – except in the sense that the devil dwells in all of us – but in the circumstances under which they had to live and fight. The conflict in Vietnam combined the two most bitter kinds of warfare, civil war and revolution, to which was added the ferocity of jungle war. Twenty years of terrorism and fratricide had obliterated most reference points from the country's moral map long before we arrived . . . The marines in our brigade were not innately cruel, but on landing at Da Nang they learned rather quickly that Vietnam was not a place where a man could expect much mercy if, say, he was taken prisoner. And men who do not expect to receive mercy eventually lose their inclination to grant it.[8]

With atrocities come guilt. The problem of 'guilt around killing, injuring, or striking a defenseless enemy' is as old as conflict itself. Ernst Simmel encountered it in German soldiers in 1918 and thirty years later a British psychiatrist wrote that 'the soldier's problem in coping with his own aggression, when war makes it legitimate and even desirable', had been underrated. A 1951 study of American veterans found that 'If enemy soldiers or noncombatants were shot when they were unarmed, or unprepared for the attack, or while in a seemingly defenseless position, great guilt was engendered.' When men returned home, 'the military code and superimposed group conscience, which gave permission to kill and destroy under certain circumstances, was quickly dissipated and replaced by the usual civilian morale and conscience, which places sharp limits on such impulses. Under such circumstances, conflict and guilt were quickly generated and difficult to master.'[9]

But not all men feel guilt; much depends on context. In Hitler's Germany, soldiers who committed terrible atrocities against Russians, Poles and Jews appear not to have carried guilt about it because they felt supported in their action by their society, culture and government. But after Vietnam, many American soldiers on returning home began to develop intense feelings of guilt about what they had done because it conflicted with the underlying Christian values of their society and because their society did not endorse what they had done. They were not given victory parades and church services; did not receive absolution. Because the war seemed to them to have no meaning, the killing was doubly sinful. The fact that they had derived *pleasure* from killing was often especially troubling later on.[10]

How, then, should the therapist treat atrocity guilt? Was the man who committed crimes in Vietnam a perpetrator or a victim? Who could judge him and whose judgement would he accept? Sarah Haley's response to these questions was guided by the practical matter of what a patient would take from a psychiatrist who hadn't 'been there', by her own sense of compassion and by Robert Jay Lifton's argument that guilt lay less with the soldiers in Vietnam than with the society which had sent them there. 'Most of the harmful behaviour that occurs in Vietnam,' Lifton declared in 1971, 'is due to the malignant environment we create there, an environment of murder. For instance the men who killed at My Lai, let's say, had no discernible or diagnosable psychiatric disease. They were, I would say, in an advanced state of brutalization and under enormous pressures. The kind of thing that could happen to any one of us, were we put under similar training and that kind of situation.'[11]

Haley was emphatic that there was no question of being judgemental. You had to put yourself in the patient's shoes – to identify with him, 'be able to feel, I could well have done that.'

It does not have to be said, just felt; but there is a clear difference between being able or not able to feel it. And the patient can tell. No matter how experienced, it is always in some measure costly to the therapist each time it is felt, but the treatment process requires that the therapist be able to. One cannot understand the trauma unless one can feel what the patient felt.[12]

Unless this effort was made, the treatment was between the 'good' therapist and the 'bad' out-of-control patient, and the patient left or stayed only because he had found the censure that he consciously or unconsciously felt he deserved.

Haley drew on the writings of Erik Erikson – Freud's former chauffeur who gave to Freudian 'ego psychology' the ideas of the life cycle and the identity crisis – and on the 'object relations' school of neo-Freudians, then gaining ground in the United States. She saw Vietnam soldiers as essentially late adolescents, still sorting out their personalities and sexual identities, subject to temporary moments of regression and in need of clear rules and consistent, caring and supportive parents and peer groups. Instead, in Vietnam, they met conditions that made them regress further. 'The continued stress of guerrilla warfare, and most often the lack of good leadership, led to regression to earlier, preadolescent, and pregenital levels of psychic organization.' The soldier, she believed, 'often turned to a single buddy, who then took on the role of the transitional object, as in childhood, the first "not me" object.' This buddy, this friend, thus served to assuage anxiety, fear and abandonment panic because of the magical belief that this buddy – as long as the soldier stayed physically close to him – could protect him.' Because so much was invested in the buddy his death could be a devastating blow, like a young child losing its mother.[13]

One of her patients, Mark, a black Marine Corps sergeant, had developed a friendship in Vietnam with a young white lieutenant, Alan. On the completion of his tour of duty there, Mark had re-enlisted to 'watch over' him – even though his wife was beginning to be unfaithful. In 1968, during the Tet Offensive, both of them were ambushed by the Viet Cong. Alan was severely wounded. Mark was temporarily blinded but managed to keep the enemy at bay. Twenty-four hours later, relief helicopters reached the group. Mark was enraged by the refusal of the triage officers to evacuate his mortally wounded friend immediately. Instead, 'restrained and comforted', he spent two hours with his friend waiting for the helicopter to return.

Their final conversation was similar to many they had had in the past: family, friends, girlfriends, memories of R & R, and ethnic slurs and jokes levelled at each other. This 'gallows humour' continued even as Alan was loaded into the helicopter and they parted, eyes riveted on each other, each saying, 'See you around.'

Alan died in the helicopter on the way to hospital. Soon afterwards, a group of Viet Cong prisoners were brought to the camp where Mark was recovering. He and some of the other survivors of the ambush surrounded them and machine-gunned them all to death. 'Mark's involvement in atrocity,' Haley wrote, had 'followed a battle of overwhelming threat to his own survival and the death of his closest friend.'[14]

Sarah Haley spent one year reliving Mark's Vietnam experiences, often suffering 'dry heaves' before the sessions, and another exploring his background and the failure of his marriage. She met, and was approved by, his mother. Then, inevitably, Mark told Haley that he loved and wanted to marry her. She congratulated him on again thinking of himself as lovable ('the return of a viable ego ideal'), but he was not fooled and punished her for the rejection: 'There followed months of rage, depression, and the revelation of his pleasure and guilt at watching atrocities, particularly ones involving women.' Haley felt increasing revulsion; felt in herself the 'negative counter-transference reaction' she had counselled others against. Then there began to be progress, talk of friendships with men and 'tentative dating', only for an accident at work to set things back again. One day, some four years after starting treatment, Mark appeared in her office with the girl he wanted to marry.

Thus, by prolonged personal therapy, Sarah Haley was able to rescue one patient. That she gave unstintingly to all her patients – and was an effective therapist – is not in doubt; her dedication may have contributed to her early death from cancer in 1989. But did the non-judgemental approach she advocated work generally? Should it provide the model for the counselling which after 1980 was made available by the Veterans' Administration? One of the first to voice doubts was Peter Marin.

Marin was not a psychiatrist, but a journalist specialising in psychology. After talking at length to a number of veterans and therapists, he concluded that the media were not helping veterans by portraying them as 'victims of the society that sent them to war' and saying that 'the solution to their problems was increased acceptance and gratitude here at home'. The veterans' real problems, Marin argued, were moral. They had a profound sense of guilt and of having sinned. They craved penance and absolution: 'We aren't just counsellors; we're almost priests,' one of the leaders of the Outreach Program told Marin. 'They come to us for absolution as well as help.' Yet psychotherapy, by its very nature, was incapable of providing this.[15]

Marin condemned the way the problem of atrocities was being dealt with by some psychotherapists. Either they skirted it altogether or they used psycho-babble – 'seemingly precise analytic terms for repressed guilt' like 'impacted grief' – to obscure from themselves and their patients the real nature of what had happened. 'Various phrases and terms' were being used 'to empty the vets' experience of moral content, to defuse and bowdlerise it.' Some VA therapists were even talking about the need to 'deresponsibilize' their patients, 'that is to get the Vietnam vets to attribute their actions to external causes rather than moral choice.' When guilt was mentioned, it was usually survivors' guilt.

Marin argued that the issue of judgement was avoided because it would not be good for funding, or because many therapists were unhappy with it – uncomfortable in judging the behaviour of others, guilty at not having been to Vietnam themselves. But, more fundamentally, it was because of 'the limits of the discipline itself, the inadequacy of psychological categories and language in describing the nature and pain of human conscience.' In its 'justifiable accent upon human needs as opposed to social obligation', psychoanalysis had 'established habits of thought that have now been honed into a morally vacuous view of human nature.'[16]

A graphic illustration of Marin's argument can be found in the readjustment programme in a Veterans' Administration hospital in 1986, as witnessed by the anthropologist Allan Young. The treatment regime in the hospital was on a rigid psychoanalytic model and patients and nurses were discouraged from talking about 'shoulds'.

That belongs to 'morality': thou shalt do this or not do this. And no talk about 'wrong' . . . look at your behaviour as a 'stress response'. It's not a question of whether it's right or wrong, but a question of what it goes back to.[17]

Morality was neutralised. Instead, this hospital's treatment programme was based on a quasi-Freudian idea of 'splitting'. Post-Traumatic Stress Disorder was seen an 'epiphenomenon of the unfused libidinal drive' caused by the split between the aggressive drive and the libidinal drive. Treatment was designed to use abreaction to bring about recovery through a 're-fusing' of the two drives. Not surprisingly, both staff and patients were mystified by this. However, in the same hospital, an alternative kind of help was available from the chaplain, who offered veterans a mixture of a lecture on neurobiology – to explain what makes most people behave 'badly' in battle – and old-fashioned absolution. The chaplain's version was that 'guilt is irreducible and is absolved through "confession" and reparation.'[18]

It's not clear from Young's account which method of treatment the patients preferred, nor what results this centre achieved. Considering that most of its patients had spent nearly two decades in alcoholism, substance abuse and social failure, the value of finding and abreacting the original traumatic experience is open to doubt.

Many therapists who have worked closely with chronic Vietnam cases emphasise the moral, spiritual side of their suffering, the way service in Vietnam involved, for many people, the 'undoing of character'. Looking for ways to help their patients, they have rediscovered the historical role of ritual in spiritually cleansing returning warriors. For example, a Boston psychiatrist compared the way that Homeric warriors used ceremonies of public grief and catharsis to channel and control the emotions aroused by war with the shabby, bureaucratic mechanisms of modern America; a Catholic theologian described how medieval warriors were made to serve a penance before being readmitted to civil society; and a group of Veterans' Administration doctors researched Native American homecoming rituals. Fascinating as these accounts are, it is difficult to see how the revival of such ceremonies can work in the modern electronic age, with its consumerist, irreligious, and antiauthoritarian ethos. Certainly, they cannot be used long after the event, to heal old wounds. On hearing of one such proposal in the mid-1980s, an embittered patient at a VA hospital declared:

I mean this rally they're planning for Washington, to 'welcome home the Vietnam Vets'. If I could arrange it I'd go there for the rally and shit in the middle of the streets.[19]

On the other hand, the Vietnam Wall in Washington DC and its equivalents around the United States – monuments erected by veterans themselves – are generally thought to have had an important redemptive role. It is noticeable, too, that the only organisations to report success with chronic Vietnam veterans are religious groups. Their claims are, of course, purely anecdotal and open to every kind of scientific objection. In the late 1980s, the journalist Shirley Dicks interviewed a score of veterans, who after years of unsuccessful treatment by the Veterans' Administration, had remade their lives after joining an organisation known as Point Man Ministries. 'In 1985 I was born into Christ, and my flashbacks, nightmares and many other PTSD symptoms disappeared,' Fred Love, a former Marine, told her, speaking for many. 'There are residues of the war that will always be with me, but I was delivered of my daily drinking problem immediately.' For these men, religion had been able to offer more than psychiatry could.[20]

It is easy to mock such statements as 'the ministry has continued from the original concept to an unfolding of the complete vision of what God has in store for Vietnam veterans and their families and all the victims of trauma'. What emerges clearly from the strange mixture of psychobabble and God-speak is that

God has supplied many of the men with the authority figure they have been searching for and psychotherapists have failed to provide.[21]

*   *   *

In recent years, right-wing revisionists have argued that the extent of atrocities in Vietnam was grossly exaggerated for political reasons by opponents of the war. Veterans, they say, often claimed to have participated in atrocities in order to 'achieve a feeling of importance and solidarity with the antiwar movement by calling attention to themselves in this way' or to win sympathy, particularly from female therapists. Some of those involved with Vietnam Veterans Against the War were not in fact veterans; many of the alleged atrocities (for example those described at the Vietnam Veterans Against the War's hearings) did not take place. Furthermore, the charge goes, psychiatrists imposed their own political agenda on impressionable young men; it has even been alleged that patients who didn't 'show sufficient guilt' were bullied until they left Robert Lifton's rap group.[22]

There is some justice to these charges but how much we will never know. Veterans' accounts of their experiences in Vietnam were seldom checked by doctors against their service records. The media were even more gullible – a veteran called Steve who featured in two documentaries in the 1980s, living in the backwoods of Washington State and unable to get over his terrible experiences, later turned out to have been a film projectionist in Vietnam. Had Sarah Haley's first patient *actually* been at My Lai? It seems unlikely. On the other hand, I doubt whether all her other patients were fabulists and attention-seekers, or that none of the incidents reported in the psychiatric literature took place.[23]

The important point is the one raised by Peter Marin. Historically, issues of responsibility for one's actions and attitudes to authority have been at the heart of the war neuroses. Vietnam made it much more difficult to confront them. Instead of forcing the men to take responsibility for their actions, the psychiatrists and American society sympathised with them and excused them. What was done in Vietnam, instead of being seen as a moral outrage, an aberration, something never to be repeated, somehow became the norm, the standard.

FROM THE FALKLANDS TO THE GULF

Armies never learn from other armies. They only learn from their own mistakes.

Drew Middleton, 1972[1]

It had been a long time since the British had been involved in a major military operation. Since Suez in 1956, there had been guerrilla war in Malaya, operations in Aden, the long, tense policing operation in Northern Ireland, but no major campaign. Then, on 2 April 1982, the Argentine junta invaded the Falkland Islands, a tiny British dependency in the South Atlantic. After three days of indecision, the British government sent a Task Force composed of Naval, Air Force and elite Army units to reconquer the islands. The main flotilla of ships sailed on 29 April.

The campaign that followed was short but savage. By the time the Argentine commander surrendered on 14 June, some 255 British servicemen and 746 Argentines had been killed. The operation was presented in the British media as a triumph of calm professionalism, yet it was apparent, even thousands of miles away, that it was a 'damned close-run thing', marked by numerous troubling moments and some alarming shortcomings of equipment (British warships struck by French Exorcet missiles burned like tinderboxes). Subsequent testimony confirmed that, for all the rigour of their training, many soldiers found it difficult to cope with the horrible reality of battle. After the years of exercises, they hadn't, for example, developed an ear for artillery fire and so couldn't tell 'incoming' from 'outgoing'; they didn't know that if you throw a real hand grenade into a tent you shouldn't stand outside it; some still had naive notions of fair play. Several episodes in the campaign were particularly disturbing. Most notably, the bombing of the troopship *Sir Galahad*, with the loss of 56 lives, was 'very dodgy' – distressing because it need not have happened. Accustomed to peacetime ceremonial and comfort, the Welsh Guards stayed on board the troopship, despite the risk of Argentine air attack, 'because they didn't want to walk the one or two miles to their positions if the ship could take them. Rather than tea and videos on board they should have got off and dug in.'[2]

Hastily improvised, the task force was very much 'a Navy Show'; no Army psychiatrists were 'invited' to come along. The Royal Navy had always been by far the most traditional of all the British services, the most determined to play down psychiatric problems, the most firmly wedded to attitudes which had seen it through in the past. The Navy's psychiatrists spent most of their time dealing with alcoholism, domestic problems and psychosis: it says something for their culture that, at the time of the Falklands war, they had simply never heard of PIE, the great universal formula of military psychiatry. They *had* heard of PTSD, but thought it was something that happened only to American conscripts, not to professionals.[3]

For whatever reason, many of the hallowed principles of military psychiatry were ignored. There was no psychological screening of the troops – most, after all, were in special forces; no psychiatrists accompanied the ground forces; and when psychiatric casualties did occur they were evacuated off the Falklands to hospital ships, as effectively removed from the battlefield psychologically as the soldiers sent back across the Channel in 1914.[4]

Yet all these decisions appeared to be vindicated. It was reported that only 3% of the British wounded suffered any psychiatric problems; that only 21 cases of primary psychiatric disorder were diagnosed (a figure later amended to 48). With an air of quiet pride, one of the psychiatrists explained the reasons for this low incidence: the troops were from elite units; they had had time to prepare; they had had an assault role; they had sustained few casualties; and they had retained group cohesion and high morale. Above all, the campaign was short.[5]

Not only did the British forces win the war; their efforts were well recognised. The military went to some lengths to reunite them quickly with their loved ones by flying them home and giving them leave; returning British troops were greeted as heroes by the media and the public. Services of thanksgiving were held – including one in St Paul's Cathedral where the Archbishop of Canterbury annoyed the Prime Minister, Mrs Thatcher, by praying for the Argentinian dead.

But about five years later, stories began to surface about Falklands veterans having problems. The British media, now becoming aware of Post-Traumatic Stress Disorder, began to ask whether soldiers were suffering from this new affliction. Whitehall adamantly denied that there was any such problem. The British Ministry of Defence was still locked into the mindset which, it believed, had served it well in the past. Publicly to acknowledge the emotional after-effects of battle was felt to be 'damaging to fighting spirit' and bad for recruitment; mental casualties, when they did appear, were regarded as a man's own business or, if he was beyond recovery, the concern of service charities or civilian doctors. If some individuals got a raw deal, that was too bad; the important thing was collective morale. This view was held strongly by service doctors, particularly at a time when financial cuts were forcing the military to consider its priorities.[6]

What Whitehall failed to take into account was a change in public opinion. Although the Falklands campaign had been flag-wavingly popular (and had secured triumphant re-election for the Thatcher government), the media's reporting of war and its aftermath had become much more critical (the watershed in Britain having been crossed at Suez in 1956, when the government, by lying to both Parliament and people, forever lost the simple trust it had previously enjoyed). The emphasis now was as much on the effects on the individual as on collective glory. Also, medical issues which earlier generations had left to doctors were now a regular part of the media's diet, with much space given to 'wrenching accounts of patients' suffering'. Equally, the legal climate had changed, issues such as nuclear testing having created a precedent for suing the state.[7]

Somewhere in the middle of all this were the British military psychiatrists. But, although they finally recognised the term Post-Traumatic Stress Disorder in 1986, they were not of one mind. Some psychiatrists were thought to have overstated their case in order to be heard, or to have used the issue of PTSD as a platform 'for individual reputations'. In 1990, a British Army officer found that 'PTSD had become a rather tedious subject regarded with varying degrees of scorn or indifference, even as an indication of weakness of character.' One lecturer at the Staff College referred to it as 'Compensation-itis'.[8]

Some of these tensions surfaced publicly. In 1986, a Naval psychiatrist, Dr Morgan O'Connell, published an article calling for research on post-traumatic stress in Falklands veterans, with a disclaimer from the Ministry at its top. A year later, a newspaper report claimed that O'Connell had himself conducted a survey of 924 officers and ratings who had served in the Falklands and found that one in eight had war-related psychiatric problems.[9]

By this time, Falkland veterans who had returned to civil life were going to see doctors. In January 1987, two Welsh psychologists reported three cases they had come across 'by chance'. A 19-year-old Welsh Guard had been 'blown out of a below decks compartment' on *Sir Galahad* by a bomb blast and returned to find the 'mutilated remains of his best friend'. Although injured himself he had heroically helped with the wounded, but on returning to Wales suffered from feelings of guilt and rage, especially when seeing television programmes about *Sir Galahad*. A man in his thirties, as a first-aid orderly on HMS *Antelope*, had seen his friend decapitated by a faulty fuse. Another Welsh Guard had suffered terrible burns. Although seen on television coping heroically with his burns, he drank a lot on his return and 'it was only when drunk that he could talk of his guilt at surviving'. While drunk he revealed that his worst hand injuries had been sustained while trying to rescue his friends but he had had to leave them eventually. The doctors wondered whether these cases were the tip of an iceberg, pointing out that all three had found it impossible to get help in the services.[10]

In 1987 two Army doctors did carry out a study, eventually published in 1991, of 64 veterans still serving in the British Army, compared with a group of matched controls. 'Half of the veterans reported some symptoms of PTSD and 22% were rated as having the complete syndrome.' They found an association between symptoms and intensity of combat and early emotional difficulties on returning from the war. Yet puzzlingly, these researchers could detect little 'actual disability in this group of people'. They didn't spontaneously complain of symptoms and seemed to be functioning normally. 'The men either did not see themselves as ill, or had not decided to consult [a doctor].' The authors speculated that, by staying in the military, these men had a 'milieu in which there is commonality and an acceptance so that members are supported'. But there might also be dangers: 'it may tend to perpetuate symptoms and prevent resolution of conflict'.[11]

Some people argued that all the mysteries could be cleared up if the Ministry of Defence carried out a thorough epidemiological survey of all Falklands veterans to see what their incidence of PTSD was; help could then be given where needed and lessons for future wars learned. Roderick Ørner, a civilian psychologist who had worked with Falkland veterans, accused the Ministry not only of failing to carry out such a survey itself but of declining to co-operate with outside researchers such as himself. Ørner compared the 'shameful record' of the British to the elaborate follow-up studies of veterans of the 1982–5 Lebanon War carried out by the Israelis. The Ministry of Defence had no intention of carrying out such a survey, which it perceived as an open invitation to ex-servicemen to sue for compensation.[12]

By the end of the decade, the situation was becoming increasingly polarised: the authorities denying that there was a problem, yet refusing to carry out surveys; critics claiming that about one in five Falklands veterans were suffering from nightmares, depression, alcohol or drug abuse and other mental disorders directly related to their war experiences. Television programmes highlighted case histories to show the effects that even a short, well-conducted campaign could have on a trained, professional soldier and veterans spoke publicly of their symptoms. Stephen, for example, was a Marine Officer who came from a military family and had always wanted to be a soldier. In the Falklands he had commanded a team of specialist commandos landed at night behind enemy lines to knock out key points of opposition prior to the British landings at San Carlos Bay. Outwardly, all went well. The operation was a complete success and Stephen was decorated for his courage and leadership. Inwardly, though, he suffered from 'constant anxiety' that his mission would fail, hated being cold and wet for days on end and felt terrible loneliness. When he returned to England, ordinary life seemed much more complicated and stressful; he began to have nightmares, not directly about the Falklands, but featuring 'various sorts of stressful situations, one of which was particularly upsetting was being a man condemned to death.' He also began to suffer from depression.[13]

Despite these symptoms, Stephen kept his difficulties to himself and performed the duties of a junior officer well enough to gain further promotion. He was convinced that his problems were unique, and it was only when he married a doctor with some psychiatric experience that he found the courage to recognise his condition and insist on treatment for it. When, in the summer of 1989, he was finally told that he was suffering from PTSD, it was a great relief. He left the military soon after.

If Stephen's problems stemmed from the stresses of command, Mike's derived from the horrors he had seen at first hand as a medical orderly with the paras: a helicopter crew sliced to pieces by their rotor blades; a young soldier burned alive till he looked like 'a log that had just come off the camp fire'; an officer with his brains hanging out of the back of his head. Almost immediately after Mike's return to England, his nightmares started. On one occasion he found himself sitting up in bed at four in the morning:

I could actually see someone . . . he was . . . shimmering white and transparent walking into the room. It was one of the guys who had died in the Falklands and he stood at the bottom of my bed and he looked at me and I remember screaming at him. 'What do you want? What do you want?' I eventually woke up fully and of course I was in the room by myself.

Mike tried to drown his memories in alcohol and marijuana; his marriage collapsed and subsequent relationships fell apart. He left the Army but was unable to hold down a job.[14]

Other veterans had different areas of disquiet: the 'dirty' way some battles had been fought or the abrupt transition from the heightened horrors of the battlefield to the tender banalities of home life (it emerged that units that returned more slowly by sea – giving their men a couple of weeks to relive their battlefield experiences in the alcoholic company of their peers – later reported fewer difficulties than those flown straight back to Britain).[15]

Public pressure did bring some response from the military. In late 1988 serving soldiers began to be offered help. Mike, the Falklands medical orderly, was given group therapy at a military hospital and made good progress before the psychiatrist treating him was abruptly transferred abroad. But the facilities provided were so inadequate that two leading Army psychiatrists resigned in despair. By the 1990s Falklands veterans were beginning to sue the Ministry of Defence for medical negligence, on the grounds that, by failing to detect and provide adequate counselling for PTSD at the right time, it had failed in its 'duty of care'. The Falklands war had introduced a new mood into military service.[16]

* * *

In August 1990, the Iraqi dictator Saddam Hussein invaded his oil-rich neighbour, Kuwait. To punish this act of aggression, an elaborate diplomatic alliance was mobilised and an immense military force assembled in Saudi Arabia, dominated by the United States but with contingents from Nato and Arab countries. By early 1991, the American commander in the Gulf, General Schwarzkopf, had an immense superiority of men and material. He was, though, constrained by a wish to minimise Allied casualties and by worries that Saddam Hussein might deploy against the Allies the chemical and biological weapons he had already deployed with murderous effect on Kurdish rebels and Iranian troops. Neither side had used gas in the Second World War, aware of the retaliatory power of the other, yet for seventy years the threat of chemical (and latterly biological) warfare remained a potent threat, something against which troops could not be completely protected by their cumbersome 'Noddy suits' and unpleasant antidote medications.[17]

To minimise these risks, General Schwarzkopf relied mainly on air power; only after 39 days of preparatory bombing – 'one of the heaviest air campaigns in history' – did he launch his ground offensive on 24 February 1991. Little opposition was encountered, Kuwait was soon liberated and columns of Iraqi soldiers retreating to Baghdad were mown down from the air.

The campaign seemed, from the Allied point of view, a model of clinical efficiency; British troops described it as 'fun'. Although some 697,000 United States, 45,000 British and 4,500 Canadian troops had been involved – and casualties as high as 45,000 had privately been predicted – only 148 men were killed in action and a further 467 injured among American troops. Aware of past mistakes and the new sensitivity of public opinion, the military went to considerable lengths to provide psychiatric counselling to the troops before the battle. The Americans appointed large panels of psychiatric worthies to give them advice; the British, mindful of the post-Falklands backlash, provided psychiatric treatment at the divisional level – a policy unheard of since Burma in 1944.[18]

Yet despite all these measures, early in 1991 reports began to emerge of chronic illnesses ranging 'from headaches and fatigue to motor neurone disease, heart conditions and cancer', contracted by both American and British veterans of the campaign. The press began to talk of a 'Gulf War Syndrome' and to highlight cases like that of Corporal Robert Lake, before the war a strapping 15-stone, now a wasting figure of 8-stone confined to a wheelchair.[19]

What could have caused these symptoms? Suspicions focused on four factors: the enriched uranium shells, which (it emerged) had been used in large quantities and handled by many servicemen; the vaccines given to the troops to protect them from Saddam's chemical and bacteriological weapons; the organo-phosphate chemicals which had been sprayed around with some abandon during the campaign; and, finally, Iraqi nerve agents in a bunker blown up by Allied troops. In Corporal Lake's case, the illness appeared to date from the moment he was given his inoculations for polio, typhoid, cholera, tetanus, pertussis and anthrax. Despite collapsing after being given his second anthrax injection, he had (like all British and American troops) also taken anti-nerve agent tablets (NAPS) every eight hours during his tour of duty. This 'chemical cocktail', it was argued, had somehow damaged his immune system and made him allergic to everyday life.[20]

On both sides of the Atlantic, efforts to uncover the truth were frustrated by the inadequacy of surviving military records (some of which were deliberately destroyed) and by foot-dragging in the bureaucracy. Only in October 1996 did a British minister finally admit that, contrary to his own earlier statements to the House of Commons, British troops in the Gulf *had* been exposed to organophosphate pesticides. He claimed to have been 'misled' by his officials.[21]

The political response to Gulf War Syndrome was fragmented. In the United States, many in the Pentagon and Veterans' Administration were initially dismissive. 'There's been mass hallucinations. There's been mass post-traumatic stress disorder,' the chief of the Houston VA Medical Center announced. But President Clinton and Congress both appeared more sympathetic to veterans' claims and more prepared to spend large sums of money investigating them. The politicians had learned that the most effective way to counter emotional press reports focusing on individual cases was to commission elaborate epidemiological surveys. The scientific community, at first very sceptical about Gulf War Syndrome, took it much more seriously when the scale of research funding became apparent (ultimately it would exceed $115m). By the mid-1990s numerous epidemiological studies were under way.[22]

One trend soon emerged. The high-profile cases reported in the media tended to be suffering from neurological damage that might have been caused by exposure to some specific chemical or biological toxin; some patients were ill or visibly dying, others appeared to have passed birth defects on to children conceived since the war. Yet the symptoms described in large-scale surveys of Gulf War illness tended to be much vaguer, with the interpretative emphasis put more on psychophysiological factors. For example, a panel of experts appointed by President Clinton found no evidence that the long-term effects reported by veterans could have been caused by low-level exposure to toxins, but substantial evidence of affects caused by 'stress'. Stress, they went on,

is known to affect the brain, immune system, cardiovascular system and various hormonal responses. Stress manifests in diverse ways, and is likely to be an important contributing factor to the broad range of physical and physiological illnesses currently being reported.[23]

This argument was taken a stage further by Elaine Showalter, a Professor of English at Princeton and feminist historian of hysteria. Gulf War Syndrome, said Showalter, was an 'hysterical epidemic', very similar to those attacks of paranoia and conspiracy theory to which Americans had always been prone, but spread with lightning speed by the media and that new vector of hysteria, the internet. Despite the blunders, cover-ups and deceit of the government, 'in this case, reason, science, and history are all on the side of psychological rather than chemical causes for the syndrome'. She was immediately attacked as a 'fascist', a tool of the government 'trying to bolster a flagging career in academia'.[24]

Showalter argued that Gulf War Syndrome was just a new name for the standard psychosomatic legacies of wartime tension; many of its symptoms, after all, were remarkably similar to those of Soldiers' Heart in the Great War and Effort Syndrome in the Second. She thought that just as the problems of soldiers in the trenches had been caused by their immobility and passivity, so those of Gulf War veterans had been caused by the 'months of fearful anticipation' of being poisoned and fanned by the lavish (and sometimes real-time) news coverage of the war and by irresponsible reporting afterwards (by the summer of 1995, over 200 newspapers stories on Gulf War Syndrome had appeared in the British press). The military and its medical men have also tended to take this line – that all wars have produced such symptoms but only in the media-conscious, compensation-minded, conspiracy-seeking 1990s have we chosen to make much fuss about them. It was also pointed out that 'large increases in reportage of symptoms corresponded to periods of intense media coverage.'[25]

By the end of the millennium there were still few clear answers to the questions raised. Researchers seemed agreed that there was no 'Gulf War Syndrome' as such, but that Gulf War veterans were roughly twice as ill as comparable soldiers who had served in Bosnia or in Britain. There was evidence, too, that the vaccines were the likeliest cause of illness and that taking vaccines in the Gulf, rather than in Britain or Germany, was likely to cause problems – the combination of vaccine and stress being somehow potent. On the other hand, the same researcher believed that Gulf War veterans were actually functioning just as well as their peers; the difference was in how they *felt* about themselves. He also believed that nearly all their symptoms had been found in previous wars and, indeed, in patients in his South London clinic who had never been out of England.[26]

Other doctors remained unconvinced by the 'this is what happens in all wars' line. They believed that the Gulf War was a uniquely toxic environment, posing enormous risks to the human system, and that their patients were genuinely ill. Further revelations may appear, but it seems unlikely that a smoking gun will emerge.[27]

None of the parties involved – military, politicians, media and public opinion – comes out of the Gulf War episode well. Ironically, for all the millions of dollars spent, neither the Pentagon nor Whitehall has had to face the kind of detailed and thorough official enquiry into their medical practices (aspects of which clearly were negligent), from which lessons for the future might be learnt. But perhaps in the age of the spin-doctor, such dispassionate searching after truth has become impossible.

THE CULTURE OF TRAUMA

I did have nightmares. But what is this post-dramatic stress?

Russian woman, 1998[1]

The 1980s saw a 'rediscovery of trauma'. The concept of Post-Traumatic Stress Disorder created a standardised model of how victims respond to trauma, a 'single syndrome that appears to be the final, common pathway in response to severe stress'. This made it possible to build bridges between the 'trauma of war' and other kinds of trauma such as rape, child abuse, and civilian disasters, which were then attracting attention. Military psychiatry, instead of languishing in an obscure medical ghetto, became part of a burgeoning socio-medical movement that aimed to bring into the open society's 'collective secret' and finally to reverse decades of wilful ignorance of traumatic acts and denial of post-traumatic suffering.[2]

In 1985 the International Society for Traumatic Stress Studies was formed; soon afterwards *The Journal of Traumatic Stress* began to appear; trauma books proliferated. Some 295 academic papers were submitted to the Society's 8th Annual Congress at the Beverley Hilton in Los Angeles in 1992, and over a thousand delegates attended. Three obvious categories were discernible among them: bearded men in their forties, wearing jeans – Vietnam veterans turned therapists; power-suited women specialising in rape and child abuse; and assertive, well-dressed Ivy Leaguers specialising in the 'biology of trauma'.

The rapid growth of 'traumatology' within medicine was helped by the authority which Post-Traumatic Stress Disorder quickly acquired by being included in the American Psychiatric Association's *Diagnostic and Statistical Manual* (*DSM-III*) in 1980. Not only was there now a 'Chinese menu' of its symptoms, easy for both doctor and patient to read, there were also standardised packages of diagnostic questionnaires and psychometric devices. No longer need the doctor struggle to understand his patient's life history and personality, assess his ability to cope, make a 'subjective' judgement on his state. Now, the checklist of symptoms told him at a glance whether the patient's condition was PTSD or not; it was all 'objective', taken out of the clinician's hands.[3]

Although in its origins PTSD was 'as much a socio-political as a medical response to the problems of a particular group at a particular point in time', it soon mutated. As Derek Summerfield has written, 'the mental health field rapidly accorded it the status of scientific truth, supposedly representing a universal and essentially context-independent entity. This was to say that from the beginning of history people exposed to shocking experiences had been liable to a psychiatric condition which only in 1980 had been fully discovered and named.' Learned articles uncovered the symptoms of PTSD in the Bible, the works of Shakespeare, and Samuel Pepys' diary.[4]

Initially an American phenomenon, PTSD spread round the world very quickly, its adoption in Britain hastened by the 1982 Falklands War and the spate of man-made disasters in the later years of Margaret Thatcher's premiership: in 1985, 53 people died in a football stadium fire in Bradford; two years later a cross-channel ferry sank with the loss of 193 lives; and a fire on the London Underground killed 31 more. In 1988, 167 people perished on an oil-drilling rig in the North Sea and a further 270 were killed when terrorists blew up a PanAm aircraft over the Scottish town of Lockerbie. The following year, bad crowd management at a football game in Sheffield claimed another 95 lives.[5]

The Bradford fire was a 'turning point in the way health-care professionals and the public view[ed] disasters'. Thanks to television, millions of viewers witnessed this horror and 'were able to identify more easily with the victims and their families, recognising the psychological and longer-term consequences of such an event.' After Bradford, the emergency services used the term 'post-trauma stress' for the first time and made the 'first attempt to mount a proactive outreach service by a statutory body'. Whereas in the 1940s people were left alone after such experiences and assumed to be managing unless they came forward for help, now 'potential clients' were contacted directly, 'rather than waiting for them to refer themselves'. By the time of the Zeebrugge ferry disaster in 1987, the 'Assistance Unit visited each victim who did not actively refuse a visit'; indeed there began to be 'convergence' on victims 'when agencies, both statutory and voluntary, descend in rapid succession on potential clients'. 'When I saw the twelfth person coming down the garden path,' said the widow of a man drowned at Zeebrugge, 'I hid.'[6]

Television companies were quick to see the potential of 'trauma'. The emotions provoked by fear and stress had long since ceased to be private and shameful; in the new confessional age, they were commodities to be traded in the marketplace of deregulated television and tabloid journalism. 'Trauma' became one of the staples of the daytime talk shows, the cheapest form of entertainment. Disaster survivors seemed happy to tell interviewers 'how they felt' and, by the end of the 1980s, often used a garbled version of the PTSD checklist to describe their symptoms.

If the media vectored PTSD into the public consciousness, the law, too, was quick to take it up. By 1990, British personal injury lawyers were obtaining substantial sums in compensation on behalf of traumatised victims of disasters, though claims on behalf of loved ones watching at home were eventually rejected by the courts. Members of the emergency services now began to claim compensation for the 'trauma' they suffered doing their job and 14 policemen who worked at the Hillsborough football stadium tragedy – caused by police incompetence – were awarded £1.2 million for psychiatric damage.[7]

Partly because of these new legal pressures, there was a mushroom growth in 'counselling'. By the 1990s it was normal for large employers like the police and emergency services to hire 'counsellors', therapists brought in from outside to 'debrief' survivors of disasters (and to ward off the threat of suits of negligence). Their procedures soon became standardised and 'debriefing' – a one-off event carried out in a highly structured and disciplined manner with the possibility of a follow-up at a later stage – became routine. 'I would make debriefing mandatory for anyone exposed to a very distressing event,' the director the Tavistock Clinic's Trauma Unit told journalists in 1995. 'I want to remove the idea that to ask for help after a stressful event is wimpish. Eventually, wine, women and song will not do as therapy.' The same year, the BBC announced that reporters covering the gruesome West murder trial would receive 'stress counselling'. 'What nonsense,' retorted a retired crime reporter who had covered every sensational trial of the last forty years. The best counselling, Reginald Blenkinsop believed, 'came in the pub with colleagues over a pint . . . or two . . . or three.'[8]

'Trauma' was also exported to the Third World. By the 1990s, Western 'experts' working for international agencies were using 'trauma programmes' which assumed that there was a 'universal trauma response' that could be measured by giving victims checklists of symptoms devised by American PTSD doctors. UNICEF workers surveyed 3,000 Rwandan children using the 'Impact of Events Scale' and the 'Grief Reaction Inventory' and concluded that they had high levels of PTSD which needed immediate treatment to 'restore a sense of hopefulness about their future and to prevent long-term sequelae such as depression and anxiety disorders.'[9]

During the 1980s an enormous quantity of time and money was spent in investigating Post-Traumatic Stress Disorder. The resulting literature was infinite, but in several ways odd. We have seen that most psychiatrists who worked closely with Vietnam veterans (and wrote old fashioned 'anecdotal' papers based round individual case histories) emphasised socio-psychological problems like guilt and self-hatred, and alcohol and drug use. Yet the clinical papers published after 1980 nearly all addressed a completely different agenda, concerned with the 'biology of trauma'. Written by doctors with an interest in 'biological' psychiatry working with chronic PTSD cases in Veterans' Administration hospitals, they said as much about clinical fashion and funding as about human need.

The emphasis was on the timelessness of PTSD and the hopelessness of the patient:

A highly decorated veteran . . . has led a life tortured by fear and anger since his return from Vietnam more than twenty years ago. He is unable to close his eyes in the shower because of the dread that someone will grab him. He has impulses to shoot, stab or strangle everyone he encounters.

He panics at the ring of a doorbell. Being kept waiting in line can send him into a rage. He washes his hands compulsively and repetitively checks the stove and the locks on the doors.[10]

The overall starting point for these researchers was the 'paradoxical' pattern of symptoms first noticed by Abram Kardiner at the VA hospital in the Bronx in the 1920s – paradoxical because the patient is at once bombarded by intrusive images recalling the original trauma yet does everything possible to avoid anything reminiscent of it and also becomes extremely irritable – what is sometimes known as 'a triad of intrusion, avoidance, and arousal'. To find the neurobiological explanation for these symptoms, researchers deployed a battery of tools to measure and compare heartbeat, blood pressure and the complex hormonal interactions between brain and nervous system. Quantitative tools like the 'Mississippi Scale for Combat-Related Post-Traumatic Stress Disorder', the 'Peritraumatic Dissociation Experiences Questionnaire', the 'Dissociative Experiences Scale' were wielded; modern neuroscience and experimental psychology were pressed into service. But behind the high-tech facade, much of this writing was both naive and superficial. The origins of the PTSD were seldom explored, phrases like 'combat veterans' were used with gay abandon (few attempts being made to check veterans' accounts against their service records) and patients were invariably lumped together – '20 male combat veterans with PTSD' is a typical grouping – and nothing was ever said about personality before going to Vietnam or their functioning since. The patients were just passive victims of PTSD whose symptoms can be measured.[11]

Of course, interesting hypotheses emerged. Dr Lawrence Kolb, a distinguished psychiatrist of the World War Two generation, spent some time subjecting veterans to 're-arousal' – making them watch war movies or listen again to jungle noise – and measuring their physiological responses. He concluded that 'any intense life threatening experience perceived by the exposed individual as a mortal threat . . . [was] associated with arousal of unusually intense emotional responses of fear/terror. Within the central nervous system, repeated high intensity emotional signals lead eventually to neural change, which in turn leads to hypersensitivity and impaired potential for habituation and learning.'[12]

Younger doctors have drawn on the work of neuroscientists like Joseph LeDoux to produce bold hypotheses about the way, in terrifying situations, the brain interacts with the nervous and endocrine systems to create memories that will not go away or will be re-triggered if the body is exposed again to the same environmental pressures. LeDoux updated the work of Pavlov and Cannon by showing that a part of the brain known as the amygdala acts as what Daniel Goleman has called an 'emotional sentinel, able to hijack the brain system'. Thus the arousal of the amygdala seems to imprint in memory most moments of great emotional intensity with an added degree of strength.[13]

According to Dr Roger Pitman, horrible emotional experiences may generate activity in the endocrine system which 'engraves' powerful and recurring memories in the brain. He explains the striking 'timelessness' of PTSD by arguing that traumatic events stimulate endogenous stress hormones to the point where there is 'overconsolidation of the memory trace', a process which he calls 'overconditioning'. This leads to the formation of deeply engraved memories and conditioned responses. You then get a 'positive feedback loop' in which recollection of a stress releases more stress hormones which further engrave the memory. Other researchers have found that PTSD produces changes in the axis between the brain and the pituitary and adrenal glands.[14]

These bold and exciting ideas remain hypotheses. There is no proof that they are true, nor have the findings of biological abnormality derived from chronic patients in VA hospitals been much replicated elsewhere. There are also complex issues of 'co-morbidity', of the overlap in symptoms between PTSD and other disorders such as alcoholism and depression. The fundamental objection, however, is that these hypotheses do not explain why some people are affected by traumatic events and others are not. There is still no 'Grand Unified Theory that can explain in a single sentence or equation' the cause of PTSD.[15]

Nor have the biological researchers so far produced any therapeutic breakthroughs. At a workshop in 1998, Dr Rachel Yehuda gave a bravura account of her work yet could offer little practical help to coal-face therapists. Another leading PTSD researcher has admitted that 'we can better identify, evaluate and even predict PTSD than effectively treat this disorder'.[16]

Underpinning nearly everything written about, or done to, veterans since 1980 is the notion of 'traumatic memory' – the 'professional consensus that PTSD is a freezing of the normal traumatic stress reaction and recovery process'. Indeed PTSD was distinguished from previous formulations such as 'shell-shock' by this emphasis on traumatic memory and by offering a standardised model of how traumatic memories operate across time. Traumatic memory, some have argued, is the glue that holds together the diverse symptoms of PTSD.[17]

Originally the model used was very much Freud's – of trauma followed by repression. However, in the 1980s Freud was becoming unpopular with feminists just as Henri Ellenberger's influential history of psychoanalysis, *The Discovery of the Unconscious*, was offering the first thorough account in English of the work of his long-forgotten rival, Pierre Janet. The result was a sudden rediscovery of Janet (largely ignored outside France since the First World War), and of Janet's notion of dissociation. It is arguable that Janet's original patients, simple servant girls in Paris, better approximate to the modern model than Freud's highly sophisticated Viennese *haute bourgeois*. In the same way Janet's dissociation, which 'resulted from the *passive* falling away of mental contents from an ego too weak to retain them in consciousness' better fits the age of television than Freud's '*active* repression of undesirable and emotionally painful mental contents by an ego that was strong enough to banish them from conscious awareness'. In all events, there was a revival of interest in Janet's work.[18]

'Traumatic memory' became much more than a piece of clinical shorthand, however, with the publication in 1988 of Ellen Bass and Laura Davis's book *The Courage to Heal*, which sold some 750,000 copies. Building on earlier clinical work, Bass and Davis popularised the idea that abuse in childhood caused victims to 'dissociate', leaving behind 'hidden memories' in their minds, which could then be 'remembered', years later, in psychotherapy. There then followed a number of well-reported incidents where grown-up children brought suits against their parents, using as evidence such 'recovered memories'. Clearly some genuine child abuse, for example in orphanages, was brought to the surface, but by 1995 a counterblast was under way, spearheaded by Mark Pendergrast's book *Victims of Memory*, which argued that most of the grotesque incidents of childhood rape and ritual abuse recollected by adult (mostly female) patients had simply never taken place; they were instead 'false memories' planted by therapists in the minds of highly suggestible patients.[19]

By and large, the controversy over 'false memories' was independent of the work being done with PTSD patients. But it provoked fierce criticism of the very notion of 'traumatic memory' and of Freud and Janet's theories of repression and dissociation on which most therapy with Vietnam veterans – and indeed much of twentieth-century military psychiatry by the likes of Rivers, Kardiner and Grinker – is based. It also sowed seeds of doubt about the role of therapists.[20]

Those doubts were reinforced by increasing evidence that 'de-briefing', the bureaucratic mechanism of counselling after traumatic events, systematically embraced across Western society in the late 1980s, did not actually work and probably caused as much PTSD as it prevented. Debriefing programmes seemed to do more to meet society's collective need to be seen to help victims than to address the clinical needs of the individual patients themselves. 'Why,' it was asked, 'was debriefing so successful as a social movement and so believed in as an ideology', when there had been no adequate demonstrations that it did victims any good or prevented post-traumatic illness?[21]

Given the huge social investment in 'debriefing' and its wider social function, it showed no signs of going away. Yet some leading figures in the profession were convinced of its harmfulness. 'Early and excessive hope that debriefing alone could prevent stress disorders from occurring' had been replaced, Dr Arieh Shalev wrote, by an awareness that these 'interventions' were 'stress-management functions, rather than preventive interventions'. In a talk in 1999, Bessel van der Kolk, one of the most charismatic of the PTSD doctors, emphasised the need *not* to talk to acute trauma patients about their traumatic experiences. It was much better, he said, to give them experiences which renewed their sense of pleasure and purpose in life, gave them back their capacity to function on their own. He sounded for all the world like a Victorian psychiatrist sending his patients off on a long sea voyage.[22]

Not only have methods of treating trauma begun to revert to the past; over the last decade, much of the theoretical underpinning of Post-Traumatic Stress

Disorder has also been unravelling. PTSD was originally seen, in 1980, as something that happened after extreme life-threatening events; by implication, if the stressor was severe enough, to everyone. But, for all their erudition, the makers of PTSD drew more on the pathological literature than on the overall record. They overlooked the central fact that not everyone *does* suffer in the wake of trauma. It has taken psychiatry two decades painstakingly to rediscover this basic truth; in 1995 two highly-regarded PTSD researchers announced, with great earnestness, that 'PTSD is not an inevitable consequence of trauma'. Any front-line medical officer on the Western Front, never mind William Brown in 1919 or T. A. Ross in 1941, could have told them that.[23]

Detailed studies have shown that while rates of PTSD are uniformly high after certain stressors such as rape, they are much more variable after combat, and comparatively low in workers in the emergency services. At the same time it has emerged that some people develop the symptoms of PTSD after exposure to quite minor stressors, just as in 1917 doctors found the symptoms of shell-shock in people who had never left England. Thus PTSD, if there is such a thing, is not an extreme form of the normal reaction to stress but something qualitatively quite different. In the face of this evidence, the simple, uniform model of 'trauma' adumbrated in 1980 has been fragmenting into different categories – acute and chronic PTSD, simple and complex PTSD, even male and female PTSD. At the same time, the old issue of 'predisposition' or 'vulnerability', anathema in the 1970s, has resurfaced.[24]

By the end of the century, the mood among the godfathers of PTSD was humbled, chastened, reflective. Even as the trauma bandwagon rumbled on in the wider society, some of its builders were trying to get off it. Far from seeing PTSD as the culmination of everything that had gone before – pure, scientific and ahistorical – there was now an acceptance that it was just as much a product of its time and place as anything else, probably more so. How difficult it was, Nancy Andreasen reflected in 1995, 'to precisely and empirically define subtle psychological constructs, particularly when they are vulnerable to overuse'.

The original concept of PTSD [she maintained] was a rich one, derived from broad-based research on combat, civilian catastrophes and natural disasters, conducted by many of the pioneers of psychiatry who were interested in studying mind/body relationships . . . somehow it became difficult to distil their wisdom into diagnostic criteria. We live in a world that places a high premium on standardization and objectivity; subtlety and complexity are imperilled in that world.[25]

Mardi Horowitz too, voiced concerns about 'the exclusive and reductionist' way the 'biological stuff' was being used. He re-emphasised that it was the 'psychological meaning of the life event which produced changes' and that such meaning must relate to 'pre-existing personality features'.[26]

Inevitably, in this more sceptical mood, doctors began asking what 'twenty years of passionate rhetoric about trauma' had actually *done* for its original constituency, America's Vietnam veterans.

In 1981, it will be recalled, it had seemed that a new era was dawning for the vets. Their problems were finally getting the recognition they deserved. Particular hopes rested on the Outreach Program of out-patient clinics, to be run by an able and energetic psychiatrist and veteran, Arthur S. Blank, Jr. 'At the time it was created, the hope was that a Vet Center system could be put in place quickly, do its job, and then be dismantled'. But it didn't quite work like that. 'Over its first years of operation . . . vets began coming to Vet Centers – and kept coming in. As a result, Congress renewed the program in 1981 and 1983.' By the mid-1980s, Vet Centers were treating about 150,000 vets a year and another 28,000 were in treatment for PTSD in one of the172 Veteran Administration Hospitals, thirteen of which had special PTSD units. Far from declining, the problem seemed to be growing; the 'true extent of PTSD' was now said to be between 500,000 and one million and, significantly, the numbers of 'psychological casualties . . . without war activities' were 'increasing'. 'We still haven't seen the peak,' the clinical psychologist at one Vet Center told a journalist. The Outreach Program had just been expanded to some 189 Vet Centers.[27]

In an attempt to sort out once and for all the contentious issue of numbers, Congress commissioned in 1983 'a specific and comprehensive study' of the 'mental health status and general life adjustments of Vietnam veterans', to which the future of the Vet Center programme was to be tied. After spending some $9m, the survey finally reported in 1988 that 15 years after the last American combatant had left Vietnam, 479,000 of the 3.14 million men who served there still had PTSD and almost a million people in all had had 'full-blown' PTSD. Yet, of those, only some 300,000 had actually been in combat.[28]

Politically, this exercise enabled the Vet Center programme to survive the arrival of the Reagan administration, but it was hardly the last word on the subject, not simply because of the enormous disparity between its figures and those of other surveys. Its methodology also aroused profound scepticism. In the past, follow-up studies had used crude, common sense yardsticks – assuming for example, that a man holding down a job and a relationship could be said to be managing. Now, in the quantitative age, questioners were given an enormous shopping list of symptoms and trained to probe until they found them. Nor were the implications of the numbers who had not been in the battle zone claiming PTSD addressed.[29]

At the 1992 Traumatic Stress conference, the mood of weary pessimism among those actually working therapeutically with veterans – and the papers on 'therapist burnout' – were in striking contrast to the loud confidence of the PTSD researchers. By 1997 a review of the effectiveness of current procedures (in the house journal of PTSD) concluded that most of the current 'treatment protocols' were not working and, in particular, that long-stay in-patient programmes by the Veterans' Administration in the United States had been a disastrous failure. These programmes, a VA doctor conceded, were 'grounded in a distinctive historical moment when Americans were seeking to come to terms with the Vietnam War and to settle a deeply felt debt to the nation's Vietnam veterans'. It was time, a distinguished Israeli psychiatrist wrote, to replace 'naivete' with 'maturation'.[30]

There was now also a rising chorus of complaint from outside psychiatry, claiming that the invention of PTSD had simply turned a generation of veterans into hopeless, dependent, welfare junkies. In a long-delayed right-wing counterattack to the offensive in the 1970s by Chaim Shatan, Robert Lifton, Sarah Haley and others that led up to the creation of PTSD, revisionists claimed that anti-war psychiatrists had screwed up a generation of Americans by feeding to the media a stereotype of the Vietnam veteran as a crazy, dysfunctional time bomb, when most veterans were just regular guys getting over a war. These critics made use of one potent new weapon, the Freedom of Information Act, to prove that numerous celebrated cases of PTSD (including many who had told heart-rending stories on national television of the horrors they had witnessed in combat in Asia) had never been to Vietnam or had served in rear-echelon units there.[31]

There was also renewed criticism of the Outreach Program for Veterans – the Vet Centers finally created in 1979. Quite early on, there had been those who questioned whether making therapy available on the clients' terms, with an emphasis on 'rap groups' – on veterans being with and treated by their peers – would necessarily encourage a return to work and family responsibilities, to facing the world. 'The talk of angry veterans who feed off each other may be temporarily enjoyable,' a psychologist who had served in Vietnam wrote in 1985, 'but ultimately it is counterproductive.' He warned of the danger of promoting the 'Vietnam veteran syndrome' – an identity which allowed men to use Vietnam as an alibi for their own faults of character and social failures – and cited the case of a patient who 'had taken on the role of the punished victim and appears to be using the Vietnam issue as an excuse for not taking responsibility for his life.'[32]

The general 'hope of therapy' which Vet Centers offered is well conveyed in Aphrodite Matsakis's 1987 book *Vietnam Wives*:

In order for a veteran to overcome the paralyzing and destructive effects of his war experiences, he needs to reconsider his Vietnam experiences in three levels: 1. the cognitive or mental, 2. the emotional, and 3. the moral and spiritual. Group therapy with other Vietnam veterans, led by a qualified, caring therapist knowledgeable about PTSD and the nature of the Vietnam war, is often recommended.

In order for healing to begin, the Vietnam veteran needs to 'uncover the trauma'. The specific events which were traumatic to him need to be brought out of repression and into his conscious awareness, then shared in group or individual therapy. There he can be helped to understand the meaning of these events in his life. Often these events involve incidents where the veteran's action or inaction led to the injury or death of another human being.[33]

While acknowledging that some veterans did not feel guilt, Dr Matsakis (a Vet Center psychologist) believed that, in many cases, the veteran's memories were 'distorted in the direction of unreasonable guilt'. The therapist and other veterans could help him 'evaluate the incident more objectively and relieve him of "long held guilt".'

Matsakis found that wives were often disappointed when therapy didn't 'fix their husbands as rapidly as they desire[d]'. Women who had 'waited ten or fifteen years for their husbands to finally seek help' were often 'dismayed to discover that the healing process can be painfully slow', usually at least a year. Furthermore, Matsakis warned, there were limits to what therapy could achieve. It would never remove Vietnam from the veteran's memory, but it might return him to his pre-war level of functioning, able to support a job or a career.[34]

Such cautions were certainly illustrated by the 'successful' case she cited. Rita's husband was a 'well paid, highly functional professional' whose PTSD 'never expressed itself in job problems' but who suffered from depression and an inability to relate to others. He invariably rebuffed Rita's attempts to help with the line, 'You can't understand. You weren't there.' Initially Rita went into group therapy herself, hoping thereby to find a way to 'heal' her husband. When that failed, she eventually persuaded him to seek help himself, as a way of paying back the government that had 'ripped him off'. When he finally agreed she was jubilant.

When your husband goes into therapy, you think, 'Hurrah! The problems are finally over with.' Well, guess what? There are more nightmares, more holes in the wall, more anger at you.[35]

Rita soon discovered that 'it gets worse before it gets better'. Her husband began drinking more than ever and, at one point, was taught by the group to be more 'assertive, rather than passive or aggressive, which were his usual styles'.

Here I was [Rita said] holding in everything for years and not being assertive so he wouldn't get upset and quit therapy, and here he was, practising his group's assertiveness training on me. Then, when I objected, he accused me of undercutting his therapy.[36]

It took six months of going to a group before Rita's husband shared his Vietnam experiences. Then, one night he went out drinking and the next night he 'cried on [her] lap all night long, just like a baby. Then he cried for almost a whole week afterwards, too. He couldn't even go to work.'

'Am I going crazy?' he'd ask [her].
'No, honey, you're just feeling your pain.'[37]

Eventually, he achieved 'considerable relief' from his PTSD symptoms and began to behave differently towards Rita. 'Now he wants to have a "real relationship" with me,' she said. 'But I've forgotten how to be relaxed around him.' In all, it took three years of therapy – 'his therapy, my therapy, couples therapy – the works' for their relationship to improve.[38]

That, remember, is a successful outcome, and a case where the veteran was holding down a job before he even went into therapy. What about more complex and difficult cases? Doubts about the programme's success with less motivated individuals crystallised eventually into the charge that it was becoming an enormous scam. Far from doing its job and going away, the Outreach Program had continued to grow – in 1994, there were 201 Centers costing some $58 million a year; and, the accusation went, the reluctance of the VA to challenge any veteran's claim to having PTSD or seriously to investigate his service record had made them a 'haven for malingerers'. Critics pointed, for instance, to a 1993 publication, *Posttraumatic Stress Disorder: How to Apply for 100 Percent Total Disability*, which offered guidance to claimants:

Tell them all about the symptoms you have that you read about . . . Tell them about your marriage(s). Tell them about your anger and rage. Tell how you don't trust people. ESPECIALLY THE GOVERNMENT! . . . Let the tears start to come if you are able. Tell them how screwed up life has been since you got back from 'Nam. And, tell them for some reason, things seem to be getting worse for you, harder to handle . . . Tell them sometimes you just think you can't take much more of this life.[39]

On the other hand, the booklet urged claimants to say as little as possible about their childhood, because a childhood 'trauma' might affect their disability rating:

Don't volunteer any information about your childhood. You had a normal childhood. Even if you didn't, for the purpose of the interviews you did.

Some doctors with extensive VA experience shared this view of the Centers as 'havens for malingers'. Dr Richard Burns, who had served with Special Forces in Vietnam, believed that 'out of the fifty or so patients he saw a month who claimed they were Vietnam veterans with disabling PTSD, about five – *only 10%* – truly suffered from the symptoms.' He reckoned to have seen 'only a handful of real combat vets who actually were disabled by PTSD'. 'I doubt if five of the hundred I've seen deserved 100% compensation,' he said. Burns thought most of them were 'just damn lazy. They're doing drugs, drinking alcohol, they don't want to get jobs . . . Wouldn't you rather be diagnosed a hero suffering from a war trauma and given three thousand dollars a month than diagnosed as somebody who's got an anti-social disorder?'[40]

How will history judge the lengthy aftermath of Vietnam, a saga dragged out over three decades? That Chatan, Lifton and their colleagues acted from the best of motives and genuinely believed they were helping the veterans is not in doubt. Nor is their naivety and lack of appropriate experience.

No purpose is served by taking up the cudgels in this debate and trying to blame either side. The Americans, for understandable reasons, repeated many of the socio-political mistakes they had made in the 1920s. Just as many Great War veterans had become chronic patients by the time the gleaming VA hospitals became available to treat them in 1922, so many Vietnam veterans had become irretrievably lost by the time Vet Centers were conjured up in earlier 1979. In both episodes, the long rhetorical interval – with Tom Salmon's biblical sonorities in the one case and Shatan and Lifton's overheated neo-Freudian formulae in the other – served to magnify rather than reduce the problem.

What happened between 1970 and 1980 was as much a social negotiation as a clinical programme, with psychiatry mediating between, on the one side, aggrieved veterans, and, on the other, an American public guilty at having sent them to a dirty unwinnable war. Yet history shows that to appease veterans' groups, to give them what they want, can be damaging both to veterans and to the wider society.[41]

The Vet Center programme was probably the most ambitious attempt at collective psychotherapy in history, based on an idealistic hope that mass treatment could transform the lives of up to half a million people. Yet, not only is the effectiveness of psychotherapy far from proven, American experience in the 1920s – which, apart from Kardiner's writing was, for some reason, completely ignored – had shown that once war veterans become chronic patients they tend not to recover, just as large caregiving bureaucracies, once assembled, tend not to dismantle themselves. Despite considerable evidence that those who went to Vietnam were not very well selected, the issue of 'vulnerability' was never seriously addressed because that 'would be interpreted as blaming the soldier rather than the war' – politically impossible in the climate of the times. Nor was the inherent difficulty of applying a model of 'trauma' based on the stresses of battle to hundreds of thousands of people who clearly had not been in battle ever really addressed.

It would, I repeat, be senseless to blame one group or set of individuals: it happened. Equally, though, the American post-Vietnam experience was clearly both *sui generis* and a model to be avoided rather than followed by other nations. Yet, thanks to the sheer volume of the PTSD literature, the avidity with which the European media lunge at every new transatlantic medical fashion and the ubiquity of American cultural models in the 1980s, it was eagerly taken up.

*   *   *

However, by the end of the century, there was a growing awareness among leading psychiatrists of the importance of social and cultural, rather than medical, responses to 'trauma' and to war. Critics began to peel off the layers of arrogant ignorance involved in sending 'trauma programmes' to places like Rwanda and Bosnia, of assuming that a quantitative measure of 'trauma response' developed in 1970s California was common to all societies and cultures. It was absurdly simplistic, the British psychiatrist Derek Summerfield wrote, to imagine that 'war collapses down in the head of an individual survivor to a discrete mental entity, the "trauma", that can be meaningfully addressed by Western counselling or other talk therapy.'[42]

Closer to home, it was becoming clear that enormous changes in social values since the Second World War had redefined the role of emotion and stress in Anglo-Saxon public culture. Those changes have been lucidly summarised by the American historian Alan Brinkley. 'Where once society organized itself around a cluster of powerful and widely shared values, many of them emphasizing restraint, self-discipline and personal responsibility,' Brinkley has written, 'now it is dominated by a new and more permissive ethos that emphasizes personal fulfilment, desire and identity.' A 'set of essentially bourgeois standards, rules and truths' had been displaced by 'what was once a dissenting subculture, the world of the bohemians of the early twentieth century . . . and the countercultural Left of the 1960s'. Conservatives argued that 'while some good things came from these changes, most notably, perhaps, the assault on racial injustice – most of its results had been dismaying and socially destructive'; others felt the gains outweighed the losses.[43]

The effect of these new values, according to a psychiatrist running a British 'trauma clinic' was that, whereas 'in past decades an almost military heroism, or at the very least a reticence in discussing fear, [had] appeared to be the cultural norm,' now 'a younger and better informed generation ha[d] begun to look on stress as a quality-of-life issue, and ha[d] taken a more consumerist attitude to treatment for stress-related disorders.' The most obvious shift in values was a feminisation of public life. Already noticeable in the media agenda and the style of politicians like Blair and Clinton, this was startlingly revealed in Britain by the 'week of self-indulgence and sentimentality that followed the death of the Princess Diana' in September 1997 – 'not a good month,' the journalist Ian Jack wrote, 'for those who imagined that human society is, or might one day be, governed by reason.' Like others of the 'Stoical Tendency', Jack was horrified by 'the willingness of young men to grieve publicly in a "feminine" way'; the abandonment of Protestant restraint for Catholic, Latin kitsch; the mood of public hysteria in which 'touchy-feely fascists' terrorised those felt to be showing insufficient grief; and the depth of emotional investment in someone known only from the television screen. This glimpse of the nation's 'Mental Hygiene', after two decades of getting its moral teaching from confessional television, left pundits reaching for 'the plain dignity of emotional continence' and 'the decent drapery of life'. Others pointed out how Princess Diana, victim and celebrity, fitted into the new therapy culture.[44]

What impact this shift in values will have on those who have to go to war in the future is hard to say. One psychiatrist working with war-damaged men believes that 'men today are incapable of fighting war without psychological damage.' David Alun Jones believes that 'Masculinity, with society, has changed too much. Men today are too vulnerable.' In truth, though, the link between masculinity and war was uncoupled much earlier. 'With the advent of nuclear weapons,' Sir Michael Howard has written, 'the belief in war as a "test of manhood" has sharply diminished, though it remains in the fantasy-world of science-fiction, as well as the glorification of such organizations as the SAS. There has indeed been a seismic, cultural shift, though to what precisely it is difficult to see.'[45]

Others decry the effect of the compensation culture on the service ethos. One of the most liberal and intelligent of British generals, Lord Carver, a veteran of the Western Desert and of Normandy, has deplored the way in which the old military culture, in which risk and hazard were assumed to be part of the job, has given way to a new ethos 'encouraged by instant media reporting which plays to a sentimental public, and . . . exploited by a certain type of lawyer'; a culture in which counselling and compensation are expected for any 'adverse effect they claim results from their military service.' The 'idea that the answer to stress is professional counselling' might, Carver warned, 'tend to undermine support for the serviceman's own strength of will to overcome his anxiety to fears, so retaining the respect of his colleagues'.[46]

It may seem odd to conclude this book with an anecdote that has nothing to do with psychiatrists. But one of its recurring themes has been that military psychiatry is often done best, not by psychiatrists, but by doctors, officers or soldiers who understand the principles of group psychology and use the defences in the culture to help people through traumatic situations.

Many of these cultural defences would not be acceptable today – for example, racial pride. In a book on *Shipwreck Survivors* published in 1943 the neurologist Macdonald Critchley wrote:

Race has been mentioned as a factor in mood and behaviour. The Anglo-Saxon emerges creditably in such ordeals, no doubt because of the high standards of demeanour and conduct which are so important in his social code. The disapproval of emotional extravagances, and more particularly of emotional display, conduce to an equipoise which counts for a great deal in circumstances such as these.[47]

But one also catches glimpses of other traditional techniques, deeply rooted in popular culture, for handling psychological pressure: ritualised violence – the two men in Cyril Joly's tank who started a mock fight on the way into battle; dissociation – while commanding a tank, Joly would deliberately spend hours remembering jaunts in the Somerset countryside; displacement; sex; and, above all, singing, humour and alcohol.

In Eric Joysmith's 1943 story 'The Crew of the *Jackdaw*', two North Sea trawlers are racing for port when one hits a mine and blows up.[48]

It was raining heavily and all blowing off to leeward and in the air were men – men with flying arms and legs, and there were pieces of wood and the wheelhouse floating all by itself . . .

The *Jackdaw* stops and the crew retrieve the bodies from the water.

The skipper radioed in and they said to proceed to the harbour and they'd have an ambulance waiting.
    'An ambulance and a butcher's cart is what they need,' said Sticks, and he was right.

The deck of the trawler is now covered with bodies and bits of bodies:

they was all mixed up, they lay up against the rail with the old cod-end over them and lashing all round to keep 'em from rolling.

The narrator realises this is upsetting the crew:

I saw the boys' faces, standing there by the wheelhouse looking and I said 'You bastards 'ud better sing' and I began to sing 'Rose of Tralee' that I always like and Sticks came in with me, then the little cook that we call the Duke because his name is Wellington – he joined in. After that we had 'Roll out the Barrel' and then the stoker pipes up with 'I'm the man that makes the Smoke come o' the lum – choo! choo!'and we followed that with 'They all get on to the fireman when the ship is very slow' – and we were singing fine, with never a hymn to make us sad, when we came in between the pierheads . . .

[The survivors are removed] but they had a hell of a job to fit the other boys into the stretchers, and in the end they just put 'em in a canvas sling.

[After that] we had our sheggie – and that was well laced with rum – yes they must have drained the bloody jar to make it that way. I slept good after it.

NOTES

Abbrevations Used in the Notes

Ahrenfeldt	R. H. Ahrenfeldt, *Psychiatry in the British Army in the Second World War* (London, 1958)
AJO	*American Journal of Orthopsychiatry*
AJP	*American Journal of Psychiatry*
Arch GenPsy	*Archives of General Psychiatry*
BJP	*British Journal of Psychiatry*
BMFRS	*Biographical Memoirs of Fellows of the Royal Society*
BMJ	*British Medical Journal*
Bull H Med	*Bulletin of the History of Medicine*
Butler	A. G. Butler, 'Moral and Mental Disorders in the War of 1914–18, in *Australian Army Medical Services in the War of 1914–1918,* Vol. 3 (Canberra, 1943)
C&M	T. Copp & B. McAndrew, *Battle Exhaustion: Soldiers and Psychiatrists in the Canadian Army*, 1939–1945 (Montreal, 1990)
CMAC	Contemporary Medical Archive Centre, Wellcome Institute for the History of Medicine.
E-F, MRC	T. R. Elliott and W. M. Fletcher Correspondence, Medical Research Council
IWM	Imperial War Museum
JAMA	*Journal of the American Medical Association*
JCH	*Journal of Contemporary History*
JHBS	*Journal of the History of the Behavioural Sciences*
JMH	*Journal of Modern History*
JMS	*Journal of Mental Science*
JNMD	*Journal of Nervous and Mental Disease*
J&R	W. Johnson & R. G. Rows, 'Neurasthenia and War Neuroses', in *History of the Great War Based on Official Documents: Diseases of War,* Vol. 2 (London, 1923)
JRAMC	*Journal of the Royal Army Medical Corps*

JTS   Journal of Traumatic Stress
LC/UL   Liddle Collection, University of Leeds
LH/KCL   Liddell Hart Centre for Military Archives, King's College, London.
MH   Mental Hygiene
Mil Med   Military Medicine
Myers, SSIF   C. S. Myers, Shell Shock in France 1914–1918 (Cambridge, 1940)
NPWW1   The Medical Department of the United States Army in the World War, Volume X: Neuropsychiatry (Washington, DC, 1929)
NPWW2   A. J. Glass et al (eds), Neuropsychiatry in World War Two, 2 vols (Washington, DC, 1966, 1973)
PRO   Public Record Office
PRSM   Proceedings of the Royal Society of Medicine
RWOCIS   Report of the War Office Commission of Enquiry into 'Shell-Shock' (London, 1922)
Scott, Politics   Wilbur J. Scott, The Politics of Readjustment: Vietnam Veterans Since the War (New York, 1993)
Shorter, HoP   E. Shorter, A History of Psychiatry (New York, 1997)
USVBMB   United States Veterans' Bureau Medical Bulletin

Introduction

1. H. W. Hills. [Wartime Reminiscences], n.d. LC/UL.
2. A. Feiling, 'Loss of Personality from "Shell Shock"', Lancet (1915), ii, pp. 63–6.
3. D. D. Bond, The Love and Fear of Flying, pp. 100–101.
4. PRSM 31 (1946), p. 141.
5. RWOCIS p. 43; W. Brown, Talks on Psychotherapy, 1923, p. 58.
6. M. Culpin, Psychoneuroses of War and Peace, p. 121; idem, Recent Advances in the Study of the Psychoneuroses, p. 38.
7. D. Morton and G. Wright, Winning the Second Battle, p. 75.
8. E. Mapother, PRSM 29 (1935) p. 855. Mapother was Medical Director of the Maudsley Hospital and Psychiatric Adviser to the Ex-Service Mental Welfare Society.
9. A. Kardiner, 'The Traumatic Neuroses of War' in S.Arieti (ed.) American Handbook of Psychiatry (New York, 1959) 1, p. 295
10. E. Leed, E. Showalter, The Female Malady, M. Stone.
11. S. Sassoon, Sherston's Progress (London, 1936); W. H. R. Rivers, Conflict and Dream, P. Barker, Regeneration; The Eye in the Door; The Ghost Road. See also B. Shephard, Times Literary Supplement, 22 March 1996 and A. Young, 'Rivers and the War Neuroses', JHBS 35 (1999), pp. 359–78.
12. e.g. 'How Armed Forces Forgot Lessons of the Western Front'. Daily Telegraph, 22 April 2000.

13. P. J. R. Davis, 'Divisional Psychiatry', *JRAMC* 86 (1944), pp. 254–74.
14. Scott, *Politics*; A. Young, *Harmony of Illness*
15. A. Shalev, 'Discussion: Treatment of Prolonged [PTSD]', *JTS* 10 (1997) pp. 415–23; J. D. Bremner, 'Acute and Chronic Response to Psychological Trauma: Where do we go from Here', *AJP* 156 (1999) p. 351.
16. K. Douglas, *Collected Poems* (London, 1966), p. 144.

Prologue

1. C. S. Myers, 'A Contribution to the Study of Shell Shock', *Lancet* (1915), i, pp. 316–20.
2. For details see H. Merskey.
3. H. Cushing, *The Life of Sir William Osler* (Oxford, 1925), 2, p. 484; W. Osler, 'Medical Notes on England at War', *JAMA* 64 (1915), p. 2001.
4. D. Forsythe, 'Functional Nerve Disease and the Shock of Battle', *Lancet* (1915), ii, pp. 1399–1403.
5. M. Howard, *War in European History* (Oxford, 1970) p. 120.
6. F. W. Mott, 'High Explosive and the Central Nervous System', *Lancet*, (1916), i, p. 337; A. Bowlby, 'Wounds in War', *Lancet* (1915), ii, p. 1385.
7. Ashmead-Bartlett, quoted in Mott, 'High Explosives', p. 336.
8. *RWOCIS*, pp. 4–6.

Chapter 1: Doctors' Minds

1. V. Brittain, *Testament of Youth* (1933; London, 1978), p. 91.
2. *17th International Congress of Medicine* (London, 1913).
3. Unattributed quotes in this chapter are from *The Times* for August 1913.
4. The section was called 'Neuropathology'; to avoid confusion, some terms have been standardised.
5. E. Jones, *Free Associations.* (London, 1959), p. 123; 'Insanity', *Encyclopaedia Brittanica* (11th Edn, 1912).
6. The poet Heine and the musicians Robert Schumann and Scott Joplin were among numerous victims of G.P.I. H. Klawans, *Newton's Madness* (London, 1990), pp. 161–75.
7. Anon, 'Nerves and Nervousness', *Spectator* 72 (1894), pp. 11–12. The writer was a little behind in his history. Precisely this division was noted in Dr Johnson's *Dictionary*. W. F. Bynum, 'The Nervous Patient in Eighteenth- and Nineteenth-Century Britain' in W. F. Bynum *et al* (eds), *The Anatomy of Madness*, 2 vols (London, 1985).
8. T. C. Allbutt, 'Nervous Diseases and Modern Life'. *Contemporary Review* 67 (1895), pp. 210–31.
9. R. B. Aird, *Foundations of Modern Neurology. A Century of Progress* (New York, 1993); J. Spillane, *The Doctrine of the Nerves* (London, 1981).
10. G. Holmes, *The National Hospital, Queen Square* (Edinburgh, 1954); M. Critchley, *BMJ* (1960), i, pp. 1829–37.

11. W. Haymaker and F. Schiller, *The Pioneers of Neurology* (2nd Edn, Springfield, Illinois, 1970); C. D. Aring, *JNMD* 141 (1966), p. 499.

12. Jones, *Free Associations*; J. Purves-Stewart, *Sands of Times* (London, 1935).

13. Quoted in E. Shorter, *Bedside Manners: The Troubled History of Doctors and Patients* (New York, 1985), p. 14. In the 1900s, many doctors wrote of 'functional nervous disorders' rather than of 'psychoneuroses'.

14. W. A. Turner and G. Stewart, *A Textbook of Nervous Diseases* (London, 1910), p. 522; W. Gowers, *A Manual of Diseases of the Nervous System* (2nd Edn, London, 1893), pp. 984–1030; 'Hysteria', *Encyclopaedia Britannica* (11th Edn, 1912); M. Micale, *Approaching Hysteria: Disease and its Interpretations* (Princeton, 1995).

15. E. Showalter, *The Female Malady* (London,1987), pp. 145–164. C. Goetz *et al.*, *Charcot: Constructing Neurology* (Oxford,1996) pp. 184–8. J. Goldstein, *Console and Classify. The French Psychiatric Profession in the Nineteenth Century* (Cambridge, 1987) stresses Charcot's positivist and anti-clerical agenda.

16. Gowers, *Diseases of the Nervous System*, pp. 984–1030; S. A. K. Wilson, 'Some Modern French Conceptions of Hysteria', *Brain* 33 (1910–11), p. 298.

17. S. Wessely and T. Lutz, 'Neurasthenia' in G. Berrios and R. Porter, *History of Clinical Psychiatry* (London, 1995) pp. 509–44.

18. E. Shorter, *From Paralysis to Fatigue* (New York, 1992), p. 278; A. Proust and G. Ballet, *The Treatment of Neurasthenia* (English translation London, 1902).

19. J. Oppenheim, *'Shattered Nerves': Doctors, Patients and Depression in Victorian England* (New York, 1991) pp. 265–92.

20. Wessely, 'Neurasthenia' p. 516; Bumke, quoted in Shorter, *From Paralysis*, p. 231. The French psychiatrist Pierre Janet came up with an alternative to neurasthenia called 'psychasthenia'. Psychasthenics had obsessions or compulsions to act in particular ways, phobias and anxieties and were characterised by a feeling of 'psychological incompleteness'. Although taken up by some doctors, it did not displace neurasthenia. Oppenheim, *'Shattered'*, pp. 312–4.

21. E. Ash, *Medical Times* 37 (1909), pp. 35–54; *BMJ* 1912 (ii), p. 1459.

22. H. Lee, *Virginia Woolf* (London, 1997), pp. 175–200; S. Trombley, *All That Summer She Was Mad* (London, 1982); A. Caesar, *Taking It Like A Man* (Manchester, 1993), p. 41; F. M. Ford, *Return to Yesterday* (London, 1931), pp. 266–72. Ford claimed to have been cured by Joseph Conrad's family doctor, 'an eccentric, unkempt man called Dr Albert Tebb', who told him, 'with a hollow and mournful vindictiveness', that he would be dead within the month. 'As soon as he was gone, I jumped up, dressed myself and . . . took a hansom to Piccadilly Circus. I walked backwards and forwards across the Circus for an hour and a half. I kept saying: "Damn that brute. I will not be dead in a month"'; T. Lutz, *American Nervousness,1903: An Anecdotal History* (Cornell, 1991).

23. Quoted in P. Gay, *The Tender Passion* (New York, 1987) pp. 331–9.

24. Allbutt, 'Nervous diseases'; de Coubertin quoted in R. Nye, 'Degeneration, Neurasthenia and the Culture of Sport in Belle Epoque France'. *JCH* 17 (1982), pp. 51–68.

25. Shorter, *HoP*, p. 143; R. Harris, *Murders and Madness: Medicine, Law and Society in the* Fin de Siecle (Oxford, 1989), p. 178.

26. Shorter, *HoP*, pp. 140–3; *idem, From Paralysis to Fatigue*, pp. 246–51.

27. A. Hurst, *A Twentieth Century Physician* (London, 1949), pp. 99–108.

28. *ibid.* E. Trillat, *Histoire de l'hysterie* (Paris, 1986) pp. 199–212.

29. J. Collie, 'Malingering', *BMJ* (1913), ii, p. 647; C. L.Tuckey, Introduction to H. Crichton Miller, *Hypnotism and Disease: A Plea for Rational Psychotherapy* (London, 1912), p. 8. E. M. Forster's *Maurice*, finding that the family physician brushes aside his confession that he is 'an unspeakable of the Oscar Wilde Sort' with the words 'Rubbish, rubbish!', visits a hypnotist in Welbeck Street, who attempts to 'cure' his condition, by putting him into a trance and showing him images of a music-hall actress, projected on to his consulting room wall. The treatment fails; Maurice is unable to resist the gardener, Scudder.

30. H. Ellenberger, *The Discovery of the Unconscious* (New York, 1970), pp. 331–417. 'Hysterics are patients who are easily managed, who talk willingly, who are not dangerous, on whom one can experiment without any great fear, and who, lastly, like to observe, and readily lend themselves to observations'. P. Janet, *The Major Symptoms of Hysteria* (2nd Edn, New York, 1920), p. 7. The term 'psycho-analysis' was coined by Freud and Breuer in 1896.

31. S. Freud and J. Breuer, *Studies in Hysteria* (1895; English translation, 1909).

32. E. Jones, *The Life and Work of Sigmund Freud* (1953–7); P. Gay, *Freud: A Life for our Time* (London, 1988).

33. For example, *BMJ* (1913), ii, pp. 13–17, 23–4, 1213–18; H. C. Thomson. 'Mental Therapetics in Neurasthenia', *The Practitioner*, May 1911, pp. 76–83.

34. R. Roberts, *The Classic Slum* (Manchester, 1971), p. 97.

35. E. S.Turner, *The Shocking History of Advertising* (Harmondsworth, 1975), p. 132; *Daily Mirror*, 12 July 1915.

36. Secret Remedies' *Edinburgh Review* 442 (1912); Roberts, *Classic Slum.* p. 97. The exhilaration of selling 'slightly injurious rubbish' to the public' at 'one-and-three-half pence a bottle' is wonderfully caught in H. G. Wells' *Tono-Bungay* (1909).

37. *More Secret Remedies: What they Cost and What they Contain* (London, 1912), pp. 45–70.

38. Turner, *Shocking History,* pp. 161–5.

39. W. Thorburn, 'The Traumatic Neuroses', *PRSM* 7 (1914), pp. 1–14.

40. J. Collie, *Malingering.* (London, 1913), p. 133; J. Purves Stewart, *The Diagnosis of Nervous Diseases* (5th Edn, London, 1920), p. 362. See M. Trimble, *Post-Traumatic Neurosis* (Chichester, 1981); T. Keller, 'Railway Spine Revisited', *Journal of the History of Medicine and Allied Sciences* 50

(1995), pp. 507–24 ; E. M. Caplan, 'Trains, Brains, and Sprains', *Bull H Med* 69 (1995), pp. 387–419.

41. *Lancet*, (1907), i, pp. 30–1.
42. Quoted in M. Howard, *Lessons of History* (Oxford, 1990), p. 78 'In 1845, 105 men per thousand recruited for the army had been under the standard height of 5'6". In 1900, 565 per thousand were under this height. In 1901, the army had finally obtained permission to enlist men down to a minimum height of 5 feet.' B. Gilbert, *Bull H Med* 39 (1965), p. 143.
43. T. Turner in H. Freeman (ed.), *A Century of Psychiatry* (London, 1999), p. 14; *Fortnighly Review*, 112, p. 854; Lord Meath, *Essays on Duty and Discipline* (London, 1910).
44. P. Addison, *Churchill on the Home Front* (London, 1992), p. 125. An Act of 1913 required the mentally retarded to be confined in homes – though not, in Britain, to be sterilised. M. Thomson, *The Problem of Mental Deficiency* (Oxford, 1998).
45. T. Travers, 'Technology, Tactics and Morale: Jean de Bloch, the Boer War, and British Military Theory, 1900–1914. *JMH* 51 (1979), pp. 264–86; M. Howard, 'Men Against Fire', in *idem, Lessons of History* (Oxford, 1990).
46. Travers, 'Technology', p. 283.
47. Letter, 16 October 1997. With thanks to Sir Michael Howard.
48. P. Parker, *The Old Lie. The Great War and the Public School Ethos* (London, 1987), p. 41.
49. J. Springhall, 'Building character in the British boy', in J. A. Mangan and J. Walvin (eds), *Manliness and Morality* (London,1987), p. 70.
50. M. J. Clark, 'The Rejection of Psychological Approaches', in A. Scull (ed), *Madhouses, Mad-Doctors and Madmen. A Social History of Psychiatry in the Victorian Era* (Philadelphia, 1981).
51. E. M. Forster, *The Longest Journey* (1907; Harmondsworth, 1968), p. 58.
52. J. Harris, *Private Lives, Public Spirit: Britain 1870–1914* (Harmondsworth, 1994), p. 6.

Chapter 2: Shell-Shock in France.

1. J&R, pp. 1–2.
2. C. S. Myers, 'Diary, 1914–15'. With thanks to Joan Rumens.
3. C. S. Myers, 'Autobiographical Notes'; F. C. Bartlett, *BMFRS*, 5 (1948); *idem, American Journal of Psychology* 50 (1937); L. S. Hearnshaw, *A Short History of British Psychology* (London, 1964); Haddon papers, Cambridge University Library; *Nature* 68 (1903), pp. 409–10; H. Kuklick, 'Darwinian biogeography and British anthropology'. *American Ethnologist* 22 (1996), pp. 611–38.
4. C. S. Myers, *A Textbook of Experimental Psychology* (Cambridge, 1909); *idem, An Introduction to Experimental Psychology*, (Cambridge, 1911).
5. Myers, 'Diary'; *idem, SSIF,* p. 14
6. Myers, 'Diary'; *idem, SSIF,* p. x.

7. E. Jones, *Free Associations* (London, 1959), pp. 244–5; T. R. Elliott 22 January 1917, E-F, MRC.

8. R. McLaughlin, *The Royal Army Medical Corps* (London, 1972); J. S. G. Blair, *Centenary History of the RAMC* (Edinburgh, 1998); Butler, p. 231. M. Harrison, 'Medicine and the Management of Modern Warfare', *History of Science* 34 (1996), pp. 379–410.

9. M. Finucane, 'General Nervous Shock . . . in the South African Campaign, *Lancet* (1900), ii, pp. 807; A. G. Kay, 'Insanity in the Army', *JRAMC* 18 (1912), pp. 146–58; H. E. M. Douglas and H. St. M. Carter, 'Observations made during the Serbo-Bulgarian War, 1913'. CMAC. RAMC 446/6; Myers, *SSIF*, p. 17.

10. *BMJ*, (1936), ii, pp. 317–8; R. B. Haldane, *An Autobiography* (London, 1929).

11. *Who Was Who?*, *BMJ* (1923) ii, 1088–91; H. Cushing, *From A Surgeon's Journal* (Boston, 1936); E-F, MRC; Myers, *SSIF*, p. 11.

12. J. Charteris, *At GHQ* (London, 1931), p. 129; M. Gilbert, *Winston S. Churchill*, vol. 3. Companion vol. Part 2 (London, 1972), pp. 1353–4; E-F, MRC.

13. R. C. Money quoted in I. Beckett and K. Simpson (eds), *A Nation in Arms*. (Manchester,1985), p. 68; see also O. Sitwell, *Great Morning* (London, 1949).

14. F. Richards, *Old Soldiers Never Die* (London, 1933); *idem, Old Soldier Sahib* (London, 1936).

15. *RWOCIS*, p. 9; J. Baynes, *Morale* (London, 1987).

16. J&R, p. 54; E. Mapother, *PRSM* 29 (1936) p. 108.

17. Lt.-Col H. Clay, *RWOCIS*, p. 41.

18. *RWOCIS*, pp. 160–70, 16, 18, 72.

19. J&R, p. 10; H. Dearden, *Medicine and Duty*. (London, 1928), p. ix.

20. Myers, *SSIF*, pp. 76–101. Myers' 'Contributions' on shell-shock in the *Lancet* discussed 'loss of memory, vision, smell and taste' (February 1915), treatment by hypnosis (January 1916), 'Disorders of cutaneous sensibility' (March 1916), 'Disorders of speech . . . and their relation to malingering' (September 1916) and 'unsettled points' (January 1919).

21. Myers, *SSIF*, p.90.

22. P. Fussell, *The Great War and Modern Memory* (1975); S. Hynes, *A War Imagined* (1990); Butler, p. 94.

23. *RWOCIS*, pp. 4–6; J&R, p. 9.

24. J. C. Dunn, *The War The Infantry Knew* (1938; London, 1987), p. 250; *Daily Mirror* 7, 8, 22, 29 July 1915; *Daily Mail* throughout September 1915.

25. *The Times*, 25 May 1915.

26. Myers, *SSIF*, pp. 93–101.

27. Myers, *SSIF*, p. 95; *RWOCIS*, p. 141.

28. Myers, *SSIF*, p. 96–7.

29. F. W. Mott, 'The effects of high explosives on the central nervous system',

Lancet (1916), i, pp. 331–8, 441–9, 545–53; 'Special discussion on shell shock without visible signs of injury', *PRSM* 1916 (Section of Psychiatry), pp. 1–44.

30. H. Wiltshire, 'A Contribution to the Etiology of Shell Shock', *Lancet*, (1916), i, pp. 1207–12.
31. Myers, *SSIF*, p. 25–29.
32. 'Special discussion on shell shock', *PRSM* 1916.
33. Myers, *SSIF*, p. 92; J&R, p. 2. The Australian medical historian A. G. Butler, a doctor on the Western Front, believed that 'The idea and the name of "shell-shock," though propounded in good faith as a helpful medical hypothesis, [became] through military and social exploitation and mass suggestion – a devastating menace'. Butler, p. 93.

Chapter 3: Trench Work

1. A. Alfands to Lord Northcliffe, Northliffe Papers, British Library.
2. Lord Moran (Charles Wilson), *The Anatomy of Courage.* (London, 1945), p. 27–40.
3. J. Terraine (ed.), *General Jack's Diary* (London, 1964), p. 65; G. Chapman, *A Passionate Prodigality* (London, 1933), pp. 86–7; D. Judd, *Ford Madox Ford* (London, 1990), pp. 290–1.
4. William Strang, 3 August 1916, LC/UL. Strang later ran the Foreign Office.
5. Chapman.
6. *RWOCIS,* p. 60; A. Osburn, *Unwilling Passenger* (London,1932), pp. 291–2.
7. Hiram Sturdy papers, IWM.
8. Moran, *Anatomy*, pp. 33–4.
9. F. Manning, *The Middle Parts of Fortune* (1929; London, 1986). According to his PRO file, Manning was evacuated from France suffering from alcoholic poisoning.
10. Tyrrell, *RWOCIS*, pp. 88–91; Tyrrell papers, IWM.
11. Robert Wingham, LC/UL.
12. Dr Charles McKerrow,19 July 1916. LC/UL.
13. W. H. Round, LC/UL.
14. Hiram Sturdy, IWM.
15. CMAC/RAMC 739/4
16. Moran, *Anatomy* p. 75.
17. *NPWW1*, p. 507; R. D. Ritchie, 'One History of Shell-shock', PhD thesis, University of California, San Diego, 1986.

Chapter 4: The Somme

1. G. Powell, Diary, IWM, quoted in M. Eksteins, *Rites of Spring: The Great War and the Birth of the Modern Age* (1989; London, 1990), p. 238.
2. PRO WO 95/415; H. Somervell, *After Everest* (London, 1936), pp. 25–6.

3. Somervell, op.cit. pp. 26–7; PRO WO 95/415. War Diaries of other CCSs are in WO 95/344, 412– 6, and 498–501.

4. PRO WO 95/344.

5. J&R, pp. 16–17.

6. Butler, p. 102.

7. J&R, pp. 8–9; W. G. Macpherson *et al, Official History of the War: Medical Services; General History*, vol. 3 (London, 1924), p. 41.

8. G. Holmes, *RWOCIS*, p. 41.

9. P. Gibbs, *The Realities of War* (London, 1920), p. 304; R. Blake (ed.), *The Private Papers of Douglas Haig, 1914–19* (London, 1952), p. 133; T. Travers, *The Killing Ground* (London, 1990), pp. 170, 158.

10. W. Brown, *PRSM* (1916), Section of Psychiatry, p. xxx; W. Johnson, *RWOCIS*, p. 82.

11. 'V. M.', *Records of the 11th (Service) Battalion, Border Regiment (Lonsdale)* (Appleby-in-Westmoreland, 1916). Unusually for one of his rank, Colonel Machell had stayed with his men in the trench and, 'watching the progress of his men,' had decided to lead the attack himself. He was killed 'as soon as he left the trench,' M. Middlebrook, *The First Day of the Somme* (Harmondsworth, 1984), pp. 164, 330. This account is taken from 'Extract from proceedings of a Court of Enquiry'. CMAC, RAMC 446/11.

12. PRO WO 95/45; B. Gammage, *The Broken Years.* (Ringwood, Victoria, 1975) p. 163.

13. Gammage, *Broken Years,* p. 166; P. Charlton, *Pozieres* (London, 1986).

14. C. E. W. Bean, quoted in Butler, p. 103; *loc. cit.* The writer, J. A. Raws, was killed soon after.

15. Butler, pp. 102–13 (with detailed figures); Gammage, *Broken Years*, p. 170. Col. C. G. Manifold quoted in Butler, pp. 110–12. Manifold's first report was written in September 1916, his second in February 1918.

16. Montgomery-Massingberd papers, Liddell Hart Centre for Military Archives, King's College London (M-M, LH/KCL).

17. M-M, LH/KCL. Similar criticism came from General Furse: 'Nothing will persuade me', he wrote, 'that in the long run it is good business to put large numbers of infantry into areas that are bound to be heavily shelled by the enemy before such numbers can protect themselves by digging from such a bombardment.'

18. M-M, LH/ KCL.

19. M-M, LH/KCL. Sir Reginald Stephens. 'Lessons from the Recent Offensives', September 1916, IWM 69/70/1. Stephens also complained about 'slightly wounded men and people with shell shock [who] have not the stoutest of hearts' being allowed to leave the ranks: 'They are also retailers of terrible stories of the dangers they have undergone. They do a lot of harm by frightening men fresh from England with yarns of the terrors before them. Officers have got to be hard-hearted with these sort of people.' After the war, Lord Gort, V.C. (Grenadier Guards) asserted that 'among the regular battalions with a good class of men . . . there were few cases of real "shell

shock"' and Colonel Burnett (Gordon Highlanders) said that 'in pre-war Regular battalions so long as the officer himself did not go back with a nervous breakdown very few of the men would'. *RWOCIS*, pp. 49,45. On the other hand, Lt.-Col. F. Maxwell, VC, CO of a 'Kitchener' batallion, wrote on 26 July 1916: "Shell shock" is a complaint which, to my mind, is too prevalent everywhere; and I have told my people that my name for it is fright, or something worse, and I am not going to have it. Of course, the average nerve system of this class is much lower than ours, and sights and sounds affect them much more. It means . . . that they haven't got our power of self-control, that's all. Quoted in H. Cecil and P. H. Liddle (eds), *Facing Armageddon: The First World War Experienced.* (London, 1996) p. 305.

20. Travers, *Killing Ground*, pp. 77.

21. F. Wilson (1936), General Furse (1916), both quoted in Travers, *Killing Ground*, pp. 20–3.

22. CO, X Corps. 19 August, 1916. M-M, LH/KCL.

23. PRO CAB 34/145. Several people described going to see their superior officer and being told 'I know why you're here, you want to get this attack cancelled. It's no good we've already tried ourselves.' On one such occasion a brigadier said, 'I can't send your request in. I shall lose my job.' When the attack failed, he lost it anyway.

24. J. F. C. Fuller, *RWOCIS*, pp. 73, 28.

25. Travers, *Killing Ground*, p. 173.

26. DGMS (Sloggett), PRO WO 95/45; DMS, 4th Army – WO 95/447; DMS, Reserve Army – WO 95/532; DDMS,1st Anzac Corps – WO 95/996

27. PRO WO 935/532; WO 95/658; J&R, pp. 10–11.

28. *RWOCIS*, pp. 123–5. This is fairly similar to 'PIE' – 'Proximity, Immediacy, Expectancy' – the formula of frontline treatment devised in the 1950s.

29. Myers, *SSIF*, pp. 19–20.

30. War Diary, DMS, L. of C, 1, 8 Jan. 1917. PRO WO 95/3980; Myers, *SSIF*, p. 21.

31. Myers, *SSIF*, p. 20.

32. B. G. Parsons-Smith, in F. C. Rose and W. F. Bynum (eds), *Historical Aspects of the Neurosciences* (New York, 1985), pp. 357–70; F. Walshe, *BMFRS* 12 (1966); C. D. Aring and D. Denny-Brown, *JNMD* 141 (1966), pp. 497–504; M. Critchley, *The Divine Banquet of the Brain*, (New York, 1979) pp. 228–34. Interviews, Kathleen Holmes, 1991; Jim MacGregor, July 1990.

33. H. Cushing, *From A Surgeon's Journal.* (London,1936) p. 57; C. Blakemore, *Mechanics of the Mind* (Cambridge,1977), pp. 63–4.

34. G. Holmes, 'The Sexual Element in the Neurasthenia of Men,' *The Practitioner*, 86 (1911) pp. 55–60; J. Purdon Martin, 'Reminiscences of Queen Square', *BMJ*. (1981) ii, pp. 1640–2; J. MacGregor interview.

35. BMJ (1919), I, p. 711; F. Kennedy. *The Making of a Neurologist.* (London, 1981), p. 62; *idem*, 'The Nature of Nervousness in Soldiers', *JAMA* 71 (1918), p. 17.

36. *RWOCIS*, pp. 123–5. In *Shell Shock In France* this passage reads 'restore his self-knowledge, self-confidence, and self-esteem'. (p. 55).
37. C. S. Myers, 'Certain Cases Treated by Hypnosis', *Lancet*, (1916), i, p. 69.
38. W. Brown, 'The Treatment of Cases of Shell-Shock in an Advanced Neurological Centre', *Lancet*, (1918), ii, pp. 197–200.
39. Myers, 'Certain Cases'. Interview, Brigadier Emund Myers, 1992.
40. Myers, *SSIF*, p. 105; *PRSM* 29 (1935), p. 855.
41. R. D. Hinshelwood in G. E. Berrios and H. Freeman (eds), *150 Years of British Psychiatry* (London, 1991), p. 201.
42. Myers-Rivers, August 1917, Psychology Department, Cambridge University.

Chapter 5: Psychiatry at the Front, 1917–18.
1. C. Edmunds (Charles Carrington), *A Subaltern's War* (London, 1929), p. 133.
2. C. R. M. F. Cruttwell, *A History of the Great War, 1914–1918* (Oxford, 1934), p. 342; E. Blunden, *Undertones of War* (1928; Harmondsworth, 1982), p. 187.
3. D. Woodward, *Lloyd George and the Generals* (Newark, Dela., 1983), p. 230.
4. *RWOCIS*, p. 40.
5. Butler, p. 122; *RWOCIS*, p. 39; J&R, pp. 10–11; PRO WO 95/532.
6. PRO WO 95/532.
7. Rogers, *RWOCIS*, p. 67.
8. *RWOCIS*, pp. 39, 81.
9. Myers, *SSIF*, p. 101; Butler, p. 127; Lawrence Gameson, 'Memoirs', IWM.
10. Butler, p. 128.
11. Rogers, *RWOCIS*, pp. 62–8. Rogers' practice of marching with his men, 'great coolness and utter disregard for personal safety', and 'personality and devotion to duty' earned him 'the affection of all men and officers'. Returning from sick leave in 1917, he 'met with a great welcome from all ranks'. A. G. Wauchope, *History of the Black Watch in the Great War* (London, 1926), II, pp. 12, 20, 80.
12. Wilson, *RWOCIS*, p. 76
13. Butler, p. 128.
14. C. Symonds, quoted in R. Symonds, 'The Life of Sir Charles Symonds' (unpublished).
15. Tyrrell, *RWOCIS*, p. 32.
16. Fuller, *RWOCIS*, p. 39.
17. R. D. Ritchie, 'One History of Shell-Shock', PhD Thesis, University of California, San Diego (1986).
18. Henry Head, *RWOCIS*, p. 68. According to Johnson, 'Any soldier above the rank of corporal seemed possessed of too much dignity to become hysterical', J&R, p. 18.
19. L. Macdonald, *They Called It Passchendaele* (1978; London, 1983), p. 146.

20. H. Cushing. *From A Surgeon's Journal,* (London, 1936) p. 127.

21. *BMJ* (1949), i, p. 593; *Lancet,* (1949), i, p. 589.

22. Johnson, RWOCIS, pp. 81–2.

23. J&R, p. 9.

24. This description is of Dr Henry Yellowlees, but Johnson followed similar techniques. M. Culpin, *Recent Advances* (London, 1931), pp. 15–16.

25. *RWOCIS,* p. 39.

26. *RWOCIS,* pp. 39–40; J&R, p. 35.

27. Cushing, *Surgeon's Journal* pp. 233–4; J&R, p. 34. 'The patient was intensely introspective and was full of complaints to an almost nauseating degree.' Passchendaele figures: *RWOCIS,* pp. 40, 80; J&R, pp. 12–13.

28. *RWOCIS,* pp. 39–41, 80–2; J&R, pp. 41–5; J. Tippett, *BMJ* (1939), ii, p. 742.

29. *BMJ* (1952), i, p. 1136; *Lancet,* (1952), i, pp. 1073, 1119. During the war, Brown served in Alexandria (at the time of Gallipoli), at Maghull Hospital near Liverpool and the Maudsley in London.

30. W. Brown, *Talks on Psychotherapy* (London, 1923), p. 22.

31. W. Brown, *Psychology and Psychotherapy* (3rd Edn, London, 1934), pp. 92–3.

32. W. Brown, C. Myers, and W. McDougall, 'Discussion: 'The Revival of Emotional Memories and its Therapeutic Value'. *British Journal of Medical Psychology* 1 (1920), pp. 16–33; H. Owen and J. Bell (eds), *Wilfred Owen: The Collected Letters* (Oxford, 1967), p. 455.

33. W. Brown, 'The Treatment of Cases of Shell Shock in an Advanced Neurological Centre, *Lancet* (1918), i, pp. 197–200; Myers, *SSIF,* p. 110; J&R, pp. 10–11, Butler, p. 128–30. D. Englander, 'Discipline and Morale in the British Army, 1917–18' in J. Horne (ed.) *State, Society and Mobilization During the First World War* (Cambridge,1997); J. G. Fuller, *Troop Morale and Popular Culture in the British and Dominion Armies 1914–18* (Oxford, 1992).

34. R. Harris and J. Paxman, *A Higher Form of Killing* (London, 1983), p. 21.

35. PRO WO 142/1101. Quoted, Harris and Paxman, *Higher Form,* p. 18.

36. Harris and Paxman, *Higher Form,* pp. 21–4.

37. *ibid.,* pp. 24–5.

38. *ibid.,* pp. 14–17; *RWOCIS,* pp. 62–3. 'Poor devils!' wrote Dr Harvey Cushing on 23 July 1917, after witnessing gas cases, '. . . their eyes bandaged, led along by a man with a string while they try to keep to the duckboards. Some of the after-effects are as extraordinary as they are horrible – the sloughing of the genitals, for example.' *Surgeon's Journal,* p. 166.

39. H. Allen, quoted in D. Winter, *Death's Men* (Harmondsworth, 1979), p. 121.

40. Butler, p. 128–9. 31.5% of American battle casualties from the war were from gas. After the war, 300,000 veterans applied for war relief because of 'gas disability', while gas casualties only came to 224, 089, *loc.cit.*

41. Moran, quoted in Winter, *Death's Men,* p. 126; T. R. Elliott, 7 April 1918. E-F, MRC.

42. Elliott-Fletcher, *loc. cit.*

43. D. Mumford, 'Somatic Symptoms and Psychological Distress in the *Iliad* of Homer', *Journal of Psychosomatic Research*, 41 (1996), pp. 139–148; H. J. Starling 'Discussion on Effort Syndrome', *PRSM* 34 (1941), pp. 541–2; R. McN. Wilson, 'The Irritable Heart of Soldiers', *BMJ* (1916), i, pp. 119–20; O. Paul, 'Da Costa's Syndrome' *British Heart Journal* 58 (1987), pp. 306–15; P. W. Skerritt, 'Anxiety and the Heart – a Historical Review', *Psychological Medicine* 13 (1983), pp. 17–25.

44. J. M. Da Costa, 'On Irritable Heart', *American Journal of the Medical Sciences*, 61 (1871), pp. 17–52.

45. Da Costa, 'On Irritable Heart'; J. Hay, in W. G. Mapherson *et al* (eds), *Medical Services: Diseases of the War*, vol. 1 (London, 1924), pp. 504–5.

46. Hay, in Macpherson, *Medical Diseases*, 1, p. 506.

47. J. D. Howell. 'Soldier's Heart', *Medical History*, Supplement 5 (1985), pp. 34–52; A. J. Christophers, 'Heart Disease Amongst British Soldiers During [WW1],' *War & Society* 15 (1997), pp. 53–72.

48. T. Lewis, *The Soldier's Heart and the Effort Syndrome* (2nd Edn, London, 1940).

49. H. J. Starling, *PRSM* 34 (1941), pp. 541–2; Howell, 'Soldier's Heart', p. 42.

50. Christophers, 'Heart Disease'. Many of the claims of physiological abnormality were dropped from the second (1940) edition of Lewis's *Soldier's Heart.*

51. M. Culpin, *BMJ* (1952), ii, p. 956; Paul, 'Da Costa's Syndrome'. p. 310.

52. Lewis, *The Soldier's Heart*, quoted in M. Jones; 'Physiological and Psychological Responses to Stress in Neurotic Patients'. *JMS* 94 (1948), p. 392; Howells, 'Soldier's Heart'.

53. Opinions vary as to whether 306 or 307 soldiers were executed during the war. The figure of 324, sometimes quoted, covers the period from 4 August 1914 to 31 March 1920. A further 700-odd Indian soldiers were executed. A. Babington, *For the Sake of Example* (London, 1983); J. Putkowski and J. Sykes, *Shot At Dawn* (London, 1992). The British record is defended by J. Peaty, 'Haig and Military Discipline' in B. Bond and N. Cave (eds), *Haig. A Reappraisal 70 Years On* (Barnsley, 1999).

54. Letter to Andrew MacKinlay, MP, quoted in the *Independent*, 16 August 1993. Five years later, Dr John Reid, Armed Forces Minister in the Labour government, used similar arguments. 'What had convinced' him that 'a general pardon could not be justified legally', Reid said, 'was the impression that shell-shock had been taken into account'. Of the 20,000 personnel convicted of military offences for which the death penalty could have been imposed, only 3,000 were sentenced to death. But 89% of those had their sentences commuted by their commander-in-chief and 'one can assume that shellshock and trauma, as we would call it today, were taken into account, although most of the medical records were destroyed', *The Times*, 25 July,1998. Both men were echoing the words of the Deputy Adjutant-General, Sir Wyndham Childs, who in 1921 said (quite mendaciously) that

'the greatest care was taken by the Commander-in-Chief not to confirm any . . . sentence until the prisoner's case had been fully examined by experts in nervous disorders. The procedure controlling the court-martial procedure [sic] was put in force in the autumn of 1914'. *RWOCIS*, p. 88. See also W. Childs, *Episodes and Reflections* (London, 1927).

55. *Independent,* 16 August 1993. PRO WO 71/509.

56. PRO WO 71/539, 541, 542, 587, 591, 609, 625, 627, 630, 657.

57. Babington, *For the Sake*, p. 142.

58. Lawrence Gameson, 'Memoirs', IWM.

59. *ibid.*

60. Babington, *For the Sake*, pp. 140–1.

61. *ibid.,* p157.

62. *ibid.,* pp. 158–9.

63. J. G. Fuller, *Morale and Popular Culture in the British and Dominion Armies* (Oxford, 1992), S. P. Mackenzie, *Politics and Military Morale* (Oxford, 1994); R. Blake (ed.), *The Private Papers of Douglas Haig* (London, 1952), p. 277.

64. Wilson, *Myriad Faces,* p. 576; H. W. Hills, (Recollections), LC/UL. Charles Myers, too, found himself 'endeavouring to save soldiers being shot . . . who were clearly not wholly responsible for their acts'. *SSIF*, p. 135.

65. Hills, 'Recollections'. One British doctor believed that 'most cases of desertion and absence without leave were 'the subject of simple hysterical fugues'. The medical term 'fugue' refers to 'those instances in which a person disappears from his accustomed haunts and reappears at some distant place, astonished and puzzled to find himself there, and unable to give any account of himself in the period between his disappearance and his reappearance . . . the actual fugue realises some fantasy previously generated by a repressed desire for such escape from the scene'. Nearly all were soldiers who had walked away from the front towards the principal Channel port, Boulogne, and were arrested in or near that town. Dr W. D. Chambers thought it astonishing 'that so many profoundly dissociated cases mananged to elude the numerous and inquisitive military police as long as they did . . . it argues a very considerable degree of unconscious alertness and cunning'. Some fugueurs were undoubtedly shot, but most were not prosecuted. (W. D. Chambers, 'Mental Wards with the [BEF]', *JMS* 65 (1919), pp. 152–80; W. McDougall, *Outline of Abnormal Psychology*, (New York, 1926), p. 257. Fugues had enjoyed great vogue in French neurology in the 1900s. See I. Hacking, *Mad Travelers*, (Charlottesville, Va., 1998).

Chapter Six: Home Fires

1. Myers, *SSIF*, pp. 120–7.

2. Viscount Knutsford, *In Black & White* (London, 1928), pp. 268–70; P. J. Leese, 'A Social and Cultural History of Shellshock'. PhD thesis, Open University (1989); M. Stone. 'Shellshock and the Psychologists' in W. T.

Bynum *et al* (eds), *The Anatomy of Madness*, vol. 2, (London, 1985).

3. W. A. Turner, 'Arrangements for the Care of Cases of Nervous and Mental Shock Coming from Overseas', *Lancet* (1916), i, 1073–5.

4. T. W. Salmon, 'The Care and Treatment of Mental Disdeases and War Neuroses ("Shell Shock") in the British Army' in *NPWW1*, pp. 507–9; J&R, p. 55.

5. W. Hutchinson, *The Doctor in War* (London, 1919), pp. 109–16; L. MacDonald, *The Roses of No Man's Land* (1980; Harmondsworth, 1993), pp. 213–9; *RWOCIS*, p. 83.

6. Hutchinson, *Doctor in War*, p. 112.

7. MacDonald, *Roses*, *loc.cit*. Gunner McPhail, 'Just Shell Shock', *Springfield War Hospital Gazette*, September 1916.

8. MacPhail, 'Just Shell Shock'.

9. J. Collie, 'The management of neurasthenia', *Recalled to Life*, 2 September 1917; Salmon, 'Care and Treatment', p. 511.

10. Salmon, 'Care and Treatment', p. 515.

11. Salmon, 'Care and Treatment', p. 505; *Truth*, 9 February 1916.

12. Myers, *SSIF*, pp. 119–21.

13. Salmon, 'Care and Treatment', p. 522.

14. J&R, p. 9; C. Read, 'Survey of War Neuropsychiatry, *Mental Hygiene* 2 (1918), pp. 353–87; E. F. Buzzard, 'Warfare on the Brain', *Lancet* (1916), ii, pp. 1095–9.

15. A. Hodgkin, *BMFRS* 25 (1979); R. D. Ritchie, 'One History of Shell-Shock', PhD thesis, University of California, San Diego, 1986.

16. E. D. Adrian and L. R. Yealland, 'The Treatment of Some Common War Neuroses', *Lancet* (1917), i, pp. 867–72.

17. E. D. Adrian, 'Freud Without Tears' (Unpublished talk,1919. Thanks to Lord Adrian); Adrian and Yealland, 'Treatment'.

18. Adrian and Yealland, 'Treatment'.

19. L. R. Yealland, *Hysterical Disorders of Warfare* (London, 1918) pp. 7–15.

20. *ibid.*

21. *ibid.*

22. *War Neuroses* (1918), British Pathe; A. F. Hurst, *PRSM* 11 (1918) pp. 39–42.

23. A. Hurst, *A Twentieth Century Physician* (London, 1949) pp. 40–108.

24. *Lancet,* (1944), ii, pp. 329– 30; *Guy's Hospital Reports*, 89 (1939), 94 (1945); C. Symonds, *Studies in Neurology* (Oxford, 1970) p. 10.

25. Symonds, *Studies*; A. F. Hurst and J. Syms, 'The Rapid Cure of Hysterical Symptoms in Soldiers', *Lancet* (1918), iii, pp. 139–41.

26. Hurst and Syms, 'Rapid Cure'.

27. *ibid.*; *Seale Hayne Neurological Studies* (1918–20).

28. Osler, preface to *Seale Hayne Neurological Studies*; *BMJ* (1939), ii, p. 742; *BMJ* (1940), i, pp. 499–500; Interview, Dr S. MacKeith, 1990.

29. Adrian, 'Freud Without Tears'.

30. [Lord] Adrian, 'Hysteria'. Unpublished talk 1967. Thanks to Lord Adrian.

31. B. Shephard, 'R. G. Rows and Maghull', in H. Freeman and G. E. Berrios, *150 Years of British Psychiatry, Volume II: The Aftermath* (London, 1996).

32. T. H. Pear, 'Some Early Recollections'. *Journal of the Royal Anthropological Institute* 90 (1960), pp. 227–37.

33. W. R. Dawson (ed.), *Sir Grafton Elliot Smith* (London, 1938), p. 61.

34. J&R, p. 51.

35. R. G. Rows, 'Mental Conditions Following Strain and Nerve Shock', *BMJ* (1916), i, pp. 441–3.

36. *ibid.*

37. *ibid.*

38. W. H. R. Rivers, *Conflict and Dream* (London, 1923), p. 6.

39. T. H. Pear, 'Reminiscences' (with thanks to Dr Alan Costall); T. A. Ross, 'Shellshock' in H. Joules (ed.), *The Doctor's View of War* (London, 1938).

40. Salmon, 'Care and Treatment', p. 511; J&R. pp. 45–65.

41. Myers, 'Autobiographical Notes' p. 15. McDougall was not based at Maghull, but took some part in discusssions there. See Shephard, 'Rows'.

42. R. Slobodin, *W. H. R. Rivers* (New York, 1978); A. Young, 'W. H. R. Rivers and the War Neuroses', *JHBS* 35 (1999), pp. 359–78.

43. A. C. Haddon, *Head Hunters. Black, White and Brown* (London,1901), p. 124.

44. F. C. Bartlett, *The Eagle* (1967) pp. 156–60; Pear, 'Some Early Recollections'.

45. W. H. R. Rivers, *Conflict and Dream*, (Cambridge, 1922), pp. 5–7.

46. J. Stallworthy, *Wilfred Owen: A Biography* (1974; Oxford, 1977), p. 192.

47. S. Sassoon *Sherston's Progress* (1936; London, 1988), pp. 16, 50–51.

48. W. H. R. Rivers, 'Freud's Psychology of the Unconscious', in *idem, Instinct and Unconscious* (Cambridge, 1922).

49. D. Eder, 'The Psychopathology of the War Neuroses,' *Lancet* (1916), ii, pp. 264–8.

50. *ibid.* When told under hypnosis that the fight was over and he could let go of the rifle, this soldier immediately relaxed his hand. Eder was an early socialist (rioting in Trafalgar Square in 1887), graduate in psychology and for 15 years a doctor and traveller in Africa and South America. He then pioneered 'medicine for the poor' with a 'queer little practice in Soho among foreign waiters', helped to found the Labour Party, befriended D. H. Lawrence and took up Freud and Jung. Jones, *Free Associations*, pp. 137–9.

51. D. Eder, *War Shock* (London,1917) p. 100–5.

52. Eder, *War Shock*, loc. cit; A. F. Hurst, *Medical Diseases of the War* (2nd End, London, 1918), p. 75.

53. Rivers, 'Freud's Psychology'.

54. W. H. R. Rivers, 'Psychotherapeutics' in J. Hastings (ed.), *Encyclopaedia of Religion and Ethics*, vol. 10 (Edinburgh, 1920); Rivers, *Conflict and Dream*, pp. 32–7.

55. B. Hart, *BMJ* (1920) i, pp. 207–11; W. H. R. Rivers, 'The Repression of War Experience'. *Lancet* (1918), i, pp.173–7.

56. Rivers, 'Repression'.

57. Rivers, *Conflict and Dream*, pp. 165–180.

58. S. Sassoon, *Sherston's Progress*. Its power was immediately recognised by Rivers' sister. 'So glad you called him Rivers,' she wrote to Sassoon in 1936. 'Now his name "liveth forever more on earth"'. Sassoon papers, IWM; R. Hart-Davies (ed.), *Siegfried Sassoon, Diaries*, (London,1983); R. Graves, *Goodbye to All That* (London, 1929); P. Fussell, *The Great War and Modern Memory* (Oxford, 1975). Biographies by Jean Moorcroft Wilson and John Wilson appeared in 1998 and 1999.

59. Sassoon, *Sherston's Progress*, p. 51. In his diaries, however, Sassoon described his fellow patients as '160 more-or-less dotty officers, a great many . . . degenerate-looking'. He spent his time walking the Pentland hills and 'slogging golf-balls' around Edinburgh's 'delightfully unfrequented' links. *Sassoon, Diaries*, pp. 183–96.

60. Rivers-Sassoon,1 February 1918. Sassoon papers, IWM; Adrian Caesar argues that guilt over his homosexuality made Sassoon 'angry, violent and sado-masochistic.' *Taking It Like A Man* (Manchester, 1993).

61. Rivers, *Conflict and Dream*, pp. 171–80. Much of the imagery of Rivers' dreams came from his student days in Germany.

62. 'Notes on Craiglockhart staff', Sassoon papers, IWM.

63. Stallworthy, *Wilfred Owen*; D. Hibberd, *Owen the Poet* (London, 1986); *idem, Wilfred Owen, The Last Year 1917–1918* (London,1992); J. Breen, 'Wilfred Owen . . . His Recovery from "Shell-Shock"'. *Notes & Queries* 23 (July 1976), pp. 301–5.

64. H. Owen and J. Bell (eds.), *Wilfred Owen: Collected Letters* (Oxford,1967), pp. 427–8.

65. *ibid.*, p. 458.

66. *ibid.*, p. 452.

67. *ibid.*, p. 453.

68. Hibberd, *Owen the Poet*, pp. 71–8.

69. Breen, 'Wilfred Owen'. Owen's description of Brown as 'a wizard' was quoted earlier.

70. Hibberd, *Owen the Poet*, p. 17. The modern sleep researcher, Ernest Hartman, belives that 'nightmare sufferers' fit a particular personality pattern – creative, sexually ambivalent, prone to schizophrenia – rather like Owen. See D. Barrett (ed.), *Trauma and Dreams* (Cambridge, Mass., 1997).

71. C. Day Lewis (ed.), *The Collected Poems of Wilfred Owen* (London, 1974), p. 55.

72. *ibid.*, loc. cit.

73. *ibid.*, p. 61.

74. On battle dreams see W. McDougall, *Outline of Abnormal Psychology* (New York, 1926); Eder, *War Shock*; F. W. Mott, *Lancet* (1916), i, pp. 547–8; (1918), i, pp. 127–8.

75. Hibberd, *Owen The Poet*, pp. 84–94, 195–6; *idem, Wilfred Owen: The Last Year*, pp. 22–9; A. J. Brock, 'The Re-Education of the Adult: The

Neurasthenic in War and Peace', *Sociological Review* 10 (1918), pp. 25, 40.

76. Brock, 'Re-education'; Notes on Craiglockhart Staff, Sassoon papers,IWM.

77. Brock, 'Re-Education'.

78. Hibberd, *Wilfred Owen. The Last Year*, p. 22. A picture of the two giants wrestling hung above Brock's desk, and he saw in the story a metaphor for his own work.:'Surely every officer who comes to Craiglockhart recognises that, in a way, he is himself an Antaeus, who has been taken from his Mother earth and well-nigh crushed to death by the war-giant or military machine. ..Antaeus typifies the occupation cure at Craiglockhart. His story is the justification for our activities'.

79. *ibid.* p. 35.

80. Day-Lewis, *Collected Poems of Wilfred Owen*, p. 61.

81. Hibberd, *Owen the Poet*, p. 115.

82. Owen and Bell, *Owen Collected Letters*, p. 521; *ibid*,p. 533–4.

83. Day-Lewis, *Collected Poems of Wilfred Owen*, p. 35–6. The 1917 poems were of course revised in 1918.

84. Jon Stallworthy sees Owen's flowering as a poet arising naturally out of his earlier life. To Philip Larkin,however, the 'instant maturity legend' remained 'a convenient shorthand for the evidence as we have it'. The three crucial influences on Owen, for Larkin-according to Andrew Motion- were 'belonging to a common enterprise' in the Manchester regiment; the 'encounter with Sassoon'; and, in 1918, the 'association with homosexuals [which] introduced him to an emotional climate that at that time he found liberating and relevant'. A. Motion, *Times Literary Supplement,* 6 November 1992.

Chapter 7. Europeans

1. B. Ulrich and S. Ziemann(eds) *Frontalltag im Ersten Weltkrieg: Wahn und Wirklichkeit* (Frankfurt-am-Main,1994), p. 103.

2. The French introduced such legislation in 1898. G. Roussy and J. Lhermitte, *The Psychoneuroses of War* (English translation, London, 1918), p. xxxi.

3. M. O. Roudebush, 'A Battle of Nerves: Hysteria and Its Treatment in France During World War 1'. PhD Thesis. University of California at Berkeley, 1995; D. Kaufman, 'Science as Cultural Practice: Psychiatry in the First World War and Weimar Germany', *JCH* 34 (1999), pp. 125–44.

4. J. Brunner, 'Psychiatry, Psychoanalysis and Politics During the First World War', *JHBS* 27 (1991), pp. 352–65.

5. Roudebush, 'Battle', p. 88.

6. Dr Chiray, April–May 1916, quoted Roudebush, 'Battle', p. 109.

7. P. F. Lerner, 'Hysterical Men: War, Neurosis, and German Mental Medicine, 1914–1921', PhD thesis, Columbia University, 1996. pp. 81–148; *idem,* ' German Neuropsychiatry in World War 1' in M. Berg and G. Cocks (eds), *Medicine and Modernity* (Washington DC, 1997).

8. Lerner, 'Hysterical Men', pp. 81–148.

9. M. W. Browne and F. E. Williams, *Neuropsychiatry and the War* (New York, 1918).

10. M. Nonne, *Anfang und Ziel Meines Lebens* (Hamburg, 1971), pp. 177–8.

11. *loc. cit.*

12. Nonne 'had patients always undress to complete nakedness, since I found that one could thereby increase their feeling of dependence or helplessness'. Nonne quoted in Brunner, 'Psychiatry', p. 355.

13. Lerner, 'Hysterical Men', pp 185–204; K. R. Eissler, *Freud as an Expert Witness. The Discussion of War Neuroses Between Freud and Wagner-Juaregg* (Madison, Ct., 1986), pp 302–10.

14. D. Kaufman, 'Science as cultural practice' p. 139.

15. Ulrich and Zieman, *Frontalltag*, p. 107; Eissler, *Freud*, pp. 304, 107.

16. Lerner, 'Hysterical Men, pp. 149–225.

17. M. Messerschmidt, ' German Military Law in the Second World War' in W. Deist (ed.) *The German Military in the Age of Total War.* (Leamington Spa, 1985), p. 324. Lerner, 'Hysterical Men' pp. 226 68; W. Mayer-Gross, *Lancet* (1939), ii, pp. 1327–30. C. Jahr's important comparative study of British and German military justice, (*Gewöhnliche Soldaten*, (Göttingen, 1998), appeared too late to be used here.

18. Gaupp, quoted Ullrich and Ziemand, *Frontalltag*, p 102.

19. Lerner, 'Hysterical men', pp. 269–77; R. Binion, *Hitler Among the Germans* (New York, 1976), pp. 6–7. Binion revived the beguiling theory (dating from the 1930s) that Forster, when working near Berlin in November 1918, treated a young soldier suffering from hysterical gas blindness and by his forceful therapy, converted Adolf Hitler from a failed water-colorist into a charismatic leader of men. Although Forster committed suicide soon after Hitler came to power in 1933, the evidence is inconclusive. Joachim Fest and Ian Kershaw's biographies dismiss the idea.

20. Roudebush, 'Battle', p. 89.

21. *ibid.* Roudebush has a richly nuanced account of the arguments among French neurolgists.

22. Clovis Vincent is described as a 'toreador' by Roudebush, 'Battle' p. 134 ; M. O. Roudebush,' A Patient Fights Back:Neurology in the Court of Public Opinion in France during the First World War', *JCH* 35 (2000), pp. 29–38.

23. Roudebush, 'A Patient fights back'

24. Roudebush, 'Battle', p. 207.

25. Roudebush, 'Battle', p. 222; *idem*, 'A Patient fights back'. See also D. Englander, 'The French Soldier, 1914–18', *French History* (1987) and S. Audoin-Rouzeau, *Men At War, 1914–1918* (Providence, R. I, 1993).

26. Roudebush, 'Battle', p. 162.

27. Roudebush, 'Battle', pp. 182–3. Dr Roussy, who ran the Salins hospital, evidently toned down his methods after the Deschamps affair. *The Psychoneuroses of War*, published in English in 1918 but written in 1916, describes the 'cure of a psycho-neuropath' as a 'mental contest, resulting in the victory of the physician', in which the patient's mind is 'mastered and finally

conquered'; and speaks of applying electric current to sensitive parts of the skin such as the lips and scrotum. The patient 'lies absolutely naked on the bed', pp. 159–71.

28. E. Jones, *The Life and Work of Sigmund Freud* (Harmondsworth, 1964), pp. 424–47; L. Hoffman, 'War, Revolution and Psychoanalysis', *JHBS* 17 (1981) pp. 251–69.

29. S. Ferenczi, *Selected Writings* (Harmondsworth, 1999), p. 130; Hoffman, ' War', p. 264.

30. E. Simmel, 'War Neuroses' in S. Lorand (ed.), *Psychoanalysis Today* (London, 1948) pp. 243–4.

31. Simmel, 'War Neuroses', p. 244.

32. E. Simmel, in S. Ferenczi *et al.*, *Psycho-Analysis and the War Neuroses* (London, 1921) pp. 30–43.

33. Simmel, 'War Neuroses', p. 245.

34. Hoffman, 'War'; Brunner, 'Psychiatry'; Lerner, 'Hysterical Men', pp. 304–23.

35. Ferenczi, *et al.*, *Psycho-Analysis and the War Neuroses*, p. 39.

36. Simmel in, Ferenczi *et al.*, *Psycho-Analysis and the War Neuroses*.

37. Ferenczi *et al.*, *Psycho-Analysis*, pP. 1–4, 47–8. Jones was not at the Budapest conference. His paper was given in London in April 1918.

38. S. Freud, *On Metapsychology* (Harmondsworth, 1991), p. 301.

39. *ibid.*, p. 304.

Chapter 8: Arguments and Enigmas, 1917–18

1. B. Pogson, *Maurice Nicoll. A Portrait.* (London, 1961), p. 58.

2. M. Stone, 'Shellshock' in W. F. Bynum *et al.* (eds) *The Anatomy of Madness*, vol 2. (London, 1985); M. Culpin, *Occupational Psychology* 23 (1949).

3. P. J. Leese, 'Social and Cultural History of Shellshock', Open Universoty PhD Thesis, 1989; Myers, *SSIF*, p. 116.

4. J&R, pp. 47–8; Leese, 'Social and Cultural history'.

5. J&R, p. 54.

6. J. T. MacCurdy, *War Neuroses* (Cambridge, 1918), pp. 4–7.

7. G. E. Smith and T. H. Pear, *Shell-Shock and Its Lessons* (2nd Ed, Manchester, 1918) pp. 87–88. It was dedicated to Ronald Rows and the sections on British asylums were lifted wholesale from his pre-war writings .

8. *Nature*, 100 (1917), pp. 1–3; J. Wolfsohn, 'The Pre-Disposing Factors of War Psycho-Neurosis', *Lancet* (1918) i, 177–80.

9. F. W. Mott, 'Two Addresses on War Psycho-Neuroses', *Lancet* (1918) i, pp. 127–9, 169–72.

10. ibid.

11. W. B. Cannon. *Bodily Changes in Pain, Hunger, Fear and Rage* (New York, 1915). 'Adrenalin' was originally the trade name; Cannon hated the word. During the war, Cannon worked in France on surgical shock, but took no part in the arguments over shell-shock.

12. D. W. Carmallt Jones, 'War-Neurasthenia, Acute and Chronic', *Brain* 42 (1919), pp. 171–213. This Queen Square-trained doctor claimed to have frequently found 'the type known to neurologists as "degenerate", which contains many epileptics in its ranks, with the physicial characteristics of narrow palate and crowded teeth, simian hand and coarse skin', among his patients. He had 'come to regard a narrow palate as indicating a bad prognosis' p. 176.

13. Mott, 'Two Addresses'; W. Brown, 'War Neuroses. A Comparison of Early Cases seen in the Field with those seen at the Base'. *Lancet* (1919) i, pp. 833–6; For attempts to use drugs in this way see Shephard, 'R. G. Rows', pp. 452–3.

14. Brown, 'A Comparison'.

15. F. Buzzard. *PRSM* 8 (1914–15), Neurological section, p. 66.

16. J. Brophy and E. Partridge, *The Long Trail* (3rd Ed, London 1965) p. 189.

17. Moran, *Anatomy of Courage*.

18. *RWOCIS*, pp. 140–4. Another complicating factor, scarcely explored in the literature, was that in 1917 'nearly one-third of all admissions into medical wards from Home Forces [were] for neurasthenia'. F. W. Burton-Fanning, 'Neurasthenia in Home Forces', *Lancet* (1917), i, pp. 907–11.

19. J. H. Butlin Papers, IWM.

20. 'J. W. Roworth' (Edward Casey) 'The Misfit Soldier', IWM, as quoted in R. D. Ritchie, 'One History of Shellshock' (1986). A selection has also been published as J. Bourke (ed.) *The Misfit Soldier* (Cork, 1999). Casey's spelling and punctuation have, with some regrets, been tidied up here.

21. A. Horne, *Macmillian 1894–1956* (London, 1990), p. 43.

22. H. Crichton-Miller, quoted in *NPWW1*, p. 511; W. McDougall, in C. Murchison (ed.) *History of Psychology in Autobiography* (New York, 1930), 1, pp. 191–233.

23. W. H. R. Rivers, 'A Case of Caustrophobia' in *Instinct and the Unconscious* (1920; 2nd Ed, Cambridge, 1922), pp. 17–84.

24. W. McDougall, *Outline of Abnormal Psychology* (New York, 1926), pp. 289–92. A Cambridge contemporary of Myers and Rivers, McDougall had accompanied them on the Torres Straits expedition. Perhaps the most prolific and influential British psychologist before the war, known for his theory of instincts, he was also renowned among his peers for his arrogance, Roman nose and drawling voice. Yet he found working with shell-shocked soldiers (at Netley and then Oxford) a humbling and rewarding experience. 'Sympathetic rapport with the man was the main thing,' he later wrote. McDougall in *History of Pyschology in Autobiography*.

25. A. F. Hurst in *Seale Hayne Neurological Studies* 1 (1918), pp. 91–5.

26. *War Neuroses*, 1918.

27. McDougall, *Outline*, pp. 292–8.

28. C. Stanford Read, 'A Survey of War Neuro-Psychiatry', *MH* 2(1918), pp. 359–87; A. Young, 'Rivers and the War Neuroses', *JHBS* 35(1999), pp. 359–78. Rivers' return to his neurological past may have been influenced by

the fact that Henry Head, with whom he was then working, was republishing the writings of Hughlings Jackson in the neurological journal *Brain* .

29. J. Miller, 'The Dog Beneath the Skin', *The Listener*, 20 July 1972.
30. *ibid.*

Chapter 9: 'Skirting the Edges of Hell'

1. E. D. Bond *Thomas W. Salmon, Psychiatrist* (New York, 1950), p. 104.
2. E. T. Dean, *Shook Over Hell: Post-Traumatic Stress, Vietnam, and the Civil War* (Cambridge, Mass., 1997)
3. Bond, *Salmon*, pp. 17–49.
4. *ibid*, pp. 31–44; T. W. Salmon, 'Immigration and the Mixture of Races in Relation to the Mental Health of the Nation' in W. A. White and S. E. Jelliffe (eds), *The Modern Treatment of Nervous and Mental Diseases.* (Philadephia, 1913). For a harsher verdict, see G. N. Grob, *Mental Illness and American Society* (Princeton, 1983), pp. 156–7.
5. Bond, *Salmon*, p. 91; N. Dain, *Clifford W. Beers. Advocate for the Insane* (Pittsburgh, 1980), pp. 165–186.
6. Bond, *Salmon.* pp. 50–69.
7. T. W. Salmon, 'The Care and Treatment of Mental Diseases and War Neurosis ("Shell Shock") in the British Army', (originally published *MH* 1 (1917), pp. 509–47); reprinted in *NPWWI*, pp. 499–523.
8. *ibid.*, p. 506.
9. *ibid.*, p. 513–23.
10. *NPWWI*, p. 71–85.
11. *ibid.*, pp. 58, 84–5
12. R. Schaffer, *America in the Great War* (New York, 1991), pp. 133–9; M. Thomson, 'Mental Deficiency in the First World War', in R. Cooter *et al.* (eds), *War, Medicine and Modernity* (Stroud, 1998), pp. 149–66.
13. S. J. Gould, *The Mismeasure of Man* (Harmondsworth, 1984).
14. Thomson, 'Status'.
15. Bond, *Salmon*, pp. 100, 102.
16. Bond, *Salmon*, p. 136.
17. Bond, *Salmon*, pp. 126, 93
18. Bond, *Salmon*, p. 144.
19. Bond, *Salmon*, pp. 90–146, 149.
20. *NPWWI*, p. 306.
21. *ibid.*, pp. 313–24.
22. *ibid.*, pp. 314.
23. *ibid.* p. 318; Bond, *Salmon*, p. 97.
24. J. H. Rhein, 'Neuropsychiatric Problems at the Front during Combat', *Journal of Abnormal Psychology*, 14 (1919), pp. 9–14.
25. *ibid.*, p. 11.
26. *ibid.*, p. 13.
27. *NPWWI*, pp. 330–4; see also E. A. Strecker, 'World War I', in G. Zilboorg

(ed.), *American Psychiatry, 1844–1944.* (Washington, D. C, 1944)

28. *ibid.*, pp. 294–5.
29. *ibid.*, pp. 296–7.
30. Bond, *Salmon*, pp. 110–111.
31. *NPWW2*, pp. 355–67.
32. *loc. cit.*
33. *RWOCIS*, p. 182 According to Strecker, 'the total number of [American] neuropsychiatric disabilities in World War I was 69, 394'. ('World War I', p. 403). Modern estimates by Lerner and Leese suggest that the British and Germans both had about 200, 000 psychiatric casualties. Roudebush offers no figures for the French. Such statistics should be treated with great caution.

Chapter 10: Inquests

1. Quoted in E. Bethge, *Dietrich Bonhoeffer* (London 1970), p. 17.
2. P. Lerner, 'Hysterical Men. War, Neurosis and German Mental Medicine'. PhD thesis, Columbia, 1996, pp. 354–76; *idem*, 'Hysterical Cures', *History Workshop Journal* 45(1998) pp. 79–95; R. Whalen, *Bitter Wounds.* (Ithaca, 1984) p. 116
3. N. Davies, *Europe . A History* (London, 1997), pp. 921–5; W. Deist, 'The Military Breakthrough', *War in History* 3 (1996); H. Strachan, 'The Morale of the German Army', in H. Cecil and P. Liddle (eds), *Facing Armageddon* (London, 1996)
4. Lerner, 'Hysterical Men' p. 360.
5. D. Kaufman, 'Science as Cultural Practice', *JCH* 34 (1999), p. 141.
6. Lerner, 'Hysterical Men', p. 359.
7. C. Clarens, *The Horror Film* (London, 1967), pp. 38–40; S. Kracauer, *From Caligari to Hitler* (Princeton, 1947).
8. K. R. Eissler, *Freud as Expert Witness. The Discussion of war neuroses between Freud and Wagner-Jauregg* (Madison Conn., 1986).
9. *ibid.*, pp. 14–15.
10. *ibid.*, pp. 15–16.
11. *ibid.*, pp. 32–4, 165–219.
12. *ibid.*, pp. 36–42. This was certainly true of Ullstein in the 1970s.
13. *ibid.*, pp. 129–35; 202–8.
14. *ibid.*, pp. 38–45, 55.
15. *loc. cit.*
16. *ibid.*, pp. 49–52
17. S. Freud, 'Memorandum on the Electrical Treatment of War Neurotics' in *idem, Standard Edition*, Volume 17 (1955), pp. 211–15.
18. Eissler, *Freud as Expert Witness*, pp. 58–61.
19. *ibid.*, pp. 70–1.
20. *ibid.*, 97. Occupational therapy is equated with psychotherapy.
21. *ibid.*, p. 99.
22. C. Wilson letter, *The Times*, 22 September 1920; T. Bogacz, 'War Neurosis

and Cultural Change in England 1914–22: The Work of the War Office Committee of Enquiry into "Shellshock"', *JCH* 24 (1989), pp. 227–56.

23. Myers, *SSIF,* p. 141.
24. *RWOCIS,* p. 88.
25. *RWOCIS,* pp. 59–62;K. Simpson, 'Introduction' to J. C. Dunn, *The War the Infantry Knew* (1938; London, 1987); *RWOCIS,* p. 31; Tyrrell papers, IWM.
26. *RWOCIS,* pp. 89–91, 18.
27. *RWOCIS,* pp. 190–5.
28. A. Babington, *For the Sake of Example* (London, 1983) pp. 202–14.
29. *ibid.,* p. 211.
30. K. Simpson, in B. Bond (ed.) *The Great War and British Military History* (London, 1991), p. 145.
31. Express Newspapers, *Covenants with Death* (London, 1934).

Chapter 11: 'Will Peace Bring Peace'?

1. Quoted in D. Winter, *Death's Men* (Harmondsworth, 1979), p. 242.
2. R. Dahl, *Boy* (Harmondworth, 1986), pp. 108–118.
3. P. Gibbs, *The Realities of War* (London, 1920), p. 452.
4. Ahrenfeldt, p. 10; T. Lewis, *Soldier's Heart* (1940); T. J. Mitchell and G. M. Smith. *Casualties and Medical Statistics* (London, 1931), p. 255.
5. P. Gibbs, *Realities of War* (London, 1920), p. 452
6. R. Graves, *The Long Week-End,* p. 27
7. Winter, *Death's Men,* pp. 235–63; Judd, *Ford Madox Ford.*
8. *Lancet,* (1919), i, p. 702; J. S. Milne, *Neurasthenia, Shell Shock, and a New Life* (Newcastle-on-Tyne, 1918), pp. 17, 25.
9. Milne, *Neurasthenia,* p. 9; the recovery of memory is marvellously described in Ford Madox Ford's *Parades' End.*
10. E. Leed, *No Man's Land* (1979); E. Showalter, *The Female Malady* (1985); S. M. Gilbert, 'Soldier's heart: Literary Men, Literary Women, and the Great War', *Signs:* 8 (1983), pp. 422–50; D. L. Sayers, *Some Unpleasantness at the Bellona Club* (London, 1925), p. 84.
12. Gilbert, 'Soldier's Heart'
13. V. Brittain, *Testament of Youth* (1933; London, 1978), p. 143.
14. Aldington, quoted in P. Parker, *The Old Lie* (London, 1987), p. 175.
15. Hiscock quoted in Parker, *The Old Lie,* pp. 175–6; C. Carrington, *Soldier From the Wars Returning* (1964; London, 1970), pp. 178–88, 280–1. The 'strong and unattractive streak of misogyny' which certainly runs through the literature of the war – the most famous example being Robert Graves's savage attack on 'the little mother' – is nearly always the work of homosexuals like Sassoon and Owen who found warmongering women at home an obscene contrast to the 'honest masculine world at the front'.
16. Gilbert, 'Soldier's heart, p. 429; *Daily Mail,* 5 June 1918.
17. quoted in C. Haste, *Rules of Desire* (London, 1992), p. 65.

18. Ferenczi and German doctor quoted in Leed, *No Man's Land* pp. 183–4; R. Hall (ed.), *Dear Dr Stopes. Sex in the 1920s* (London, 1978), p. 143.

19. H. Somerville, 'The War-anxiety Neurotic' *JMS* 69 (1923), pp. 173, 176.

20. In Gilbert Frankau's popular novel, *Peter Jackson* (1920) the hero is salvaged from shell-shock when his wife boldly takes the sexual initiative.

21. D. Lessing, *A Small Personal Voice* (London, 1994), p. 92.

22. M. Culpin, 'The Problem of the Neurasthenic Pensioner', *British Journal of Medical Psychology* 1(1921), p. 326.

23. E. E. Southard, 'Shell shock and after', *Boston Medical and Surgical Journal,* 179 (1918), pp. 73–93; N. Fenton, *Shell Shock and Its Aftermath* (St Louis, 1926), pp. 85–8.

24. quoted in Bogacz, 'War Neurosis', *JCH* 24(1989), p. 235; Culpin, 'Problem' p. 326; see also E. W. White *BMJ* (1918), i, pp. 421–2.

25. Fenton, *Shell Shock* p. 92; W. Sargant, *The Unquiet Mind* p. 89.

26. *JAMA* 72 (1919), p. 537; E. Weiss, *The Eyewitness* (English translation, Boston, 1977).

27. T. J. Mitchell and G. M. Smith, *Casualties and Medical Statistics* (London, 1931), pp. 307–14; *BMJ* (1920), i, p. 36.

28. Discussion in *JMS* 67 (1921), pp. 525–32; T. Salmon, 'Some Problems of Disabled Ex-Service Men'. *MH* 6 (1922), p. 7; D. A. Thom, 'The Patient and his attitude toward his neurosis', *MH* 7 (1923), pp. 234–47; Culpin, 'Problem'.

29. Mitchell and Smith, *Casualties*, p. 341. The Australian historian broadly agreed: 'the first few years after the war saw great activity among the psychiatrists in the treatment of the various classical types of neurosis. . . gradually they were cured, or became "incurable", and in their place there appeared-especially in the years of the financial depression, 1930–1935 – a manifestation of the same tendencies which were at the root of acute shell-shock' [a flight from reality into neurotic illness]. Butler, pp. 142–5. In the United States, Dr Douglas Thom distinguished between an 'active' group of 'inherently unstable individuals' who sought refuge in neurosis and a much smaller 'passive' group who did not seek, but were 'overtaken by their neurosis'. Thom, 'The Patient'.

30. Mitchell and Smith, *Casualties*, p. 341.

31. PRO. PIN 15/2401. B. Shephard, *History of Psychiatry* 10 (1999), p. 503.

32. T. A. Ross *The Common Neuroses*, quoted in Leese, 'Social and Cultural History' p. 205.

33. *RWOCIS*, p. 80. Tom Salmon disagreed. 'Compensation, wisely, skilfully and humanely awarded', could, he argued, be made to serve 'not as a means of prolonging invalidism and discouraging initiative but of making good the inroads in earning power created by disease and helping to insure medical or social recovery'. Millais Culpin doubted whether there were many cases where simply stopping the pension would lead to recovery. This might be so with a very few hysterical cases, but 'few psychotherapists would like to diagnose them'.

34. Myers, *SSIF,* p. 139; P. Lerner, 'Hysterical Men' PhD thesis, 1996; R. Whalen, *Bitter Wounds* (Cornell, 1984); L. B. Kalinowsky, *AJP* 107 (1950), p. 341.
35. PRO PIN 15/1632.
36. A. G. MacDonnell, *England, Their England* (London, 1933), p. 21.
37. E. D. Bond, *Thomas W. Salmon. Psychiatrist* (New York, 1950), p. 166–7.
38. *ibid.*; K. Mayo, *Soldiers What Next!* (London, 1934).
39. T. Skocpol, *Protecting Soldiers and Mothers: The Political Origins of Social Policy in the United States* (Cambridge, Mass., 1992).
40. Thom, 'The Patient'; G. H. Hyslop, 'The Relation of Compensation to Neuropsychiatric Disability' *USVBMB* I:2 (1925), pp. 14–19; L. C. Woods, 'What is to Become of the Psychoneurotic?' *USVBMB* I:5 (1925), pp. 17–19; *NPWW1*, pp. 477–87.
41. A. Kardiner, *My Analysis with Freud* (New York, 1977).
42. ibid.; A. Kardiner, *The Traumatic Neuroses of War* (New York, 1941).
43. Kardiner, *Traumatic Neuroses,* pp. 43–51.
44. Kardiner, *My Analysis,* pp. 109–11. 'T' bore Kardiner no ill will and, as a sign of gratitude for his efforts, even offered to 'bump off' anyone Kardiner might nominate. Though tempted, Kardiner never took him up on this.
45. Kardiner, *My Analysis* p. 112–6. For a sophisticated, psychoanalaytic interpretation see R. Leys, 'Death Masks: Kardiner and Ferenczi on Psychic Trauma', *Representations* 53 (1996), pp. 44–73.
46. A. Kardiner, *The Individual and His Society* (1939).
47. A. Kardiner, 'The Neuroses of War', *War Medicine* 1 (1941), pp. 219–26.
48. ibid.
49. To remedy this defect, Kardiner collaborated with Herbert Spiegel on a second edition of his book, retitled *War Stress and Traumatic Illness* (New York, 1947).
50. Kardiner's chapter on 'Traumatic Neuroses of War', in S. Areti (ed.), *American Handbook of Psychiatry* (New York, 1959), proved more influential.
51. PRO MH 106/2214. I owe this file to Dr Peter Barham, who is working on a history of 'service patients'. This soldier was said by a doctor in France to have 'a very narrow, high-arched palate'
52. P. Barham, 'The Forgotten Lunatics of the Great War: Insane "Service Patients" in Britain, 1914–39'. Unpublished paper. Thanks to Dr Barham.
53. W. Robinson, 'The Future of Service patients in Mental Hospitals'. *JMS* 65 (1921) pp. 40–8.
54. R. Eager, *JMS* 64 (1918), pp. 295.
55. Barham, 'Forgotten Lunatics'; Mitchell and Green, *Casualties,* p. 328.
56. E. Leed, *No Man's Land,* (Cambridge, 1979), p. 189.
57. Barham, 'Forgotten Lunatics'.
58. Barham, 'Forgotten Lunatics; M. Stone, 'Shell-shock and the Psychologists', in W. F. Bynum et al., *Anatomy of Madness,* vol. 2 (London, 1985); P. Gibbs, 'A Plea for Nerve-strained Victims of the War', *Overseas,* January 1927, pp.

39–42. The Society was also helping at least 25, 000 neurasthenic ex-servicemen unable to suport themselves.

59. M. Hurd, *The Ordeal of Ivor Gurney* (Oxford 1978); R. K. R. Thornton (ed.), *Ivor Gurney Collected letters* (Ashington, 1991).

60. *Gurney Letters*, p. 337.

61. ibid., p. 395.

62. ibid., pp. 416–8.

63. Hurd, *Ordeal*, pp. 122–6.

64. Hurd, *Ordeal*. Gurney's case continues to arouse debate: A. Rattenbury, 'How the sanity of poets can be edited away', *London Review of Books*, 14 October 1999.

65. 'War Stress and Some of Its Sequels', *Lancet* (1936), ii, pp. 93–5.

66. *Mail on Sunday*, 8 November 1998.

Chapter 12: The Lessons of Shell-Shock

1. G. E. Smith and T. H. Pear, *Shell-Shock and Its Lessons* (Manchester, 1918), p. xv.

2. L. S. Hearnshaw, *A Short History of British Psychology* (London, 1964); K. Jones, *History of the Mental Health Services* (London, 1972).

3. For a masterly assessment of Foucault's influence, see C. Sangoopta, 'Michel Foucault', in H. Freeman (ed.), *A Century of Psychiatry* (London, 1999).

4. H. C. Cameron, 'Sir Maurice Craig', *Guy's Hospital Reports* 85 (1935), pp. 251–7.

5. H. Dicks, *Fifty Years of the Tavistock Clinic* (London, 1970), pp. 1–5, 12–33.

6. P. Allderidge in G. Berrios and H. Freeman (eds) *150 Years of British Psychiatry* (London, 1991); A. Lewis, 'Edward Mapother', *BJP* 122 (1969) p. 1349.

7. T. Lidz, 'Adolf Meyer', *AJP* 123 (1996), pp. 320–3; G. Grob, *The Mad Among Us* New York, 1994), pp. 142–6; M. Gelder, 'Adolf Meyer and his influence on British Psychiatry' in G. Berrios and H. Freeman (eds), *150 Years of British Psychiatry* (London, 1991).

8. E. Slater, 'Psychiatry in the 'Thirties', *Contemporary Review* 226 (1975), pp. 70–5; Mrs Angela Lawrence, interview 1992.

9. F. I. de la P. Garforth, *Occupational Psychology* 19 (1945), p. 103.

10. W. H. Auden, *Selected Poems* (London, 1979), p. 93.

11. McDougall believed Freud had 'done more for the advancement of psychology than any student since Aristotle' but found much current psychoanalytic doctrine 'ill-founded and somewhat fantastic', W. McDougall, *Outline of Abnormal Psychology* (New York, 1926), p. viii.

12. A. Phillips, 'Bombs Away', *History Workshop Journal* 45 (1998) p. 183–98.

13. J. Padel, *Oxford Companion to the Mind* (Oxford, 1987), p. 270.

14. P. Fuller, Introduction to C. Rycroft, *Psychoanalysis and Beyond* (London, 1991), pp. 13–14. The disagreements between Anna Freud and Melanie Klein came to a head in 1942 : 'It takes more than a world war to stop

analysts fighting each other', L. A. Limentani, 'Psychoanalysis during the war years', *International Review of Psycho-Analysis* 16 (1989), p. 6.

15. R. Graves and A. Hodge, *The Long Week-End*, (London, 1940), p. 102; R. Cooter (ed.), *In the Name of the Child: Wealth and Welfare 1880–1940* (London, 1992)

16. quoted from F. G. Alexander and S. T. Selesnick, *The History of Psychiatry* (London, 1967), pp. 388–97.

17. E. Shorter, *From Paralysis to Fatigue* (New York, 1992), pp. 259–61.

18. Dicks, *Fifty Years*, pp. 76–8; J. A. C. Brown, *Freud and the Post-Freudians* (Harmondsworth, 1987), p. 98.

19. Sir Ronald Adam, PRO WO 32/11972.

20. B. Shephard, '"Pitiless Psychology": The role of prevention in British military psychiatry in the Second World War', *History of Psychiatry* 10 (1999), pp. 491–524; PRO PIN 15/2401.

21. Rivers had died suddenly in 1922, of a strangulated hernia, when about to embark on a new career, as a politician. The same year, Myers had left Cambridge to found the National Institute for Industrial Psychology. Myers had been a pupil of Rivers; McCurdy and Riddoch, medical colleagues of his during the war. William Brown, probably the most effective British psychotherapist in the Great War, was not involved in the 1939 discussions at all, possibly because of a curious incident in 1937 when he had told an academic gathering that Hitler was 'the greatest psychotherapist of the nations'. In 1940 he explained that 'at that time I was trying to get an interview with Herr Hitler and therefore could not stress the defects of his qualities such as were already becoming apparent'. (*Lancet* [1940], i, pp. 194–5, 243, 344). Brown seems to have believed that 'if he could only have the opportunity of a two-hour talk with Hitler . . . he could divert him from his mad course of destruction' (S. Zuckerman, *From Apes to Warlords* (London, 1988), p. 97). It is not clear how far this scheme progressed.

22. PRO PIN 15/2401.

23. Shephard, '"Pitiless Psychology"', pp. 507, 514. 'Trauma does not cause neurosis', Ross told doctors in 1940. 'It is not followed by neurosis unless there is some advantage to be gained', T. A. Ross, *Lectures on War Neuroses* (Oxford, 1941), p. 32.

24. Shephard, '"Pitiless Psychology"', p. 507.

25. J. R. Rees, a Medical Officer in the First World War, took over the Tavistock in 1933. He was a skilful administrator, with a genius for public relations and for 'firing the enthusiasm of collaborators'.

Chapter 13: Dunkirk, the Blitz and the Blue

1. R. Collier, *The Sands of Dunkirk* (London, Collins, 1961), p. 244.

2. ibid.; A. Rhodes, *Sword of Bone* (1942; London, 1986), pp. 208–35.

3. Collier, *Sands*, p. 129–30. Collier used material from 1070 eye-witnesses, as described in his *The Past Is A Foreign Country* (London, 1996).

4. Collier, *Sands*, pp. 100–490.

5. A. J. Barker. *Dunkirk: The Great Escape* (London, 1977), p. 107.

6. Collier, *Sands*, pp. 103, 141.

7. J. L. S. Coulter, *Royal Naval Medical Service, Vol 2, Operations* (London, 1956), p. 328.

8. ibid., p. 327.

9. A. Calder, *The People's War* (London, 1969), p. 109.

10. W. Sargant, *The Unquiet Mind*, (London, 1967), pp. 86–7; T. A. Ross, *Lectures on the War Neuroses* (Oxford, 1941), pp. 59–60.

11. Dr John Wishart, interview, 1992.

12. J. Bowlby and K. Soddy, letter, *Lancet* (1940), ii, pp. 343–4; Bowlby, interview, 1990.

13. Bowlby, interview, 1990; Bowlby papers, CMAC.

14. R. Blythe, *Private Words* (1991); P. Fussell, *Wartime. Understanding and Behaviour in the Second World War* (New York, 1990)

15. C. Day-Lewis, 'Where Are the War Poets?' *Penguin New Writing* 3 (1941).

16. J. R. Rees, *The Shaping of Psychiatry by War* (New York, 1945), p. 16; M. Bragg, quoted in Fussell, *Wartime*, p. 136.

17. R. K. Webb, *Modern England* (2nd Edn. London, 1980), p. 550; C. L. Mowat, *Britain Between the Wars* (London, 1968), pp. 512–3; H. J. Starling *PRSM*, 34 (1941), p. 542.

18. A. Bryant, *The Turn of the Tide* (1957; London, 1958), p. 188; H. Moran, *In My Fashion* (London, 1946) p. 135.

19. C. Hardyment, *Dream Babies* (London, 1983), p. 170.

20. L. MacNeice, *The Strings Are False* (1965; London, 1996), pp. 95–112.

21. H. Moran, *In My Fashion*, p. 136.

22. Bryant, *Turn of the Tide*, p. 132; 'Captain X', *The Soldier Looks Ahead* (London, 1944).

23. Blythe, *Private Words*, p. 189. Psychiatrists heard this line frequently. G. W. B. James, 'Narrative Concerning the Middle East Force'. Unpublished MS. Thanks to Philip James.

24. G. Orwell, *Collected Essays*, vol 2 (Harmondsworth, 1970), p. 84; M. Carver, *Out of Step* (London, 1988), p. 178.

25. T. Harrisson, *Living Through the Blitz* (Harmondsworth, 1978), pp. 19–30;

26. R. M. Titmuss, *Problems of Social Policy* (London, 1950), pp. 3–11.

27. Titmuss, *Problems*, pp. 4–5.

28. Harrisson, *Blitz*, pp. 40–1.

29. W. Trotter, 'Panic', *BMJ*, (1940), i, p. 270; J. Rickman, 'Panic and Air Raid Precautions', *Lancet* (1938), i, pp. 1291–5.

30. P. Lewis, *A People's War* (London, 1986), p. 12; 'Problems of the Evacuee Child', *PRSM* 33 (1940); J. Macnicol, 'The Evacuation of Schoolchildren' in H. L. Smith (ed.) *War and Social Change* (Manchester, 1986). In December 1939, three psychiatrists had warned of the psychological consequences of evacuation. A. Philips, *Winnicott* (London, 1988), p. 62.

31. D. K. Henderson and R. D. Gillespie, *Textbook of Psychiatry* (7th Edn,

Oxford, 1950), p. 615.

32. Effort Syndrome, it will be recalled, had previously been known as 'Soldier's Heart', 'Disordered Action of the Heart', etc. See Ahrenfeldt for references to the immense World War Two literature.

33. Calder, *The People's War*, pp. 167–227.

34. Lewis, *A People's War*, p. 54.

35. Harrisson, *Living Through the Blitz*, pp. 81–2.

36. Calder, *The People's War*, p. 179–87.

37. N. Balchin, *Darkness Falls from the Air* (1942); E. Waugh, *Men At Arms* (1952); H. Green, *Caught* (1943); G. Greene, *The Ministry of Fear* (London, 1943); *Independent*, 27 September 1994. J. Strachey, *Post D* (1941) and B. Nixon, *Raiders Overhead* (1943) are brilliant factual accounts.

38. A. Calder, *The Myth of the Blitz* (London, 1991); Monsarrat quoted in Fussell, *Wartime*, p. 289.

39. Harrison, *Living Through the Blitz*, pp. 132–41.

40. *ibid.*, p. 139

41. Calder, *Myth of the Blitz*, p. 218

42. I. L. Janis, *Air War and Emotional Stress* (New York, 1951), p. 71.

43. Titmuss, *Problems of Social Policy*; Harrison, *Living Through the Blitz*.

44. E. Glover, *International Journal of Psychoanalysis* 23 (1942), pp. 17–37.

45. A. Lewis, 'Incidence of Neurosis', *Lancet* (1942), ii, pp. 175–83; D. Billany, *The Trap* (London, 1947); J. Mack and S. Humphries, *London at War* (London, 1990); C. Webster and N. Frankland, *The Strategic Air Offensive Against Germany* (London, 1961), 1, pp. 331–2.

46. Lewis, 'Incidence'.

47. Glover, op. cit.

48. C. P. Blacker, *Neurosis and the Mental Health Services* (London, 1946).

49. For the medical literature of the Blitz, see Janis, *Air War*, pp. 260–4.

50. F. Brown, 'Civilian Psychiatric Air-Raid Casualties', *Lancet* (1941), i, pp. 686–691.

51. Mack and Humphries, *London at War*; Titmuss, *Problems of Social Policy*.

52. Titmuss, *Problems of Social Policy*; J. Symons, 'The brief possibility of a different kind of history'. *London Review of Books*, 12 September 1991.

53. Shephard, '"Pitiless Psychology"', pp. 514–6.

54. H. Wilson, 'Mental Reactions to Air-Raids', *Lancet* (1942), i, pp. 284–287.

55. Ross, *Lectures*, p. 106.

56. F. Brown, 'Civilian Psychiatric Casualties'.

57. *ibid.*

58. N. McCallum, *Journey With A Pistol* (London, 1957), p. 42.

59. M. Carver, *Dilemmas of the Desert War* (London, 1986).

60. C. Joly. *Take These Men* (1955; London, 1985), pp. 132–3.

61. *ibid.*, pp. 71–2, 103.

62. R. Maugham, *Come To Dust* (London, 1945), p. 78.

63. James, 'Narrative', p. 258. James offered no explanation for this behaviour.

64. *BMJ* (1968), iii, 333; G. W. B. James, 'Reflections on the Army of the

Future'. Unpublished MS (thanks to Philip James).

65. *Inter-Allied Conferences on War Medicine* (London, 1947), p. 243; 'Psychiatric Casualties. Hints to Medical Officers', [Cairo, March 1941] IWM.

66. James, 'Narrative'; G. W. B. James, 'Psychiatry in the Middle East Force' in Z. Cope (ed.), *United Kingdom Medical Services: Medicine and Pathology* (London, 1952), pp. 371–81.

67. James estimated that '40% of the psychiatric casualties . . . could have been foreseen by a careful psychiatric survey or even a reasonably careful medical history'. 'Narrative', p. 76.

68. PRO WO 177/324; James, 'Narrative'.

69. James, 'Narrative', p. 148.

70. James, in Cope, *Medicine and Pathology*, p. 378; talk to engineers quoted from J. Lucas, *War In the Desert*, (London, 1982), pp. 114–120.

71. Lucas, *War in the Desert, loc. cit.*

72. Lucas. *loc. cit.*

73. James, Narrative, p. 224

74. *ibid.*

Chapter 14: 'We Can Save Those Boys from Horror'.

1. *PRSM* 36 (1943), p. 257.

2. *Lancet* (1936), ii, p. 93; J. R. Rees, *BMJ*, (1943), pp. 1–6.

3. T. F. Main, interview with T. Harrison (1984). Thanks to Tom Harrison.

4. M. Howard, in B. Bond and I. Roy (eds) *War and Society* (London, 1975), p. 223; *Lancet* (1940), ii, p. 299; G. W. B James, *Lancet* (1945), ii, p. 801.

5. Adam papers. LH/KCL; S. P. Mackenzie, *Politics and Military Morale* (Oxford, 1992); A. Danchev, 'The Army and the Home Front 1939–1945', in D. Chandler (ed.), *The Oxford History of the British Army* (Oxford, 1994); T. F. Rodger, Tribute to Ronald Hargreaves, Rodger papers, University of Glasgow.

6. According to Dr Tom Main, 'I gave him Raven's matrices. With the version we had there, you couldn't get top marks. Like any good intelligence test no one could get top marks. It was a 40-minute version. He did it in 12 minutes and got every one right.' [Adam then] said, "It's a good idea, isn't it?"' Main interview with Harrison.

7. J. C. Raven, *Lancet*, (1942), i, pp. 115–117; *idem, Mental Health* 1(1941), pp. 10–18. Progressive Matrices were originally designed to test for schizophrenia.

8. PRO WO, 165/129.

9. *PRSM* 36(1943), p. 260.

10. *Personnel Selection in the British Army*, film 1944. IWM; Rodger, Hargreaves tribute, p. 8; E. Waugh, *Unconditional Surrender* (Harmondsworth, 1964), p. 31.

11. Rodger, Hargreaves tribute; J. Bowlby interview; S. MacKeith interview.

12 . H. Moran, *In My Fashion* (London, 1946), p. 141; C&M, pp. 27–43.

13. Ahrenfeldt, pp. 29–50.
14. In the end, 'after a long, hard pull', Sherriff did become an officer; the huge losses in France had forced the authorities to 'lower their sights and accept young men outside the exclusive circle of the public schools'. Indeed, by the end of the war many officers were former sergeants and corporals who had proved themselves in battle. G. A. Panichas. (ed.), *Promise of Greatness: The War of 1914*–1918. (London, 1968), pp. 133– 154.
15. E. Anstey, *The Psychologist*, November 1989, pp. 475–478.
16. U. Geuter, *The Professionalization of Psychology in Nazi Germany* (Cambridge, 1992); H. Eysneck, *Uses and Abuses of Psychology* (Harmondsworth, 1953) pp. 138–59.
17. Adam papers, LH/ KCL; R. Gal and A. D. Mangelsdorff (eds), *Handbook of Military Psychology* (Chichester, 1991) p. 64.
18. W. R. Bion, 'The Leaderless Group Project' *Bulletin of the Menninger Clinic* 10 (1946) pp. 77–81; G. Bléandonu, *Wilfred Bion.* (London, 1994).
19. S. Bidwell, *Modern Warfare* (London, 1973) p. 118; A. Jones, 'Psychologists and Military Officer Selection' in Gal and Mangelsdorff, *Handbook of Military Psychology*, p. 73; H. Vinden, 'The Introduction of Leaderless Groups', in B. Bond and I. Roy (eds) *War and Society* 2 (1977).
20. Bowlby interview .
21. M. Davie. (ed.), *The Diaries of Evelyn Waugh* (London, 1982), p. 212.
22. G. Fitzpatrick, *JRAMC* 84, 1945. pp. 75–8.; F. I. de la P. Garforth, *Occupational Psychology.* 19 (1945), pp. 97–108; S. W. Gillman, ' Methods of Officer Selection in the Army', *JMS* 93 (1947) pp. 101–11; F. McLynn, *Carl Gustav Jung* (London, 1997), pp. 70–71.
23. Gillman, 'Methods', p. 105; H. Murray *et al.*, *Explorations in Personality* (New York, 1938), pp. 530 – 45.
24. P. E. Vernon and J. B. Parry, *Personnel Selection in the British Forces* (London, 1949), p. 65; P. Ustinov, *Dear Me* (Harmondsworth, 1978), p. 159.
37. Gillman, 'Methods'.
26. H. Harris, *The Group Approach to Leadership Testing* (London, 1949), pp. 159–62; Gillman, 'Methods'; A. Bowlby, *The Recollections of Rifleman Bowlby* (1969; London, 1989), p. 84. Other questions were 'Both your parents are neurotic, aren't they?, 'What do you most like in life', and 'What would you feel if you bayonetted a German?'; Ahrenfeldt; John Bowlby interview.
27. PRO WO 32/11972
28. P. Addison, *The Road to 1945.* (London, 1977), 190–1; Vinden. 'Introduction of [WOSBs]'; PRO WO 32/11972.
29. PRO WO 32/11972; Privy Council Office, *Report of an Expert Committee on the Work of Psychologists and Psychiatrist in the Services* (London, 1947) .
30. W. S. Churchill, *History of the Second World War, vol 4* (London, 1951), p. 815.
31. Rodger, Hargreaves tribute, p. 12; PRO WO 32/11972; Danchev, 'The Army and the Home Front', p. 304.

32. P. Young, *Storm From the Sea* (London, 1958), p. 21. Durnford-Slater trained the Commando 'very much as if it were a horse'; *Dictionary of National Biography*; J. Verney, *Going to the Wars* (1955; London, 1957), p. 110.

33. F. Maclean, *Eastern Approaches*. (London, 1949), p. 195, M. R. D. Foot, *SOE in France* (London, 1996), credits Mayne with half that number; A. Beevor, *Crete: The Battle and the Resistance* (Harmondsworth, 1992), p. 251

34. Verney, *Going to the Wars*, p. 140; Young, *Storm*, p. 15; T. Royle, *Wingate* (London, 1995), p. 238.

35. R. S. Greene, 'The Role of the Psychiatrist in World War II' (Columbia University, PhD thesis, 1977); W. C. Menninger, *Psychiatry in a Troubled World* (New York, Macmillan, 1948); A. Deutsch, 'Military Psychiatry: World War II' in *One Hundred Years of American Psychiatry* (New York, 1944); I. C. Berlin and R. D. Waggoner, in *NPWW2,2*.

36. Menninger, *Psychiatry*, p. 267. Deutsch, 'Military Psychiatry', p. 424.

37. A. Kardiner *War Medicine* I (1941), pp. 219–26; Greene, 'Role', pp. 124–6.

38. H. S. Perry, *Psychiatrist of America: The Life of Harry Stack Sullivan* (Cambridge, Mass., 1982); Greene, 'Role', pp. 104–16.

39. H. S. Sullivan. *Mental Hygiene* 25 (1941), pp. 7–15; Greene, 'Role', p. 97.

40. H. S. Sullivan, *Psychiatry* 4 (1941), pp. 201–17.

41. *ibid.*, p. 208

42. 'Practical Psychiatric Diagnosis', *Psychiatry* 4 (1941), pp. 265–83.

43. Greene, 'Role'.

44. Menninger, *Psychiatry*, pp. 266–80; Green, 'Role'.

45. 'Youth in Crisis', *March of Time* 1942. Thanks to Vicki Wegg-Prosser.

46. E. Ginzberg, *Psychiatry and Military Manpower* (New York, 1953); L. Kennett. *GI: The American Soldier in World War II* (1987; Norman, Okl., 1997), p. 29; C. W. Heath *et al.*, 'Personnel Selection', *Annals of Internal Medicine*, 19 (1943).

47. E. Ginzberg. *The Ineffective Soldier: The Lost Divisions* (New York, 1959); J. Ellis, *The Sharp End: The Fighting Man in World War II* (1980; London, 1993), pp. 10–11.

48. Greene, 'Role', pp. 183–95.

49. *ibid.*, pp. 259–322.

50. *ibid.*, pp. 323–76.

51. *ibid.*, pp. 350–66.

52. Menninger, *Psychiatry*, p. 289.

53. K. L. Artiss, *Mil Med* 128 (1963), pp. 1011–5; L. I. Bland (ed.), *The Papers of George Catlett Marshall*, vol. 4 (Baltimore, 1996), pp. 221–5; N. J. Hale Jr, *The Rise and Crisis of Psychoanalysis in the United States* (New York, 1993), pp. 201–2; *NPWW2* 1, pp. 131–6.

54. Marshall, *Papers* 4, p. 224.

55. L. J. Friedman, *Menninger: The Family and the Clinic* (New York, 1990).

56. B. H. Hall, *A Psychiatrist for a Troubled World*, 2 Vols (New York, 1967), 1, p. 5.

Chapter 15: Front-line Psychiatry

1. F. Majdalany, *Patrol* (1953; London, 1972), p. 138.
2. W. Sargant, *The Unquiet Mind* (London, Heinemann, 1967), pp. 86–87.
3. L. Thomas, *The Youngest Science* (Oxford, 1985), pp. 20–50; H. Cushing, *The Life of Sir William Osler* (Oxford, 1924).
4. L. Thomas, 'Biomedical Science and Human Health: The long-range prospect', in B. Dixon (ed.), *From Creation to Chaos* (London, 1989), pp. 258–61.
5. Shorter, *HoP*, pp. 207–24, has an excellent summary and references.
6. *ibid.*, pp. 225–9. Sargant's *Unquiet Mind* vividly recalls the excitements and dilemmas created by the new treatments.
7. Discussion, 'Prolonged narcosis in Mental Disorder', *JMS* 80 (1934).
8. W. Sneader, *Drug Discovery: The Evolution of Modern Medicines* (Chichester, 1985), pp. 29–31; Shorter, *HoP*, pp. 200–7; W. J. Bleckwenn, 'Narcosis as Therapy', *JAMA* 95 (1930), pp. 1168–71; C. P. Wagner, 'Pharmacological Use of Barbiturates', *JAMA* 125 (1933), pp. 1787–92; E. Lindemann, *AJP* 11 (1932), p. 1083. For opposition, W. Wilcox, *PRSM* 20 (1927), pp. 1479–99.
9. J. S. Horsley, *Lancet* (1936), i, p. 55; *idem*, 'Narco-Analysis', *JMS* 82 (1936), pp. 416–22; *idem*, *Narco-Analysis* (Oxford, 1942).
10. H. A. Palmer. 'The Value of Continuous Narcosis', *JMS* 83. (1937), pp. 635–78; R. D. Gillespie, 'Narcosis Therapy'. *Journal of Neurology and Psycho – pathology*, 2 (1939), p. 45; H. D. Palmer and F. J. Braceland, 'Narcosis Therapy'. *AJP* 94 (1937), pp. 37–57.
11. Sargant, *The Unquiet Mind*, pp. 1–13; Interviews, Ann Dally, Stephen MacKeith; A. Dally, 'William Sargant', in H. Freeman (ed.), *A Century of Psychiatry* (London, 1999), pp. 177–9; W. Sargant and E. Slater, *An Introduction to Physical Methods of Treatment in Psychiatry* (Edinburgh, 1944), p. 4.
12. Sargant, *The Unquiet Mind*, p. 87.
13. *ibid.*, p. 88.
14. W. Sargant and E. Slater, 'Acute War Neuroses', *Lancet* (1940), ii, pp. 1–2.
15. G. Debenham *et al.*, 'Treatment of War Neurosis', *Lancet* (1941), i, pp. 107–9; 'War Neuroses', *Medical Press and Circular*, 12 February 1941, pp. 131–48.
16. W. Sargant. 'Physical Treatment of Acute War Neuroses,' *BMJ* (1942), ii, pp. 574–6
17. W. Sargant and E. Slater. 'Amnesic Syndromes in War', *PRSM* 34 (1941), pp. 757–764. Sargant conceded that 'men admitted to us months after Dunkirk have seemed to benefit from the restoration of lost memories . . . The better the personality the more is the lack of knowledge of what happened in an amnesic period a source of worry to the patient.' His antipathy to psychotherapy derived from his impatient temperament, Mapother's influence and a year spent at the Massachusetts General Hospital in Boston in 1938 where, as he saw it, Freudian conformity was taken to

ludicrous lengths, *The Unquiet Mind,* p. 59.

18. Wilde, *BMJ* (1942), ii, p. 6.
19. J. L. Clegg, *BMJ* (1942), ii, p. 140.
20. C. Burns, *BMJ* 1942, ii, p. 295.
21. Dr John Wishart, interview; *NPWW2*, vol. 2, p. 4 (footnote 5).
22. J. R. Rees, *Reflections* (New York, 1966), p. 54; Ahrenfeldt, p. 183.
23. M. Blumenson, *Rommel's Last Victory* (London, 1968).
24. Fraser, *And We Shall Shock Them* (London, 1988), p. 250; Wishart, interview; CMAC RAMC 465/6 (1).
25. *JRAMC* 91 (1948), p. 94.
26. S. A. MacKeith, *JMS* 92 (1946), pp. 542–50; Wishart, interview; 'Recent Experience of War Neurosis', Algiers, 5 June 1943, *BMJ* (1943), ii, p. 336–7.
27. 'Recent Experience'.
28. Blumenson, *Rommel's Last Victory*, p. 157; General Fredendall 'proved a shocking commander', C. d'Este, *Bitter Victory* (London, 1988), p. 59.
29. Blumenson, *Rommel's Last Victory*, pp. 189–90.
30. *ibid.,* p. 211.
31. At Queen Square, he had watched Gordon Holmes's 'anger with neurotic patients'. R. R. Grinker, *Fifty Years in Psychiatry* (Springfield, Illinois, 1979) p. 5; *idem*, 'Reminiscences', *Journal of the American Academy of Psychoanalysis* 3 (1975) pp. 211–21; *idem*, *Neurology* (Springfield, Illinois, 1934).
32. Grinker, *Fifty Years*, pp. 9–11; *idem*, 'Reminiscences of a Personal Contact with Freud', *American Journal of Orthopsychiatry* 10 (1940), pp. 850–4. By this stage, cancer of the mouth obliged Freud to wear a prosthesis.
33. Grinker, *Fifty Years.*
34. John P. Spiegel taped recollections. With thanks to Heli Meltsner.
35. According to John Spiegel, only fortunate chance led to its publication; the manuscript, submitted 'through channels', ended up on the Washington desk of the Surgeon General of the Army Air Force, where it happened to be seen by the medical director of the Macy foundation which had already funded several psychiatric publications. Intrigued by its title, he read it overnight, and insisted it be published and distributed at the foundation's expense. It seems more likely that Grinker, an inveterate networker, arranged the whole thing. D. R. Jones, 'The Macy Reports: Combat Fatigue in [WW2] Flyers', *Aviation, Space and Environmental Medicine* 1987, pp. 808–9.
36. R. R. Grinker and J. P. Spiegel, *War Neuroses in North Africa: The Tunisian Campaign January-May 1943.* (New York, 1943).
37. John Spiegel recollections.
38. Grinker and Spiegel, *War Neuroses*, p. 160.
39. *ibid.,* p. 161.
40. *ibid.,* p. 162.
41. *ibid.,* p. 165.
42. *ibid.,* pp. 198–208.

43. *ibid.*, p. 158.

44. *BMJ* (1943), ii, p. 336–7. For other criticisms of 'narcosynthesis':*NPWW2* 2, 771, 906.

45. A. J. Glass, 'Psychotherapy in the Combat Zone', *AJP* 110 (1954), p. 727. Grinker and Spiegel conceded that less than 2% of their patients returned to the front line. *War Neuroses*, p. 235.

46. *NPWW2*, 2, pp. 3–9; interview, Dr E. A. Weinstein; C&M, p. 25.

47. F. R. Hanson, 'The Factor of Fatigue in the Neuroses of Combat', *Bulletin of U. S. Army Medical Department* 9 (1949), pp. 147–50.

48. *ibid.*

49. R. R. Grinker and J. P. Spiegel, 'Brief Psychotherapy in War Neuroses', *Psychosomatic Medicine* 6 (1944), pp. 123–31.

50. *Medical Department, United States Army, Internal Medicine in World War II, vol. 1, Activities of Medical Consultants* (Washington DC, 1961), p. 165.

51. E. D. Cooke, *All But Me and Thee* (Washington DC, 1946), pp. 151–5; Herbert Spiegel interview, 1994.

52. *NPWW2*, 2, pp. 10–11.

53. G. W. B. James, 'Narrative', unpublished MS; 'An Experimental Forward Psychiatric Unit'. 31 December 1943, PRO WO 222/1492; H. A. Palmer, 'The Problem of the P & N Casualty – a Study of 12, 000 Cases', CMAC RAMC 466/49; *idem*, 'Military Psychiatric Casualties – Experience with 12,000 cases, *Lancet* (1945), ii, pp. 454–7, 492–4; *idem*, 'Abreactive Techniques – Ether', *JRAMC* 84 (1945), pp. 86–7; On his wedding day, Palmer walked up the aisle in Manchester cathedral 'the same way he walked through the ward. With a heavy step.' Interview, Dr John Wishart.

54. Harold Anstruther Palmer (1906–1981) educated in Manchester. Before the war, assistant physician at Woodside Hospital. *BMJ* (1981), i, p. 2063. Interviews, Dr Stephen MacKeith and Dr. R. S. Morton.

55. Palmer, 'The Problem of the P & N Casualty'.

56. CMAC RAMC 466/49. p. 11.

57. *ibid.*, pp. 2–3. Palmer estimated that 65% of his cases were 'low morale and 35%, 'high-morale'. Some 45% had broken down soon after going into battle for the first time. The high morale cases had been worn down by the strain of prolonged fighting or traumatised by some battlefield horror.

58. W. Needles, *Psychiatry* 9 (1946), p. 171. Needles also claimed that 'the British in their African campaign set a high-water mark for returns-to-duty' by 'return[ing] to duty psychotic patients, epileptic patients, severely neurotic patients'; [Sir Ronald Adam] 'The Health of the Army', December 1943, CMAC RAMC 446 /38, p. 4; Wishart interview.

59. Interview, E. A. Weinstein; C. H. Jonas, *AJP* 102(1946), p. 819.

60. C. D'Este, *A Genius for War: A Life of General George S. Patton* (London, 1996), pp. 521–46; M. Howard, *Times Literary Supplement*, 8 February 1996.

61. D. Hunter, 'A Corps Psychiatrist in[Italy]', *JRAMC* 86 (1946), pp. 127–30.

62. XIII Corps had transferred from the Adriatic Front a few weeks earlier.

C. d'Este, *Fatal Decision: Anzio and the Battle for Rome* (London, 1991), pp. 349–54. According to the cameraman's 'dope sheet', the boys are mostly cases of 'inadequate personality' or 'unstable mental defectives'. The men have 'acute depression', mild or severe acute anxiety states, mild acute anxiety, or 'anxiety state in man of good personality'. Department of Film, IWM.

63. S. Milligan, *Mussolini: His Part In My Downfall* (Harmondsworth, 1980), pp. 276–88; *idem, BMA News Review*, January 1991.

64. S. Milligan, *Where Have All the Bullets Gone* (Harmondsworth, 1986), pp. 11–22. In 1942, G. W. B. James reported increasing difficulty in finding work for men 'whose category has been lowered for psychiatric reasons'; the reluctance of white South African soldiers to 'lose face' by doing 'Kafir work' was a particular problem. James, 'Narrative', pp. 95–7.

65. E. A. Weinstein interview, Bethesda, 1992; S. W. Ransom, 'The Normal Battle Reaction' *Bulletin of U. S. Army Medical Department* 9 (1949).

66. Fraser, *And We Shall Shock*, p. 304; P. Davis, *A Child At Arms* (London, 1970); P. Ziegler, *Mountbatten* (London, 1986), pp. 251–2; B. L. Raina (ed.), *Medical Services: Medicine, Surgery and Pathology* (New Delhi, 1955), pp. 335–84; F. A. E. Crew, (ed.), *United Kingdom Medical Services: Army Medical Services Campaigns*, vol. 5 (London, 1966), p. 682.

67. E. A. Bennet, 'Psychiatry in India and Pakistan', *Mental Health* (London)7 (1947), p. 3; P. Scott, *The Towers of Silence* (1971; London, 1996), pp. 378–9.

68. Raina, op. cit.; CMAC RAMC 814; P. J. R. Davis, *JRAMC* 86 (1946), pp. 254–74.

69. *JRAMC* 86 (1946), pp. 254–74.

70. Raina, p. 366; CMAC RAMC 814.

71. Morison quoted in W. Manchester, *Goodbye Darkness* (London, 1982), p. 191; *ibid.*, p. 209.

72. T. Lidz, 'Psychiatric Casualties from Guadalcanal', *Psychiatry* 9 (1946), pp. 193–213.

73. *ibid.*; T. Lidz, 'Nightmares and the Combat Neuroses', *Psychiatry* 9 (1946), pp. 37– 49.

74. *NPWW2* 2, pp. 458–63; 623–38.

75. *ibid.*, pp. 463–5; T. Lidz, letter to the author 1996.

76. G. E. Gifford (ed.), *Psychoanalysis, Psychotherapy and the New England Scene 1894–1944* (New York, 1978), pp. 346–53; P. Roazen, *Helene Deutsch* (New Brunswick, New Jersey, 1992), p. 280.

77. *NPWW2*, 2, pp. 465–71; Lidz letter, 1996.

78. M. R. Kaufman and L. E Beaton, 'A Psychiatric Program in Combat', *Bulletin of the Menninger Clinic* 11 (1947), pp. 1–14.

79. Kaufman and Beaton, 'Program', p. 4; Gifford, *Psychoanalysis*, p. 400.

80. *NPWW2*, 2, pp. 639–739.

81. *ibid.*

82. *ibid.*

83. *ibid.*, But see J. V. Coleman, in *NPWW2*, 2, pp. 635–6 for a shrewd critique. P. Solomon, *Archives of Neurology & Psychiatry* 57(1947) describes work with Marines on Okinawa. E. Sledge, *With the Old Breed* is a classic account of the battle.

84. Sargant, *The Unquiet Mind*, p. 113.

85. W. Needles, 'The Regression of Psychiatry in the Army', *Psychiatry* 9 (1946), pp. 167–85.

86. *ibid.*

87. P. S. Wagner, *Psychiatry* 9 (1946), pp. 341–64.

88. Needles, 'Regression'.

Chapter 16: New Ways of War

1. R. Blythe (ed.), *Private Words* (Harmondsworth, 1993), p. 185.

2. *The Times, Independent*, 23 November 1994.

3. R. Farrant, *Winged Dagger* (1948; London, 1998), p. 96.

4. I. McD. G. Stewart, *The Struggle for Crete* (1966; Oxford, 1991), p. 329.

5. C. Barnett, *The Audit of War* (London, 1986); P. Addison, *The Road to 1945* (London, 1975).

6. G. Orwell, *Collected Essays, Journalism and Letters, 2* (London, 1968), *passim*; S. P. Mackenzie, *Politics and Military Morale* (Oxford 1992).

7. D. Fernbach, 'Tom Wintringham and Socialist Defense Strategy', *History Workshop* 14 (1982), pp. 63–91.

8. 'Captain X', *A Soldier Looks Ahead* (London, 1944). The author, W. C. Shebbeare, died in a tank in Normandy in 1944.

9. Adam Papers, LH/ KCL; Mackenzie, *Politics*.

10. P. Ustinov, *Dear Me* (Harmondsworth, 1978), p. 147; J. A. English, *The Canadian Army and the Normandy Campaign* (New York, 1991), pp. 107–23.

11. English, *Canadian Army*.

12. D. Forman, *To Reason Why* (London, 1992),

13. Forman, *To Reason*, p. 40; BBC Archives.

14. Main interview with Harrison, 1984. Both the British and the Americans continued to show footage of Japanese atrocities to troops being sent to fight against them. J. Dower, *War Without Mercy* (New York, 1986)

15. F. A. E. Crew (ed.), *The Army Medical Services Campaigns*, vol 1 (London, 1956), pp. 631–2; R. E. Tunbridge, 'Psychiatric experiences in Malta', *Lancet*, (1945), ii, pp. 587–90; PRO W0 222/239; G. Greer, *Daddy We Hardly Knew You* (London, 1989)

16. S. Bidwell, *Modern Warfare*, (London, 1973), p. 136; Crew, *Campaigns*, 1, p. 632.

17. Ahrenfeldt, pp. 199–90; Tunbridge, 'Psychiatric Experiences'.

18. S. A. Stouffer *et al.*, *The American Soldier*, vol 2 (Princeton, 1949), p. 196.

19. F. L. McLoughlin and W. M. Millar, 'Employment of Air Raid Noises in Psychotherapy', *BMJ* (1941), ii, pp. 158–9; Forman, *To Reason Why*, p. 42.

20. R. Grinker and J. P. Spiegel *Men Under Stress* (Philadelphia, 1945), p. 135.
21. Fussell, *Wartime*, p. 274,
22. S. L. A. Marshall, *Island Victory* (Washington D.C., 1944).
23. S. L. A. Marshall, *Men Against Fire* (New York, 1947), p. 149.
24. *ibid.*, p. 78.
25. *ibid.*, pp. 157–202.
26. D. E. Graves in D. A. Chartes *et al.* (eds), *Military History and the Military Profession* (Westport, Conn., 1992); R. Spiller, *RUSI Journal* 133 (1988); Forman, *To Reason Why*.
27. Forman, *To Reason Why*, pp. 197–204.
28. *loc. cit.*
29. *ibid.*, pp. 205–17.
30. FM Viscount Montgomery, 'Morale in Battle', *BMJ*, (1946), ii, pp. 702–4.
31. M. Howard, *Journal of Military History* 55 (1991), p. 379.
32. A. Cooper, *Cairo During the War* (London, 1989) pp. 188–9. D. French, 'Discipline and the death penalty in the British Army in the war against Germany during the Second World War', *JCH* 33 (1998), pp. 531–45.
33. French 'Discipline'.
34. Cooper, *Cairo*, p. 214.
35. A. Bowlby, *The Recollections of Rifleman Bowlby* (London, 1989), pp. 51–2.
36. *ibid.*, pp. 58, 109.
37. French, 'Discipline'; WO 277/16. J. Sparrow, 'Morale'.
38. P. Hart, *The Heat of Battle* (Barnsley, 1999), p. 142; E. Morris, *Circles of Hell* (London, 1993), p. 399; C&M, pp. 107–8.
39. WO 277/16
40. C&M, pp. 106–7.
41. French, 'Discipline'; WO 277/16; M. Lindsay, *So Few Got Through* (London, 1946), p. 263.
42. WO 277/16.
43. French, 'Discipline'; C. D'Este, *Fatal Decision* (London, 1991), p. 311; Ellis, *Sharp End*, pp. 243–5.
44. Bowlby, *Recollections*, Lindsay, *So Few* and Hart, *Heat of Battle* have frank accounts of the desertion problem.
45. G. Rosen, 'Nostalgia', *Psychological Medicine* 5 (1975), pp. 340–54; D. J. Flicker and P. Weiss, 'Nostalgia', *War Medicine* 4 (1943), pp. 380–7; E. T. Dean, *Shook Over Hell* (Cambridge, Mass., 1997), pp. 128–30.
46. Blythe, *Private Words*, pp. 61–2; G. W. B. James, 'Narrative', p. 53. Numerous contributors to *NPWW2* discuss nostalgia in American troops.
47. Main interview with Harrison.
48. W. R. D. Fairbairn, 'The War Neuroses', *BMJ* (1943), i, pp. 183–6; WO 277/16. One group felt to be immune from this problem were torpedoed sailors seen in a New York out-patients clinic. Most 'had gone to sea early in life' and 'many had run away from home or . . . gone in spite of parental objections . . . The motivation seemed to be a strong, inarticulate need to get away from home and to get way from the disciplined social authority and

regimentation of life on land'. Even after being torpedoed, many declined to visit their families. Others would 'go home eagerly, but within a few days would find a tide of restlessness rising which would soon make it impossible to stay . . . One man said "I go home. I say I never go to sea again till the war is over. They make big fuss. My mother, she so good to me, I can't stand it. In two days I go back to sea".' S. Margolin, *et al., War Medicine* 3 (1943), pp. 393–408.

49. Greene, 'Role', p. 391; J. W. Appel, 'Preventive Psychiatry', in *NPWW2* 1, pp. 373– 415.

50. H. Spiegel, in *NPWW2,* 2, p. 115 (originally published 1944).

51. 'The Group' was, of course, one of the great buzzwords of the 1930s intellectual Left; both London and New York had 'Group Theatres'. Appel, 'Preventive Psychiatry'; interviews: E. A Weinstein, H. Spiegel; T. A. Wilson, 'Who Fought and Why? The Assignment of American Soldiers to Combat' in P. Addison and A. Calder, *Time to Kill* (London, 1997).

52. J. W. Appel and G. W. Beebe, *JAMA* 131 (1946), pp. 1469–75.

53. S. Ambrose, *Citizen Soldiers* (New York, 1997), pp. 273–89; G. Cosmas and A. Cowdrey, *Medical Services in the European Theatre of Operations* (Washington, DC, 1992), p. 617. G. W. B. James reckoned officers and NCOs could do a year; men, 'probably two years' ('Narrative' p. 151). Despite paying more attention to exhaustion, the British had problems of their own. An officer at Anzio in early 1944 reported that most long-serving NCOs in his Battalion were 'bomb-happy'; a private who seemed 'to have lost all his bounce lately' was 'showing 'all the symptoms of the first stages of bomb-happiness. R. Trevelyan, *The Fortress* (Harmondsworth, 1979), pp. 40, 51. See: Ellis, *Sharp End,* pp. 296–7, Hart, *Heat of Battle.*

Chapter 17: D-Day and After

1. PRO WO 165/129.
2. *ibid.*
3. *ibid.*; S. MacKeith interview, 1990.
4. T. F. Main, interview with T. Harrison, 1984; *idem,* 'The Soldier Abroad'; PRO WO 165/129; Ahrenfeldt; Forman, *To Reason Why.*
5. Main interview; J. Crang, *The British Army and the People's War* (Manchester, 2000).
6. C&M, p. 109; Main interview.
7. C&M, pp. 110–112; F. Crew (ed.) *The Army Medical Services. Campaigns.* 4 (London, 1962)
8. Jennifer Johns, letter 1992; C&M, p. 109.
9. Main interview
10. R. F. Fidler, 'A Psychiatrist's Observations in the B. L. A', *JRAMC* 88 (1947), pp. 186–191; interview, Dr John Wishart, 1992.
11. R. Miller, *Nothing Less Than Victory* (London, 1993).
12. *World At War,* Thames Television, 1973.

13. PRO WO 177/925; quoted in C&M, p. 224.

14. C&M, p. 114; PRO 165/129.

15. C. D'Este, *Decision in Normandy* (London, 1984); M. Hastings, *Overlord* (London, 1993); J. Keegan, *Six Armies in Normandy* (Harmondsworth, 1983).

16. Keegan, *Six Armies*, pp. 241–4.

17. D. Holbrook, *Flesh Wounds* (1966; London, 1987), p. 189.

18. *ibid.*, p. 158.

19. C&M, pp. 114–5; D'Este, *Decision*, pp. 274–6; Hastings, *Overlord*, pp. 177–9; F. M. Richardson, *Fighting Spirit. Psychological factors in War* (London, 1978) p. 117–183.

20. Hastings, *Overlord*, p. 178.

21. C&M, pp. 131.

22. PRO WO 177/321; PRO WO 177/133; Hastings, *Overlord*, p. 345.

23. Fidler, 'Psychiatrist's Observations'.

24. D'Este, *Decision*, pp. 281–2.

25. PRO WO 171/1306

26. *ibid.*

27. *ibid.*, Italics added. On 13 July, the Divisional Commander General Thomas visited the Battalion and 'spen[t] most of the time in a slit trench owing to mortar fire'. Four days later, a British Typhoon aircraft attacking German positions dropped a few bombs short on the Hampshires' position. Only one man was injured but one officer and six men were evacuated with shell-shock.

28. J. A. English, *The Canadian Army and the Normandy Campaign* (New York, 1991); C&M, pp. 110–26.

29. C&M, pp. 121–7.

30. PRO. WO 177/321.

31. C&M, pp. 141–8.

32. PRO WO 165/129.

Chapter 18: A Tale of Two Hospitals

1. CMAC PP/ SHF.

2. M. Silverman, *Psychiatric Bulletin* 16 (1992), pp. 385–6.

3. T. Harrison, *Bion, Rickman, Foulkes and the Northfield Experiment* (London, 2000).

4. S. H. Foulkes, *Introduction to Group-Analytic Psychotherapy* (1948; London, 1991), p. 43.

5. *ibid.*, p. 44.

6. Harrison, *Bion, Rickman*, pp. 24–54; G. Bléandonu, *Wilfred Bion* (London, 1994).

7. W. R. Bion and J. Rickman, 'Intra-Group Tensions in Therapy', *Lancet*, (1943) ii, pp. 678–81.

8. M. Pines (ed.), *Bion and Group Psychotherapy* (London, 1985).

9. Bion and Rickman, 'Tensions'.

10. *ibid.*; Pines, *Bion*, p. 110.

11. J. Carey, *The Intellectuals and the Masses* (London, 1993).

12. R. Heppenstall, *The Lesser Infortune* (London, 1953), pp. 22, 68, 72, 71, 113. While Great War writers like Sassoon idealised the common soldier, literary types a generation later often despised him, partly in reaction against the ceaseless talk of a 'People's War'.

13. ibid., p. 132. Maclaren-Ross, the model for Anthony Powell's character, X Trapnel, makes no mention of Northfield in his *Memoirs of the Forties*.

14. ibid., p. 143.

15. Foulkes, *Introduction*, pp. 46–7.

16. CMAC PP/SHF.

17. Hargreaves–Foulkes, 27 October 1944 and 30 August 1945. CMAC PP/SHF; S. H. Foulkes, 'Some Autobiographical Notes', CMAC PP/SHF.

18. Hargreaves-Foulkes, 30 August 1945. CMAC. PP/SHF.

19. Foulkes, 'Autobiographical Notes'. Ignoring advice that he anglicise his name from Fuchs to Fox, he had 'welshified' it to Foulkes.

20. T. F. Main interview with Dr Tom Harrison, 1984; P de Maré, in Pines (ed.), *The Evolution of Group-Analysis* (London, 1983), pp. 218–9; E. J. Anthony, ' in ibid., p. 30.

21. Anthony, in Pines, *Evolution*; patient discussions, Northfield, 28 October and 5 December 1944, CMAC PP/SHF.

22. Group Meeting, Northfield, 2 August 1945. CMAC PP/SHF.

23. CMAC. PP/SHF.

24. Anthony, in Pines, *Evolution*, p. 30.

25. Foulkes, *Introduction*, pp. 87–91.

26. Foulkes, *Introduction*, pp. 95.

27. S. H. Foulkes, 'A Memorandum on Group Therapy', July 1945, CMAC PP/ SHF.

28. J. Kovel, *A Complete Guide to Therapy* (London, 1978), pp. 230–2; Foulkes, *Introduction*, p. 115; Foulkes's elaborate notes on Moreno, CMAC PP/SHF. During the war Moreno himself worked with sailors at St Elizabeth's Hospital in Washington, DC. N. G. Hale, *The Rise and Crisis of Psyhoanalysis in the United States* (New York, 1995), p. 281.

29. Foulkes, 'Some Autobiographical Notes', CMAC PP/SHF. Foulkes,

30. 'Discussion of Group Therapy', 3 May 1945, CMAC PP/SHF.

31. M. Dewar, BBC interview, 1994. With thanks to Alastair Wilson. Tom Main was also sceptical in retrospect, quoting a Dorothy Parker review of a Broadway play: 'It's sad. It's bad. But, boy, is it psychological.' 'A psychodrama's like that,' said Dr Main: 'ah, boy, is it *psychological.* But it didn't help.' Main, Harrison interview.

32. H. Bridger, 'Northfield Revisited,' in Pines, *Bion*, pp. 87–107; *idem*, 'The Northfield Experiment', *BMC* 10 (1946), pp. 71–76; Bridger interview with Sabine Strich, 1990, CMAC PP/SHF.

33. Bridger interview.

34. Bridger, in Pines, *Bion*.

35. CMAC PP/SHF.
36. Foulkes, *Introduction*, pp. 90–131.
37. *ibid.*; Bridger interview.
38. Dewar, BBC interview; Staff Discussion, 29 August 1945, CMAC. PP/SHF.
39. Discussion, 29 August 1945, CMAC PP/SHF.
40. Bridger interview with Strich CMAC PP/SHF.
41. Main, Harrison interview.
42. Dewar, BBC interview.
43. Main, Harrison interview.
44. *ibid.*,
45. Dewar, BBC interview.
46. L. H. Bartemeier *et al.*, *JNMD* 104 (1946) p. 496.
47. Main, Harrison interview.
48. M. James, *British Medical Students' Journal*, spring 1950. Thanks to Jessica James; *Personnel Selection* film 1944; Dewar, BBC interview.
49 W. Holden, *Shell Shock: The Psychological Impact of War* (London, 1998), pp. 120–1; Harrison, *Bion, Rickman*.
50. The concept of 'group dynamics', applying the laws of modern physics to relationships in groups, had been developed just before the war by the sociologist, Kurt Lewin. Staff discussion. 24 May 1945, CMAC PP/SHF.
51. October 1945, CMAC PP/SHF.
52. CMAC PP/SHF.
53. Rickman–Foulkes, 29 October 1944, CMAC PP/SHF; V. Scannel, *The Tiger and the Rose* (London, 1983).
54. J. T. Robinson, 'Group Therapy', *JRAMC* 91 (1948), pp. 66–79.
55. 15 November 1945, CMAC PP/SHF.
56. W. C. Menninger, *Psychiatry in A Troubled World* (New York, 1948), p. 293.
57. 'The Returning Veteran', *March of Time*, 1945.
58. Menninger, *Psychiatry*, pp. 293–300.
59. J. Huston, *An Open Book* (1981; London, 1988), pp. 122–6.
60. Wonderfully spoken by Walter Huston, the director's father. Unattributed quotations in this section are from the soundtrack of *Let There Be Light*. Thanks to Paul Sargent and the IWM Department of Film.
61. *NPWW2*, 1, pp. 623–5, 675–83, 701–17; B. Simon, *Medical Clinics of North America* (March 1946), pp. 459–72.
62. Herbert Spiegel interview, 1994; Huston, *Open Book*, p. 125.
63. *NPWW2*, 1, pp. 701–17; on American group psychotherapy see Hale, *Rise and Crisis of Psychoanalysis in the United States*, pp. 199–200, 429–30 and Leo Rosten's fine novel, *Captain Newman, M. D.* (1961).

Chapter 19: The Helmeted Airman

1. Quoted in Fussell, *Wartime*, (New York, 1990), p. 132.
2. M. Middlebrook, *The Berlin Raids*. (Harmondsworth, 1988), pp. 29–76; C.

Webster and N. Frankland, *The Strategic Air Offensive Against Germany*, 1939–1945 (London, 1961), 2, p. 193.

3. M. Middlebrook, *The Schweinfurt-Regensburg Mission* (Harmondsworth, 1985).

4. Sir John Salmond, *RWOCIS*, p. 84.

5. Webster and Frankland, *Strategic Air Offensive*; M. Hastings, *Bomber Command* (London, 1979); J. Terraine, *The Right of the Line: The Royal Air Force in the European War, 1939–1945* (London, 1988).

6. This view has recently been challenged by R. J. Overy, *War and Economy in the Third Reich* (Oxford 1994).

7. W. F. Craven and J. L. Cate. *The Army Air Forces in World War II* (Chicago, 1949); R. Schaffer, *Wings of Judgment: American Bombing in World War II* (New York, 1985).

8. *Pathe News*, 1942.

9. E. Partridge, *A Dictionary of R. A. F. Slang* (London, 1945).

10. M. Middlebrook, *The Nuremberg Raid* (Harmondsworth, 1986), p. 318.

11. D. W. Hastings *et al.*, *Psychiatric Experiences of the Eight Air Force* (New York, 1944), p. 3; Craven and Cate, *Army Air Forces*, vol. 7, p. 401.

12. M. Wells, *Courage in Air Warfare* (London, 1995), pp. 101–4; Terraine, *Right*, p. 527; Wells, *Courage*, pp. 125–6.

13. Harris, quoted Terraine, *Right*, p. 536; Hastings, *Psychiatric*, p. 35–67.

14. Hastings, *Psychiatric*, pp. 209–307; D. Stafford-Clark, 'Morale and Flying Experience', *JMS* (1949), pp. 10–50.

15. Stafford-Clark, 'Morale', p. 12.

16. *ibid.*

17. The consultant psychiatrist to the Eighth Air Force in England believed that 'narcosis therapy' – just putting an airman out for a few days breaking the cycle of worry and 'push[ing] the traumatic events further into the background, so that their impact on the personality is lessened', but without any 'uncovering' therapy to get at underlying psychological factors – was effective. Interview, Bernard C. Glueck 1996. Roy Grinker, the prophet of narcosynthesis, was adamant that it was not. R. Grinker and J. P. Spiegel, *Men Under Stress* (Philadelphia, 1945), pp. 389–400.

18. R. D. Gillespie, 'War Neuroses after Psychological trauma', *BMJ* (1945), i, pp. 653–6; interview, Dr J. MacGregor.

19. Stafford-Clark, 'Morale', p. 20.

20. R. Kee, 'Mercury on a Fork', *Listener*, 18 February 1971, p. 208.

21. Terraine, *Right*, p. 522; F. Dyson, *Disturbing The Universe* (London, 1981), pp. 19–32.

22. J. Steinbeck, *Once There Was a War* (London, 1990), pp. 39–41; Fussell, *Wartime*, p. 49.

23. Stafford-Clark, 'Morale', p. 16; Middlebrook, *Nuremberg*, p. 52.

24. Douglas Harvey quoted Fussell, *Wartime*, pp. 100–1.

25. Hastings, *Bomber Command*, 217–22.

26. M. Tripp, *The Eight Passenger* (London, 1969).

27. Terraine, *The Right*, 520–37.

28. W. Holden, *Shellshock* (London, 1998), pp. 110–11. Some 80% of LMF cases were non-commissioned aircrew. On the ground, such men did not 'mix' with officers – even if they were members of the same crew. This 'palpably unfair practice' (Terraine, *Right of the Line*, p. 466) was bad for morale but, despite Canadian protests, the RAF refused to give commissions to all aircrew. That would have altered the elite social character of the service.

29. Lord Balfour of Inchrye, quoted in Wells, *Courage* p. 194; J. McCarthy, 'Aircrew and [LMF in WW2]', *War & Society* 2 (1984), pp. 87–101.

30. Terraine, *Right*, pp. 534–5; Hastings, *Bomber Command*, p. 214; Dyson, *Disturbing*, p. 23; Wells, *Courage*, p. 204–5.

31. Terraine, *Right*, p. 552–4. Air Vice-Marshal Don Bennett quoted in Webster and Frankland 2, pp. 19—211; Middlebrook, *Berlin Raids*.

32. Middlebrook, *Berlin Raids*, pp. 312–20; B. Greenhous *et al.*, *The Crucible of War* (Toronto, 1994). According to W. Johnston, *War & Society*, 14 (1996), p. 91, 'the Canadian government's insistence that Canada have its own bomber formation (6 Group) caused heavy casualties among Canadian aircrew . . . If Canadians had been mixed in with other crews in squadrons and groups, they would probably have learned the skills necessary for survival from other more skilled crews and commanders and would probably have had a better chance to complete their thirty-mission tours of duty.'

33. Middlebrook, *Berlin Raids*, pp. 318–9.

34. Hastings, *Bomber Command*, p. 214. This is denied by Wells, a serving USAF officer (*Courage*, p. 135), but confirmed by Dr Bernard C. Glueck (taped recollections, 1996). 'There certainly was [a problem of morale in October 1943]. The feeling was "they're going to keep us flying until we're all killed off". It was then that . . . we saw a majority of the men getting to serious enough trouble so that they were referred for treatment.' The arrival of massive reinforcements of crew and aircraft soon turned the situation round. On 'crashlanding', Hastings, *Bomber Command*, p. 269; 'Whispers in the Air', Channel 4 Television, 1989. Again, Wells dismisses this charge (*Courage*, p. 114).

35. R. Symonds, 'The Life of Sir Charles Symonds' (unpublished); C. Symonds, *Studies in Neurology* (Oxford, 1970), pp. 1–23; D. Williams, Introduction to Moran's *The Anatomy of Courage* (London, 1984) pp. ix-xxii; CMAC. PP/CPS; C. P. Symonds and D. Williams, *Psychological Disorders in Flying Personnel of the Royal Air Force 1939–1945* (London, 1947). Interviews: Henry Rollin, 1996; David Stafford-Clark, 1996; Peggy Jay, 1992.

36. R. Symonds, 'Life', pp. 81–3.

37. D. K. Henderson, *Guy's Hospital Report*, 95 (1946), pp. 1–6; *Guy's Hospital Gazette* (1946), pp. 284–6.

38. D. K. Henderson and R. D. Gillespie, *A Text-Book of Psychiatry* (1927).

39. D. Stafford-Clark interview 1996; *Lancet*, 1939, ii, pp. 576, 622.

40. Stafford-Clark interview.

41. C. Symonds, *Studies*, p. 18.

42. Symonds, quoted in A. S. English, 'A Predisposition Towards Cowardice?', *War & Society* 13 (1995), p. 26.

43. Neurologist interview, 1994; Dr J. MacGregor interview 1990, letter, 1995.

44. Stafford-Clark interview. In 1944 the official line was slightly softened. It was recognised that 'in some cases, owing to the less robust constitution of an individual or his subjection to special strain operational strain, earlier relief will be necessary'. The Unit Medical Officer, 'if he sees the man shewing signs of strain in the latter half of his operational tour', could recommend 'accelerated relief employment'. PRO AIR 20/10727. It is not clear how widespread this practice was.

45. Dyson, *Disturbing the Universe*; T. M. Gibson and M. H. Harrison, *Into Thin Air: A History of Aviation Medicine in the RAF* (London, 1984), pp. 238–54; R. D. Gillespie, *The Psychological Effects of War* (New York, 1942). Dr Bernard Glueck recalls that at medical meetings in London in June 1943 Gillespie stood out from his RAF colleagues by 'taking the psychodynamic line' and showing a willingness 'to treat us as fellow doctors and psychiatrists rather than looking at the rank on our shoulders'. Symonds, by contrast, was 'very polished but rather austere', much too grand to talk to a mere Second Lieutenant. Telephone interview, 6 September 1996.

46. Wells, *Courage*, pp. 89–114.

47. Craven and Cate, *Army Air Force*, 7, pp. 403–7. The official history's sketch of a flight surgeon's day has him rising at 4 a.m. for a mission briefing, and dealing with patients soon after – a man with diarrhoea is grounded and a pilot shocked by a runway crash given a drink and sedative. By 10 a.m. the planes have gone for the day; the flight surgeon is visiting aircrew in hospital, deciding that a pilot with minor abdominal wounds has 'had it'. After lunch he goes over to another hospital and persuades the staff not to send a pilot from his unit to see the psychiatrist – 'He's an iron man and his crew idolises him – he needs a psychiatrist like I do.' Then he persuades a Disposition Board that a mechanic's headaches were caused by 'rotten moonshine' and not 'hostility to his lieutenant' and gives some phenobarb and a little rest to a man who's just got a 'Dear John'letter. By now, it's 4 p.m., fog is coming down and the planes are begining to return from the day's mission. One crash-lands safely but a second catches fire and the co-pilot is lost. An hour later the flight surgeon hands out medicinal whisky to a few needy crewmen: 'No one very edgy except Lt . . . who has just lost the second roommate in a fortnight . . . Later at the club I played gin rummy with him and we philosophized about luck and life and things'. After dinner comes evening sick call, disposing of the body of the dead co-pilot and a meeting with other doctors. In bed at 11 the flight surgeon is awakened: 'one of the armourers has DTs and is sitting in his bed shooting the snakes with his . 45'. After taking away the gun the doctor gets him back to the surgery for a shot of sodium amytal.

48. *ibid.*, pp. 403–4.

49. Basil Embry, in Symonds Papers, CMAC PP/CPS/2.

50. Cheshire, quoted by Embry, *loc. cit.*
51. Written by USAAF staff officers Beirne Lay and Sy Bartlett, the film was based on the experiences of Colonel Frank A. Armstrong. See B. L. Gravatt and F. H. Ayers, Jr, *Aerospace Historian*, September 1988, pp. 204–8.
52. R. Morris, *Guy Gibson* (London, 1994), pp. 132–8, 158.
53. *ibid.*, pp. 249–307.
54. A. Boyle, *No Passing Glory* (London, 1955), p. 169; Symonds, *Studies*, p. 21.
55. Boyle, *No Passing Glory*, p. 170.
56. Webster and Frankland, *Strategic Air Offensive*, 3, p. 156; Boyle, *No Passing Glory*, p. 232.
57. Symonds, quoted in Boyle, *No Passing Glory*, pp. 237–8.
58. Boyle, *No Passing Glory*, p. 295.
59. C. Foxley-Norris, *Independent*, 31 August 1992.
60. D. D. Bond, *The Love and Fear of Flying* (New York, 1952), pp. 19–23.
61. ibid., p. 25–31; D. R. Jones, 'Flying and Danger, Joy and Fear', *Aviation, Space and Environmental Medicine*, February 1986, pp. 131–6.
62. Bond, *Love*, p. 20; Magee was killed at nineteen. His poem was quoted by President Ronald Reagan in his speech after the Challenger disaster.
63. Bond, *Love*, pp. 32–41.
64. *loc. cit.*
65. Glueck interview.
66. H. R. Rollin, *Festina Lente: A Psychiatric Odyssey* (London, 1990) p. 38.
67. R. D. Gillespie, 'War Neuroses after Psychological Trauma', *BMJ* (1945), i, pp. 653–6.
68. *BMJ* (1945), ii, p. 708; Rollin interview.
69. Letter to the author, 29 June 1999. Thanks to Dr Frankland.

Chapter 20: Learning from the Germans?

1. H. Binneveld, *From Shell Shock to Combat Stress* (Amsterdam, 1997), p. 91.
2. *International Review of Psycho-Analysis* 16 (1989), pp. 27–31.
3. L. B. Kalinowsky, 'Problems of War Neuroses in the Light of Experiences in Other Countries', *AJP* 107 (1950), pp. 340–6; Shorter, *HoP*, p. 221.
4. PRO WO 177/316.
5. A Bryant, *The Turn of the Tide* (London, 1958), p. 101; *idem, Triumph in the West* (London, 1959), p. 141.
6. D. Fraser, *And We Shall Shock Them* (London, 1988), p. 108.
7. M van Creveld, *Fighting Power: German and U. S. Army Performance 1939–1945* (London, 1983).
8. Theo J. Schulte, 'The German Soldier in Occupied Russia', in P. Addison and A. Calder (eds), *Time To Kill* (London, 1997), ably summarises the debate on the role of the Wehrmacht; H. Oosterhuis, 'Medicine, Male Bonding and Homosexuality in Nazi Germany', *JCH* 32 (1997), pp. 187–205.
9. V. L. Lidtke, *Bull H Med* 65 (1991), p. 285; R. Gaupp, 'The Development

of Psychiatry in Germany', *AJP* 108 (1952), pp. 721–5; G. Cocks and M. Berg (eds), *Medicine and Modernity* (Cambridge, 1997); G. Cocks, *JMH* 64, suppl. (1992), S204–16; G. Aly *et al.* (eds), *Cleansing the Fatherland: Nazi Medicine and Racial Hygiene* (Baltimore, 1994); P. Weindling, 'Medicine in Nazi Germany', *Bull H Med* 65 (1991), pp. 416–9; *idem*, 'Psychiatry and the Holocaust', *Psychological Medicine* 22 (1992), pp. 1–3.; *idem*, *Health, Race and German Politics between National Unification and Nazism, 1870–1945* (Cambridge, 1989); M. Burleigh, *Social History of Medicine* 7 (1994), pp. 213–28.

10. R. Proctor, *Racial Hygiene: Medicine Under the Nazis* (Cambridge, Mass., 1988); R. J. Lifton, *The Nazi Doctors* (London, 1986).

11. E. Bethge, *Dietrich Bonhoeffer* (London, 1970); W. D. Zimmermann and R. G. Smith (eds), *I Knew Dietrich Bonhoeffer* (London, 1966); M. Burleigh, *Death and Deliverance* (Cambridge, 1994), p. 12; P. Riedesser and A. Verderber, '*Maschinengewehre hinter der Front': Zur Geschichte der deutschen Militärpsychiatrie* (Frankfurt am Main, 1996), p. 102. Weindling's account is more nuanced and sympathetic than that of modern German historians.

12. G. Cocks, *Psychotherapy in the Third Reich: The Göring Institute* (New York, 1985); F. G. Alexander and S. T. Selesnick, *The History of Psychiatry* (London, 1967), pp. 407–9; F. McLynn, *Carl Gustav Jung* (London, 1997), pp. 344–67; Jung, quoted in J. Masson, *Against Therapy* (London, 1989), pp. 140–1.

13. Cocks, *Psychotherapy*; Weindling, *Health, Race.*

14. Van Creveld, *Fighting Power*, p. 91; Riedesser and Verderber, '*Maschinengewehre*', pp. 101–16.

15. Kalinowsky, 'Problems'. For a detailed discussion of the pensions issue, see P. Lerner, 'Hysterical Men' (PhD thesis, Columbia, 1996), pp. 377–411.

17. There had already been some killing of child patients. By 24 August 1941 over 70, 000 adult mental patients had been murdered. Proctor, *Racial Hygiene*, pp. 176–222; Burleigh, *Death*; U. Schmidt, 'Reassessing the Beginning of the Euthanasia Programme'. *German History* 17(1999), pp. 543–50.

18. D. Young, *Rommel* (London, 1961), pp. 25–26.

19. Van Creveld, *Fighting Power, passim.*

20. J. Keegan, *Six Armies in Normandy* (Harmondsworth, 1983) p. 231.

21. F. von Senger and Etterlin, *Neither Fear Nor Hope* (London, 1963), pp. 208–9, 259.

22. *ibid.*, p. 219

23. A. Horne, *To Lose A Battle* (London, 1967), pp. 46–7.

24. Quoted from O. Bartov, 'German Workers, German Soldiers', *German History* 8 (1990), pp. 46–65. See also T. J. Schulte, *The German Army and Nazi Politics in Occupied Russia* (Oxford, 1989).

25. O. Bartov, *Hitler's Army* (Oxford, 1992), pp. 106–78; S. G. Fritz, 'Ideology and Motivation in the Wehrmacht on the Eastern Front', *Journal of Military History* 60 (1996), pp. 683–710.

26. M. Messerchmidt, 'German Military Law in the Second World War', in W. Deist (ed.), *The German Military in the Age of Total War* (Leamington Spa, 1985); G. L. Weinberg argues the 'true figure is above 30,000'. *Journal of Military History* 62 (1998), pp. 371–8. Some 442, 000 Red Army soldiers served in penal battalions and over 158, 000 were either shot by their own side or killed in penal battalions. R. Overy (*Russia's War*, London, 1997), p. 160; A. Sella, *The Value of Life in Soviet Warfare* (London, 1992).

27. O. Bartov, 'The Conduct of War', *JMH* 64 suppl. (1992), S 32–45.

28. L. Alexander, 'Report on German Military Neuropsychiatry', 2 August 1945, US National Archives (With thanks to Ulf Schmift), pp. 47, 66; R. Schneider, 'Military Psychiatry in the German Army', in R. Gabriel (ed.), *Military Psychiatry: A Comparative Perspective* (Westport, Conn., 1986).

29. F. von der Heydte, *Daedalus Returned* (London, 1958), pp. 58, 79.

30. Alexander, 'Report', p. 59. 'Gastric' cases were seen by physicians not psychiatrists, *ibid.*, p. 78.

31. Bartov, *Hitler's Army*, p. 21.

32. ibid., p.19.

33. Schulte, *German Army*.

34. Consultant Psychiatrist, Army Group South, 'Quarterly Report, March–June 1943', 10 July 1943, Federal Military Archives, Freiburg, quoted in van Creveld, *Fighting Power*, p. 92; *ibid.*, p. 94.

35. Alexander, 'Report', p. 110; PRO 177/316.

36. H. Spaeter and W. Ritter von Schramm, *Die Geschichte des Panzerkorps Grossdeutschland* (Bielefeld, 1958), quoted in Bartov, *Hitler's Army*, p. 26; Riedesser and Verderber, '*Maschinengewehre*' pp. 159–60. 'Psychasthenia' was of course Janet's alternative to 'neurasthenia'.

37. Van Creveld, *Fighting Power*, pp. 91–4.

38. J. Galvin, 'German Psychiatry during the war', *AJP* 106 (1950), pp. 703–7.

39. Riedesser and Verderber, '*Maschinengewehre*', pp. 126–30

40. *ibid.*, pp. 145–9; Alexander, 'Report', p. 76.

41. Alexander, 'Report', p. 61.

42. B. Muller-Hill, *Murderous Science* (Oxford, 1988), p. 42.

43. Cocks, *Psychotherapy*, pp. 217–23. In 1945 one German doctor attacked the Luftwaffe's 'rather evasive and confused way' of handling the problem of flying fatigue – 'by means of long leaves in rest homes in rural surroundings, with facilities for outdoor sports such as hunting and fishing'. Alexander, 'Report' p. 117. When asked about abreactive treatments, Dr Kurt Schneider 'stated he had never heard of such a thing . . . he was on principle opposed to the use of barbiturates'. *ibid.*, p. 49.

44. Cocks, *Psychotherapy*, pp. 225–6.

45. Schneider, 'Military Psychiatry', p. 140–1.

46. C. D'Este, *Bitter Victory* (London, 1988), p. 341; Messerschmidt, 'German Military Law'; O. Hennicke quoted in Schulte, *The German Army*, p. 243; Böll, quoted in P. Fussell (ed.), *The Bloody Game: An Anthology of Modern War* (London, 1992), pp. 633–4.

47. Cocks, *Psychotherapy* p. 227; Schneider, 'Military Psychiatry', pp. 139–40; K-H. Roth, 'Die Modernisierung der Folter in den Beiden Weltkriegen', *1999*, July 1987, p. 72.

48. For a different view see E. Shils and M. Janowitz, 'Cohesion and Disintegration in the Wehrmacht in World War II', *Public Opinion Quarterly* 12 (1948) pp. 280–315.

49. M. Gellhorn, *The Face of War* (London, 1985), p. 176.

50. M. Thomson, in M. Gijswift-Hostra and R. Porter (eds), *Cultures of Psychiatry* (Amsterdam, 1999), p. 53; N. Annan, *Changing Enemies. The Defeat and Regeneration of Germany* (London, 1996), pp. 201–12; Burleigh, *Death*, pp. 291–2.

51. Burleigh, *Death*, p. 416.

Chapter 21: Prisoners of War

1. Coombs papers. IWM.

2. B. Moore and K. Fedorowich (eds), *Prisoners of War and their Captors in World War II* (Oxford, 1996); G. McCormack and H. Nelson, *The Burma–Thailand Railway* (St Leonard's, 1993); R. Overy, *Russia's War* (London, 1997), p. 297.

3. A. T. M. Wilson, 'The Serviceman Comes Home', *Pilot Papers* 1 (1946), pp. 9–28; PRO. W0 165/129; Interview, Dr Stephen MacKeith.

4. 1,000 RAMC officers and men were exchanged in 1943. L. van der Post, introduction to E. E. Dunlop, *The War Diaries of Weary Dunlop* (Ringwood, Victoria, 1990); A. L. Cochrane, 'Notes on the Psychology of [POWs]', *BMJ* (1946), i, pp. 282–4.

5. Cochrane, 'Notes'; G. Daws, *Prisoners of the Japanese* (New York, 1994).

6. P. Newman, 'The Prisoner-of-War Mentality', *BMJ* (1944), i, pp. 8–11.

7. A. W. Vaughan Eley, *BMJ* (1944), i, pp. 403–4. 'Every prisoner,' wrote Robert Kee, 'suffered from cycles of depression, more frequent but almost as regular as the changing seasons. With some people the effect was just numbing: the man would lie on his bed all day like a piece of dead wood. With others it brought a violent distress of spirit often visible on faces for days on end.' *A Crowd is not Company*. (1946; London, 1990), p. 116.

8. Newman, 'PoW Mentality'.

9. Captain Mustardé, 'Adjustment and Mal-Adjustment within the Camp' (Talk to Psychiatrists' conference, 7–8 October, 1944), CMAC RAMC 466/49.

10. *ibid.*

11. *ibid.*; J. Witte. [Memoirs], IWM; Dan Billany and David Dowie's novel *The Cage* (1949), written in an Italian camp in 1943, wrestles with the question of whether homosexual love is better than no love at all.

12. Kee, *Crowd*, p. 78; Crawley, *Escape From Germany* (London, 1985), pp. 3–7. Only a tiny minority succeeded: of the 10, 000 Royal Air Force prisoners in permanent camps in Germany less than thirty ever reached British or neutral territory.

13. Newman, 'POW Mentality'.

14. Wilson, 'Serviceman', CMAC RAMC 466/49.

15. A. T. M. Wilson–J. Rickman, 22 February 1944, Rickman papers, Archives of the British Psycho-Analytic Society.

16. Wilson, 'Serviceman'; Ahrenfeldt, p. 240. The figure of 60% refers only to ex-POWs from Germany. D. Rolf, *Prisoners of the Reich* (London, 1988), p. 191, says 'a third of all' repatriates volunteered for CRUs (p. 191).

17. Goodman, quoted in W. Capps, *The Vietnam Reader* (New York, 1991), pp. 51–2; M. G. Bavin, 'The Repatriated [POW]', *British Journal of Social Psychiatry* 1 (1947), pp. 29–35; Ahrenfeldt, p. 300.

18. A. T. M. Wilson, *et al.*, 'Group Techniques in a Transitional Community', *Lancet* (1947), i, pp. 735–8

19. A. Curle and E. Trist, *Human Relations* 1(1948), pp. 42–58, 240–88. Those who volunteered for CRUs were, it could be argued, more highly motivated than those who did not. Not always though: Robert Kee avoided the CRUs, 'having a wish to be shot of anything like a camp for good'. Letter, 6 October 1994.

20. B. Bettelheim, 'Individualism and Mass Behaviour in Extreme Situations', *Journal of Abnormal Psychology* 38 (1943). Some Freudians tried to link the sadistic behaviour of the Japanese to their rigid toilet training. J. Dower, *War Without Mercy* (1986; New York, 1993), pp. 123–32. Letters from John Kelnar, Rickman Papers. Archives of the British Psycho-Analytical Society.

21. Sir J. Grigg, House of Commons, 26 September 1944.

22. PRO WO 165/129.

23. E. Lomax, *The Railway Man* (London, 1995), pp. 206–7; Dunlop, *War Diaries*. R. Braddon, *The Naked Island* is a classic account; H. Nelson, *Prisoners of War: Australians Under Nippon* (Sydney, 1885), a vivid oral history.

24. T. F. Rodger [two-page fragment from 1945 report]; Rodger papers, Glasgow; interviews, Adam Curle, Pat de Maré, 1995. On the internal economies of the camps and the behaviour of officers see Dunlop, *Diaries*. A doctor watching POW patients walking into a hospital in South India noticed that 'all showed emaciation, and some had swellings on their legs, but their morale can only be described as terrific. There was great superficial gaiety, but beneath this was a deep-rooted fear which showed itself when their faces were at rest. The frequent blinking and the shaking hand were a legacy of what they had been through. Their condition was aptly described as that of the whipped dog returning to his master.' *BMJ* (1945), ii, pp. 241.

25. K. W. Todd, 'European into Coolie', *JRAMC* 86(1946), p. 185; E. E. Dunlop, *BMJ* (1946), ii, p. 485.

26. Coombs papers, IWM; Lomax, *Railway Man*; J. Fletcher Cooke, *The Emperor's Guest* (London, 1975); L. van der Post, *The Night of the New Moon* (London, 1970; H. Goulding, *Yasmé* (London, 1988).

27. B. Shephard, 'A Clouded Homecoming', *History Today*, September 1996.

28. Goulding, *Yasmé*; Lomax, *Railway Man*, p. 206.

29. I. Watt, 'The Liberty of the Prison', in G. Moir (ed.), *Beyond Hatred* (London, 1969), pp. 139–56.
30. *ibid.*
31. *ibid.*
32. *ibid.*
33. 'Editorial', *Mental Health* 7 (1947), p. 2; J. Kirman, *JMS* 92 (1946), pp. 808–13; P. Watson 'Report on the Post-Captivity Health of Ex-[POws} of the Japanese', February 1985, unpublished. My thanks to Dr Watson.
34. Watson, 'Report'.
35. Ahrenfeldt; Rolfe, *Prisoners*, p. 195; J. H. Walters *et al.*, a FEPOW survey (Queen Mary's, Roehampton, *c.* 1975); letter from Dr Peter Dally, 1995.
36. [Anonymous] 'War Baby', *Guardian*, August 1995. Psychiatrists found that some patients identified their wives with Japanese guards.
37. Watson, 'Report'; Jack Chalker, interview, 1995.

Chapter 22: A Good War?

1. R. Blythe, *Private Words* (Harmondworth, 1991), p. 307; Michael Howard, *Times Literary Supplement*, 6 January 1995.
2. P. Fussell, *Wartime* (New York, 1990), p. 142; *idem*, 'The Real War', *Atlantic Monthly*, August 1989, pp. 32–9.
3. H. L'Etang, 'A Citicism of military psychiatry in the Second World War', JRAMC 97 (1951), pp. 236–44, 316–27; N. Balchin, *The Flight of the Sparrow* (London, 1955), p. 21. The novelist Nigel Balchin was an Army psychologist .
4. W. C. Menninger, 'Psychiatric Experience in the War', *AJP* 103 (1947), pp. 577–86; F. J. Braceland, 'Psychiatric Lessons from [WW2]', ibid., pp. 587–93.
5. J. Keegan, *The Face of Battle* (Harmondsworth, 1978), p. 335.
6. F Crew, *The Army Medical Services Campaigns*, vol. 4 (London, 1962), p. 558; J. R. Rees, *The Shaping of Psychiatry by War* (New York, 1945), p. 119; J. W. Appel *et al.*, 'Comparative Incidence of [NP] casualties in WW1 and WW2', *AJP* (1946), pp. 196–9. Appel's boss thought that American soldiers in World War Two confronted stronger weapons for longer and that psychiatrists now had 'greater knowledge of personality disorders'. W. Menninger, *Atlantic Monthly*, September 1945.
7. *Mail on Sunday*, 12 April 1998.
8. D. Englander, 'Soldiers and Social Reform in the First and Second World Wars', *Historical Research* 57 (1994), pp. 318–26; P. Addison, *Now The War Is Over* (London, 1995); B. Turner and T. Rennell, *When Daddy Came Home* (London, 1995); P. Shapiro, *British Journal of Psychiatric Social Work*. 2 (1948), pp. 61–70. The Marriage Guidance Council, formed in 1938, became the National Marriage Guidance Council in 1948.
9. *Lancet* (1947), i, 728; W. F. Mellor, *Casualties and Medical Statistics* (London, 1972). The Annual Reports of the Ministry of Pensions do not

distinguish between different categories of medical pensioner – no doubt for shrewd bureaucratic reasons. The War Pensions Agency, in a remarkable display of British official *glasnost,* refused to provide *any* statistics or statement of its policy guidelines in this area, but insisted that its policy was coherent and humane. (Correspondence with Dr Anne Braidwood, 1999).

10. J. R. P. Edkins, 'Further Developments in Abreaction', in N. G. Harris (ed.) *Further Developments in Psychological Medicine* (London, 1947), pp. 265–88.

11. 'Whatever Happened to the Veterans?' *Time,* 5 January 1959.

12. *ibid.*; S. M. Hartman, 'Prescriptions for Penelope: Literature on women's obligations to returning World War II veterans'. *Women's Studies* 5 (1978), pp. 223–39; B. Friedan, *The Feminine Mystique* (London, 1963), pp. 182–3.

13. R. England, *Twenty Million Veterans* (London, 1950), p176; Hartman, 'Prescriptions', p. 225.

14. Goldman, quoted in J. L. Brand, *Bull H Med* 39 (1965), pp. 231–45; O. M. Bradley, *MH* 30 (1946), pp. 1–8; R. Severo and L. Milford, *The Wages of War* (New York, 1989), pp. 283–314; L. J. Friedman, *Menninger,* pp. 168–9.

15. Menninger, *Psychiatry,* p. 380; R. Greene, 'Role of the Psychiatrist' (PhD thesis, Columbia 1978), p. 531. The fact that the VA provided the only publicly funded medical care in the United States, 'regardless of service connection', means that these statistics must be interpreted with caution. R. Kracke, 'The Medical care of the veteran', *JAMA* 143 (1950), pp. 1321–31.

16. N. Q. Brill and G. W. Beebe, *A Follow-up Study of War Neuroses* (Washington, DC, 1955); H. S. Ripley and S. Wolf, 'Long-term study of combat area schizophrenic reactions', *AJP* 108 (1951), pp. 409–16.

17. S. Futterman and E. Pumpian-Mindlin, 'Traumatic War Neuroses five years later', *AJP* 108 (1951), pp. 401–8'. This study was repeated at five year intervals.

18. H. Dicks, *Fifty Years of the Tavistock Clinic* (London, 1970), p. 6; W. Sargant and H. J Shorvon, *Archives of Neurology and Psychiatry* 54 (1945), pp. 231–40. The comparative rarity in World War Two of the hysterical conversion cases so common a generation before was generally attributed to more mobile warfare, better selection of soldiers, higher standards of education and the abolition of the death penalty for cowardice. Hysterical cases tended to be found in distinct ethnic groups (such as Hispanic Americans, Indians and West Africans) or in units with a strongly macho culture, like paratroops or the Brigade of Guards. E. Weinstein, 'Conversion Disorders', in F. D. Jones (ed.), *War Psychiatry* (Falls Church, Va., 1995); James, 'Narrative'.

19. 'Don Cesar Beach Resort and Spa'. Press Pack, 1997; E. D. Cooke, *All But Me and Thee* (Washington, DC, 1946); The USAAF eventually took over most of the hotels in Miami Beach, 'for the use of depleted and nerve shattered flyers'. J. Jones, *WWII* (London, 1975), p. 84; R. R. Grinker and J. P. Spiegel, *Men Under Stress* (Philadelpia, 1945).

20. Grinker and Spiegel, *Men Under Stress.*

21. A. Adler, 'Two Different Types of Post-Traumatic Neuroses', *AJP* 102 (1945), pp. 237–40; E. Lindemann, 'Symptomatology and Management of Acute Grief', *AJP* 101 (1944), pp. 141–8.

22. G. Grob, *The Mad Among Us* (New York, 1994), pp. 191–2.

23. *ibid.*, pp. 196–7; G. E. Gifford (ed.), *Psychoanalysis, Psychotherapy and the New England Medical Scene* (New York, 1978), p. 394.

24. N. G. Hale, Jr, *The Rise and Crisis of Psychoanalysis in the United States* (New York, 1995), pp. 276–84.

25. Hale, *Rise*, p. 278.

26. Hale, *Rise*, p. 280 .

27. R. Michels, *Partisan Review*, Fall, 1997.

28. *ibid.*

29. T. F. Rodger, Tribute to G. R. Hargreaves, Rodger Papers, Glasgow University.

30. J. R. Rees, *The Shaping of Psychiatry by War* (New York, 1945), pp. 117–39.

31. E. Glover, interview with *Cavalcade* magazine. Quoted at meeting of British Psycho-analytical Society, 2 February 1944. E. R. Zetzel papers, Schlesinger Library, Radcliffe College, box 4/no. 160.

32. Rodger, Hargreaves tribute.

33. D. W. Millard, 'Maxwell Jones and the Therapeutic Community', in H. Freeman and G. Berrios (eds), *150 Years of British Psychiatry, Vol. 2: The Aftermath* (London, 1996); for Tom Main's later career, see T. F. Main, *The Ailment and other Psychoanalytic Essays* (London, 1989).

34. W. Sargant and C. M. Stewart, 'Chronic Battle Neurosis Treated with Leucotomy', *BMJ* (1947), ii, pp. 866–9.

35. *BMJ* (1943), ii, p. 829; (1944), i, pp. 60–1, 94, 126–7, 159–60, 197, 234–5, 305–6, 469, 537–8.

36. E. S. Valenstein, *Great and Desperate Cures: The Rise and Decline of Psychosurgery and other Radical Treatments for Mental Illness* (New York, Basic, 198), pp. 167–198; *idem.* 'Therapeutic Exuberance: A Double-Edged Sword', in A. Harrington (ed.), *So Human A Brain: Knowledge and Values in the Neurosciences.* (Boston, Birkhauser, 1992). On leucotomy, see Shorter, *HoP* and A. Clare, *Psychiatry in Dissent* (London, 1976).

37. Valenstein, *Great*, p. 172.

38. Valenstein, *Great*, p. 182.

39. D. Shutts, *Resort to the Knife* (New York, 1982), pp. 136, 198–9, 225–6.

40. *PRSM* 39 (1945–1946), pp. 443–458; W. Sargant and E. Slater, *Physical Methods of Treatment in Psychiatry* (Edinburgh, 1944), p. 143; Valenstein, *Great*, p. 178; W. McKissock, 'Rostral Leucotomy', *Lancet*, 1951, ii, 94.

41. McKissock, quoted Sargant and Slater, *Physical Methods*, pp. 137–9.

42. Sargant and Stewart, 'Chronic Battle Neurosis'.

43. CMAC/PP/WWS. E3/4. Incontinence was a common side-effect.

44. W. Sargant. 'Ten Years' Clinical Experience of Modified Leucotomy Operations', *BMJ* (1953), ii, pp. 800–3; A. A. Baker and L. Minski, 'Social Adjustment of Neurotic Patients after Prefrontal Leucotomy', *BMJ*, (1951),

ii, pp. 1239–43. W. Sargant, 'Leucotomy in Psychosomatic Disorders', *Lancet* (1951), ii, pp. 87–91.

45 Shorter, *HoP*, p. 228. Sargant was exceptional in continuing to carry out leucotomies long after 1954. There has recently been a revival in the use of leucotomy but modern neurosurgical techniques allow the procedure to be much more localised than was possible fifty years ago. It is also much more sparingly used. My thanks to Mr Peter Schurr and Drs John Crammer, Alex Baker, Ann Dally and Jonathan Bird for clarification.

Chapter 23: Vietnam Doctors

1. 'Disguised' case quoted in N. M. Camp, 'The Vietnam War and the Ethics of Combat Psychiatry', *AJP* 150 (1993), pp. 1000–10 – the essential text, with full bibliography. See also N. M Camp *et al.*, *Stress Strain, and Vietnam* (New York, 1988). I thank Dr Camp for his generous help.

2. R. Kulka *et al.*, *Trauma and the Vietnam War Generation* (New York, 1990), pp. v, xxvii. Vietnam, the first 'computer war', has few hard statistics. In 1978 it was estimated that 2. 15 million went to Vietnam. More recently, the VA's 'Vietnam warriors: a statistical profile' puts the figure at nearly 2. 6 million. G. de Groot, *A Noble Cause? America and the Vietnam War* (Harlow, 2000), pp. 311–2. There are no agreed figures for the numbers 'in combat'.

3. W. J. Tiffany and W. S. Allerton 'Army Psychiatry in the Mid-'60s', *AJP*, 123 (1967), pp. 810–21; P. Bourne, 'Military Psychiatry and the Viet Nam Experience', *AJP* 127 (1970), pp. 481–8.

4. Three-quarters of Vietnam veterans were 'volunteers'. Many, though, had enlisted in order to pre-empt the draft.

5. R. Glasser, *365 Days* (London, 1971); J. L. Estep, *Company Commander Vietnam* (Novato, Cal., 1996).

6. M. Hastings, *The Korean War* (London, 1987), pp. 110, 150, 194.

7. *ibid.*, p. 210.

8. D. B. Peterson and R. E. Chambers, 'Restatement of Combat Psychiatry', *AJP* 109 (1952), pp. 249–54.

9. A. J. Glass, 'Psychotherapy in the Combat Zone', *AJP* 110 (1954), pp. 725–31; *idem*, 'Principles of Combat Psychiatry', *Mil Med* 117 (1955), pp. 27–33.

10. Peterson and Chambers, 'Restatement'.

11. *ibid.*

12. K. L. Artiss, 'Human Behavior under Stress – from Combat to Social Psychiatry' *Mil Med* 128 (1963), pp. 1011–5.

13. W. Haussman and D. Rioch, 'Military Psychiatry. A prototype of Social and Preventive Psychiatry in the United States'. *Arch Gen Psych* 16 (1967), pp. 727–39; W. C. Westmoreland, 'Mental Health-An Aspect of Command', *Mil Med* 128 (1963), p. 213; A. K. Daniels, 'Military psychiatry: The Emergence of a Subspecialty', in E. Freidson and J. Lorber (eds), *Medical Men and their Work* (Chicago, 1972).

14. F. D Jones, 'Experiences as a division psychiatrist in Vietnam', *Mil Med* 132 (1967), pp. 1003–8; de Groot, *A Noble Cause?*, p. 151.

15. Casualties were seen first by a specially trained medic at an 'outpost' receiving up to a week of 'cursory and of necessity relatively superficial psychiatric management'. Cases which didn't respond reached Bloch's team and received an 'intensive though brief psychiatrically sophisticated attempt to restitute someone'. S. Bloch, 'Army Clinical Psychiatry in the Combat Zone – 1967–1968', *AJP* 126 (1969), pp. 189–98. There were some 100 technicians in Vietnam. D. R. Bey and W. E. Smith, 'Mental Health Technicians in Vietnam', *Bulletin of the Menninger Clinic*, 24 (1971), pp. 363–71.

16. 'George', quoted in M. MacPherson, *Long Time Passing: Vietnam and the Haunted Generation* (New York, 1984), p. 130; L. M. Baskir and W. A. Strauss, *Chance and Circumstance* (New York, 1978), p. 6.

17. J. Fallows, 'What did you do in the class war, Daddy?', in W. Capps (ed.), *The Vietnam Reader* (New York, 1991); *Time* 16 November, 1970; *AJP* 127(1971), pp. 1236, 1238.

18. I. M. Frank and F. S. Hoedemaker, 'The Civilian Psychiatrist and the Draft', *AJP* 127 (1970), pp. 497–502; Baskir and Strauss, *Chance*, pp. 122–31; MacPherson, *Long Time Passing*, pp. 558–62.

19. Baskir and Strauss, *Chance*, pp. 7–10; de Groot, *Noble Cause*, pp. 275, 315–6. The passions aroused by this issue can be sampled in C. G. Appy, *Working Class War. American Combat Soldiers in Vietnam* (Chapel Hill, N. Carolina, 1993); Dean, *Shook Over Hell*, pp. 184, 297–8; and B. G. Burkett and G. Whitley, *Stolen Valor* (Dallas, 1998), pp. 56–9, 452–65.

20. R. J. Arthur, 'Reflections on Military Psychiatry', *AJP* 135 (July 1978), suppl., pp. 2–7.

21. *ibid.*; Camp, 'Vietnam War', p. 1004. One respondent to a 1983 survey of Vietnam psychiatrists replied, 'What [ethical] dilemma? I evac'd them all to Japan'.

22. G. S. Livingston, 'Letter from a Vietnam veteran' *Saturday Review*, 20 September 1969, pp. 22–3.

23. E. M. Colbach, 'Ethical Issues in Combat Psychiatry', *Mil Med* 150 (1985), pp. 256–65.

24. *ibid.*

25. *ibid.* An Australian doctor in Vietnam later wrote, 'Look I'm no hero. I wasn't prepared to take on the whole army. I didn't want to be court martialled and stuck in some gaol up there. I used to say, "What a shit war" and wait for the home-time and the housing grant.' Barry Kavanagh, quoted in J. Bourke, *An Intimate History of Killing* (London, 1999) p. 200.

26. Colbach, 'Ethical Issues'; Bey and Smith, 'Mental Health Technicians', make no reference to drugs.

27. N. M. Camp interview, Washington, 1994. N. M. Camp [Recollections of Vietnam service], unpublished MS, p. 13. My thanks to Dr Camp.

28. T. C. Bond, 'The Why of Fragging', *AJP* 133 (1976), pp. 1328–331; H. W.

Fisher, 'Vietnam psychiatry:portrait of anarchy', *Minnesota Medicine* 55 (1972), pp. 1165–7.

29. T. Maier, *AJP* 126 (1970), p. 1039; H. J. Friedman, *Arch Gen Psych* 26 (1972), pp. 118–23; R. J. Lifton. *Home From The War* (1973; Boston, 1992), p. 417; *AJP* 128 (1971), pp. 138–9.

30. S. Howard, *American Journal of Psychotherapy* (1976), p. 121.

31. W. J. Tiffany, 'The Mental Health of Army Troops in Viet Nam', *AJP* 123 (1967), pp. 1585–6; Tiffany and Allerton, 'Army Psychiatry', pp. 813–8; P. Bourne, quoted in R. Holmes, *Firing Line* (Harmondsworth, 1987), p. 263; W. Bey, 'Division Psychiatry in Viet Nam', *AJP* 127 (1970), pp. 146–50.

32. R. Viner, 'Putting Stress in Life: Hans Selye and the Making of Stress Theory', *Social Studies of Science* 29 (1999), pp. 391–410; J. W. Mason, 'A Historical View of the Stress Field', *Journal of Human Stress* 1(1975), pp. 6–12, 22–36; H. Selye, *The Stress of Life* (New York, 1956). In many ways, 'Stress' filled the placed vacated when 'Neurasthenia' finally disappeared in the 1930s in Britain and America. In Germany, though, it lived on.

33. Viner, 'Putting Stess'; P. Bourne (ed.), *The Psychology and Physiology of Stress* (New York, 1969).

34. Bloch, 'The Psychological Adjustment of Normal People During a Year's Tour in Vietnam', *Psychiatric Quarterly* (1970), p. 624. The flip side of this was the isolation of the 'FNG' or 'fucking new guy' on arrival at his unit.

35. J. A. Renner, Jr, 'The Changing Patterns of Psychiatric Problems in Vietnam', *Comprehensive Psychiatry* 14 (1973), pp. 169–81.

36. T. Maier and S. Bloch, *AJP* 126 (1970), pp. 1039–40.

37. Bey and Smith, 'Mental Health technicians'.

38. S. Mirin and G. McKenna. 'Combat Zone Adjustment: Role of Marihuana Use', *Mil Med* 140 (1975), pp. 482–6; M. D. Stanton, 'The Hooked Serviceman', in C. R. Figley (ed.), *Strangers at Home* (New York, 1975); H. C. Holloway, 'Epidemiology of Heroin Dependency among Soldiers in Vietnam', *Mil Med.* 139 (1974), pp. 108–13; J. Char, 'Drug Abuse in Vietnam', *AJP* 129 (1972), pp. 463–5.

39. Richard A. Ratner, 'Drugs and Despair in Vietnam'. *University of Chicago Magazine* 64 (1972), pp. 15–23; Stanton, ' Hooked Serviceman'; R. L. Nail *et al.*. 'Black-White Differences in Social Background and Military Drug Use Patterns', *AJP* 131 (1974), pp. 1097–1102; E. Marcovitz and H. J. Myers, 'The Marihuana Addict in the Army', *War Medicine* 6 (1943), pp. 382–91.

41. Ratner, 'Drugs and Despair'.

42. Ratner, 'Drugs and Despair', p. 16; Holloway, 'Epidemiology', p. 111.

43. J. Ladinsky, review of J. Helmer, *Bringing The War Back Home: The American Soldier in Vietnam and After* (New York, 1974), in *Armed Forces & Society* 2 (1976), pp. 435–67.

44. N. M. Camp interview 1994; Holloway, 'Epidemiology'.

45. Ratner, 'Drugs and Despair'.

46. N. M. Camp interview, 1994; Stanton, 'Hooked Serviceman'; Holloway, 'Epidemiology', pp. 111–2; Unpublished paper by H. Holloway,

summarised in E. G. Howe and F. D. Jones, 'Ethical Issues in Combat Psychiatry' in F. D. Jones *et al.* (eds) *Military Psychiatry.* (Falls Church, Va., 1994), p. 122.

47. M. J. Horowitz and G. F. Solomon, 'A prediction of delayed stress response syndromes in Vietnam veterans', *Journal of Social Issues* 31 (1973), pp. 67–80.

Chapter 24: From Post-Vietnam Syndrome to Post-Traumatic Stress Disorder

1. A. S. Blank, Jr. 'On the central role of advocacy in the traumatic stress field'. *Stresspoints* 11(1997), p. 4.

2. R. Ørner, *The Psychologist,* August 1997, p. 351; Shorter, *H of P,* p. 304; E. T. Dean, Jr, *Shook Over Hell* (Cambridge, Mass, 1997), pp. 182–202; B. G. Burkett and G. Whitley, *Stolen Valor* (Dallas, 1998), pp. 139–61.

3. C. Hussey, 'Chaim Shatan: Helping Vietnam Veterans to help themselves', *McGill News,* February 1983. Thanks to Dr Shatan.

4. Hussey, 'Chaim Shatan'; Wilbur J. Scott, *The Politics of Readjustment: Vietnam Veterans Since the War.* (New York, 1993), pp. 1–4, 14–18. This chapter is heavily indebted to Scott's important study.

5. C. Shatan, 'The Grief of Soldiers: Vietnam Combat Veterans' Self-Help Movement', *AJO* 43 (1973), pp. 640–53; A. Egendorf, 'Vietnam Veteran Rap Groups '. *Journal of Social Issues* 31 (1975), pp. 111–24

6. R. W. Eisenhart, 'You Can't Hack It Little Girl', *Journal of Social Issues* 31 (1975), pp. 13–23. William Manchester, Eugene Sledge and Philip Caputo have classic accounts of Marine training. Oral histories of the Vietnam War record the place of *The Sands of Iwo Jima* in the collective male consciousness. C. M. Cameron, *American Samurai* (Cambridge, 1994) is a disappointing examination of Marine mythology.

7. Smith, Egendorf, quoted in Scott, *Politics* 17; Bly, quoted in W. Capps (ed.), *The Vietnam Reader* (New York, 1991), p. 85.

8. Scott, *Politics,* p. 23–4.

9. J. Nordheimer, *New York Times,* 26 May 1971.

10. C. Shatan, 'The Post-Vietnam Syndrome', *New York Times,* 6 May 1972; *idem,* 'Grief of Soldiers' p. 648; *idem,* 'Stress Disorders Among Vietnam Veterans: The Emotional Content of Combat Continues' in C. Figley (ed.), *Stress Disorders Among Vietnam Veterans* (New York, 1978), pp. 46–7; Robert Jay Lifton, *Home From the War* (1973; Boston, 1992), pp. 420, 447–8; Scott, *Politics,* p. 42.

11. J. Borus, 'Incidence of Maladjustment in Vietnam Returnees', *Arch Gen Psych* 30 (1974), pp. 554–7; *idem,* 'Reentry I', *Arch Gen Psych* 28 (1973), pp. 501–8; *idem,* 'Reentry II' *AJP* 130 (1973), pp. 850–4; *idem,* 'Reentry III', *Psychiatry* 36 (1973), pp. 428–39.

12. According to Dr Jonathan Borus, there were six factors which 'eased reentry': 1. gradual return; 2. reorienting combatants to civilian routines; 3. giving formal acknowledgement to the soldier; 4. access to the immediate

group unit in sharing experiences and facilitating readjustment 5. fore-warning the veteran of likely stresses 6. Making 'the continuing non-combat role meaningful to the veteran'. Few of these steps were taken. P. Sgroi, 'To Vietnam and Back', in Capps, *Vietnam Reader*, p. 29. Sgroi committed suicide in 1987, two years after writing this essay.

13. S. E. Ambrose, *Nixon 2. 1962–1972* (New York, 1989), pp. 465–6; Shatan, 'Grief of Soldiers', pp. 652–3. Nixon's Cabinet, finding no evidence of communist subversion behind the anti-war protests, blamed them on permissive child-rearing practices and psychiatrists who had left the middle-class young, 'rudderless in a world from which they demanded certainty without sacrifice' (Henry Kissinger). 'They don't know who they are,' Kissinger told members of his staff. 'They need fathers, not brothers . . . They are going through an identity crisis . . . This is like dealing with thumb-sucking.' 'Vietnam is only symptomatic,' he informed Nixon. 'When that issue is gone, another will take its place.' Nixon's speech-writer thought they were engaging in 'an orgy of right-brain indulgence'. T. Wells, *The War Within. America's Battle over Vietnam* (Berkeley, 1994), pp. 315–7.

14. C. R. Figley and S. Leventman (eds), *Strangers At Home* (New York, 1980), p. 363.

15. P. Novick, *The Holocaust in American Life* (New York, 1999). For many years, the most influential accounts were B. Bettelheim. 'Individual and Mass Behaviour in Extreme Situations', *Journal of Abnormal and Social Psychology* 38 (1943), pp. 417–52, based on experience in Dachau and later heavily criticised by Primo Lévi and others; E. Cohen, *Human Behaviour in the Concentration Camp* (London, 1954) and V. Frankl, *Man's Search for Meaning* (New York, 1959) – all written by psychonalysts/victims.

16. L. Eitinger, 'Concentration Camp Survivors in the Postwar World,' *AJO* 25 (1961), pp. 367–75; *idem*, 'Pathology of the Concentration Camp Syndrome' *Arch Gen Psych* 18 (1961), pp. 371–9. Eitinger argued that the survivors' irritability, inability to concentrate, impotence, and sleeplessness were 'the result of organic changes in the brain'; W. G Niederland, 'The Problem of the Survivor: The Psychiatric Evaluation of Emotional Disorders in Survivors of Nazi Persecution', *Journal of Hillside Hospital* 10 (1961), pp. 233–47.

17. W. G. Niederland, 'Clinical Observations on the "Survivor Syndrome"', *International Journal of Psychoanalysis* 49 (1968), pp. 313–5. The son of a rabbi, William Niederland (1904–1993) was born in East Prussia, arrived in the United States in 1940, and qualified as an analyst in 1953. *The Times*, 12 August 1993.

18. Niederland, 'The Problem'.

19. S. Davidson, in H. Dasberg *et al.*, *Society and Trauma of War* (Maastricht, 1987), pp. 14–32 – a wise and inspiring book; S. Davidson, *Holding on to Humanity: The Message of Holocaust Survivors* (New York, 1992); P. Matussek *et al.*, *Imprisonment in Concentration Camps and its Consequence* (Berlin, 1971).

20. Shatan, 'Grief'; *idem*, 'Stress Disorders'; H. Glover, 'Survival Guilt and the Vietnam Veteran', *JNMD* 172 (1984), pp. 393–7.
21. Lifton, in C. Caruth (ed.), *Trauma: Explorations in Memory* (Baltimore, 1995), pp. 133–47; R. J. Lifton, *Home From the War* (New York, 1972).
22. Caruth, *Trauma*.
23. Scott, *Politics*, pp. 7–9; R. Severo and L. Milford, *The Wages of Fear* (New York, 1989), pp. 347–417.
24. Scott, *Politics*, pp. 9–12.
25. R. Bitzer, 'Mentally Disabled Veterans and the [VA]', in C. Figley and S. Leventman(eds), *Strangers At Home: Vietnam Veterans Since the War* (New York, 1980), pp. 305–23.; T. van Putten and W. H. Emory, 'Traumatic Neuroses in Vietnam Returnees', *Arch Gen Psych* 29 (1973), pp. 695–8.
26. J. F. Borus, 'Incidence of Maladjustment in Vietnam Returnees' *Arch Gen Psych* 30 (1974), pp. 554–7; B. Boman, 'The Vietnam Veteran Ten Years On', *Australian and New Zealand Journal of Psychiatry* 16 (1982), pp. 107–27.
27. Scott, *Politics*.
28. G. Grob, 'Origins of *DSM-I*: A Study in Appearance and Reality', *AJP* 148 (1991), pp. 421–31.
29. G. E. Berrios and R. Hauser, 'Kraepelin', in G. E. Berrios and R. Porter (eds), *A History of Clinical Psychiatry: The Origin and History of Psychiatric Disorders* (London, 1995), p. 280; Shorter, *HoP*, p. 299.
30. Grob, 'Origins'.
31. Shorter, *HoP*, pp. 246–255.
32. ibid., pp. 255–62, 280–1.
33. S. B. Guze, 'Biological psychiatry: is there any other kind?', *Psychological Medicine*, 19 (1989), pp. 315–23; B. Charlton, 'A critique of biological psychiatry', *Psychological Medicine* 20 (1990), pp. 3–6.
34. Grob, 'Origins'; M. Wilson, 'DSM-III and the Transformation of American psychiatry', *AJP* 150 (1993), pp. 399–410; Scott, *Politics*, pp. 28–34.
35. Scott, *Politics*, p. 34, 50, 62.
36. ibid., p. 59.
37. Quoted in Burkett and Whitley, *Stolen Valor*, p. 148; *New York Times*, 27 May 1975. *Penthouse* campaigned on behalf of its large veteran readership. Wicker later acknowledged the mistakes in his article. For press coverage, see E. T. Dean, Jr, 'The Myth of the Troubled and Scorned Vietnam Veteran', *Journal of American Studies* 26 (1992), pp. 59–74; B. Boman, 'Are All Vietnam Veterans like John Rambo?', in M. E. Wolf and A. D. Mosnaim (eds), *PTSD, Etiology, Phemonenology and Treatment* (Washington, DC, 1990); D. A. Pollock *et al.*, 'Estimating the Number of Suicides among Vietnam Veterans', *AJP* 147 (1990), pp. 772–6; Dean, *Shook Over Hell*, p. 246–7.
38. Burkett and Whitley, *Stolen Valor*, p. 163. Neither movie was really about Vietnam. *Taxi Driver* derived from scriptwriter Paul Schrader's low-life experiences. David Morrel's 1972 novel, *First Blood*, was based on the

tormented later life of the World War Two hero Audie Murphy. It passed through innumerable rewrites, acquiring 'layers of falsehood' (and Sylvester Stallone) before reaching the screen. S. Faludi, *Stiffed: The Betrayal of the Modern Man* (London, 1999), pp. 359–406.

39. C. Shatan, *Psychiatric Opinion* 11 (1974), p. 8; J. Wilson, Introduction to National Vietnam Veterans Survey (New York, 1985), p. x; Egendorf, *Healing*, p. 2; J. I. Walker and J. O. Cavenar, Jr, 'Vietnam Veterans: Their Problems Continue', *JNMD* 170 (1982), p. 174. As we have seen, there are no agreed statistics on the numbers who went to Vietnam or fought there.

40. Burkett and Whitley, *Stolen Valor*, p. 149, quoting *Los Angeles Times*, 11 November, 1975. In a 1980 Harris poll 71% of Vietnam veterans said they were 'glad' they went, 74% 'enjoyed' their tour and 66% said they would happily serve again. S. Karnow, *Vietnam* (London, 1990), p. 480.

41. Dean, *Shook Over Hell.* Between 1965 and 1971, US armed forces sprayed over eleven million gallons of the herbicide Agent Orange in Vietnam. By 1979, some 500 Vietnam veterans were claiming that explosure to the chemical while in Vietnam almost a decade before had pronounced health abnormalities among themselves and their children. After a prolonged medico-politico-legal battle, during which the scientific issues were never resolved, the chemical companies agreed a settlement of some $200m. See Scott, *Politics*, pp. 75–230.

42. M. J. Horowitz, *Stress Response Syndromes* (Northvale, N. J., 1978); interview, M. J. Horowitz, San Francisco, 1994.

43. See A. Young, *The Harmony of Illusions* (Princeton, 1995) for a masterly analysis.

44. Scott, *Politics*, p. 238.

45. Figley and Leventman, *Strangers*, p. 366.

Chapter 25: 'When the Patient Reports Atrocities . . .'

1. H. S. Hughes, 'Emotional Disturbance and American Social Change', *AJP* 126 (1969), pp. 21–8.

2. C. F. Shatan, ' "A True Child of Trauma" -- Sarah Haley: 1939–1989', *JTS* 3 (1990), pp. 477–81; S. Bloom, 'Origins of the [ISTSS]', in A. Shalev *et al.* (eds), *International Handbook of Human Response to Trauma* (New York, 2000).

3. Haley interview with Wilbur Scott, 1988. Scott, *Politics*, p. 5.

4. S. Haley, 'Some of My Best Friends Are Dead; Treatment of the PTSD Patient and his Family' in W. B. Kelly (ed.), *Post-Traumatic Stress Disorder and the War Veteran Patient* (New York, 1983), p. 63.

5. S. Haley, 'When the Patient Reports Atrocities', *Arch Gen Psych* 30 (1974), pp. 191–6; Cases quoted from H. Hendin and A. P. Haas, *Wounds of War* (New York, 1982), pp. 81, 136–7, 179.

6. N. Fergusson, *The Pity of War* (London, 1998), pp. 373–84; *Atlantic*, quoted in Burkett and Whitley, *Stolen Valor*, p. 122.

7. W. B. Gault, 'Remarks on Slaughter', *AJP* 128 (1971), pp. 450–3; H. P. Langner, 'The Making of a Murderer', *AJP* 127 (1971), pp. 950–3; R. P. Fox, 'Narcissistic Rage and . . . Combat Aggression'. *Arch Gen Psych* 31 (1974), pp. 807–11; J. Yager, 'Personal Violence in Infantry Combat', *Arch Gen Psych* 32 (1975), pp. 257–61.

8. P. Caputo, *A Rumor of War* (London, 1978), pp. xvi–xvii.

9. E. Simmel in S. Ferenczi *et al.*, *Psycho-Analysis and the War Neuroses* (London, 1921) p. 40; J. R. P Edkins, in N. G. Harris (ed.), *Modern Trends in Psychological Medicine* (London, 1948); J. R. Rees, *Shaping of Psychiatry by War* (New York, 1945), p. 15; S. Futterman and E. Pumpian-Mindlin. *AJP* 108 (1951), pp. 401–8.

10. C. Browning, *Ordinary Men*. (New York, 1992); E. Cohen, *Human Behaviour in the Concentration Camp* (London, 1954). It seems, though, that some 20% of the Germans involved in killing did suffer symptoms such as anxiety, nightmares and tremors. After 100 people were shot in Minsk in 1941, SS Obergruppenführer Erich von dem Bach-Zalewski said to Himmler, 'Look at the eyes of the men in this Kommando, how deeply shaken they are! These men are finished for the rest of their lives.' Bach-Zalewski himself had similar symptoms. J. Glover, *Humanity*. (London, 1999), p. 345.

11. R. J. Lifton, Testimony 1971, quoted in Figley, *Strangers*, pp. 308–9.

12. Haley, 'When the Patient'.

13. Haley, 'Some of My Best Friends'.

14. *ibid.*

15. P. Marin, 'Living in Moral Pain', *Psychology Today*, November 1981, reprinted in Capps, *Vietnam Reader*, pp. 40–53.

16. *ibid.*,

17. A. Young, *The Harmony of Illusions: Inventing Post-Traumatic Stress Disorder* (Princeton, 1995), p. 248. Elsewhere, the medical director of the hospital gets very touchy with a nurse who is unhappy treating in one-to-one sessions a patient who has committed atrocities. She replies: 'Well, this is how I feel. I'm very angry. Oh, shit! I do believe in the model. The thing is, my moral judgment gets in the way'. *ibid.*, p. 261. Young's brilliant verbatim account of protracted therapy in an institutional setting is probably the best single thing in the whole post-PTSD literature.

18. ibid., pp. 207– 9.

19. J. Shay, *Achilles in Vietnam: Combat Trauma and the Undoing of Character* (New York, 1994); B. J. Verkamp, *The Moral Treatment of Returning Warriors in Early Medieval and Modern Times* (Scranton, Pa., 1993); D. R. Johnson *et al.*, 'The Therapeutic Use of Ritual and Ceremony in the Treatment of [PTSD]', *JTS* 8 (1995), pp. 282–298. See also, A. Egendorf, *Healing From the War: Trauma & Transformation after Vietnam* (Boston, 1995); quote from Young, *Harmony of Illusions*, p. 254.

20. R. Atkinson, *The Long Gray Line* (London 1990); S. Dicks. *From Vietnam to Hell*. (Jefferson, North Carolina, 1990), p. 84.

21. Dicks, *From Vietnam*, pp. 51–3.
22. G. Lewy, *America in Vietnam* (New York, 1985), quoted in Dean, *Shook Over Hell*; Burkett and Whitley, *Stolen Valor*, p. 145.
23. Burkett and Whitley pursue this point at obsessive length.

Chapter 26: From the Falklands to the Gulf
1. In Thames Television's *World At War*, 1973.
2. M. Middlebrook, *Operation Corporate: The Falklands War 1982* (London, 1985), pp. 382–4; H. McManners, *The Scars of War* (London, 1993), pp. 118–35. R. O. Moro, *The History of the South Atlantic War* (New York, 1989), p. 324, gives Argentine dead as 635, of whom 323 were on the cruiser *General Belgrano*.
3. H. H. Price, 'The Falklands: Rate of British Psychiatric Combat Casualties Compared to Recent American Wars', *JRAMC* 130 (1984), pp. 109–113; M. O'Connell, Talk at Wellcome Institute for the History of Medicine, 1996.
4. In fact, under the Geneva Convention, casualties evacuated to hospital ship cannot be returned to combat.
5. Price, 'The Falklands'; A. Scott-Brown, 'The Hospital Ship Psychiatrist: Falkland Islands 1982', Paper to World Conference on Military Psychiatry, Vienna, 1984.
6. R. Ørner, 'Falklands War Veterans'. *The Psychologist*, August 1997, pp. 351–5.
7. E. Shorter, *From Paralysis to Fatigue* (New York, 1992), p. 392.
8. McManners, *Scars*, p. 12.
9. M O'Connell, 'A naval psychiatrist's personal view of the Falklands conflict', *Stress Medicine* 2 (1986), pp. 307–14; *Sunday Times*, 5 April 1987.
10. G. H. Jones and J. Lovett, 'Delayed psychiatric sequelae among Falklands war veterans', *Journal of the Royal College of General Practitioners* 37 (1987), pp. 34–5.
11. L. S. O'Brien and S. Hughes, 'Symptoms of [PTSD] in Falklands war veterans five years after the conflict', *BJP* 59 (1991), pp. 135–41.
12. Ørner, 'Falklands War Veterans'. The Israelis assessed 'longitudinal PTSD rates, general psychiatric symptomatology, social functioning, somatic complaints, effects of repeated exposure, reactivation of PTSD, delayed onset of PTSD, onset of subclincial PTSD and delayed help-seeking'.
13. *Eyewitness*, London Weekend Television, 1990.
14. *ibid.*
15. *Guardian*, 8 February 1995 and 19 August 1997; Interview, John Mackenzie, 20 December 1999.
16. R. Ørner *et al.*, 'Long-term stress reactions in British Falklands war veterans', *British Journal of Clinical Psychology* 32 (1993), pp. 157–9.
17. F. D. Jones, 'Neuropsychiatric Casualties of Nuclear, Biological and Chemical Warfare', in F. D. Jones (ed.), *War Psychiatry* (Falls Church, Va., 1995).

18. R. Atkinson, *Crusade* (New York, 1993); M. Kelly, *Martyrs' Day* (New York, 1993); N. Schwarzkopf, *It Doesn't Take A Hero* (New York, 1992); Stephen E. Straus, 'Bridging the gulf in war syndromes', *Lancet* (1999), i, pp. 162–3. The elaborate British psychiatric arrangements are described in W. Holden, *Shell Shock* (London, 1998), pp. 166–70.

19. *Guardian*, 27 May 1995. Lake was diagnosed with anorexia nervosa. See also 'Gulf Babies maimed at birth', *Guardian* 23 December 1993.

20. P. J. Landrigan, 'Illness in Gulf War Veterans', *JAMA* 277 (1977), pp. 259–61; A. David, 'Gulf War Illness', *BMJ* (1977), i, pp. 239–40.

21. Armed Forces Minister Nicholas Soames; 'Gulf war illness. Why it took so long to decide to investigate', *BMJ* (1997), i, p. 1041.

22. 'Marching to the Veterans' Drum', *New Scientist*, 25 June 1994; *idem*, 19, 26 October, 30 November, 21 December 1996, 18 January 1997.

23. Presidential Advisory Committee on Gulf War Veterans' Illnesses, Final Report (Washington, December 1996).

24. E. Showalter, 'First Casualty of the Gulf War', *Guardian*, 17 May 1997; *idem, Hystories. Hysterical Epidemics and Modern Culture.* (London, 1998), p. x.

25. Howard Fienberg, letter *The Times*, 2 March 1999, referring to a study in *American Journal of Epidemiology* in August 1998

26. S. Wessley, lecture, King's College London, 27 January 2000. See also C. Unwin *et al.*, 'Health of UK servicemen who served in Persian Gulf War, *Lancet*, 1999, i, pp. 169–78; Landrigan, 'Illness in Gulf War Veterans'; David *et al.*, 'Gulf War Illness'; K. Hyams *et al.*, 'War Syndromes and Their Evaluation: From the US Civil War to the Persian Gulf War', *Annals of Internal Medicine* 125 (1996), pp. 398–405. According to British accounts, French troops in the Gulf were not given the same chemical cocktail as British and American soldiers and suffered almost no after-effects. For some reason, British medical opinion refuses to pursue this point.

27. M. Hooper, 'Report on Gulf Health Research Meeting', held at Royal Society of Medicine, London, 10 December 1998. Telephone interview with Professor Malcolm Hooper, November 1999.

Chapter 27: The Culture of Trauma

1. C. Merridale, 'The Collective Mind: Trauma and Shell-Shock in Twentieth-century Russia', *JCH* 35 (2000), pp. 39–55.

2. B. van der Kolk, lecture, Royal College of Psychiatrists, London, 1995, J. L. Herman *Trauma and Recovery: From Domestic Abuse to Political Terror* (New York, 1992); J. Wilson *et al.* (eds), *Human Adaptation to Extreme Stress: From the Holocaust to Vietnam* (New York, 1988); B. Raphael, *When Disaster Strikes* (London, 1986).

3. I have stolen the phrase 'Chinese menu' from G. E. Vaillant, 'The disadvantages of *DSM-III* outweigh its advantages', *AJP* 141 (1984), p. 543.

4. D. Summerfield, *Social Science & Medicine* 48 (1999), p. 1450; R. J. Daly,

'Samuel Pepys and [PTSD]', *BJP* 143(1983), pp. 64–8; M. R. Trimble, '[PTSD]: History of a Concept', in C. R. Figley (ed.), *Trauma and its Wake* (New York, 1985), pp. 5–14; B. Gersons and I. Carlier, '[PTSD]: The History of a Recent Concept', *BJP* 161 (1992), pp. 742–8.

5. *Independent,* 2 May 1990. Many of these calamities were due to government deregulation and corporate underinvestment.

6. D. Sturgeon, *Guardian,* 11 November 1988; P. Hodgkinson, 'Technological Disaster – Survival and Bereavement', *Social Science & Medicine* 29 (1989) pp. 351–6. Television news bulletins frequently showed disaster survivors cowering in their hospital beds when the Prime Minister and her handbag came to visit.

7. C. R. Pugh and M. Trimble, 'Psychiatric Injury after Hillsborough', *BJP* 163 (1993), pp. 425–9. Five law lords later blocked payments to other officers, saying it was unfair for them to receive compensation when some of the bereaved received nothing.

8. F. Parkinson, *Post-Trauma Stress* (London, 1993), p. 147. The architects of Critical Incident Stress Debriefing were the Norwegian Atle Dyregrov and the American J. T. Mitchell. See also, M. J. Scott and S. G. Stradling, *Counselling for Post-Traumatic Stress Disorder* (London, 1992) and L. Miller. *Shocks to the System: Psychotherapy of Traumatic Disability Syndromes* (New York, 1998), *Guardian,* 1995; *The Times,* 12 October 1995.

9. D. Summerfield, 'A critique of seven assumptions behind psychological trauma programmes in war-affected areas'. *Social Science & Medicine* 48 (1999), pp. 1449–62.

10. R. Pitman *et al.,* 'Once Bitten: Twice Shy: Beyond the Conditioning Model of PTSD', *Biological Psychiatry* 50 (1994), pp. 7–9.

11. Kardiner, of course, did not use the term PTSD. B van der Kolk *et al.,* 'Inescapable Shock, Neurotransmitters, and addiction to Trauma: Toward a Psychobiology of Post Traumatic Stress', *Biological Psychiatry* 20 (1985), pp. 314–25. The vast PTSD literature can be found in E. L. Giller Jr (ed.), *Biological Assessment and Treatment of [PTSD]* (Washington, DC 1990); J. R. T. Davidson and E. B. Foa, *[PTSD] DSM-IV and Beyond* (Washington, DC, 1993); B. van der Kolk *et al..* (eds), *Traumatic Stress. The Effects of Overwhelming Experience on Mind, Body, and Society* (New York, 1996).

12. L. C. Kolb, 'The Psychobiology of PTSD', paper given to ISTSS conference, 1991. My thanks to Dr Kolb. See also, *idem,* 'A Neuro-psychological Hypothesis Explaining [PTSDs]', *AJP* 144 (1987) pp. 989–95.

13. D. Goleman, *Emotional Intelligence,* pp. 17–21. See also, J. LeDoux, *The Emotional Brain* (London, 1998), pp. 256–8.

14. R. K. Pitman, '[PTSD], Hormones, and Memory', *Biological Psychiatry* 26 (1989), pp. 221–3; R. K. Pitman and S. Orr, 'The Black Hole of Trauma', *Biological Psychiatry* 27 (1990), pp. 469–71; A. Y. Shalev *et al.,* 'Conditioned Fear and psychological trauma', *Biological Psychiatry* 31 (1992), pp. 863–5.

15. L. S. O'Brien, *Traumatic Events and Mental Health* (Cambridge, 1998), pp. 108–9. The best overview of the subject.

16. R. Yehuda, PTSD Workshop, London 1998; A. Shalev, *JTS* 10 (1997) p. 416.

17. A. Blank, in S. Sonneberg *et al.* (eds), *The Trauma of War* (Washington, DC, 1985), p. 236; Young, *Harmony of Illusions.*

18. Quoted from J. C. Nemiah, 'Janet Redivivus,' *AJP* 146 (1989), pp. 1527–9 (italics in original); H. F. Ellenberger, *The Discovery of the Unconscious* (New York, 1970); F. Putnam, 'Janet and Modern Views of Dissociation', *JTS* 2 (1989), pp. 413–29; B. van der Kolk and O. van der Hart, 'Janet and the breakdown of adaptation in psychological trauma. *AJP* 146(1989), pp. 1530–40; Supplement on 'Dissociation' *AJP* 153(July 1996). In 1999, the actress Gwyneth Paltrow told an interviewer that she had 'dissociated' the 'traumatic experience' of winning an Oscar.

19. M. Pendergrast, *Victims of Memory: Incest Accusations and Shattered Lives* (London, 1996); E. Loftus and K. Ketcham, *The Myth of Repressed Memory: False Memories and Allegations of Sexual Abuse.* (New York, 1994).

20. F. Crews, *The Memory Wars: Freud's Legacy in Disrepute* (New York, 1995).

21. B. Raphael *et al.*, 'Does debriefing after psychological trauma work?', *BMJ,* (1995), i, pp. 1479– 80.

22. A. Y. Shalev *et al.*, 'Historical Group Debriefing After Combat Exposure', *Mil Med* 163 (1998), pp. 494–8; B. van der Kolk, Trauma Workshop, London, 2 February 1999.

23. R. Yehuda and A. McFarlane, 'Conflict Between Current Knowledge about [PTSD] and Its Original Conceptual Basis', *AJP* 152 (1995), pp. 1705–13.

24. Yehuda and MacFarlane, 'Conflict'; O'Brien, *Traumatic Events,* pp. 53–82, 83–118.

25. N. C. Andreasen, '[PTSD]: Psychology, Biology, and the Manichean Warfare Between False Dichotomies', *AJP* 152 (1995), pp. 963–5. Dr Andreasen had played an important role in getting the framers of *DSM-III* to accept PTSD in 1979 (Scott, *Politics,* pp. 61–3).

26. M. J. Horowitz, interview, San Francisco, 1992.

27. C. R. Figley, 'Editorial Note' to R. A. Kulka *et al.*, *Trauma and the Vietnam War Generation.* (New York, 1990) pp. xxix–xx; A. S. Blank, Jr, 'The [VA's] Viet Nam Veterans Outreach and Counselling Centers', in S. Sonnenberg *et al.* (eds), *The Trauma of War* (Washington, DC, 1985); A. Matsakis, *Vietnam Wives* (Kensington, Md., 1988).

28. Kulka *et al.*, *Trauma and the Vietnam War Generation,* pp. v–vi, pp. 265–75; G. de Groot, *A Noble Cause?* (Harlow, 2000) p. 345.

29. Young, *Harmony of Illusions,* pp. 129–35 has a masterly discussion of these complex issues; Burkett and Whitley, *Stolen Valor,* p. 227.

30. Rosenheck *et al.*, 'Inpatient Treatment of War-Related [PTSD]', *JTS* (1997), pp. 407–13. A. Shalev, 'Discussion: Treatment of Prolonged [PTSD] – Learning From Experience', *JTS* 10(1997), pp. 415–23; *idem,* 'Treatment of [PTSD]: A Review', *Psychosomatic Medicine* 58 (1996), pp. 165–82.

31. E. T. Dean, Jr, *Shook Over Hell: Post-Traumatic Stress, Vietnam and the Civil War* (Cambridge, Mass., 1997); Burkett and Whitley, *Stolen Valor.*

32. R. H. Fleming, 'Post Vietnam Syndrome: Neurosis or Sociosis?', *Psychiatry* 48 (1985), pp. 122–39.
33. Matsakis, *Vietnam Wives.*
34. *ibid.*
35. *ibid.*
36. *ibid.*
37. *ibid.*
38. *ibid.*
39. Burkett and Whitley, *Stolen Valor,* pp. 232, 243–4.
40. *ibid.*, p. 261.
41. Stephen Garton argues in *The Cost of War: Australians Return* (Melbourne, 1996) that Anzac veterans were allowed to overinfluence Australian national identity.
42. R. J. Kleber *et al.* (eds) *Beyond Trauma: Cultural and Societal Dynamics* (New York, 1995); M de Vries, 'Trauma in Cultural Perspective' in B. van der Kolk *et al.* (eds), *Traumatic Stress* (New York, 1996), pp. 398–413; K. Nader *et al.* (eds), *Honoring Differences: Cultural Issues in the Treatment of Trauma and Loss* (New York, 1999); D. Summerfield, 'A critique'. See also, *idem,* 'The Psychological Legacy of War and Atrocity', *JNMD* 184 (1996), pp. 375–7. Summerfield and F. De Vries debate the effectiveness of trauma programmes in Bosnia in *Lancet* (1997), i, p. 1568. *Lancet,* (1998), i, pp. 1579–80.
43. A. Brinkley, *Times Literary Supplement,* 21 January 2000.
44. J. Thompson, *BJP* 166 (1995), pp. 682–4; I. Jack *et al.*, 'Those Who Felt Differently', *Granta* 60 (1997); A. O'Hear, in D. Anderson and P. Mullen (eds), *Faking It: The Sentimentalisation of Modern Society* (Harmondsworth, 1998); R. McKibbin, 'Mass Observation in the Mall', *London Review of Books,* 2 October 1997.
45. Jones quoted Holden, *Shell Shock,* p. 175; Howard, letter to author, 16 October 1997. With thanks to Sir Michael Howard.
46. Quoted, Holden, *Shell Shock,* p. 180.
47. Critchley goes on to say that Anglo-Saxons haven't always behaved in this way. 'Older accounts of shipwreck disasters will ring strangely to modern seafaring people who take for granted a restrained and discipline behaviour under stress. [They tell of] "shrieks of anguish and despair" and [of] "tears rolling down the faces of officers and men as they flung themselves on their knees in despairing prayer and supplication. M. Critchley, *Shipwreck Survivor* (London, 1943), p. 73.
48. E. Joysmith, 'The Crew of the *Jackdaw*', in D. Davin (ed.), *Short Stories from the Second World War* (Oxford, 1982)

SELECT BIBLIOGRAPHY

R. H. Ahrenfeldt, *Psychiatry in the British Army in the Second World War* (London, 1958)

A. Babington, *For the Sake of Example: Capital Courts Martial 1914–1920* (London, 1983)

——*Shell-Shock: A History of the Changing Attitudes to War Neurosis* (London, 1997)

P. Barham, *The Forgotten Lunatics of the Great War* (forthcoming)

P. Barker, *Regeneration* (London, 1991)

——*The Eye in the Door* (London, 1993)

——*The Ghost Road* (London, 1995)

D. Barrett (ed.) *Trauma and Dreams* (Cambridge, Mass, 1996)

H. Binneveld, *From Shellshock to Combat Stress: A Comparative History of Military Psychiatry* (Amsterdam, 1997).

D. D. Bond, *The Love and Fear of Flying* (New York, 1952)

E. D. Bond, *Thomas W. Salmon: Psychiatrist* (New York, 1950)

J. Bourke, *Dismembering the Male: Men's Bodies, Britain and the Great War* (London, 1996)

——*An Intimate History of Killing: Face-to-Face Killing in Twentieth-Century Warfare* (London, 1999)

P. G. Bourne, *The Psychology and Physiology of Stress with Reference to Special Studies of the Viet Nam War* (New York, 1969)

R. Brook, *The Stress of Combat: The Combat of Stress* (Brighton, 1999)

W. Brown, *Talks on Psychotherapy* (London, 1923)

——*Psychology and Psychotherapy* (London, 1921)

——*Psychological Methods of Healing: An Introduction to Psychotherapy* (London, 1938)

B. G. Burkett and G. Whitley, *Stolen Valor: How the Vietnam Generation was Robbed of its Heroes and Its History* (Dallas, 1998)

A. G. Butler, 'Moral and Mental Disorders in the War of 1914–1918', in *The Australian Army Medical Services in the War of 1914–1918*, Vol 3. (Canberra, 1943)

N. M. Camp *et al.*, *Stress, Strain and Vietnam. An Annotated Bibliography* . (New

York, 1988)

W B. Cannon, *Bodily Changes in Pain, Hunger, Fear and Rage* (New York, 1915)

W. Capps (ed.), *The Vietnam Reader* (New York, 1991)

C. Caruth (ed.), *Trauma: Explorations in Memory.* (Baltimore, 1995)

T. Copp and B. McAndrew, *Battle Exhaustion: Soldiers and Psychiatrists in the Canadian Army, 1939–1945* (Montreal, 1990)

A. E. Cowdrey, *Fighting for Life: American Military Medicine in World War II* (New York, 1994).

J. Crang, *The British Army and the People's War, 1939–1945* (Manchester, 2000)

H. Crichton-Miller (ed.), *Functional Nerve Disease: An Epitome of War Experience for the Practitioner* (London, 1920)

M. Critchley, *Shipwreck Survivors* (London, 1943)

M. Culpin, *Psychoneuroses of War and Peace* (Cambridge, 1920)

———*The Nervous Patient* (London, 1924)

———*Recent Advances in the Study of the Psychoneuroses* (London, 1931)

H. H. Dasberg, *et al., Society and Trauma of War* (Maastricht, 1987)

E. T. Dean, Jr, *Shook Over Hell: Post-Traumatic Stress, Vietnam and the Civil War* (Cambridge, Mass., 1997)

J. Dejerine and R. Gauckler, *The Psychoneuroses and their Treatment by Psychotherapy* (English translation. Philadelphia, 1913).

H. V. Dicks, *Fifty Years of the Tavistock Clinic* (London, 1970)

E. Dinter, *Hero or Coward* (London, 1985)

G. F. Drinka, *The Birth of Neurosis: Myth, Malady and the Victorians* (New York, 1984)

D. Eder, *War Shock* (London, 1917)

A. Egendorf, *Healing from the War: Trauma and Transformation After Vietnam.* (Boston, 1985)

K. R. Eissler, *Freud as Expert Witness. The Discussion of War Neurosis Between Freud and Wagner-Jauregg* (English translation, Madison, Conn., 1986)

N. R. Fenton, *Shell Shock and its Aftermath* (St Louis, 1926)

C. R. Figley (ed.), *Stress Disorders among Vietnam Veterans* (New York, 1978)

——— and S. Leventman, *Strangers at Home: Vietnam Veterans Since the War* (New York, 1980)

R. Gabriel, *No More Heroes: Madness and Psychiatry in War* (New York, 1987)

——— (ed.), *Military Psychiatry: A Comparative Perspective* Westport, Conn., 1989)

S. Garton, *The Cost of War: Australians Return* (Sydney, 1996)

R. D. Gillespie, *Psychological Effects of War on Citizen and Soldier* (New York, 1942)

E. Ginzberg *et al., The Ineffective Soldier* (New York, 1959)

A. J. Glass *et al.* (eds) *Neuropsychiatry in World War Two*, 2 vols (Washington, DC, 1966, 1973)

R. S. Greene, 'The Role of the Psychiatrist in World War II', PhD thesis, Columbia University, 1976

R. R. Grinker and J. P. Spiegel, *War Neuroses in North Africa: The Tunisian*

Campaign (New York, 1943)

────── *Men Under Stress* (Philadelphia, 1945)

J. A. Hadfield, *Psychology and Morals* (London, 1923)

────── *Introduction to Psychotherapy* (London, 1967)

B. Hart, *The Psychology of Insanity* (Cambridge, 1912)

────── *Psychopathology: Its Development and its Place in Medicine* (Cambridge, 1927)

H. Hendin and A. P Haas, *Wounds of War: The Psychological Aftermath of Combat in Vietnam* (New York, 1984)

J. L. Herman, *Trauma and Recovery* (London, 1992)

W. Holden, *Shell Shock: The Psychological Impact of War* (London, 1998)

J. Holmes (ed.), *Textbook of Psychotherapy in Psychiatric Practice* (Edinburgh, 1991)

A. F. Hurst, *Medical Diseases of War* (London, 1917)

C. Jahr, *Gewöhnliche Soldaten: Desertion und Deserteure im deutchen und britischen Heer 1914– 1918* (Göttingen, 1998)

F. D. Jones *et al.* (eds), *Military Psychiatry: Preparing in Peace for War* (Falls Church, Va., 1994)

────── *War Psychiatry* (Falls Church, Va., 1995)

A. Kardiner, *The Traumatic Neuroses of War* (New York, 1941)

────── *My Analysis with Freud* (New York 1977)

────── and H. Spiegel, *War Stress and Neurotic Illness* (New York, 1947)

E. Leed, *No Man's Land* (Cambridge, 1979)

P. J. Leese, 'A Social and Cultural History of Shellshock'. PhD thesis, Open University, 1989

P. Lerner, *Hysterical Men: War, Neurosis and German Mental Medicine, 1914–1926* (forthcoming)

────── (ed.), *Traumatic Pasts* (forthcoming)

R. Leys, *Trauma: A Genealogy* (Chicago, 2000).

R. J. Lifton, *Home from the War* (New York, 1973)

J. T. MacCurdy, *War Neuroses* (Cambridge, 1918)

W. McDougall, *An Outline of Abnormal Psychology* (New York, 1926)

H. McManners, *The Scars of War* (London, 1993)

M. MacPherson, *Long Time Passing: Vietnam and the Haunted Generation* (New York, 1984)

S. P. Mackenzie, *Politics and Military Morale* (Oxford, 1992).

W. C. Mennninger, *Psychiatry in a Troubled World.* (New York, 1948)

H. Merskey, 'Shell-Shock' in G. E. Berrios and H. Freeman (eds) *150 Years of British Psychiatry, 1841–1991* (London, 1991)

E. Miller (ed.), *The Neuroses in War* (London, 1940)

W. Moore, *The Thin Yellow Line* (London, 1974)

Lord Moran, *Anatomy of Courage* (London, 1945)

D. Morton and G. Wright, *Winning the Second Battle: Canadian Veterans and the Return to Civilian Life* (Toronto, 1987)

F. W. Mott, *War Neuroses and Shell-Shock* (London, 1919)

C. S. Myers, *Shell Shock in France, 1914–1918* (Cambridge, 1940)

L. S. O'Brien, *Traumatic Events and Mental Health* (Cambridge, 1998)

J. Putkowski and J. Sykes, *Shot at Dawn* (London, 1992)

J. Radkau, *Das Zeitalter der Nervosität: Deutschland zwischen Bismarck und Hitler* (Munich, 1998)

J. R. Rees, *The Shaping of Psychiatry by War* (New York, 1945)

———— *Reflections* (New York, 1966)

F. Richardson, F*ighting Spirit . Psychological Factors in War* (London, 1978)

P. Riedesser and A. Verderber, *'Maschinengewehre hinter der Front', Zur Geschichte der deutschen Militärpsychiatrie* (Frankfurt-am-Main, 1996)

R. D. Ritchie, 'One History of Shell-Shock'. PhD thesis, University of California, San Diego, 1986

W. H. R. Rivers, *Instinct and the Unconscious: A Contribution to a Biological Theory of the Psycho-Neuroses* (Cambridge, 1920)

———— *Conflict and Dream* (Cambridge, 1922)

M. O. Roudebush, 'A Battle of Nerves: Hysteria and its Treatment in France during World War I'. PhD thesis, University of California at Berkeley, 1995

T. A. Ross, *The Common Neuroses* (London, 1923)

———— *Lectures on War Neuroses* (Oxford, 1941)

———— 'Shellshock', in H. Joules (ed.), *The Doctor's View of War* (London, 1938)

———— 'Anxiety Neuroses of War', in A. F. Hurst, *Medical Diseases of War* (3rd Edition, London, 1941)

G. Roussy and J. Lhermitte, *The Psychoneuroses of War* (English translation, London, 1918)

T. Salmon *et al.* (eds), *The Medical Department of the United States Army in the World War Vol. 10: Neuropsychiatry* (Washington, DC, 1929)

W. Sargant, *The Unquiet Mind* (London, 1967)

———— E. Slater, *Physical Methods of Treatment in Psychiatry* (Edinburgh, 1944)

W. J. Scott, *The Politics of Readjustment: Vietnam Veterans Since the War* (New York, 1993)

J. Shay, *Achilles in Vietnam. Combat Trauma and the Undoing of Character* (New York, 1995)

B. Shephard, 'The Early Treatment of Mental Disorders: R. G. Rows and Maghull 1914–1918'. in H. Freeman and G. E. Berrios (eds), *150 Years of British Psychiatry, Volume II: The Aftermath* (London, 1996)

———— 'Shell-Shock', in H. Freeman (ed.), *A Century of Psychiatry* (London, 1999)

E. Shorter, *From Paralysis to Fatigue: A History of Psychosomatic Illness in the Modern Era* (New York, 1992)

———— *A History of Psychiatry* (New York, 1997)

E. Showalter, *The Female Malady: Women, Madness & English Culture* (New York, 1985)

———— *Hystories* (London, 1997)

G. E. Smith and T. H. Pear, *Shell-Shock and Its Lessons* (Manchester, 1917)

S. Sonnenberg *et al.* (eds), *The Trauma of War: Stress and Recovery in Vietnam Veterans* (Washington, DC, 1985).

M. Stone, 'Shellshock and the Psychologists', in W. Bynum *et al.* (eds), *The Anatomy of Madness*, Vol. 2 (London, 1985)

J. M. Tanner (ed), *Stress and Psychiatric Disorder* (Oxford, 1960)

M. Thomson, *The Problem of Mental Deficiency: Eugenics, Democracy and Social Policy in Great Britain, c. 1870–1959.* (Oxford, 1998)

E. Trillat, *Histoire de l'Hysterie* (Paris, 1986)

M. Trimble, *Post-Traumatic Neurosis* (Chichester, 1981)

B. J. Verkamp, *The Moral Treatment of Returning Warriors in Early Medieval and Modern Times* (Scranton, Pa., 1993)

B. van der Kolk *et al.* (eds), *Traumatic Stress: The Effects of Overwhelming Experience on Mind, Body and Society* (New York, 1996)

War Office, *Report of the Committee of Enquiry into 'Shell-Shock'* (London, 1922)

T. Williams, *Post-Traumatic Stress Disorders: A Handbook for Clinicians* (Cincinnati, 1987)

L. R. Yealland, *Hysterical Disorders of War* (London, 1919)

A. Young. *The Harmony of Illusions: Inventing Post-Traumatic Stress Disorder* (Princeton, 1995)

INDEX

etimología de nervel 7
auge de nervril al mismo tiempo ge nacimiento de psychoanalysis
División de diagnósticos de nerosis x dolel 8-9
teatricalidad de histericas en po fesor de Freud 7
tratamiento "+ efectivo" en mujeres (10)
literary people "more prone" to nervous breakdowns (12
responses to modernity 10-15 (psydive)
                                        culture of
vr 28 para shell-shock coming from m "nerver" y diferencias
de disursos. para diff audiencies
coherence ≈ mod -ef/ 28)
expertos lo quieren quitar y se adopta en lo lay (31)
        ("shell - shock)
management of fear (55) ni topic of literature
vr: fear with → reconocer en otro el miedos en
battlefield
54 VR medica de nuess en shell-shock ver FORM!
        (gve tan pervirso el)
54 vr faking / lying ; soldien. being delivered.
58 fear transformed into hysteria
vr: yo como los doctores ge prmeter se hacen amigos los
69 discharge y medical rechains prede ser un placeholder
 si desearos ≈ desertion
persona de 7   pasa rade x   (NPR)
    shell shok   nivel de tortura